Mr. Flagler's St. Augustine

UNIVERSITY PRESS OF FLORIDA

Florida A&M University, Tallahassee
Florida Atlantic University, Boca Raton
Florida Gulf Coast University, Ft. Myers
Florida International University, Miami
Florida State University, Tallahassee
New College of Florida, Sarasota
University of Central Florida, Orlando
University of Florida, Gainesville
University of North Florida, Jacksonville
University of South Florida, Tampa
University of West Florida, Pensacola

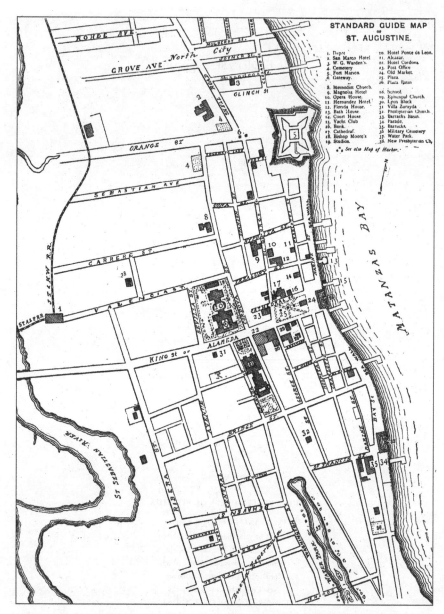

Map of the town in the *Standard Guide to St. Augustine,* 1894. Four-pointed Fort Marion is at the top. The Hotel Ponce de Leon is in the center, with the Hotel Alcazar below it across the street marked "King St. or Alameda." The unfilled part of Maria Sanchez Creek is at the bottom right. From the collection of the St. Augustine Historical Society Research Library.

Thomas Graham

MR. FLAGLER'S
ST. AUGUSTINE

UNIVERSITY PRESS OF FLORIDA

Gainesville · Tallahassee · Tampa · Boca Raton
Pensacola · Orlando · Miami · Jacksonville
Ft. Myers · Sarasota

A Florida Quincentennial Book

Copyright 2014 by Thomas Graham
All rights reserved
Published in the United States of America

First cloth printing, 2014
First paperback printing, 2022

27 26 25 24 23 22   6 5 4 3 2 1

Library of Congress Cataloging-in-Publication Data
Graham, Thomas, 1943–
Mr. Flagler's St. Augustine / Thomas Graham.
pages cm
Mister Flagler's Saint Augustine
Includes bibliographical references and index.
ISBN 978-0-8130-4937-3 (cloth) | ISBN 978-0-8130-6873-2 (pbk.)
1. Saint Augustine (Fla.)—History. 2. Flagler, Henry Morrison,
1830–1913. 3. Florida—History. I. Title.
F319.S2G695 2014
975.9'18—dc23
2013044110

The University Press of Florida is the scholarly publishing agency for the State University System of Florida, comprising Florida A&M University, Florida Atlantic University, Florida Gulf Coast University, Florida International University, Florida State University, New College of Florida, University of Central Florida, University of Florida, University of North Florida, University of South Florida, and University of West Florida.

University Press of Florida
2046 NE Waldo Road
Suite 2100
Gainesville, FL 32609
http://upress.ufl.edu

To Edward N. Akin
Who left us all too soon

Contents

Preface

Two monumental statues stand facing each other in downtown St. Augustine at opposite sides of a plaza once known as the Alameda. One is Don Pedro Menéndez de Avilés, who founded St. Augustine in 1565. He stands triumphantly, holding a sword in his hand and wearing the steel breastplate of a Spanish conquistador. The life of Pedro Menéndez ended in the year 1574 when he was fifty-five years old. The other statue depicts Henry Morrison Flagler. He stands more casually, his right foot advanced just half a pace, wearing the long duster coat of a traveling man, his eyes fixed on the horizon and his right hand in his pocket—counting his change, say the carriage drivers who pass by every day carrying tourists through the oldest European city in the continental United States. Flagler came to St. Augustine in 1885 at the age of fifty-five and began to transform the ancient city into a modern municipality. Perhaps no man, single-handedly, did more to make over a city than did Henry Flagler. Indeed, he is said to have transformed the entire East Coast of Florida, changing it from a remote frontier wilderness into the winter playground of America.

This book tells the story of Henry Flagler's enterprises in St. Augustine and, to some extent, of his activities along the entire East Coast from Jacksonville to Key West—and even beyond to Nassau. He built the Florida East Coast Railway and a chain of luxury winter resort hotels along the Atlantic seaboard, but his initiatives took him into many other fields. This account also explores sympathetically the personal story of a great, enigmatic man who kept his distance from most people and attempted to conceal his private life from the world. He was foremost a businessman who engaged his mind and energy almost every day in the details of actively managing his many ventures. In his first business career he partnered with John D. Rockefeller to build Standard Oil Company into the greatest corporation the world had ever seen. He became fabulously rich—a 1901 calculus ranked him the sixth wealthiest man in America, and a 1905 estimate placed him twelfth—but in his second career in Florida, Flagler spent money in prodigious amounts on ventures that benefited the state and its people but not necessarily Flagler himself.[1] He usually justified his business undertakings on commercial principles, yet almost certainly much of what he attempted in Florida was done as a personal adventure. It seems that the challenge of creating something new outweighed the desire to make money. One might hazard the speculation that he saw continuing innovative activity, ever moving on to the next endeavor, as a way of maintaining his vitality. When he finally reached Key West, he died.

In some respects the visage of a stone-faced captain of industry that Flagler habitually maintained reflected his inner personality. His difficult childhood, followed by a strenuous battle to rise to the top of a mercilessly competitive business world, must have shaped his character profoundly. Raised in a Presbyterian household, he developed a strict personal code of self-restraint but also a sense of obligation to do good for his fellows. In public Flagler appeared as a modest, quiet man. He never used swear words, never danced, and drank alcoholic beverages only in moderation, but he did habitually smoke little Cuban cigars.

In his first career the hard, disciplined part of his character predominated, while in Florida he could play the role of philanthropist, albeit a philanthropist who believed that the best way he could serve others was by being a successful entrepreneur who created work and wealth for them. "If it wasn't for Florida," Flagler would joke in his old age, "I'd be quite a rich man today."[2]

Flagler was a man of his times. He imbibed the economic and social values of Social Darwinism, while tempering its cold-blooded calculus with Christian concern for the misfortunes of others. He accepted the attitudes and social norms of racial segregation and the political disfranchisement of black citizens, yet he seemed embarrassed when obliged to enforce the color bar on his trains. He was a conservative William McKinley Republican and hated progressive reformer Teddy Roosevelt. His tastes in art and music were prosaic, yet he patronized some of the greatest artists of his day.

Flagler married three times. His first two marriages ended in heartbreak. His first wife died young, and his second wife went insane. His relationship with his third wife began before he managed to secure a divorce from the second, which he arranged by having the legislature change the state of Florida's divorce law. This became a major political controversy because it appeared that a wealthy man had induced the legislature through corrupt means to do his will. Yet in his adopted state he had many defenders who sympathized with his plight.

There were other tragedies in his life. His two daughters died at young ages, and his only son deserted him in his old age. He maintained only a few close friendships. One man who dealt with him said, "I think that he was the most lonely man, inwardly, that I have ever known."[3] His friend and pastor in Palm Beach, George Ward, explained that Flagler simply could not reach out to others: "He craved especially the companionship of youth, the gaiety of light and color, yet he had been trained so long to hold himself in check, had been self-repressed so long, he could not go half way."[4]

This book is also the story of other people in the Flagler orbit: Dr. Andrew Anderson, a native of St. Augustine who played the role of civic leader and became perhaps Flagler's closest friend after John D. Rockefeller; the architects John Carrère and Thomas Hastings, who created some of the most significant buildings in the United States; and James McGuire and Joseph McDonald, Flagler's builders. Other key figures include Abbie Brooks, a popular writer who promoted St. Augustine a decade before Flagler and also became an early historian of Spanish Florida; Frank P. Thompson, black headwaiter at Flagler's first hotel and a black rights leader in an age when the tide of racism in America had reached its height; and Captain Henry Marcotte and his wife Anna, both journalists, who recorded the happenings in St. Augustine society during the Flagler era. It is often said that if you stay in St. Augustine long enough, the world will come to your doorstep, and indeed in Flagler's day the rich, famous, and powerful of the world came to stay at his St. Augustine hotels.

Today Henry Flagler's mortal remains are entombed in a mausoleum attached to Memorial Presbyterian Church. Flagler built this church in commemoration of his daughter Jennie Louise, but today it stands as his own monument as well. Next door is Flagler College, its campus built around Flagler's Hotel Ponce de Leon. This, too, is a tribute to the memory of Henry Flagler. To an extent, the city of St. Augustine can itself be seen as a monument to two men from different worlds and ages who dreamed dreams of Florida's future: Pedro Menéndez de Avilés and Henry Morrison Flagler.

Mr. Flagler's St. Augustine

When completed in 1841, the Anderson family home, Markland, on King Street, displayed simple architectural lines. From the collection of the St. Augustine Historical Society Research Library.

1

Dr. Anderson of
St. Augustine, 1839–1880

If there is one sin I detest it is meanness.

—Andrew Anderson to his mother,
December 28, 1863

The antique village of St. Augustine, Florida, was the birthplace of Andrew Anderson. Returning there after spending the Civil War years in his father's former home, New York City, he found circumstances much changed. He entered Florida by way of Jacksonville, the river-crossing town that had fairly prospered before the war. Now it lay half in ruins, having been deliberately burned alternately by Secessionists and Union army forces as the town changed hands several times during the fighting. From there he took a steamer up the broad, placid St. Johns River to Picolata, the remote riverbank landing where the Spanish had once maintained a small blockhouse. Second Lieutenant W. T. Sherman had once been briefly stationed there in 1840, during what was then called the Florida War, now designated the Second Seminole War. The rustic stagecoach carrying passengers from Picolata to St. Augustine passed through an open landscape of wiregrass flatlands under a canopy of ancient longleaf pines where as a boy, not so many years earlier, Anderson had explored on his pony. At the San Sebastian River on the outskirts of St. Augustine the stage rolled onto a flatboat that served as a ferry to reach the east bank. A bridge had stood there before the war, but it had fallen casualty to the skirmishing.

From that point on Anderson was home: the King Street causeway, lined with coquina stone seawalls on either side, carried him quickly across the San Sebastian salt marshes. These mud flats, scattered with patches of marsh grass, had served as the town's first line of defense in olden days, for their deep, sucking clay mud could not be crossed on foot by any living thing heavier than a marsh hen. Once over this barrier Anderson reached the front gate of his home, Markland.[1]

In contrast to the devastation Anderson had witnessed along his journey south, Markland looked more prosperous than he remembered it. The live oak trees planted along King Street by his mother years earlier had grown to over-arch the sandy roadway. The orange grove, which in his boyhood had consisted of disease-stunted trees, had leafed into a green forest, abundant with golden orbs—both ornamental and, more important, profitable when shipped in win-tertime to shivering Yankees up North. Four years before his birth, the Great Freeze of 1835 had blasted the trees down to their roots, and just as they started to recover, the orange coccus, a scale insect that sucked the life from citrus trees, withered the struggling shoots. But in recent years something marvelous had happened; some disease or predator bug had eradicated the coccus, and the trees erupted in celebration. In the midst of the grove stood Markland House, a mod-est enough dwelling of two stories, with tall verandas all around, but imposing in its garden setting. Like so many of the older Spanish buildings in town—and Spain's fortress, the *castillo*—it was constructed of local coquina stone, the shells of tiny beach mollusks compacted by time into a soft limestone.

Anderson's mother, Clarissa Fairbanks Anderson, welcomed her only child home with great joy. All his years away had been a torment to her, and she had expressed her concern, as mothers do, with a stream of letters admonishing him about his studies, his pipe smoking, his possible drinking of wine, his attendance at what she imagined must be rowdy parties, and his gradual escape from the re-straints under which he had been raised. In her letters Mrs. Anderson expressed special concern for the state of Andrew's immortal soul, for despite her repeated pleas, he had refused to stand up and profess his faith in Jesus as his savior. But now he was safely at home again, and Andrew could resume life with his doting mother.

During his years away his mother had presided over the grove, supported by a small corps of servants, some of whom had been family slaves before the war. Clarissa Fairbanks had come to St. Augustine from Boston in 1837 to care for the children of the first Dr. Andrew Anderson, whose wife Mary had recently succumbed to tuberculosis. Like so many newcomers to St. Augustine, the An-dersons had arrived from New York City in 1828 because of Mary's invalidism, with the hope that mild winters and bracing salt air would work as a curative. Sometimes it did, and sometimes it did not. Mary's death left her husband with three daughters: Hannah, Emily, and Mary. Just six months after Clarissa's arrival to tend the girls, her status changed from governess to wife, and a year later in 1839 the baby Andrew was born in a rented house on Hospital Street (now Aviles Street). "It was entirely a family party as to the patient, Doctor & nurses," Dr. Anderson Sr. informed relatives up North.[2]

The first Dr. Andrew Anderson had been one of St. Augustine's leading citizens. As so often was the case in those days, Anderson found that doctoring did not pay as well as other enterprises. He purchased a schooner and engaged in direct trading with New York City, his brother Smith acting as his agent there. Growing and shipping oranges had been his most profitable business up until the 1835 freeze, and after that he got caught up in a craze for propagating mulberry trees to supply a prospective silk industry in the South. This hysteria soon crashed, as did all Dr. Anderson's other ventures into coastal shipping, banking, canal digging, and a railroad proposition that died due to lack of investment capital.

Yet he stood as one of the town's leading citizens, justice of the peace, pillar of the Presbyterian Church, and president of the temperance society. (He wrote to his brother Smith regarding St. Augustine's citizenry: "If they would only banish Rum in all its forms, I believe they would all die of old age or starvation, for we are the laziest pack in Christendom.")[3] Then Florida's great inexplicable natural curse, yellow fever, overwhelmed the community in 1840 and carried Dr. Anderson away along with the unlucky among his patients.

Left without a husband and far from her family in Boston, Clarissa Anderson put her Yankee virtues to work and bustled to make a life for herself in her adopted home. Her husband's will provided that his estate be divided equally among his four children, but she would have free use of the property until her death. She finished construction of Markland House, which had just commenced when her husband died, but the house was built to only half the size originally envisioned. This house would be linked to the fortunes of the Anderson family for three generations, partly because Clarissa fiercely tied her life to this home and its surrounding grove.

To make ends meet she resorted to various stratagems, the most important of which was turning Markland into a boarding house for northern visitors during the winter season. She also began selling off some of the slaves she had inherited when her husband died, and sometimes she hired out one or two of her remaining slaves to anyone who needed temporary help. Her northern relatives expressed disapproval of her ownership of slaves but could offer no solution for her predicament other than that she act on Christian principles. Like so many southern owners, Clarissa sometimes adopted euphemisms when referring to her slaves, calling them "our colored friends"; and as also often happened, she developed close personal ties to a few of her servants. Her chief house servant Aunt Matilda assumed major responsibilities around the premises and became chief caretaker when Mrs. Anderson was away during summers.

Another source of income for the Andersons was a trust fund set up by

Andrew's grandfather James, who had established himself as a shoemaker on Broadway just after the American Revolution. Like one of his neighbors, John Jacob Astor, James Anderson had had the foresight—and perhaps luck—to purchase a fair amount of Manhattan Island real estate that became very valuable as the city's population mushroomed. This small flow of money represented a tangible link between the Andersons in St. Augustine and New York City—an important New York connection shared by other St. Augustinians.

By the 1850s the young Andrew's three half-sisters had moved away from home to pursue married lives, leaving Andrew alone with his mother. In 1854 mother and son set off for a two-year tour of Europe as part of Andrew's education. In letters home to America, Clarissa expressed disapproval of Europe's scandalous theaters, drinking of wine and (in Germany) beer, dancing, Popish religion, and desecrations of the Sabbath. Yet she admired the parks, museums, and boulevards of Paris—and at the same time judged it a "wicked city."

Upon their return Andrew Anderson was enrolled at Princeton College, which had a reputation as being a "safe" school for gentlemen from the South whose families did not want to risk exposing them to the radical ideas they feared to be circulating at Harvard or Yale. By this time Andrew had grown into a handsome young man: solidly built, with thick dark hair, brown eyes, and a complexion so swarthy that people sometimes mistook him for one of Florida's Spaniards. At Princeton he cultivated a luxuriant moustache that would become one of his most distinguishing features for the remainder of his life.

Into his busy life as a scholar dropped a bolt from the clear sky that changed Anderson's outlook on life forever: a letter arrived from home in the spring of 1859 bringing the totally unexpected news that "sweet and lovely" Nellie Baldwin, Anderson's secret fiancée, had died suddenly of typhoid fever. Staggered by the news, Anderson wrote to tell his mother that he would drop out of Princeton and return to Europe. His mother replied that he should remain in school, and she admonished him that Nellie's death sent a warning for him to turn his eyes toward God. Andrew replied softly but bitterly: "How can it seem otherwise than cruel?" He continued, "I feel as if, were it possible, I would never fix my affections upon any-one, for the end thereof is pain and sorrow."[4] After a short time Anderson resumed his normal routine and continued with his life, but evidently this loss deeply scarred his personality. He seemed destined to remain forever a bachelor.

In the fateful year of 1860 the states of the North elected Abraham Lincoln president (without a single recorded vote for Lincoln from any citizen of Florida). In the uncertainty of the moment, many observers wondered whether St. Augustine, with its strong social and economic connections to the North and foreign Minorcan immigrant inhabitants, might be able to resist secession mania.

Surprisingly, it turned out to be no contest: St. Augustine enthusiastically enlisted in the independence movement. Young Andrew joined with his fellow young townsmen in a local militia unit but then thought better of it and quietly slipped out of town, headed for personal neutrality in the North. He almost failed to make it out of the state, blundering into a Federal raiding party sent to burn docks and warehouses at the port of Cedar Key on the Gulf Coast. However, the small schooner on which Andrew sailed ducked into the mangrove marshes and escaped to Cuba and then New York City, where Anderson enrolled in the College of Physicians and Surgeons to train for the medical profession.

Left alone in St. Augustine, Clarissa Anderson kept to herself on her farm and remained unmolested despite her well-known Union opinions. Indeed, she counted among her friends Frances Smith, mother of Confederate general Edmund Kirby Smith, who, like her son Andrew, had been born in a house on Hospital Street, a decade and a half before Andrew. In March 1862 Federal troops landed from black-hulled United States Navy warships and would occupy the town for the rest of the war. Now it became time for rebel sympathizers to stay home and keep to themselves. As secessionist Hannah Jencks noted, "We are beginning the game of rise Ladies and change your places, and between two stools your humble servant is coming to the ground."[5]

Although there would be no fighting in the town, tiny, isolated St. Augustine suffered grievously from the war. Many of its men marched off to confront General U. S. Grant's invading army at Shiloh, Tennessee, in April 1862, and some were still in the ranks at Appomattox three years later. Many never came home, and those who did found St. Augustine turned upside down. Slavery, of course, had ended—in St. Augustine long before most places in the South. Rebel property had been confiscated for nonpayment of taxes. Most of the trees, fences, and many old frame houses had been chopped into firewood by Federal occupation troops, who seldom dared leave the confines of town for fear of Rebel bushwhackers lurking in the surrounding countryside. The Presbyterian Church was stripped of its wooden pews—which were not needed anyway since there were no services during the war.

To this scene of desolation Andrew Anderson returned after the war. At the age of twenty-six—now Dr. Anderson—he assumed the role of leading citizen once held by his father. He thought of himself primarily as an orange grove manager, but he did some doctoring and looked for other ways to wring money out of an isolated region with no industry, no mining, and no extensive agricultural hinterland beyond town. In 1869 Anderson built a substantial frame house fronting on King Street, just east of Markland House. During the winter season he and his mother would live in this house and rent the more spacious and attractive Markland to northern visitors. The new house, called Anderson Cottage, stood just on the edge of the marshes of Maria Sanchez Creek, which formed the western boundary of old colonial St. Augustine. In the 1820s a narrow causeway and coquina stone bridge had been constructed across the marsh, and at high tide water flowed under King Street and up to an earthen berm Anderson had built to keep salt water out of his grove. The Andersons and others who lived west of Maria Sanchez, including the black residents of Lincolnville, considered themselves as living "in the country" even though a country boy could throw a rock all the way across the marsh.

Renting rooms to invalid northern "strangers" during the winter season had long been one of the primary ways of infusing outside money into the rickety St. Augustine economy. The town had two old hotels, the Magnolia and the Florida House, and smaller boarding houses opened their doors on just about every one of the narrow unpaved streets. (According to a local joke, the Spanish should have named the town "Sand Augustine.") In February 1869 the *St. Augustine Examiner* published a clarion call for construction of a new, modern hotel to attract visitors to town. The editor declared that passengers journeying on steamboats along the St. Johns were being told to bypass St. Augustine because it lacked proper accommodations. In response Frank H. Palmer raised the St. Augustine Hotel on one of the town's prime parcels of real estate, with its front on the bay, its sunny southern porches overlooking the Plaza, and its back to the old Catholic church.[6] The four-story building made no gesture toward architectural elegance, save for upcurving finials on the corners of its roof that gave it a vaguely Oriental pagoda aspect.

Palmer must have run into financial difficulties because the next summer he brought Anderson and Edward E. Vaill in as partners, with each investing $11,000 and agreeing to share equally in any profits. Anderson soon converted his one-third of the partnership into a mortgage, and Vaill, a former ship captain with a marvelous gift for profanity, became sole proprietor of the hotel.[7]

This brush with the hotel business must have given Anderson some insights that would prove beneficial when another investor came to town with a proposal to build a hotel.

Anderson felt a strong sense of civic responsibility for the curious little city of his birth, and so it was only natural that among the first things he did upon his return after the war was to accept a position as one of the five trustees of the Presbyterian Church, assuming a responsibility once carried by his father. He joined his mother in the frustrating toil of attempting to keep a small congregation together under what amounted to frontier conditions. Clarissa Anderson and a small cadre of stalwart matrons had labored for many long years to maintain the simple coquina stone church building on South St. George Street, where attendance swelled in the winter season and shriveled during the long, hot "dull season." Mrs. Anderson loved the church and particularly cherished its ministers, an infatuation with parsons that both bored and exasperated her son. Interestingly, although a trustee of the church, Andrew was not a member of it, refusing on principle to affirm any comprehensive belief in the Apostles' Creed.

In another expression of civic duty Anderson adopted St. Augustine's black population as the particular object of his attention, and they reciprocated by accepting him as a special patron. In an age when a black man needed a white man to vouch for him in law and business, Dr. Anderson became the advocate of many black men. This commitment received institutional structure in 1872 with the establishment of the Buckingham Smith Benevolent Association, which was dedicated to the welfare of needy and aged black residents. Buckingham Smith had been the Andersons' next-door neighbor, owning a grove adjoining Markland on the north side. A Harvard-trained lawyer and judge, Smith had gone to Spain in the 1850s as secretary to the United States legation, and while there he had begun assembling and making copies of documents relating to the epic history of Spanish Florida and its northernmost outpost, St. Augustine. Later in the 1860s he returned to Spain to continue his research. Then in 1871 the habitually disheveled statesman-scholar suffered a stroke on a sidewalk in New York City. The police threw him into the drunk tank, and by the time authorities realized the true nature of his condition, it was too late. Only a chance identification by a friend prevented his body being consigned to a pauper's grave.

When Smith's will was read in St. Augustine, it provided that the bulk of his small estate go to assist impoverished, ill, and aged black people. Thus the Benevolent Association was created, with Dr. Anderson as a board member and attending physician. As with the Presbyterian Church, he would remain on its board until his death more than a half-century later. In Anderson's view such charity represented simply the duty of a Christian gentleman. In writing a letter to his mother during the war about the stinginess of an acquaintance, Anderson said: "If there is one sin I detest it is meanness & especially in one who is rich & who can afford to be generous without inconveniencing himself."[8]

In politics Dr. Anderson was a Republican, the party of the Union but also the party of sound money and a sober, honest government that protected people's property and encouraged commerce. In the Reconstruction South he would be considered a scalawag, a southerner who cooperated with the hated Republican carpetbag state government; but Anderson's status in town seems to have inoculated him against hostility from the unreconstructed Democratic majority. Thanks to a new postwar Florida constitution, power was concentrated in the hands of the governor in Tallahassee, and Republican governors appointed

Anderson a county commissioner for three terms in the 1870s. He also served an appointed term as tax collector as well as being elected a town alderman in 1875. However, Anderson certainly did not consider himself a politician but only a citizen serving his community during a time of unusual exigency.

In January 1880 St. Augustine basked for a few moments in the national spotlight when former President U. S. Grant and his wife Julia Dent Grant spent two weeks in town while on a tour of the South. Grant came to St. Augustine because his wife's brother, General Frederick Dent, commanded the troops stationed at St. Francis Barracks, an old Franciscan convent on the south side of town that had been turned into a military base. Dr. Anderson was among the small delegation of St. Augustinians sent to the river town of Palatka to escort Grant into St. Augustine.

A steamer from Palatka dropped the Grant party off at Tocoi, western terminus of the St. Johns Railroad that connected the river to St. Augustine, sixteen miles to the east. The railroad had supplanted the old Picolata stage line. Harriet Beecher Stowe, who passed that way in 1872, wrote of Tocoi that it "consists of a shed and a sand-bank, and a little shanty."[9] Construction of the railroad had begun before the war but had not reached completion. Dr. John Wescott, originator of the railroad, had attempted as a major in the Confederate Army to prevent Yankee invaders from occupying Tampa, but now his railroad brought Yankees to St. Augustine.

Dr. Anderson later recalled: "St. Augustine was connected with the St. Johns by a wooden tramway, on which a primitive car with calico curtains was drawn by a mule; the mule afterwards gave place to a home-made engine which acted like a mule, for you never knew what it was going to do; it burnt holes in the calico curtains and in the clothes of the passengers and once burnt up the baggage."[10] By the time Grant's party made the trip over the Tocoi line, improvements had been made, but evidently the changes did not end the Tocoi railway's reputation for dreadful service. Just about every traveler over this railway, St. Augustine's primary link to the outside world, had some tale of approbation: stops to grease the wheels, delays to load up with firewood, derailments, trips of over two hours long, and more.

When Grant arrived at the railroad depot on the west bank of the San Sebastian, he was met by a delegation of local dignitaries led by Mayor George Greeno, a relative newcomer who had arrived with the Fourth New Hampshire Regiment to occupy St. Augustine during the war and had returned to open a grocery business. The parade of carriages crossed over the San Sebastian on a newly rebuilt bridge, but it lost some of its dignity in splashing through calf-deep water over the causeway across the marshes, flooded by high tide and recent rains. Nonetheless, the procession of fine carriages proceeded along King Street, followed by a rag-tag assemblage of humble carts, horses, and mules carrying St. Augustine's black citizenry boisterously welcoming their liberator. In front of Markland an arch spanned the road with the message: "Our Oldest City Welcomes Our Greatest General." At the St. Augustine Hotel a band struck up "Hail to the Chief," and the general settled in for a fortnight-long round of dinners, receptions, and visits to the historic sites.

Many years later Anderson recalled the trip to Palatka to meet President Grant on his tour of Florida: "In the evening seated in the office of the little hotel in Palatka, the taciturn General discoursed enthusiastically on the future of Florida. He said that railroads would penetrate the State in every direction, and that thousands of emigrants would flock hither, and that its growth would be phenomenal. I listened with unbelieving ears. Had I not lived in the State all my life and had I seen any growth? Very little. At the time, you must remember, there was no railroad south of Jacksonville, and there was an almost unbroken wilderness south of Palatka."[11]

2

Visions of the Ancient City,
1869–1880

America is now wholly given over to ... scribbling women.
—Nathaniel Hawthorne to his publisher, 1855

St. Augustine's first big promoter with dreams of an extravagant future for Florida arrived in town in 1869. He was John F. Whitney, and he represented the prototype of the modern Florida land developer. Born a grandson of the famous Eli Whitney, the younger Whitney became an acquaintance of Abraham Lincoln, William Cullen Bryant, and P. T. Barnum. He started newspapers in Boston and New York City, and when he came to the old city he founded the *St. Augustine Press*. Whitney distributed copies of his newspaper around the country to publicize his adopted hometown and published the booklet *A Brief Account of St. Augustine and Its Environs*, in which he declared that St. Augustine made an ideal place to settle year-round. His son-in-law W. W. Palmer became Dr. Anderson's partner in the St. Augustine Hotel. Whitney himself invested in a large tract of land on the west bank of the San Sebastian that he named Ravenswood, where with P. T. Barnum flair he named a freshwater seep Ponce de Leon Spring. The road to the spring became a favorite route for winter visitors out for leisurely carriage rides in the countryside.[1]

By the 1870s Whitney was not the only one advancing St. Augustine's claim to the country's attention. Harriet Beecher Stowe paid a visit and rhapsodized about the land of June in winter. The Georgia poet Sidney Lanier commended the town's languid atmosphere as ideal for passing the time in repose. (Boss Tweed of the Tammany Hall Democratic Party machine passed through town incognito in 1869 in his flight to Cuba to avoid prosecution for corruption in New York City, but he had no intention of letting anyone know where he was.) The two most influential writers in defining the image of St. Augustine were a pair of remarkable women who captured its essence as America's unique Ancient City and suspended that image forever in amber in the American mind.

The first was Constance Fenimore Woolson, grandniece of James Fenimore Cooper. She came to St. Augustine with her widowed mother and spent several winters during the 1870s. She penned a long story for *Harper's Magazine,* employing her considerable talents as a writer and her vivid imagination as a novelist to draw her readers into the exotic atmosphere of the old Spanish town, redolent both of moss-covered decay and the pungent, sweet aroma of orange blossoms. The steel-plate engravings printed in *Harper's* of narrow streets overarched with balconies etched an indelible image into the nation's consciousness. "All those in search of health, all endowed with romance and imagination, all who could appreciate the rare charming haze of antiquity which hangs over the ancient little city," she wrote, would fall in love with St. Augustine.[2]

Following her mother's death in 1879, Woolson removed to Europe and spent the rest of her life there, wandering with the seasons from England to Germany to Italy. She used St. Augustine as the setting for her 1886 novel *East Angels.* Woolson became a close friend of the novelist Henry James, and their relationship gave rise to speculation that they might also be lovers. In 1894, depressed and delirious with fever, she either fell or jumped to her death from an apartment window in Venice. Shortly before her death Woolson had written that she hoped to return to Florida, buy a plot of land, plant orange trees, and live out the rest of her life quietly.[3]

During her lifetime Woolson earned well-deserved fame as a creative talent, but the other woman who shaped the image of St. Augustine lived her life in an anonymity of her own making.

"Sylvia Sunshine" hid her identity behind a pretty pseudonym when she published *Petals Plucked from Sunny Climes* in 1880. The only two clues to her identity embedded in the text were the fact that Southern Methodist Publishing of Nashville brought out her book and her revelation that her journey to Florida began from Atlanta. Hence she might have been a southern woman. Other than that, the only suggestion of her identity was her obvious talent as a writer, as evidenced by the sprightly journalistic prose of *Petals.* In 1888 she turned up in St. Augustine again, once more in the guise of Sylvia Sunshine, to write about the opening of Henry Flagler's Hotel Ponce de Leon for North Carolina's *Charlotte Chronicle.*[4]

More than any other guidebook or contemporary description of St. Augustine, *Petals Plucked from Sunny Climes* captures the sights, smells, and distinctive textures of the Ancient City.

Sylvia Sunshine, like almost all other travelers, reached St. Augustine by way of the Tocoi railway. The arrival of the train from Tocoi marked a highlight of the day for strangers already safely ensconced in their hotels and boarding houses. For one thing, it provided a vignette of the human spectacle in the form of another band of bedraggled refugees who had just survived the ordeal of travel. Passing under the visual inspection of already established visitors constituted an informal rite of initiation for newcomers. Also, the appearance of the train meant a bag of fresh mail from the North. After the horse-drawn omnibus from the depot arrived, a crowd of people would cluster around the post office in the Plaza (the old Spanish governor's house) and then queue up at the general delivery window to inquire if any mail had arrived for them. If not, they could at least talk with acquaintances who had been fortunate enough to receive a missive from back home or perhaps a recent northern newspaper.

Newcomers arriving in town had a choice of three large hotels: Captain Vaill's new St. Augustine Hotel on the Plaza, the Florida House just a half block to the north, or the Magnolia another half block farther north, fronting on St. George Street, the town's thoroughfare to the City Gates at the northern limit of the old Spanish town. All were barracks-like structures built of heart-pine, clearly designed for housing large numbers of people and without much pretense at architectural distinction. Miss Sunshine, however, mentions the smaller, newer Sunnyside House as having "taken a front seat for first-class accommodations with all its patrons."[5] The Sunnyside stood at King Street on a lot sold to Captain Thomas F. House by Dr. Anderson in 1876. Behind the little hotel spread the marshes of Maria Sanchez Creek, and at high tide the salt water lapped at the coquina stone causeway that carried King Street across the marsh flats and past the higher ground to the west in front of Dr. Anderson's Markland home and orange grove.

Many of the winter strangers coming to town were victims of the great pandemic of the nineteenth century—tuberculosis—for which there was no known cure but which might be assuaged by spending the winter months in a warm clime. Thus St. Augustine was, to a great degree, one large sanitarium. The quiet darkness of the nights was punctuated with the coughing from a sad host of diseased lungs accompanied by the melancholy strains of flute playing—recommended by doctors for keeping bronchial passages open. Adding to the evening noises, prowling alley cats caterwauled, and out-of-sync roosters crowed at midnight. All this could be heard over the faint whisper of ocean breakers washing up on the beaches of Anastasia Island across the bay.

Miss Sunshine included in her guidebook some of the stilted, pseudomedical wisdom expected in advice to invalids seeking a health resort: "The powerful chemical ingredients, which exist in the atmosphere on the sea-coast, act as a neutralizer to disease. The chloride of sodium, compounded in the laboratory of

King Street ran in front of the Sunnyside House over a narrow causeway lined with a coquina stone sea wall that held back the water of Maria Sanchez Creek. By permission of State Archives of Florida.

the great saline aquarium and respired without effort, is freighted with the germs of health, which are productive of beneficial effect in many forms of pulmonic complaints."[6]

From this prosaic base she vaults into poetic endorsement of St. Augustine's virtues for the infirm: "Like Ponce de Leon, they visit St. Augustine in search of the famous waters which would give back their youth, restore and strengthen their feeble limbs with renewed vigor, that would be perpetual as the verdure and beauty by which they are surrounded. Nor are they disappointed in all respects; for if they do not grow younger, they prolong their days to enjoy more of God's pure air and sunlight, mingled with the perfume of flowers and singing of sweet birds, than they would in their own homes."[7]

St. Augustine's other claim to distinction, complementing its Mediterranean climate, was its Spanish heritage, evidenced in the hoary stone vestiges left behind from ancient times. Miss Sunshine gives her readers descriptions of the major "sites" in town, adding commentaries that show her respect for preserving relics from the past as well as her practical appreciation that such remnants constituted a major commercial draw for curious visitors from the outside. "The ancient fortress of Castle San Marco, the name of which has been improperly changed to Fort Marion, is considered one of the most attractive and interesting objects in St. Augustine. It was constructed in the style of the strong castles in Europe during the Middle Ages."[8]

On her narrative walk through the town she visits one of the most sketched, painted, and photographed remnants in town, the City Gates—by common usage the name is almost always made plural. "On the north side of the town, near the fort, stands what is left of the city gates, the most interesting relic that remains from a walled city. The gates are gone, the architecture of the two towers, or pillars, remaining being purely arabesque, surmounted by a carved pomegranate. Like the relics at Mount Vernon, if a protection is not built around these pillars, the hand of vandalism will soon have them destroyed, as so many careless visitors are constantly chipping off fragments. The sentry-boxes are much defaced, their foundation being a cement, the art of making it now being lost."[9]

Her reference to cement was unintentionally prescient, considering the revolution in concrete construction that loomed less than a decade ahead for St. Augustine. She was correct in observing that the Spanish had routinely employed *tapia* or "tabby" concrete in local buildings. Such concrete was made by mixing water with sand and lime created by burning oyster shells. This humble concrete followed the much grander tradition of the Romans, who had built great structures such as the Pantheon in Rome wholly from concrete. However, that tradition had been lost for centuries, only to be revived with the discovery of Portland cement in the early nineteenth century. Even as Miss Sunshine wrote, revolutionary developments in concrete construction were emerging both in Europe and in the United States.

West of the City Gates ran Orange Street, built atop what had once been an earthen and log wall extending from the fort to the San Sebastian marshes. A moat had once paralleled this wall, but now there remained only a shallow, sandy ditch that served mainly as a nuisance. Outside this ditch stretched an empty lot. In earlier days it had constituted an open area providing a field of fire for soldiers guarding the wall against invaders from the north—first the English and later the Americans. The old moat or ditch was known as "the lines," and it constituted a barrier to the expansion of the city northward since permission had to be obtained from the federal government for any "encroachment" passing over the lines, such as a road, gas main, or railroad track.

Other than the fort and the relatively modest Catholic cathedral, St. Augustine possessed nothing pretending toward monumental architecture, and Miss Sunshine acknowledged as much: "There is nothing now remaining of courtly splendors. A few only of the ancient tenements are left, some of them tumbling down by degrees; those having occupants are a class of persons struggling for an existence, with adverse circumstances surrounding them which cannot be overcome, but must be borne in silent submission. Our imagination before visiting declining architecture is always to conceive that they have an air of the picturesque—a softness reflected on them by moonlight, or a panorama with dulcet strains floating somewhere in our fanciful dreams."[10]

St. Augustinians devised some additional "attractions" to intrigue visitors from the North. Several houses advertised themselves as "oldest" or just "old." The story goes that a photographer thought he would sell more souvenir pictures of the Public Market if he labeled it the "Old Slave Market," and the name stuck. (The Public Market primarily served farmers, fishermen, and butchers in its day, but a slave sale did take place there from time to time. At any rate, the "Slave Market" would serve as the stage for a speech by Martin Luther King in 1964 when he led protests in St. Augustine that advanced the passage of the landmark Civil Rights Act of 1964.)

By the time Miss Sunshine arrived in St. Augustine, the town had attracted enough attention to experience noticeable growth from northerners moving in to live there year-round, or at least to build winter cottages. The contrast between the crumbling coquina stone Spanish houses and the freshly painted new wood-frame Yankee homes was great, as Miss Sunshine noted: "St. Augustine, unlike the European cities, bears no record of great prosperity or vanished splendors in the display of colossal buildings, or fine scientific skill, as the present period boasts of more fine houses than at any time anterior to this."[11]

She added: "A good cart was formerly the highest ambition of the natives, while now elegant carriages, with liveried drivers, roll around the streets, decked with the trappings of wealth and show of fashion."[12]

The grandest landaus and victorias seen on the sandy byways of St. Augustine were owned by George L. Lorillard of the Lorillard tobacco empire. A tall, athletic man, trained in medicine at Yale, Lorillard found his health beginning to deteriorate from rheumatoid arthritis as he aged. He sought relief in the warmer winter temperatures of St. Augustine, where he walked slowly and painfully with heavy canes and sometimes with crutches. Lorillard built an impressive home on a large lot facing St. George Street. His villa employed the popular stick style

Narrow, sandy Bay Street has become today's four-lane Avenida Menendez, and the old sea wall now lies buried under the street's median. Capo's Bath House over the water would long remain a landmark on the bay front. By permission of Library of Congress.

architecture imitating European half-timbered designs. Behind it stood a tall windmill that pumped water up into a tower tank, from which a strong flow of irrigation water could be used to cultivate a veritable tropical garden of exotic plants. A noted yachtsman and owner of a stable of racehorses, Lorillard brought both to St. Augustine. He built a racetrack west of town that attracted an upscale clientele. During the summers up North his horses—flaunting the colors orange and blue—won the Preakness five times in a row, the Belmont Stakes three times, and the Travers twice. He named one of his most popular thoroughbreds "St. Augustine."[13]

Another northerner who made his winter home in St. Augustine was James Renwick, the New York architect whose mammoth unfinished St. Patrick's Cathedral had already been under construction for nearly two decades. Renwick, whose sorrowful eyes peered out between a high forehead and a full gray beard, purchased the old Fishman Warf Lot on South Bay Street at Artillery Lane. He also bought the Rodriguez Grant making up the scrub dunes near the northern tip of Anastasia Island, save for a five-acre lot that had been purchased in 1871 by the United States government as the site for a new lighthouse, which would soon be under construction. In 1872 Renwick sold both his town and island properties to his father-in-law, William Henry Aspinwall, whose eldest daughter Anna was Renwick's wife. In 1873 the Aspinwalls built a fine town house on the Bay Street lot and a cottage called "Glimpse of Glory" on the Anastasia property—the first house in the area of the new lighthouse.[14]

Aspinwall was a man of legendary proportions. Back in the 1840s he had imported tea from China in fast clipper ships with speed that ensured his customers would purchase the freshest tea, if not the least expensive. His *Sea Witch* set a record on the China to New York route that has never been equaled by any sailing ship. During the California gold rush his vessels carried Forty Niners from New York to the gold fields, and then, to shorten the distance between the Atlantic and Pacific coasts, he built the railroad across the Isthmus of Panama. After the Civil War he helped found a precursor of the New York Public Library and, as a serious collector of European art, the Metropolitan Museum of Art.

When Aspinwall built his home, the *St. Augustine Examiner* editorialized: "It is a sure sign of the future prosperity of this place, that gentlemen of wealth and enterprise . . . are all erecting their winter residences here, and where such men lead, the crowd is sure to follow."[15]

Another pioneer from the uppermost level of society ranked as perhaps the richest man in America: William Astor, grandson of the patriarch John Jacob Astor. Burdened with a diffident personality, William Astor loved nothing more than cruising on his seagoing yacht, managing a stable of thoroughbred horses, and rusticating during the winters in wilderness Florida. In 1874 he purchased a huge tract of land in the interior of the state that had once belonged to old-time St. Augustine citizen Moses Levy. Astor built two hotels on the banks of the upper St. Johns River to accommodate prospective land purchasers. (The tiny river landing of Astor survives on the site to this day.) Unlike the reclusive William, his wife Caroline relished the whirl of Manhattan high society and engaged in society affairs as if they were a blood sport.[16]

Astor seems not to have built a winter home in St. Augustine, since he ordinarily lived on his yacht. As late as 1886 he showed up at the old Magnolia Hotel on St. George Street, and it was "rumored" that he might build a house in town.[17] However, to make access to St. Augustine more convenient for travelers, back in about 1870 his father William Sr. had purchased the rickety Tocoi railway. Following his father's death, William Jr. rebuilt the roadbed, added new iron rails, and put two locomotives and new passenger cars to work on the line. When the first of the new locomotives chugged into town, a crowd of people turned out to see this wonder of modern technology. Many St. Augustine denizens had never seen a locomotive before. As a major landowner and railroad operator, Astor pointed the way for later, more engaged businessmen to develop the state.[18]

The stark contrast between the northern visitors' splendid coaches and the natives' humble ox carts formed an integral part of the warp and woof of society in St. Augustine. Their relationship constituted the fundamental nexus of the community's economy. As Miss Sunshine told it: "The little boy replied to the Northerner who asked him how the people all lived down here in this sandy country. The lad replied, 'Off from sweet taters and sick Yankees.'"[19]

Among the native population, the Minorcans formed the most distinctive element. Their ancestors had been brought to Florida as indentured servants back in the 1760s. By this time few continued to speak Spanish, but they did maintain a somewhat separate identity, and outsiders liked to consider them a foreign remnant of the old Spanish populace. Miss Sunshine thought of them that way as well, writing: "They are a quiet, frugal people, retiring in their manners, and simple in their ways—the very opposite in every respect of the grasping, bustling, overreaching Yankee—devoted Catholics, warm in their friendship, but timid toward strangers. The young girls in the community have a type of feminine beauty which can be seen at no other place, except on the shores of the Mediterranean, or in the Madonnas of the Italian masters—in short, St. Augustine is an Italian town on the shores of America, and in that respect differs from any on the Western Continent."[20]

The natives enjoyed only a brief four-month window of opportunity during the winter season to earn their livelihoods—resulting in something like an air of desperation in the natives' attempts to extract money from their guests. Miss Sunshine paints this verbal picture: "Many complain of the manner in which they are annoyed by all kinds of professions, from the boot-black—who screams in your ears, 'Shine, sah!' until you feel like elevating him somewhere among the shining orbs, from which point he would not soon return—to the hotel bills. 'Four dollars a day, if no baggage, in advance.' Then the carriages—'Ride, sir? take a nice ride?' The pleasure-yachts come in for their share of attention—'Take an excursion over on the beach? I takes over pleasure-parties.' These all swoop down on the defenseless travelers, like birds of prey over a fallen carcass, to the amusement of some, and the annoyance of many more. There is no lack of attention from interested parties, if you have the money to spend."[21]

St. Augustine's black inhabitants added to the curiosity of the place for Yankee visitors, intensifying the exoticism of the setting with a tincture of darkest Africa. Generally whites treated the black population with benign paternalism, shaded with frustration whenever blacks either failed or refused to play their assigned role as laborers in the lowest, sweatiest jobs. A profound assumption of black inferiority undergirded the social mindset of almost all white people. One component of the racist mentality held that black people were particularly suited to play the role of comic relief in the drama of resort life. This theater could be witnessed every day in the streets, as one New York observer reported to readers back home: "After dinner the inhabitants congregate on the long porch of the St. Augustine Hotel and bask in the sun, *à la* alligator, while the little darkies, whose name is legion, are induced, at the sight of five cents or a dime, to cater to our amusement by turning somersaults, tumbling about in a bag-race, bumping their hard heads together, or, as occurred here last week, climbing a greased pole and chasing greased pigs."[22]

Many black men earned their living by carrying sailing parties across the half-mile expanse of Matanzas Bay to Anastasia Island, where carriages and later a tramway transported amusement seekers to the beach. Few visitors dared to attempt bathing in the Atlantic surf, especially during the winter chill, but walks on the beach were an expected part of the St. Augustine experience. The old Spanish lighthouse, its base being undermined by the waves, stood on a northern shore of the island, with the new brick lighthouse more safely inland a short distance. Around the lighthouses could be found the quarries from which the town mined coquina stone. Besides these installations the island remained almost uninhabited by humans, but white-tailed deer, wild cattle, and untamed Spanish ponies called "marsh tackies" roamed in abundance.

Back in town, sojourners were required to spend some time shopping for keepsakes to carry home as mementos of their sojourn. Miss Sunshine gives us an idea of the variety of souvenirs offered for sale: "The celebrated Florida curiosities are a great source of traffic, from the June-bugs to the head of a Jew-fish, including stuffed baby alligators that neither breathe nor eat, tusks from the grown ones, mounted with gold; birds of beautiful and varied plumage, relieved by the taxidermist of every thing but their coat of feathers and the epidermis, looking at you from out glass windows, through glass eyes; screech-owl tails and wings; pink and white curlew-feathers; saws from sword-fish of fabulous length; sharks' heads; sea-beans, supposed to have grown on Anastasia Island, but drifted from the West Indies; and the palm, wrought in so many varied and fanciful forms of imaginary and practical utility as scarcely to be identified as a native of the Florida wilds, whose rough and jagged stalks seem to defy an assault from the hand of the most expert explorer, being upheld by its roots of inexplicable size and strength."[23]

The orange, of course, represented Florida's signature gift of nature. Visitors learned the lore of the various varieties of oranges and the ways in which they might be consumed. One writer offered this vignette of orange culture in the hotels: "Stepping out on the veranda in the early morning we find everybody sucking oranges in the most solemn business-like fashion. The gentlemen go at it with a will, and generally work through a whole basketful of the golden fruit; they make a hole at one end and suck with inflated cheeks, like a bevy of ancient cherubs blowing a trumpet, and suck in sweet silence, seemingly oblivious of all that is passing round them as they take their morning dose of this delicious nectar. Some of the ladies peel them with white slim fingers, and extract the juice as daintily as the bee extracts honey from the flower; some of the uncompromising feminine family, 'who have no nonsense about them,' pull the orange to pieces, mangle its delicate tissues, and disembowel it with ruthless teeth. Some work as though they were sucking for a wager, and others go through their heap with slow, solemn enjoyment. Those who have not eaten a fresh gathered orange in Florida don't know what an orange is."[24]

By March the visitor season would be at its apex and the weather at its most delightful. Blossoms for next year's orange crop exploded into bloom. To entertain its guests, the town got up a variety of amusements. The Yacht Club sponsored a regatta, with Matanzas Bay providing an excellent sheet of water about three miles long suitable for races. On shore Minorcan boys mounted on marsh tackies raced around the fort reservation, and other men vied in pedestrian races. Included among the contestants in 1877 were a visiting professional walker from the North, local boys, and some of the imprisoned Western Indians then living in the fort (but allowed freedom of the town). Black boys vied in a wheelbarrow race across the Plaza, with one overly enthusiastic competitor ending up somersaulting into the boat basin at the east end of the Plaza. All the while the army brass band from St. Francis Barracks kept up lively tunes to accompany the action. The main festival day was capped off with a greased pole climb, with a ham and greenbacks planted atop the pole as prizes.[25]

With the arrival of April, the exodus to the North accelerated. Miss Sunshine observed, "Many speak of this favorably as a summer-resort, but when the season advances into May, the winter-visitors all leave. Then a painful silence pervades every thing, unbroken only by an occasional yawn from the residents, who are tired of doing nothing."[26]

Another lady visitor, Julia Newberry, wrote this epitaph to her visit: "I like St. Augustine, and every one does, and generally without knowing why; one is bored to death half the time, & yet fascinated with the place; it is so quaint, old, and different from any other place in America. . . . I am glad to go home, and yet sorry to leave this interesting spot; it is a queer place, and its charm lies in being queer. It will be horrid when they have a railroad, more hotels, and a bridge instead of a Ferry."[27]

3

The Private Henry
Morrison Flagler, 1830–1883

I was hard on Flagler, but I would rather be my own tyrant.

—Henry Flagler to newsman James Morrow, 1906

In 1903 Henry Morrison Flagler concluded a letter of reply to John F. Forbes, president of Stetson University in Deland, Florida, with an admonition: "I note that the envelope containing your letter bore the imprint of the President's office of the Stetson University. I think it would be more prudent if you would do as I do, use plain envelopes."[1]

The letter is revealing of Henry Flagler's habitual mode of thinking. He had just donated money for the construction of a building at Stetson that would be called simply Science Hall, with no acknowledgment that Flagler had provided the funding. Typically, he wished to maintain this high level of confidentiality in his philanthropies, but far beyond that, Flagler also desired to keep his entire private life sealed in a "plain envelope."

One of his chief lieutenants was once asked to give an assessment of Flagler's character, and he offered a few cursory observations before giving up, saying, "I do not know if I have helped you to form an estimate of Mr. Flagler. His innermost self? I don't know it. He keeps it under lock and key."[2]

Henry Flagler never wrote a book, never put down his memoirs, and seldom submitted to interviews by journalists. In fact, only twice did he volunteer information on his personal life story for publication.

The first time, in 1906, newspaperman James B. Morrow managed to land an interview with Flagler in the Standard Oil Building at 26 Broadway. (The second interview would be given to Wall Street, reported Edwin Lefevre in 1909.) Morrow left this description of his encounter:

"Twelve stories up I found Mr. Flagler in a large corner room from the windows of which could be seen the North River, its hurrying ships and its fleets of hungry gulls, winged scavengers of the water. Seventy-six years old is this business giant, but in body and intellect a tall, erect and handsome man in the full sweep of his powers, and with no sign of uncertainty or unsoundness. A major general of cavalry, you might say, trained to ride the field. Excellent head; fine gray eyes; short white hair parted in the center; straight, classic nose; closely trimmed mustache. That is his picture. In familiar discourse ready and brusque with philosophy, reflection, experience and the sense of humor."[3]

At the start of the interview, Flagler, as was his rule, informed Morrow that the talk would be limited to questions relating to his business career. "No one can understand how I dislike to see my name in print," said Flagler. "But my work is another matter. It concerns the public. Flagler's personal history doesn't." Still, Morrow managed to insert some queries of a personal nature into the dialogue, opening a crack in Flagler's wall of silence.

Flagler began the interview with a simple enough answer to the safe question of where he was born: "In a little village south of Rochester and near the town of Canandaigua. State of New York." (The settlement was Hopewell and the year 1830.)

When asked about his family background, Flagler responded with a story: "My father was a preacher, but away from the pulpit he was a reserved, I might say, a silent man. When my mother died the editor of the town in which we lived printed a notice of her death and funeral. I remember that while I was wrapping up a number of papers for friends and relatives my father came in. After watching me for several minutes, he said I might send one to a married woman in Indiana whose address he gave. In five minutes he mentioned the name of another woman. I had never heard of them, and so asked: 'Who are they?' 'My sisters,' he replied. He hadn't seen either of them for thirty years."

Flagler offered the opinion that he had inherited his reticence from his father. During his conversation with Morrow, Flagler did not mention the names of either his father or his mother, nor did he even so much as allude to the three women who had been his wives during his lifetime.

In a letter written some sixteen years earlier, Flagler had been equally unhelpful to a woman who had inquired about his ancestry: "I left my home when I was fourteen years of age, and have never had time to look up my relatives; consequently, my knowledge of the Family Tree is very limited. I have a Family Record, which I have not seen for many years, and it is my impression that my grandfather's name was Solomon, but I am not certain."[4]

In reality, Flagler's family tree branched in many confusing directions because of multiple marriages, deaths, and remarriages among his forebears. His father, whose name was Isaac Flagler, was married three times, and his mother Elizabeth also married three times. Such blended families were not uncommon in a day when untimely death visited households frequently.

Isaac Flagler's ancestors immigrated to New York from Germany in the early 1700s. His father, whose name was indeed Solomon, had changed the spelling of the family name from Flegler to Flagler. Although Isaac had no formal seminary training, he was ordained as a Presbyterian minister at age twenty-one and began a humble ministry that carried him over the years to several places in New York and Ohio. When he married Elizabeth in 1828, he had already lost two wives, and she had by then buried two husbands.[5]

Henry Flagler's mother Elizabeth's first husband had been Hugh Morrison, and from him Henry received his middle name. However, his mother's relatives from her second marriage to David Harkness would play the most important part in Flagler's life. When Elizabeth married David Harkness in 1820, he already had a son from a previous marriage, Stephen V. Harkness; and then together Elizabeth and David produced a son, Daniel Harkness. In addition, David had a brother named Lamon G. Harkness, who had been trained in medicine but who had become a major real estate developer and merchant in the area around Bellevue, Ohio. When David Harkness died in 1825, Elizabeth moved back to New York state with her son Daniel, where she married Isaac Flagler.

Henry Flagler, like Abraham Lincoln before him, had no warm memories to share with newspaperman Morrow of a bucolic childhood life in rustic, agrarian America. His minister in Palm Beach, George Ward, recalled, "He used to say that his only schooling had been that of adversity. Many a time he has told me of the hardships of his boyhood. He used to even say that he had no boyhood."[6]

At Morrow's prompting, Flagler gave the only account of his early life that he would ever offer. In answer to the stock question about where he went to school, Flagler responded, "All the training I ever got in school was obtained before I was fourteen years old. At that age I concluded that my mother and sister needed the lean pay which my father received for preaching. So I left home and walked nine miles to the town of Medina, carrying a carpetbag in my hand."

Although Flagler did not mention it to Morrow, when he left home Flagler was heading west to join his mother's Harkness relatives in Ohio. His half-brother Dan Harkness had already located there; both boys likely realized that prospects were much brighter among the prospering Harkness clan than with the humble Flaglers.

At Medina Flagler took passage on a slow freight boat heading west on the Erie Canal to Buffalo. From Buffalo, Flagler explained,

I took vessel for Sandusky, Ohio. I was on Lake Erie for three days in a dreadful storm. I was seasick, lonely, and very wretched. My mother had put some lunch in my carpetbag and of that I ate, when I ate at all, during my gloomy journey over canal and lake."

I remember I went ashore early in the morning. Weak and dizzy, I staggered along the wharf between piles of cordwood, and was mortified to think some one might see me and believe I was drunk. I paid twenty-five cents for a hot breakfast and felt better.

From there Flagler pushed on overland to Republic. He arrived with just a small assortment of change in his pocket: a nickel, four pennies, and a French five-franc piece that exchanged locally at the value of a dollar. Flagler informed Morrow that he kept the five-franc coin at home in his desk as a souvenir of those days.

In Republic Flagler went to work in a country store owned by Lamon Harkness and managed by Flagler's older half-brother Dan Harkness. Flagler had placed his foot upon the first rung of a ladder that would carry him to far greater success in business than his modest first position as store clerk presaged. His salary amounted to five dollars a month, plus board. It was said that he slept under the counter, wrapped in crinkly package paper to insulate himself from the cold.[7] As in most general stores, "We sold everything from a pint of molasses to a corn plaster." Clerking in the store enlarged Flagler's world, as frontier Ohio's parade of humanity entered and exited through the front door. Conducting face-to-face retail business taught him something of "the vanities and infirmities of human nature." To illustrate the point, Flagler explained that in the basement was a keg of brandy, and orders for all customers were filled from that same single keg, but the price varied depending on what Dan thought the customer would be willing to pay. "The keg taught me to inquire somewhat closely of that which is offered for sale."

Lacking a large income, Flagler accumulated capital by adopting a parsimonious style of living. As he would later write to one of his colleagues, "Don't forget that a dollar saved is sure profit."[8] To Morrow he explained of his youth, "I hesitate to say it, but I recollect when I wore a thin overcoat and thought how comfortable I should be when I could afford a long, thick ulster. I carried a luncheon in my pocket until I was a rich man. I trained myself in the school of self-control and self-denial. I was hard on Flagler, but I would rather be my own tyrant than to have some one else tyrannize over me."

Many years later, when Flagler was living comfortably in Palm Beach as one of the richest men in America, his private secretary entered Flagler's office and found him painstakingly removing a postage stamp from a spoiled envelope. "If

I can get this stamp the rest of the way off, we shall save two cents," declared Flagler.[9]

After four years of labor in the Republic store, Flagler had so impressed his distant relation Lamon Harkness that Harkness called young Henry to his headquarters in Bellevue and put him on a salary of four hundred dollars a year. Flagler later noted that so long as he worked as an employee of another, his salary never exceeded four hundred dollars a year. His term as a salaried employee ended in 1852 when Lamon and Dan Harkness brought Flagler into a new mercantile company as a partner.

The partnership developed a personal dimension when, also in 1852, Dan married Lamon's oldest daughter Isabella, and in 1853 Henry married the younger daughter Mary. He was twenty-three, and she had just turned twenty.

Flagler's long-time friend Charles Foster, later governor of Ohio, wrote an account of the Flaglers' honeymoon trip to New York: "Henry Flagler and I were married on the same day. I was married in Fremont and he in Bellevue. . . . We took the same train for our wedding trips east and with our wives were in a railroad wreck near a small town in Pennsylvania. The little tavern in the village was not half large enough to accommodate the passengers. I remember we sat up the balance of the night with our brides sitting on our laps to save space for the others."[10]

A photograph of Henry Flagler with the Harkness sisters, probably taken about the time of the marriage, shows Henry as a handsome, clean-shaven young man gazing into the camera lens with a great deal of confidence. Mary seems small and pensive in comparison. As a member of the wealthy Harkness family, Mary had grown up in a quite different situation from that endured by her new husband. The Bellevue newspaper reported: "Her father was able to afford his children every advantage in life any child could have, and these, with the benefits of travel, were improved to the uttermost by his daughter Mary. She became as accomplished as she was lovely, and was the idol of a large and devoted circle of friends."[11]

Mary's health had already become a concern to her parents while she was young. They sent her to school in the South in order for her to escape the winter winds that swept across Lake Erie. A letter written by Lamon Harkness to Mary in January of 1852 has survived. Mary was then in a boarding school in Savannah, Georgia, almost as far south as one could go at the time and still enjoy the amenities of civilization. In the letter father admonishes daughter to keep the family informed of her well-being: "Let us know exactly how your health was from day to day."[12] However, once married to Henry, Mary would spend the winters at home in Bellevue.

The Harkness-Flagler firm became a major buyer and seller of wheat and corn

Henry Flagler cut a dashing figure. With him are his wife Mary Harkness, standing, and his sister-in-law Isabella Harkness (early 1850s). © Flagler Museum Archives.

from the fertile lands of the Ohio River Valley, which was already becoming the breadbasket of America and Europe. Flagler shipped many carloads of wheat to Cleveland to be sold by commission merchants there, most prominently one John D. Rockefeller of the firm of Hewitt & Tuttle. (Years later Henry Flagler would cross paths with a member of the Tuttle family, Julia Tuttle, in Florida.)

Flagler and the Harkness family also went into the distilling business in a large and profitable way. Converting grain into a less bulky commodity—whiskey—before transporting it east had long been practiced in the West, and Flagler later defended the practice as an acceptable one. Yet ultimately he gave up the liquor trade, he said, because of his personal reservations about its morality.[13] In his later career as owner of pleasure resorts in Florida and as manager of a railroad employing thousands of workmen, Flagler would continue to struggle with the perpetual alcoholic drink question.

Possibly Flagler's parents influenced his decision to abandon the distillery, for by this time his father had retired from the ministry, and the elder Flaglers moved to Bellevue to be near their son. Henry's older half-sister Ann Caroline, known as Carrie, came as well and was incorporated into the family circle. Both father and son became involved in the Sunday school department of the Bellevue Congregational Church, there being no local Presbyterian church. Despite her poor health, Mary cheerfully presided over the family home.

By this time the Flaglers had produced two daughters: Jennie Louise, born in 1855, and Carrie, who followed in 1858. Sadly, young Carrie passed away in 1861 at the age of three. Flagler's mother also died that same year, leaving elderly and infirm Isaac Flagler with the family for another fifteen years until his death in 1876.[14]

By the time of the outbreak of the Civil War, Henry Flagler had accumulated a small fortune of $50,000. He had risen to become a rich man, yet the hammer of adversity had already forged his essential character. As Flagler put it: "When I was young I was too poor to indulge in bad habits. By the time I was able to afford them, it had become a fixed habit to live simply."[15]

Flagler's manner of living might have been conservative, but his ambitions to advance in the business world continued to drive him. Having established himself as a successful, respected businessman with a family and place in the community, Flagler could have rested on his accomplishments. Yet, as he told James Morrow, "I was contented, but not satisfied. I have always been contented, but I have never been satisfied. To be dissatisfied means that you are ambitious to advance, to do things, not that you may be richer, but that you may be useful and take a part in the work of the world."[16]

During the war the Union's huge armies generated a vast demand for salt to use as a preservative for the pork and beef that fed soldiers in the field. Seeing an opportunity both to aid the cause of the Union and to enrich himself, Flagler relocated to Saginaw, Michigan, to engage in the mining and selling of salt. It was a totally new field and an educational experience. Flagler learned about the cutthroat nature of business in the booming, frantically competitive world of salt production and saw how some of his fellow manufacturers attempted to maintain prices and create some sort of order by organizing into a cooperative— lessons Flagler would soon apply to the petroleum industry. However, when the war ended and the armies disbanded, the government's need for salt abruptly plummeted, and most of Saginaw's salt manufacturers collapsed into bankruptcy. Flagler claimed that he not only lost his original $50,000 investment but also went $50,000 into debt.

Returning to Ohio, Flagler decided to relocate to Cleveland and resume business as a grain merchant. Some of his Harkness relatives lent him money, at 10 percent interest, to pay off his salt venture debts. In Cleveland Flagler discovered that his fellow grain trader John D. Rockefeller had also moved into a new commercial activity during the war: the refining of petroleum. Flagler's office was in the same downtown Cleveland building as Rockefeller's. "John D. and William Rockefeller and Samuel Andrews had started a small oil refinery in Cleveland on the side of a hill," said Flagler in explaining the origins of Standard Oil.[17]

For his part, Rockefeller remembered, "When the oil business was developing and we needed more help, I at once thought of Mr. Flagler as a possible partner, and made him an offer to come with us and give up his commission business." When Andrews and the Rockefellers needed additional capital to build a second refinery in 1867, Stephen V. Harkness, half-brother of Flagler's half-brother Dan, backed the deal by investing $100,000—evidently on the condition that Flagler join the partnership. Rockefeller accepted, later saying, "And so began that lifelong friendship which has never had a moment's interruption."[18] The addition of Henry Flagler to the company set the stage for the revolutionizing of the oil industry—indeed, of all industry.

The collaboration of John D. Rockefeller and Henry Flagler functioned seamlessly because the two were well matched. So much alike in their personalities were they that a description of one might aptly suit the other also. Rockefeller was nine years younger, having been born in 1839. Like Flagler he had started life in New York and moved to Ohio, where he began his career in business near the bottom, and like Flagler he burned with boundless ambition to better himself. When Flagler first knew him, Rockefeller had a thin, emotionless face, with light brown hair, a reddish moustache, and blue eyes. Of the two men Flagler had received the sterner tests in his early life, and perhaps for this reason Flagler possessed the more flint-like resolution. Both men were meticulous in advancing toward their goals. Nothing was ventured without first carefully analyzing the perils and possibilities of any enterprise. Both obsessed over efficiency, order, and the details of business.[19]

Rockefeller paid tribute to Flagler's daring spirit in a 1906 memoir: "The part played by one of my earliest partners, Mr. H. M. Flagler, was always an inspiration to me. He invariably wanted to go ahead and accomplish great projects of all kinds, he was always on the active side of every question, and to his wonderful energy is due much of the rapid progress of the company in the early days."[20]

Flagler took the lead in buying out competing refineries and in negotiating the lowest possible rates for transporting the partnership's products over the railroads. Rockefeller even gave Flagler credit for conceiving of the Standard Oil Trust: "I wish I'd had the brains to think of it."[21] Flagler attributed Standard's rise to a consistent policy of paying low dividends to its stockholders and plowing most of the profits back into expansion of the company—the same strategy of economy and investment that Flagler had employed in his personal career. He later recalled, "We worked night and day, making good oil as cheaply as possible and selling it for all we could get."[22]

Flagler and Rockefeller became best friends. They lived near each other on Euclid Avenue, rough-hewn Cleveland's most fashionable street, in similarly attractive new homes. Nearby, in the most pretentious house on the avenue, lived Amasa Stone, Ohio's most prominent railroad builder and a major stockholder in the Western Union Company and in Standard Oil. His son-in-law John Hay, Lincoln's wartime private secretary, also lived along the way. Hay would later write a novel, *The Bread Winners*, which he published anonymously to avoid criticism that might derail his aspirations for a political career. In the narrative, which received generally approving reviews, Hay described the "thin culture" of Euclid Avenue and the great labor union strikes of the 1870s. Amasa Stone would commit suicide in 1883 after the bloody collapse of one of his railroad bridges, and Hay took his place on Western Union's board of directors. At some point Flagler also became a director of Western Union, putting himself in a position to see how a monopoly operated.[23]

Looking back on his Euclid Avenue days, Rockefeller remembered, "For years and years this early partner and I worked shoulder to shoulder, our desks being in the same room. Mr. Flagler drew practically all our contracts. We both lived on Euclid Avenue, a few rods apart. We met and walked to the office together, walked home to luncheon, back again after luncheon, and home again at night. On these walks, when we were away from the office interruptions, we did our thinking, talking, and planning together."[24]

One day in the winter of 1874 Rockefeller burst into the Standard office crying and giving Flagler a hearty embrace. His wife Laura had just given birth to an infant son, the first boy after a line of girls. This little vignette from the birth of John D. Rockefeller Jr. is one of the very few times we see Rockefeller and Flagler openly and enthusiastically displaying emotion.[25] Interestingly, over the coming years while Flagler addressed his letters to Rockefeller with the friendly salutation "Dear John," he would not let down the barrier of formality that shielded his inner person from the world, even for his closest partner, and signed himself "H. M. Flagler," as he did to everyone.

While they were building the largest corporation in the world, the Rockefellers and Flaglers lived conventional middle-class lives. John D. was, if anything, the more conventional of the two, his life blending harmoniously with typical midwestern folkways. Rockefeller seldom read books and had limited interests outside of business affairs. At home in the evenings the family sometimes entertained themselves singing around the piano. However, Rockefeller did have two quite different passions that stirred his blood. The first was the Baptist Church, where Rockefeller dedicated himself to the Sunday school. Second, he loved fast horses, and Rockefeller maintained a large stable of fine trotters in the rear of his house. He reveled in the exhilaration of speeding along some suburban avenue in his carriage behind a handsome pair of matched ponies.[26]

Flagler, the Presbyterian, also owned horses and a carriage, but his interest in horseflesh was more restrained. The Flaglers were also stay-at-homes, and Flagler once said he had gone out only twice in the evenings in seventeen years. His wife Mary's poor health kept them tied to the house. Friends and family often stopped by and even spent weeks as guests to enliven the family hearth. During the evenings when they were alone, after dinner, by the light of a Standard Oil kerosene lamp, Flagler would read to Mary, or if she were too tired, he would retire to the adjoining room to read alone.[27]

Only Flagler's most intimate friends were aware of the important role that reading played in his life. In public Flagler appeared only as a highly focused businessman devoted to his commercial enterprises, but in private he lived a rich vicarious life through the printed page. He never took the grand tour of Europe. "If ever the Lord made a man who hated traveling, I am that man," Flagler told journalist Edwin Lefevre.[28] Thus books served as his means of escape from the prosaic here and now. The *Ocala Banner* editor Frank Harris, who became his friend in Florida, explained that there was a hidden side to Flagler's character: "Despite the fact that all his life Mr. Flagler was interested in commercial business affairs, he early developed a love for literature and there was a romantic and poetic side to his nature. . . . He was fond of literature, was possessed of a good memory, and was an interesting and entertaining conversationalist."[29]

His Palm Beach minister and friend George Ward testified: "He was one of the widest readers I ever knew. Many of the books I treasure most dearly are books he first discovered and read. He was catholic in his literary preferences, as in all else. We would read together philosophy, science, the humorous (He dearly loved 'David Harum'), and, above all, the Bible."[30]

Flagler's appreciation of Edward Noyes Westcott's 1898 novel *David Harum* is easy to understand, since Flagler must have seen much of himself and his tumultuous business career in the homespun tales of a fictional elderly New York country banker who imparted wisdom in colloquial dialect. The book's protagonist, Harum, elucidated the intricacies of the "horse trading" business and explained that the ethics of it were not quite the same as conventional morality. Harum's version of the Golden Rule went: "Do unto the other feller the way he'd like to do unto you, an' do it fust."

We know of just a few other books that Flagler read. In 1902 he sent two books to an acquaintance in Richmond, Virginia. One was *The Fortunes of Oliver Horn*, a collection of short stories about the life of an artist in New York City, and the other was *Stage-Coach and Tavern Days*, a book about cross-country travel in the time before the railroads. In that same year Flagler ordered a seventeen-volume set of Francis Parkman's epic history of the French exploration and settlement of America.[31] Parkman's highly romanticized sagas entertained thousands of readers in the United States who were hungry for an American history equal in dramatic scope to Walter Scott's novels of Europe's fabled past.

The testimony differs on Flagler's interest in history. Editor Harris wrote that Flagler could become caught up in the romance of historical tales, and journalist Lefevre elaborated: "Antiquity and the works of antiquity had for him a peculiar fascination. You must bear in mind also that there is a well-developed vein of sentiment in him."[32] However, his minister Ward said, "History he did not care for. You see it was the past. His only interest was in the present, and, above all, the future. He literally lived for the future." However, in 1903 Flagler did pay five dollars to become a member of the Florida Historical Society.[33]

During the 1870s Rockefeller and Flagler hurried America into the future, modernizing both the oil industry and the way in which corporate America organized itself. Every day presented new challenges to the leaders of Standard Oil, and their lives were swept along as months turned into years in the heady commotion of making petroleum products and accumulating money.

Rockefeller paid tribute to one of Flagler's attitudes about doing business that would continue when Flagler struck out on his own in Florida: "Another thing about Mr. Flagler, for which I think he deserves great credit, was that in the early days he felt that, when a refinery was to be put in, it should be different from the flimsy shacks which it was the custom to build. Everyone was so afraid that the oil would disappear and that the money expended in the buildings would be a loss that the meanest and cheapest buildings were erected for use as refineries. This was the sort of thing Mr. Flagler objected to. While he had to admit that it was possible the oil supply might fail and that the risks of the trade were great, he always felt that if we went into the oil business at all we should do the work as well as we knew how; that we should have the very best facilities; that everything should be solid and substantial; and that nothing should be left undone to produce the finest results."[34]

Along with Flagler's burgeoning accomplishments in the business world came an unexpected new development at home. On December 2, 1870, after a lapse of twelve years since the birth of the Flaglers' second child Carrie, thirty-six-year-old

Mary gave birth to a son. They named him Henry Harkness Flagler, but he would be forever known as Harry. Young Harry would grow up to be very much like his father, at least in outward demeanor, and by the time Harry arrived at his maturity it was clear that Flagler viewed him as heir to the estate. But that lay in the future.

The Flaglers celebrated another happy family occasion when daughter Jennie Louise married John Arthur Hinckley on the evening of April 26, 1876, in the First Presbyterian Church of Cleveland. Hinckley had begun his career as a cashier for a railroad headquartered in Chicago, but his father-in-law saw to it that he found employment within the Standard Oil empire.[35] Flagler evidently assured Hinckley's financial security by giving him a substantial number of shares in Standard Oil, as later became apparent in Hinckley's estate. Jennie Louise and John made their home in New York City.[36]

The lives of the remaining Flagler family circle—Mary, Henry, seven-year-old Harry, and Henry's half-sister Carrie—began a momentous transformation in the early winter of 1877 when they left the familiar neighborhood of Cleveland's Euclid Avenue to test the prospects of a new life in the throbbing commercial hub of New York City. Flagler had already begun the process of shifting his home base to New York in the preceding years as he was called there more frequently on Standard Oil business. New York was rapidly becoming the financial capital of the world, and as the largest business organization in the world, Standard needed to have its nerve center located there. The Flagler family lived at the Buckingham Hotel and later the Windsor Hotel, the two hotels where the Rockefellers also lived. Both residential hotels combined modern conveniences with opulent living accommodations, providing both an educational experience and a sort of apprenticeship for Flagler's future career as a hotel man in Florida.[37]

Meanwhile, a Connecticut-based contractor renovated a house at 685 Fifth Avenue as the Flaglers' new home. Typically, Henry fussed over every detail of the building process, urging his contractor to "crowd" the suppliers and workers into faster action.[38]

The Flaglers' home on Fifth Avenue stood in an area that was rapidly being transformed from farmland into a residential neighborhood, although much of the land remained vacant lots. Flagler's neighborhood stood to the north of the old city of New York and just south of the recently established Central Park. W. K. Vanderbilt's French Renaissance chateau rose just two blocks south of the Flagler's residence, across Fifth Avenue. The Vanderbilt mansion set an exultant standard for what was developing into an extravagant collection of architecturally diverse fashions: Greek Revival, Gothic, French Renaissance, Italian Renaissance, Norman, and others all stood shoulder to shoulder along the avenue. John D. Rockefeller's four-story brownstone—like Flagler's home, unremarkable in size or exterior architectural adornment—stood just one house away, across the cobblestones of Fifth Avenue at 4 West 54th Street. Rockefeller purchased it from Arabella Worsham, who had just married Collis P. Huntington, builder of the Central Pacific Railroad. She had elaborately refurnished the interiors, and years later the Rockefeller family would donate two of these artistic period rooms to the Museum of New York City. Since neither Rockefeller nor Flagler hosted lavish entertainments for New York high society, there was no need for anything more than large, comfortable homes for their families and gatherings of friends and business associates.

Both Flagler and Rockefeller owned fine trotting horses, with stables to accommodate them and an assortment of carriages. In fact, Flagler's stable and carriage house was reputed to be the largest in New York City. It turned out to be larger than he needed, so he sold it to his friend Rockefeller, who took a greater fancy to fast horseflesh. In exchange Rockefeller sold the stable beside his house to Flagler, for less than half of what he paid Flagler for the larger one. Harry Harkness Flagler later wrote: "Earlier father owned several fine trotting horses which he used to drive in Central Park, New York and also on Seventh Avenue above the Park, which in those days was a street where fast driving and racing was permitted."[39]

The elite of New York society did not recognize midwestern provincials such as Rockefeller and Flagler. When Ward McAllister, social counselor to William Astor's wife Caroline—the "Mrs. Astor" who set herself up as arbiter of polite society—drew up his "authorized, reliable, and the only correct list" of the charmed Four Hundred, it included only those whose families had held their money long enough for it to acquire a patina of gentility.[40] Anyone who had recently earned wealth or notoriety through labor in business, science, politics, or the arts simply did not measure up to the test of membership in the leisure class.

Many of the men living in Flagler's neighborhood, whose lives intertwined with his, also fell into the category of not-comfortably-reliable-enough for admission into Mrs. Astor's ballroom. Nearby stood the residences of Henry B. Plant, Jay Gould, Roswell P. Flower, Russell Sage, Chauncey Depew, Henry H. Rogers, and William Rockefeller.[41] Only Depew merited a place on McAllister's privileged roll. (Interestingly, McAllister may have condescended to visit Flagler's Hotel Ponce de Leon when it opened. William and Caroline's son John Jacob Astor IV and his bride honeymooned at the Ponce de Leon in 1891.)[42]

During their second year in New York, in the winter of 1878, both Henry and Mary Flagler suffered from deteriorating health. Henry was worn out from continuing struggles of Standard's shipping wars with the railroads, and Mary's doctors had at last diagnosed her condition as tuberculosis—usually a slow, cruel death sentence in those days. Leaving instructions with headquarters to keep him informed on current affairs, Flagler set off for Florida in late February accompanied by Mary and Harry. In Virginia the railroad changed from the standard gauge employed in most of the North to a wider gauge, necessitating either hoisting the car up and switching the wheels or simply changing trains. The various roads south of Virginia suffered from poor connections, so that travel from New York to Jacksonville required three or four days—and at that time Pullman cars or sleeping cars were unheard of in the South.[43] In other words, travel remained a primitive ordeal. In Jacksonville the Flaglers stayed at the newly built St. James, the premier hotel in the state, which stood on a rise overlooking the rough warehouses and docks crowding the banks of the St. Johns River.[44]

Flagler decided to try an excursion up river to pay a visit to America's storied Oldest City. He later summed up his first trip to St. Augustine in a few pithy sentences: "I did not form a very favorable first impression, I must admit. I came here from Jacksonville by way of the river and the Tocoi railway and got here just at night. The accommodation was very bad and most of the visitors here were consumptives. I didn't like it, and took the first train back to Jacksonville."[45]

It was hardly an auspicious introduction to St. Augustine. In fact, the Flaglers cut short their visit to Florida and hurried back to New York City, where by mid-March Henry returned to the boardroom wars at Standard Oil.

The next three years swept by quickly as Standard Oil matters concentrated Flagler's attention on an ever-changing series of conflicts, crises, and, ultimately, triumphs. Meanwhile, Mary's health continued to worsen. In the winter of 1880 Flagler considered a return trip to Florida, but Mary's doctors warned that the arduous trip south might do more harm than good by draining her dwindling resources. Mary's friends watched helplessly "with deepest anxiety the too painful evidences of her failing health."[46] Following another hard winter in New York, Mary passed away on May 18, 1881.[47] She was buried in a simple brick tomb in the fashionable Woodlawn Cemetery north of Manhattan, where many of New York's most distinguished deceased established permanent residence.

Flagler's spinster half-sister Carrie, long a resident member of the family circle, moved into the home on Fifth Avenue to help look after ten-year-old Harry. Jennie Louise, Harry's much beloved older married sister, lived nearby and also helped to fill the void left by Mary's death.[48]

Perhaps to divert his mind from grief, in the summer of 1881 Flagler rented a home on Long Island Sound in the community of Mamaroneck, a short commute from Manhattan on the New Haven Railroad. One writer described Mamaroneck as a village where "the air is that of refinement and retirement rather than display." The place Flagler rented had been given the name Satan's Toe decades earlier by Constance Fenimore Woolson's great uncle James Fenimore Cooper.

Flagler would call it Satanstoe or Lawn Beach. The following year Flagler purchased the rambling forty-room dark-wood house, which had broad porches and a square tower that afforded a panoramic view of the water and the Larchmont Yacht Club to the west. When Flagler acquired the thirty-two-acre estate, mud flats surrounded its higher ground, and at high tide it became an island. Over the years Flagler would add a causeway, seawall, and sand beach to refine the site. Visitors followed a winding drive through a small grove of trees, hay meadow, and landscaped lawns to the house. He hired the prestigious New York firm of Pottier and Stymus, which had refurbished some rooms in the White House for President Grant, to redecorate the interiors. On one side stood several outbuildings: a billiard room, a cottage for the gardener, a carriage house, and a stable for the horses. To amuse himself, Flagler built a quarter-mile track where he could exercise his trotters and a wharf and breakwater near which yachts could anchor.[49]

For the first time in his life Flagler spent significant money and time on a personal indulgence. A new dimension of thinking and acting seems to have been added to Flagler's habitually restrained manner of living.

He became a yachting enthusiast, joining the New York Yacht Club and the Larchmont Yacht Club. His first boat was probably a fifty-one-foot sloop called the *Eclipse*. Flagler may have gotten more enjoyment out of this small vessel than his later yachts, as he told a friend, "the nearer you are to the water the more fun you have."[50] His second craft was the noted racing schooner *Columbia*, which had won the Americas Cup in 1871. In coming years the *Columbia* would attract attention when it moored in summer resorts such as Shelter Island, Newport, and Martha's Vineyard. In the summer of 1885 Flagler's daughter Jennie Louise went on a sailing tour in the company of friends, including Martha Benedict, the daughter of her father's friend Elias C. Benedict—and, as it turned out, the sister of the man who would become Jennie Louise's second husband, Fred H. Benedict, after her divorce. Two years later Flagler wrote enthusiastically, "We had a delightful 'fourth,' and lovely weather on Long Island Sound."[51]

Back in Manhattan, Flagler encountered another dimension of conflict as governments joined private interests in attacking Standard Oil. In December of 1882 the Select Committee on Corners of the Senate held hearings at the Metropolitan Hotel to inquire into what had become a heated issue of public concern: the formation of large business combinations to control trade and competition. The era of giant corporations had arrived, and no company better exemplified the supposed evils of monopolies than Standard Oil. Rockefeller and Flagler, the two largest individual shareholders in Standard, appeared voluntarily before the committee on successive days, with Flagler going first. Samuel Dodd, who had

recently been hired as counsel to guide Standard Oil through the increasing en-
tanglements of government regulations and law suits, advised Flagler and Rockefeller that the committee lacked power to compel testimony into the affairs of a
private corporation—advice that neither Flagler nor Rockefeller really needed.

Reporters for the *New York Times* and the *New York Sun* gave similar accounts
of the inquiry, but the *Sun*'s correspondent supplied some graphic images to go
along with quotes from the verbal jousting. After a long series of questions about
the organization and financing of Standard Oil Trust—to which Flagler repeatedly replied, "I decline to answer"—the exchange between Senator Boyd and
Flagler heated up:

"Do you decline to answer because the question would tend to subject you to
prosecution?"

"I decline to answer."

"How am I to understand that answer?"

"You may understand it as you please. I consider the question improper and
beyond the scope of the committee's power."

Senators Boyd and Browning explained to the witness that they considered
the questions proper and elicited by Mr. Flagler's voluntary testimony given to
the committee. Mr. Dodd, the counsel for Mr. Flagler, instructed him that any
inquiries relating to personal transactions he was not bound to answer.

"I have but little," began Mr. Chittenden [lawyer for the committee].

"I do not know what you call little," observed Mr. Flagler.

"You had better be civil," retorted Mr. Chittenden.

"You had better keep your advice to yourself. I am not paying you for it," replied Mr. Flagler.

"And I am not paying you for robbing the community," replied Mr. Chittenden.

Mr. Flagler turned pale, got up from the witness chair, and walked away to
his counsel. Mr. Chittenden made a speech to the committee to the effect that
the Standard Oil Company controlled 90 per cent of the oil business, and it was
a question of whether that was a public curse or a public blessing. At the close
of Mr. Chittenden's speech, Mr. Dodd said he would advise Mr. Flagler not to
answer any questions because what Mr. Chittenden had referred to was not the
object of the committee.

Mr. Chittenden then asked a series of questions relative to the organization
of the different oil companies, all of which Mr. Flagler declined to answer. After
declining to answer twenty questions, he took up a newspaper and yawned behind it.

Flagler's attorney, Mr. Dodd, concluded the proceedings by stating that Standard Oil Trust owned stock in various refining companies, that it was an advisory

body only, and that during the time the trust had been in existence, the price of refined oil had dropped from twenty-five cents a gallon to seven cents a gallon.[52]

By the time the Senate committee held its hearings, Flagler had already begun slowly withdrawing from active day-to-day management of Standard Oil Corporation. His departure would be gradual and would not be complete for another two decades, but by this time Standard Oil amounted to a challenge that had been met—an endeavor that had been completed. The headaches of defending Standard Oil from sniping by politicians lacked the visceral appeal that the creation of Standard Oil had once offered. It had always been part of Henry Flagler's character to seek out new challenges. His Palm Beach pastor George Ward later summed it up: "He loved to overcome obstacles and once they were conquered they lost their charm."[53]

In 1882 Flagler took a step with portents for the future. He became one of nine board members of the Plant Investment Company, a railroad consortium established by one of his neighbors who lived just one block south on Fifth Avenue, Henry Bradley Plant. Although Connecticut-born, Plant had made his career rebuilding railroads in the South after the war. In the 1880s Plant began to extend his interests from Georgia southward into the Florida peninsula. He needed associates with deep pockets to help finance his undertakings. Another of Plant's partners, Henry Sanford, a former diplomat, had become owner of an extensive winter vegetable plantation in Central Florida. There can be no doubt that Flagler's attention had been drawn to Florida, but whether he entertained any ideas at the time about taking a more active, independent role in so remote a frontier region is unknown.

Flagler's personal life took a decided turn on June 5, 1883, when he married Ida Alice Shourds in a private ceremony at the residence of the bride's mother, Margaret Leek Shourds. Rev. O. H. Tiffany, a Methodist minister who had recently been transferred from Philadelphia to New York, performed the ceremony. This information was conveyed to the public in a tiny announcement in the *New York Times*.[54] The marriage of one of the wealthiest, most powerful men in America attracted no more open notice than that.

Ida Alice Shourds had lived all her life in humble anonymity. Her father, John H. Shourds, was described as a Methodist Episcopal minister of very limited income who died in 1873, leaving Alice, her mother, two brothers, and one sister to make do as best they could. By one account Margaret Shourds kept a country store in Tuckerton, New Jersey, a coastal town east of Philadelphia where many members of the Shourds family lived.[55] By the time of the 1880 census Alice and her mother were living in Manhattan. The census record lists no occupation for Alice.

In the late 1940s Sidney Walter Martin, a University of Georgia history profes-

The only surviving photograph of Ida Alice Flagler shows the hourglass figure of the former actress; details about her are elusive. By permission of Flagler College.

sor, attempted to unravel the mystery of Ida Alice Shourds when he researched his biography of Flagler. Martin was fortunate to be able to interview two elderly people who had known Henry Flagler.[56] He also talked with Anna Fremd Hadley, the daughter of William Fremd, whom Martin described as "one of Flagler's closest friends." Most important, Martin spent a week with seventy-eight-year-old Harry Harkness Flagler in his New York apartment. However, Martin later wrote that he got very little out of Harry Flagler. "I could never get him to commit one way or another upon the case of Ida Alice Shourds. . . . He would always shy away from that second marriage, and I am frank to admit that none of my information about that came from him."[57]

Most of what Martin wrote about Alice's early relationship with Flagler seems to have come from Anna Fremd Hadley. "This Mr. Fremd" Martin explained "had lived with Flagler since before his first wife died, and naturally was in a position to know many of the personal stories about his life. I took it as truth since it came from that source, and I have reason to believe that it is true."[58]

However, Martin was wrong in his assumptions about William Fremd. A young immigrant from Germany, Fremd began working as gardener for Flagler at Satanstoe in January 1883, almost two years after Mary Flagler's death, not before her death. Although Fremd would go on to be head gardener for Flagler's Palm Beach hotels, it is doubtful that he was "one of Flagler's closest friends." He may have been the person longest in the employ of Henry Flagler, but it is impossible to judge the reliability of his testimony about Flagler's personal life—which Martin received secondhand through Fremd's daughter Anna.[59] In his book *Florida's Flagler*, Martin established the portrait of Ida Alice Flagler that has persisted down to the present. He wrote that Alice had once been an aspiring actress of limited talent and then a practical nurse attending Mary Harkness Flagler during the time before her death. Martin described Ida Alice as a beautiful, self-centered, luxury-loving, and socially insecure woman who craved the attention and acceptance of polite society. He also wrote that she possessed a hot temper to go with her red hair.[60]

After the publication of Martin's book, Dr. Howard Lee of Memorial Presbyterian Church in St. Augustine contacted Harry Flagler about a biographical sketch of Henry M. Flagler that he was putting together, and Harry Flagler strongly denied Martin's characterization of Alice as a nurse for Mary. Dr. Lee then wrote to Martin to get his response, saying: "Mr. Harry Flagler states in his letter to me that 'this has not the slightest foundation in fact' and that she had not been known to anyone in their home until Henry Flagler made the announcement to the family of his intention to marry Ida Alice Shourds."[61]

Martin responded to Dr. Lee by saying, "I am not going to argue the point with Mr. Flagler. . . . I rather doubt that he knows much about it, since he was only a very young boy at the time, and from all I can gather, he spent a good bit of time with his aunt, Miss Carrie Flagler."[62] Harry was twelve years old when his father married Ida Alice.

In addition to his letter to Dr. Lee, Harry Flagler also composed a two-page typewritten critique of Martin's book as well as writing marginal notes in a copy of the book. He did not dispute that Alice had once been an actress, and this is attested to by several newspaper stories published years later during the time of her insanity, when reporters were attempting to uncover her personal history. However, regarding whether she was ever a nurse to the first Mrs. Flagler, Harry again declared: "No truth whatever in this statement. . . . We never heard the name of Ida Alice Shourds until my father told us he was to marry: we never saw her until, after his announcement, my sister and Aunt Carrie and I paid her the usual visit of courtesy."[63]

Harry disagreed with just about every other description Martin gave of Ida Alice. He doubted that his father married Ida Alice for her good looks. "I never got the impression that he thought she was beautiful; in fact she was rather plain of face, but had red hair of an attractive hue and a beautiful figure."[64]

Today only one photograph of Ida Alice is known to exist, and in it her face is set in a constricted expression—possibly because of a corset laced tight in hourglass form.

As to Ida Alice's ungovernable temper, Harry wrote, "I never saw any exhibition of violent temper on her part." On her supposed desire for acceptance into high society: "I never felt she wanted or tried for social recognition in New York." Regarding living in opulence at Satanstoe, Harry said, "There was no display of splendor and wealth. The home was comfortably and well furnished according to the taste of the day, but there was nothing ostentatious about it." He questioned the statement that she was "self-centered and interested in social standing," and he was puzzled by Martin's assertion that she wanted to be the center of attention at social affairs.[65]

Unfortunately, having demolished Martin's portrayal of Ida Alice Flagler, Harry Flagler did not leave any positive depiction of his own. Thus Ida Alice fades into obscurity.

Martin had written that Flagler was too absorbed with business to go on a honeymoon immediately after his wedding, and their honeymoon came when they journeyed to Florida six months later. Harry wrote that the idea of a delayed honeymoon six months later was absurd—and simply wrong: "They *did* go away on a wedding trip, I think to the middle West, of what length I cannot remember, but it was one of more than a few days—possibly of ten days to two weeks."[66]

Shortly after his marriage, Flagler transferred 1,060 shares of Standard Oil stock to his new wife. These would be valued at almost two million dollars today. Flagler and Rockefeller signed the certificate as treasurer and president of the company. By permission of Don Robbins and Flagler College.

Following Flagler's marriage, his sister Carrie moved out of the house on Fifth Avenue and into her own apartment in New York, leaving the newlyweds and Harry alone with just the house servants.[67]

During his marriage to Alice, Flagler evidently had little interaction with her family, although he and Alice were in touch with her two brothers, Stephen and Charles, and her surviving sister Martha. Alice's other sister, Mary, had passed away in 1864, leaving three sons, but their whereabouts were unknown since Mary's husband, Edward W. Taylor, unable to cope with the children, had given them up to a children's asylum, which apprenticed them to farm families out West. Henry found it necessary to give financial assistance to Stephen Shourds for a number of years, but Charles was doing quite well for himself as a businessman in Boston.[68]

When Henry Flagler married Ida Alice, he was fifty-three years old and she was a month short of thirty-five, an age difference not all that unusual in Victorian times. Unlike Flagler's first marriage into the wealthy Harkness family, which had made sound economic sense, his marriage to Alice is a mystery, but it fits into what was becoming a pattern in Flagler's life: an attempt by a middle-aged man to recapture his youth.

4

Coming to Florida,
1883–1885

Mr. Flagler dreamed dreams.
—Newspaper editor Frank Harris, May 1913

In December 1883 Henry and Alice Flagler traveled to Florida accompanied by John D. and Laura Rockefeller, taking trains southward to the end of the line in Jacksonville. At the station they were greeted by Dr. Andrew Anderson of St. Augustine.

When Flagler had first met Anderson is not known, but they may have been introduced sometime earlier in New York. Flagler once wrote that the mother of one of his best friends in New York had been a close friend of Clarissa Anderson.[1] In any case, Flagler and Anderson would soon become warm friends. As Flagler explained in a letter written a few years later: "Dr. Anderson is a particular friend of mine. He is a bachelor. A little slow to get acquainted with but a down right good fellow in every sense of the word." Years later James Ingraham, one of Flagler's chief lieutenants, would write, "Perhaps no one possessed Mr. Flagler's entire confidence and esteem to a greater extent than Dr. Anderson."[2] At the Jacksonville docks Anderson escorted the party on board the *Sylvan Glen*, one of the crack steamers of the DeBary-Baya "Fast Line." A single-stack side-wheeler, the *Sylvan Glen*, with its sleek battlecruiser hull, made the run upriver to Palatka and back to Jacksonville every day.

Evidently the New Yorkers stopped at Green Cove Springs along the way; perhaps they spent a night at the new, high-toned Magnolia Springs Hotel. We know the Rockefeller-Flagler party made a stopover somewhere along the St. Johns River because they took passage on the DeBary-Baya's other elite steamer, the *John Sylvester*, to complete their run upriver to Tocoi. From there they endured the slow chug to St. Augustine over the St. Johns Railroad.

That evening around the fireplace of Anderson's modest cottage, Rockefeller, Flagler, and Anderson were joined by George Lorillard, who came over from his villa on St. George Street for a conversation that likely touched upon St. Augustine's prospects for the future. Possibly the Rockefellers and Flaglers, or just the Flaglers, spent a while as Anderson's guests. The Flaglers would remain in St. Augustine for the better part of the season, perhaps because weather reports coming in from New York told of frigid, miserable storms in the North. Not until March did they return home.[3]

The next winter Flagler came back to St. Augustine. His impulse derived from the long-established motive of strangers who came there: a desire to recover his health. Years later Flagler's cousin John H. Flagler, president of the Cottonseed Oil Company, took credit for sending Henry Flagler to Florida. He explained that his cousin badly needed a rest, and only for this reason was John able to persuade him, reluctantly, to abandon his business in New York City to seek recuperation in Florida.[4]

Henry Flagler himself told a newspaper reporter that he decided to return "because my liver became disordered."[5] In his extended interview with Edwin Lefevre, given years after the fact, Flagler said in passing that he was accompanied by his daughter Jennie Louise, who was also not well.[6]

Flagler's doctor had advised him to go to St. Augustine, but Flagler's earlier experiences with the town's second-rate lodging and hotel food made him hesitant. However, a new resort hotel had just opened in St. Augustine, and Flagler decided he would risk another visit to the Oldest City. He wired ahead for reservations, but he was obliged to stay in Jacksonville, probably at the St. James, until February 27 since he could not get rooms in St. Augustine until then. On this visit the final leg of the trip would be easier because a new railroad had been built directly linking Jacksonville and St. Augustine.[7]

Flagler and Ida Alice (and perhaps Harry and Jennie Louise, too) stayed at the new San Marco Hotel, which stood just inland from Fort Marion and enjoyed views of the fort, the town, and the placid waters of Matanzas Bay. The San Marco had become St. Augustine's new landmark, its white walls and red trim visible from miles away looming over the rooftops of the town. It stood five stories tall, topped with three mansard-roofed towers. Built of longleaf pine harvested in the surrounding flatlands, it offered what was called "solidly fashionable" accommodation in a "homelike" atmosphere. Its interior walls and ceilings were painted in light colors, with no decorative cornice work or other fancy ornamentation and only commonplace framed pictures hanging on the walls. Typically awful Victorian furniture filled spaces around the parlor, with lace doilies on the backs of the chairs. Perhaps to keep guests from treating the hotel too much like home, its stationery included the printed notice: "Dogs not permitted in the hotel." It

NO. 12 HOTEL SAN MARCO, ST. AUGUSTINE, FLA.

The Hotel San Marco opened a new era in winter resort hotels in St. Augustine. By permission of Florida Historical Society.

embodied the simplicity of the typical seasonal resort hotel, except that it featured all the modern amenities save for electric lights.[8]

Flagler later told the *Jacksonville News-Herald* of his arrival in 1885:

I was surprised when I got here. There had been a wonderful change in the former state of things. Instead of the depressing accommodations of nine years before I found the San Marco, one of the most comfortable and best kept hotels in the world, and filled, too, not with consumptives, but that class of society one meets at the great watering places of Europe—men who go there to enjoy themselves and not for the benefit of their health. . . . I liked it well enough to stay. Well, I couldn't sit still all the time and I used daily to take walks down St. George Street, around the plaza to the club house [the Yacht Club], and back to the hotel again. I found that all the other gentlemen did the same thing, with the same apparent regularity, and then, as now, that was all there was to do for recreation and amusement. But I liked the place and the climate, and it occurred to me very strongly that some one with sufficient means ought to provide accommodations for that class of people who are not sick, but who come here to enjoy the climate, have plenty of money, but can find no satisfactory way of spending it.[9]

Flagler's description of his reaction to St. Augustine is important, for it gives the most succinct rationale for the genesis of his future career in Florida. (In this interview he skipped mention of his 1883–84 visit.)

On another occasion Flagler explained that he undertook his hotel business with the same careful planning he had employed at Standard Oil: "It does seem singular that I, a busy man, who never had time for leisure trips or rest, should build a hotel practically for rich people alone. But I thought at the time that somebody should consider and satisfy their wants as to a winter home in Florida. I found it necessary, or at least desirable, that I should, with my family, spend a part of the winter South, and I studied and investigated the question of climate and location as I would a purely business matter. I found that St. Augustine filled every requirement, and so I invested here and built these hotels."[10] Flagler's explanation of his decision to embark on a hotel building enterprise in St. Augustine stressed its business rationale.

His partner Rockefeller, looking back from the vantage of many years, similarly saw Flagler's efforts as a labor of creation, at least in part, much like building up Standard Oil: "It was to be expected of such a man that he should fulfill his destiny by working out some great problems at a time when most men want to retire to a comfortable life of ease. This would not appeal to my old friend. He undertook, single handed, the task of building up the East Coast of Florida. . . . This one man, by his own energy and capital, has opened up a vast stretch of country, so that the old inhabitants and the new settlers may have a market for their products. He has given work to thousands of these people. . . . Practically, this has been done after what most men would have considered a full business life, and a man of any other nationality situated as he was would have retired to enjoy the fruits of his labor."[11]

Rockefeller, of course, knew that Flagler's Florida project was more than just a business proposition. "Think of pouring out all that money on a whim," Rockefeller pondered. "But then Henry was always bold."[12] What Rockefeller called a "whim," Flagler's lieutenant James Ingraham termed a "hobby." "I am convinced," Ingraham wrote, "that he did not regard his Florida properties in the same light as he would have looked upon a commercial enterprise. Mr. Flagler erected the Ponce de Leon Hotel, which was the beginning of his work in Florida, as a hobby."[13]

Frank Harris, editor of the *Ocala Banner*, felt sure that Flagler's coming to Florida was an expression of a quixotic element of his personality that Flagler carefully concealed from public view. "He became so infatuated with the legends and traditions of the state that he conceived the idea of giving a partly classic, partly commercial, tinge to the visions that are supposed to have haunted Ponce de Leon and those Spanish cavaliers who crossed the ocean with him and found the savage aborigines in his romantic quest for the revivifying water of the Fountain of Youth. . . . Mr. Flagler dreamed dreams." To Harris it was not surprising that Flagler built hotels that looked like castles.[14]

Edwin Lefevre seconded Harris's assertions about Flagler's romantic fantasies, skipping lightly over the commercial elements: "And so this man of fifty-five, so rich that his most serious problem was how to invest his income, this man who had read a great deal and *had never traveled*, went to St. Augustine. It was the oldest city in the United States. He saw the old slave market, he saw the old *Spanish* fort; he saw the old city gates! He saw what you and I saw when we went to Pompeii or first gazed on the Pyramids! He saw palms—*palms*—this man who had grown up in Ohio amid wheat. St. Augustine was a magic pool; he steeped his soul in the glamour and romance of antiquity. It was to him, logically enough, the most interesting place he had ever seen, the most unusual, the most un-American. . . . This *Spanish* city was three-hundred years old; and the city of Cleveland, Ohio—why, he was as old as Cleveland, almost."[15]

Although Flagler stressed that his Florida enterprises were business propositions, he offered a couple of whimsical explanations for his midlife change of course. His first comment, to Lefevre, was no explanation at all: "Oh, it's just one of those things that just happen. I happened to be in St. Augustine and had some spare money."[16]

Flagler also had a story that he evidently told many times: "There once was a Deacon Brown who shockingly stood up for himself over his 'lordly drunkenness' disturbing the congregation. Upon being upbraided by his astonished pastor, Deacon Brown explained, 'The fact is that having served the Lord faithfully, constantly for forty-five years, I thought I would take a day off for myself.' And that's the way with me. Having devoted my head and heart and hands and time and thought and service to my business for a lifetime, I thought I would indulge in a little personal gratification."[17]

Another witticism he sometimes used went along the lines that a friend explained Flagler's coming to Florida by saying, "Flagler, I was asked the other day why you were building that hotel in St. Augustine, and you replied that you had been looking around for several years for a place to make a fool of yourself in and had at last selected St. Augustine as the spot."[18]

In the same vein, Flagler once wrote to a pastor, "When I commenced operations in Florida, my business friends at the North set me up (figuratively speaking) on a pedestal, on the base of which they engraved the words 'Pro bono publico,' and beneath this legend, in smaller letters but large enough to read, 'a——fool.'"[19]

Flagler's decision to come to Florida was influenced by a northerner, Franklin W. Smith, who had recently decided to locate in St. Augustine. His home facing

Franklin W. Smith's exotic Villa Zorayda helped inspire Flagler's creative imagination. By permission of Library of Congress.

King Street near Dr. Anderson's Markland definitely stood out—in striking contrast to the wooden houses flanking it, Smith's house was an outlandish vision of Oriental opulence. The "Villa Zorayda" had been named for a princess in Washington Irving's popular romance novel *Tales of the Alhambra*. It looked like a miniature Alhambra, with Moorish arches, columns, and crenulated ramparts around the top. At first glance the villa appeared to be made of stone, but a closer inspection revealed it to be a solid monolith of concrete. Above the door, in Arabic, was the inscription: "There is no conqueror but Allah." Inside was a glass-roofed courtyard where banana plants grew and vines climbed the columns. Luxurious divans were placed about—scattered with exotically embroidered pillows—and Oriental rugs covered the floor, while brass ornaments hung on the walls and exotic bric-a-brac from North Africa filled every niche. The house exemplified Victorian Exoticism carried to the ultimate extreme.[20]

Smith, who cultivated his gray sideburns into enormous muttonchops, presided over his palace like a Turkish pasha. Flagler would introduce Smith to a friend a few years later thus: "Mr. Smith is a Boston Yankee pure and unadulterated. He is the owner of the 'Lion' of St. Augustine to wit, 'the Moorish house,' pictures of which I believe I have shown you. I hope he won't 'talk you to death.'

He is a man of extensive information, has traveled all over the world and is very entertaining."[21]

Smith had been born in Boston in 1826 into the Puritan aristocracy of Beacon Hill. One of his ancestors had been a president of Harvard College. He and his older brother Benjamin operated a large hardware company that supplied goods to merchant shipping companies. Smith actively supported the Baptist Sunday School movement and helped to form the YMCA into a national organization. An abolitionist, he joined the new Republican Party in its earliest months. Just days before Lincoln's inauguration, Smith married Laura Bevan, the very attractive daughter of a wealthy Baltimore family, and the new Mrs. Smith wore her fresh wedding gown to the inaugural ball, attracting a great deal of attention. When the Civil War broke out, Smith and his brother put their company's services to work for the United States Navy.[22]

During the war Smith made himself notorious with the Navy Department and certain merchants in Boston for loudly criticizing what he said were corrupt practices, sometimes putting his accusations into the form of pamphlets. A U.S. Senate committee investigating fraud in navy contracts called upon him to testify. Two weeks after his testimony Smith and his brother Benjamin were arrested on the orders of Secretary of the Navy Gideon Welles, who was evidently convinced that the Smith brothers were sanctimonious hypocrites who themselves had defrauded the government. The arrests and subsequent trial of the Smiths in military court caused a national sensation. Massachusetts Senator Charles Sumner accused Welles of going after the Smiths simply because they had exposed

Franklin W. Smith epitomized the ideal nineteenth-century gentleman. He was a successful businessman, patriot, world traveler, and amateur scholar. From the collection of St. Augustine Historical Society Research Library.

incompetence and theft in the navy. For his part, Welles thought the Smiths were guilty and were benefiting from the protection of Republican politicians in Massachusetts, Baptist Church leaders, and Boston high society, which protected its own. Ultimately, Abraham Lincoln himself nullified the proceedings against the Smiths in one of his last acts before his assassination. Perhaps to show its support for Smith, Boston selected him to preside over the city's memorial service for Lincoln.[23]

Smith would later declare that fighting the criminal case had cost him much of his fortune in legal expenses and that the emotional strain had ruined his health. He turned his attention to world travel and became an amateur student of architecture. (A woman visitor to St. Augustine once recognized Smith as a man she had first met inside the burial chamber of the Great Pyramid of Giza.) When he returned from his journeys, he built elaborate scale models of the monumental structures he had visited. In about 1882, "seeking a more gentle climate," Smith visited St. Augustine, and in early 1883 he began construction of the Villa Zorayda. He had just witnessed construction of a concrete building in Switzerland, and he decided to revive the ancient use of concrete practiced by the Romans two thousand years earlier.[24]

Smith was an active member of the St. Augustine Yacht Club, and Flagler's decision to come to Florida may have been influenced by other men he met and fraternized with at the yacht club. Its membership adopted a clear self-description: "The St. Augustine Yacht Club was originally founded by gentlemen of leisure, members of the prominent Yacht and Social Clubs of the principal cities of the Country, for the purpose of securing during a winter residence in this State (while promoting the interests of yachting) a center for recreation and social enjoyment among themselves and with others of congenial tastes similarly situated who might join them."[25]

This unusual boldface declaration of social snobbery may not have been quite as fierce in practice as it sounds, for the club's membership seems to have included a diverse assemblage of notables, including the architect James Renwick. Local hotel man and retired sea captain E. E. Vaill was a founding member, as was Dr. Anderson, who became honorary "fleet surgeon." In 1885 the yachtsmen numbered 114 active associates, but members were allowed to add "guests" for a season. It is highly probable that Flagler came in as Anderson's guest.

Their clubhouse stood on piers just off the seawall north of the Plaza, allowing small sailboats to tie up on the adjacent dock. The building was described as "one story in height and not more than forty feet in length, its floor covered with matting and furniture of rattan, comfortable and cozy, but without the least effort for display or elegance." Without a kitchen or even a bar, the members used the club simply to talk, read newspapers, or play cards. When high tides flooded

Bay Street, the august members of the club were required to make an indecorous totter across wooden planks laid to traverse the puddles. Receptions sponsored by the club ranked as highlights of the winter, and their March gala marked the climax of the season.[26]

The 1885 gala took on a historical character dedicated to celebrating Juan Ponce de León's discovery of the Land of Flowers at Easter time in 1513. Dr. DeWitt Webb, president of the St. Augustine Historical Society, headed the celebration committee, while George R. Fairbanks, the leading scholar of Florida history, agreed to give the keynote oration honoring Florida's discoverer. (St. Augustine claimed Ponce for itself, although recent studies suggest that he landed much farther south down the peninsula.) The two days of festivities came off brilliantly. On Friday many businesses closed for the day, hanging from their eaves a variety of flags and banners representative of Florida's storied past. Local notables in the guise of conquistadors landed at the fort from a ship, the Catholic Church celebrated a mass, Fairbanks spoke, and afterward everyone in costume or representing a military unit, brass band, or fraternal organization paraded down Bay Street. The next day sailboats raced on the bay, and in the evening the army's Third Artillery Band filled the air around the bay front with music. Hundreds of dollars' worth of fireworks, launched from a barge anchored in the water, rent the darkness with brilliant flashes while the steamer *Seth Lowe* towed a procession of gaily lighted yachts in review before the seawall.[27]

On the eve of the celebration Henry Flagler was elected a regular member of the St. Augustine Yacht Club, and a few days later, upon the nomination of Philip Ammidown, whom Flagler described as "a capital good fellow," Flagler was honored as a life member. It was the first tangible indication that he had made a commitment to establish himself firmly in St. Augustine.[28]

In February, during the time leading up to the Ponce de Leon celebration, J. S. Cowdon, the regular local correspondent of the Jacksonville-based *Florida Times-Union*, had written, "It has crossed my mind that it would be a just thing to abandon the celebration, for what is the use to have people come here when they can't be cared for?" He noted that although St. Augustine had many hotels, any increase in visitation to the city would strain accommodations beyond their limits. "St. Augustine needs another hotel as large as the San Marco."[29]

At the time that this article appeared, Flagler was almost certainly thinking the same thing.

On March 22, 1885, Flagler paused to write a letter to Rockefeller on Hotel San Marco stationery. He commented on a stock transaction he had read about in the newspaper, hoped for better health for a friend, and wrote, "I trust that Mrs. Rockefeller and the children are getting through this *miserable* month without illness or discomfort. May I be very kindly remembered to them all." Nowhere did he broach the subject of his thinking on a hotel project. Instead he said, "My rheumatism hangs on with an uncomfortable grip, and as I should do nothing but quarrel with you all if were there, I have decided to remain until 1st here."[30]

So secretive about his plans was Flagler that he would not even hint at them to his closest friend. One crucial reason for this silence had to do with acquisition of the land needed for the hotel and its surrounding grounds. From his Standard Oil days, Flagler knew it was vital to control as much of the environment of operations as possible to achieve optimal results. If any hint of Flagler's interest in St. Augustine real estate leaked out, the cost of acquisitions would skyrocket. Hence the need for absolute silence.

Dr. Anderson was certainly among the first persons with whom Flagler talked about his plans to build a hotel in St. Augustine. Intriguingly, on February 2, 1885, two weeks before Flagler arrived in town, Anderson, Mrs. Frances Ball, Mrs. Lucinda House, and others presented a petition to the St. Augustine City Council to widen and straighten Tolomato Street, which formed the western boundary of the old colonial town and bordered Anderson's property on the east. This proposal may not have had anything to do with Flagler's decision to build his hotel—but on the other hand, it may indicate that Flagler and Anderson had already been quietly making plans. At the time Tolomato was little more than a footpath along the eastern bank of the Maria Sanchez marsh, and making it into a real street would be important for development of the properties that eventually became the site of Flagler's—and Smith's—hotels. Anderson hired Fort Marion's "keeper," Frederick Bruce, the only engineer in town, to survey the street line, and in April the city council agreed to the new street.[31]

At first Flagler's goals seem to have been much more modest than they eventually turned out to be. He approached Anderson and said he would build another big hotel like the San Marco if Anderson would sell him the easternmost portion of his property, which consisted mostly of the upper marshlands of Maria Sanchez Creek. Flagler made his proposal contingent upon purchase of both the Sunnyside House property and the Ball orange grove. The Sunnyside stood at the southeast corner of Anderson's estate. The Ball grove stood just on the north border of Anderson's property.

Anderson explained to Flagler that both the Sunnyside and Ball lands were available since they were owned by women seeking to sell out. However, he warned Flagler that his own property was under a cloud since the estates of his three deceased half sisters were contesting ownership of his Markland property, and this applied also to the Sunnyside lot. Flagler decided to move ahead anyway since the Sunnyside and Ball properties might not continue to be available for long.[32]

Soon after this Flagler and Anderson sat down with Franklin W. Smith in Smith's Villa Zorayda to discuss the hotel proposal. The site lay just across King

Street from Smith's place. Flagler wanted some St. Augustine gentlemen, primarily Anderson and Smith, to become on-the-ground administrators of the hotel-grove enterprise, since Flagler himself would not be in town most of the time, and he was still actively involved in Standard Oil. Flagler would invest $150,000, and Smith would put up $50,000 in the joint venture. Flagler also wanted Smith to oversee cultivation and sale of the orange crop from the Ball grove.[33]

In the late winter and spring Anderson and Smith, acting in the interest of Flagler and Smith, quietly began negotiations to purchase various properties around the site of Flagler's proposed hotel. Maintaining a veil of secrecy over their activities would prevent property owners from raising the asking prices for their land. Whenever Flagler found it necessary to telegraph Anderson, he used coded messages, a practice he had employed in earlier years at Standard Oil.[34]

Anderson bought the Sunnyside property from Mrs. Lucinda House on May 9, 1885, for $20,000. On the northwest corner of King and Tolomato streets, it had originally been a part of Anderson's Markland estate, but in the early 1870s his mother had sold the lot to Captain Thomas F. House, lately of the U.S. Army. A Vermonter, House had come to St. Augustine in 1868 seeking to restore his health. He immediately established himself as the town's prime building contractor, erecting Captain Vaill's St. Augustine Hotel, George Lorillard's villa, and other important buildings. He built Sunnyside in 1876 as a thirty-room boarding house and later transferred ownership to his wife. However, Thomas House was a dying man when his wife sold Sunnyside to Anderson. On May 12, three days after Anderson bought Sunnyside, he resold it to Henry Flagler for $20,000.[35]

At the same time that Flagler bought the Sunnyside House and lot from Dr. Anderson, Flagler also purchased the Ball estate. This fifteen-acre tract had belonged to the historian Buckingham Smith. Following Smith's death, Henry and Frances Ball, wealthy New Yorkers, had purchased it, and in 1874 they erected an impressive mansion in the middle of the grove of oranges. When Henry Ball passed away in 1878 Mrs. Ball began looking for a buyer and finally found a willing one in Flagler. Since the expansive "Ball Place" ran all the way west to the San Sebastian marshes, it gave Flagler access to the location where the town's new railroad station would soon be built. There was no public discussion of extending the railroad tracks to this location at the time, but it is virtually certain that Flagler and others had already thought of this logical next step.[36]

At the same time Flagler purchased the new skating rink on the south side of King Street across from the Anderson lands. It stood partly on stilts over the Maria Sanchez marshes. This large arena had been built to satisfy the local public's interest in roller-skating, a newfangled mania at the time, but it also served as a place for dances and other large gatherings. Thanks to Flagler, however, its operating life would be short.[37]

Adding to Flagler's initial haul of properties, he acquired three small lots on south Tolomato Street belonging to Dr. Alba, John Britt, and Frank Andreu. These lots, too, extended into the Maria Sanchez marshes.[38]

All this activity alerted the press to what had been going on, and on May 23 a story appeared in the *St. Johns Weekly* trumpeting a "boom era" for the Oldest City. The story declared that Smith and Flagler, agents of the "Money God," had bestowed $100,000 on sundry property owners in the vicinity of the Maria Sanchez marshes. The story gave foremost credit for this effort to enhance St. Augustine to the well-known Smith, not the stranger Flagler. Three days earlier the *Times-Union* in Jacksonville had published a story in a similar vein, adding that a "million dollar" hotel larger than the San Marco would be built. It also attributed the endeavor to "a company of Northern capitalists," led by Smith.[39]

Flagler took another man into his confidence at an early point: Osborn Dunlap Seavey, manager of the San Marco Hotel, where Flagler stayed. Seavey enjoyed a reputation as one of the most knowledgeable and experienced resort hotel managers in the country.

Described as "a thorough hotel man," Osborn Dunlap Seavey had literally been born in a hotel—the Central Hotel in Unity, Maine, where his father was manager. As he grew up, Seavey learned the hotel business from the ground up, from back in the kitchen to up front at the reception desk. Eventually he became manager of a small hotel and then took a demotion to the position of night clerk in order to join the staff of a large metropolitan hotel on Broadway in New York City. An old friend wrote that he first met "Os" Osborn at this hotel in 1873, standing behind the counter looking as though he owned the place. "He was a sort of revelation to me, for he had the diamond pin, the copyrighted smile, and all the customary *bonhomie* of the 'upper ten' hotel clerks of that period."[40]

Having served his internship in a big city hotel, Seavey went to Boston to manage the Brunswick Hotel, and this move brought him under the eye of Isaac Cruft, a Boston-based international merchant who had made a fortune importing tea from China. Cruft hired Seavey to upgrade the Maplewood Hotel in the summer mountain resort colony of Bethlehem, New Hampshire.

In 1881 Cruft and Seavey ventured to Green Cove Springs, Florida, on a scouting expedition, looking for a spot to erect a winter resort hotel. They liked this idyllic setting under spreading live oak trees on the bank of the St. Johns River and decided to build. The resulting Magnolia Hotel ranked second only to the St. James in Jacksonville in the grandness of Florida accommodations. At the time the St. Johns River provided the main transportation artery into the interior of East Florida, with flotillas of steamboats taking travelers as far south as Sanford in Central Florida and as far inland as Silver Springs, where excursionists could behold one of the great wonders of the natural world. Green Cove Springs enjoyed boom times. Seavey later recalled, "I have stood on the dock on arrival of steamers telling would-be guests not to get off as there were no rooms."[41] Within a few years the railroads of Henry Plant and Henry Flagler would end the St. Johns River's days as the premier transportation lifeline of East Florida and would turn Green Cove Springs into a backwater community.

When Flagler came to stay at the Hotel San Marco in St. Augustine, Seavey was dividing his time between St. Augustine and Green Cove Springs, managing both of Cruft's hotels. Flagler caught Seavey at the apex of his powers. A flattering description of him from this period of his life epitomizes the way Seavey was appreciated by his contemporaries: "To his experience and business judgment are added good taste and all the qualities that make up the gentleman and the popular man. He has a high appreciation of the humorous and a vein of his own which is indescribable. In height Mr. Seavey is about five feet seven or eight inches, is of a complexion approaching the blonde, has bluish gray eyes, wears a full beard, and is a little inclined to be stout. His address is the finest possible, and his dress is always stylish and in the very best taste."[42]

Flagler also brought the builders of Cruft's San Marco into his orbit. They were James McGuire and Joseph McDonald: an irascible Irishman and a dour Scotsman.

James Alexander McGuire had been born in St. John, New Brunswick, Canada, in 1838, the second of eleven children in a family of Irish Catholic immigrants. As a youngster he traveled to New York City and found work in the shipyards building wooden ships. At night he took advantage of free classes offered at Cooper Union to develop his technical skills in practical engineering. A few years later in the seafaring town of Mystic, Connecticut, he met Joseph McDonald.[43]

Joseph Albert McDonald was born in the maritime province of Prince Edward Island, Canada, in 1842. His only formal education came in the local public schools, and like McGuire, he grew up learning the skills of a ship carpenter. As a young man searching for work, he moved to Connecticut, and there he encountered James McGuire.[44]

In 1880 McGuire went to Green Cove Springs to build an Episcopal church and took McDonald with him as his foreman. It was in Green Cove that Cruft and Seavey discovered McGuire and McDonald (now organized as partners) and hired them to build the Magnolia Hotel and, immediately after that, the San Marco.

McGuire's and McDonald's chilly northern qualities never seem to have thawed out completely, even in the South. As a young man McDonald wore a handlebar mustache too large for his slim face and was once described as "a very austere man, not overly good-looking, but very busy."[45] McGuire was "a man of rugged health and rather taciturn disposition, but he was recognized as a man of unusual ability." McDonald married happily and fathered three children, but McGuire remained a lifelong bachelor. McGuire presented a direct, no-nonsense façade to the world, but one of his nephews remembered, "He was jolly and witty with his friends."[46]

Flagler appreciated genius in others and recruited such men into his ventures. In this case he simply hired Cruft's highly successful team away from him. McGuire & McDonald would build Flagler's resort hotel, while Seavey acted as expert advisor on practical hotel arrangements.

Flagler charged Seavey with the task of working with the designers and builders in planning the hotel. His knowledge and practical experience would prove invaluable in working with Flagler's architects and builders in the design of the Hotel Ponce de Leon. Seavey was given particular credit for originating the layout and equipping of the kitchen and culinary departments and for selecting the "greater part" of the hotel's furniture. When the time came to staff the hotel, Seavey assumed responsibility for hiring all the various department heads and seeing that they filled their divisions with reliable, expert employees.[47] Once the hotel was complete, Seavey would preside over the establishment as manager.

For nearly the next three decades the lives of these men would be inextricably linked to Flagler's Florida enterprises. A great deal of Flagler's success as a hotel man can be attributed to the knowledge and acumen of these men.

At the same time that Flagler stayed at the San Marco, pondering the idea of putting down roots in Florida, another famous man, Thomas Alva Edison, also stopped in at the hotel on an expedition in search of a place for a winter home. Although he would return to St. Augustine in 1886, Edison decided to make his Florida residence in the far-off southwestern reaches of the state at a tiny settlement called Fort Meyers.[48]

Whether Edison and Flagler ever met we do not know, but in 1886 Theodore H. Whitney, son of the St. Augustine promoter John F. Whitney, wrote to Edison saying Flagler planned to visit Edison in his New Jersey headquarters to see about ordering an electric plant for the Hotel Ponce de Leon. The younger Whitney, who had worked with Edison for a while after Whitney's father introduced them in 1878, now hoped to be put in charge of installing Edison's system in Flagler's new hotel; he would be disappointed in that quest.[49]

5

Architects Carrère
and Hastings, 1885

We've got a million dollar hotel to build.

—Tom Hastings to John Carrère, 1885

Having decided to build a hotel in St. Augustine, Flagler returned from New York in May 1885 to meet with Dr. Anderson and Franklin W. Smith, attend to the details of his property acquisitions, and sign the attendant legal documents. He brought with him an expert real estate man from New York to evaluate the properties he had purchased and those he intended to buy. He also brought twenty-five-year-old Thomas Hastings. Flagler meant for this young man to supply the creative spark for the design of his hotel. The trio of northerners stayed at Markland as the guests of Dr. Anderson while they did their investigations and discussed their plans for the future.[1]

Thomas Hastings was the son of Flagler's close friend and former pastor Thomas S. Hastings. Flagler and his family worshiped at the church where Hastings had been pastor, West Presbyterian Church on 42nd Street, a dozen blocks south of the Flagler home. Each Sabbath more than a thousand worshipers filled its large auditorium. West Presbyterian was known as the "brokers' church" or the "millionaires' church." Its membership included Jay Gould, Russell Sage, and Elias Cornelius Benedict.

The church stood just off Fifth Avenue overlooking Bryant Park, named after the poet William Cullen Bryant. The impressive West Presbyterian building had been constructed in the popular red-brick Gothic Revival style with square towers and a slender steeple. At the east end of the park, facing Fifth Avenue, loomed the massive fortress-like walls of the Croton Reservoir, the source of water for lower Manhattan. The supervising engineer for construction of the reservoir had been young James Renwick, who in his subsequent career as architect followed the Gothic revival style in designing the Smithsonian Institution's "Castle" head-quarters on the National Mall in Washington D.C. and in his great St. Patrick's Cathedral on New York City's Fifth Avenue.

Thomas Hastings's father, Thomas S. Hastings, was a descendent of one of the Puritan founding families of Massachusetts. For the first quarter century of West Presbyterian Church's existence, the elder Hastings had ministered as its pastor, and then in 1881 Hastings became a professor of homiletics at Union Theological Seminary. He soon rose to become the seminary's president. The Reverend Doctor Hastings's career placed him in successive positions of eminent respectability and prestige that partly counted for money in the calculus of social standing. Beyond that, he had married into a family from the old Manhattan Dutch aristocracy, which also opened doors to the higher echelons of New York society.[2]

Years later Harry Harkness Flagler would describe Dr. Thomas S. Hastings as "a very old friend of my father's."[3] Between 1895 and 1902 Flagler would hold a position on the board of Union Theological Seminary (and was presumably a financial supporter), although he was an inactive member.[4] Flagler's friendship with Hastings would have tremendous impact on Flagler's future and on that of Hastings's son.

Young Thomas Hastings was born in 1860, the fourth of five children. A delicate child, he grew up in a family of intellectuals and musically talented relatives. (Hastings's grandfather, another Thomas Hastings, an albino, had been a prodigious composer of hymns, including the American version of Rock of Ages.) As a child Thomas evinced a gift for drawing. "He drew insistently from an early age, constituting himself something of a nuisance as he decorated pages of books and other surfaces not intended to be used as drawing paper."[5] His parents showed sensitivity to his talents, and after he had spent a while at a college prep school, at age seventeen Thomas was apprenticed to Herter Brothers, the interior decorating firm that had furnished the Hastings residence. Christian Herter's talents as an interior decorator had won him commissions from many of the city's well-to-do families. The architect attached to Herter's firm, Charles Atwood, introduced Hastings to the discipline of the drafting table. One of Hastings's co-workers recalled him as "all electricity, on the nervous *qui vive*, enjoying every minute and constantly laughing."[6]

Hastings joined a "sketch club" of architects who met biweekly to amuse themselves by hashing over design problems. Then Herter Brothers gave Hastings his first real assignment: devising the interior decoration for one room of the Seventh Regiment Armory.[7] The red-brick Gothic structure on Park Avenue served as headquarters for the "Silk Stocking Regiment" and was erected by contributions from high society New Yorkers. In addition to Herter Brothers, other interior decorating firms received invitations to display their talents by

Busts of Thomas Hastings (*left*) and his partner John Carrère occupy niches facing each other in the foyer of the New York Public Library, their firm's most famous architectural creation. Author's photos.

decorating various rooms. The prize assignment, the large Veterans Room, went to Louis C. Tiffany and his soon-to-be company, Associated Artists. Pottier and Stymus, the city's leading furniture and decorating company, also took a hand in adding ornaments. Within a decade Hastings, Tiffany, and Pottier and Stymus would once again combine their talents in the creation of the Hotel Ponce de Leon.

With the encouragement of his friends at Herter Brothers, Hastings ventured off to the top of the architectural world: the École des Beaux Arts in Paris, the preeminent school of architecture. Thomas Hastings arrived in Paris in 1880 at a time when France's capital basked in glory as the most beautiful city in the world. Emperor Napoleon III and his chief engineer Georges Haussmann had transformed the grimy medieval city into a modern municipality of wide boulevards, convenient railroad stations, green park spaces, tastefully designed building façades, and efficient sanitary sewers.

Following some preliminary study with a pair of veteran French architects, Hastings gained acceptance into the École in August. At the school students sat through lectures on history, art, architectural theory, and construction, but the serious work of learning was done in the *ateliers*, or studios, of master architects, who guided their charges through intensively competitive monthly projects that forced students to come up with solutions to problems they would be likely to encounter in their future careers. Hastings chose the studio of Jules André, a popular master who had mentored a number of American students.

The École taught that architecture is the science of solving problems. True to the modern French spirit, it stressed order and efficiency. The school maintained the classical Greek ideal that mathematically correct proportions and symmetry are inherently pleasing to human sensibilities. Ornamental Renaissance French and Italian styles embellished both exterior and interior surfaces, but underneath this veneer of adornment lay a foundation of logical order. The École abhorred German Gothic architecture, with its deliberate imperfections and its foundations in the Dark Ages. Romanesque buildings also belonged in the Middle Ages, not the modern world. Likewise, the English naturalistic sensibilities of the John Ruskin school were viewed as disconcertingly untidy, although the French did pay homage to Nature as the supreme architect.[8]

During his three years at the École Tom Hastings did not shine as an outstanding talent. But he learned to speak French well enough (with casual Anglo-Saxon indifference to the Gallic idea that nouns have gender) and thrived in the challenging environment, emerging in 1883 a confirmed lover of all things French.[9]

Hastings's years of study at the École des Beaux Arts overlapped those of two other men destined to play roles in his career. In the spring of 1882 Hastings welcomed another American to share his apartment on the Rue Saint-Michel—Bernard Maybeck. His new compatriot, a couple of years younger, possessed a whimsical smile and a flair for unconventional apparel. "Ben" Maybeck had come to Paris to work as an artisan in the studio affiliated with Pottier and Stymus, where his father headed the woodcarving department. Pottier and Stymus occupied a leading place in American woodworking, furniture making, and interior decorating. Earlier, while apprenticed as an office boy in the New York factory of Pottier and Stymus, the young Maybeck found the prospect of laboring as a craftsman for the rest of his life unappealing and raised his sights to becoming an architect. While a student at the École, Maybeck haunted the medieval cathedrals of Paris seeking spiritual communion with the humble stone carvers and masons who had erected these great gray monuments to the mystical presence of the living God.[10]

The other student Hastings encountered in Paris was John Carrère. They crossed paths only once while in Paris, because the more cosmopolitan Carrère attached himself to a different studio from Hastings, apart from the American students. Hastings paid no attention to Carrère until Carrère requested a meeting to discuss an architectural competition being held in New York. "I had seen him quite frequently," explained Hastings, "but had always taken him to be a Frenchman. He both looked and spoke like a Frenchman."[11]

John Merven Carrère had been born in Rio de Janeiro, Brazil, in 1858, making him two years older than Hastings. His father John Merven Carrère Sr. came from a prominent Baltimore family. The elder Carrère had lived in Brazil while managing trade accounts in coffee and had married a Brazilian woman, Anna Louisa Maxwell, whose ancestors had immigrated from Scotland and Portugal. As a boy Carrère grew up in an internationally diverse culture. He spoke English and French fluently and probably knew German and Portuguese as well. His family sent him to boarding school in Switzerland, and from there he progressed to the École des Beaux Arts. Like Hastings, he did not stand out as a prize-winning scholar, but he departed from the École in 1882, a year earlier than Hastings, with full honors—except for a degree, which the school granted only to French citizens.[12]

The paths of Carrère and Hastings came together again unexpectedly in New York City when they both secured positions as draftsmen for the firm of McKim, Mead and White, the company that was rapidly becoming famous for leading an "American Renaissance" in architecture. They joined the firm in October 1883.[13] Both Carrère and Hastings—but especially Hastings—possessed the pedigrees and social connections requisite for employment in a company that dealt exclusively with an elite clientele of wealth and elevated class status.

Charles Follen McKim, himself a Beaux Arts graduate, had established his firm in 1872. Prior to this he had been an associate of the country's leading architect Henry Hobson Richardson, a specialist in Romanesque style. As the firm's leading partner, McKim welcomed Hastings into the fold, and they would become fast personal friends for life.[14]

William Rutherford Mead had been McKim's original partner when the firm was established, bringing engineering skills to the company. His sister Elinor was married to the writer William Dean Howells, whose novel *The Rise of Silas Lapham* examined the transformation American manners and mores in a country rapidly moving from a rural society into an urban society—and sometimes into a social order of great wealth.

Stanford White, another former associate of H. H. Richardson, joined the partnership in 1877. White was responsible for managing the office and coordinating the activities of the staff. The son of a Shakespearian scholar, White led a life outside his professional career that would become the stuff of tabloid sensation. He enjoyed the company of Bohemian artists, intellectuals, bon vivants, and showgirls. His escapades made him notorious—and would eventually cause his demise. Yet Thomas Hastings, a thoroughly decent person of Puritan ancestry, counted White as one of his closest friends.

One assignment from McKim, Mead and White took Carrère to his father's hometown of Baltimore to work with the client and contractors on construction of the Ross Winans mansion.[15] Hastings remained behind in the New York office refining plans for the same house. Thus from the beginning of their association, Carrère and Hastings had already fallen into a pattern they would maintain for the rest of their collaboration: Carrère handling people, practical issues, and business affairs, while Hastings remained in the studio toiling with calipers, ruler, pencil, and drafting paper.

Working together on the Winans house gave Carrère and Hastings the idea of forming a separate partnership of their own. Hastings saw that Carrère possessed executive and practical abilities that would be necessary in running a business. Thus late in 1884 they formed a partnership based on just a handshake. Since Carrère ranked first in seniority, being twenty-six years old to Hastings's twenty-four, the firm's name became Carrère and Hastings.

With the blessings of their employers, they set up shop in two small rented rooms at the back of the McKim, Mead and White headquarters at 57 Broadway in lower Manhattan. At first they struggled to find clients. McKim, Mead and White helped them pay the rent by hiring them to do some drafting work.

Hastings and Carrère possessed strengths that overlapped and complemented each other. Hastings was the more artistically inclined of the two. An early photograph shows him as a refined young artist: lean faced, dark hair carefully parted in the middle, pince-nez glasses, stylishly luxuriant mustache, and full lips over a high starched collar and silk bow tie. His 1932 *Dictionary of American Biography* entry, written shortly after his death, describes him as being of medium height, energetic, and carrying himself with military bearing.[16]

David Gray, whose play *The Best People* enjoyed a long run on Broadway in the mid-1920s, wrote a short laudatory memorial biography of Hastings shortly following the architect's death. In it he said of Hastings: "Yet his personality was curiously perplexing. The man and the artist seemed inexplicably detached one from the other. So to speak, one never met them both at the same time. . . . As artist he was single-purposed, concentrated, intense, withdrawn into himself, obeying the mystic guidance of his genius with an almost ruthless energy and devotion. As a man in his human relations his qualities were those of a lovable child, generous, affectionate, sunny-natured."[17]

He enjoyed laboring for long hours over a drafting board, spinning out fanciful designs for new projects. In fact, it was joked that his partner Carrère had to purloin drawings from Hastings's drafting table to terminate endless adjustments to the plans. "With every piece of work in which Hastings became absorbed, there came a point at which on one pretext or another the drawing had to be physically removed from his table or he would have restudied indefinitely."[18]

After hours of effort, his drawings became refined "hard line" designs with specific details. When these had matured to Hastings's satisfaction, he consulted with Carrère, made further alterations, and then handed them on to his staff.

Later on, after Carrère and Hastings had established themselves, John Carrère spent most of his time managing the office, supervising the staff, dealing with local government officials, and negotiating with clients and contractors. Interestingly for a man whose job involved so much personal interaction, Carrère was famous for his brusque, no-nonsense persona, spiked with a tendency to lose his temper. A heavy-set, olive-skinned man, Carrère cut an imposing figure. Donn Barber, a fellow architect, offered this assessment of the colorful Brazilian American: "He possessed a high order of intelligence, a well organized mentality and sterling integrity which made him a good executive. He was at the same time childlike in his capacity for enthusiasm. He was saturated with the spirit of devotion and sincerity to his art."[19]

The newly minted firm of Carrère and Hastings did not have to wait long before Henry M. Flagler launched their company upon a meteoric rise. Several other members of West Presbyterian Church would follow Flagler as clients of Carrère and Hastings in later years. Carrère gave this account of receiving the news that Flagler had hired them:

> I remember how I felt when Mr. Hastings and myself secured our first job, which was a hotel. One afternoon about twenty-three years ago we and our sole assistant, an office boy, were sitting in our office waiting for something to turn up, when Mr. Hastings received a note from Mr. Henry M. Flagler asking him to go around to Mr. Flagler's office. Mr. Hastings was gone about an hour. I meanwhile holding the fort with our only employee. As Mr. Hastings had done some small things for Mr. Flagler, I supposed that he had been sent for in connection with these.
>
> Suddenly I heard a great commotion in the hall. It seemed to me as if every door was being slammed, and the first thing I knew Mr. Hastings had opened and slammed our door and was standing in the office and I saw the New York directory flying through the air at my head. I just managed to dodge that when I had to duck again to allow a T-square that was flying in my direction to pass without hitting me. Then I began to pick up things from my desk and throw them at my partner, until above the din and the confusion I heard Mr. Hastings shout, "We are going to Florida! We've got a million dollar hotel to build there!" Then we simply proceeded to smash everything we could lay hands on, our office boy ably assisting us. Of course, we didn't know anything about hotels.[20]

Thomas Hastings drew this rendering of the Flagler monument that would be erected in Woodlawn Cemetery. The monument was demolished after the bodies of Mary Harkness Flagler and Jennie Louise Flagler Benedict were removed from Woodlawn and placed in the mausoleum at Memorial Church in St. Augustine. "Monument," *American Architect and Building News*, November 25, 1882, 255.

The "small things" Hastings had previously done for Flagler consisted of two undertakings: he designed a library for Flagler's new country home at Mamaroneck, but probably before this, while still living in Paris, Hastings conceived the plan for a Flagler monument at Woodlawn Cemetery. Hastings's drawing of the memorial appeared in the November 25, 1882, issue of *American Architect* and had appeared in a French journal prior to that. It replaced the small marker originally erected at Mary's grave and was intended to be the central monument around which Flagler's whole family would someday be interred.[21]

A contemporary description captures the impressive scale of the memorial column: "Probably the most costly, as it is the most elaborate Woodlawn monument, is that belonging to Henry M. Flagler, the Standard-Oil millionaire. It is a massive granite cylinder, surmounted by a dome, upon the apex of which is a cross, standing upon a circular granite platform. It is covered in nearly every part with the most delicate carvings and traceries. On opposite sides of the shaft are found sunken panels, framed with light columns, and arched over with semicircular porticoes of carved granite. Scripture texts are carved on these panels, and the name Flagler is in raised letters upon the base of the shaft. The monument stands on an eminence that makes it the most conspicuous object in this part of the cemetery."[22]

For a man who valued his privacy so highly, this elaborate display represents something of an enigma; but then Flagler was also a man who sought permanence, and this stone memorial may have been his way of ensuring that the memory of Henry Flagler would persist after his death. As it turned out, Flagler would later remove the column and erect even grander memorials to his family and himself in St. Augustine.

When Flagler first approached Hastings, he explained that he wanted the young architect's help creating a resort hotel in Florida. Flagler expected only that Hastings and Carrère would draw a "pretty picture" of the building and that McGuire and McDonald would then undertake actual planning and construction of the hotel.[23]

However, Hastings evidently proposed that he and his partner undertake the whole design of the building, and he doubtless rejected the idea that simply drawing an elevation of the façade constituted a good use of his talents. Hastings knew that the front elevation of a building cannot be separated from the whole of a structure. He would later write: "It is, generally speaking, amateurish to use the perspective for any other purpose than to explain a building to a layman."[24]

Hastings proposed undertaking the whole process of architectural creation. Flagler probably soon recognized in Hastings the same impatience with anything less than the comprehensive that characterized Flagler's own work. There was much more to Hastings than a talent for creating gossamer dreams.

This preliminary drawing of the Hotel Ponce de Leon from the summer of 1885 is probably the image that Flagler first requested from Hastings. It shows that Hastings arrived at the basic concept of the hotel at a very early date. By permission of Avery Architectural and Fine Arts Collection, Columbia University.

Flagler's initial interaction with Hastings may have gone something like the scenario described by Henry Clay Frick's private secretary when Hastings was designing Frick's palatial townhouse on Fifth Avenue, several blocks north of Henry Flagler's home. Frick's subordinate wrote: "I spent a delightful hour with Mr. Hastings and caught much of his enthusiasm. He is a wonderful combination of idealism and practicality—a personified blend of the artistic and the useful. At first I thought him governed solely by instinct, his feelings for the beauties of his art was so spontaneous, but soon I discovered that every detail of his conception had a scientific basis and that the placing of even a window ledge must conform to the laws of light and shade."[25]

Within a short period of time Flagler had decided to hire Carrère and Hastings as architects for his hotel with comprehensive powers that included such things as letting subcontracts and watching over shipments of materials south. The young pair agreed not to undertake any other employment until the hotel was completed.

Carrère's friend and former employer William Mead later recalled fearing at the time that the two young men might have bitten off more than they could chew. "The opportunity seemed to me a dangerous one for men just starting in their profession."[26] Hastings's biographer David Gray thought the same thing of Henry Flagler: "With characteristic intrepidity he entrusted the building of the first of his St. Augustine hotels to his friend's son, a highly educated but wholly untried young architect."[27]

Of course, almost two decades earlier Flagler had formed a partnership in the oil refining business with the twenty-eight-year-old youngster John D. Rockefeller.

Years later, in 1910, Flagler would write John Carrère a short letter briefly reminiscing on the beginning of their association: "To me, it is most gratifying that you and Tom have had such a wonderful successful career in your profession, and it is also very gratifying to feel that through accident I may have had some small part in giving you both the start you so richly deserved." Thomas Hastings was one of the very few people Flagler called by his first name.[28] In May 1885 when Thomas Hastings accompanied Henry Flagler to St. Augustine, he rode in a private railroad car, and along the way Hastings made a preliminary sketch for the prospective hotel. Hastings's first steps down into the sandy streets of St. Augustine brought him back to earth. As Hastings later recalled, "When Mr. Flagler led me to the spot where he wanted the Ponce de Leon to stand I was discouraged for it was low and marshy—in fact, a continuation of Maria Sanchez Creek."[29] A short while later John Carrère visited St. Augustine, and he would add his judgment of the situation: "In the Ponce de Leon Hotel we found an unusual opportunity," wrote Carrère. "In the first place, it was to be built in one of the most individual towns in the United States, a simple little Spanish city. When we looked over the ground we realized that by putting up an incongruous structure we might destroy forever the individuality and charm of that old Spanish community. Mr. Hastings had traveled much in Spain, and I was born in one of the cities of South America. Yet it was not so much our predilection for Spanish architecture as our conscientious scruples against destroying the characteristic atmosphere of St. Augustine that guided us in adopting the Spanish style for the Ponce de Leon."[30]

Hastings said the same thing: "I spent much time roaming around St. Augustine endeavoring to absorb as much of the local atmosphere as possible. I wanted to retain the Spanish character of St. Augustine and so designed the buildings with the architecture of the early houses here with their quaint over-hanging balconies."[31] In the promotional book Carrère and Hastings later produced for Flagler, they bluntly condemned the architecture recently constructed in St. Augustine. They compared the typical hotel to "a huge bandbox or a slightly exaggerated Saratoga trunk with windows. Sometimes the hotel may be very fair architecturally, as in some parts of Switzerland, but it is an architecture quite repugnant to the spirit of the place." The "bandbox" characterization would aptly fit the old Florida House and the Magnolia, while the large San Marco, with its French mansard towers, would be seen as inappropriate for its Florida locale.

Similar criticisms were heaped upon recently constructed private residences Carrère and Hastings deemed incongruous in their location and simply in bad taste: "Specimens of this exotic architecture have obtruded themselves on our stroll, in the shape of smart little Queen Anne villas, with an impudent gable here and a meaningless turret there, strongly suggesting that Queen Anne has gone staring mad and has attired herself like a dude on Easter Day."[32]

Henry Flagler and his architects planned to correct these travesties imposed upon Florida's tropical setting and Spanish heritage by supplying old St. Augustine with the "courtly splendors" of monumental buildings that Sylvia Sunshine had found absent when she penned *Petals Plucked from Sunny Climes*.

Two decades after Carrère and Hastings did their work, writer Edwin Lefevre testified to the success of the architects' strategy: "They fit, these beautiful edifices, Spanish in architecture and gloriously successful in the utter un-Americanness of their environment and general effect. Barely twenty years old, they look as if they had always been there, in that precise spot. They 'belong' very decidedly."[33]

The second major question to be settled was selection of the building material for the hotel. Brick could not be manufactured nearby for lack of red clay, and it would be expensive to import. Local sawmills turned out an abundance of pine lumber, but Carrère feared it would be too green to be used with confidence. Both Carrère and Hastings decided that nature had already dictated the material to be used: coquina. The Spanish had been using it for centuries, and this gray stone was a defining element of St. Augustine's essential character. Hastings took a sailboat over to Anastasia Island to explore the quarries with a pick and shovel. He declared coquina "a suggestion from nature not to be overlooked."[34]

Soon Hastings returned to New York, elaborating his sketches into intricate drawings, studies, and plans. The first known image of the Hotel Ponce de Leon, presumably the "pretty picture" Hastings presented to Flagler for his consideration, is a watercolor sketch dated August 1885 and bearing the notation "a work on these lines, Carrère and Hastings." The sketch looks very much like the Ponce de Leon as it finally emerged, although the towers are bulkier. A few details differ from what became reality. A carriage is shown emerging from the courtyard gate, and within the courtyard a towering geyser of water from an artesian well shoots above the wall; neither of these fanciful ideas was implemented.

As was his wont, Henry Flagler stayed intimately involved in the planning. He later declared that deciding upon the architectural style of the Hotel Ponce de Leon was his most perplexing decision in Florida. "How to build a hotel to meet the requirements of nineteenth-century America and have it in keeping with the character of the place—that was my hardest problem."[35] Yet both the architects and Flagler himself testified to the free hand that Flagler gave his young artisans. Carrère later declared: "To Mr. Flagler also should be given the credit for having given us, twenty-three years ago, when we were still unknown, a free hand to experiment within the measure of our ability to produce something artistic and beautiful."[36]

Flagler observed that it made him glad to afford Carrère and Hastings the opportunity to transform their grandest architectural "day-dreams" into reality. "So I just turned 'Tom' Hastings loose, and the result is the Ponce de Leon. Whatever beauty and merit it has belongs to him. The only credit I claim is that I am cheerfully enduring pen-paralysis or rheumatism brought on by signing checks to pay for it."[37]

Yet it was not quite that simple. Flagler could not restrain himself from interjecting on some details, as attested by a penciled note on one of the surviving architectural drawings: "Stop work above this point until Mr. Carrere comes down as Mr. Flagler is not yet decided about roof."[38]

With Flagler's go-ahead in hand to create the Hotel Ponce de Leon, Carrère and Hastings required a much larger working space; they vacated their back rooms at McKim, Mead and White and moved two blocks away to 3 Bowling Green, off Broadway near Battery Park. In a row of renovated colonial era

A drawing of the gate to the grounds of Grace Methodist Church bears a notation asking the builders to delay adding the roof because "Mr. Flagler is not yet decided about roof." Evidently Flagler decided against adding the roof; the two columns remain today without the final touch Hastings planned. Carrère and Hastings Digital Collection, University of Florida. By permission of Flagler College.

buildings occupied by the offices of steamship companies, Carrère and Hastings set up shop in an attic, with open oak rafters and dormer windows that Hastings recalled gave him a view up Broadway.[39]

With "youthful and impetuous enthusiasm" Hastings and his new partner went to work. Flagler's expansive demands on their talents "brought us closely together," Hastings remembered, "working with great sympathy, each gradually finding his own sphere. The necessarily strenuous character of our work in these early days brought about because of our having so little help and because of our lack of experience made it necessary for each of us to find or drift into that portion of our work for which he seemed best fitted, and this without any prearranged understanding. Responsibility thrust upon us in this way forcing us sometimes into the solution of new problems, gave us unusual opportunities for quick development."[40]

One of the first things they did was to place a shot-in-the-dark request in the country's leading architectural journal: "To the Editors of the American Architect:—Gentlemen—can you inform us if there are any books or pamphlets now published giving general information about the construction of large-sized hotels, their requirements, arrangement, plans, etc. and if so where they can be had. You will greatly oblige us by sending any data you may possess on the subject or informing us where we can procure the same. Yours truly, John M. Carrère."[41]

Carrère captures some of the amusing aspects of their early research into the arcane aspects of planning a building in which hundreds of people would live together, it was hoped, in harmony. "We spent hours and days," he wrote, "interviewing different hotel men, and we found only two points of agreement among them. Each thought that all other hotel men knew nothing at all about hotels, but all agreed that the size of every apartment in a hotel should be some multiple of twenty-seven inches—at that time the measurement of a standard width of carpet."[42]

Flagler had already selected O. D. Seavey as the architects' chief resource on the practical side of hotel planning. One of Seavey's ideas, which influenced both the design of the building and the layout of the grounds, was to have the primary functional entrance at the rear of the hotel. Travelers arriving at the Ponce de Leon would not disembark from their carriages or omnibuses at the great arched entranceway at the front of the hotel; instead, carriages would approach along a driveway running behind the central building and under the Dining Room. A small foyer, decorated with a golden "Bien Venido" welcoming mural, would receive guests and lead them up a stairway to the rear of the Rotunda. Meanwhile, their baggage would be whisked into the basement and from there into the freight elevator, to appear later outside their guest rooms. This arrangement afforded arriving vacationers some privacy. As one newspaperman explained, "The dusty traveler will not be obliged to alight at the main entrance before a balcony full of people, and then move across the office under the gaze of all who chance to be there. . . . This arrangement will be appreciated by ladies in particular, for they dislike to appear in public clad in traveling clothes."[43]

Carrère and Hastings, although utter novices in such a large undertaking, brought a wealth of training and talent to the task of designing the Hotel Ponce de Leon. In his later writings Hastings took considerable pride in his workmanship on this, his first big commission. Years afterward, addressing fellow architects, he explained that a building should be designed with meticulous attention to the relationships among all its various parts so that each would integrate harmoniously into a unified whole. He started his designs from the inside and progressed outward—beginning from the ground and working up. With the Hotel Ponce de Leon, he commenced from the general layout of the building.

Hastings sketched two figures in his drawing of the columns in the Dining Room, to show their scale in relation to the height of a person. At the bottom he indicated the ten-inch iron structural columns enclosed within the wooden columns. Carrére and Hastings Digital Collection, University of Florida. By permission of Flagler College.

"Fully three quarters of the time that we spent studying this building before beginning the foundations," Hastings later wrote, "was devoted to the first floor plan; not merely to arrange the rooms, but rather to determining the general scheme, and the relation of one part to another."[44]

Hastings pointed out that the floor plan determines two of the three dimensions of any structure, and development of a sound layout makes it possible for the rest of the building to flow naturally from the initial scheme. His floor plan for the Ponce integrated Beaux Arts ideas such as symmetry, good proportion, regular distribution and repetition, and radiation from central points. The plan allowed for convenient, logical flow of foot traffic from one part of the building to the next.[45] Hastings also incorporated typical Beaux Arts devices such as transitional spaces between the major units of the hotel: guests entering the hotel pass through a low-ceilinged foyer before walking into the high-domed Rotunda. From the Rotunda the hotel spreads out along four axes: north, south, east, and west. A visitor continuing through the Rotunda ascends a flight of steps leading to a dark, narrow passageway before stepping into the wondrous vista of the vaulted Dining Room.[46]

Although the Hotel Ponce de Leon was intended to be a building of monumental proportions, Carrère and Hastings honored the Greek ideal that man should be the measure of all things. The building aimed to inspire people—not overwhelm them with its massive size. Hastings instructed his students: "Before beginning to work, it is well to sketch a man at one side of the paper, drawing him at the scale to be adopted; this is for comparison and guidance." Railings of balustrades should be about three feet high. Stair steps should rise an easy six inches, with wide twelve-inch treads.[47] After all, the building was intended to be a temporary home for travelers, and therefore it should impart a feeling of domestic comfort and security.

At the same time that Carrère and Hastings were determining the floor plan, they were also mindful of the elevation or, as they called it, "support" of the building. This involved consideration of how thick the walls would be and how high the various units of the building would rise. At this point reflection on how the building would look from the outside came into play. The height and bulk of the elements of the building determined how it would look in silhouette. In the Ponce de Leon, Hastings pointed out, the towers stood tallest, followed by the central dome, then the four small tower rooms on the front, and lastly the roof over the entrance to the courtyard. The size and height of each of these components had to relate harmoniously to the others in order to form a coherent, pleasing entirety.[48]

Explaining the plan from the point of view of a pedestrian entering the Ponce de Leon's front gate, Carrère and Hastings show how the elevations all fit together: "The country about is flat and monotonous, hence our building must be as varied in outline as possible. The eye travels from the gateway in the centre of the one-story portico up to the corner turrets of the wings, then back to the high walls of the main part of the building, and up to the great dome surmounted by

This watercolor front view of the proposed Hotel Ponce de Leon was painted by architect Emmanuel Masqueray, who worked for Carrère and Hastings before going on to make his reputation as a builder of churches in Minnesota. Swales, "Master Draftsmen VII," *Pencil Points*, 1924, 66.

its graceful lantern, and so finally on and up to the huge corner towers that rise one hundred and fifty feet into the clear blue sky."[49]

The final consideration—although it had already been determined and held in abeyance throughout the design process—was the styling and decoration of the exterior. Carrère and Hastings called it "Spanish Renaissance," and it was revolutionary for its time. At a moment when counties across America were building new courthouses in red-brick neo-Gothic and McKim, Meade and White were popularizing French Renaissance, Carrère and Hastings struck out on a totally novel path. Of course, a Spanish theme was perfectly natural for St. Augustine, and Florida builders have followed "Mediterranean" forms ever since; but at the time the decision was radical. The red barrel–tile roof (actually a new element in St. Augustine, but not in Spain or Mexico), the overhanging balconies, the central courtyard, the broad eaves that sheltered the walls from intense sunlight—all broke new ground in monumental building in America.

America's most influential architect, H. H. Richardson, also a product of the École des Beaux Arts, would surely have approved of how Carrère and Hastings used "honest" gray concrete as the basic fabric of the walls and its bold contrast with the colorful salmon terra-cotta as decoration. The thick, solid medieval walls and round arches also had a "Richardsonian Romanesque" aspect. However, the grand man of American architecture died in 1886 and never had a chance to see what the next generation of architects would produce.

Although the towers of the Ponce de Leon exemplify the vertical portion of the design, the hotel's general aspect accentuates the horizontal—as befits the level landscape of coastal Florida. Playing dual roles as both businessman and design arbiter, Henry Flagler later explained that a taller building would have afforded more rooms to rent, but he noted: "Two more stories, or even one, would have ruined it as a work of art, and I could not consent to sacrifice it.... It is true that two additional stories would have been desirable from a financial point of view, but I did not build it as a money-making speculation, and it will never, while I own it, be conducted with that special purpose. I am entirely satisfied, however, on that score, and have no doubt of the future."[50]

Thus by the fall of 1885 Flagler had found his architects, and they had found their milieu. On paper the prospective hotel was already assuming vast proportions, but paper dreams are just that. Flagler had work to do before his dream had any chance of becoming reality.

6

Remaking the Oldest City, 1885

The scheme has outgrown my original ideas.

—Henry Flagler to Franklin Smith, October 16, 1885

During the summer of 1885, after Flagler had already purchased extensive tracts of land in St. Augustine and commenced serious planning for his hotel, his whole enterprise threatened to come unraveled when Dr. Anderson could not secure a clear title to the site of the hotel. By September Flagler appeared to be on the brink of walking away from the entire venture.

The trouble stemmed from the will of Anderson's father, who had passed away more than forty years earlier. His will gave lifetime tenure to his widow Clarissa, but after her death, which came in 1881, the estate was to be divided among his four children. Dr. Anderson's three half-sisters were dead by this time, but their heirs, the Northrop and Crafts families, requested three-quarters of the value of the fifteen-acre Markland estate. Anderson was, of course, reluctant to surrender what he regarded as his inheritance to people who were almost strangers to him. As a result the Northrops and Crafts brought suit against Anderson, and that suit remained unsettled when Flagler arrived on the scene.

Since Flagler could not wait for the court's decision, whenever that might come, Anderson decided to make an agreement hastily with the Northrops and Crafts to sell just the five-acre marsh lot that Flagler wanted and split the proceeds—with Anderson receiving only a one-quarter share. This agreement, of course, compromised Anderson's claim to the whole of the estate, but he felt that considering the need for immediate action, he should make this compromise. At first Anderson thought his proposition satisfied everyone, but by the end of July negotiations bogged down.[1]

In August William Crafts bypassed Anderson and contacted Flagler directly with a proposal to settle with the Crafts and Northrops for $5,500 each as their share of the marsh lot. Flagler took up the role of intermediary, and he and Dr. Anderson met with the Northrops and Crafts to discuss the matter. Evidently no final agreement was reached at this meeting. Soon thereafter Flagler's lawyer C. M. Cooper traveled to Charleston to meet with the Northrops and Crafts, but he was unable to gather all of the principals together in one place at the same time to sign an agreement. Cooper then called off the negotiations and declared that the court case should be settled in two or three weeks, and that would decide things.[2]

On the first of September Flagler wrote two letters suggesting that he was just about at the end of his rope. To O. D. Seavey, who was spending the summer as manager of the Maplewood Hotel in New Hampshire, he explained that Anderson's legal troubles "seem to have come to a termination without putting him in a position to make a title to the hotel site. What may come of the matter hereafter is impossible to say at present." To William Crafts he wrote that "further delay will be fatal to the plans I have entertained."[3]

The next day Flagler wrote to his lawyer Cooper and declared that he had decided to accept the agreement with the Crafts and Northrops rather than wait for the decision on the court case. He repeated his dire assessment of the situation: "Further delay will be fatal to my work." The next day he sent Cooper another letter in which he praised Anderson for giving up three-quarters of the purchase price in order to see that the hotel project would continue. At the time Anderson still hoped to win his suit against the Crafts and Northrops. In the same envelope with the letter Flagler enclosed a check for $11,000.[4]

Still Flagler remained uncertain that all the various members of the Northrop and Crafts clans would put their signatures to the agreement so that a proper deed of ownership could be secured. On September 22 he wrote to his builder James McGuire asking him to delay the start of work on construction until Flagler held firm legal title to the land. Finally, on September 25, he could write to tell Anderson that the Northrops and Crafts had each been sent their $5,500 checks after all the necessary signatures had been secured.[5] The final major barrier to securing the main site for the hotel had been cleared. Flagler now owned the five-acre hotel site and the adjacent Ball estate—the properties he had deemed essential from the start.

The decision in the case of *Northrop v. Anderson* was handed down by the circuit court on November 14, 1885, and it went totally against Anderson. The court allowed Flagler's purchase to stand, subject to review by a court-appointed master, but Anderson was ordered to pay the Northrops and Crafts three-quarters of the value of the remainder of the Markland estate. Anderson would appeal the decision to the state supreme court, but its decision in 1891 reaffirmed the lower court's judgment.[6]

While the critical negotiations over the hotel site proper dragged on during the summer and fall of 1885, Henry Flagler and Franklin W. Smith continued to accumulate properties around the hotel lot at a brisk pace, but at the same time complexities of various sorts began to pile up. It is a tribute to Flagler's diligence and persistence that he eventually achieved all he had first aimed for—and much more.

Acquisition of one particular parcel proved to be a difficult, time-consuming proposition. Olivet Methodist Church occupied a spot that was essential to the full realization of Flagler's plan. The Methodists' simple native pine-wood building perched on stilts overhanging Maria Sanchez Creek at the intersection of King and Tolomato streets. Considering its awkward location, the Methodists should have been more than willing to sell out and move to a more desirable place, but evidently a number of the church's aldermen, for unknown reasons, refused to deal with Flagler.

Olivet Methodist Church had been established in 1882 by Samuel D. Paine, an English-born former soldier, who was criticized at the time for purchasing a "mud hole" as the site for the church; however, with the advent of Flagler's hotel venture, suddenly that decision looked very farsighted. Rumors published in the newspaper had it that Flagler wanted either to buy the church and property or to buy just the property and move the church building to another location. Evidently the majority of the church trustees at some point agreed to a deal that swapped the church building and its lot for the promise of a new church to be located elsewhere on Flagler's property, probably on the Ball estate. However, the opposition of some trustees prevented the deal from being legally consummated. Meanwhile, for the next two years the Methodists would continue to worship in their little chapel while Flagler filled the marsh and construction work went on all around them. During that time Flagler would donate a total of $2,665 to the church, an amount that constituted more than three quarters of the church's budget.[7] Final legal transfer of the Olivet church property to Flagler would not take place until two years later in the fall of 1887, after one group of church trustees sued another group to clear the way for the church corporation to grant Flagler title to the land.[8]

In September Flagler added another important piece to his hotel project puzzle when he purchased the corner lot diagonally across the King Street–Tolomato Street intersection from the Hotel Ponce de Leon site where the Sunnyside House stood. This large lot was bought from a widow, Ellen Ryall, whose summer home was in New Jersey.[9] In November Flagler resold the Ryall lot to Franklin Smith, and at the same time he sold the Sunnyside building to Smith and had it moved to the Ryall lot, where Smith would continue to operate it as a small hotel.[10]

These transactions signaled a change in Flagler's relationship with Smith—and in Flagler's commitment to St. Augustine. In the middle of October Flagler composed a long letter to Smith in which he reviewed their association from the time when they had first sat down with Dr. Anderson in the Villa Zorayda to discuss Flagler's dream of a $200,000 hotel. Flagler explained that after a few months he realized Smith would not be able to contribute the $50,000 that Flagler had expected; so Flagler decided to go ahead and purchase property on his own—committing far more money than he had originally planned—and investing much more of his time and himself into the venture. "I saw then that the whole investment, together with the burden of detail, must fall upon my shoulders. . . . Thus, you see, the scheme has outgrown my original ideas." Flagler proposed that Smith withdraw any financial commitment to Flagler's enterprise and concentrate his efforts on the Sunnyside and properties south of King Street that Flagler had just sold him.[11]

That was the way things worked out over the next two years. Smith continued to be Flagler's close associate and confidant, but the two men proceeded in pursuit of different dreams. Smith began speaking of erecting his own hotel, to be called Casa Monica. Flagler attempted to discourage him, saying that running the Sunnyside House would pay him quite as well in return for money invested as would establishing a whole new hotel. However, Smith—a man who, like Flagler, mixed strong will with elaborate schemes—would not be content to operate Sunnyside, an ordinary boarding house. He wanted his own great building that would express his grandiose vision of Moorish architecture. Thus Smith pushed ahead, and in spite of his reservations, Flagler facilitated Smith's efforts by purchasing the two lots east of the Ryall property. These encompassed all the land fronting King Street up to the Lyon property on the corner of St. George Street—prime St. Augustine real estate opposite the western section of the Plaza where the old Spanish governor's house, now the post office, stood. Eventually Flagler would sell this land to Smith to allow him to build his Casa Monica on a large scale.[12]

Smith hoped Flagler would help him acquire sand and lumber for the Casa Monica at a reduced cost by conjoining his purchases with Flagler's, but Flagler would have nothing to do with such an arrangement. As Flagler wrote to one of his lieutenants about McGuire's and McDonald's relations with Smith: "While I am willing they should extend to him every courtesy and favor possible, I do not want them to be involved in any adjustments between Mr. Smith and parties furnishing him with supplies. . . . While I don't doubt Mr. Smith's credit and integrity, I want him to 'paddle his own canoe.'"[13]

Meanwhile Flagler continued trying to buy up all the Maria Sanchez marshlands lying south of King Street. For one thing, he wanted to eliminate an unsightly and potentially unhealthy swamp from the front doorstep of his luxury resort hotel. For another, Thomas Hastings had already proposed, perhaps at the request of Seavey or Flagler himself, erection of some sort of entertainment casino on this additional extensive stretch of land.

Flagler purchased the long, narrow creek bottom of Maria Sanchez itself—totaling just one acre—from the state of Florida for the sum of one dollar—perhaps not an unreasonable price for a completely submerged piece of real estate.[14]

Flagler had attempted to buy George Atwood's marsh lot on Bridge Street in the spring of 1885 but failed. In September he tried again, using St. Augustine mayor John G. Long as an intermediary. Long wrote telling Flagler that Atwood had offered him the property but that he would not stand in the way if Flagler wanted it: "You are doing too much for St. Augustine for any of her people to offer an obstacle or stand in the way; we appreciate too highly the advantages to result from your investments there." Long bought the lot and turned it over to Flagler.[15]

The portion of Maria Sanchez marsh lying just south of the skating rink property belonged to the Buckingham Smith Benevolent Association, which operated a home for indigent black people in a large building standing on the west side of the marsh. Fortunately for Flagler, the most prominent man on the board of the association was Dr. Anderson, and as both Anderson and Flagler expected, in March 1886 the board agreed to a sale of the marshland. Although Flagler had not yet obtained all the property he wanted, he told Anderson that with the Benevolent Association land and the Olivet Church property, "I can put up about all that was contemplated in Mr. Hastings's original sketch."[16]

This early reference to a Hastings-designed building intended for the south side of King Street indicates that Hastings and Flagler had already been thinking of an ancillary building to augment the Hotel Ponce de Leon. Whether the concept of what would finally become the Hotel Alcazar, baths, and casino complex had already emerged as a full-blown design is not known. However, the word *casino* was already being spoken in connection with Flagler's plans for the Maria Sanchez tract. Flagler advised Anderson to avoid using the word *casino* when dealing with locals, since it might make property owners reluctant to sell. Flagler suggested using *park* instead, since it implied less intrusive activities.[17]

When Philip Ammidown refused to sell his piece of marsh property, Flagler wrote to Smith that he might simply drop the whole idea of building south of King Street, since he already owned plenty of land north of the hotel site. In his letter to Smith he labeled the casino the "Zacastine," perhaps a name being considered as a blend of Alcazar and Augustine. He vented his frustrations to Smith.

"My thought was to make King St. the 5th Avenue of St. Augustine," he wrote, "but I don't feel disposed *to coax and pay, both*." However, he concluded on a hopeful note: "I believe that, with the example I am inaugurating we can make St. Augustine the Newport of the South."[18]

Flagler also shared his annoyance with his Standard Oil associate W. G. Warden: "Those St. Augustinians think they have a bonanza and are working it for all it is worth."[19]

The *St. Augustine Evening News* editorialized on Flagler's attempt to purchase the Maria Sanchez watercourse, addressing those who refused to sell: "It is therefore a question of doubt whether the Maria Sanchez creek, between King and Bridge streets, will be filled in and beautified, or remain an eye-sore for another decade. We believe our citizens as a rule, are inclined to manifest the most liberal spirit toward the projector of the great work, now in progress in our city, and we deeply regret that any should be so short-sighted, selfish and unwise, as to withhold property that may at any time be condemned as a public nuisance, for, we suppose, no other purpose than to extort unreasonable sums for the ownership of the same."[20]

Before Flagler could build his hotel or his casino, he needed to turn the Maria Sanchez marsh into high, dry land. To assist him in this important undertaking, he hired the only trained civil engineer in town, Captain Frederick W. Bruce, who worked for the federal government as the "fort keeper." Bruce's chief charge was to see that Fort Marion and its grounds were properly maintained; from time to time he was allowed to do work on his own—such as his earlier survey of Tolomato Street for Dr. Anderson. In May 1885 Bruce was hired by Franklin W. Smith to survey Maria Sanchez from King Street south to Bridge Street (as it turned out, the extent of the Alcazar complex grounds) and to calculate the volume of material needed to fill it in. At the same time he made a survey of the five-acre Hotel Ponce de Leon site for Flagler and offered to supervise filling of the marsh north of King Street. Flagler accepted this offer.[21]

Anderson, playing the role of leading citizen, appeared in June before the city council to request permission to fill the marsh on the hotel site, and three weeks later the city gave the go-ahead.[22]

In order to obtain the soil necessary to begin filling the marshes, Flagler purchased a tract of land north of town called the Bradford property. The land included both sand hills and marsh. Common opinion held that swamp muck, with its mix of putrefying vegetation, spawned lethal miasmas. But Bruce expressed his view that there was no health preference between the dry sand and the mud from the marsh. He added that Flagler could excavate from a pit in the marsh at any time except for a three-hour period around the high tides.[23]

The next problem was getting the fill material to the hotel site, and to do this an obstacle had to be overcome. The fill would have to be hauled over two pieces of property belonging to the federal government: the shallow ditch along Orange Street, a sad remnant of the old Spanish moat; and the Old Powder House Lot, a large parcel of land where the Spanish had once maintained a munitions store. Flagler believed, correctly it seems, that he actually did not need permission from the government to cross these areas if he bypassed them by staying below the high water line in the San Sebastian River marshes. He nevertheless asked the War Department for permission, explaining that "owing to the deep sand of which the roads and streets of St. Augustine are constructed a haul of said material from the railroad terminus to the hotel site would be slow, tedious, and ruinously expensive." He requested permission to run a temporary railroad track along the marshes and promised to take up the track after his fill was completed. The War Department agreed to this proposal.[24]

Meanwhile Flagler had already put Bruce to work surveying the marshes on the east bank of the San Sebastian River all the way from Orange Street on the north to King Street on the south.[25] Dr. Anderson's Markland estate and Flagler's newly purchased Ball property bordered this marsh to the east, but other properties, including the Powder House Lot, also fronted the marsh.

At this time the rail line from Jacksonville terminated at a small station north of Orange Street behind the San Marco Hotel. However, on September 20, before permission had been given by the government, workers for the Jacksonville railroad began building a bridge across the marsh where the government's ditch emptied into the San Sebastian, and then they continued southward. By October Anderson had secured permission from the army general in charge of Florida to build the railroad, giving the new railroad legitimacy.[26] The tramway ran along the edge of the San Sebastian marsh until it reached the Ball estate, where it turned eastward to the Hotel Ponce de Leon site. By October carloads of sand and marl were being hauled to the headwaters of the Maria Sanchez marshes.

After months of frustrating delays that had threatened to derail his plans, Flagler was now in a position to begin the transformation of St. Augustine into an American Riviera.

In December 1885, as that momentous year drew near its close, a writer for the *Chicago Daily National Hotel Reporter* visited St. Augustine to describe its accommodations to readers in the hotel trade. He visited the St. Augustine Hotel on the Plaza, encountering its manager, the crusty former merchant sailor and U.S. Navy officer Edward E. Vaill. He reported, "Captain Vaill was suffering from the gout, one of his feet bundled and resting on a footstool. He was irritated, not alone with the gout, but because he would soon have competition of a rival hotel. He was prolific in his adverse adjectives regarding one—Flagler who was starting to build a hotel in the swamp!"

Flagler built a rail line for hauling in dirt to fill Maria Sanchez Creek. Olivet Methodist Church and a roller-skating rink stood where the marshlands met King Street. These buildings would be removed to create space for a plaza Flagler called the Alameda. From the collection of the St. Augustine Historical Society Research Library.

His curiosity aroused, the reporter walked into the Plaza, where he encountered a "smartly dressed Negro," who turned out to be the servant Frank, steward of Flagler's yacht *Columbia*. Flagler praised Frank as "a bright intelligent man, a first class servant."[27] Frank directed the Chicagoan to the "villa" (probably Markland) where Flagler was staying. After introducing himself, the reporter was ushered into the parlor by Flagler, who proceeded to show him the Carrère and Hastings plans for the hotel. The newspaperman dubbed the diagrams "Flagler's Dream" and proceeded to give a remarkably detailed description of what would eventually become a reality. Thus at Christmas time, 1885, the whole universe of hotel operators could read about the prospect of the Hotel Ponce de Leon.[28]

7

First, Buy the Railroad,
1885–1886

The papers have considerable to say about
the "Flagler Syndicate."
—Henry Flagler to J. B. Higbee, February 6, 1886

During the formative years of Standard Oil, Henry Flagler had been the company's railroad specialist, bargaining with various railroads in Ohio, Pennsylvania, and New York and negotiating contracts to secure the most favorable shipping rates for Standard's products. In fact, the company's success could be attributed in large part to Flagler's hardnosed tactics. So ruthless had his methods been that laws were passed to prohibit the "rebates" and "drawbacks" that Standard had extracted from the railroads to drive down shipping rates and drive competitors out of business. When Flagler began his operations in Florida, he understood very well the vital role that railroad connections with the North would play in the success of his plan to turn St. Augustine into a winter Newport. He also possessed abundant knowledge and experience in railroad operations. Thus it is hardly surprising that his hotel enterprise quickly became a railroad venture as well.

When Flagler arrived in St. Augustine in 1885 the rickety old St. Johns Railroad from Tocoi had been supplanted as the primary artery to town by the Jacksonville, St. Augustine, and Halifax River Railway that ran directly south from Jacksonville. Only a short ferry crossing over the St. Johns River in downtown Jacksonville broke continuous rail connections with the North.

Construction of this railroad had been started in 1881, and by May 1883 the railroad was completed to the northern city limits of St. Augustine. At that spot the railroad built a small temporary wooden depot near the site of today's main branch of the St. Johns County public library. A little over a year later the track was extended to a new two-story wooden station on Orange Street behind the

San Marco Hotel. (That station is long gone, but it stood near the site of the present-day Ketterlinus school gymnasium.) This was the situation in the summer of 1885 when Flagler started working with the Jacksonville railroad in extending a temporary track to transport fill dirt to the site of the Hotel Ponce de Leon.[1]

Just when Flagler decided to purchase the Jacksonville, St. Augustine, and Halifax River Railway is not known, but it did not take him long to make up his mind. All his experience in the oil business had taught him the desirability of commanding as much of his environment as possible, and that meant gaining control of the railroad linking his hotel with the outside world. A few years later Flagler would write, "I don't know of a hotel that I would want to take as a gift except I owned the transportation lines that reached it."[2]

As early as the spring of 1885 Charles Green of Utica, New York, the principal owner of the railroad, had informed St. Augustine's Mayor Long that he would be willing to sell the road.[3] At the time Flagler did not act, but as the months went on he became more and more dissatisfied with the service provided by the Jacksonville railroad. Finally he confided in a letter to McGuire and McDonald, "I must confess I am becoming disgusted with the unfulfilled promises on the part of the 'J. St. A. & H. R. R.,' and unless there is an early improvement in the condition of affairs, I shall take decided measures to correct the evils complained of."[4]

By the time Flagler wrote this letter he was deeply involved in negotiations to purchase the railroad. Green had written in early September reminding him of earlier discussions about the sale of the road, but Flagler put him off by saying that he was too involved in other matters to give it proper attention. Soon, however, Flagler went into motion to acquire the line. Before leaving for a trip to St. Augustine, he asked Green to instruct the road's superintendent, William L. Crawford, to supply him with all pertinent information on the road's operations and finances so that Flagler might make a proper valuation of it.[5]

Interestingly, before entering into discussions with Crawford, Flagler wrote to James McGuire asking him to inquire into Crawford's drinking habits, having heard rumors from several gentlemen that Crawford was hitting the bottle pretty heavily.[6] Evidently McGuire gave a favorable report on Crawford; Flagler kept him on after purchasing the road.

Flagler's October trip to St. Augustine gave him a chance to ride the Jacksonville railroad both ways and experience its shortcomings firsthand. On November 6 he wrote to tell Green he would purchase the road if a price could be agreed upon. Ten days later Flagler sent his lawyer to negotiate the details, and on December 9 Green and his board, meeting in Utica, elected Flagler a director of the railroad so that he would have standing when the board met again to confirm the deal officially. The day after Christmas Flagler and Green agreed on a price of $300,000. On December 31 Flagler and Green met in the luxurious Fifth Avenue Hotel in Lower Manhattan to shake hands and exchange cash for securities. The next day the board met to receive the resignations of Green's men and ratify the election of Flagler's representatives. Henry Flagler was then named the new president of the Jacksonville, St. Augustine, and Halifax River Railway. He was now a railroad man.[7]

In a side deal, Flagler allowed the owners of the Jacksonville, Tampa, and Key West Railway, which operated a line on the west side of the St. Johns River, to buy some of the stock in his railroad. He did this as part of an agreement that allowed them to oversee day-to-day management of the railroad.[8] Many people assumed from outward appearances that the Jacksonville, Tampa, and Key West Railway had purchased the road to St. Augustine.

Writing to J. B. Higbee of Daytona, a man he knew from earlier years in Bellevue, Ohio, Flagler explained: "The papers have considerable to say about the 'Flagler Syndicate.' *Confidentially*, this is all 'bosh.' 'The Flagler Syndicate' consists of H. M. Flagler. In the Railroad matter, however, I joined with some personal friends, who are interested in the 'J.T. & K.W.R.R.' They put in 1/7 of the money, as I did not want to bother with the administration of the road." He added that he had too many irons in the fire to devote personal attention to management of the railroad.

Then he went on to address Higbee's reason for contacting him: the question of extending the railroad to the Daytona area. Flagler wrote to say simply that extending the road that far south had not yet been considered seriously but that he hoped to visit Daytona in a few weeks and wished to speak with Higbee then.[9]

The Jacksonville, St. Augustine, and Halifax River Railway's charter from the State of Florida awarded it grants of land that accrued to the company as it continued its line into the Ormond-Daytona region. Thus when Flagler purchased the railroad, he also acquired an incentive to extend the Florida frontier southward past St. Augustine. In December 1885, while Flagler labored mightily to turn St. Augustine into the ultimate winter resort for the wealthy, he was already laying the groundwork for the development of South Florida that would ultimately undermine the preeminence of St. Augustine as a winter destination. This grand vision of the future would not have been more than a glimmering in the minds of a few optimistic pioneer boosters at the time. Most settlers in the wilds down the peninsula just wanted a railroad to transport oranges to market from their isolated groves.

One of the first things Flagler did upon purchasing the railroad was to assign a share of stock to his friend Dr. Anderson and have him elected to the board of directors. As a practical matter, it gave Flagler someone in Florida who could represent him. Upon informing Anderson of his elevation to the directorship of the railroad, Flagler wrote: "I suggest that you look over your largest file of red feathers, & select one which you think will be best adapted to this new degree to be conferred upon you." In years thereafter, Flagler often jokingly referred to the railroad as "Dr. Anderson's railroad."[10]

Although Flagler did not wish to manage the railroad actively, he was not averse to expressing his wishes to the men who did run the road. To general manager George W. Bentley he suggested lowering passenger rates on the St. Augustine route to encourage more visitors to come to St. Augustine and more St. Augustine residents to travel to Jacksonville. He instructed superintendent Crawford to make sure that the passenger accommodations were kept as clean as possible, although Flagler admitted there was not much that could be done immediately to improve the second-rate roadbed and make the ride more comfortable.[11]

The thirty-six-mile journey between Jacksonville and St. Augustine remained something of an ordeal. The road's lightweight iron rails could not bear the weight of more powerful locomotives, and its narrowly spaced tracks caused the passenger cars to rock like boats as they passed along. The smoke-billowing locomotive engines burned fat pine logs chopped by local woodsmen from the forests that lined both sides of the tracks. During the summer, no matter how high the temperature, the railcar windows had to be kept closed to keep out clouds of mosquitoes and sand flies. Enterprising boys came through the cars selling insect repellant. Whenever the weather turned dry, the train stirred up a fine white dust that settled over everything. Upon arrival in St. Augustine the final duty of the black porter would be to whiskbroom the passengers' shoulders as they prepared to disembark. This also signaled that the time had come to press a quarter into the palm of the ever courteous and grateful porter.[12]

Flagler's railroad enterprise and his land filling efforts converged on the broad bank of the San Sebastian River west of St. Augustine. He purchased this hitherto worthless expanse of mud flats and salt marsh from the estate of William Bradford—although the legitimacy of this purchase would later be disputed.[13] It was intended to become the site of a new railroad station that would link his Jacksonville line with the St. Johns Railroad to Tocoi and with a new line, the St. Johns and Palatka Railway, just then being completed to connect St. Augustine with Palatka to the southwest. Filling this site, which consisted of four or five times as much land as the Maria Sanchez marsh he was already filling, would be a monumental assignment, unprecedented in Florida history.

The first task to be undertaken was construction of a railroad bridge across the river to the north of the existing King Street bridge. This would allow the Tocoi and Palatka railroads to move their station from the west bank of the river to its east bank. (Today Depot Street is the only remaining evidence of the old depot on the west bank.) In September 1885 Fredrick Bruce surveyed the route of the new bridge and the location of a new station. By January construction of the bridge trestle had reached halfway across the river, and by summer the new station was ready for use.[14]

Flagler had given the Tocoi and Palatka railroads right of way and use of his land for their station at no charge, since these roads would connect his St. Augustine hotels with points in the interior of Florida. When Richard McLaughlin, superintendent of the Tocoi and Palatka railroads, brought up the question of temporary working arrangements with Flagler's railroad, Flagler responded, "What would you think of some more permanent arrangement for operating your road under our management?" Flagler already had plans to erect a much larger Union Station on the banks of the San Sebastian as soon as filling operations were completed and he could extend his line from Orange Street to link up with the Tocoi-Palatka lines.[15]

While Flagler harbored designs to extend his own railroad interests southward, he also entertained some broader musings in that direction. He began plans for a large dock south of King Street on the San Sebastian, where ships and barges could dock and make connections with his railroad. This might be important, he explained, if the canal then being dredged along the East Coast "ever amounts to anything."[16] (The coastal canal would not be completed until 1912, well after Flagler demolished his seldom-used dock in 1903.)[17]

Longer-term designs aside, Flagler's plans for St. Augustine itself had begun to take visible shape. The original idea of a resort hotel, or two hotels and a casino, was evolving into the concept of a whole winter resort village, with handsome cottages replacing the orange groves that stood behind the site of the Hotel Ponce de Leon. A winter Newport beckoned. To achieve this dream, Flagler needed to expand his realm northward beyond the Anderson and Ball properties. In July and August 1885 he acquired a large tract of land to the north of the Ball grove and south of the old Catholic Tolomato Cemetery.[18] However, between this tract and the Ball property stood the U.S. government's Powder House Lot. Its acreage was approximately as large as either the Anderson or Ball grove, and adding it to his holdings would complete Flagler's ownership of a whole neighborhood. Across Tolomato Street from the Powder House Lot stood the government's smaller Dragoon Barracks Lot, and Flagler hoped to net this as well.

In 1884 Congress had passed a law permitting the federal government to sell surplus property to private individuals at auction, and Flagler hoped to use this to acquire both the Powder House and Dragoon Barracks lands. However, his plans encountered an unexpected obstruction. Some leading citizens of St. Augustine, evidently ignorant of Flagler's ambitions, also coveted these lots as possible sites for municipal buildings, a school, a library, or perhaps a public park. The backward little town of St. Augustine lacked both land for public uses and the tax money to buy such real estate. Thus a petition had been gotten up and sent to U.S. Senator Wilkinson Call asking that the government donate the Powder House and Dragoon Barracks lots to the people of St. Augustine. This petition led Senator Call to introduce a bill transferring ownership of the properties to the city—and the bill collided with Flagler's efforts to acquire the land for himself.[19]

Flagler turned to Dr. Anderson to resolve the conflict. He instructed Anderson to tell Mayor John Long and the men who had signed the petition that "if I am fairly treated the City of St. A is likely to get a great deal more help from me than from the general government." Flagler told Anderson he had arranged for Call to amend his bill to apply only to the Dragoon Barracks Lot, leaving Flagler free to contend for the Powder House Lot. "Very *confidentially*," Flagler told Anderson, "I don't believe there is a 'ghost of a chance' of passing Call's bill, but . . . I don't want to antagonize any of the Citizens of St. A." He added that if the signers of the petition did not cooperate with him, "I must *try* to defeat it. Of course *you must not say this out loud*."[20]

It turned out well for Flagler in the end. Anderson prevailed upon most of the petition signers to withdraw their support, and Flagler's lobbyist in Washington, a Standard lawyer named John H. Flagg, visited Senator Call to explain that Flagler and St. Augustine's leading men were now in agreement on the disposal of the Powder House Lot. In August 1886 Flagler purchased the lot at public auction at the Gainesville Land Office.[21]

Immediately after the sale, having succeeded in consolidating his holdings, Flagler began dumping railroad carloads of fill dirt into the San Sebastian marshes. During the next three years the residents of St. Augustine would grow accustomed to "Mr. Flagler's gravel trains" rumbling from borrow pits north of town into the marsh to discharge their loads.[22]

Meanwhile, filling the hotel site was taking longer than Flagler hoped since superintendent Crawford could not build the temporary tram railway to the hotel site as quickly as anticipated. "Until Crawford completes his track," Flagler wrote to McGuire and McDonald, "he ought to bear the expense of carrying all material from the depot to the Hotel site. Get him to do this and he will then have a double motive for completing his track at the earliest moment possible." Two months later Flagler was still not sure that the railway had been completed, and he wrote to Crawford: "I trust that you will have the track laid to the hotel grounds by the time this reaches you."[23]

All these workmen dumping and spreading fresh muck into the local marshes aroused concern in the minds of some among the local citizenry, since folk wisdom held that any disturbance of the soil could unleash an outbreak of malaria or yellow fever. Swamps were blamed for fevers, but prevailing theory held that filling a swamp might also trigger an eruption of disease. One resident complained to the *Times-Union* that a member of his family had contracted typhoid fever from a stagnant pond on the Powder House Lot. He blamed the standing water on Flagler and complained that the Board of Health would not address the issue for fear of offending Flagler. Ten days later the *Times-Union* reported that Flagler was filling the Powder House Lot, eliminating "what for years has been a bed of pestilence and an eyesore to the public." Apparently Flagler's men read the newspapers and reacted to public censure.[24]

Flagler evidently gave some credence to these prevailing suppositions about disease, and he clearly realized that the feelings of the citizenry needed to be placated since some would seize upon any pretext to criticize him. After all, one of St. Augustine's prime assets was its reputation for health, and anything that cast doubt on the town's wholesome atmosphere rose to the level of a very serious civic concern.

Franklin W. Smith had more reason than most to fear disease since he lived across the street from the activities on the hotel site. In December he wrote a letter to Flagler expressing his anxiety about the possibility of malaria being released by the deep trenches being dug for the Ponce de Leon's foundations. Flagler wrote to Dr. Anderson, telling him of Smith's concerns, saying that "it would be very unfortunate if sickness should be caused by our excavations, as it would give other hotels a good opportunity to promulgate theories adverse to the locality, which might be hard to suppress." He asked Anderson to consider the matter, and if he thought it advisable, to direct the builders to spread lime over the site as a disinfectant.[25]

All this wrong-headed concern over the cause of disease came to nothing, of course, yet the fear of disease was rightly appropriate, because the possibility of an epidemic held catastrophic potential. The baffling force that brought on malaria and yellow fever was not yet understood as mosquito-borne virus transmission. Like an unseen malevolent presence, it was thought to lurk in marshes, in the underbrush of woods, in dank alleyways, in the rotting wood of houses, and even in dirty bed linen. The nation's best medical knowledge seemed as impotent as the speculations on the street or the bizarre myths of conjurers. Only the first frost of winter could be counted on reliably to banish the threat until the winter passed and warm weather returned.

But in 1885 the mysterious deadly scourges did not appear. It had been quite a year for Henry Flagler. By year's end he owned the site for his hotels, and he was proprietor of a railroad connecting his enterprise to the great, wide world. Now, with the preliminaries out of the way, the work of building could begin.

8

Construction of the Ponce de Leon, 1885–1887

A hundred years hence it will be all the same to me, and
the building the better because of my extravagance.

—Henry Flagler to McGuire and McDonald,
December 26, 1885

Henry Flagler was a man in a hurry to accomplish great things. Once he had decided to go ahead with his hotel scheme, he rushed to acquire the real estate needed for the hotel site and surrounding properties. Although he had been remarkably successful in acquiring what he wanted, the delays in getting his hands on the Anderson site and Powder House Lot frustrated him. McGuire and McDonald had told him it would take eighteen months to construct a building such as the one that Carrère and Hastings envisioned. Flagler could count the months ahead and realized that this schedule would put the completion date of the hotel well into 1887—too late for that year's winter season. That meant another year's delay until the 1888 season came around. Flagler resigned himself to this situation and pushed ahead.[1]

In spite of the delays, progress continued toward bringing the hotel to reality. On November 7, in New York City, Hastings showed Flagler the complete plans for the Hotel Ponce de Leon. And in St. Augustine on November 10 McGuire and McDonald started preliminary work on the five-acre hotel site.[2] As soon as a copy of the intricate Carrère and Hastings plans arrived, McGuire and McDonald staked out the footprint of the building in the sandy soil—and found to their consternation that the plans were all out of kilter. This raised a dismaying and potentially disastrous complication, for it brought Carrère and Hastings's competence into question before the first spade of dirt had been turned.

The builders and architects exchanged telegrams, and then Carrère and Hastings appealed to Flagler for a chance to "vindicate" their design. Quickly Carrère set off for St. Augustine carrying Flagler's letter of introduction to Dr. Anderson. From his brief experience with McKim, Mead and White, Carrère was already experienced in troubleshooting difficulties with clients. Hastings later explained the situation: "When Mr. Carrère arrived he found that in laying out the plans on the grounds, they had started at one corner of the work and followed all the way round the silhouette of the plan, each time arriving within a few inches away from the corner where they had started, so that there was naturally a discrepancy owing to the inaccuracy of the instrument and the work on the grounds. After this Mr. Carrère immediately surveyed the center lines, and figures right and left, completing the layout on the ground, showing that our work was correct, and this was the beginning of our final employment to supervise the work until its completion."[3]

Thus Flagler could finally rejoice in getting down to work on the mammoth project. "On the first day of December, 1885, we commenced the digging of the excavation for the foundations of the Hotel Ponce de Leon in St. Augustine."[4] During the summer there had been considerable discussion of just what sort of foundation was required. Engineer Frederick Bruce reported to Flagler that he had been in consultation with McGuire and McDonald, and Bruce felt that wooden pilings would be useless in the sandy soil unless driven to a great depth. Bruce recommended what he called a "floating foundation," and this was the path followed.

A building with a floating foundation "floats" upon the earth in the same way that a ship floats on water. The building displaces a weight of earth equal to the weight of the building, just as a ship displaces a volume of water equal in weight to the heaviness of the ship. Also, just as a ship must have a sound hull, the building must have a robust foundation. In the case of the Hotel Ponce de Leon the walls become thicker at their base, forming a foundation of solid concrete sunk deep into the earth.[5]

In order to produce the concrete that would go into the hotel's foundations and walls, two local materials were required: sand and coquina shell to serve as aggregate. Getting these required extensive, careful negotiations, land dealings, and purchases.

Flagler had three options as sources for coquina. His preference was simply to take coquina from the federal government's old King's Quarries south of the lighthouse. Visitors can walk into one of these quarries today near the entrance to Anastasia State Park. The Spanish had used blocks of solid stone made from the naturally compacted shells of thousands of tiny coquina shellfish to build the Castillo de San Marcos. Flagler, on the other hand, needed just loose coquina shells for his concrete. His second option was a quarry owned by a descendent of Francisco Xavier Sanchez, progenitor of the oldest surviving European family in the United States. The third was the land of the Aspinwall family.

From the beginning of this enterprise Flagler realized that taking free coquina from the government's quarries presented difficulties since the War Department had recently frowned upon such giveaways. He wrote to Franklin Smith instructing him to investigate the Aspinwall quarry as an alternative source for coquina should the War Department prohibit them from exploiting the King's Quarries.[6] However, a month later things began to look up for the government option. James McGuire wrote to Flagler: "I have been to the Island today. Arranged with W. A. Harn for shell. . . . He will look after our interests on the Island. . . . I see no trouble about the shell; believe it will be all right." William A. Harn had been stationed in Fort Sumter during its bombardment in April 1861 at the onset of the Civil War. A few years after the war he became keeper of the St. Augustine lighthouse, with the honorary title of major. In addition to maintaining the light, his responsibilities extended to overseeing all government property in its vicinity. Flagler reported this development to Anderson, writing offhandedly, "I am glad to know that McGuire has 'captured' the Major, and unless the theft reaches the ears of the Sec'y of War, I guess we are all right."[7]

Unfortunately for Flagler, that was just what happened. Flagler soon learned that "certain parties" in St. Augustine were raising objections to his "foraging on the coquina beds," and he presumed that their objective was to force him to purchase private land in order to obtain the shell he needed. He instructed McGuire to investigate the opposition discreetly and, at the same time, to explore the purchase of private land as a fall-back option should the government's quarries be closed to him.[8]

It turned out that one of the men objecting to Flagler's removal of government shell was Venancio Sanchez, an old man who offered to sell Flagler his quarry lands for $20,000. Flagler considered this price far too high, particularly since Sanchez's title to all the land he claimed remained suspect. Flagler thought $10,000 came closer to the property's real value. As often happened, Anderson acted as his go-between with Sanchez. Flagler explained to Anderson: "Mr. Sanchez can make more money out of me by being friendly, and not interfering with the removal of the shell than by taking the opposite course—I hope he will be wise enough to act friendly."[9]

As it happened, just as negotiations with Sanchez stalled, the Aspinwall property became available, and Flagler turned to this third option to get his shell.

William H. Aspinwall, the old merchant captain and Panama railroad builder (see chapter 2), had passed away ten years earlier in 1875, and his widow Anna had recently died in January of 1885. Following her death the Anastasia property

The Aspinwall quarry stood on the beach side of Anastasia Island just north of the site of the old lighthouse, which appears in this 1870s vintage engraving. Today, homes stand on the quarry site along the east side of the Lighthouse Park neighborhood. From the collection of the St. Augustine Historical Society Research Library.

passed to their son, Rev. John A. Aspinwall, a New York minister who still maintained the winter home on Bay Street just a few paces south of the Plaza. Then, in September, John Aspinwall sold his twenty-nine-acre tract to Moses R. Bean, who intended to turn the land into a subdivision called Anastasia. Bean's partners in this venture were Milo Cartter of St. Louis and Dr. Charles Carver, a local dentist who resided in what had long been known as the "Oldest House" on St. Francis Street. Carver opened his residence as a curiosity for tourists, and it has remained such ever since.[10]

McGuire made a deal with the new owners to mine coquina shell from the Aspinwall quarry, a turn of events that, as Flagler triumphantly reported to Anderson, made him "independent of Sanchez." Flagler formalized the agreement with the partners on November 19, assuring himself the right to transport coquina on a tramway across their property to a dock on the Matanzas River. As part of his dealings with Carver, Bean, and Cartter, Flagler bought lots number 1 and 2 in their Anastasia development, placing his property right under the shadow of the lighthouse. The purchase also put him on top of and adjoining the island's northernmost vein of coquina shell and stone, a seaside quarry familiar to many strangers who walked the beach to view the picturesque outcroppings of this unusual stone.[11]

To handle his mining operations Flagler erected a boarding house in the area and brought in a gang of Italian workers who would excavate coquina and haul it to lighters that ferried the material across the bay to town.[12] There is no precise record of just where Flagler mined his coquina shell, but the most likely area is the land just north of the lighthouse along what is today called Salt Run. A newspaper story from 1898 refers to this general area as the "Ponce de Leon quarries." Before Flagler's time, large outcroppings of coquina could be seen there, but today that land is flat, suggesting that Flagler's quarrymen stripped a layer of coquina off the top of the terrain.[13]

To haul the coquina shell from the quarry site to Matanzas Bay, Flagler built a tramway along what is today Old Quarry Road to Quarry Creek. From this landing, which the Spanish had probably also used in earlier days, flat-bottom lighters that McGuire and McDonald had built, pulled by a steam tug, ferried the coquina across the bay to the seawall at the Plaza.[14]

During his complex negotiations Flagler discovered that ownership of most of Anastasia Island remained an unsettled question. Back in Spanish colonial days a local entrepreneur named Jesse Fish had obtained a grant from the king of Spain for most of the island south of the Rodriguez and Sanchez grants. Fish built a plantation home on a point across the bay from the town and raised oranges on the site. In Flagler's time the ruins of Fish's homestead were a popular winter visitor destination known as Fish Island. After the transfer of Florida to the United States, Fish's heirs, who lived in South Carolina, did not take steps to confirm their claim with the U.S. government until interest in the land picked up during the 1880s. Flagler invested in extensive tracts of property on the island, claiming that the land belonged to the U.S. government. Thereupon a Fish heir named Charles M. Furman brought suit to set aside the purchases made by Flagler and others.

As the Furman suit dragged on for years, Flagler lost interest in Anastasia Island and turned his attention to Palm Beach and Miami. Eventually in 1901 the Supreme Court of the United States declared the Fish grant invalid. Flagler's Model Land Company was confirmed as the owner of large tracts of property on the island, and the suit also opened the way for others to develop modern Anastasia Island.[15]

While his extended search for coquina was going on, Flagler looked to Moultrie Creek about two miles south of town to obtain sand for his concrete mix. The coarse-grained sand on this site was deemed suitable for use in concrete. Flagler built a wharf on the south side of the creek near its tall bluffs to ship out the sand. Robert Oliver, whose father operated a sawmill on the creek, gave this description of Flagler's sand removal operations: "To get the sand Mr. Flagler put in tram-cars, running on narrow-gauge tracks, he built a pier and carried the sand to lighters, which, without power, and taking advantage of high tide, steered them to the seawall at the foot of King Street and then hauled to the construction site. Then at rising tide the lighters were steered back to Moultrie Point to reload."[16] Flagler's barges ferrying sand and coquina shell over the waters of the Matanzas River became as familiar a sight to St. Augustine residents as the gravel trains hauling fill dirt to the marshes.

To receive Flagler's lighters and move the sand and shell from the seawall to the hotel lot, McGuire and McDonald built a dock at the foot of the Plaza and ran a tramway along King Street. This dock and railway would also be used to transport other building materials, such as the thousands of red bricks that came in on seagoing schooners from the North. McGuire and McDonald built another temporary railway from George W. Atwood's property on South Street, near the mouth of Maria Sanchez Creek, up to the hotel property, running along the eastern side of the marsh.[17]

To oversee the concrete work that went into his hotel, Flagler hired the country's foremost expert on concrete, William Kennish, who had just supervised the concrete construction of the large pedestal building upholding the Statue of Liberty. Kennish's father had been chief engineer for one of the companies involved in the French attempt to build a canal across the Isthmus of Panama to supplant Aspinwall's railroad. Kennish himself had built two huge concrete dry docks on Lake Erie. He went to St. Augustine, where he found McGuire and McDonald already busy collaborating with Franklin W. Smith on experiments to determine the strength of concrete. They cast a large number of concrete bricks of various compositions and tested their capacity to withstand pressure. A brick would be placed on a stage and then barrels of dry cement would be stacked atop it until the brick crumpled. Some of the world's most innovative experiments in concrete construction were being performed in the tiny, remote village of St. Augustine, Florida.[18]

From his office in New York City, Flagler took a direct interest in the process. He wrote to McGuire and McDonald: "Mr. Hastings brought in here today a model for the forms in which to cast the concrete walls. The thing was gotten up between Kennish and Carrère and Hastings." Flagler hoped that the procedure of building the walls could be speeded up and offered some ideas for McGuire and McDonald to consider.[19]

To mix his concrete Flagler was required to design and build his own cement mixers, most likely the largest in the world up to that time. In September architect Hastings and builder McGuire accompanied Kennish to the Statue of Liberty, where they watched a revolving cement mixer at work. Using Kennish's design, Flagler ordered construction of two giant steam-powered mixers, each capable of holding a ton of material. Kennish felt that concrete should be used as quickly as possible after mixing, and these machines would accelerate the process. By December the mixers were on the ground in St. Augustine.[20]

The blend of concrete that went into the foundations of the Hotel Ponce de Leon consisted of a particularly strong mixture made up of one part Portland cement, one part sand, and three parts coquina shell. This ate up an enormous amount of expensive cement at a staggering rate: more than twelve thousand barrels by the middle of March 1886. The day after Christmas, Flagler wondered in a letter to McGuire and McDonald if he could afford to complete the hotel at the rate they were consuming cement. Then he added, "I think it more likely I am spending an unnecessary amount of money in the foundation walls, but I comfort myself with the reflection that a hundred years hence it will be all the same to me, and the building the better because of my extravagance."[21]

The letter reflected Flagler's deep yearning for permanence, even as he admitted his own mortality. But he was correct about the strength of the foundations; after more than a century they stand as solidly as granite, and the building continues to "float" on an absolute even keel.

Fortunately for Flagler's pocketbook, the blend of concrete used in the upper walls required less Portland cement: one part cement to two parts sand and four or five parts shell aggregate. This concrete was not as strong as that in the foundation, but it did not need to be. Each of the giant concrete mixers had its own supervising engineer to oversee the mixing process. The freshly produced concrete would be poured into wheelbarrows and rolled to a large steam-powered elevator that had been erected inside what would become the hotel's courtyard. The elevator would lift four wheelbarrows at a trip. Then workers pushed the wheelbarrows around the walls to the point where pours were currently being made into the wooden forms fixed atop the previous pours. Each new course of concrete would be allowed to cure for two days, and then the wooden forms were removed and reassembled at the next higher level to receive another layer of fresh concrete.

Compared to modern concrete, Flagler's mix contained less water. McGuire later explained that their experiments had shown that when wet mixes dried out, air pockets would be trapped inside. Flagler worried that unless the concrete formed solidly, water would seep into the walls, giving the hotel a damp atmosphere. To eliminate these voids, Flagler's men used a relatively dry mix, followed by vigorous tamping of the fresh concrete to ram it into the bottoms of the wooden forms. Once the walls were up, workmen fixed eight-inch wooden studs along the interiors and covered these with lath and plaster to create an insulating air pocket that would keep moisture out.[22]

We do not have an account of the laborers doing the tamping work on the walls, but this description from a few years later must catch the spirit of the workers: "Scores of visitors stopped in their daily walks near the Ponce de Leon yesterday to listen to a weird negro chorus of about twenty voices, the men being engaged in pounding down the concrete mixture used as a base for the asphalt pavements on King street. They kept perfect time with the 'thump, thump' of their mauls, much after the manner of sailors in 'getting the anchor' and could be heard distinctly several blocks away."[23]

In contrast to modern concrete buildings, Flagler's hotels and churches used little iron reinforcement. For the most part they stand simply on the strength of their thick, massive walls. However, Carrère and Hastings were familiar with the innovative use of iron in building construction, and they employed some iron reinforcement. Over windows, doors, and arches the builders would drop three-quarter-inch round iron rebar into the wet concrete mix to add strength. Since Flagler also had lots of lightweight railroad track iron on hand, salvaged from his railway, McGuire and McDonald sometimes substituted railroad track for the round rebar. It worked quite well. Twenty-three years later James McGuire sent Carrère and Hastings some iron removed from a wall during renovations. The iron showed virtually no rust.

McGuire and McDonald even thought of using concrete in the floors of the loggias surrounding the hotel's courtyard. They made a slab of concrete with a grid of flat iron slats molded inside to test the practicality of the concept. When the slab had cured, the builders suspended it between two supports and piled barrels of cement on top of it to measure its strength. The concrete sagged only one-quarter of an inch. Ultimately, however, they decided to construct the floors of the loggias, as well as the floors in the rest of the building, from conventional wooden beams.[24]

The end of the year arrived with work well under way, and Flagler looked forward to finding great progress when he arrived for the 1886 winter season. "As soon as the foundation walls are completed," he wrote to McGuire and McDonald, "I shall be disappointed if I do not see the best part of Anastasia Island on the hotel site, when I come down."[25]

Anderson did his part to smooth Flagler's path in St. Augustine by getting himself elected mayor in November. He defeated the sitting mayor John Long by a vote of 652 to 480. In the previous year's election the total vote for all candidates had amounted to only 570 votes. Anderson called attention to this increase in population in his inaugural message to the city council: "During the past two years our population has probably doubled and the city has spread in every direction." He laid out a program for the town that addressed three primary needs: a new city jail, street improvements, and an enhanced fire department. Of streets he said, "It appears to me this problem has but one answer, 'Asphalt.' It is almost indestructible in this climate and will last for years without repair. It is as smooth as a floor and is superior to any other pavement from a sanitary point of view." He issued a prescient warning about the city's fire-fighting capabilities: "In case of fire, the machinery is not efficient and the water supply is reported inadequate."

Anderson offered a challenge and a vision for the future of St. Augustine: "The past year has witnessed a revolution in our City which no one could have anticipated. Hundreds of thousands of dollars have been spent and are being spent in our midst.... The crowning enterprise, the building of the Ponce de Leon Hotel, will make St. Augustine famous.... Our city bids fair therefore to become the Nice, as well as the Newport of America."[26]

As mayor, Anderson could act to further Flagler's good relations with the St. Augustine community. When one of Flagler's wagon drivers was accused of beating a mule to death, Flagler thanked Anderson for appearing in the mayor's court to defend his employee, and added, "Under no circumstances would I uphold overworking a beast." He advised McGuire and McDonald: "As a matter of principle, as well of respect to the sentiment of the community, I desire that you should do no Sunday work about the hotel grounds. If it is absolutely necessary to make any repairs on that day, try to do it as it will not be observed."[27]

Then matters took a potentially serious turn.

In January 1886 tempers boiled over at the construction site, causing Flagler to wonder if he would have to make drastic changes in the team managing his building project. Franklin W. Smith and Kennish, who both regarded themselves experts on concrete construction, became embroiled in an argument. McGuire and McDonald took Kennish's side, and in trying to smooth over the controversy, Anderson fell into the wrangling as well. From his isolated vantage in New York City, Flagler fired off a series of letters aimed at either mollifying the combatants or eliminating some of them. First he wrote to Smith to say that he valued Kennish and wanted to continue to engage him in future building projects. Flagler attempted to soothe Smith's feelings by saying that Anderson had perhaps made a simple blunder in taking sides with McGuire and McDonald.

To Anderson he wrote that Smith seemed to have the better side in the argument on the concrete, and he even wondered if perhaps McGuire and McDonald lacked the executive capacity to handle such a large undertaking. Finally, he wrote to John Carrère telling him to investigate the situation on his next trip to St. Augustine. Flagler suggested that in dealing with Smith, "we should make considerable allowance for our friend's idiosyncrasies, yet it will not do to ignore his practical knowledge." He added that if Carrère found Kennish to be in the wrong, he had Flagler's authority to fire Kennish.[28]

Fortunately, the controversy seems to have passed without further incident, and Flagler's team continued their work. However, Flagler found other issues to worry about. He asked Smith to check into the drinking habits of two contractors, and when Smith returned an unfavorable report, Flagler responded: "I regret exceedingly that the brothers of this firm are addicted to the use of liquor. Unless this is corrected, I will make short work of them when I arrive."[29]

Flagler, along with Alice, Harry, and Harry's tutor, came to St. Augustine in mid-February and took a suite of rooms in the San Marco. He immediately set about impressing his will on the situation. He was by no means a novice at major construction projects, having overseen construction of the Standard Oil headquarters building at 26 Broadway a few years earlier. Flagler and Rockefeller had become famous for the efficiency of their oil refinery operations, and Flagler wanted the same standards upheld in Florida. A few days spent in St. Augustine, he told Anderson, convinced him "that there is a great lack of system; that more intelligent driving foremen [are] essential, and that with them very much more work can be obtained from the day laborers."[30]

When Flagler arrived in St. Augustine the foundation walls were nearly completed, and between three hundred and four hundred men swarmed over the construction site. Along Tolomato Street winter guests paused to inspect progress, as a correspondent for the local press reported: "The busy scene of work on the new Ponce de Leon draws the attention of all our visitors, who watch with wonderment the multifarious kinds of work continuously in operation."[31]

On the west side of this activity McGuire and McDonald had erected a large wooden building as their headquarters, with space for Carrère and Hastings as well. Hastings came down a few weeks later in February to walk around the grounds with Flagler, although usually it would be Carrère who visited to watch over the interests of their firm. John W. Ingle, an architect with a degree from Columbia University, remained on site constantly as the supervising architect representing Carrère and Hastings. At one end of McGuire's building Flagler set up an office for himself where he could issue commands and act as the final court of appeals for any of the parties engaged in the enterprise. Workmen built a wooden walkway from the back door of Dr. Anderson's Markland home to the headquarters building. This feature suggests that Flagler spent a good deal of time at Markland during his visits to St. Augustine.[32]

In the midst of this major building project, John Carrère took time to attend to a personal matter. He married Marion Sidonia Dell of Jacksonville. Her father,

This photo of the Hotel Ponce de Leon under construction, taken from the corner tower of the Hotel Casa Monica, shows a locomotive parked at the intersection of Cordova and King streets. Flagler ran temporary tracks over his property to haul in fill dirt and building materials. By permission of Flagler College.

Colonel Charles Dell, had served in the Second Seminole War. Marion had grown up in Texas and California, but evidently she had returned to Florida, where she met Carrère during one of his trips to St. Augustine.[33]

On the last day of February, Henry and Alice attended a ball at the San Marco Hotel with Franklin W. Smith, his wife, and their daughter Nina, who was just as beautiful as her mother. They were also accompanied to the dance by William G. Warden and his wife. Warden was an oil man who had run Philadelphia's largest refinery until 1874, when he was prevailed upon to enlist in the Standard empire. Flagler seems to have inspired Warden to join his St. Augustine venture: in the summer Warden and Anderson went in together with another investor to form the St. Augustine Gas and Electric Company to furnish gas for the city. In years thereafter Warden and his family would become leading citizens of the town during the winter season, erecting their own Moorish castle of concrete just north of the Fort Marion reservation.[34]

By the time the Flaglers departed for New York at the end of March, work had commenced on the second story of the hotel, and carpenters had moved in to initiate framing of the woodwork of the ground floor.

Across King Street the major task of filling in the southern reaches of Maria Sanchez commenced. Flagler emphasized to his builders: "It is quite important for the future reputation of the hotel, that we remove, at as early a day as possible, every vestige of the marsh near King St."[35]

McGuire and McDonald extended their temporary railroad all the way across the hotel lot and over King Street to the proposed site of Hastings's casino. By the summer of 1886 what for centuries had been Maria Sanchez marsh, on both sides of King Street, had become an expanse of white sand on which Flagler erected a bustling warren of workshops, built warehouses, and kept construction equipment.[36]

April 1886 found Flagler back in Florida. The walls of the hotel continued to rise quickly, with the red brickwork around windows and in arches adding color to the mass of concrete. People wondered if the hotel might be completed in time for the next winter's season. A reporter for the *Florida Times-Union* managed to extract a few comments from Flagler as he stopped in Jacksonville at the Windsor Hotel. Flagler averred to the newspaperman that he hoped the hotel would be finished in time to open in 1887. He added that the "work was growing on his hands" and that he was obliged to give a great deal of his personal attention to details of construction. At the same time, privately, he confirmed his earlier estimate that the building would not be ready until the 1888 season. "I have decided not to undertake the completion of the 'Ponce de Leon' until a year from next winter," he wrote to a friend in New York.[37]

The general public knew nothing of this timetable and, instead, marveled at the rapidity with which the work progressed. "Surprisingly easy does the mammoth structure rise heavenward," declared the *Times-Union*, "and in each angle and curve is seen that proportion of artistic beauty and design that the plans are developing."[38] By the first week of June the walls of the second story were almost up. By the third week of July the third story neared completion. The middle of August found carpenters framing in the roof, while others were beginning to bring the Dining Room area into shape. The New York City firm of Pottier and Stymus surfaced the floor in a kiln-dried white oak known as "Fifty year old oak." In December window frames were being placed into the window openings. The pace had been fantastic, yet by the end of the year it had become obvious to all that there remained much still to be done—and the winter season had arrived.[39]

In November Flagler came down from New York in a private car, accompanied by Carrère and Anderson, who had spent some time in the North as Flagler's guest. Saying he was pleased with progress on the hotel, Flagler returned to New York to spend the Christmas season at home.[40] In January and then again in March 1887 Flagler returned to St. Augustine to check up on advances in the building. While in town he consulted with O. D. Seavey on matters relating to the interiors of the hotel.[41]

Even though he had known all along that there was little hope of opening in 1887, it must have been disappointing for him to wait another whole year. After all, time was flying, and as Flagler held, "time is life."[42]

It may have been during this visit when a little incident occurred that has become part of the Flagler legend in St. Augustine.

His chief builder, James McGuire, a crotchety bachelor, employed an old black woman as his cook and her daughter as his housekeeper. The daughter had a son named Amos Phillips, who became at first McGuire's errand boy and eventually, over the years, something of a surrogate son.

Phillips had gone on the payroll of the hotel company on November 28, 1885, just days before work began on the foundations of the Ponce. At the age of seventeen he assumed whatever duties McGuire assigned to him.[43] At some stage of work on the hotel, McGuire stationed his young major domo Amos in a room of the Ponce de Leon where some valuable materials had been temporarily stored, instructing him to keep everyone out of the room and by no means to allow anyone to smoke in the vicinity. While Amos was on duty at his sentry post, an important-looking gentleman wandered up smoking a small cigar, and Amos promptly informed him that he must get out immediately and take his smoke with him. "Who gave you these orders, boy?" asked the man calmly. "Mr. McGuire," answered Amos, vowing with all the heat he could muster that he aimed to see those orders carried out.

The man was, of course, Henry Flagler, and he went to McGuire's office and asked, "Who is that young Negro working at the hotel?" McGuire answered, "That's Amos Phillips. I brought him from Magnolia Springs with me. Why, has he done something wrong?" "Wrong!" replied Flagler, "He's the best worker we have, and I want to see that he gets paid for his efficiency and trustworthiness." Flagler would come to know Philips well over the years, and on one occasion, Phillips recalled, Flagler took off his coat and rolled up his sleeves to demonstrate the proper technique for "laying a fire" in one of the hotel's fireplaces.[44]

Phillips would continue to be employed by the East Coast Hotel Company for fifty-one years, retiring in 1936 to great acclaim for his service.[45]

9

Transforming
St. Augustine, 1887

He does not want it known in St. Augustine, even at the
bank, what he gives. . . . We must keep his secret.

—Bishop John Moore to Edward Pace, July 28, 1887

A new hotel did open in St. Augustine for the winter season in January 1887—
Franklin W. Smith's Casa Monica. However, this building represented just the
first installment of the much larger hotel he envisioned.

Smith erected his hotel in conjunction with the Lyon Building, which occupied the corner of King and St. George streets. Walter Lyon had long operated
a grocery store on this corner, but he had passed away, and his heirs decided to
replace the old wooden store with a large, modern business building of concrete.
When the imposing four-story structure opened in November 1886, the Lyon
Building represented the first of the great innovative concrete structures to be
completed—and the harbinger of even greater things to come.[1]

Smith's Casa Monica abutted the Lyon Building on its west side, making the
two structures appear as one continuous concrete edifice. Smith marked the
opening of his hotel by issuing a little leaflet praising its exotic architecture—
with "battlements like those in Toledo left by the Moors" and "kneeling balconies designed by Michael Angelo." Otherwise there seems not to have been any
great public recognition of the Casa Monica's debut; guests just started arriving,
while a ladies' apparel shop and the telephone company's office moved into the
ground floor. Looking toward the future, Smith's flier stated: "Its first section is
completed and a more elaborate remainder will soon follow."[2]

Franklin Smith made a new departure in the type of concrete used in the Lyon
Building and Casa Monica. Perhaps he did this out of necessity, for he lacked the
sand and coquina quarries that Flagler had secured for his buildings. To obtain

sand, Smith simply dredged it from the sandbars of Matanzas Bay and omitted shell or stone aggregate from his concrete mix. Although a few scattered coquina and even scallop shells happened to find their way into the blend, this new all-sand formula resulted in a smoother, more uniform texture than the coarse concrete Smith had utilized in the Villa Zorayda and Flagler was then using in the Ponce de Leon. The new concrete turned out to be extremely dense and fabulously strong. If a workman struck it with a hammer, the hammer would recoil as if striking iron.[3]

In April 1887, as the winter season drew to its conclusion, Smith closed the Sunnyside and Casa Monica. Immediately workers dismantled the Sunnyside and moved two of its wings to West Augustine, where one remnant of the old house still survives at 525 West King Street. Smith cleared several other buildings from the west side of his property to make way for the remaining section of the Casa Monica, which would dwarf the original building in size. Laborers began pouring the concrete foundations within weeks, and by mid-June the concrete walls had risen as far as two stories. A month later they reached three stories. Smith's workers seemed to be racing to match Flagler's preparations for the opening of the 1888 season.[4]

The Lyon Building, the first of the great concrete commercial buildings, opened in late 1886. Today it holds shops on its ground floor and apartments on its upper floors—very much as it did from the beginning. By permission of the Florida Historical Society.

The first section of the Hotel Casa Monica opened in 1887. This early section with its balconies, hipped roof, and two chimneys stands between the Lyon Building on the left and the square tower of the newer part of the Casa Monica that was completed in 1888. By permission of Flagler College.

Across the way Flagler's men appeared to be far in advance of Smith's efforts, with the walls and roof of the Ponce de Leon already in place when Smith had just commenced his work on the Casa Monica extension. Inside the walls of the Ponce de Leon, Flagler's architects and builders employed some innovative materials as well as some time-honored elements. Iron and steel had already come into use in New York and Paris a decade earlier, but Carrère and Hastings were not far behind with their use in Flagler's buildings. In the heart of the Ponce de Leon, surrounding the open rotunda area, they placed a circle of eight iron structural support columns planted on concrete foundations deep in the cellar. These columns helped hold up the mezzanine floor and extended all the way up to the dome to support it as well. To span the thirty-seven-foot-wide galleries of the Grand Parlor, they utilized steel I-beams.[5]

Much of the structural fabric of the floors and roof of the Hotel Ponce de Leon, on the other hand, consisted of traditional wooden framework, with which McGuire and McDonald had been familiar since their days as ship builders. The wood came from the primeval forests of the surrounding Florida countryside: yellow pine, also called longleaf pine, which, when sawed into lumber, became known as hart pine. Heavy with resin, this wood resisted rot, was impervious to insects and, when dried, became strong and tough.

McGuire and McDonald built the vaulted ceiling of the Ponce de Leon's Dining Room using traditional building methods employing wooded trusses. On the right, the wooden forms holding freshly poured concrete can be seen at the top of the utility wing of the hotel. By permission of Library of Congress.

McGuire and McDonald purchased lumber wherever they could find it, but most came from a sawmill at the south end of town on the San Sebastian River known as the English Mill or Sloggett's Mill, for its manager Dr. Henry C. Sloggett. The mill belonged to an English firm, the East Florida Land and Produce Company, which owned thousands of acres and even built a railroad twelve miles into the interior for chasing pine trees. Sloggett was a British subject who had trained as a physician in Scotland and served as ship's surgeon on the HMS *Challenger* when it made a scientific voyage to the Pacific in the 1870s. Sloggett himself owned a 130-acre orange grove on Pellicer Creek south of St. Augustine (including what is today Princess Place Preserve, a state park). Sloggett lived in a large residence on the bank of Matanzas Bay at the south end of town.[6]

The fatal flaw of yellow pine lurks in its rich amber resin, which, when set afire, burns like a torch. With so many of the South's buildings constructed of this pine, massive conflagrations became an inevitable matter of course. Everyone knew this full well, and warnings to be prepared were not scarce. The *Jacksonville Morning News* advised St. Augustinians to take heed of a recent fire in the town of Sanford: "St. Augustine is now crowded with wooden structures of all sizes and descriptions, should a fire start in St. Augustine now it is reasonable to suppose that the city would be almost if not totally destroyed." When the city council took up a proposal to buy another fire engine, the problem of how to pay for it stymied action, leading the *Times-Union* to opine: "The question of fire protection is again agitating the minds of the City Fathers and the public, and no doubt will be left to slumber until a fire comes along while they are sleeping, leaving nothing but ashes for monuments to their apathy."[7]

Early in the still morning hours of April 12, 1887, fire broke out in the boiler room of Captain Vaill's St. Augustine Hotel, and within minutes the whole building glowed with orange flames that shot sparks high into the air to ignite adjacent buildings. Soldiers from St. Francis Barracks and workers from Flagler's building projects came running to help townspeople remove valuables from inside structures in the path of the fire, creating piles of furniture and household goods in the Plaza and on Bay Street along the seawall. The major effort centered upon preventing the flames from spreading across narrow Treasury Street to the Florida Hotel and the northern part of town. The roof of the old market in the Plaza went up in smoke, and then the fire reached the Catholic cathedral. Its roof caught fire and eventually collapsed into the interior, gutting the building down to its thick coquina stone walls. The church's clock in the façade valiantly chimed the hours and half-hours until 5:30 and then fell silent. Fortunately the air remained calm during the night, making the work of the firefighters ultimately successful. The fire consumed just the single town block north of the Plaza.

Since the winter season had passed, few guests occupied the hotel's rooms, and only one unfortunate woman perished in the conflagration. Another guest of the hotel, the architect James Renwick, lost the roof over his head.

One of the firemen exclaimed: "The one and only Mansfield fire engine was a marvel. How it shook and coughed and danced from side to side, but it faithfully kept the water flowing under good pressure until the fire was extinguished."[8]

The day after the fire McGuire and McDonald suspended work on Flagler's buildings so that their laborers could assist in cleaning up debris in the burned district, and Flagler continued to pay his workforce at a rate of more than a thousand dollars a day. He also pledged to aid financially in the rebuilding effort.[9]

A month after the fire, the city council belatedly authorized purchase of a new, more powerful Silsby fire engine for $4,000, with Flagler picking up one-fourth of the cost. When the new engine arrived in July the city handed it over to the care of the newly formed Ponce de Leon Steam Fire Engine and Hose Company, which had been organized by McGuire and McDonald. Some local citizens objected that the Flagler men were not true residents of the city, but Flagler got his way since he had put up the money. The old Mansfield engine went to the "colored" volunteer fire company, and the town's other white volunteer fire fighters went without an engine.[10]

In the aftermath of the fire, Catholic bishop John Moore established a subscription fund to raise money for rebuilding the cathedral, and during the summer he traveled north to solicit funds. He achieved meager results until he called on Henry Flagler in New York, who extended his good will and donated $5,000. Flagler deposited the money into an account in a northern bank from which Moore could draw as needed. Moore explained Flagler's desires to his rector Edward Pace back in St. Augustine: "He does not want it known in St. Augustine, even at the bank, what he gives, and therefore does not like to send his checks there. We must keep his secret." Later it would be said that Flagler donated a total of $75,000 to rebuild and enhance the church, but just how much money Flagler gave the church is a secret that Bishop Moore and Henry Flagler have managed to keep down to the present.[11]

Flagler's generosity to the church was not entirely altruistic. The church owned a large block of property just to the east of the Hotel Ponce de Leon that Flagler wished to acquire to ensure that its use would comport with the refined atmosphere of his luxury resort. The lot ran all the way from St. George Street to Tolomato Street. Bishop Moore agreed to transfer the property to Flagler. In the middle of the lot stood the old St. Mary's Convent, which Flagler would later lease as a cigar factory. At the western side of the lot, the St. Augustine Transfer Company, which carried passengers to and from the railway station, would have its headquarters, conveniently across the street from the hotel.[12]

Immediately after the fire, James Renwick volunteered to prepare plans for rebuilding the cathedral, and Bishop Moore was very pleased to accept the services of the distinguished architect who had designed St. Patrick's Cathedral, the most monumental church in America. In addition to modernizing and expanding the church, Renwick added a magnificent bell tower to the side of the simple church's façade. For himself, Renwick took great pride in having this opportunity to contribute his skills to the enhancement of such a venerable edifice as the old Spanish church.[13]

Henry Flagler and Renwick do not seem to have had a close relationship, although they were both New Yorkers and yachtsmen who belonged to the same yacht clubs in New York City, Larchmont, and St. Augustine. When Flagler's Hotel Ponce de Leon opened, almost a year after the cathedral fire, Renwick received a personal tour of the building conducted by John Carrère.[14] It is remarkable that five of the leading architects in America—Renwick, Hastings, Carrère, and the Carrère and Hastings associates Bernard Maybeck and Emmanuel Louis Masqueray—were all working on projects in tiny St. Augustine at the same moment.

Other citizens who had been victimized by the fire also immediately set about rebuilding, this time using fireproof concrete. Captain Vaill borrowed $38,000 from Flagler and replaced his hotel with a business block that went up quickly. It rose only one story high and reflected the Moorish influence of the Villa Zorayda. The building still stands today, although thoroughly modernized, with only the tavern fronting 124 Charlotte Street maintaining most of its original appearance. Mrs. Sophia Carr, widow of B. E. Carr, one of the town's elder citizens from before the war, lost her "old fashioned residence" fronting Bay Street, but she likewise rebuilt in concrete, almost exactly duplicating the appearance of her original home. This building also still stands, at 46 Avenida Menendez, and is used as a restaurant. The city council voted to reroof the old "Slave Market," but for almost the whole of the next year it would be covered with palm thatch until blue slate could be purchased to do the job properly.[15]

Although the city's tardy effort to restore the Slave Market illustrated the town's typical inability to act quickly, it also demonstrated the city fathers' recognition that historic landmarks defined the character of St. Augustine. A general feeling prevailed that the traditional atmosphere of the town should be preserved and that "progress"—personified by Henry Flagler's mammoth projects—represented almost as great a threat to the city as did fire. Commenting on the "great improvements" in town, one writer declared: "It is regretted by many that this work so often necessitates the tearing down and demolishing of so many of the old houses that here always provided the charm for the visiting tourist. New and modern palaces may always be erected, but there is no artisan, no matter how perfect his skill, who can ever produce, when once destroyed, any of these quaint old Spanish landmarks."[16]

An editorial in the *Florida Weekly Times* of Jacksonville reads as if written in the spirit of the modern preservation movement. Comparing the improvements of recent years to acts of "Vandals of modern architecture," it called upon the city council to establish an organized movement "to control and direct with a view to the future the buildings and other improvements that shall hereafter be erected. In no place in America should the 'eternal fitness of things' be more highly valued. Above all things immediate steps should be taken to preserve and restore the older buildings and walls." The writer proposed that new buildings should be erected in locations that did not require the destruction of old houses and that they be constructed of materials and in architectural styles compatible with the existing ambiance of the "Ancient City." This could be done without sacrificing modern conveniences and only required sensitivity to the architectural requirements of "old Spanish styles of construction." With this approach St. Augustine could be made more interesting and attractive to visitors than ever before.[17]

Meanwhile, Flagler continued his work of transforming St. Augustine. Having filled the northern reaches of the Maria Sanchez marsh for his two hotels, Flagler continued his operations southward another long block to the modern terminus of filled land at today's Maria Sanchez Lake. To obtain additional sand he purchased a farm located about a mile north of town belonging to David Batewell. He ran a temporary spur rail line to the farm. It was commonly called the Moses Tract, a name corrupted from the original Mose. Fort Mose, founded by the Spanish in 1738, had been a settlement of refuge for runaway black slaves who had escaped from British colonies to the north. Today it is a state park commemorating the first free black town in the United States. However, all but the extreme eastern tip of the Fort Mose site is now tidal marsh, almost certainly testimony to Flagler's excavations. Only a small portion of the location of the original fort and its successor fort survived Flagler's dredging.[18]

At the Fort Mose site, Flagler built a temporary camp alongside the rail line to Jacksonville where a gang of 125 men lived and labored to fill a train of eleven carloads of sand and marl for runs to town several times a day. Every few days some workmen would be allowed to ride the train to town for a break, but the superintendent required each man to take a swig of quinine before leaving, supposedly to protect him from any fever that might be brought on by the heavy drinking he was expected to engage in while in town. One day the workmen at the sand pit killed a rattlesnake measuring eight feet, three inches long; if this length is accurate, it would be the longest rattler ever recorded in Florida—and perhaps the United States.[19]

Much of the sand from the Batewell farm went to fill the east bank of the San Sebastian River. By the end of summer all of the salt flats north of King Street had been filled and graded. This would be the site for Flagler's new Union Station, with plenty of additional room for other structures. Along the east side of the filled land, workmen created a new street called Ribera, preserving the old Spanish name for the riverbank that had existed there. Over time common English usage transformed Ribera into Riberia, as the street is called today.[20]

During the spring and summer of 1887, work continued in the center of town according to the usual routines on the site of Flagler's hotels. Some discontented skilled laborers—the men doing the plasterwork, the carpenters, and the plumbers—asked for higher wages. A number of them received increases, while others were fired. The carpenters organized a union, and McGuire and McDonald thereafter gave the union recognition.[21] To keep spirits up, McGuire and McDonald once chartered a train to take workers to the beach in Jacksonville. They always gave the whole workforce a couple hours off at noon during the hottest time of the day. Interestingly, Flagler's men operated on a different clock than the rest of town, and sometimes this resulted in a confusing disconnect between "Flagler Time" and the local time traditionally set by the clock in the Catholic church and by local merchants.[22] Workers received their pay every two weeks, with skilled mechanics (mostly white men) being paid on one Friday, and unskilled day laborers (mostly black men) getting their money on the following Friday. Newspaper estimates of the weekly payout ran from $8,000 to $20,000. Whatever the numbers, it amounted to a spectacularly unprecedented infusion of cash into the traditionally meager local economy—especially during the summer "dull season."[23]

A black craftsman from Jacksonville, who identified himself only as "W. S.," gave this testimony of his experience working on the Ponce de Leon: "They first put me with what they called the Negro gang, on the rough part or back end of the building, the white men were on the front part. Some of the white men were not fit for hod carriers. Of course, they were very soon fired if they could not hold up and compete with their white brothers; they saw from my work I was a good mason; they carried me to the front and put me to work on a piece of work that every white mason had failed on and I completed my job satisfactorily. The whites then made complaint to the foreman that they did not want to work with a Negro; they then arranged to keep me on the front on a difficult job to myself, that being the order of the general boss [probably McGuire]. The foreman hated a colored man worse than he would a snake, and although he kept me on the front work until the job was finished, but would never raise my wages up with the white masons, yet I did the best work and most difficult jobs on the hotel."[24]

Even as the bricks were being laid and the concrete poured, Carrère and Hastings began to incorporate decorative terra-cotta elements into the walls. This salmon clay ornamentation added color to an otherwise austere building. Terracotta had come into use in the United States during the 1870s as a much less expensive substitute for carved stone—and was criticized at the time for being a cheap, manufactured imitation of stone sculpture. The liquid terra-cotta clay would first be poured into molds and then, when dry, pulled out of the forms by craftsmen who would sand off parting seams and add a few finishing details by hand. Finally the pieces would be fired in a furnace to give them the hardness of brick. Earlier in the decade McKim, Mead and White had used both orange and blonde terra-cotta in their buildings; thus Carrère and Hastings were already familiar with it. The terra-cotta in the hotel came from a company in Perth Amboy, New Jersey. By March 1886 crates of terra-cotta pieces with cherubs, dolphins, and coats of arms were stacked on the hotel grounds ready to be put in place. The orange terra-cotta decorations and orange brick window surrounds provided a pleasing contrast to the stark, gray concrete walls.[25]

To enrich the interiors and create an exotic atmosphere, Carrère and Hastings used heavy wooden ornamentation that became particularly elaborate in the Rotunda, the Dining Room, and other major public areas. In the Rotunda, the eight sturdy iron columns supporting the mezzanine and dome were concealed by encasing them with carved oak in the form of Greek caryatids. The commission to accomplish this expansive undertaking had gone to Pottier and Stymus, a leading interior decorating and furniture-making firm that occupied an immense, rambling six-story factory in midtown Manhattan.[26] Although their craftsmen could—and did—create custom-made furniture and decorations in a wide variety of styles, they were commonly associated with the garish, over-stuffed Egyptian and Oriental styles so popular in those days and that today have come to epitomize the bad taste of the high Victorian age.

Pottier and Stymus employed hundreds of workers, many of them recently arrived from Europe with craftsmanship skills learned in the old country. Among these was Bernhardt Maybeck, whose parents had sent him to America after the failed liberal revolution of 1848 in Germany. He married Elisa Kern, daughter of another German revolutionary, and they settled in Greenwich Village, where their son Bernard was born in 1862. The elder Maybeck operated a woodworking shop of his own for several years but then joined Pottier and Stymus in the 1870s to become foreman of the woodcarving department. During construction of the Hotel Ponce de Leon, Bernhardt came to St. Augustine to supervise installation of the woodwork.[27]

Pottier and Stymus took great pride in their contributions to Flagler's hotel. Their entry in a New York City business guide boasted: "Much of the finest work in the gorgeous Ponce de Leon Hotel, at St. Augustine, came from this wonderful repository and manufactory."[28]

By coincidence, but perhaps not such a great coincidence considering the relatively small universe of architects, artists, and artisans in the New York City area, Bernhardt Maybeck's labors on the wood carvings going into the Hotel Ponce de Leon brought him into close working relations with his son Bernard, who was engaged on the same project.

In 1886 Bernard Maybeck had returned from Paris after completion of his studies at the École des Beaux Arts and joined his old schoolmates Hastings and Carrère. It is likely that the young firm of Carrère and Hastings, deeply immersed in Henry Flagler's expansive St. Augustine program, needed additional help and saw Maybeck as a congenial personality whose training at the École fitted him to work as a collaborator on the elements of architectural design.

Unfortunately, no documentation of Maybeck's creative work with Carrère and Hastings has survived, so it is impossible to identify any original contributions he may have made to the Flagler buildings in St. Augustine. The design of the Ponce de Leon was well advanced by the time Maybeck joined the firm; any work he did would more likely have been focused on the Alcazar, Grace Methodist Church, and Memorial Presbyterian Church. The medieval aspects of the Methodist church closely parallel some of the designs Maybeck later executed in California, but attributing these to Maybeck is merely conjecture; we do not know precisely what he did.[29]

Years later, in 1952, architect Frederick Nichols called upon ninety-year-old Bernard Maybeck on the sunny patio of his home in California. The bearded, barefoot Maybeck reminisced about his sixty-plus years as an architect, recalling the Hotel Ponce de Leon, "with which he was particularly pleased for he mentioned it several times." Maybeck's wife Annie gave Nichols a letter in which Maybeck explained how he had worked with Carrère and Hastings on the Ponce de Leon: "Hastings made the preliminary drawings and explained the scheme. These drawings were given to the draftsmen to draw up, putting the practical work on paper. Then Hastings or Maybeck 'studied' proportions, etc. The drawings were corrected accordingly and turned over to the main office for engineering, electrical, and plumbing drawings. Then the whole thing went to Carrère."[30]

Maybeck's portrayal of working arrangements among the architects bears the ring of truth. Thomas Hastings would not likely have turned over creative leadership to anyone else in his firm, yet he certainly would have needed practical professional assistance in the myriad of details involved in the Flagler projects. Carrère's stepping in at the end of the process when planning reached the actual brick-and-mortar stage also fits with what is known of his role in the company.

Maybeck's employment at the firm lasted only about three years, and then he departed for California, where he became a leading figure in the arts and crafts movement. One can speculate that Maybeck, with his interest in medieval culture and his commitment to honest, craftsman values, did not fit in well with the more elevated ideals espoused by Carrère and Hastings. His working-class background, lack of money, and, perhaps, lack of aspiration to associate with high society may also have contributed to his departure for the West. Perhaps he simply wanted to be his own boss.[31]

During the summer of 1887, decorative stained glass went into the windows of the Dining Room and Rotunda of the Ponce de Leon. This art glass came from the newly formed Tiffany Glass Company, which Louis C. Tiffany had established on December 1, 1885, to produce glass on a commercial scale for homes and buildings. It is likely that Flagler was the company's first important client. Tiffany was no stranger to Thomas Hastings, who had known him at least as far back as the days of working on the Seventh Regiment Armory, and Tiffany knew St. Augustine well. In the winter of 1883, Tiffany had come to Florida with his gravely ill first wife Mary. While in town, Tiffany set up a studio and painted, among other things, a scene of Fort Marion and the rear loggia of the Kirby-Smith house.[32]

The contribution of Tiffany himself to the Hotel Ponce de Leon is something

Tiffany Glass Company
provided the decorative glass for
the Hotel Ponce de Leon, but
it is not known which artist(s)
actually designed the windows.
Author's photo.

of a mystery. Contemporary newspaper accounts say nothing of the windows, while Flagler's own publicity, amazingly, never even alludes to the windows. The only authentication of Tiffany's involvement is contained in a brochure Tiffany produced for the 1893 Chicago World's Fair that lists "ornamental windows" and "decorations" for the Hotel Ponce de Leon. "Decorations" poses another problem. During the 1870s and early 1880s Tiffany had been deeply involved with interior decorating, having done, most famously, the Mark Twain house in Hartford and renovations to President Chester Arthur's White House. But what contribution he made to the interior decoration of the Ponce de Leon is unknown. Compilations published by the Tiffany company in later years lack any further reference to the Hotel Ponce de Leon.[33]

Exactly who executed the artistic designs for the extensive and marvelous collection of windows in the hotel is thus unknown. When Tiffany started his company, he listed eight other artists who worked alongside him in fashioning the images to be executed in glass.[34] A strong candidate for at least some of the artistic effort that went into the Tiffany windows of the Ponce de Leon is David Maitland Armstrong.

Armstrong sprang from old New York ancestry, and this connection served him well when his uncle, Secretary of State Hamilton Fish, named him U.S. consul to the Vatican State in 1869 so that young Armstrong could study art in Rome. There he met the sculptor Augustus Saint-Gaudens, who would become a lifelong friend. In Paris he met George W. Maynard, and back in New York he became an associate of John LaFarge as well as a collaborator with LaFarge's competitor in stained glass, Louis C. Tiffany. From about 1880 until 1887 Armstrong worked closely with Tiffany, later working independently designing stained glass under his own name.[35]

A tantalizing piece of evidence supporting Armstrong's connection with the glass in the Hotel Ponce de Leon is contained in a novel by Armstrong's daughter Margaret Armstrong. In *Murder in Stained Glass*, published in 1939, she has one of the characters in her mystery story, a stained glass artist, travel to St. Augustine to see about a commission to supply stained glass for a new resort hotel. Could she have created this fictional incident from her knowledge of her father's actual work?

If the Hotel Ponce de Leon's stained glass windows present something of a mystery, at least St. Augustinians can be sure of two windows in Trinity Episcopal Church. In this church on the Plaza both Tiffany and Armstrong signed their respective windows.

During that busy spring and summer of 1887 a plastering contractor sent teams of artisans into the Ponce de Leon to cover the wood lath sheeting of the walls and ceilings with a thick coat of white plaster. They began with the great public rooms and then moved on to the hallways and private guest chambers. As soon as the plasterers vacated the great rooms, teams of mural artists began to fill the empty spaces with intricate designs that would eventually cover almost all of the walls and ceilings of the major public rooms. Unfortunately for the long-term survival of this art, they applied their paint to dry plaster, and so it is not a true fresco painting, embedded into the plaster. The member of the artistic team who attracted the most attention from the press was a "beautiful model" who posed for the allegorical female images around which the decorations revolved.[36]

Thomas Hastings himself claimed credit for the overall conceptual design of the murals; however, he also gave recognition for these decorations to George Willoughby Maynard, then in his mid-forties and entering the maturity of his artistic career.

Maynard had been born in Washington, D.C., son of Dr. Edward Maynard, one of the country's leading oral surgeons, but most recognized as inventor of the Maynard Carbine, a breech-loading rifle used by Union cavalry in the Civil War. The younger Maynard, a balding, bearded, hawk-nosed bachelor, possessed a mouth that turned down in a scowl, giving him a fierce look.

Maynard lived in a hotel for unmarried men facing Washington Square in New York City. His friends the sculptor Augustus Saint-Gaudens and stained glass artist D. Maitland Armstrong maintained studios nearby. The whole neighborhood was filled with artists and literary people. Maynard enjoyed evenings smoking cigars and playing low-stakes card games of skill with other young gentlemen. In 1876 he and Saint-Gaudens worked with John LaFarge in decorating Trinity Church in Boston. Then he traveled to Paris for two years of study. Returning to New York, in 1885 he was elected to the National Academy of Design as a "rising young artist."[37]

While Maynard and the mural artists were busy on their scaffolding, James McGuire would sometimes take visitors through the building to see the latest work in progress. Guests first encountered Maynard's art as they gazed upward into the dome of the Rotunda. The experience, then as today, is like peering into the depths of an amber jewel, with each facet of the gem painted in shimmering gold details. The most prominent artistic components of the ceiling consist of

George W. Maynard painted the allegorical figures that are focal points of the murals in the Rotunda of the Ponce de Leon. Author's photo.

The festive themes of the murals on the ceiling of the Dining Room are drawn from history and mythology. Author's photo.

eight allegorical female figures representing the ancient Greek elements of Earth, Fire, Air, and Water; they are joined by Discovery, Civilization, Adventure, and Conquest. Each occupies a separate angle of the ceiling encircling the central opening of a dome rising to a clear oculus three stories above. Maynard painted the figures on a flat, pale gold surface in a Pompeian style that presents each figure in isolation, placidly facing the viewer.[38] Maynard signed his art unobtrusively by working the message "Maynard fecit 1887" into the gold-embroidered neckline of Discovery's blue gown. This sly signature would not be discovered until workmen came across it while restoring the art in the early 1990s.

The secondary elements of the decoration consist of a myriad of painted floral garlands and other symbolic images filling every empty space: harps, swans, cow skulls for the Europeans, and deer skulls for the Native Americans. The names of conquistadors appear at the cardinal compass points: Jean Ribault, Hernando de Soto, Pánfilo Narváez, and, in the foremost position, Ponce de León. The least prominent features of the Rotunda decorations are the heraldic shields of Spanish kingdoms, with their names lettered above them.

These secondary embellishments are most likely the work of an artist who labored without receiving public credit from the hotel's publicists but whose contributions were known at the time: Herman Theodore Schladermundt.[39]

The Hotel Ponce de Leon would be just the first of many commissions on which Schladermundt would collaborate with either Maynard or Carrère and Hastings.

Schladermundt had been born in 1863 into the family of a Lutheran minister then living in Milwaukee but who nomadically migrated from church to church, carrying his family with him. As a teenager, Herman, already known to his friends as "Pete," apprenticed himself to an architect in Buffalo, then found a place at the firm of Burnham and Root in Chicago until he secured a position with the new partnership of Carrère and Hastings when he was just past twenty years of age. An early photograph of him reveals a slim-faced youth, hair neatly parted in the middle, with his bow tie askew and head off kilter to the right. In later portraits, after he had cultivated a beard and handlebar mustache, he fixes a penetrating gaze on the camera. Visitors to the hotel, moving upstairs into the great vaulted Dining Room, find that the wall and ceiling murals continue the themes of the Rotunda: allegorical women, conquistadors' galleons with billowing sails, and the coats of arms from various Spanish kingdoms. Swags of floral decorations are painted to fill intermediate spaces, although large expanses of the great pale gold central vault are left open to enhance the feeling of height. The symbolic women, two versions of the four seasons placed on either side of the vault, are clearly the work of Maynard. The Spanish royal crests and mermaids amid sinuous strands of foliage may be Schladermundt's; he employed such devices in his later works. Of course, the directing imagination of Thomas Hastings must be in the mix as well. A reporter from the *Jacksonville News-Herald* who visited the hotel in November 1887 found Hastings, Maynard, and Schladermundt in the Dining Room. He reported: "Mr. Hastings has been engaged of late in painting designs for the decorations of the ceilings."[40]

In a circular medallion over the north orchestra balcony appear the dates "1885–1887," the years of the hotel's construction. In a less prominent place in a side alcove is "1512," the supposed date of Juan Ponce de León's discovery and naming of La Florida. At the time, most history books erroneously placed the date at 1512, when it was actually 1513.

Maynard and Schladermundt employed a small team of journeymen artists to assist them in the monumental labor of covering the hotel's ceilings and walls with artistic designs. The process of mural painting would begin by reproducing the artists' original studies on large sheets of paper. These "cartoons" would then receive rows of pinpricks made by rolling a tracing wheel along the major lines of the composition. After this the cartoons would be fixed to the wall or ceiling and a pouncing bag loaded with chalk dust would be dabbed over the paper. When the paper was removed, faint lines of chalk dots would be left in place on the plaster for artists to trace over in reproducing the major lines of the design. Then the painting could begin.

Along the curve of the Dining Room's central vault a series of proverbs appears, perhaps intended to amuse the guests dining below. Translated from Spanish, they impart such wisdom as: "Old friends and old wines are the best. The ass that brays most eats least. A change of pastures makes fat calves."

At each end of the Dining Room a frieze in green and cream depicts cherubs exuberantly dancing around flaming cauldrons in a happy bacchanal. The flaming basins repeat the image employed in the decorative glass of the semicircular clerestory windows. The green-backed frieze differs from the golden-hued walls elsewhere in the room, and while this frieze may represent the work of a different artist's hand, it may simply serve as a transition from the airy ceiling to the dark wooden wainscoting of the floor level.

Meanwhile, as artistic decoration proceeded inside and heavy construction began drawing to a conclusion outside, Flagler started to landscape the grounds around the hotel. His architects Carrère and Hastings, as well as Flagler himself, thought of the Ponce de Leon and Alcazar hotels as the centerpieces of a much grander design for renewing the old town of St. Augustine. Having lived in Paris amid the results of the Second Empire's all-embracing urban revitalization program, Thomas Hastings and John Carrère welcomed the opportunity to remake at least the areas bordering the hotels according to the tenets of modern urban planning and landscape architecture. Henry Flagler, the man who had brought order and rationality to the oil industry, wanted to control as much as possible the environment surrounding his enterprises in St. Augustine.

Wide boulevards and expansive parks made up the heart of the architects' vision. For starters, they wanted King Street widened and paved to create an efficient thoroughfare for traffic passing between the hotels. Next, Carrère and Hastings set the Hotel Alcazar well back on its lot so that the front of its grounds could be turned into an open mall, echoing St. Augustine's old Spanish Plaza, the southwest corner of which just touched Flagler's new plaza. They gave the new plaza the grand name "the Alameda." However, their proposal to change the name of King Street to the Alameda was too much for the citizens of the city council to swallow. The council did accept changing Bronson Street, on the west side of the Hotel Alcazar, to Granada Street, while the awkward-sounding Tolomato Street along the east side of the hotels (strangers had called it "Tomato Street") received the more pronounceable name Cordova Street.[41]

Carrère and Hastings decided to place the front of the Hotel Ponce de Leon close to King Street, with its left side hard against Cordova Street. Flagler owned plenty of real estate behind the hotel, so one might wonder why the great hotel was not situated in the middle of an expansive park with lawns all around it. Carrère and Hastings had good reasons for placing the Ponce where they did. First, their placement honored the ancient Spanish tradition that houses be built right against the street line in front, with yard and patio space situated in the rear for privacy. Second, the Alameda across the way served as an open space from which the Hotel Ponce de Leon could be admired with an unobstructed view.

A few years later, in 1890, Flagler was able to create a second park adjacent to his hotels when the U.S. government donated what was then officially known as the Customs House Lot to the City of St. Augustine for use as a park. Flagler made a deal with the city fathers whereby he would build a decorative fountain matching the one in front of the Alcazar and would landscape and maintain the park for a period of ten years.[42] Popularly known as Post Office Park, the area formed the west end of the Spanish Plaza.

In those days Government House consisted only of the north wing of what is today a much larger building, so someone walking in the eastern end of the Plaza near the Slave Market enjoyed a long vista all the way through to the Hotel Ponce de Leon. Today an expanded Government House and the growth of spreading live oak trees obscure the fact that the Plaza continues beyond Government House, just as they obscure the view of Flagler's hotels. The fountain Flagler built has lost its once prominent place, although the city did rehabilitate it to working operation in 2009.

In his treatment of the Ponce grounds, Hastings followed principles that he would later apply to many of his town houses. He felt that placing a building in the center of its lot divided the available space into segments that were too small for any practical use, whereas locating the building to one side of the lot left a larger unified space on the other side that could be devoted to a lawn or courtyard where people might gather for outdoor activities.[43] In the case of the Hotel Ponce de Leon, Hastings clearly had in mind preserving as much of the Anderson and Ball orange groves as possible to the rear of the hotel. The spacious western lawn of the hotel also afforded newcomers arriving along King Street or Valencia Street a sweeping first prospect of the hotel from that vantage.

In Flagler's promotional book *Florida: The American Riviera*, Carrère and Hastings wrote: "The Ponce de Leon is fortunate in finding a site near the most beautiful garden in St. Augustine. The orange groves of the Ball estate are famous, and these are now included in the hotel grounds. In this beautiful garden one can find realized all his dreams of Southern splendor. Nothing can be more luscious than to stroll at noon under the dense canopy of the Orange Archway or Lovers' Lane, where the trees, planted close together and meeting above, complete a tunnel over the head." They added that guests at the windows of their hotel rooms could "look down over a sea of glossy, brilliant green, dotted thickly with the golden oranges and combining richly with the deep Southern sky."[44]

Hastings surrounded the grounds immediately about the Hotel Ponce de Leon with a low concrete fence, punctuated at close intervals by concrete pedestals with concrete balls balanced on top. Higher semicircles of concrete wall interrupt the course of the low main wall. These small arcs may have been intended to pay homage to the recently destroyed Rosario Lunette, a curved bastion of coquina stone that had stood at the west the of the Plaza until torn down in the widening of Tolomato Street.

This fence not only defined the perimeter of the hotel; the fill dirt behind the wall also served to raise the level of the land surrounding the hotel about twenty inches above sidewalk level. However, this fence did not completely enclose the property of the hotel. The northwest corner of the grounds was left unobstructed so that guests of the hotel could wander into the orange grove that Carrère and Hastings wished so much to exploit for its romantic atmosphere.

This vision of continuing the old St. Augustine tradition of walks though the orange groves eventually fell victim to practical considerations. According to local legend, Flagler was once asked if he intended to save "Lovers' Lane," and he replied, "Yes, I was young myself once." However, he ran Valencia Street just south of the path of Lovers' Lane to provide direct access to his new railroad station, and later other streets and house lots obliterated the romantic path, except for a portion of it that remained on Flagler's Kirkside estate in a woodsy area next to Ribera Street. The hotel manager's house and Memorial Presbyterian Church erased more of the Ball grove. Beyond this, Mother Nature came down with a heavy hand. An orange tree blight—the curse that periodically visits Florida's groves—caused the citrus trees to waste away, and those that struggled to survive were wiped out in the Great Freeze of 1895.[45]

Interestingly, Carrère and Hastings's desire to leave the orange grove in its natural state went against both their training and ordinary inclinations. Since the success of Frederick Law Olmsted's Central Park in New York City, the conventional wisdom among landscapers held that urban dwellers wanted to bring the pastoral countryside into the city. Olmsted's rolling hillsides, meandering paths, and rustic ponds provided models for the landscaping of both city parks and country estates. However, Hastings believed that the landscape surrounding a building comprised an integral part of the architectural composition, and, as with the design of his buildings, Hastings strove for a more formal, controlled arrangement of the setting. He advocated geometric patterns, balanced design, and carefully articulated merging of all the various elements of the outdoor environment.[46] As Hastings once explained: "This landscape work is to surround and to support the building, serving as both frame and pedestal. The immediate accessories of the architecture such as the terraces, balustrades, paths, fountains, or open spaces and vistas which come nearest to the building, are really a part of the building itself."[47]

At the Hotel Ponce de Leon the process of framing the building began with the surrounding concrete fence, which served both to lift the structure above street level and to ornament the grounds adjacent to the walls. Visitors entering the courtyard through the great arched entryway encountered a view of the hotel building resting atop a raised terrace that encompassed the second half of the court. A concrete pathway directed walkers straight toward the front door of the hotel. The layout of the courtyard garden followed strict geometric designs: a circular pathway circumscribed the insides of the courtyard square; then right-angle walks from the centers of the four sides intersected in the middle, where a large decorative fountain stood inside another circle. The left and right side walkways angled upward toward the side entrances, while the path beyond the fountain ascended a stairway to the terrace and then another stairway led to the front door. Every component part could be described with a compass and ruler. There were no natural hillside slopes, only ramps and staircases; no rustic pond, but a formal classical fountain, with water-spewing terra-cotta turtles and frogs surrounding a central pedestal fountain decorated with tiles of glass and clay. However, the retaining wall of the upper courtyard terrace was constructed of natural coquina stone blocks—the only place in the hotel where ordinary coquina stone was used. The coquina stones used here had been salvaged from the old Catholic cathedral when it was reconstructed after the great fire of 1887.[48]

Although Hastings later claimed to have designed the courtyard, and although it conforms to his expressed philosophy of landscaping, this central garden and its companion, the Alameda, in front of the Hotel Alcazar, cannot confidently be attributed entirely to his hand.[49] Carrère and Hastings had employed another man to play a role in the shaping of the Flagler hotel grounds—one of the nation's leading landscape architects: Nathan Frank Barrett.

A native of Staten Island, born in 1845, Barrett had entered into the gardening profession in 1869 by working in his brother's nursery. He acquired his training in "landscape engineering" through the practical process of reading whatever books he could find on the subject, watching Olmsted develop Central Park, and visiting every country house under construction in the surrounding region. Then in 1879 George M. Pullman, manufacturer of the Pullman Palace Cars, hired Barrett to lay out his model company town of Pullman, just south of Chicago. This made Barrett's reputation and also made Pullman a lifelong friend of his.[50]

Barrett's outlook on landscaping closely paralleled that of Carrère and Hastings. He believed that good design resulted from the mixing of opposites: "The division as applied to my art means the formal gardens and the naturalistic instinct." Most of the time his inclinations led him toward the formal side. He once wrote, "The formal garden is a gem, therefore should be an attachment, a pendant, to the house."[51] These sentiments could have been spoken by Thomas

Thomas Hastings laid out the courtyard of the Ponce de Leon with mathematical symmetry, and Nathan Frank Barrett planted it with tropical plants and trees adapted to the climate. By permission of Library of Congress.

Hastings. Barrett added that formal gardens "belong quite as much to the profession of architecture as to the art I represent."[52]

Today, examining the gardens of the Hotels Ponce de Leon and Alcazar, it is impossible to say just how much derives from Hastings and how much from Barrett. A reporter for the *Jacksonville News-Herald*, writing in the summer of 1887 while the landscaping was being done, explained the relationship this way: "The beautifying of the grounds will be designed by Messers. Carrere and Hastings, the architects of the Ponce de Leon and Alcazar, and will be laid out under the immediate supervision of Mr. N. F. Barrett, a famous landscape artist."[53] This statement is probably very near the truth: Hastings provided the design and Barrett infused it with the trees, plants, and flowers that gave it life.

For his part, Barrett complained that the only garden he ever wholly designed was the one surrounding his own home in New Rochelle, New York. He observed that clients and architects tended to meddle in the way landscapers executed their commissions. On a small note, he did express a preference for gravel walks over "the cold, dull, materialist cement" that was used at the Hotel Ponce de Leon and in which Henry Flagler showed so much interest.[54]

A few years after the opening of the Ponce de Leon, Hastings and Barrett would team up again to plan and design an exhibition for the National Sculptural Society held in the building of the Fine Arts Society on West Fifty-Seventh Street in New York. The exhibition featured statues standing amid landscaped settings and even employed a stairway to an elevated terrace, as in the garden of the Hotel Ponce de Leon.[55]

A congenial, pipe-smoking character, Barrett would go on to become a respected elder statesman among landscape architects. He was a founding member and early president of the American Society of Landscape Architects and on his death in 1919 was venerated as the oldest living landscape architect in the country.[56] In a memorial essay, Carl Parker wrote of Barrett: "He claimed to be the earliest exponent of the formal garden in America, the Ponce-de-Leon Hotel in Florida and the estate of R. G. Dunn at Narragansett Pier containing his first efforts along these lines."[57] The gardens of the Ponce de Leon and Alcazar hotels may well be the earliest formal gardens created in the United States after colonial times.

The courtyard of the Hotel Ponce de Leon did not evoke the same feelings as the fine-textured, well-watered flower gardens of Maine or Pennsylvania. Barrett had pointed out that the tropical climate of Florida demanded "a different study" of what could be done in the way of plantings.[58] Many shrubs and flowers that grew well during the temperate summer months in the loamy soils of the North simply would not survive in the sands and searing summer heat of Florida. Carrère and Hastings wished to emphasize this difference by fashioning a courtyard filled with trees, shrubs, and flowers of a "richly tropical character" that would be exotic to northerners. In *Florida: The American Riviera*, they described the effect they aimed to produce on guests entering the front gate of the hotel: "The first impression is one of tropical splendor. Palms, vines, roses, as well as plants and flowers strange to a Northerner, fill the great court."[59]

The Ponce de Leon's courtyard, properly for a winter resort, turned its face south so that the low winter sun would shine in, while the bulk of the hotel building blocked out the chill north wind. This afforded a warm, sheltered environment both for vegetation and for winter guests occupying the green chairs on the open loggias surrounding the court.

However, in the summer of 1887 and on into January when the hotel opened, the dominating feature of the courtyard was sand. Many small plants and shrubs had been planted, and perhaps some ground cover, but no growing thing had yet managed to establish itself sufficiently to overcome the general impression of a

Harper's Weekly (July 21, 1888, 528) published these images of what the rooftop gardens of the Hotel Ponce de Leon and Alcazar were expected to look like.

sandy yard still under construction. Several examples of Florida's emblematic palm, the cabbage or sabal palm, stood in the quadrants of the garden, but they were yet small and straggly. Canary Island date palms, common in local yards, would soon appear, if they had not already been planted at the beginning. Some large century plants (*Agave americana*) stood out prominently, with their long succulent and spiked leaves. A few arrowroot or *zamia* ferns had been planted, and their thick glossy green fronds would in later years present themselves luxuriantly. Photos from that first year also show thin bushes, perhaps Florida wax myrtle or holly.

Overall the selection of plants and trees represented hearty flora known to thrive in the St. Augustine climate, where long dry spells and cold snaps in the winter alternated with scorching heat and torrential rains during the summer. This led to an ambiance more semi-arid than the lush Xanadu of Hastings's imagination.

The grounds to the east and west of the Ponce de Leon received minimal attention from Hastings and Barrett. Two coquina shell walks paralleled the building, running south and north in precise, straight lines, with the eastern one leading to Grace Methodist Church. On the west side a curved arc—equally precise—carved a path through the orange grove on the northwest side of the building. These paths carried traffic efficiently from the entrances of the hotel to the rear of the grounds with no pause for interesting diversions. In the evenings after dinner, gentlemen smoking their cigars—exiled from indoors (except for one smoking room)—would make the circuit of these paths.

Flowering annuals appeared in abundance growing in pots balanced on the railings of the loggias and in beds scattered across the courtyard. Eventually in a yearly routine beginning in late summer, in preparation for the coming season, a company employee (and later James McGuire himself) would order seeds for flowers. Geraniums led the list, but other common flowers were ordered by the hundreds: forget-me-nots, pansies, daisies, sweet peas, poppies, asters, dianthus, carnations, marigolds, and more.[60]

In late 1887, as the time for opening the hotels loomed closer, orders for potted plants that could be counted on to bloom in January went out, with instructions to "send express to St. Augustine at once."[61]

10

Electricity, Water, and
Final Touches, 1887

[We'll search] until a depth of two-thousand feet is
reached, unless the inhabitants of China demur.

—Drilling superintendent, quoted in
Times-Union, January 28, 1887

While the architecture and gardens of the Hotel Ponce de Leon may have har-kened back to the past, Flagler wanted the most up-to-date utilities for his hotel, including electricity. It was not the first place in Florida to enjoy electricity. That honor probably belongs to steamships plying Florida's waters. The floating palace steamer *H. B. Plant* attracted a crowd of spectators when it docked at Jacksonville in December 1882 with brilliant electric lights blazing. By the following December both the Carleton House and St. James Hotel in Jacksonville glowed with incandescent lights. When the Hotel Ponce de Leon opened, however, it would be the second largest free-standing structure in the United States ever electrified, surpassed only by the Dakota apartments in Manhattan.[1]

Thomas Edison promoted the use of electricity as a major improvement over gas for illumination. One of his advertising brochures stated: "The traveling pub-lic soon learns to appreciate in the hotels the advantages of a light which, while it throws out no heat, smoke or noxious gases, is a pleasant, soft and steady light, and above all, gives assurance of the maximum immunity from danger of fire or asphyxiation."[2]

Flagler's decision to employ electricity in his hotel may have been influenced by the fact that Thomas Hastings's brother Frank S. Hastings had joined Thomas Edison as his executive secretary in 1883.[3]

In 1887 the Edison Electric Company shipped equipment for an electric generating power plant to St. Augustine for the Hotel Ponce de Leon. The generators were manufactured by the Edison plant in Schenectady, New York, and, like all Edison dynamos, produced direct current that could not be transmitted over long distances—thus the need for individual or neighborhood plants. The four generators placed in the Ponce de Leon were 45-kilowatt, 125-volt machines, driven by three Armington & Sims steam-powered engines. The steam came from four Babcock & Wilcox boilers, which also supplied steam for the radiators heating the hotel. The boilers were housed in a large building right under the hotel's tall smokestack, while the generators were next door beneath the rear of the utility wing of the hotel. Across an adjacent courtyard stood several arched bays that held coal for the boilers. When all systems in the hotel were up and running, the boilers' firebox stokers shoveled in eight tons of coal a day.[4]

Thomas Edison sent one of his closest associates, William J. Hammer, to supervise installation of the electric plant and comprehensive electrical system. At the time Hammer was twenty-nine years old but already an old hand in the innovative field of incandescent lighting. Hired by Edison in 1879, he had taken part in most of the early experiments with electric lamps. Hammer was an inveterate note taker and collector; his records and collection of early incandescent light bulbs are the best in the world today. After assisting with the setup of the Pearl Street Station in the business district of New York City, Hammer went to London to establish the English Edison Electric Light Company. The plant in London actually started operation shortly before the Pearl Street Station, making it the world's first electric power plant. After initiating Edison's electric system in Germany, Hammer returned to the United States. It was only natural that Edison would send him to St. Augustine for the Flagler hotel project, especially when Hammer was also a close friend of Frank Hastings.[5]

Wiring the hotel was a complex process involving the laying of perhaps 50,000 feet of insulated wire—mostly placed into grooves in plaster or strung along porcelain insulators nailed to floor and ceiling beams. Along the hallways, Hammer placed panels with circuit switches and circuit breakers to control flow and prevent overloads. Outside the building, wires with a waterproof coating were buried underground. Altogether Edison claimed that there were 4,100 electric lamps in the Ponce de Leon and Alcazar hotels.[6] Most of the lights were sixteen-candlepower bulbs. (It is impossible to convert the luminosity of candlepower ratings to common modern units, but the prevalence of twenty-five-watt bulbs ordered as replacements in later years is suggestive of a modest light output per bulb.)

Hammer served as chief engineer during the hotel's first season, and every season thereafter the hotel employed an engineer to oversee the generators and electrical system. The chief engineer was assisted by a helper who watched over the system during the night, including checking up on the power room firemen to make sure that they were keeping the boilers stoked with coal. The assistant engineer and his helpers also circulated through the building replacing burned-out bulbs, a routine necessitated by the short service life of most bulbs in those days, although some bulbs might continue burning for years.[7]

In addition to electricity, Flagler also needed an abundant supply of water for his large hotels. Historically the small population of St. Augustine had obtained drinking water by digging shallow wells and by catching rainwater from rooftops and storing it in brick cisterns next to their homes. Obviously these simple methods would not yield nearly enough water. However, already in recent years local people had been hiring well drillers using modern machinery to put down deep wells into underground reservoirs. Wells drilled deep enough tapped into layers of water naturally charged with intense pressure from geologic forces, and from these wells gushed forth water in huge quantities. Unfortunately, the water from these artesian wells contained high concentrations of sulfur, salt, and other minerals. This sulfur water both rusted iron pipes and eventually choked the insides of pipes with deposits—and it smelled like rotten eggs.

Flagler's quest for good water began in the late fall of 1886 when workmen commenced drilling a well with a twelve-inch bore—twice as large as usual for a large utility well. He intended to drill deeply enough to find a stratum of rock, sand, or clay producing mineral-free water. The local newspapers were curious to see what he would find and kept up a running commentary on the progress of the well: 180 feet on December 14, 550 feet on December 31, 750 feet on January 11, 1887, 910 feet on January 19, and on January 27 the drill passed 1,000 feet. All the time the temperature of the water continued to increase until it was warmed to more than 80 degrees by geothermal energy. The drillers maintained an office in a wooden shed where glass jars with water samples from various levels were shelved for analysis. The superintendent declared that the search for sweet water would continue "until a depth of two-thousand feet is reached, unless the inhabitants of China demur."[8]

Flagler shipped barrels of well water to the firm of James B. Clow & Son of Chicago to analyze it and propose a method of removing the impurities. With typical thoroughness he demanded a detailed explanation of the mechanisms and chemicals that Clow proposed to employ in his Jewell Patented Water Purifier. Unfortunately for Flagler's needs, his 1,490-foot-deep well was found to produce water carrying even more dissolved minerals than his 450-foot well. In the end, Flagler ordered a filter to be used on the water fed into the steam boilers of the hotel, since preventing the buildup of mineral encrustations was most critical there.[9]

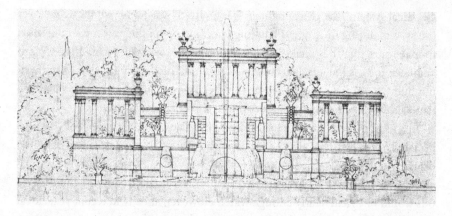

Thomas Hastings designed the Cascade with Greek colonnades at the top and on either side of the mid-level. In this front view, water is shown flowing down a central flight of steps—which Hastings wanted made with glass risers and illuminated with electric lights from behind. After flowing into a raised basin, the water would continue into a lower pool. A geyser of water from an artesian well spouts from the center of this pool. However, Hastings's spectacular idea never got beyond the drawing board. Carrère and Hastings Digital Collection, University of Florida. By permission of Flagler College.

Flagler's great well was such a novelty that it rated a front-page story in *Scientific American*. The picture accompanying the feature showed a fountain of water shooting twenty feet into the air, and the text explained that the well produced seven thousand gallons of water a minute or ten million gallons a day. Drilling had stopped at 1,490 feet when the drill bit was lost. Interestingly, the engineers suggested that the warm water might be piped through the hotel for heating purposes, and the flow of water might be used to drive a dynamo for production of electricity.[10]

Thomas Hastings had another idea of an artistic nature: why not build a water feature, a fountain and cascade such as beautify the grounds of Versailles and other elegant European gardens? He would locate his cascade directly behind the Ponce de Leon on the Ball property. The artists' studios that Hastings had placed at the rear of the hotel would overlook this water park. *Scientific American* painted a picture in words that might have been copied from Hastings: the plan would create "terraces of colored glass lighted by electricity, and after the water gushes forth as an impetuous geyser it will be conducted over these illuminated terraces, producing with prismatic effect a most gorgeous cascade."[11]

The cascade would never be built, but several more modest decorative fountains did add interest to the grounds of Flagler's hotels. One of these spraying fountains also served the utilitarian purpose of aerating the sulfur water before it was pumped up into four large iron tanks in the towers of the Ponce de Leon. These tanks were open to the air on top so that more of the sulfur smell might dissipate before the water went into the plumbing system. In addition, each tower contained a concrete cistern to hold rainwater caught from the roof. Altogether it amounted to an ingenious system, although still unsatisfactory. The high mineral content of the water damaged the pipes, and a faint whiff of sulfur lingered. The biggest problems for the plumbing, however, came from men flushing cigars down the toilets and women rinsing long strands of hair down drains.[12]

The water served at the dinner tables and in the pitchers supplied to rooms came from local well water that had been "distilled" to remove impurities. Also, guests could choose to purchase bottled waters, such as that ubiquitous resort hotel staple, Poland Spring Water. (Perrier would not appear until 1907.) Thus guests had choices in drinking water, just as they had choices in other beverages. The great hotels had wine rooms presided over by expert wine stewards who could provide patrons with just the alcoholic beverages they desired. In the fall of 1894, for example, thousands of dollars' worth of Bordeaux wines passed through the local customs house on the way to Flagler's hotels.[13]

One of the water tanks in each of the towers serviced another modern utility of the hotel—hydraulic elevators. Otis Brothers of New York furnished a freight elevator and two passenger elevators. Each tower tank provided water pressure for large cylinders in the basement powering pistons that would push the elevator cars upward. These elevators were delicately counterweighted so that water pressure from the tanks atop the towers was easily sufficient to raise several hundred pounds of either people or baggage. A uniformed operator in the polished wood passenger car managed the controls in delivering guests to their desired floors. The freight elevator descended all the way down into the basement so that baggage could be handled there, far out of the sight and hearing of the hotel's patrons.

The population of Florida when Henry Flagler arrived in the mid-1880s totaled a sparse 350,000—approximately same as the number of Tequesta, Calusa, Timucua, and Apalachee Indians who were living in Florida when Juan Ponce de León landed in 1513. Later on, the Seminole Indians were able to hold out against the U.S. Army for years because white men feared venturing into Florida during the sweltering summer months—the unhealthy season. Fear of malaria and yellow fever restrained settlers from pioneering homesteads in Florida. Rumors of yellow fever outbreaks circulated during the summers with the persistence of afternoon thundershowers, and evaluation of such rumors ranked as something of a folk science—a mixture of skepticism and dead serious respect. In June 1887 two men died in Key West in confirmed cases of yellow fever, and several illnesses in Tampa were attributed to the disease. Lacking knowledge of the cause of the disease and of any way of combating it, communities resorted in self defense to quarantines against regions where the disease was known to exist.

On June 6, 1887, the St. Augustine Board of Health declared that no one would be allowed to come into town from Palatka and points southward toward Tampa. Ten days later it issued an order that no one could enter town from Jacksonville without a clean bill of health signed by a physician.[14]

Fortunately for Flagler's hotel and railroad projects, the "scare" had little effect on St. Augustine's population, and only a few of McGuire and McDonald's workers elected to head north for home. However, the reciprocal restrictions on travel between St. Augustine and Jacksonville did hurt passenger travel on the Jacksonville, St. Augustine, and Halifax River Railway. From New York, Flagler wrote to Dr. Anderson in St. Augustine to get a reading on the situation in Florida. Although Flagler regretted the loss of passenger traffic, he added, "Of course, the health of St. Augustine is the first thing to be considered and business interests must suffer if necessary." In a subsequent letter he added a bit of black humor: "I have no doubt that you will make the Cemetery 'one of the attractive points' of St. A."[15]

On the first of July the cities of St. Augustine and Jacksonville lifted their travel controls, and St. Augustine's quarantine against Palatka was converted to a system in which all persons coming to town were required to pass under the eye of health wardens. St. Augustine proclaimed that it had never been in a better state of health and cleanliness and that it was open to receive travelers.[16]

Near the end of July 1887 Flagler visited St. Augustine to inspect his hotel now that its construction was nearing the final stages. He could look up to the scaffolding surrounding the pointed spires of the towers and see that the decorative sunburst weather vanes were almost ready to be put in place as a fitting signal that another milestone of construction had been achieved. After a brief visit, he returned to New York, taking Anderson with him. Flagler had written to the doctor a few weeks earlier about going to New York in July. "By that time I think the hot weather and mosquitoes will have reduced you to such a state of abject submission that I will have no difficulty in succeeding with my 'devilish' purpose of bringing you north." Anderson was one of the few people with whom Flagler felt sufficiently comfortable to maintain a tone of friendly banter. By mid-October Anderson was back in St. Augustine, having spent two months at Mamaroneck.[17]

A few days before Anderson's return, a train arrived in St. Augustine from Palatka with rumors that fever had killed several people in Tampa. Some of the passengers who had come in on the train were conducted to houses in the sand hills west of town to wait under quarantine until they were proven to be free of the disease. With the winter vacationer months approaching, all of St. Augustine understood the stark reality that if the fever appeared in St. Augustine, all hope of a prosperous season would evaporate. Flagler's and Smith's new hotels would have been built in vain.[18]

As mayor, Anderson supported a strict quarantine and did what he could do to cope with the situation. McGuire and McDonald offered to construct a house of refuge for fever sufferers out of town, should the epidemic penetrate the town's defenses. However, this proved unnecessary, and within a few weeks some northern early birds began to show up in town. On November 12, even before the first freeze of the winter, the Board of Health lifted the quarantine. St. Augustine emerged from the episode relatively unscathed.[19]

In the fall of 1887, to publicize the imminent opening of his hotel, Flagler sent copies of a promotional book titled *Florida: The American Riviera, St. Augustine: The Winter Newport* to individuals listed in the social registers of America as well as to every family enrolled in England's society record, *The Landed Gentry*.[20] The book had been put together by John Carrère and Thomas Hastings, who held the copyright.

The book opens with a typical overblown promotional piece on the healthfulness of Florida, in prose worthy of Sylvia Sunshine. It warns northerners that expending vitality battling the rigors of winter shortens life, while in St. Augustine people luxuriate in sunshine worthy of Egypt or Spain, and "the best loved west wind sighs through the pine barrens with sweet and hallowed tone, bearing to the invalid resinous and healing odors."[21] A chapter follows taken from Duffus Hardy's guidebook *Down South*, published in 1880.

The core of the book consists of lyrical descriptions of the Ponce de Leon, Alcazar, and Casa Monica hotels. Interestingly, some of the features planned by Carrère and Hastings made their way into the book but were never executed in reality. For example, they had planned an aviary of tropical birds for the Ponce courtyard. On the other hand, some elements that were brought to life—the elaborate courtyard fountain, for instance—do not appear in the engravings that form the most enduringly important part of this book. Some of the illustrations were created by Otto Bacher, a popular painter and engraver of the day and friend of James McNeill Whistler.[22]

At the back of *Florida: The American Riviera*, most of the major companies that had contributed to the Hotel Ponce de Leon placed cards to advertise their participation in the building of this landmark edifice. Today this section of the book is valuable to researchers wishing to better understand the various elements that went into the hotel.

For two years the area around King Street, between the Ponce de Leon and Alcazar hotel sites, had been an unsightly construction area, with temporary railroad tracks crossing it and a random collection of wooden buildings and sheds scattered across the lot. These buildings had to be removed to make way for the opening of the hotel. Most significantly, Anderson's frame cottage on King Street was put on rollers and moved north and west to a spot behind Markland house, facing the west side of the Ponce. It is still there today as part of Flagler College's Crisp-Ellert art complex. The frame building used as offices for Flagler, the architects, and McGuire and McDonald was moved to the rear of the hotel, where in later years it may have become the office of McGuire and McDonald. The stables of the Ball estate were removed. A large building that had once served as a general store, which had been moved to a spot right between the Ponce de Leon and Alcazar—as well as smaller work and storage sheds in front of the Alcazar—were demolished or moved out of sight.[23]

In the fall the concrete crews started working on the perimeter wall that would surround the hotel. Since it involved some fairly intricate work piecing together curves and pillars, curious spectators would pause for a while to see just how the liquid cement went into the wooden forms. When progress on the wall reached around to the west side of the hotel, along King Street, the temporary railway that had run across the grounds and down to the west side of the Alcazar had to be pulled up to make way for the fence. The ties and rails were moved over to Cordova Street. Here the railway would continue to serve the essential function of conveying materials to the hotel, but it also created an eyesore. When the hotel opened, every visitor arriving from the train depot would bump over this ugly obstacle upon entering the carriage way.[24]

Once the wall had been put in place, a concrete sidewalk—a novelty in St. Augustine—was laid along King Street and then up Cordova Street. Workmen widened King Street to accommodate the expected increase in traffic.[25]

As we have seen, in October and November work on the landscaping of the Ponce de Leon's courtyard commenced. This undertaking had been held in abeyance until near the last moment so that construction equipment and materials could continue to be placed conveniently in this central location. Palm trees and other local plants were excavated from local farms and brought within the confines of the courtyard. A local newspaper correspondent reported: "Mr. Barrett, the landscape gardener in charge of the landscape decorations of the Hotel Ponce de Leon, is beautifying the court of the hotel in a manner well worthy of his reputation. Gardeners are busy from morning 'til night planting the choicest of shrubs and flowers, and when the work is finished it will be a gem of beauty in the way of a flower garden."[26]

Once the heavy work on the courtyard landscape had been finished, the last part of the building itself, the front entranceway to the courtyard, could be completed. The last scaffolding came down on December 29. The roofing tiles were put in place and a white plaster decorative frieze completely surrounded the entrance pavilion.[27]

December found the mural artists still hard at work on the ceilings of the Rotunda and Dining Room. It seems that Thomas Hastings himself rolled up his sleeves and donned an apron to "take a hand" with the decorations. Hastings may have had this in mind when later on he spoke of "the enthusiasm of youth" in decorating the interiors.[28]

As the year drew to a close the rush to complete the hotel continued seemingly unabated. "The lawn just east of the hotel is a perfect wilderness of cases, crates, and boxes," reported a newspaperman, "another force of men and teams being engaged in breaking them up and carting off the lumber."[29]

An advance force of sixty servants who would remain as part of the staff after the hotel opened arrived in December to help place materials in their proper places inside the hotel. They were the first people to sleep under the roof of the Hotel Ponce de Leon. On December 29 the first of the kitchen help arrived, sixty strong.[30]

Of course, as the great building neared completion, the public's desire to get inside and see the interiors became tremendous. McGuire and McDonald did consent to take a privileged few among the curious on personal tours, but everyone else was told to stay away. Partly to pacify the public clamor, McGuire and McDonald announced that everyone would be invited into the hotel at a later date for a public visitation.[31]

Whether the hotel would be completed on time remained one unanswered question, and another was whether anyone would show up. Skeptics had long and loudly opined that Flagler's and Smith's hotels would never be filled, and many people were rightly concerned that the grumblers might be right. The previous summer's yellow fever epidemics downstate in Key West and Tampa, accompanied by travel quarantines, certainly seemed likely to scare Yankees away from Florida. Veteran local politician William A. MacWilliams recalled years later: "There was quite a question whether the hotel would open by reason of a yellow fever scare."[32]

Yet in the fall of 1887 a great rumbling began in the North. Railroad booking agents began to receive an unprecedented number of inquiries about travel to Florida, and published timetables that had formerly concluded their listings with Jacksonville now made St. Augustine their terminus. Wonderful tales of what Flagler was doing in St. Augustine became a focus of conversation among the resort set in New York. So the omens—both ominous and hopeful—waxed indecisive.[33]

To encourage good press coverage Flagler "liberally endowed" Allan Forman, editor of the newspaper trade magazine the *Journalist,* to promote the hotel. This covertly planted seed money led to a long story by Forman in the *New York Evening Post* that described the Hotel Ponce de Leon as "without doubt the finest piece of hotel architecture in the country—probably the finest in the world."[34]

The day after Christmas the *Florida Times-Union* reported that every room in the Ponce de Leon had already been engaged. This clearly exaggerated things, but in St. Augustine McGuire and McDonald began hurriedly converting rooms on the fourth floor of the Ponce that had been planned for servants' quarters into rooms for paying guests. At the same time they sent a gang of seventy-five workers to south Cordova Street at the St. Frances Street intersection, where filling operations on Maria Sanchez Creek had come to a stop, and they quickly erected an eighty-room wood-frame barracks for male hotel employees. Obviously Flagler and his lieutenants were confident that an overflow crowd was on its way.[35]

During the hectic days of November, Henry Flagler spent three weeks in St. Augustine personally overseeing operations. He lived as Anderson's houseguest at Markland, from which it was just a short walk through the orange grove to the scene of the action on the hotel grounds. Several years later the *Tatler* society magazine published "an amusing legend that bears the impress of truth—The delay in the arrival of a schooner load of furniture made willing hands necessary when it was finally landed, and Mr. Flagler took off his coat and worked to get it into place. One of the men who witnessed this and taking him for a fellow workman, said, 'This Flagler is a pretty good fellow.' Raising his eyebrows Mr. Flagler asked, 'Are you one of the workmen?' 'Oh yes; I have been here a long time and it is the best loafing place I know. You see the old man does not come around often, and when he does we work like beavers.'"[36]

Flagler knocked off work in mid-December and returned to New York for the Christmas season.[37] While in the North he paid a visit to Boston, perhaps to check on the hotel's order for linens, and on the return train he shared the coach with a number of passengers, including three newlywed couples eagerly engaged in conversation with each other and with other travelers. One groom said he and his bride would go to St. Augustine to the Hotel Ponce de Leon if the hotel opened. He inquired if anyone had recent news of developments in St. Augustine. No one spoke up.

One of the passengers in the car happened to be a reporter for the *New York Daily Graphic,* and he gave this account of another traveler in the railroad car: "In the corner of the car sat an aristocratic-looking man—tall, about fifty I should judge, his head covered with silvery hair, his profile purely Grecian, the outline aided somewhat by a gracefully equipped moustache. He read the entire trip, spoke to no one and seemed entirely content whether the train was at full speed, as it was part of the time, or lagging as it was much of the time. We entered the depot and one of Chauncey M. Depew's numerous retainers walking by my side said, pointing to the tall, self-poised, quiet-mannered man above described, 'There goes Flagler.'"[38]

On Christmas Eve in one of St. Augustine's older hotels, the architects John Carrère and Thomas Hastings and the builders James McGuire and Joseph McDonald sat down to a festive dinner along with other leading men who had brought the hotel into being. They had a lot to celebrate—and still a lot of final work to accomplish. January 10 had been set as the opening day for the hotel.[39]

Flagler returned to St. Augustine on December 29 and took up residence in the Hotel Ponce de Leon—making him the hotel's first guest. He may have stayed in the suite occupying the corner of the third floor overlooking the Villa Zorayda; he would use those rooms from time to time in later years. The third floor had been the first one to be completely finished and furnished. Flagler also ate meals prepared for him in the kitchen by the staff. We do not know whether Ida Alice accompanied him—the newspaper mentions only Flagler as being there. He may have walked the long, empty hallways by himself in those dark December days.[40]

If Henry Flagler had much to worry about as 1887 drew to a close, his problems seemed light in comparison to the multitude of woes besetting Franklin W. Smith. In the case of the Casa Monica, it really did appear likely that it would not be ready to receive guests in January.

In late September Smith had returned from Europe, where he had reportedly been "searching the Old World for features that might lend new beauty" to the Casa Monica.

He went back and forth between St. Augustine and New York in November.[41] As late as November things appeared to be going well on the Casa Monica construction site. The St. Augustine correspondent of the *Times-Union* wrote in early November: "The Casa Monica, since the removal of the scaffolding and frames, towers up among the prominent improvements with majestic splendor and beauty."[42]

Then reports appeared in the press indicating that the situation had turned very serious at the Casa Monica. On December 9 the usually reliable *Jacksonville News-Herald* carried an article saying that Smith had informed all his contractors that work on the hotel would stop on January 1, and anything not completed by that time would be put off until after the season. The *Times-Union* reported a week later that workers employed on the interiors of the hotel were hurrying to a finish in a rushed, slipshod manner, and much of the interior would have to be ripped out at the conclusion of the season. A few days later the *Times-Union* expressed the opinion that not enough laborers were engaged to be able to

When the Hotel Casa Monica opened in January 1888, the Hotel Alcazar (*right*) remained unfinished, with scaffolding still encircling its towers. By permission of P. K. Yonge Library of Florida History, University of Florida.

finish the Casa Monica by the first of January. All these reports proved essentially true. Thus, just when—and if—the Casa Monica would open became an open question.[43]

Although Flagler could be fairly confident that the Ponce de Leon would open on time, he had a second hotel under construction, and its opening seemed much more doubtful.

The concept of a second auxiliary structure to complement the Hotel Ponce de Leon had arisen shortly after planning for the Ponce commenced—if indeed it had not been in Flagler's or Hastings's mind from the very beginning. This companion building would offer multiple diversions to occupy the leisure time of guests staying at the Ponce de Leon. The front section of the complex would house businesses on its ground floor, where patrons could enjoy the pleasures of shopping for higher-class souvenirs, objects of art, and other sightseer fare in what Hastings envisioned as a "cosmopolitan bazaar." Some of the business offices would serve more mundane purposes, such as a parcel express service. In the floors above would be guest rooms to handle the overflow from the Ponce should it be filled to capacity or should some guests not require or desire the first-class accommodations of the Ponce de Leon.

Following the custom of European spas and St. Augustine's tradition as a health resort, those seeking relief from their various ailments could patronize hot baths and other such therapeutic services. From this plan of diverse baths, according to Thomas Hastings, evolved the idea of adding a huge indoor swimming pool for enjoyment as well as healing. Hastings, in his typical lyrical fashion, envisioned the pool as a place for evening entertainments, with electric lights, fountains of water, boats afloat—"a beautiful water scene."[44]

Work had begun in March 1887 on what had previously been referred to as the "casino" or Ponce de Leon "annex." It now received the regal name Alcazar—the House of Caesar.

As in the Hotel Ponce de Leon, the floor plan of the Hotel Alcazar followed Beaux Arts principles, with a strong central axis running the length of the complex. The nature of the available land also dictated this approach, for the bed of Maria Sanchez Creek provided Hastings with a long, narrow building lot. Thus Carrère and Hastings's plan for the Alcazar ended up with a three-part division: a hotel in front, followed by a bath area, and terminating in the rear with the casino with its swimming pool.

The Spanish Renaissance inspired the outward character of the building. Its twin towers echoed the larger towers of the Ponce de Leon across the way, while terra-cotta ornamentation and red tile roofs continued the pattern set by its more majestic neighbor. The front entrance to the second hotel would be partly enclosed by a semicircular loggia decorated with elaborate terra-cotta work. This loggia would provide an intermediate architectural elevation, easing the transition upward from the front garden to the four-story façade of the hotel. The hotel itself surrounded an intimate courtyard with a large decorative pool in its center.

Before construction could be commenced on the elaborate Alcazar complex, the San Marco Skating Rink and Olivet Methodist Church had to be removed to make way. Workmen dismantled the rink at the end of February, while the little church on stilts was jacked up onto rollers and made a short journey to a spot south of the Alcazar site. To lift the congregation's walk to church above the sand and mud of Cordova Street, Flagler constructed a wooden sidewalk to their new front door.[45]

Unlike the Ponce de Leon, with its floating foundation, the Alcazar would be constructed on pilings. Commencing on April 2, Jacksonville contractor J. P. Coughlin put a pile driver to work pounding pine tree trunks into the sand of what had formerly been Maria Sanchez marsh. He would not be finished until October, by which time nearly four thousand piles had been rammed into the earth.[46] Late in May, about the time concrete work was finished on the Ponce de Leon and while the pile driver still hammered away at the rear of the site, laborers began pouring concrete for the foundation of the Alcazar.[47]

An elevation drawing of the Hotel Alcazar shows the semicircular loggia that Carrère and Hastings planned for the front of the building. To Hastings's enduring dismay, the loggia would never be built. Carrère and Hastings, *Florida: The American Riviera*, insert 16.

Work progressed rapidly, although a few untoward episodes slowed progress. In June stories of yellow fever in Tampa caused some workers to depart for their northern homes, and the Board of Health ordered a ban on any excavations in the city, acting on the usual supposition that disturbing the soil released dangerous vapors. McGuire and McDonald put new men on the payroll to replace those who had left and rushed work just in case a verified yellow fever epidemic caused the Board of Health to order a quarantine of travel into town. In June they had 250 men at work on the walls.[48]

The threat of yellow fever did not deter Flagler and Hastings from coming down for a brief visit in July to inspect work on the Ponce de Leon, Alcazar, and Grace Methodist Church—all of which were coming along propitiously. When he departed Flagler took with him his friend Dr. Anderson to spend some weeks enjoying the refreshing breezes of Long Island Sound at his Mamaroneck home.[49]

By August the walls of the Alcazar had risen to a height that led spectators to believe that at least the front part of the building—the hotel—would soon be complete. Then in October a combination of torrential rains and exhaustion of the Portland cement supply on hand forced McGuire and McDonald to lay

Many observers found the compact, restrained basilica-style architecture of Grace Method-ist Church to be more pleasing than Flagler's larger, more ornate buildings. By permission of Library of Congress.

off some of their workers. However, a schooner loaded with barrels of cement arrived the in mid-October, and workers again had material available to resume construction.[50]

By the beginning of October the first shipment of terra-cotta decorations had arrived and could be put in place on the towers and chimneys. These finishing touches led the correspondent of the *Times-Union* to announce, prematurely as it developed, that the Alcazar "no doubt will be ready when the Ponce de Leon opens."[51]

In some respects the Alcazar did seem ready for opening. Several of the ground floor stores had already been rented. Foremost among these stood Greenleaf and Crosby, a Jacksonville jewelry store that would occupy the front left side of the entrance for the rest of the Flagler era. Dr. F. Fremont Smith had reserved an-other room for his office, with a pharmacy located next door. A store selling Cin-cinnati Art Pottery and another offering furniture and art shared the west side of the building with the Southern Express Company, which stood adjacent to the driveway where carriages from the railroad station dropped off and picked up hotel guests.[52]

As January 1888 approached, it seemed barely possible that Flagler might have not just one but two hotels to open for the winter season. Or perhaps optimists were putting wishful thinking in place of hard analysis.

One Flagler building did open on time: Grace Methodist Church. The previous summer Dr. Anderson had ventured inside to watch the work in progress and had written to tell Flagler he approved of what he saw. "I am glad to know that the interior of the M. E. Church is so pleasing," replied Flagler. "I have not the slightest idea as to how it looks."[53]

During the evening of December 31, 1887, the Methodists held one last service in Olivet Church to say farewell to their wood-frame place of worship on Cordova Street. The next morning they gathered in the exquisite concrete basilica church building that Carrère and Hastings had designed for them one block north of the Ponce de Leon. The relative simplicity of the exterior elicited favorable comments in comparisons with Flagler's hotels. The interior of unadorned pine and basswood seemed appropriate for the straightforward tastes of Methodism. The official dedication would not take place until January 15, when Flagler added his congratulation by sending his hotel band over to play for both the morning and afternoon services.[54]

11

Opening Day, 1888

The expressions of wonder and admiration burst
involuntarily from their lips.

—*Jacksonville News-Herald*, January 11, 1888

When the citizens of St. Augustine awakened on the morning of January 1, 1888, the long-awaited dawning of a new epoch in the history of the Ancient City at last was at hand. The celebrated Hotel Ponce de Leon, more than two years in the making, appeared ready to receive guests. Yet activity around the building and grounds seemed more frantic than ever. As January 10 approached, eight hundred workmen and women scurried in and out of doorways tending to a thousand different finishing touches requisite for the hotel's unveiling. "It will be a close call," McGuire told a reporter. He stationed himself in Jacksonville to receive shipments from the North arriving by rail or ship, directing materials south in order of their priority for finishing the hotel. The Jacksonville, St. Augustine, and Halifax River Railway ran thirty-five boxcars of freight southward on some days.[1]

The heavy scaffolding had just come down in the Rotunda, but artists were still scaling a movable ladder, adding more detail to the dome paintings. Teams of regular house painters worked twelve-hour days on the walls of the guest rooms and hallways. Carpenters and joiners were fitting wainscoting in place on the walls and securing the last planks of oak into the dining room floor. The baggage elevator operated efficiently, but one of the passenger elevators still needed work. As soon as craftsmen finished tacking down carpet in guest rooms, other workers rushed in to put furniture in place, and maids hung just-hemmed draperies in the windows. Light fixtures were among the last items to be installed. Then maids carried in armfuls of bedding and linen. The hundred yards of King Street fronting the hotel received a pavement of asphalt. At night the evening sky glowed from fires burning up packing crates and other debris left behind in the rush to completion.[2]

As the final strokes were applied to the Hotel Ponce de Leon, hundreds of construction workers received their final paychecks, and in their places a new force of employees who would run the hotel arrived. Almost all of them were professional hotel men and women who spent their summers in mountain or seaside resorts in the North. They left Jersey City in a special train of six passenger cars, traveled overnight, and arrived in Jacksonville in time for breakfast at the Everett Hotel. Then they departed for St. Augustine, where their arrival was awaited with great anticipation both by the townspeople and by colleagues who had preceded them. The train bypassed the passenger station on Orange Street and proceeded all the way to the Cordova-King Street intersection, where a large crowd had gathered. "As the train approached the mammoth hotel, the car windows were crowded with eager faces anxious to take a first peep at the great building of which they had heard so much." As soon as the employees disembarked and made their greetings, they were marched away to their various living quarters. It had been quite an event—and the hotel was not yet open. Some folks in the crowd expressed disappointment that the members of Joyce's Military Band (lately of Saratoga Springs), who came down on the train, did not uncase their instruments and play a tune for everybody.[3]

A few days later a more elegant train departed from the Pennsylvania Railroad's Jersey City station carrying some of the honored guests to Flagler's grand opening. (In the days before digging of the tunnel under the Hudson and the opening of Penn Station in Manhattan in 1910, travelers from New York City took the Pennsylvania Railroad ferry to Jersey City to catch a train to Florida.) A crowd turned out for the landmark departure. This was the first of the awkwardly named "vestibule trains," so called because the cars were connected with each other by accordion-fold rubber diaphragms that enclosed the spaces between cars. This allowed a passenger to pass from one car to another "precisely as he passes from one room to another in his own house." The diaphragm walls and carpeted floors sealed out cold, rain, and dust from the interior. A traveler could walk from a passenger car to the parlor car and continue comfortably to the dining car, which was usually located at the end of the train. All the comforts of home, including electric lights, made the trip south a pleasure caravan "to keep up with the desires of these opulent, fastidious, luxury-loving travelers."[4]

The train bore a placard reading: "Special Florida Vestibule Train." It was a high speed "flier" with cleared right-of-way through to Jacksonville and with a minimum of stops, at Philadelphia, Washington, Wilmington, Charleston, and Savannah. The major southern railroads had finally converted to standard gauge, eliminating the necessity of changing trains multiple times on the way south.

George M. Pullman himself was on board to savor the excitement, although he apparently got off in Philadelphia rather than proceeding to Florida.[5]

On the last leg of their journey, from the landing on the south side of the St. Johns River, Flagler's guests traveled aboard the Jacksonville, St. Augustine, and Halifax River Railway's two elite passenger cars, the Governor Bloxham and the Governor Perry. It took fifty-seven minutes to pass from the south bank of the St. Johns River in Jacksonville to the station on Orange Street. From here the visitors climbed aboard carriages and rolled in a cloud of dust down Cordova Street. A reporter for the *Jacksonville News-Herald* had been invited along to record the proceedings. "It was dark," he wrote, "and the Hotel Ponce de Leon was brilliantly lighted by electricity. As the carriages turned sharply into the private driveway, the expressions of wonder and admiration burst involuntarily from their lips. The carriages moved slowly through the great arched porte cochère. The Spanish 'Bien Venido' greeted the guests from the arched ceiling of the vestibule."[6]

From this relatively modest carriage entrance, the guests climbed stairs into the Rotunda, where the enchantments commenced. While the ladies gazed up into the Rotunda dome to admire the murals and examined the carved wood ornamentation, a little informal ceremony took place at the registration desk. The first person to step up and sign the large registration book was New York financier Michel Charles Bouvier (whose grandniece Jacqueline Bouvier Kennedy would in 1961 become first lady of the United States). However, the first line in the register had been left blank for a man who was already in town and would arrive later for dinner, Captain A.V.W. Leroy of the St. Augustine Yacht Club, who was regarded as having the longest-running record of wintertime residence in St. Augustine among the northern strangers. Mrs. Deborah Shedd, a widow from Stamford, Connecticut, also signed the register; she would be a regular winter guest.[7]

After freshening up in their rooms, the guests made their way to the Dining Room. On the stair landing they found a poem, supposedly selected by Henry Flagler himself, composed by the English poet William Shenstone.[8]

> Whoe'er has travell'd life's dull round,
> Where'er his stages may have been,
> May sigh to think he still has found
> The warmest welcome at an inn.

Eighty invited friends and associates shared dinner with Flagler in the western alcove of the Dining Room. For all it ranked as a great triumph, and for some it came as a relief. One of those present later recalled: "There had been innumerable delays, goods required in the finishing touches had not arrived, furniture had gone astray, and here and there the sound of the hammer was heard, the suggestion of oil and varnish occasionally caught; the parlors were in the hands of the decorators."[9] Yet these were trivial annoyances that evening. A mood of jubilation prevailed. Joyce's band provided music for dining. Flagler played the genial host, shaking hands and accepting congratulations. "Every visitor was impressed with the modest bearing of the man whose wealth had made this beauty possible, as quietly he returned the greetings and congratulations of friends."

McGuire and McDonald received heaps of praise. Mural artist George W. Maynard "attracted much attention, although when spoken to in regard to his work, blushed like a school boy."[10] John Carrère and his wife bore honors with modesty. The Reverend Doctor Thomas S. Hastings and his wife occupied a place of distinction. They had been in town for a week, the doctor having delivered a sermon at the Presbyterian Church the previous Sunday. A spectator commented, "It was beautiful to see the pride with which they inspected the beauties their son's brains had designed and executed." As for their son Thomas: "A bright, nervous creature, every movement suggestive of genius, was here, there and everywhere, it was his gala day, but it is doubtful if he realized it. The strain of the brain work had not yet relaxed, and, as he said, later, 'I only realized that the work of brains and hands was mine no longer, that when I leave on the morrow I bid it goodbye, and it saddens as though parting from a loved child.'"[11]

The man who had been present at the genesis of the hotel project and who had labored on it the longest, O. D. Seavey, received no such reprieve as Hastings with the opening of the hotel. His work as manager of the Hotel Ponce de Leon had just commenced. Before, during, and after the dinner Seavey dodged here and there attending to details, hardly having time to sit down with his wife and enjoy the meal and festivities. Those who wanted to congratulate him had to catch him on the fly. "It was doubtful if it was a time of pleasure to him," noted an observer. As another sacrifice of pleasure, for the duration of the season Seavey laid aside his Havana cigars so that the odor of tobacco would not linger on his clothes and breath.[12]

Each guest at dinner received a souvenir menu, freshly minted from the hotel's own in-house print shop. *Hors d' oeuvres* consisted of Blue Point oysters, a choice of two soups, and shrimp croquets. Guests had their choice of main courses: broiled shad, roast beef, turkey with cranberry sauce, ham in Madeira sauce, lamb chops, chicken sauté, or broiled plover on toast. With coffee came a selection of fruit, cheeses, and desserts—vanilla pudding, apple pie, coconut pie, chocolate éclairs, assorted cakes, fruitcake, vanilla ice cream, and—for the diet conscious—calf's foot jelly (the precursor of Jell-O).[13]

After the meal, at 8:00 p.m., the dinner party took up chairs in the center of the vaulted Dining Room to listen to a concert by Joyce's band, stationed in the east alcove. They were wearing their new navy blue uniforms, tasseled with gold, and twenty-dollar caps with the crest of the Ponce de Leon in gold and silver on the crown. At ten o'clock it all concluded. "Everything was in perfect keeping with the retiring character of the owner," noted a newspaper reporter.[14]

Two days later, on Thursday, January 12—as Flagler had promised—the doors of the Hotel Ponce de Leon opened to admit anyone who wished to inspect the hotel. To residents of St. Augustine, it was a chance to see for themselves just what Henry Flagler had bestowed upon their modest village. Joyce's band played for the edification of the thousands who gathered on the new asphalt pavement out front on King Street awaiting their chance to go in. For a few hours the hotel belonged to every Floridian, white, black, or Minorcan, as much as to the Yankee aristocracy. The Grand Parlor remained closed because the decorators were still applying final enhancing elements to the interior, and a few other public rooms also remained unfinished and closed off.

Commenting on the similar grand opening of two years later, the correspondent of the black newspaper the *New York Age* observed with a certain wonder this momentary lowering of the color bar: "A striking example of social equality in the South was seen in the parlors of the Ponce de Leon Hotel on the opening night when the doors were thrown open to the public and several adventurous pickaninnies were discovered enjoying with great satisfaction the dazzling array of splendor seen and heard on every side in the midst of the broadcloths, silk and satin of the guests of the hotels in the city."[15]

On the evening of the twelfth, after the common throng had been ushered out of the building, hotel guests enjoyed dinner in the Dining Room. Flagler and a small assembly of intimates took seats at a long table in the west alcove, apart from the other diners. Joyce's "orchestra" (as bands were often called in those days) took a position in one of the lofts in the vault overlooking the central hall of the Dining Room. From time to time one of the performers would offer a solo vocal selection. After dinner five hundred invited guests came in and took seats in the Rotunda to enjoy a concert presented by Joyce's orchestra from a place on the mezzanine balcony. The first number, "Greetings from St. Augustine," had been composed for the occasion.

A few days later Bartolo Genovar, a leading merchant and operator of the Opera House on St. George Street, met Flagler at a little ceremony in the Ponce de Leon and presented him with a morocco-bound case containing a heavy gold medallion. Inscribed on its face was the salutation: "To H. M. Flagler, From the 'Natives' of St. Augustine. Our gates will always be open and a hearty welcome extended to the progressive spirit of the new 'Ancient City.' January 10th 1888." The reverse side bore the image of the City Gates. It represented a fine gesture

Residents ("Natives") of St. Augustine presented Flagler with this medallion as a token of their appreciation for the improvements he had made to their city. © Flagler Museum Archives.

from the old Minorcan families and other "natives" of town; relations between Flagler and some of the local inhabitants would not always be blessed with such cordiality.[16]

The Hotel Ponce de Leon had been fittingly opened for its first season and the beginning of a seventy-nine-year career that would encompass a mixture of glory, triumphs, trials, and misfortunes.[17]

With Flagler's Hotel Ponce de Leon now splendidly unveiled, attention turned toward Franklin Smith's Casa Monica across the way. The hotel's manager, Eli N. Wilson, had moved his office into the building on January 2 to watch over the carpenters and finishers who were rushing to put the last touches on stairways, doors, and paneling. At the same time, cleaning women and chambermaids were preparing guest rooms for occupancy.[18]

The first venturesome guests of the hotel went to sleep in their rooms on the evening of January 17, although they were obliged to share the hotel with workmen still hurrying to complete their tasks. The general public did not get a chance to go inside to inspect Smith's creation until January 30, when the hotel was finally declared complete.[19]

The Casa Monica enjoyed sparse patronage, as might be expected considering its uncertain prospects for opening on time. To counter negative rumors, Smith took out an advertisement in the *Florida Times-Union* affirming: "Reports to the contrary notwithstanding, this Superb New Hotel is in complete running order and open for reception of guests. . . . Inspection invited."[20]

Unlike the strictly symmetrical and logical architecture Carrère and Hastings followed in the Ponce de Leon, Franklin Smith, who acted as his own architect, designed the Casa Monica to be deliberately irregular. He wanted it to look as if it had evolved over centuries as new appendages were adjoined to older remnants. While the vision of the Ponce de Leon sprang from the Renaissance, the Casa Monica drew upon the spirit of the Middle Ages. In an expansive mood, Smith explained that his house exemplified the "Spanish castellated and the Hispano-Moresque forms."[21]

The interiors exposed Smith's shallow pocketbook: while Flagler dressed his hotel with imported oak and painted his guest apartments and hallways in white and pastels, Smith used native pine throughout, giving the interiors a dismal ambiance, particularly at night under gas lights. Flagler employed nationally famous artists to decorate his hotel, while the best Smith could do was hang copies of Spanish masters on his walls.[22]

Guests entered the Casa Monica under an impressive archway that faced the Plaza and the post office across King Street. A large lobby extended along the front of the building, but if visitors walked straight through the entrance they would find themselves in the Sala del Sol, a glassed-over patio that served as a sort of greenhouse for tropical plants and a sitting room for guests. The house's ten-piece orchestra played there in the mornings.[23] The eccentric arrangements

The Casa Monica's Sala del Sol (sun room) featured a glass ceiling and Franklin Smith's typical Moorish architecture. From the collection of the St. Augustine Historical Society Research Library.

of the guest chambers puzzled one visitor. The entrance to his suite, which was in one of the hotel's five towers, led immediately into the bed chamber, through which he was required to walk to reach the sitting room.[24] Nevertheless, the Casa Monica had managed to open its doors for customers, and it occupied one of the most favored locations in town with unsurpassed views of its more impressive Flagler neighbors.

Now that Flagler and Smith had thrown wide the doors to their hotels, would the expected host of shivering Yankees show up in St. Augustine? Two weeks after opening day, O. D. Seavey reported that the Ponce held two hundred guests, and he declared this a good start to the season. A week later, in New York City, a reporter for the *New York Times* wrote that worry over yellow fever had "completely choked" travel to Florida for a time but then added: "The recent terrible weather [in the North] has caused a sudden and remarkable increase of travel."[25]

"Sudden and remarkable" it turned out to be. The usual February rush arrived with a vengeance. On February 8 the Ponce reported a house count of 350. The San Marco and St. George declared increases of 30 and 25 percent over the previous year. The Magnolia and Florida House said they were almost full. At this point the Ponce de Leon began turning away customers. The Casa Monica benefited from the diverted traffic.[26]

For winter visitors, arrival in St. Augustine invariably provided a spectacle that could be both entertaining and frustrating. A lady visitor left this account: "'St. Augustine!' The cry rang through the car. We were all ready; the porter had been assiduously brushing the coats of the masculine portion of the passengers, the numerous invalids had tied up shawl straps, bags, and satchels, and all the children were on the que vive. As the train rolled into the station we all crowded to the door, eager for a glimpse of the old town. The sun was shining brightly; the air redolent with the perfume of orange blossoms, and before us lay St. Augustine. When we alighted we were instantly surrounded by a swarm of aspirants for our luggage, and by omnibus drivers shouting the names of their different houses!"[27]

Another narrator takes up the story: "An almost deafening shout of 'Hotel Ponce de Leon,' 'San Marco,' and 'Magnolia Hotel' arose from the throats of two or three dozen bus and carriage drivers."[28]

Municipal law required the hack drivers to remain behind a yellow line painted across the landing platform of the Orange Street station. Later the new Union Station had a fence separating the coachmen from their quarry. Major Argrett, a noted carriage driver, was once hauled into the mayor's court for crossing the "dead line," but the passenger who had hired Argrett appeared in court and explained that he had requested Argrett to come across to retrieve his baggage, and the charge was dropped. Argrett's son, Major Argrett Jr., would become

St. Augustine's most famous carriage driver. After he retired in the 1970s a memorial to him would be erected on the bay front just south of the Castillo.[29]

Although the hackmen, almost all of them black, with their brass-button coats and tall stovepipe hats, were famous for their "metallic cheek and unvarnished impertinence," the passengers were often in just as much of a rush to find a conveyance. The hotel men constantly reassured guests to remain calm because arrangements for their passage to the hotels were complete, so there was no need to hurry. A uniform fare for everyone was set by law at twenty-five cents per person.[30]

Flagler maintained the most splendid omnibuses for guests staying at the Ponce de Leon, but as the most important patron of the largest transfer company, he was sensitive to complaints that carriage drivers steered potential customers to his hotels. Flagler demanded that the drivers employed by the transfer company maintain an absolute impartiality in giving information to arriving passengers who had not already engaged rooms in advance at some hotel. They were forbidden to mention rates charged at the various hotels. Hotels were often accused of bribing hack drivers to steer customers to their doorstep. However, the drivers sometimes performed a useful service for newcomers without bookings, for the hackmen were intimately familiar with all the rooming establishments. They knew which hotels were full and which still had vacancies, and they could usually make a good estimate of what class of hotel their passengers might be able to afford.[31]

Prior to the opening of the Ponce de Leon, Flagler contracted with Louis A. Colee, a local man, to provide transportation from the railroad depot to the hotel. Colee and his father had operated the stage line from Picolata to St. Augustine in the 1870s, and he later claimed that he had driven Flagler around town in a carriage to show him the sights before Flagler decided to build his hotel. With his lucrative contract in hand, Colee purchased additional horses from Kentucky and bought an elegant black and maroon omnibus with a polished oak interior from a company in Wisconsin to serve as the primary conveyance to the Ponce de Leon.[32]

Colee knew well the carriage drivers' reputation for rough manners, so he enforced a policy of no smoking and no profane language. He advertised "intelligent and polite drivers" available for hire to take visitors on scenic drives around town or excursions into the country.[33]

Colee's company received a large infusion of capital for the 1889 season when J. T. Brundage and Charles W. Miller became the primary owners of the St. Augustine Transfer Company. Colee remained manager. Brundage and Miller ran a similar transport company in Niagara Falls, New York, and each year Colee and the company's horses and carriages made the trek from North to South and back again. Flagler built a large stable south of King Street near the San Sebastian River to shelter the horses, carriages, and equipment. The transfer company's downtown headquarters was located in the west wing of the Hotel Alcazar and later on the corner of Cordova Street and Cathedral Place, next door to the Ponce de Leon. Any guest of the Flagler hotels wishing to hire a carriage could simply place a request with the uniformed transfer company agent stationed near the hotel's office, and a driver would bring a carriage to the hotel's doorstep.[34]

Newly arrived visitors coming to the Hotel Ponce de Leon would be delivered to the rear of the hotel along the carriage drive that stretched in a straight line from Cordova Street through the hotel grounds to Sevilla Street, passing under the looming walls of the hotel. Stopping in the enclosed place under the hotel, sheltered from rain and wind, guests would check their baggage with the "luggage busters," who then carried steamer trunks and bulky cases through a freight door into the cellar. They might handle as many as four hundred trunks a day, since each guest usually arrived with multiple bags. No unsightly luggage would ever mar the refined ambiance of the Rotunda. A servant would then escort guests through a modest entrance and up either of two flights of stairs to the Rotunda, where the ladies would be ushered into a small waiting room while the men checked in. Then the servant would direct the newcomers to the passenger elevator and thence to their assigned apartment. Once inside, the servant would take the trunk checks and rush downstairs to direct the luggage handlers to bring their burdens up by way of the freight elevator to the proper room. It all happened quickly, efficiently, and with a minimum of stress to weary travelers.[35]

The interior decorations of the guest rooms were done with feminine touches intended to make ladies feel at home and comfortable. Most rooms were painted

Henry Flagler stands in the carriage way behind the Hotel Ponce de Leon. Most guests arrived and departed from this drive to avoid having to make their way through the courtyard garden at the front of the hotel. © Flagler Museum Archives.

white with gold trim.[36] Not a single early photograph has been found recording the look of the hotel's private apartments, but *New York Times* correspondent William Drysdale provided this verbal picture of his room:

No. 112 is a room perhaps fifteen feet long by twelve feet wide, with another room at the back, the alcove, in which is the bed, the sleeping room being ten or twelve feet square and separated from the front room by curtains. In the front room we have velvet carpet; in the back room a Brussels of the same pattern. The window sashes are divided in the middle and open outward on hinges, and there are two shades—one of cream color, and the other a dark green. On one side of the window a low mahogany dressing case, with a very fine glass; on the other side a mahogany chest of drawers, with a mirror on top to shave by. In the centre of the room a table covered with a heavy rug; on the right a mahogany writing desk, full of pigeonholes and little compartments. To the right of this a fireplace, tiled with very small tiles, and furnished with bright brass andirons and tongs. Over the mantel a mirror set in the wall, framed with a circular procession of plaster angels, also set in the wall. A rich upholstered sofa and four or five chairs to match complete the list. In the bedroom nothing but the soft bed and a chair or two. Electric lights enough to make the room bright as day— two over the dressing case, four in the chandelier, and two in the sleeping room—eight in all. But there is no washstand. Can it be that the millionaire guests never wash? Investigation discloses the fact that we have only to shove aside the top of the writing desk, which works upon a pivot, and we find that the lower part is a washstand, well supplied with soap, towels, and water. This was the furniture, barring a printed notice fastened to the inside of the door that 'the price of this suite is $15 a day.' This price included board for one or two persons, and for the accommodations and the service it was probably none too high. The moment the room was unoccupied it was put in order, pitchers of ice water were constantly coming up fresh and cold, the supply for the night being a pitcher containing one large block of ice, which, melting slowly, kept cold till morning. The morning's hot water appeared upon the touch of the bell, and fine stationary for the asking. It would be hard to find as good service anywhere.[37]

The head of housekeeping, Miss Annie McKay, a veteran associate of O. D. Seavey, carried a good deal of the responsibility for making this system operate smoothly. She supervised a cadre of several dozen housemaids who maintained order in the rooms.

Interestingly, Henry Flagler's old acquaintance from Cleveland, Julia Tuttle, had inquired about the position of head housekeeper for herself more than a year before the hotel opened. Tuttle wrote to John D. Rockefeller asking him to act as her intermediary in applying for the job. Rockefeller replied: "I have spoken to Mr. Flagler. He will not give any personal attention to the running of his hotel when it is completed, and is of the opinion that his Manager, O. D. Seavey, has arranged in respect to the position you refer to."[38]

This letter is illustrative of Flagler's management philosophy. He appointed competent people in whom he had confidence to run his various enterprises and then allowed them authority to administer as they saw fit. Tuttle's approach also illustrates the way in which petitioners attempted to thwart Flagler's system by going around his lieutenants and appealing directly to Flagler. His usual response was simply to turn the supplicant back to the responsible department head. Of course, Flagler often violated his own system and directly intervened in details of operations, but it was still useful for him to use his executives as shields between himself and outsiders.

Miss McKay, a redoubtable spinster, received high praise for her professionalism: "She is thoroughly conversant with the duties, has a watchful eye over her large number of employees, and as carefully guards the interests of the owner and manager as she would were they her own."[39] McKay would be among the first of the hotel staff to arrive at the Ponce de Leon in December of each successive year, with a team of professional white women resort workers, in order to unpack all the bed linen, window curtains, toiletries, and other furnishings of the guest rooms. They would also clean the rooms, oil the floors, and polish the furniture. At the end of the season they would reverse the process, being among the last employees to depart the hotel.[40]

Henry Flagler valued McKay very highly. One Christmas he sent a vase and four framed pictures from New York to James McGuire in St. Augustine with instructions for him to deliver the gifts, along with a personal letter from Flagler, to McKay on Christmas morning. McKay lived in a large shingle cottage at 18 Valencia Street, just behind the hotel and next door to O. D. Seavey's residence at 20 Valencia. As McGuire, another Ponce de Leon veteran, explained, "Some of our employees have been with us for fifteen and twenty years, and when we get the proper man we usually take care of him."[41]

McKay would continue in her position as head housekeeper of the hotel until her death in 1913. She was the last surviving member of the original hotel staff, and Flagler would remember her with a bequest in his will. Unfortunately, she died just months before Flagler did.[42]

When visitors staying in Miss McKay's hotel domain awakened in the morning, they were obliged to walk down the hallway to the community bathrooms located at the end of the hall to find toilets and bathtubs. Guests accepted this inconvenience as simply a standard feature of hotel life at the time.

Hungry patrons heading for breakfast could take the elevator or stairs to the Rotunda and then venture up the flight of marble stairs to the foyer of the Dining Room, where they would be greeted at the door by the headwaiter, who would select a button from the rows of a hundred buttons on the electric enunciator board to alert the waiters in the kitchen that a new party was being ushered to a specified table in the Dining Room. The menu offered the possibility of a gargantuan breakfast. Starting with oyster stew and clam fritters, the selections continued through a veritable fish house of marine dishes: bass, whiting, mackerel, codfish, shad, salmon, and even that local Minorcan staple, the humble mullet. Eggs could be prepared in any of six different ways or served in six varieties of omelets. Meat plates included virtually anything: from kidneys and sautés au Champagne to broiled pig's feet, English mutton chops, sirloin steak, corned beef hash, calf's liver, fried tripe, chicken liver en brochette, or tongue—and a few more. Potatoes came eight different ways. There were all kinds of hot cereals, muffins, and griddle cakes—including, for the health food faddist, rolls and pancakes made from Graham flour. Beverages ran the gamut from coffee to English tea, green tea, Oolong tea, chocolate, cocoa, and broma, a light cocoa drink then popular. Of course, oranges could be had in abundance, as could Malaga grapes and various preserves.

French travel author Paul Blouet, who wrote under the pen name Max O'Rell, found the breakfasts stupendous—large enough for dinner, to a Frenchman. "You see women come down at eight to breakfast in silk attire, and decked with diamonds, and what a breakfast!" He thought Americans ate too much generally, with less regard for quality than quantity. At the Ponce de Leon, he observed, guests spent much of their time during the day sitting in rocking chairs waiting for the next meal.

On the porticoes of the Ponce de Leon the men tended to congregate in one area and the women in another. For the men, reading a newspaper often came as the first order of the day, the reading being interspersed with commentary on current events and politics to anybody nearby. Afterward a walk around town might be in order, to complete an errand or just to see the sights and take the salt air. An outing by carriage into the countryside could fill the rest of the morning, or perhaps a leisurely and sociable game of croquet would serve as a diversion. Time was one commodity that winter visitors ordinarily had in large measure.[43]

Blouet thought Americans tended to stick too close by their hotels. He explained: "In Europe, the hotel is the means to an end. In America, it is the end. People travel hundreds, nay, thousands, of miles for the pleasure of putting up in certain hotels. Listen to their conversation, and you will find it mainly turns, not on the fine views they have discovered, or the excursions and walks they have enjoyed, but on the respective merits of the various hotels they have put up at.

The loggias of the Ponce de Leon overlooked the courtyard on the sunny south side of the massive building, where north winds never intruded. By permission of Flagler College.

Hotels are for them what cathedrals, monuments, ruins, and beauties of Nature are for us."

However, to Blouet, Flagler's hotel embodied something special: "I have almost always accepted with reserve the American superlatives followed by the traditional *in the world*; but it may be safely said that the Ponce de Leon Hotel, at St. Augustine, is not only the largest and handsomest hotel in America, but in the whole world. Standing in the prettiest part of the picturesque little town, this Moorish palace, with its walls of onyx, its vast, artistically furnished saloons, its orange walks, fountains, cloisters, and towers, is a revelation, a scene from the *Arabian Nights*."

As a popular writer for the traveling public, Blouet offered a tip on how to sample the Hotel Ponce de Leon without actually paying to rent an apartment there. "It is not everybody who can afford the luxury of the Ponce de Leon Hotel," he wrote (perhaps including himself), "but it is everybody who likes to be seen there in the season. You must be able to say, when you return to the north, that you have been at the Ponce de Leon. This is how it can be managed. In the evening, dressed up in all your diamonds, you glide into the courtyard of the great caravansary. Another step takes you to the great rotunda where the concert is going on. You stroll through the saloons and corridors, and, taking a seat where you can be seen of most of the multitude, you listen to the music. About ten or eleven o'clock, you beat a retreat and return to your own hotel."[44]

Another travel writer, Julian Ralph, found the grandeur almost too much to bear. "I know of no place, public or private," he wrote, "where the power of wealth so impresses itself on the mind as this group of Florida hotels. . . . It is the spot itself—the finding of a group of palaces in such strong contrast with all the rest of Florida. . . . To live in the Ponce de Leon is as if we had been invited to stop at a royal palace. . . . It is its general effect, rather than its details, that charms the beholder, and that effect can be expressed in a sentence—it is a melody or a poem in gray and red and green. . . . It is all too fine for some persons, too dear for others, too artificial for others, and for another class not sufficiently restful. Many find the life too closely like what they left behind in New York, or they see the same club and business friends from whom they wish to get away." Ralph found his heart lifted when he left St. Augustine and entered a country hotel beside a river where he could wear flannels and relax.[45]

Strangers came to Florida to escape the toils of routine life in the North, yet part of the attraction of St. Augustine came from the fact that you were never too far from contact with home. In an emergency, you could be back at your home or office in less than two days. Thus a visitor passing though the Rotunda might pause to send a telegram from the hotel telegraph office or—more likely—just walk to the newsstand to purchase a newspaper. Fresh papers came in daily from Jacksonville with the morning train, along with two-day-old papers from back home. Later in the day visitors would return to see if any mail had come in for them, since the newsstand also served as the hotel's post office.

During the hotel's first season, George T. Flynn presided over the newsstand. A young man, he stood only four-feet-three-inches tall but made up for his lack of stature with a grandiose, formal "Chesterfieldian" manner. Everyone in the hotel knew him as "General" Flynn. Caroline Seavey had discovered him at I. D. Whitney's linen store in Boston, where her husband ordered fabric goods for the hotel.[46]

As the days passed during the first season, additional areas of the hotel that had been unfinished on opening day became available for use. The Gentlemen's Reading Room opened just two days later. Located at the far end of the east hallway, on the ground floor, it aimed to provide the comfort and solid decorum found in private clubs up North. The walls and ceiling were painted terra-cotta, while cream paint enhanced the wainscoting, fireplace mantle, and window trim. A thick olive-colored carpet covered the floor, and a long, carved cherry table occupied the center of the room, with a large brass chandelier overhead. Newspapers from the United States and Europe could be found arranged on the table.

In one corner stood a large writing desk. Today this room is the Board Room of Flagler College.[47]

Toward the end of January the Ladies Billiard Room opened just across the hallway from the Gentlemen's Reading Room. The Ladies Billiard Room (as well as reading and writing rooms) had originally been planned for the hallway adjacent to the Grand Parlor to bolster that region of the hotel as a ladies' province, but for some reason the billiard parlor was moved to the opposite side of the hotel. Perhaps the rooms originally intended for the ladies' uses were converted to regular guest rooms in order to increase the hotel's capacity. The Ladies Billiard Room contained six billiard tables and two pool tables made by the Brunswick and Balke Company. The skills of the ladies impressed some male visitors who crossed the hallway to peek in. Today the Ladies Billiard Room serves as the office of the president of Flagler College.[48]

During the second week of the hotel's life the interior decorator finally moved out, and the Grand Parlor opened. It had clearly been designed as a domain for the ladies. While the Rotunda and Dining Room displayed masculine tones of russet in their wood paneling and mural paintings, with light filtered into muted

The pastel and gold décor of the Grand Parlor appealed to the hotel's female clientele. From the collection of the St. Augustine Historical Society Research Library.

Virgilio Tojetti painted the large canvases that cover the four corners of the Grand Parlor. Tojetti spent most of his time in New York in the 1880s, but his Ponce de Leon work is signed "Paris." Author's photo.

hues through opaque stained glass, the Parlor shimmered with gold leaf details highlighted against white and cream-colored walls. The carpet, cream with pink and olive floral accents, had been woven in Scotland. Heavy cornices and a huge shield medallion in the center of the central salon's ceiling testified to the talents of the artists who worked in plaster. In the four corners of the ceiling, paintings by Virgilio Tojetti enlivened the room. These charming sky views of cherubs sporting with doves offered a Victorian version of Juan Ponce de León's vision of a celestial land of eternal youth.[49]

Tojetti's father, a noted Italian artist who had been honored by the Vatican for his work, had immigrated to America in the 1860s with his two sons. His son Edward settled in California, becoming a successful painter, while Virgilio settled in New York City. For a while Virgilio Tojetti kept a studio on Fifth Avenue three blocks north of the Flagler residence, and one of his early commissions involved painting some of the decorations inside W. K. Vanderbilt's mansion just down Fifth Avenue on the other side of the Flagler home. About the time Flagler started building the Hotel Ponce de Leon, Tojetti was executing a major commission to paint allegorical figures inside the dome of the Academy of Music in New York City. Thus Tojetti would have been well known to the circle of artists involved in the creation of the Hotel Ponce de Leon. One of Tojetti's canvases in the Grand Parlor is signed "Paris," so Tojetti may have been living in France when he executed the ceiling paintings on canvas. They would have been rolled up for transportation to Florida and then fixed to the ceiling.[50]

Hastings conceived the Grand Parlor in the ornamented French Renaissance form favored by the Beaux Arts school, yet he showed restraint in not overdoing it. Compared to other interiors of the day, the Parlor's walls are "flat" and the decorative enrichments limited. To make the large floor space more intimate

The massive fireplace and mantel in the central salon of the Grand Parlor served as the centerpiece of the large room. By permission of Library of Congress.

and comfortable, he divided the room into three salons by throwing two arched partitions across the width of the hall. A massive fireplace with an exquisite onyx face demanded the attention of anyone in the central salon.

The open wall spaces created a gallery for displaying the paintings that Flagler purchased from northern agents, most notably Knoedler, a company that helped other wealthy Gilded Age connoisseurs form their personal collections. Flagler showed no great personal interest in art—no desire to own Old Masters or prescient interest in modern art—and his collection could be characterized as prosaic. However, a set of eight pastels of Shakespeare's heroines by Jozi Arpad Koppay stand out from the run of Oriental scenes, idyllic landscapes, and European genre paintings.

The most interesting painting Flagler purchased for the hotel was, appropriately, Thomas Moran's "Ponce de Leon in Florida." Moran, who is today noted for his Western landscapes, had offered the monumental painting to the U.S. House of Representatives, which declined to purchase it, and after it had been shown at several exhibits, Flagler purchased it for his hotel. It is not known when Flagler bought the painting, but it was hanging in the Hotel Ponce de Leon in 1890. Later Flagler transferred the Moran to his home Whitehall in Palm Beach, and after his death it passed through the hands of a variety of owners before returning to Florida in 1996 to the Cummer Museum of Art in Jacksonville.[51]

Guests wishing to enter the Grand Parlor were ushered in by a uniformed doorman who opened the heavy wooden doors that separated the Parlor from the bustle of the Rotunda. One of those visitors, Morris Phillips, editor of the *New York Home Journal*, gave the Parlor his imprimatur of approval. Phillips's magazine, later renamed *Town and Country*, served as arbiter of good taste for fashionable society, while at the same time serving up lively gossip about and for the best people. He wrote that the Parlor, "of magnificent proportions . . . is not rivaled by any other hotel in the world. To call it palatial is no complement to 'the Ponce' parlor, for I have seen no apartments in royal palaces that are more pleasing, and I have been favored with a view of many palaces in many countries."[52]

A parlor maid circulated in the Parlor to place chairs conveniently and otherwise assist patrons but also to keep watch over the premises. On rainy days she would remind guests that umbrellas were prohibited since they dripped water on the carpet, and on at least one occasion, a carelessly handled umbrella toppled a precious Satsuma vase. The Royal Worcester vases and the Mexican urns of onyx and silver displayed on the mantles were securely screwed down to the woodwork to prevent their disappearance. Then there were guests who insisted on opening windows to shout to friends outside. It seems that even the best people were no more than just people.[53]

So great was the requirement for furniture in the hotel that Flagler hired three of the country's most important wholesalers of high class furniture. The company Pottier and Stymus, which had earlier redecorated Flagler's Mamaroneck country home, was the source for the Ponce de Leon's interior woodwork for floors, paneling, and ornamentation and may also have supplied furniture. Interestingly, Pottier and Stymus was engaged in decorating Thomas Edison's house in West Orange, New Jersey, at the same time as being employed on Flagler's hotel.[54]

Nelson, Matter and Company also stood high among the ranks of companies making fine furniture. Their factory operated in Grand Rapids, Michigan, a city in the north woods that prided itself as the furniture capital of America. This company specialized in "chamber furniture," so it seems likely that many of the furnishings in the hotel bedrooms came from Nelson, Matter. The third company, Palmer and Embury of New York, listed its specialties as "Parlor, Library and Dining-Room Furniture." They operated a five-story factory standing on the wharves overlooking the East River.[55]

Virtually all the furniture in the hotel, although made to order and of high quality, failed to rise above the level of utterly conventional period furniture for public rooms. The items of furniture that have attracted the most attention over the years and that have been most closely associated with the Ponce de Leon are the heavy carved oak Dining Room chairs with their cherub-head backs. The design of the chairs was attributed to "one of the architects." This may be true, since the winged-head motif also appears in the marble archway leading into the Dining Room.[56] None of the surviving chairs bears a trademark. One brief contemporary note in the Hotel Register says that the chairs were imported from Austria. If true, this might point to Palmer and Embury as their source, for they sometimes imported furniture from Europe.[57]

The marble walls and pilasters in the Hotel Ponce de Leon were executed by the firm of Batterson, See and Eisele, of Hartford, Connecticut, one of the country's leading dealers in fine stone. After completing the Hotel Ponce de Leon, that firm would erect William K. Vanderbilt's "Marble House" mansion in Newport, Rhode Island. Both buildings employ large panels of pink Numidian marble from North Africa.

Trying to estimate the total cost of the Hotel Ponce de Leon and its furnishings is a futile enterprise. The newspapers often called it a two-million-dollar hotel. An account of the insurance Flagler took out on the building shortly after its opening offers another perspective. The policy was underwritten by a consortium of eleven insurance companies. The building, with its fixtures, furnishings, equipment, "fresco, gilding decorations of all kinds," glass, and electrical system, was insured for $200,000. A $100,000 policy covered the furniture. The building and its contents were certainly underinsured.[58]

Outside, in the days following the hotel's opening, some finishing touches that would permanently distinguish the Ponce de Leon went into place. The large ornamental fountain in the center of the courtyard received terra-cotta frogs and turtles spouting water. In those days the streams of water issuing from the frogs' mouths spurted all the way up to the raised basin high on the fountain's central column. Today the spouts of water extend only a paltry few feet into the lower basin. Each frog had been carefully crafted in a different posture, with distinctly anthropomorphic attributes. A more modest, simpler fountain went into a lunette in the perimeter wall just north of the carriage entrance. The perimeter wall received swags of black iron chains, decorated with spiked mace heads, hanging between its concrete pillars. On the thick corner posts of each lunette a wrought iron stanchion held a globe of clear glass with a gas light inside.[59]

On January 31 two large flagpoles went up on either side of the front entrance. They displayed the red and gold banners of old Spain. An even larger pole at the southeast corner of the hotel flew a huge American flag. Palm trees, then only a few feet tall, went into the small lunettes of the perimeter wall.[60]

The ornamental central fountain in the Ponce de Leon's courtyard is a focal point and one of the hotel's most distinctive features. By permission of Library of Congress.

At the beginning of March the temporary railroad track that had served Flagler so well for more than two years was taken up along Cordova Street, and a mule-pulled grader gave the street a smooth, if not yet paved, surface for carriages coming to the hotel from the railroad station.[61]

The evening of the inaugural ball of the season arrived on February 9. Invitations had been sent to the managers of all the hotels, and anyone who wished to attend might come. Of course, admission required high formal dress: swallow-tail coats for the men—preferably from Taylor's of New York City. The women arrayed themselves in gowns they had purchased weeks or months earlier and had saved for this occasion. The most desirable gowns came from the House of Charles Frederick Worth in Paris. An expatriate Englishman living in Paris, Worth set the style for each season down to his death in 1895. Other fashion houses followed the season's trends, but every woman enjoyed a dress uniquely her own since different materials, colors, and trim would be employed to achieve glorious variety.[62] Of course, each woman displayed her own personal jewelry, retrieved for the occasion from the hotel safe where it had been placed for safekeeping. Prior to the balls, women would submit a written description of their costumes to the newspaper so that their appearance could be appropriately described to society.

Patrons arrived by carriage at the front gate and stepped into the courtyard, where banners flew from the balconies, multicolored electric lights blazed from among the flowerbeds, and Joyce's promenade band played from the loggia. The band had been divided into two units for the evening. Maurice J. Joyce directed the band outside on the loggia, while his brother Thomas H. Joyce directed the orchestra in the Dining Room. Electrician William Hammer had rigged a wire so that the brothers could communicate with each other by flashing light signals. When one band stopped playing, the other would commence.[63]

Soon both the courtyard and Rotunda were filled with a milling crowd of eager society people ready for more excitement. At 9:15 bandleader Thomas Joyce, the master of ceremonies for the evening, touched an electric button provided by chief engineer Hammer, and the doors to the Dining Room opened automatically. As the guests paraded inside, the orchestra played the "Ponce de Leon March" and uniformed ushers wearing white gloves escorted patrons to rows of chairs arranged in the east and west alcoves.

There were ten dances on the program, mostly waltzes, with a gallop and one polka. Handsome young men from the army's St. Francis Barracks in dress blues added a touch of color and augmented the male contingent at the ball. A wide variety of notables attended: Franklin W. Smith, accompanied by his daughter Nina, Pierre Lorillard, George Westinghouse, Thomas Hastings, and an array of artists: Martin Johnson Heade, Frank Shapleigh, George Innis, Robert German,

Elaborate formal balls highlighted the Ponce de Leon's early seasons. Ralph, "Our Own Riviera," *Harper's New Monthly Magazine*, March 1893, 488.

and George Seavey, brother of the hotel's manager. Notably absent were Mr. and Mrs. Flagler. A happy throng packed the Dining Room, and many guests wandered into the Rotunda and courtyard to escape the crush or just enjoy the plush environment of the hotel.

At midnight, guests turned their attention to a supper spread, with a large sculpture of the Castillo de San Marcos—made of crystallized sugar and lighted from the inside with an electric bulb—in the center of the buffet table. After fortifying themselves with food, the guests happily departed either to their rooms in the Ponce or to the various hotels in town.[64]

The high point of the inaugural season came with a visit from the president of the United States, Grover Cleveland. Politicians did not necessarily command deference in resort society—Florida's U.S. senator Wilkinson Call and Governor E. A. Perry had visited in January without any particular fuss being accorded them, but a president required special handling—especially when accompanied by an attractive young wife who set styles among the ladies. (Frances Folsom Cleveland is credited with having helped send the bustle out of fashion.)

Groundwork for the presidential visit commenced in early February 1888 when Florida senators Call and Samuel Pasco, accompanied by a delegation of notables from Jacksonville, called on President Cleveland in the White House to invite him to the Sub-Tropical Exposition, Florida's attempt to showcase its assets to the nation. The president took a noncommittal attitude, saying that if he publicly declared that he would accept their kind invitation, every whistle-stop in the South between Washington and Jacksonville would deluge the chief executive's office with entreaties that he also visit their worthy cities. However, shortly afterward he admitted that he would come.[65]

When word got out that the president would extend his excursion to St. Augustine, thrilled city fathers swung into action, appointing a committee to plan a grand reception and parade for the president. He would disembark at the old train station in North City (near today's public library) and then proceed down the Shell Road to the City Gates, where artillerymen from the local garrison would discharge a twenty-one-gun salute from the ramparts of Fort Marion, and the mayor would offer President and Mrs. Cleveland the key to the city.[66]

The situation became more disturbingly complex when R. F. Armstrong from the staff of the Hotel Ponce de Leon attended the next committee meeting and explained that the president was coming to St. Augustine as the personal guest of Henry Flagler and that arrangements had already been made for his transportation and accommodations. Things got even worse a couple of days later when Daniel Lamont, Cleveland's chief of staff, telegraphed Mayor George Greeno requesting that there be no formal ceremonies of any kind. This led to a "warm debate" among the committee members, followed by a trek to the Hotel Ponce de Leon, where Flagler cordially ushered the local men into his office and said he would meet the president in Jacksonville and tell him about the city's plans for his reception, but that ultimately the president would decide what he wanted to do. The newsman present at the meeting reported, "A lengthy and not exactly humorous discussion ensued, and it was finally agreed to adhere to the original plan, and trust to the good sense of the President and his estimable wife, in accepting the courtesies offered by the citizens."[67]

On February 23 the presidential family, accompanied by Secretary of the Navy William C. Whitney and his wife, arrived in Jacksonville. After a reception at the St. James Hotel, they took the St. Johns River ferry to the railroad station on the south bank. Flagler accompanied the party in the oak-paneled parlor car *Alcazar*, the red plush upholstery of which had been accentuated with garlands of roses and orange blossoms. The exterior of the train had been festooned with strands of Florida's decoration for all occasions—Spanish moss—and portraits of the president and first lady covered the headlight and cowcatcher of the locomotive. Coming into St. Augustine, the train bypassed the old station and proceeded to Orange Street Station, where the presidential entourage disembarked and Mrs. Cleveland accepted a bouquet of flowers from some local ladies. The president and his party then strode past the nonplussed city council and Mayor Greeno—who had been pleased eight years earlier to extend the city's welcome to President Grant—and the presidential party climbed into carriages for a circuit around the town.

The president, his wife, and Flagler (but not Alice) rode in an elegant landau drawn by four grays, while Secretary Whitney and the rest of the procession followed behind. The St. Augustine Guards in their gray uniforms, army regulars in blue, volunteer firemen, police, school children, and thousands of winter guests and locals lined the seawall and streets to watch the spectacle. After two days of rain, the sun smiled brightly down on the occasion. As usually was the case, young Mrs. Cleveland attracted the most attention. After a run along Bay Street beside the seawall, past the Slave Market—which had been temporarily roofed over with palm fronds to disguise damage from the fire of the previous spring—to St. Francis Barracks, the procession returned up St. George Street to a left turn onto King Street and the short ride to the front gate of the Hotel Ponce de Leon. Along the way every hotel was decked out in colored bunting, with Franklin W. Smith's Casa Monica attracting the most attention. It streamed red and gold banners while ladies in Spanish dresses waved from the kneeling balconies.

Joyce's Military Band struck up a patriotic air as the president's carriage drew up outside the entrance to the courtyard. Tiny newsstand manager George Flynn, resplendent in a cut-away dress coat with brass buttons and beaver top hat, gave a deep bow and stepped forward to open the carriage door. As the party walked through the courtyard, students from the Deaf and Blind Institute, St. Joseph's Catholic school, and the public schools tossed flowers onto the walkways. The distinguished guests proceeded right through the Rotunda to their suites, the Clevelands to the pink bridal chamber in the west wing (rooms 38 and 40) and the Whitneys to the matching blue suite in the east wing. These extravagantly decorated bridal suites usually rented for eighty dollars a night and were furnished with crystal chandeliers and original oil paintings—and, more functionally, with the very few private bathrooms in the hotel. After freshening up and resting, the visitors were served lunch in a private room off the main dining room. Chef Joseph Campazzi was already known to the president, having prepared the dinner for Cleveland's inauguration three years earlier. After lunch Flagler and hotel manager Seavey led a tour of the hotel for the gentlemen, including a trip up into one of the towers, where a large telescope had been stationed for use by the guests. Secretary Whitney, being responsible for the U.S. Navy, asked about the depth of water over the bar at the harbor entrance. (Whitney was a cousin of St. Augustine developer John Whitney.) A second tour for the ladies followed after the men's tour.[68]

After dinner Flagler held a reception in the Rotunda for specially invited guests, including Frederick Vanderbilt, Pierre Lorillard, and the duke of Newcastle as well as local notables such as Franklin W. Smith, James Renwick, and William G. Warden (but for some reason not Andrew Anderson). Diminutive George Flynn was introduced as "General" Flynn and, with a grand flourish, shook hands with the president and first lady—who was herself noted for exuberant hand shaking.

Also in attendance were Flagler's old Euclid Avenue neighbor John Hay and the historian Henry Adams, grandson and great-grandson of presidents. They had been "aimlessly wandering" in Florida to avoid cold weather up north. Hay suffered from "chronic inflammation of the vocal chords," but Adams noted that Hay "had swarms of acquaintances, and was delightful company." Adams described Flagler's "wonderful" Ponce de Leon as "the palace just built for a hotel." Adams and Hay could appreciate the design of the Ponce since they lived in adjoining houses designed by H. H. Richardson on Lafayette Square across from Cleveland's White House. The evening before, Adams and Hay had been present at a party in the Grand Parlor attended by the whole Flagler family and about one hundred others.[69]

Following the private gathering in the Rotunda came a general reception to which "the citizens of St. Augustine and guests of the hotels" had been cordially invited. A huge crowd had assembled outside, spilling into King and Cordova streets and taxing the best efforts of the police and St. Augustine Guards to keep order. At eight o'clock the front doors were thrown open, and the excited throng rushed in. The central area of the Rotunda had been roped off, with the presidential party standing on oriental rugs inside the barrier. The president and his wife were, of course, the center of attraction; then the receiving line progressed past Secretary Whitney and his wife to Flagler, Alice (dressed in "goblin green petticoat and train, white silk brocaded heavy with gold, and a beautiful diamond necklace"), and daughter Jennie Louise Benedict.

Hay and Adams remained interested viewers of the spectacle, with Adams writing home: "I watched Mrs. Cleveland's splendid vigor in handshaking."

In the pell-mell of the crowd, rich and poor, white and black jostled each other in line, with no discrimination between the various citizens of the republic. One of the more daring of the barefoot black scamps, so common to the streetscapes of town, solemnly took his turn in line to shake hands with the president and ladies. A newsman estimated that between three thousand and six thousand people paid their respects to the chief of state.

Not among the happy throng were Mayor Greeno and members of the official reception committee. They spent the night loitering in the gloomy dimness of the Plaza. "The mayor and councilmen were quite indignant at not being introduced at the depot and refused to attend the reception in their official capacities. They expressed their disapprobation in rather forcible terms in front of the post office during the evening."[70]

During Cleveland's visit Chief Engineer Hammer pulled out all the stops in his repertoire of electrical wonders. Over the large, arched main entrance to the hotel he placed a large flashing multicolored sign spelling out the president's name letter by letter and then in full, "C-L-E-V-E-L-A-N-D: CLEVELAND." Hammer holds the dubious honor of being the inventor of the blinking electric sign, an innovation he had unveiled at a Berlin fair in 1883. Four hundred additional lights were placed around the hotel, including strings of lights around the courtyard fountain's basin, running up its central column, and finishing off with a dazzling hundred-candlepower light atop the column. Before the reception in the Rotunda, a young lady presented Mrs. Cleveland with a bouquet of flowers enclosing a light bulb powered by a small storage battery, a contrivance that made the flowers "sparkle like diamonds." During the president's tour of the hotel, Hammer escorted the president's party outside to inspect the operation of the novel artesian-well-powered electrical generator. After the reception in the evening, the president went out briefly onto the balcony overlooking the courtyard to watch an electrical light display.[71]

After the reception the Washington travelers returned to their rooms to change into their traveling clothes and then boarded a special overnight train that whisked them to Palatka and the remainder of their Florida tour.[72]

It is not known whether Flagler had ever met President Cleveland before that day in St. Augustine. Cleveland had been mayor of Buffalo and then governor of New York during the time that Flagler established himself in New York City. However, Flagler afterward maintained what was evidently a cordial but usually distant association with Cleveland. Since both men highly valued their privacy, they did not leave much of a paper trail for future historians to follow.

Flagler and Cleveland enjoyed close relationships in common with Elias C. Benedict. Cleveland often accepted Benedict's hospitality on his yacht *Oneida* to escape the heat of summer and politics in Washington. Benedict had made his money in gas and rubber before becoming a Wall Street financier. He was most noted as a boating enthusiast. A hearty man wearing a full beard, Benedict looked the part of a yacht captain. His frequent voyages included taking his own vessel up the Amazon to inspect rubber plantations.

Benedict lived near Flagler on Fifth Avenue and was a member of West Presbyterian Church. Frank Hastings, brother of Flagler's architect, had left Thomas Edison's staff to become Benedict's private secretary. However, Flagler's closest link to Benedict was the marriage of his daughter Jennie Louise to Benedict's son Frederick. Jennie Louise's first marriage to John Arthur Hinckley had ended in divorce in March 1887. (Hinckley would go on to become a noted international yachtsman, with a home in Monte Carlo. He died in 1910, leaving an inheritance of nearly two million dollars, most in Standard Oil stock.)[73]

On October 6, 1887, Jennie Louise married Frederick H. Benedict. Young Fred Benedict took after his father in being an avid sailor and horseman.[74] During the 1888 season Jennie Louise and Frederick visited the Flaglers at the Hotel Ponce de Leon.

The second ball of the year was scheduled for March 1, but some guests jumped the gun by staging an impromptu "hop" three days before. The press called it a "swell affair" that attracted most of the patrons of the hotel.[75] This renegade ball seems not to have diminished enthusiasm for the real thing that followed, as a crowd of more than a thousand invaded the hotel. The evening opened with fireworks outdoors, and when the gala company moved inside to the Dining Room they found two bands that alternated playing dance music from lofts at either end of the vaulted central hall. This time Henry Flagler and Ida Alice appeared, along with their daughter Jennie Louise and her new husband Frederick Benedict. Distinguished-looking Franklin W. Smith and his beautiful daughter Nina attracted attention. Important persons abounded. William Rockefeller, John D.'s brother, and William Warden represented a Standard Oil contingent. Some of the ladies wore newly fashionable "décolleté" gowns with swooping necklines that displayed daring expanses of shoulder and bosom.[76]

While the lights burned brightly in the Hotel Ponce de Leon, across King Street hundreds of workmen hurried to complete the Alcazar. To the disappointment of the optimists, the Alcazar had not been ready for occupancy when the Ponce de Leon opened in January. The wooden scaffolding around the Alcazar's towers proclaimed the unfinished state of the building. Thus as the days of

February ticked by, landscapers raked and leveled the sand on Alameda plaza in front of the Alcazar, while others hurried to get the hotel's courtyard scenery completed. Masons worked on the large concrete pond in the center of the courtyard. Inside, plasterers and painters furiously plied their trades.[77]

The ground floor shops were the first to be occupied, with at least a couple opening in January. Flagler generously gave one of the spaces to the St. Augustine Institute of Natural History, the precursor to the St. Augustine Historical Society. Here the society exhibited its "collection of curiosities"—bones, shells, and bits of pottery—many of which had been excavated from Indian mounds in Florida.[78]

Just as the Alcazar seemed about ready to open some of its rooms for guests, news flashed from New York City that the entire Pottier and Stymus factory had burned to the ground, destroying everything inside. Did this include the Alcazar's furniture? No, manager Seavey assured everyone, all the hotel's furniture had been shipped before the fire.[79]

This good fortune came at the right time, for as the winter season reached its peak in late February, the Ponce de Leon overflowed with guests, and Seavey anxiously awaited the moment when he could send some of this excess to the Alcazar. Finally on March 3 a few visitors could be put up in the Alcazar, and on March 5 the front desk opened its registration book.[80]

The ambiance of the Hotel Alcazar turned out to be either a fortuitous accident or a master stroke of Carrère and Hastings's genius. The scale of the building seemed just right for human sensibilities. The central court with its pond, spraying jets of water, and tropical plants—enveloped by the walls of the building—possessed an air of intimacy and exoticism that was lacking in the grander, more open courtyard of the Ponce de Leon. The entire house simply felt comfortable. The *Times-Union* correspondent sensed this right away: "There is an oddity about the place that is certainly attractive."[81]

Flagler said he had intended the Alcazar as a two-dollar-a-day hotel with a more relaxed, informal atmosphere than the high-toned Ponce de Leon. Yet he also declared, "It is every bit as good as the Ponce de Leon."[82] This was not quite true. The Alcazar lacked the Tiffany glass windows, Maynard murals, Pottier and Stymus woodwork, and overall elegance of the Ponce de Leon—but its comfortable ambiance was just what endeared the hotel to its patrons. A local observer would later write, "The people of St. Augustine are proud of the Ponce de Leon, but they love the Alcazar."[83]

Although the Alcazar in its unfinished state would be open for a only few weeks during the 1888 season, it had clearly established itself as a resort house with its own distinctive character and a future full of potential.

No Renaissance palace would be complete without the stimulating presence of a coterie of artists, and the Ponce de Leon did not disappoint in this regard. At the rear of the hotel Carrère and Hastings had built a row of seven artists' studios on the upper floor level overlooking what Hastings had hoped would be a spectacular water park. Instead, visitors walking on the balcony outside the studios had a view of McGuire and McDonald's wooden headquarters building, the tennis courts, and, across a sandy lot, Grace Methodist Church. Still, the studios provided a fascinating distraction for guests at the hotel.

St. Augustine had already attracted artists in the years before Flagler's arrival. One artist came to town in the time-honored search for health. Louis C. Tiffany's wife Mary was dying of tuberculosis when the couple arrived in January 1883. He took advantage of the months he spent in the community to do some painting, including one view of the entrance to Fort Marion and another of the back porch of the General Kirby-Smith House, today the Research Library of the St. Augustine Historical Society. As far as we know he never returned to St. Augustine in later years, although the decorative glass company he would found in 1885 played a large role in the creation of the Hotel Ponce de Leon.[84]

Another artist came at the same time as Tiffany but put down deep roots and would live the rest of his life in St. Augustine. Pennsylvania-born Martin Johnson Heade ventured into the wilderness of Florida in search of exotic vistas to put on canvas. Heade belonged to the Hudson River School of landscape painters, whose leader, Frederick Edwin Church, long shared a studio with Heade and became a lifelong friend. Heade had already passed middle age when he began exploring the American South and even Brazil on outings that included hunting, fishing, and sketching. He wrote about these ventures in *Forest and Stream* magazine, an early journal for outdoors enthusiasts.[85] In January 1883 he arrived in Florida by way of Jacksonville, took a steamer up the St. Johns River to witness in the views commonly described in the tour guidebooks, and then returned downriver to arrive at St. Augustine. Here he wrote: "I have wandered, in an unsatisfactory sort of way, nearly all over the State without finding a spot where I cared to stop until I reached St. Augustine, and that I find a fascinating, quaint old place, and is bound to be the winter Newport of this country."[86]

Heade's juxtaposition of "quaint old" with a prediction of St. Augustine's becoming the winter Newport aptly summarized his relationship with the town. He appreciated the unspoiled broad marsh and tropical river landscapes that suited his preferences in subject material, and at the same time he could see the potential for development in the area. He took note of the new Hotel San Marco, which was just then beginning construction, and the recently completed rail line north to Jacksonville—and saw that St. Augustine stood on the cusp of a real estate boom. By March he had purchased a home on the Shell Road north of the San Marco, and soon he owned another lot nearby that he bought as a real estate venture, seeing that the town was growing in a northerly direction. "A great deal has already been bought up with a view to speculation," he wrote, "and when the rush begins next season not a foot will be left, at present prices. Everything now is nicely arranged to make St. Augustine by far the most attractive winter resort in Florida."[87]

Henry Flagler would step into this picture just about two years later. It is possible that Heade was among those who influenced Flagler's decision to take a stake in St. Augustine's future. One of Heade's fellow artists, George W. Seavey, was the brother of the San Marco's manager Osborn D. Seavey, who played a large role in Flagler's early ruminations about building his own resort hotel. At the very least, the two Seaveys and Heade probably influenced Flagler's decision to build the artists' studios at the back of the Ponce de Leon.[88]

In March 1886, nearly two years before the Ponce de Leon would open, a group of artists staged a show and reception in a local hall. Paintings by George Seavey and Heade attracted attention, along with those by Frank H. Shapleigh, W. Staples Drown, Walter Paris, and M. Seymour. All but the last two artists would later occupy studios at the Ponce de Leon. Thus it is clear that Flagler's hotel did not bring the artists to St. Augustine; they arrived either before or just at the same time that Flagler did.[89]

The artists came to St. Augustine in the winter for the same reason that they went to the White Mountains or Saratoga in the summer: those were the places where well-heeled patrons of art spent the season, and they might decide to take home a nice scenic painting as a souvenir of their vacation.

In the Ponce de Leon's first winter, six of the studios were occupied. Heade held forth in the westernmost studio, number 7, which would remain his headquarters for the rest of his life. Flagler had already purchased two large paintings from Heade to hang in the hotel when it opened: *View from Fern Tree Walk*, a Jamaican landscape, and *The Great Florida Sunset*, an iconic Florida waterscape with cabbage palms that might depict many places along the St. Johns River. In the coming years he continued to paint Florida landscapes, but most of his production while at the Ponce de Leon would consist of flower studies.

George Seavey engaged Studio 1 at the other end of the gallery. Like most painters' ateliers, he filled it with curiosities to amuse anyone who might drop in: bric-a-brac, carved furniture, peacock feathers, Turkish rugs on the floor, and Japanese silks on the walls. As with Heade's work, Flagler had already purchased several of Seavey's flower paintings for the hotel and for his Fifth Avenue home. Seavey enjoyed wide popularity in the hotel community. A newspaperman assured his readers that "the fierceness of his huge mustache is neutralized by the genial good humor which lights his face."

Frank Shapleigh next door, like Seavey a Boston man, was described as "a portly and pleasant-mannered gentleman." Shapleigh could often be seen around town painting typical Ancient City streetscapes. In the summer he located himself in Crawford Notch, New Hampshire, where his woods and mountain scenes captured quite a different local color.

W. Staples Drown, "a quiet, modest young man," was the son of the rector of Trinity Episcopal Church, Edward L. Drown. To supplement his income, he taught classes in art for children in town.

Marion Foster came to St. Augustine for the all-too-common reason of poor health. A bright, petite woman with a charming studio, she often remained confined to her room at the Ponce de Leon due to sickness. A wide circle of lady folk extended their sympathy to her. Miss Foster specialized in miniature portraits, a popular item at the time.[90]

Her neighbor Robert German shared a similar story. This "tall, pale young man" had been born in Germany but immigrated to the Midwest and then, when his health broke, to Gainesville, Florida, and from there to St. Augustine, where the people who could afford to buy art spent the winter. He made miniature portraits on ivory or larger portraits executed in crayon.[91]

Friday night receptions at the artists' studios became a regular feature at the hotel. An early newspaper description perhaps overdoes the elegance of the occasions: "The artists occupying the Ponce de Leon studios donned their evening dress, their smart gowns, decked out their studios in their best attire and bade the fashionable world come and see. In answer to this, a gay throng of well-dressed, cultivated people, representing the wealth and cultivation of the continent, came, saw, and admired. Between the hours of eight and eleven the studios were thronged, and, judging from the remarks made, the pictures and the kindness in affording them the opportunity to see them, were much appreciated by the visitors."[92]

A few years later, when the throngs had perhaps thinned out somewhat, Ellen Robbins, an artist herself, offered a more modest description of a reception evening: "One had a good opportunity in these receptions of seeing the people who went for the winter to St. Augustine,—some very interesting, but a large number so uninteresting that it was depressing. The artists were very eager to sell their pictures; and these Flagler studios all being in a row, with a flight of stairs at each end,—when any one looking like a buyer came by a door, a head was quickly protruded to see what artist was fortunate enough to secure the same. Boarding at the Ponce de Leon was considered a wise thing, no matter how poor the artist, because there one was more likely to meet the rich people."[93]

The third ball of the season elevated the lofty status of the already exalted social event to an even more heady height. This time only invited guests were to be admitted. "Every one who has been fortunate enough to receive one of the talisman pasteboards is making preparations to be present," reported a newspaperman. The state's leading newspaper, the *Florida Times-Union* of Jacksonville, outdid itself in hyperbole the day after the event: "The hotel was a shining chalice of beauty, music, and fragrance. Distinguished people from all parts of the world were present, men of letters, warriors, statesman, poets, distinguished and honored in this Nation's history graced the occasion, and their wives and daughters, beautiful as houris [an Islamic nymph of paradise], made one's mind revert to stories of ancient and grand empires—where beauty and chivalry graced just such occasions—grander by far than the most imaginative eye can depict."

Thomas Joyce attracted some attention as he directed the orchestra using a baton with a bright electric light at its tip. Hammer had rigged up a small storage battery that Joyce concealed under his coat and had connected it with the baton by way of a wire running through Joyce's sleeve.[94]

The list of those sharing in the evening came close to matching the grandiose language: New York subway magnate James M. Fisk, Frederick Vanderbilt (who lived two blocks south of Flagler on Fifth Avenue), William Rockefeller, Senator Leland Stanford, and these gentlemen's wives. Elderly Julia Dent Grant—Mrs. U. S. Grant—occupied a place of deference in the great Dining Room, but other women attracted attention for their ensembles. John Carrère's wife Marion played the role of señora, dressed in "yellow silk, beautiful Spanish costume, old lace, diamonds and rubies." It seems that Henry Flagler remained away from the festivities, but Ida Alice appeared in "pink silk, Spanish lace overdress, with diamonds and sapphires." Jennie Louise and her husband Frederick were there, with Jennie Louise dressed in "black and pink striped silk, bead trimmings, radiant diamonds and sapphires." During a dance Jennie Louise dropped a diamond brooch in the form of a four-leaf clover, but another dancer spotted it glittering on the floor and, after a few inquiries, returned it to its relieved owner.[95]

The list of luminaries who called at the Hotel Ponce de Leon during its premier season includes a host of notables from all walks of life: Herman Ossian Armour, head of the "beef trust"; Isaac Singer Jr., of the sewing machine family; Robert E. Lee's nephew Fitzhugh, governor of Virginia; Henry Sanford, former diplomat and founder of the town of Sanford, Florida; Pierre Lorillard, George Lorillard's brother; editor Henry Grady of the *Atlanta Constitution*; editor Joseph Medill of the *Chicago Tribune*; the largest land owner in the country, Hamilton Disston; Henry B. Plant; William Rockefeller, president of Standard Oil; George M. Pullman, builder of the railroad cars; George Westinghouse, inventor of air brakes for railroad cars; and former secretary of war and Civil War general John M. Schofield.

The controversial Wall Street financier Jay Gould, who had once tried to "corner the gold market," arrived offshore of St. Augustine in his steam yacht

Atalanta, but his vessel drew too much water to pass over the bar; he and his family and servant came in by way of a power launch. While staying at the Ponce de Leon, Gould occupied the suite of rooms on the third floor in the southwest corner of the hotel that Flagler himself normally occupied.[96]

Although Gould was widely criticized as a Wall Street manipulator, Flagler defended him as "one of the squarest men I have ever known."[97] Gould lived near Flagler on Fifth Avenue and attended West Presbyterian Church. They both served on the board of Western Union. A few years later when Gould's daughter made her debut into society, Flagler and Alice attended the large and lavish celebration Gould threw for the occasion. Several other men and their wives among the invited company also moved in Flagler's circle: Henry B. Plant, William Rockefeller, Mrs. U. S. Grant, and Chauncey Depew. The banker J. P. Morgan, who would later provide financing for Flagler's Key West rail extension, was also in attendance.[98]

Late in March E. C. Benedict, Jennie Louise's father-in-law, returned to St. Augustine, anchoring his yacht *Oneida* in Matanzas Bay while he and his party stayed at the Ponce de Leon. The intrepid Benedict was sailing north on the Gulf Stream after a cruise through Caribbean waters. On April 7 he trimmed his yacht with flags from stem to stern and hosted a reception for folks from town. His steam launch ferried Henry Flagler, Dr. Anderson, and a few other notables out to the *Oneida*. A few days later many of them would stand on the seawall to wave Benedict goodbye.[99] One year hence the *Oneida* would play an important role in a Flagler family tragedy.

In March another celebrated guest, Julia Dent Grant, spent three weeks at the Hotel Ponce de Leon with her daughter and Senator and Mrs. Leland Stanford of California. Ex-president Grant had passed away more than two years earlier and did not have the opportunity to witness the spectacular growth of Florida he had predicted during his visit eight years before. During the stay of the Grants and Stanfords, the local army band assembled in the Plaza below their window to offer a serenade, and a delegation from the Grand Army of the Republic held a reception for Mrs. Grant in one of the private parlors of the hotel. The veterans presented her with flowers and shared recollections of wartime service with her husband, "which almost brought tears to the eyes of Mrs. Grant."[100]

Senator Stanford, an aging millionaire railroad builder, seemed to thrive in the Florida climate, looking "rugged and hearty." He was deeply intrigued with the Spanish history of old California and went shopping at the rambling St. Augustine Museum, coming away with a purchase of several hundred dollars' worth of rare books relating to Spanish times in Florida. These were doubtless intended for the museum he would open three years later at his new Stanford University. Interestingly, the museum would be built of cast-in-place concrete, and one wonders if the senator's stay at the Hotel Ponce de Leon provided some inspiration for the decision to build his museum in concrete, although letters and documents in the Stanford University archives reveal no direct connection.[101]

The hotel provided in-house entertainment on a regular basis to keep its noted guests amused. The orchestra played on the loggia both morning and afternoon—with sacred music on Sundays. The first season Flagler hired O. A. Robinson of Boston, an elocutionist, to perform dramatic soliloquies in the Grand Parlor, delivered in appropriate ethnic dialects, sometimes accompanied by musicians from Joyce's band. In the rear, below the balcony of the art studios, guests interested in outdoor sports could find a pair of wooden tennis courts.[102]

In 1888 the Ponce de Leon hosted what was called the "Tropical Championship" tennis tournament on these courts. The year before some tennis enthusiasts visiting St. Augustine had staged an impromptu tournament on Franklin Smith's wooden court behind the Villa Zorayda. Flagler promoted the 1888 tournament to attract leading players from the North to test their skills during the winter when no competing tournaments were scheduled up in cold weather country. Competition got under way on March 19, with Joyce's band playing lively tunes to please spectators seated on benches and chairs surrounding the courts. Two anonymous gentlemen provided a large sterling silver trophy reproducing the

Players in the 1888 Tropical Tennis Tournament stand on the Ponce de Leon's wooden tennis court. Oliver Campbell, three-time U.S. singles champion, stands fourth from the left. The skylights of the artists' studios can be seen in the background. "St. Augustine Lawn Tennis Tournament," *Outing Magazine*, June 1890, 180.

City Gates, onto which the winner's name would be engraved. The trophy would be given to any man who won the tournament four times. Everyone judged the tournament a success and planned for another the following year. In 1889 the matches would be played on new courts behind the Hotel Alcazar, and the Ponce de Leon's courts would be removed to make way for the construction of Valencia Street. (Years later, when the quaint wooden courts were long forgotten, Flagler College would build new courts in the same area just on the north side of Valencia Street. Now these courts also are gone.)[103]

Guests passing through the Rotunda were treated one day to an impromptu performance by one of the town's little street troubadours, who managed to slip past the guard at the entrance. A ragged Italian boy squeezed out a series of tunes on a well-worn accordion, performing a tap dance in time with the rhythm. "Mr. Flagler was among the spectators, and seemed pleased with the little fellow's audacity," reported a newsman. Afterward the youngster passed his hat and enjoyed an excellent return for his adventure.[104]

Other local boys sat on street corners offering baby alligators to passing tourists at the modest price of just a dime. Many of these tiny reptiles would be placed in cigar boxes and carried North to an always certain fate. A woman from the North told of the adventures of two young ladies: "One of them had a perfect passion for pets, often to the discomfiture of her friends. One day she purchased a chameleon, and, as matter of course, it accompanied her every where she went, even to the table, where it one day fell into a glass of milk, which our friend from Boston was raising to her lips."[105]

Late in March the bellhops of the Ponce de Leon organized a cake walk as a fundraiser for their fraternal organization, the Bell Boys Association. Seavey allowed them to use the large recreation room under the Dining Room, opposite the carriage entrance. Cake walks had long been a fixture in southern resort society—a sort of anthropological venture into the world of African American folkways for upper-class northern visitors. The cake walk offered an opportunity to sample an innocuous, staged presentation of southern black culture (although most of the hotel employees were from the North).

So large was the crowd of curious winter patrons who packed the recreation room that some who arrived too late were turned away. Henry Flagler and other distinguished guests joined the throng. The action commenced with the entrance of the bellhops and their female partners to the tune of the "Ponce de Leon March," which everyone would have recognized as the opening music to the hotel's formal balls. The hotel orchestra provided the musical accompaniment, and Maurice Joyce acted as master of ceremonies. Joyce announced the first offering: a rendition of a banjo tune composed by one of the hotel's guests,

Entertainments provided by the black employees of the hotels were a standard feature of resort life. Winners of the cake walk "took the cake." From the collection of the St. Augustine Historical Society Research Library.

one W. Shakespeare of Stratford, England, performed by two young men. Similar musical fare with a comic flamboyance followed.

A little parody called "I'll Meet Your Dar" performed by "bell-boys and their fair partners" brought the house down in gales of laughter. The play offered a caricature of the pompous white folks who inhabited the Ponce de Leon. "The costume of one of the damsels in red ribbons and white dress and a bustle that was *immense* caused bursts of wild applause." For once the black employees used their customary roles as clowns to poke a little fun at the white people.

The major attraction of the evening was the cake walk itself. Couples strolled around the stage with their most dignified posture and performed stylish turns while the band played and a jury of eminent judges assessed their flair for the fashionable and dramatic. The panel for the evening included elocutionist O. A. Robinson and "General" George Flynn, himself quite an expert on flair. W. A. Rollins, the porter at the women's entrance, won a silver-headed cane, while his partner Miss Lock was awarded an engraved gold ring—and an elaborate cake.

After the performances concluded, some guests remained behind to enjoy dancing to the music of the orchestra.[106]

Such cake walks pandered to racial stereotypes, yet in a time when racial segregation drew a more stringent and uglier line with each passing year, the cake walks afforded a moment when white people and black people could gather together in the same room to enjoy themselves and see the common humor in their shared human situation.

An example of growing racial segregation in America could be found in the raggedly organized new sport of professional baseball, where a few black players had long competed, but in which black men now increasingly found themselves excluded from the field of play. In the 1880s and 1890s St. Augustine produced some examples both of continued interracial play and of the rise of segregated baseball. The town and its hotels played a significant role in the rise of segregated black baseball; in fact, the first successful black professional baseball team, the Cuban Giants, had its origins in St. Augustine.

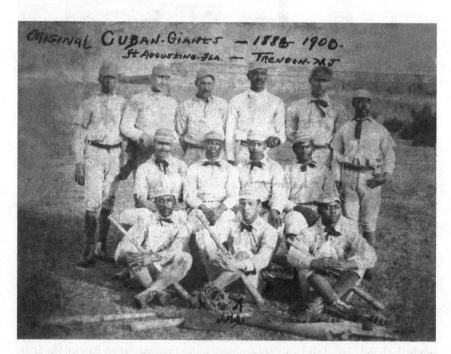

In the days of racially segregated baseball, the Cuban Giants were the most successful of the black clubs. They started by playing games on the green of Fort Marion; the fort can be dimly seen in the background of this photo. Courtesy of the Baseball Hall of Fame Museum, Cooperstown, New York.

The Hotel Ponce de Leon's manager O. D. Seavey loved sports of all kinds and saw them as a natural adjunct of resort life. Back in 1885 when Henry Flagler met Seavey at the Hotel San Marco, the hotel's black waiters were playing exhibition baseball games across the Shell Road on the grounds of Fort Marion. Since the fort's reservation had no fence, it was impractical to sell tickets to see the games, so players passed a hat to solicit donations to support their teams. The head-waiter of the San Marco, Frank P. Thompson, also served as manager of the San Marco's team, the Ancient City Athletics. When the hotel closed in April, the Athletics played games in several southern cities as they traveled north.[107]

When he arrived in Philadelphia, Thompson recruited players from other black semipro teams to form a new team called the Keystone Athletics. Later that summer the Athletics moved to Babylon, Long Island, where they were merged with the Philadelphia Orions and the Manhattans of Washington, D.C., to form the Cuban Giants. ("Cuban" was simply a euphemism for black.) Thompson ap-pears to have been one of the team's three owners when it was organized, but although the traditional history of the Cuban Giants says Thompson served as headwaiter at the Argyle Hotel in Babylon, Thompson himself did not claim to have worked at the Argyle.[108]

At the end of the season a white man, Walter Cook, bought a controlling in-terest in the team, moved it to Trenton, New Jersey, and turned it into the first financially sound black professional team. In 1887 and 1888 the Cuban Giants were declared champions among black teams, and down to the team's demise in 1899, they ruled as the most famous of the all-black squads. Thompson severed his connection with the team in the summer of 1888, citing the pressures of his career as a hotel man. On his leaving, the *Cleveland Gazette* paid tribute to him as the man "who organized the Cuban Giants and to whose ability the club is indebted for its success."[109]

In St. Augustine during the 1888 winter season, baseball games continued to be played on the fort reservation simply because it was the only large open field in town. James Mutrie, manager of the New York Giants, visited town and ar-ranged to play a game pitting his Giants against a team recruited locally, including "a number of crack players who are spending the winter."[110] Other games were played by teams made up of the employees from the various hotels, compet-ing with each other for the championship and prize money awarded to the win-ners. Three members of the Cuban Giants—Harry Johnson, Arthur Thomas, and W. White (probably Billy Whyte)—were among the hotel employees in the championship game played near the end of March. We do not know if any of these games involved mixed teams of white and black players.[111]

Most hotels in the South, like the San Marco, customarily employed black waiters to serve in their dining rooms, but in its first season the Ponce de Leon used white men to wait on tables. The hotel employed a staff of about one hundred waiters, led by their chief "Count" Julius Prokaski, who had previously been the headwaiter at Delmonico's and then at the Manhattan Beach Hotel the summer before. Most of the waiters were Irish and German immigrants.[112] They lived in the Ponce de Leon Barracks a couple of blocks south of the hotel at the headwaters of what remained of Maria Sanchez Creek. The barracks had been hastily erected of green wood, and someone got the bright idea of hastening the curing of freshly plastered walls by lighting a fire inside. Thus at midnight on January 27 workers living in the northern half of the building were awakened by shouts of "Fire!" Fortunately, the green wood and damp plaster slowed the progress of the fire, and only about a third of the building was lost. McGuire and McDonald immediately set about rebuilding, and in the meantime some of the waiters were quartered in the unfinished Hotel Alcazar.[113]

Count Prokaski's waiters made the newspapers again shortly thereafter when one of their number was shot in the thigh by a night watchman in the Alcazar. Called upon to testify in court a few days later, the waiters maintained that they had simply been walking home to their rooms after work, singing "Marching through Georgia," the anthem of General Sherman's troops in the late war. They maintained that the shooting had been unprovoked, although they implied that their assailant had been incited by their Yankee singing. The guard told a different story. He said the waiters sometimes broke into rooms of the Alcazar where work was going on to steal tools and other items. On the night in question, the watchman declared, they were trying to break down a door, and he fired a shot through the closed door as a warning. The judge believed the watchman and acquitted him of all charges.[114]

By March the waiters had earned a tarnished reputation. The kitchen help also made the daily press on St. Patrick's Day when one of the Irish employees showed up in the kitchen wearing a green ribbon. For this display of patriotism, another kitchen worker, "a burly Englishman," gave him a bloody nose.[115]

Later, after the season had concluded, manager Seavey began to receive letters from men who had been employed as waiters complaining of their treatment by Count Prokaski. They alleged that he had bullied them into paying him a percentage of the tips handed out by grateful hotel patrons. Some admitted that they had stolen silver and glassware to make up for the income they lost to Prokaski. One anonymous former waiter, who signed himself a "True Catholic," confessed that he had pilfered sundry articles from the hotel and sold them to "a colored woman" in town. He sent two dollars to pay for these, along with a box containing two shoe brushes, a bundle of toothpicks, three salt cellars, one package of macaroni, silverware, a pair of galoshes, and a set of false teeth—all lifted from the hotel and its guests.[116]

Normally late February constituted the heart of the winter season, followed by a gradual retreat of the winter visitors in March, but in the heady days of the Ponce de Leon's first year, when February turned to March and some guests began to depart homeward, new visitors arrived to replace them. At the end of March a concert in the courtyard attracted a thousand pleased listeners, and at the same time four hundred paying customers enjoyed the hotel's hospitality.[117] On just one day, March 28, eighty new guests arrived at the Ponce de Leon, and the tide continued strong. Thus Seavey and Flagler made the decision to keep the hotel open through the month of April and posted notices intended to encourage guests to remain a little longer. Although this ran counter to the usual practice for the leading hotels in town, it seemed like a good speculation. Mild, delightful weather usually prevails in northern Florida during April, making for pleasant times out of doors, while up North April usually means mud season. The railroads cooperated by continuing to run fast trains to Florida during April.[118]

Edison's electrician William Hammer staged a series of extravaganzas in April to bring the hotel's season to a colorful climax and show off the wonders of electric lighting. He used a lawn party around the Ponce de Leon's tennis courts, below the artists' studio row, to demonstrate the power of a dynamo driven by the water pressure from one of the artesian wells.

Just before the hotel's opening Hammer had connected the flow of a well to a turbine that spun a small generator at 850 revolutions per minute. His experiment demonstrated that this water-turbine-powered dynamo could light eighty-eight small sixteen-candlepower lamps, with the flow of water being so uniform that the lights maintained a steady glow. Interestingly, twenty years later Flagler would observe the ocean current rushing between islands of the Florida Keys and wonder if that tide could be harnessed to generate electricity.[119]

During the evening of the lawn party five hundred dancers waltzed on the wooden tennis courts under a huge pavilion lighted by Hammer's tiny electric lamps, while the combined Casa Monica and Ponce de Leon orchestras supplied pleasing music. Bonfires around the perimeter added to the festive atmosphere. Bunting left over from the president's visit hung from the balcony of the art studios. A crowd of townspeople stood outside the circle of light along Cordova Street watching the spectacle of rich strangers from the North enjoying themselves.[120]

Although the evening came off admirably, Hammer thought he could achieve even better results, and he quickly replaced the water turbine and connected it to a larger generator. He hoped that the hotel could achieve greater overall efficiency in its power plant by shutting down the steam-powered generators during low-demand periods and switching over to the water-powered generator. Thus during the dark hours after midnight and over the summer when the hotel was closed, it would not be necessary to burn coal and operate the steam engines to have a sufficient supply of electricity.[121] Whether the hotel ever actually used this approach is not known, but references to the water-powered generator disappear within a year.

In harsh contrast to the joy reigning at the Ponce de Leon, the Hotel Casa Monica limped through the season in quiet desperation. Although the hotel's management tried to put a good face on the situation by publicizing the notable guests who stayed under their roof, about the only truly famous patron of the Casa Monica was Franklin Smith's Boston compatriot Elisha S. Converse, the magnate of rubber-soled shoes. The Frenchman Blouet dropped by Smith's hotel to sample an evening concert and found a sprinkling of fewer than two dozen people in the audience.[122]

The hotel attempted to provide the expected amenities for its guests, such as an elevator, but no electric lights illuminated the rooms and no steam heat warmed the hallways. An impressive, brightly painted omnibus did appear to meet guests at the railroad station. A chef with a reputation in resort circles managed the kitchen. Each week the dining room would be cleared to serve as the dance floor for an informal "hop." Twice the Casa Monica hosted balls of a more elegant character that attracted guests from the other hotels in town. At the latter one, held on March 31, the Ponce de Leon orchestra came over to supply the music—indicating that Flagler was lending a hand to support the hotel's operations.[123]

On March 26 the hotel's manager E. N. Wilson was forced to issue a statement denying rumors that the Casa Monica would shut down in a day or two, but on the following day he closed two floors of rooms and laid off two or three dozen of the staff. In this condition the Casa Monica persevered until a more conventional closing date for local hotels of April 10.[124]

Three days after the Casa Monica concluded its season, word leaked out to the newspapers that Flagler had purchased the hotel from Smith. The *Jacksonville News-Herald*, which enjoyed good sources close to Flagler, broke the story and commented, "The price paid is unknown, as all the parties interested are very reticent." The *St. Augustine Evening News* put the price at $250,000. The *Times-Union* offered the opinion that probably only one dollar changed hands and wondered why "the community has remained in blissful ignorance all this time that he [Flagler] was the owner of the Casa Monica." When Flagler recorded the deed on April 20, it listed only a sale price of $325,000, with no mention of any mortgages or other encumbrances. It is possible that some of Franklin Smith's wife's family friends in Baltimore had financed the Casa Monica, entirely or in part. When Smith later sold the Villa Zorayda in 1902 it was then under mortgage to H. Ray Miller of Baltimore, a friend of Mrs. Smith's father.[125]

Many years later William A. MacWilliams, who signed the deed to the Casa Monica as one of the witnesses and may have been Smith's lawyer, gave this account of what had happened in building the Casa Monica: "After Smith had gone along with about two-thirds of the work, he became financially unable to continue.... He went to Mr. Flagler and appealed for help. Mr. Flagler agreed to take the matter off his hands and finish it, and reimburse him for the amount he had already expended."[126]

As the season drew near its conclusion, O. D. Seavey, Maurice Joyce, and William Hammer conspired together to stage a spectacular finale to the Ponce de Leon's debut. After dinner on April 3 these gentlemen ushered Flagler out to the front steps of the hotel overlooking the courtyard garden, and just as he walked out of the front door, Joyce's band struck up a celebratory anthem, red electric lights flashed atop every tower, and skyrockets launched into the evening sky from the roof. Flagler took a seat to enjoy the fireworks. Giant Japanese parasols, festooned with lanterns, stood in the garden, their electric lights flashing on and off. The St. Augustine Guards, resplendent in new uniforms, marched in and circled the fountain to perform the manual of arms. From the towers Joyce's band offered a concert to those below but also to the whole town, for the music floated eerily over the rooftops.[127]

Ten days later Henry B. Plant enjoyed the same performance.[128] Then on the last evening of April the townspeople of St. Augustine experienced the lights and music—and a new searchlight that scanned the heavens from one of the towers—as the hotel opened its gate for everyone. Once again an excited throng packed the Rotunda and elegant halls, anxious for one last glimpse of grandeur before the hotel wrapped itself in a cocoon for the warm-weather months ahead. The next morning, after the last guests breakfasted and departed, the doors closed.[129]

Shortly after the reception for Henry Plant, Flagler departed from St. Augustine for his home in New York City, concluding a hectic and triumphant four months that had witnessed the world of high society descend upon his magnificent hotel at the tail end of the railroad line on the Florida frontier. A week after returning north, Flagler found himself in Washington testifying before the House Committee on Manufactures about the alarming growth of business monopolies. He could swear honestly that on many detailed questions about the operations of Standard Oil, he could not answer, since he had not taken a hand in day-to-day operations for many years.[130] Probably he wished he were back in Florida, which, as it turned out, was exactly where he would spend the productive portion of the remainder of his life.

Already Flagler had turned his attention toward South Florida. In March, at the height of the St. Augustine season, he slipped off on an expedition southward.

He may have been accompanied by Hamilton Disston, the Philadelphia industrialist who a few years earlier had made himself the largest landowner in America by purchasing four million acres of Florida real estate. Just where Flagler went is uncertain. One report had him going to Indian River, precisely where he soon would extend his railroad. He may have been scouting the approaches to the Daytona area at this early date. Another story had him inspecting cattle ranch lands in the Kissimmee River region, where Disston was engaged in draining the swamps. At any rate, Flagler was acquainting himself with the landscape of his new homeland, probably with an eye toward the future.[131]

During the summer of 1888 Flagler undertook extensive reworking of the Casa Monica interior. Before he left for the North, he and Seavey had walked through the building to see what kind of jewel or white elephant Flagler had acquired. In July, to mark the transformation of the hotel, Flagler changed its name to the Cordova. Its former grand entranceway under the arch on King Street was converted into a store occupied by Ward Foster's El Unico curio shop.[132] Henceforth, the Cordova's front door would open on the west side facing the Alameda, bringing the focus of all three of Flagler's hotels onto the same garden.[133]

At Seavey's suggestion Flagler demolished the small freestanding kitchen that had been built behind the hotel and replaced it with a larger, better equipped kitchen. Much of the "cheap work" of the interior also had to be removed. Workers ripped up the hastily installed pine flooring and put tile in its place. Likewise, pine paneling came off the walls to be replaced with plaster.[134] Seavey ordered new furniture as well. However, the interiors still remained dark and overdone with Victorian plush and tassels and generally served as a dreadful counterpoise to the artistically enlightened interiors of the Ponce de Leon. The alterations did not amount to complete refurbishing, and changes would continue in coming years, but in its new arrangement, the Cordova stood ready to join Flagler's other hotels for the opening of the 1889 season.[135]

12

Upstairs and Downstairs, 1888–1890

Not a word is heard from the servants, except in polite
response to an order, and they glide about like dark angels.

—Morris Phillips, *Practical Hints for Tourists,* 1891

During the summer of 1888 Florida experienced a repeat of the previous year's yellow fever scare—but this time with much more serious consequences. Warning signs of trouble began early in the year, in the dead of winter, when northern newspapers published stories that yellow fever remained active in Tampa. The *Jacksonville News-Herald* condemned the account as "maliciously false" and "a base libel on Florida."[1] In April Florida's surgeon general reported the prevalence of yellow fever in the phosphate mining towns of the southwest peninsula. This elicited a blast from the *Florida Times-Union* for spreading before the world "the guesses and surmises of doctors and others as to alleged yellow fever." It predicted: "The sensation caused by Dr. Hamilton's publication of a lot of rumors gathered by one of his so-called 'experts' here in Florida, the majority of which have already been discredited, will soon die out."[2]

Far from dying out, accounts of the fever continued to accumulate as the weather grew warmer, and in St. Augustine everyone received encouragement to keep the city in a clean, sanitary condition, just in case. Then on August 9 a train from Jacksonville was stopped north of town and the passengers were forced to get off and walk to a quarantine house in the sand hills. At the same time the Board of Health imposed an embargo on all passenger traffic with Jacksonville, where the fever had now been confirmed. An estimated fifteen hundred St. Augustine residents, later described as "a panic stricken crowd," took trains to Palatka as a route of escape to the North.[3]

The town, which had withstood sieges in the past, shut its gates to the outside world. Workmen cut a cordon through the underbrush one mile north of town, along which guards armed with shotguns patrolled with military earnestness, on horseback by day and on foot by night with lanterns. One man was shot and killed by a quarantine guard—although this killing was later judged to be a personal dispute unrelated to the quarantine.[4] Yellow flags flew over the dunes near the inlet to Matanzas Bay to warn away ships, and boats patrolled the bay and rivers to stop anyone trying to enter by water. Even mail delivery between the town and Jacksonville ceased, drastically limiting communication with the outside world.

St. Augustine did send some of its old Spanish cannon to Jacksonville on loan, where they were shot off in the streets to "concuss" fever microbes.[5]

Maintaining the quarantine at least provided employment for about 350 men. By September the city council exhausted the five-hundred-dollar fund set aside to pay guards and voted to spend another five hundred dollars. Then they sent out a letter requesting donations from residents in exile for funds to keep up the quarantine.[6] Later it was reported that anonymous private donors wishing to preserve the town's reputation for health contributed $35,000 to pay for the quarantine—and only one man possessed that kind of money and that particular interest.[7]

In town an incredible dullness settled over everything. Merchants damned the Board of Health. Growlers in taverns condemned the "cowards" who had fled town. People dusted off their old medical books, looked up the supposed wisdom on yellow fever—and, no doubt, sighed and settled in to await the first frost.[8]

For the duration of the epidemic, stories about St. Augustine in the Jacksonville newspaper the *Times-Union* stopped; our main source of information from the town disappears for that interval. What impact the quarantine had on Flagler's construction projects in St. Augustine is hard to judge.

We do know that the gravel trains bringing in fill dirt from north of town ceased running.[9] Flagler's other construction projects seem to have continued apace. An adequate supply of laborers appears to have remained on hand, since the city council instructed the Board of Health that there was no need to admit any additional laborers through the quarantine.[10] Work on the Alcazar continued, and two new buildings began to rise on the newly filled east bank of the San Sebastian River: a laundry building and the railroad's Union Station.

During the Ponce de Leon's first season the laundry women had done their work in rooms on the first floor of the utility wing of the hotel, beneath the kitchen. To resolve this unsatisfactory arrangement Flagler erected a three-story, L-shaped red brick laundry building on the north side of Valencia Street, just west of Ribera Street. On the ground floor a team of women piled linen and uniforms into rows of large open tubs with wooded paddles that stirred the wash. A deep artesian well furnished water, which a boiler heated. Another boiler powered a steam engine at the rear of the building that ran all the machinery. An orderly assembly-line process sent the laundry through wash, rinse, spin, and starching processes. Drying was done both in a mechanical dryer and in a fenced-in courtyard. Then everything went into a final room for ironing and more starching.

The rest of the building served as a dormitory. The hotel band occupied a wing on the west side. White women lived on the second floor and black women on the third. A housekeeper supervised each floor. The building had its own kitchen, presided over by a cook, and dining rooms, so that the place functioned much like a second-class hotel. Those women who were employed in the hotels were instructed to walk to work along prescribed routes, to avoid the gardens, and never to be seen in the public areas of the building unless that was where their work required them to be.[11]

Flagler took advantage of the quarantine's interruption of train service between St. Augustine and Jacksonville to build a new, more substantial roadbed with heavier wooden crossties and to convert the rails from narrow gauge to standard gauge. A gang of two hundred men did the work and were happy to have the employment. The final task of laying the heavy sixty-pound steel rails and pounding the spikes came with a rush in December and January at the conclusion of the quarantine.[12]

While the transfer of rolling stock from the old track to the new one would not take place until January, and although Union Station remained incomplete, the new railroad did have one modernizing influence on St. Augustine immediately. The town's Board of Trade and then the city government voted to adopt "railroad time" or "national standard time" for the whole town, bringing the clocks of the Ancient City into line with Flagler time—and the rest of the country.[13]

The Board of Health finally lifted the quarantine in December, its members riding the first passenger train to Jacksonville on December 18 to celebrate with their medical counterparts in Jacksonville and greet St. Augustine citizens returning by steamship from exile in the North. Three days later Mother Nature put her seal of approval on the decision by sending a freeze that left ice two inches thick on puddles in the street.[14]

The people of Jacksonville had good reason to offer thanks for the passing of the yellow fever scourge, for two hundred citizens had succumbed to the disease.[15] St. Augustine escaped without a single death or even a single confirmed case of the fever, thanks to the ruthless vigilance of the city's leadership. However, St. Augustine could not avoid repercussions of the epidemic, for many northerners simply wrote off the whole of Florida as a sink of pestilence, not a possible destination for a winter vacation. Assurances that the fever never struck during cold weather often failed to reassure Yankees who decided to stay away, just in case.

St. Augustine's sandy streets had long been regarded as a quaint feature of the place, but just as often, both citizens and strangers condemned them as breeding places for disease. Mayor Long's message to the town council in the summer of 1886 put the matter bluntly: "The condition of our streets, especially St. George Street and Charlotte is a disgrace of our City Government and a reflection upon the intelligence, public spirit and enterprise of our people. Surface water with all manner of filth is allowed to accumulate and stand in stagnant pools upon principal thoroughfares of the city, sending forth their death breeding poisons and offensive odors apparently unnoticed by any City Officials. Side-Walks have entirely disappeared from any and every part of the City (except when constructed by private individuals) and no effort seems to be made to re-establish and maintain them. Pedestrians are thus forced through mud and slush, and indiscriminately out among horses, carriages, and vehicles of every size and description, at risk of life and limb."[16]

Henry Flagler was not the sort of person to put up with these conditions, and his engagement with St. Augustine initiated a revolution in street improvements that would continue for the next twenty years. He began the work by asphalting the carriage path running past the Ponce de Leon's rear entrance and the portion of King Street immediately in front of the hotel. The asphalt came into the harbor on schooners in a powdered form and was then spread upon a base of concrete, heated by a massive roller, and pounded level by a force of men with hot iron mauls. From his starting point on King Street in front of the hotel, Flagler's workmen extended the asphalt pavement all the way down Granada Street to Bridge Street, east to Cordova Street, and then north to King Street again—surrounding the Alcazar with paved streets on all sides. That completed the work for 1888.[17]

The following year Flagler asphalted the block of King Street lying between the Hotel Cordova and the post office, Cordova Street north to Valencia Street, and finally Valencia Street all the way to Union Station. Thus all Flagler's hotels were encircled by modern pavement. A writer observed that Flagler's properties appeared as an "oasis of asphalt in the center of town." At this point Flagler's venture in asphalt paving concluded.[18]

In the meantime the city government of St. Augustine undertook its own street paving program that was almost as revolutionary as Flagler's. The perpetually cash-strapped city government decided to use less expensive wooden blocks as its pavement of choice. A contractor set up a mill on the west side of the San Sebastian, where cypress logs were cut into segments about four inches thick and then forced through a trimming mold to reduce them to a uniform circumference. The streets to be paved would be leveled and covered with a layer of

Several of St. Augustine's streets, including Cathedral Place, were paved with cypress blocks as a way of saving money. From the collection of the St. Augustine Historical Society Research Library.

wooden boards to form a base upon which the circular cypress blocks would be placed. The last step in the process would be to spread white sand over the blocks to filter into the spaces between them. A writer for the *New York Herald* pronounced, "The effect is as if you walked on sawed-off tops of a crowded pine forest."[19]

Paving of St. George Street from the Plaza to the City Gates began in January 1888 and was nearing completion in April when Dr. Anderson, Dr. Smith, and Dr. Webb petitioned the city council to refrain from paving any additional streets with wood until a committee could investigate the sanitary aspect of wooden streets. They feared that moisture could saturate the wood and that filth might penetrate and become lodged in the porous surface. Some of their fears proved to apply: sweeping the streets clean turned out to be impossible, and when it rained the wood swelled and sometimes popped out of place. Horses hooves and cart wheels cut into the surface. Despite the physicians' misgivings and the drawbacks of wood as a road surface, the city paved the streets surrounding the Plaza in the winter of 1889.[20]

The Shell Road running north from the City Gates also received wooden pavement, at least for some distance, perhaps just as far as the northern edge of the Hotel San Marco's grounds. With the shell removed, some people wanted a new name for the street, and Dr. Reuben Garnett, whose orange grove standing along the road attracted visitors out for drives, suggested "San Marco Avenue" after the hotel. The city council agreed.[21]

By 1892 all the streets around Union Station, plus some other important streets—Orange, Bridge, St. Francis, and the northern end of Cordova—had been paved with wooden blocks. Most of the streets in town remained unpaved, and the wooden blocks amounted to little more than a temporary makeshift solution, but the transformation of St. Augustine into a modern city took a great step forward with these changes.[22]

The town's horses had to get used to the hard, slick new asphalt, which sometimes caused them to skid, but people on roller skates and bicycles, with their smooth-riding pneumatic tires, reveled in the new surface. In fact, in St. Augustine, as in other American cities, the advent of paved streets brought on the bicycle revolution—the precursor of the automobile revolution of a decade later. As the *Times-Union* reported: "Before Mr. Henry M. Flagler began to pave streets, there was not a bicycle in this city, and today not less than fifty bicycles are in use." The town council found it necessary to pass ordinances to control bicycle traffic, including a law to protect pedestrians by prohibiting enthusiasts from riding on the sidewalks. By contrast it would not be until the fall of 1892 that the town council prohibited cows from wandering loose on the streets.[23]

When women took up cycling, protests arose over the "impropriety" of women riding the contraptions. The *Times-Union* disagreed, saying, "A pretty sight is a squad of ladies daily availing themselves of the smooth asphalt and wooden pavements of this city by exercising on their 'safeties.'" In February 1892 women's health reformer Alice J. White made a presentation in the Alcazar complex before a crowd of women in which she "modestly illustrated her theory of dress reform" by changing into six different costumes, none of which required "artificial means" to fit her form. In her diatribe against the corset, Mrs. White asked the women to raise their hands if they felt comfortable in their present apparel. None raised a hand.[24]

Flagler also changed the face of St. Augustine by opening new streets that had never existed before. He favored opening Cathedral Place from St. George Street through to Cordova Street on the north side of the post office so that traffic around the Ponce de Leon would have another avenue of movement. More important, he wanted to make King Street from the railroad depot to the Plaza a broad, impressive thoroughfare that would make an impact on visitors coming into town. When he filled Maria Sanchez Creek, he had widened the narrow causeway across which King Street traversed the marsh, and now Flagler persuaded Dr. Anderson to give up a strip of land in front of the Markland house and grove so that King Street could be widened west of his hotels. After the enlargement of the street, the large live oak trees that Anderson's mother had planted years earlier stood in the center of the avenue.[25]

Flagler's widening of King Street brought forth no opposition since only he and Anderson sacrificed anything, but Flagler's next proposal elicited an outburst of passion that dramatically exposed the tensions between the rich northern newcomer and the old inhabitants of the town. North of King Street, Flagler had cut new streets through the old Anderson, Ball, and Powder House tracts and his more northerly properties extending up to those lots bordering Orange Street. (Later this whole area would be called the Model Land Company Tract.) The streets in question were Valencia, Carrera, Saragosa, Sevilla, Ribera, and Malaga—and also Loreda Street south of King Street. Flagler had already put in or planned to add gas lines, water lines, sewer pipes, fire hydrants, curbing, and pavements. He proposed to give these streets to the City of St. Augustine free of charge, with the following stipulations: he could repair the streets and utilities himself at his own expense, no trolley line could be placed on these streets without his permission, and no utility poles could be erected without his permission. Flagler hoped that wealthy northerners would choose to build fine houses in this area of town, and he wanted to keep out unsightly and annoying intrusions.[26]

The town council referred the proposition to its Streets and Lanes Committee. Citizens packed the next regular council meeting to see what would happen. Everyone expected fireworks. The Streets and Lanes Committee's two present members, R. L. Irwin and B. A. Masters, delivered a report recommending rejection of the offer. Hot debate ensued. Flagler's attorney W. W. Dewhurst rose to present a slightly revised version of Flagler's offer designed to soften opposition. James McDonald, the more politically adept of the McGuire and McDonald team, spoke with passion about the proposal: "Will this council refuse to accept a gift of $85,000, or will you offer insult to the generous donor? In refusing the use of the streets referred to for railroad or telegraph poles, Mr. Flagler is promoting the great and only object which he has in view, namely, to make the city of St. Augustine the grandest city of its size in the country."[27]

McDonald's speech carried the day; the council voted 4–3 to accept Flagler's offer. Councilman Irwin stormed out, asserting that he would never again return to the council. The *St. Augustine Evening News* editorialized: "THE WRANGLE in Council last evening over the proposition of Mr. Flagler to deed to the city $85,000 worth of property in improved streets, under certain conditions, was as uncalled for as it was discourteous. . . . Could the City Council afford after all Mr. Flagler had done for St. Augustine to insult him by refusing his magnificent offer?"[28]

The proposal to accept the streets became law upon its third reading on August 8, with Councilman Irwin not in attendance. This meant that in one section of town the City of St. Augustine could exercise governance over certain aspects of its own streets only with the sufferance of one private citizen. On the other hand, Henry Flagler had gained control over an important element of the environs of his properties—but at the price of growing sentiment that the people of St. Augustine were losing control of their own town.[29]

As the plague summer of 1888 advanced, the Casino section of the Alcazar complex began to take shape. In some ways this structure represented the greatest challenge for the builders because Carrère and Hastings had designed the Casino on the monumental scale of ancient Roman baths. Surrounding the large central swimming pool stood eight huge arches rising more than two stories tall and spanning twenty-two-foot-wide openings. These structural elements were built with a robust mixture of concrete that used only two barrels of coquina and one barrel of sand with each barrel of Portland cement. McGuire and McDonald buried iron reinforcement in these arches more generously than in any other parts of the hotels. At the base of the pool's corners they overlapped right-angle stacks of railroad track iron and then poured liquid cement over them to fashion a solid base. The tops of the arches contained both square and round iron rebar. Of course, once completed, all this iron encased in concrete became invisible, and the arches rose as wonders of grace and simplicity.[30]

The two floor levels surrounding the pool also employed a lot of structural iron. The flooring rested upon six-by-ten-inch iron I-beams twenty-four feet long.[31]

The upper level, or mezzanine, received a polished oak floor so that it could be used as a ballroom. The lower level was surfaced with a very solid, almost rubberlike, layer of waterproof asphaltum. On the south side of this level McGuire and McDonald built dressing rooms where patrons of the swimming pool could change clothes. The Ponce de Leon also employed asphaltum decking in several other areas where water resistant and durable flooring was required: the kitchen floors, the loggias surrounding the courtyard, the "400 Rotunda" solarium room under the dome (see chapter 17), and the roof area outside the solarium below the towers. The asphaltum floor of the Casino remains intact today.

Henry Flagler had managed to return to St. Augustine on a specially run train during the night of December 5, 1888, almost two weeks before the quarantine ended. After inspecting progress on his projects in town, he went off exploring with the president of the Jacksonville, Tampa and Key West Railway. If the newspaper account is to be believed, Flagler went as far south as Punta Gorda—well into Henry Plant's territory on the west side of the peninsula. Having satisfied his curiosity, Flagler returned to New York for the holiday season.[32]

Locals interpreted Flagler's arrival as a hopeful sign of a return to normalcy with the coming of a new year. One wrote: "The first strains of the Ponce de Leon Band will marshal in the season and leave behind all the year's worry, care, and grief." The correspondent of the *Times-Union* called on O. D. Seavey to receive reassurance that everything would come around right, and he was not disappointed. Seavey declared that none of the guest reservations made at the end of the previous season had been canceled, and more rooms had been reserved in recent weeks. He expressed his opinion that everyone understood the first frost to banish the threat of yellow fever. "The whole thing will have been forgotten in a short time, and the Florida tourists will come in unprecedentedly large numbers." He added that the Ponce de Leon had more reservations at the time than at the same time the year before. Of course, as manager of the hotel, Seavey could be expected to put an optimistic spin on his prognostications.[33]

Four days before Christmas an unusually long train of twelve coaches arrived in St. Augustine, packed with workers for the three Flagler hotels. The rest of the staff would follow this advance party in the first week of January. The quarantine had been lifted just in time. With preparations now progressing according to schedule, Seavey took time off to go quail shooting in the interior with Dr. Anderson and a couple of local men.[34]

After the trauma of the summer and fall, the Alcazar opened with a modest dinner for a few invited guests in the hotel's "swell café" on Christmas Day, 1888. Japanese lanterns and tiny electric lights amid the shrubbery illuminated the courtyard. Following dinner O. D. Seavey led an excursion around the still incomplete sections of the Alcazar complex. In the area of the Baths some of the marble paneling had not yet been put in place, and in the cavernous Casino, with its huge swimming pool, construction equipment littered the floors. Next door to the café two glass-roofed dining room additions were almost ready for use— testimony to the necessity of offering patrons all the amenities of a regular hotel.

Without the decorative portico Hastings had proposed, the Hotel Alcazar's front entrance stands bare and fortress-like. By permission of Library of Congress.

However, the Alcazar operated on the European plan that allowed guests to pay only for their rooms, purchasing dinners separately as they pleased. Thus those who wished to economize could purchase a meal for as little as twenty-five cents at the café or eat at any inexpensive restaurant in town, while those with thicker wallets and more refined tastes could walk across the Alameda to dine in luxury at the Hotel Ponce de Leon.[35]

The Cordova opened on January 8, with a front-page advertisement in the *Times-Union* proclaiming to the public: "The Cordova has recently been renovated and refurbished, and is complete in all departments." Flagler also published a little promotional pamphlet stating that since purchasing the hotel from Smith he had spent $60,000 on new furniture, a new dining room, and various other improvements. "Every room contains ample clothes closets, is handsomely furnished, has gas, steam heat and electric bells; elevator; baths on every floor—every modern convenience known to hotel art." Except for electric lights.[36] The Cordova entered this season better prepared to entertain guests, but Flagler's long-term alterations to the building had just begun.

The Ponce de Leon opened on January 10, 1889, with the same fanfare as in the inaugural opening. Joyce's band played, the portcullis rose, the bellmen stood in line at attention, and thousands of people streamed in to make the hotel's interiors their own for a few hours. The magnificence of the hotel had actually improved with a year's aging. One observer wrote: "The appearance of the hotel is greatly softened and improved. It has lost that look of newness which characterized the hotel last year. The effects of the weather have given a subdued tint to the massive walls and clinging vines have begun their journey up its sides."[37]

Flagler's other prime investment, the Jacksonville, St. Augustine, and Halifax River Railway, had also improved with the passage of another year. The light-weight narrow gauge rails had been replaced by heavier steel rails, and the width of the road was widened to standard gauge so that someday the locomotives and cars from northern railroads could continue over Flagler's road. However, Flagler maintained the common practice of laying directly on the sand the wooden crossties to which the rails were spiked without building up a gravel roadbed to hold the ties. Thus his railroad would be subject to washouts during heavy rains or rising water. Nevertheless, the road had been transformed from a rudimentary short-line railway into the initial segment of what would become a modern railroad destined eventually to reach Key West. The old engines and rolling stock were sold to the Florida Southern Railroad downstate. In their place came five huge McQueen locomotives built in Schenectady that could speed a mile a minute, four elegant parlor cars, seven passenger cars, and three cars for baggage. There were also two "combination cars," said to be "equally luxurious," that were reserved for cigar smokers and colored passengers. All these had been built by the Jackson and Sharp Company of Wilmington, Delaware, the country's largest manufacturer of rolling stock.

The interiors of the cars were finished in mahogany, with seats upholstered in blue or "old gold" velvet. At the ends of the cars were lounges that could be converted into beds for invalids. Each car had a toilet and a separate washroom for removing the dust of travel. The porter maintained his own cubicle as his headquarters. The furnace for heating was located in a separate compartment to limit the danger of fire, and a glass-front cabinet held an ax, saw, and sledge-hammer in case of an accident. Altogether it represented the epitome of travel comfort.[38]

However, the truly elite traveler went in a private car, which was both a contrivance of practical value and a prestigious ornament in that era of conspicuous consumption. Private cars ranged in style from veritable rolling palaces to plain

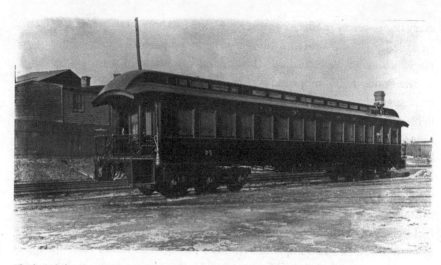

Flagler's first private rail car originally carried the number 25 and lettering of the Jacksonville, Tampa, and Key West Railway. It was called *Alicia* or *Alice* and would later be renumbered 90 and then 91. Today the car is preserved at the Henry Morrison Flagler Museum in Palm Beach. By permission of Delaware Public Archives.

utilitarian mobile residences. Some were painted in bright colors to make them distinctive, but Flagler's private car looked as ordinary as the plain envelopes in which he mailed his correspondence. Jackson and Sharp had delivered it in 1886, and Flagler christened it *Alicia*. The car afforded Flagler privacy and convenience as he traveled up and down his ever-lengthening rail line. It also proved useful in transporting distinguished guests, such as President Cleveland.

The interior of *Alicia,* with its elegant oak paneling and plush furnishings, was "suggestive of the quiet tastes of its owner." The rear compartment of the car served as an observation room, with comfortable chairs for eight people to sit and watch the countryside roll away behind them. There were two seven-by-nine-foot sleeping rooms, each with a double bed, closet, and toilet. In the floor of the hallway was a hatch that opened to an ice chest and storage pantry for the kitchen. A chef presided over the well-appointed kitchen, where first-class meals could be prepared and served in the dining room. J. W. Bunch, a black man, served as steward and had overall responsibility for the upkeep of the car.[39]

Regular service on Flagler's improved road began on February 4, and on February 24 Henry and Alice Flagler rode a special train over the line from South Jacksonville to St. Augustine in just forty-six minutes, a record time that must have pleased the yachtsman.[40] The Flaglers arrived a month later than the year before, just in time for part of the opening week of the Alcazar Casino.

Dramatic evidence of the impending opening of the Alcazar Casino came in the form of huge bonfires of construction debris burning in the streets around the structure's lofty concrete walls. Unfortunately a northeaster slammed into St. Augustine on February 21, during the night before the opening, bringing wind, rain, and chill-to-the-bone damp cold from the Atlantic. The newspaper declared it "one of the most uncomfortable days ever recorded in the annals of the Ancient City." Yet a surprisingly large crowd of people turned out to enjoy the music and dancing in the brightly lighted Alcazar café, while the Chinese lanterns outside in the courtyard whipped in the wind. The "hop" had been advertised as not requiring "full dress," and this may have led to the larger than expected turnout. Nobody wanted to get their best attire drenched on the way to the party.[41]

The following evening, visitors walking to the Alcazar were greeted by a huge multicolored electric sign reading "Alcazar" mounted between the hotel's two front towers. Electric lines strung from unsightly utility poles across the Alameda carried power from the Ponce de Leon's generators to the Alcazar. Inside the courtyard a band played as guests progressed around the loggias and back through the colonnades to the Casino in the rear. Inside the two levels of the Casino, surrounding the center pool, chairs lined the railings so that spectators could watch swimmers and listen to the Ponce de Leon band stationed on one side of the pool and the Cordova mandolin orchestra playing from the other. The colored electric lights reflecting off the water and shimmering on the Casino's pure white walls, the music, the action, and the thronging crowd produced just the pleasing exotic effect that Thomas Hastings had hoped for.[42]

Guests entering the Ponce de Leon's Dining Room in the new season encountered a distinguished-looking, portly young black gentleman, Franklin P. Thompson, standing in the doorway at the headwaiter's station. Many of the guests would have recognized him as the former headwaiter at the Hotel San Marco, and some would perhaps also have identified him as organizer of the black baseball team. After the first year's disappointing experience with white waiters, Flagler had decided to make the switch, and once again he turned to O. D. Seavey to solve the problem. Since Thompson had previously served as headwaiter for Seavey at the Magnolia Springs Hotel and then at the San Marco, his arrival at the Ponce de Leon amounted to more of a return to normal than an innovation.

Thompson was a remarkable man. Born in Charleston, Virginia, in 1855, he grew up in Carlisle, Pennsylvania, where his parents moved during his childhood. At the age of sixteen he began a nomadic career as a resort hotel waiter that carried him to summer resorts in places such as Narragansett Bay, the Catskill Mountains, and Long Island and to winter hotels including the Carlton in Jacksonville and Captain Vaill's St. Augustine Hotel. Somewhere along the way Thompson linked up with Seavey, and 1883 found him with Seavey at the Magnolia Springs Hotel.[43] In addition to serving with him in Florida, Thompson also spent many summer seasons during his long career with Seavey at the Fort

William Henry Hotel on Lake George in New York and at the Hotel Champlain on Lake Champlain. In 1901 Thompson would be managing the Champlain's baseball team, made up primarily of black college students working on their summer vacations.[44]

A flattering description of Thompson published in 1904 says this of him: "He is gifted with the essential qualifications of his calling, viz.: the faculty to grasp quickly the peculiarities of the patrons of his hotel and to dispose of difficult questions in a way to satisfy even the most exacting. Though not demonstrative, he is, naturally, a man of strong individuality, and is looked upon by his brethren in the calling as the 'Dean of the Commanders of the Dining Room.'"[45]

Many of the waiters in Thompson's crew moved with him from hotel to hotel with the change of seasons. One of his waiters, Charles E. Lee, wrote that he "is a gentleman of much experience and is liked and respected by all who serve under him, or who come in contact with him in any way. All the waiters who travel with him aim to please him, as we all realize what his friendship is to us. He has done much good for our race and is still helping, as much as possible, to place young men in such positions that they may in the future do what they can for those who will follow in later years. Those who attend schools and colleges are given work in the summer, so that when fall comes, they may be able to pursue whatever course or profession that they may have taken up."[46]

The waiters of the Hotel Ponce de Leon pose on the front steps. Frank P. Thompson is in the middle of the front row (ninth from right). From the collection of the St. Augustine Historical Society Research Library.

During his time in St. Augustine, Thompson filled a leadership role in the community of black hotel employees. In February 1889 Thompson helped organize a money-raising concert held in Genovar's Opera House on St. George Street to sustain a fund for the benefit of the nine hundred black hotel workers employed in town. He also arranged for a preacher to deliver a sermon in the Opera House to solicit contributions for the black Methodist and Baptist churches in St. Augustine. In addition, he led a singing school at St. Mary's Baptist Church. In 1891 Thompson headed a committee that held a ball to raise money for the colored ward at Alicia Hospital. White patrons attended the ball to enjoy an opening concert and some stayed longer to watch the black couples dance during the remainder of the program.[47]

Some of Thompson's activities had a sharp edge. He was described as a "race pride man" who labored for self-help among black people and at the same time favored black organization to combat racial discrimination. In 1883 Thompson wrote a letter to militant black activist T. Thomas Fortune's New York Globe saying, "Just as long as The Globe continues to crusade against race injustice, and points our citizens to the higher, grander and nobler beacon lights in the areas of education and civilization—'til you tire of this warfare—count me one of your staunch supporters."[48]

In St. Augustine Thompson addressed a meeting of black hotel workers and called for the formation of an organization to be called "The Progressive Association of the United States," which would present a series of addresses to both black workers and townspeople "upon our progress during the past twenty-five years." (This organization seems to have come to nothing.) On another occasion he spoke in the Ponce de Leon Dining Room on "the unpardonable sin of race prejudice in the South."[49] He was acutely aware of the trend toward segregation and political disenfranchisement of black Americans being vigorously pursued at the time, and he took a leadership role in attempts to organize for racial solidarity and self-improvement. "Mr. Thompson is a careful observer of current events," wrote a biographer, "and is particularly interested in everything that concerns his race. He is an optimist on what the future has in store for his race, and is always ready to help with his time and purse and enterprise undertaken for its benefit."[50]

However, for all his activism, guests entering the Dining Room of the Hotel Ponce de Leon encountered Thompson only as the polite, affable professional man that he certainly was. He possessed the valuable ability to recall the names of all the regular guests of the hotel so that he could greet each one personally. His hat-check assistant, who placed hats on the shelves lining the Dining Room foyer, enjoyed the even more remarkable gift of being able to remember "the head for every hat left in his care."[51]

As headwaiter Thompson occupied one of the elite positions available to a black man in America. Published accounts of dining at the Ponce de Leon are almost universally very high in the praise heaped on the atmosphere, the food, and the help. The Frenchman Paul Blouet considered the black waiters superior to "arrogant" white waiters. "You are served with intelligence and politeness," he wrote. "Those good negroes have such cheerful, open faces! They seem so glad to be alive, and they look so good natured, that it does one good to see them. When they look at one another, they laugh. When they look at you, they laugh."[52]

Newcomers to the Dining Room sometimes thought they were doing the waiters a favor by ordering all the courses of their meal at one time. This resulted in some of their dishes cooling off by the time that the whole dinner had been assembled back in the kitchen. Experienced diners soon learned the routine and requested one course at a time.[53]

Across King Street in the Hotel Cordova, headwaiter C. C. Randolph ran the dining room with military precision. The bullet-headed Randolph cropped his hair and mustache very closely and dressed impeccably. He also uniformed his waiters in formal suits with broad black silk sashes around their waists—and black crepe-soled shoes. Randolph's roots were in Virginia, but he had moved to New York City as a young man to enjoy the "purer atmosphere" of the North. In 1889 he brought down a crew of about fifty waiters to open the Cordova for its first season under Flagler's ownership. Randolph took pride in negotiating a contract that required the hotel company to pay for the waiters' travel expenses down, start their salaries the day they left from New York, and furnish room and board while they were employed at the Cordova. The workers were, however, required to buy their own uniforms, which Randolph supplied at cost.[54]

One day a newspaperman dropped by the Cordova between meals and found Randolph in the dining room drilling his men in their duties to ensure that they were polished in their movements and service at the tables. Randolph gave directions to his crew by way of a system of hand and finger signals he had developed so that it was not necessary to utter any verbal commands. This attention to discipline impressed Morris Phillips, author of *Practical Hints for Tourists*. "Perfect quiet reigns in the dining room," he wrote. "The waiters are governed, well governed, by a head waiter whose head is level. . . . The men, when serving dinner, wear dress coats, black trousers and white cravats. Instead of a loose waistcoat they wear a broad sash around the waist, and instead of noisy boots they wear shoes having cloth uppers and rubber soles—black tennis shoes. Not a word is heard from the servants, except in polite response to an order, and they glide about like dark angels."[55]

All hotel workers depended upon tips to supplement their salaries. One travel guide writer suggested that five dollars would be an appropriate weekly tip to the headwaiter and two or three dollars for your table waiter. He added that it would

Union Station served as the entry portal for travelers coming to St. Augustine. From this station the tracks ran north to Jacksonville and southwest to Palatka. From the collection of the St. Augustine Historical Society Research Library.

be handy to keep a pocket or purse full of silver coins to tip the bellman who brought a bucket of ice, the doorman who handled your parcels as you departed or arrived from a carriage ride, the chambermaid who fetched a box of face powder, the courtyard attendant who placed your lawn chair, and for any of the host of attentive servants who made life comfortable in a resort hotel.[56]

Monday, March 11, marked another milestone in Flagler's development of St. Augustine when the first passenger train rolled into the new Union Station on the bank of the San Sebastian River. Joyce's fifty-piece military band stirred the air with lively music, and fireworks exploded and colorful balloons lifted into the sky. A huge crowd of townspeople and northern strangers turned out to witness the event. Henry Plant and his wife were on hand to demonstrate their approval of Flagler's latest achievement.[57]

The new depot had been designed by Carrère and Hastings, although the plain wooden two-story structure made no pretense to anything other than functionality. The railroad offices occupied the second floor, while the waiting room, baggage room, and ticket office took up most of the ground floor. A broad veranda surrounded the building to shelter waiting travelers from the weather. A neat oval park with a spraying fountain ornamented the station grounds. Today a fire station near the site reproduces the profile of the station building; most of Railroad Park still remains, surrounded by its concrete wall. A row of horse-drawn carriages lined the covered platform, their drivers raising the familiar clamor to attract customers to their conveyances. When these coaches set off into town, the people of St. Augustine were treated to a novel sound—the clop-clopping of horses' hooves on pavement. Flagler had opened Valencia Street through the Ball grove and paved it with asphalt to serve as the primary road to Union Station.[58] King Street remained unpaved and unsightly.

The opening of Union Station came with a huge splash of publicity, but stealthily, without attracting public notice, Flagler had been moving to expand his railroad holdings. In the fall of 1888 he purchased two railroads from William Astor: the old road from Tocoi to St. Augustine and the newly built road from St. Augustine to Palatka that had begun operations in 1886. Flagler paid Astor $255,000 for these properties.[59] The Tocoi road was virtually worthless, having been rendered superfluous by the opening of the direct rail connection with Jacksonville, although Flagler continued to haul some lumber on the Tocoi line until he abandoned it in the late 1890s.

Purchase of the railroad to Palatka signaled a much more significant development in Flagler's Florida ventures. First, it carried his interests another twenty-five miles south and west down the peninsula, but more important, it linked him to the St. Johns and Halifax Railroad that headed southeast from Palatka to Daytona, another fifty-two miles away in largely undeveloped territory. The Daytona road had been constructed by Utley J. White, one of the true pioneers of the region. White's primary interest had been harvesting and hauling pine lumber, but Flagler saw the railroad as a pathway down the peninsula. Flagler paid White $272,300 for his line. He then converted his Astor and White railroad acquisitions to standard gauge, and on April 3, 1889, the first train pulled into the station at Daytona. However, the two halves of Flagler's railroad system lacked, for the moment, a bridge connection across the San Sebastian in St. Augustine.[60]

All this evidence of progress could not hide one glaring shortcoming: the throng of visitors on hand to enjoy the improvements had declined noticeably from the year before. The local correspondent of the *Florida Times-Union* attempted to put a hopeful face on things by admitting that the year had started slowly but that by mid-February the season had come on full blast, with "all gayety and happiness in St. Augustine." A writer for the *New York Tribune* could afford to be more blunt: "St. Augustine lies lovely and serene under the bluest summer skies. That it is extremely dull, no one attempts any longer to deny. The same story is heard from all the winter resorts—nothing going on, nothing doing, nothing done."[61]

The yellow fever epidemic of the previous summer was, of course, primarily to blame for the failure of northern visitors to show up in Florida, and moderate temperatures up North fed fears that perhaps the weather in the South had not turned cold enough to destroy the lingering risk of fever. With a mild winter in the North, there was also less push motivating people to repair southward. Another factor also came into play. In 1889 Easter came three weeks later on the calendar than in the year before. This meant that Lent also arrived three weeks later, and normally the beginning of Lent marked the end of the social season in northern cities. As one New York writer explained: "That is why so many people leave town when Lent begins. The Lenten exodus is fixed by custom, but many people rush away to escape the drab conventional days of Lenten observance. If one is in town it is customary to drop all gayeties, but if one is at some fashionable winter resort in the South, it is just as customary and conventional to enter into all sorts of social jollities."[62]

The height of social festivities for St. Augustine came in mid-March with yacht races on the bay, the Tropical Tennis Tournament, a carnival in the new Casino, and a formal ball in the Ponce de Leon. All this centered on commencing an effort to provide the city with a new, modern hospital.

The origins of the hospital dated back to the winter of 1887 when Henry Flagler began talking with the St. Johns County Medical Society about giving his support to an improved hospital for the city. That summer the St. Augustine Hospital Association was formed, with Alice Flagler named as the patroness of a movement to establish a hospital. Dr. Anderson assumed the presidency and leadership of the organization.[63]

The following year plans matured. In the midst of the celebrations surrounding the opening of the Hotel Ponce de Leon, Alice spoke with the officers of the hospital association and said she would donate land and an endowment fund for the new hospital. The hospital would become her principal charitable activity in the community. In May, after the Flaglers had departed for the North, a group of ladies convened in the Rotunda of the Ponce de Leon to charter the St. Augustine Hospital Association. Alice was named president, with Elizabeth Heade, wife of the artist, as vice-president. O. D. Seavey's wife Caroline and other female notables from the community agreed to serve on the executive committee.[64]

In 1889 the ladies outdid themselves planning and executing the Hospital Fair held in the Casino in mid-March. Described as "the swell event of the season," the fair epitomized the typical charity bazaar of the late Victorian era. The Casino ballroom on the upper level surrounding the pool was turned into a warren of little booths decorated with plants, flowers, and Japanese lanterns.

Patrons who paid a five-dollar donation at the door could pick an orange off a tree to discover a prize hidden inside the hollow orb, visit a Gypsy camp to have their fortunes told, purchase bric-a-brac or flowers, take tea in a Japanese tea house where a charming Japanese girl flirted with all the men, visit a Spanish mission to purchase lace, buy a raffle ticket for a chance to win paintings donated by the Ponce de Leon artists, sample coffee, cakes, and ice cream, or patronize any one of a number of other booths. One table sold embroidered fancy aprons made by the women of the hospital association. Guests could buy votes for their favorite businessman or professional (Dr. Anderson won "favorite physician"). Caroline Seavey had spent her summer up North soliciting donated items for the fair, and Alice Flagler had also prevailed on friends to contribute items to the fair. Her husband donated a piano to be purchased on shares and given to a worthy local cause.[65]

Joyce's band supplied background music, while a mandolin band played from an authentic Venetian gondola floating in the pool, and Antonio Jovine, the ensemble's featured tenor, sang popular songs. On the third night of the fair, rain forced the managers to shut off all the electric lights outdoors in the gardens for fear of shocks. Yet thousands had turned out, and the estimate of proceeds and donations exceeded $6,000. Afterward the true identity of the flirtatious Japanese girl was revealed, to everyone's surprise and delight, as the diminutive "General" George Flynn of the Ponce de Leon newsstand.[66]

A high-toned charity ball on behalf of Alicia Hospital, held in the Dining Room of the Ponce de Leon, offered an alternative entertainment to the Casino fair. Flagler made a rare appearance at this formal occasion, while Alice attracted attention in a gown of "lavender-watered silk, lace bodice, magnificent necklace of pearls, ostrich trimmings, and diamonds." A thousand people either danced or watched the dancers before settling down to a midnight supper.[67]

During the week of the 1889 Tropical Tennis Tournament visitors to the Ponce de Leon could inspect the massive sterling silver City Gates trophy on display in the Rotunda. The year's matches would be contested on the four new asphalt courts just completed behind the Alcazar Casino. Since Florida's common rough-textured St. Augustine grass did not suit tennis play, the courts had been made from the asphalt that Flagler was depositing so liberally both inside his hotels and on the streets around them. The asphalt proved to have the advantage that when rain showers dampened the courts, they quickly dried so that play could resume. Spectators watched from the bunting-draped railing of the Casino's broad entrance balcony, where Joyce's band was positioned to provide musical accompaniment to the festivities. Other spectators seated in lawn chairs lined the boundaries of the courts.

Intermittent showers dampened the flannel outfits and caps of the players. Then the skies opened up to drown out one day's play. But the tournament finished on an upbeat note. Oliver S. Campbell, an eighteen-year-old student at Columbia College, who played in a jaunty straw hat with a red band, received a small silver cup as his reward and had his name added to the base of the City Gates trophy. The *Times-Union* observed, prophetically: "It is predicted by them who marked the brilliant playing of Campbell that he is the coming champion of America."[68]

Baseball, a perennially popular sport, attracted attention during the 1889

Water for the Casino pool flowed from a deep artesian well. Sometimes daredevil divers would plunge into the water from the upper balcony. This upper mezzanine featured a polished wood floor for dancing and a stage for a variety of performances. By permission of Library of Congress.

season. All the games continued to be played on the fort grounds. In January the black employees of the Alcazar squared off against those of the Ponce de Leon. The *St. Augustine Weekly News* promoted interest by announcing, "As both teams possess some of the best colored baseball talent in the United States, being largely composed of the famous Cuban Giants, the game is likely to be an interesting one."[69]

Another contest a few days later between a black team from St. Augustine and one from Jacksonville resulted in a free-for-all fistfight and the arrest of several player-combatants. A month later the Standards from Jacksonville defeated the Cuban Giants 20–3, but the St. Augustine newspaper offered the excuse that several of the Giants were absent from the lineup due to illness.[70]

On the morning of March 4 President Grover Cleveland stood on the east steps of the Capitol building in Washington holding an umbrella over the head of his successor Benjamin Harrison as Harrison took the oath of office in a steady rain. Two weeks later, freed from an office that he regarded as a burden and a duty, Cleveland set off for a vacation in Florida and Cuba. Leaving Mrs. Cleveland behind, he expected to do some fishing and hunting on this, the second of what would be many future expeditions to Florida. As he had the year before,

Spectators could watch the Tropical Tennis Tournament from courtside or from the rear balcony of the Alcazar Casino. The Olivet Methodist Church building on the left had been moved to this site, where it was used as a workshop. "St. Augustine Lawn Tennis Tournament," *Outing Magazine*, June 1890, 181.

Flagler invited Cleveland to be his guest at the Hotel Ponce de Leon. (Flagler had sent a note of congratulations to Harrison upon his election but evidently bore no ill will toward Cleveland. He seems to have been willing to overlook Cleveland's Democratic affiliation since Cleveland's conservative personal political philosophy was virtually indistinguishable from that of the Republicans.)[71]

Cleveland arrived at Union Station on March 20 to be welcomed by the Hotel Ponce de Leon band and a crowd of about four hundred people—but, not surprisingly, no prominent city officials. Flagler and Alice waited unobtrusively in a carriage. With a tip of the hat from the ex-president, the party's coaches set off down Valencia Street and entered the hotel through the rear carriage entrance to avoid the crowd gathered in front of the hotel. Manager Seavey welcomed Cleveland and his party at the back doorway and led him to the guest register, where the first line had been left open for his signature. After exchanging pleasantries with some invited guests gathered in the Rotunda, Cleveland was escorted to the pink bridal suite in the west wing where he and his wife had been quartered the previous year. The whole ground floor wing had been shut off so that he could enjoy private use of the Grand Parlor, and hotel detectives patrolled the grounds outside to keep the curious away.

Former secretary of state Thomas Bayard, whose first wife had died two years earlier, accompanied the president on this stag outing. Flagler walked his guests over to the Alcazar to show off the new Casino, where Bayard donned a rented bathing suit and dived in for an enthusiastic swim. A carriage ride to see the sights around town followed; then a private reception and dinner at the Ponce came in the evening, and after that a return visit to the Casino pool to watch local daredevil Frank Greatorex perform high dives from the upper balcony. Afterward Cleveland's party returned to the Ponce de Leon for an electric light and pyrotechnic display. They witnessed it from a third floor balcony while an estimated crowd of two thousand stood in King Street below.[72]

The next morning Cleveland and Bayard boarded the train for Winter Park and Tampa. The Flaglers had intended to accompany them as far as Tampa, but an urgent message arrived that abruptly changed the Flaglers' plans: their daughter Jennie Louise was gravely ill. That evening, at ten o'clock in the dark of night, Flagler and Alice boarded a special train to carry them to Charleston, South Carolina.

At the age of thirty-three, Jennie Louise had given birth to a baby girl in her home at 8 East 54th Street, just two blocks from the Flagler residence. Born on February 9, the baby was given the name Margery and died at birth or soon thereafter. Jennie Louise's condition soon became perilous, and it was decided that a sea voyage to Florida might brace her constitution. She set off from New York on her father-in-law E. C. Benedict's ocean-going steam yacht *Oneida*, accompanied by the elder Benedict, her husband Fred Benedict, her brother Harry, three nurses, and Dr. George G. Shelton, a homeopathic physician. When her condition worsened, the yacht hove to at Norfolk, Virginia, just long enough to telegraph the Flaglers in St. Augustine to meet them in Charleston. The *Oneida* steamed south at top speed on what became a race to give Jennie Louise's father a chance to see her alive. Rather than wait helplessly on shore, Flagler engaged a motor launch and raced to meet the *Oneida* as she entered the harbor, but when he saw the flags flying at half-mast on the steamer he realized that his effort had been futile. His daughter had passed away just as the Charleston lighthouse came into sight on March 25.

The Flaglers accompanied Jennie Louise's body back to New York, where a funeral service was held in the Flagler home. Her body was interred in the Flagler family memorial at Woodlawn with her mother. In mute testimony to the delicate conventions of the day, none of the newspaper stories relating the circumstances of her death mentioned that her death had been precipitated by the birth of a child.[73]

In St. Augustine the disappointing winter season concluded with an upsurge of visitors at the end of March and in April; Lent had begun on March 12. One enterprising reporter, counting the signatures on the pages of the Ponce de Leon's house register, found that from January through the first three weeks of March an average of sixty-five people had arrived each day, and thereafter the signature count went up to one hundred per day. This filled the Ponce de Leon to capacity and required some guests to find rooms in the Cordova or Alcazar until space opened up in the Ponce de Leon. Yet the Ponce's guests-per-night total for the entire season was just 16,067, compared to 33,303 for the inaugural season, a decline of more than half. The loss might not have been as great as the count from

Jennie Louise Flagler Benedict died at sea on her father-in-law's yacht while on her way to St. Augustine. © Flagler Museum Archives.

the Ponce de Leon register seems to indicate, since in 1889 Flagler's guests could choose to stay at the Alcazar or Cordova if they pleased. The Cordova closed on April 8, and the Hotel Ponce de Leon lowered its gate on April 16, two weeks earlier than the year before. There could be no denying that it had been an "off year."[74]

A few days after the closing of the Ponce de Leon, the Flagler family returned to St. Augustine to participate in a ceremony made poignant by Jennie Louise's recent death. After years of planning and delays, work on the Presbyterian church would finally begin. At the site on Valencia Street behind the Ponce de Leon, Flagler threw the first shovel of concrete into the footing trench for the building's foundation. Alice and Harry followed, along with Jennie Louise's sister-in-law Helen Benedict, and then pastor Edwin Knox Mitchell and other officers of the Presbyterian Church added additional ceremonial shovelfuls. The following evening the Flaglers departed by train for New York. The gardeners had filled their parlor car with huge bouquets of the roses that now grew in profusion on the grounds of the Hotel Ponce de Leon.[75]

Flagler had shown interest in the Presbyterian Church in St. Augustine for a long time—not surprising, considering his church affiliation and his friendship with Dr. Anderson, the leading trustee of St. Augustine's Presbyterian church. As early as December 1885 Flagler and Anderson were exchanging letters about a possible minister Flagler had found up North who might be willing to come down and fill the pulpit in St. Augustine.[76]

When Flagler had first thought of building a new Presbyterian church, he proposed locating it on the Dragoon Barracks Lot across Cordova Street from Grace Methodist Church. During the summer of 1886 Flagler had abandoned his plan to acquire the Dragoon lot, but a year later, after the city made no attempt to buy the lot, Flagler resumed his efforts. He encountered difficulties when his Washington lobbyist could not discover which government department controlled the property: not the War Department, nor the Treasury Department. Finally it was discovered that the Interior Department held custody, but even then more problems surfaced with the paperwork. "I wonder whether our good Presbyterian friends in St. A. will *ever* get a new church," Flagler wrote to Anderson.[77]

By the summer of 1888 Flagler had managed to buy the Dragoon Barracks Lot. He removed the school for black children that stood on the property; a new school would be built in Lincolnville. In New York City Carrère and Hastings began drafting plans for the new Presbyterian church. By the winter of 1889 the plans were ready, but by that time Flagler had decided to construct the new church on the Ball estate, probably because it gave him a larger space on which to build.[78]

He chose to build the church using the same sand dredged from the sand bars of Matanzas Bay that Franklin W. Smith had used in constructing the Casa Monica. His leases on the Anastasia Island coquina quarry and Moultrie Creek sand pit had expired, and the pure sand mixture had proven stronger anyway. Carrère and Hastings also used iron I-beams in the flooring, and they embedded railroad track iron, placed vertically, into the concrete walls supporting the church's dome.[79]

Work on the structure proceeded rapidly, with the walls rising as much as ten feet above ground less than a month after the foundations were poured. Workmen who had been laid off after the completion of the Alcazar were happy to have work on another Flagler building. A force ranging from one hundred to three hundred men busied themselves with the various tasks of construction.[80] As early as the last week of May decorative blond terra-cotta and "old gold"–colored Grecian columns for the front entrance had arrived on the building site. By the third week of July the walls seemed to be complete. Then one evening, "residents in the neighborhood of the Presbyterian Church were startled from a peaceful slumber last night at 11 o'clock by a loud rumbling noise, not unlike an earthquake." Flagler's contractors raced to the scene, fearing the worst. However, the noise had been caused by the collapse of the wooden scaffolding under the dome of the church. Nothing more. At the end of the previous day, workers had hauled a large load of bricks up to the level where the masons were constructing the four large arches that spanned the wings of the church. They wanted the bricks to be available when work picked up again in the morning. But the wooden staging could not bear the weight, and eventually it gave way. Fortunately, no one was in the building at the time. What could have been a tragedy if it had happened during the day when men were at work up in the dome turned out to be nothing more than a mishap requiring cleanup.[81]

The early winter visitors who arrived in December 1889 were treated to the spectacle of the church building receiving finishing touches. "The rapidity with which this edifice is nearing completion is marvelous," declared a newspaperman. Roofers were putting red tile on the church and the attached manse, while masons installed ivory terra-cotta ornamentation around the building. The interior wooden trusses forming the tall dome had been completed and then decked over with wood. Only the final step of covering the dome with a layer of copper sheeting remained to be done. Inside plasterers were climbing over a "forest of staging" to finish the walls with a coat of white plaster.[82]

To create an unobstructed space for the new church, Flagler removed the Ball mansion from the lot just to the east of the church site. This three-story wooden home stood out as an anomaly among its Spanish Renaissance surroundings. Earlier Flagler had searched for a better name for the home than the "Ball place," and Anderson, remembering the mulberry trees planted there in his father's

Flagler moved the Ball mansion one block north to remove it from the area of the Ponce de Leon and turned it into the Barcelona Hotel. This hotel would be leased rather than operated as part of the Flagler system. From the collection of the St. Augustine Historical Society Research Library.

time, suggested that the house be called "The Mulberries." Flagler liked the name at the time, but the issue became moot once Flagler decided to move the building one block north to the newly opened Carrera Street. The move came in the summer of 1889 and was complete by October. In December, with the addition of a northern wing, the Ball place became the Barcelona Hotel. It would be leased and operated as a hotel until its demolition in 1962 to create a parking lot for Ancient City Baptist Church.[83]

On the lot vacated by the Ball mansion, McGuire and McDonald erected a two-story residence for O. D. Seavey. Wood framed, the house received a veneer of concrete with red brick trim to echo the appearance of the Hotel Ponce de Leon's walls. Interestingly, it was not designed with a kitchen or dining room, since it was presumed that the hotel manager and his wife would dine at the hotel. The house still stands at 20 Valencia Street and today holds the business offices of Flagler College.[84]

As workers toiled on the Presbyterian church during the summer of 1889, the Hotel Alcazar remained open as an experiment to see if it could make a success as a summer resort. St. Augustine had long invited Floridians from interior towns such as Gainesville and Palatka to come over to the coast and enjoy the cooling ocean breezes, and a few hotels had always stayed open to accommodate them. To justify keeping the Alcazar's restaurant and kitchen open, the hotel operated on the American plan, providing three meals a day along with a room, all for just $2.50. Seven members of Joyce's band stayed behind to keep up the twice-daily concerts in the courtyard and provide music for young folks to enjoy at occasional hops held in the Casino.[85]

A reporter counted forty patrons in the dining room one evening and thought that the crowd, although sparse, might suggest the arrival of larger numbers later. Toward the end of the summer more than one hundred members of the Florida Farmers Alliance held a convention at the hotel. The horny-handed sons of the soil seemed to enjoy particularly the novelty of swimming in the concrete swimming pool.[86]

At the end of the summer the experiment of keeping the hotel open yielded an inconclusive result, and Flagler would try it again the next summer. His head gardener Richard Dale provided the most lasting contribution to the Alcazar from that season: he deposited into the courtyard pond a container of goldfish that had been shipped in by rail, and they have continued as a charming feature of the place ever since.[87]

During the summer of 1889 the new hospital began to take shape. It would be called Alicia Hospital to honor the wife of its chief benefactor. Flagler had purchased the home of lumber mill executive Dr. Henry Sloggett at the south end of town, overlooking the bay, after Sloggett moved away in the summer of 1888. This large house would serve as the hospital's office, with a ward for white women patients upstairs. In May the Hospital Association met in Dr. Anderson's offices to reorganize as the trustees of the hospital. Anderson continued as president, a position he would hold until his death more than thirty years later. Four separate concrete buildings were constructed that summer: one for white men, one for black men, one for black women, and a laundry building. Flagler deeded all these properties to the Hospital Association, along with a block of Standard Oil stock, dividends from which would provide the hospital with a steady income. The ladies continued their charitable work to supplement this revenue, and the county government paid the hospital to treat indigent patients, whom the hospital accepted free of charge.[88]

Flagler had promised the people of St. Augustine that he would return the favor if they cooperated with him in his hotel and railroad ventures, and the hospital represented a real and important downpayment on that bargain.

During the busy summer of 1889 Flagler set out to forge the final link in his railway from Jacksonville to Daytona—the bridge across the San Sebastian at Union Station. Back in 1886 the Astor railroads leading to Tocoi and Palatka had

constructed a shared bridge across the river just north of the King Street causeway to a small depot, but this bridge and depot had been temporary expedients.[89]
The new bridge for the Jacksonville, St. Augustine, and Halifax River Railway
would be a little farther north and would cross the river at an angle, so that trains
not stopping at Union Station could continue smoothly north or south along
the line. It took hundreds of creosoted pilings, driven deep into the riverbed, to
complete the bridge. The work commenced near the end of May and finished in
the third week of July. When the bridge was completed, trains could run from
South Jacksonville through to Daytona without interruption on a line wholly
owned by Flagler.[90]

Ahead, the Lake Worth and Biscayne Bay regions beckoned—as did Flagler's
future as developer of the East Coast.

As prospective builder of a railroad system, Flagler took a trip to St. Paul, Minnesota, in the summer of 1889 to confer with other railroad men and politicians.
He took Anderson with him, and young Harry Harkness Flagler accompanied
them. In St. Paul they stayed at the West Hotel, along with Flagler's Fifth Avenue
neighbor, ex-governor Roswell P. Flower; southern railroad builder Pembroke
Jones of Wilmington, North Carolina; James J. Hill, the "Empire Builder" of the
Great Northern Railway; and a crowd of other powerful men. Their private discussions involved subjects including the highly competitive nature of the railroad industry and the growing efforts by the state and federal governments to
regulate railroads.[91]

After the summit meeting some of the rail barons headed west to Denver.
While Flagler and Anderson rolled across the windswept plains of eastern Colorado, they made an interesting and puzzling discovery: a raw one-horse town
named Flagler with a hotel bearing a sign reading Ponce de Leon.[92] Today the
pleasant little town of Flagler, Colorado, still exists. It dates its founding to 1888
and claims to be named for Henry Flagler, but no hotel named Ponce de Leon
can be found there, and beyond that local knowledge does not extend.

In late September Flagler and Anderson returned to St. Augustine, probably
having spent the height of summer at Mamaroneck. Flagler's private secretary
Jasper C. Salter, the Cordova's manager E. N. Wilson, and D. F. Jack, general manager of the Jacksonville, Tampa and Key West Railway came along in Flagler's
private car. When Flagler checked in at the Alcazar, a newly formed local coronet
band presented him with a little serenade.[93]

The purpose of Flagler's visit may have been revealed a few days later when
Flagler, railroad man Jack, Anderson, and Dr. F. F. Smith took a quick trip south
on Flagler's railroad to the end of the line at Daytona. The presence of Captain
Jack indicates that the probable purpose of the trip related to railroad business.
Perhaps Flagler was already planning on extending his road into the Indian River

region near Cape Canaveral, but actual construction southward would not come for another three years.[94]

A week later Flagler gave himself a present when his steam launch *Adelante* arrived as deck cargo on the large schooner *Marquis Edwards*, which also carried a cargo of coal for the Ponce de Leon's boilers. As soon as the launch had been winched off the deck and into the water, Flagler wasted no time in taking a party of his friends out for a brisk fourteen-knot excursion across Matanzas Bay into the inlet and past the lighthouse to the sand bars at the harbor entrance.[95]

Flagler's *Adelante* had been described as "new" back in 1885 when it was used as the judges' craft in a sail boat race sponsored by the Larchmont Yacht Club near Mamaroneck. After being transported to St. Augustine, the *Adelante* stayed there year-round, being put into commission each winter season for use by Flagler and his friends. It measured forty-three feet long but drew less than three feet of water, making it ideal for cruising among Matanzas Bay's sand bars and oyster beds. For many years it would be a familiar sight on local waters, carrying Alice Flagler and her friends to a picnic on North Beach and on another occasion to an oyster roast near Fort Matanzas down the winding river. O. D. Seavey borrowed it to go snipe hunting in the marshes of North River. Twice the *Adelante* survived brushes with destruction. Once the boathouse on the San Sebastian River in which it was kept during the off season caught fire, but some local men managed to pull it out to safety. Later a steamship attempting to moor at Flagler's dock south of King Street was pushed against the boathouse by a strong tidal current, "crushing" the boathouse. Yet the *Adelante* survived to sail again.[96]

During the long, dull summer of 1889 the people of St. Augustine and their city government engaged in a prolonged discussion of how to provide the growing but financially destitute town with a new municipal fish, meat, and vegetable market. The newly expanded police force also needed a headquarters. In addition, the mayor required an office, and the city council needed a meeting hall. Lacking a better solution, the city council decided to lease and renovate a large wooden building facing Charlotte Street; but before the city could act, a cigar maker leased the building for a cigar factory.[97]

At this point Flagler stepped in to resolve the city's quandary. He made the city council a dramatic offer, prefacing it with the remark that he had been thinking for two years of a way to "demonstrate by practical results my appreciation to our City and my desire for its prosperity." In mentioning "two years" Flagler may have been obliquely acknowledging that he had earlier thwarted the city's efforts to acquire the Powder House Lot for public purposes. He now proposed to build a large building that would encompass a market, city hall, police station, courtroom, jail, and even a fire engine house. Flagler would construct the building at his own expense and rent it to the city at a nominal cost. On the ground

The City Building continued to serve as St. Augustine's town hall until the 1960s. The fire department was located in the single-story wing to the left. People often referred to the building as the "Model Land Company Building," because Flagler's land office occupied a space on the ground floor. From the collection of the St. Augustine Historical Society Research Library.

level would be some store space that the city could lease out to recoup some of its rental expenses. It was an offer breathtaking in its scope.[98]

Three of the five councilmen reacted enthusiastically, but amazingly, one demurred and another groused that the new building, which in time would be located on St. George Street, was too far away from the seawall to be convenient for fishermen to bring in their catch. Joseph McDonald, who had attended as Flagler's representative, explained to the councilmen that Flagler desired a unanimous vote in favor of the new municipal building. Thereupon a face-to-face meeting was arranged with Flagler in his office, at which he was asked just when he would be prepared to begin construction. "Tomorrow morning," Flagler replied.[99]

He posted diagrams of the proposed City Building in the window of a drugstore on the Plaza for people to satisfy their curiosity. Some citizens complained about one aspect or another, but at their next meeting the city council voted unanimously to accept Flagler's generous offer.[100]

McDonald and Mayor W.S.M. Pinkham quickly paid visits to nearby cities to inspect their public markets, returning with a proposal that the market space be almost doubled in size. Then the firemen decided that they needed a larger fire station. Dr. Carver and other city leaders got up a petition to enlarge the building to three stories, rather than the originally proposed two, in order to provide additional office space and a hall where organizations such as the Masons and Odd Fellows might hold their meetings. Dr. Anderson signed the petition, as did about 150 others. McDonald shepherded the process along and obtained Flagler's assent to the modifications. These changes raised the total cost of the building from $70,000 to $80,000, but the city council approved the amended agreement.[101]

Interestingly, the site Flagler had selected for the new City Building did not belong to him but to the Presbyterian Church—or perhaps to the Presbytery of East Florida. The Presbyterian manse, a spacious coquina and timber structure erected shortly after the war, stood on the northwest corner of St. George and Hypolita streets. The trustees of the local church, headed by Anderson, unanimously supported trading the existing manse for the new one currently under construction as an appendage to the new church also then under construction. The question of ownership of the property was not cleared up until December, when the Presbytery of East Florida gave its consent to the swap with Flagler.[102]

Work began on the western portion of the City Building in October, while ownership of the manse remained unresolved, since that portion of the building would stand on an adjacent lot that Flagler already owned. The public market occupied this area, and by February 1890 vendors began moving into the stalls. The market had a concrete floor for sanitation, a cold storage locker for meats, and thirty-two separate stalls. It made quite a contrast to the old public market on the Plaza, the "Slave Market," which had become a sightseers' attraction rather than a functioning marketplace.[103]

While he was in town, Flagler watched progress in the move of his railroad line as it passed through the northern outskirts of town about five hundred feet westward to the margin of the San Sebastian marshes. This required Flagler to build a new segment of track a little over a mile in length and then tear up the existing tracks. This removal greatly improved property values in the growing northern part of the town, since the tracks no longer created a nuisance by running through the center of the area. All went well with the operation until fill for the tracks began to edge out into the San Sebastian marshes just north of Union Station, where the line would connect with the new bridge. As superintendent William Crawford explained to Flagler: "This morning I found about 100 feet of this embankment gone down out of sight, carrying the track with it." The sucking mud of the San Sebastian, which for so long had kept invaders at bay, had claimed another victim. Crawford brought James McGuire out to inspect the damage and offer advice. McGuire declared that the only thing to do was to keep filling—"there must be bottom somewhere." The fill took longer and cost more than expected, but it was finally done. With this project completed, Flagler had just about eliminated the makeshift nature of the railroads entering St. Augustine and furnished the city with a logical, convenient line system and terminus.[104]

One major deficiency remained in St. Augustine's railroad connections—the gap in Jacksonville across the St. Johns River, which required travelers to disembark on the north bank, take a ferry across the river, and climb aboard another train on the south bank for the final leg of the journey to St. Augustine. The river narrowed at Jacksonville, so a bridge would not have to cross a long stretch of water; however, the great depth of water at the bridge site required massive concrete pilings in order for a steel bridge structure to be erected. Overcoming such engineering hurdles was becoming routine for Flagler's builders by this time, and on December 21 the first train edged across the bridge from the south bank to the north. But the tracks connecting with the bridge from the north had not been perfected, so trains could not yet go through directly. This must have been a disappointment to Superintendent Crawford, General Manager Jack, James McGuire, and Joseph McDonald, who rode the train to meet the Flagler family arriving from the North. Flagler, Alice, and Harry made the transfer from their northern train to the St. Augustine train and could at least enjoy the thrill of passing across the first bridge of any kind to span the St. Johns at Jacksonville. By nine that night they were in St. Augustine and safely tucked away in the Alcazar.[105]

Having confirmed the success of the new railroad bridge, the Flaglers did not remain much longer in St. Augustine. Just after Christmas they set off for Daytona, where the mayor gave them a carriage ride through the orange groves and showed them the spot where a bridge would soon be built over the Halifax River to the beach. Henry and Alice made a similar visit two months later. Clearly Flagler had his eyes fixed on the extension of the rail line southward to New Smyrna and perhaps beyond. On January 3 the Flagler family set off for New York, their car decorated with flowers and with a pineapple that had been an object of interest, as it had been growing in the Sun Parlor of the Cordova. Anderson and managers Seavey and Wilson were at the station to see them off.[106]

Flagler's bridge across the river effectively ended Jacksonville's status as a winter resort destination, since it vastly improved convenience for travelers seeking warmer and more scenic havens farther down the peninsula of Florida. The old-time hotel men in Jacksonville lamented the bridge at the same time that the vacation-oriented business interests to the south rejoiced. As a writer for the *Washington Post* put it: "Jacksonville is now a way station. The glory of Jacksonville has departed and St. Augustine is the beneficiary."[107] Yet although the bridge took away resort hotel guests, it also strengthened Jacksonville's status as a transportation crossroads and the metropolis of a growing state.

13

Memorial Church, 1890

Long may he be spared to us, and whatever
he does, may it prosper.
—Rev. John R. Paxton, prayer at church dedication,
March 1890

Sometime in the closing days of 1889 Captain Henry Marcotte, U.S. Army retired, became the St. Augustine correspondent of the *Florida Times-Union*, the state's foremost newspaper. A year later his wife Anna would assume editorial control of the *St. Augustine News* and, the year after that, the *Tatler*. Both of these were weekly journals of resort society published during the winter season. Together the Marcottes became the most important chroniclers of St. Augustine during the following quarter century. However, they did more than observe the local scene, they were active players in the major developments of the day. Both were amazing people.

Henry Marcotte was born in Rome, Italy, in 1840 and emigrated to America at the age of six. That is all we know of his origins and early life. In 1861 when the southern states seceded and President Lincoln issued his call for seventy-five thousand volunteers to defend the Union, twenty-one-year-old Marcotte enlisted as a corporal in the Second New York Volunteers at Troy, New York. He marched off to war wearing the gray uniform of the local militia since the army lacked enough blue uniforms to clothe its troops at the commencement of the war. Marcotte's regiment was sent right into what was then the front line at Fortress Monroe on the peninsula outside the Union's beachhead in Virginia. In one of the war's first "battles," a confused skirmish near a church called Big Bethel, Marcotte was wounded—possibly by other Federal troops who mistook his gray-clad volunteers for Confederates.[1]

In the following two years Marcotte's service record reads like a catalog of the bloodiest battles in Virginia: Fair Oaks, Glendale, Malvern Hill, Bristoe Station,

Second Bull Run, Chantilly, Fredericksburg, Chancellorsville. There the record ends, for in the midst of the Battle of Chancellorsville, Marcotte received a wound for the third time in the war. The army sent him for surgery to a hospital in Washington, D.C. His hometown newspaper the *Troy Daily Times* reported, "Lieutenant M. was struck in the leg by a bullet injuring the bone below the knee pretty badly. He keeps up his courage well, however, and is a 'plucky soldier.'"[2]

The United States did not award medals for meritorious service during the war, save for new the newly created Medal of Honor, but instead it recognized valor by bestowing "brevet" officer commissions. For his courage in battle, Marcotte received two such advances in rank: to first lieutenant and then to captain. After recovering from his wound, Marcotte did not return to his unit because, in the words of a comrade, "he was too badly shot to pieces to continue." Marcotte was assigned to service with the 22nd Regiment, Veteran Reserve Corps, a unit created by combining surviving soldiers from regiments that had been so decimated by casualties as to be no longer serviceable. The 22nd was formed in Washington, D.C., and its men helped garrison the defenses of the capital. Following his promotion to brevet captain in the spring of 1865, Marcotte served as a staff officer, but with the effective rank, and pay, of a first lieutenant. Following the war he reentered the regular army.[3]

Sometime near the conclusion of the war or shortly thereafter he married Anna M. Hughes. We know nothing of her background except that she was born in Williamsport, Pennsylvania, in 1843. She had previously been married to Lieutenant Amos B. Rhodes (or Rhoades) of the 7th Pennsylvania Cavalry and followed his unit to the Battle of Antietam and the Siege of Nashville. On June 27, 1863, at Shelbyville, Tennessee, the 7th Cavalry made a desperate charge against a Confederate detachment led by General Joe Wheeler and routed the rebels, forcing Wheeler to escape by driving his horse into a river. The commander of the 7th, Major Charles Davis, was awarded the Medal of Honor for his gallant charge, but Lieutenant Rhodes died in the fight. After the battle Anna received a pass from the Confederates to retrieve her husband's body from beyond the lines.[4]

Years later, as an eighty-four-year-old woman, Anna Marcotte addressed a Women's Republican Club in New York on Lincoln's birthday. She told of her years in Washington during the war following the death of her husband. Marcotte said she worked in the Treasury Building on Pennsylvania Avenue near the White House and that she was accustomed to cutting across the White House grounds on her walk to and from the Treasury. Sometimes she would encounter President Lincoln outside, wearing a long overcoat with a plaid lining, and he would smile at her as she passed by. Once he sorrowfully exclaimed to her after receiving news of a battle, "Our poor, poor boys." On another occasion she went to visit an orderly who had lived in her boarding house but then had gone to a hospital to die. To her surprise, she found Lincoln in the hospital holding the hand of a soldier patient.[5]

One wonders if she met the wounded Lieutenant Marcotte in a hospital; it appears they were both living in Washington at the time of their marriage. In 1869 Brevet Captain Marcotte transferred to the 17th U.S. Infantry, and his life, and that of his new wife, became very interesting. The Northern Pacific Railroad had extended its rails deep into the Dakota Territory and wished to push on through the Yellowstone region on its way to the Pacific. Standing in the way lay a thousand miles of uncharted wilderness and an unknown number of hostile Indians. The 17th Infantry joined other U.S. troops sent to protect the railroad surveyors as they searched for a route through the deserts and mountains.

The army and railroad men made three major Yellowstone expeditions between 1871 and 1873. The winter of 1872 found the Marcottes living in tents at the construction site of Fort Abraham Lincoln (near modern day Bismarck) in temperatures of twenty below zero with Sioux war parties harassing their camp. Mrs. Marcotte learned how to use a rifle. On the third Yellowstone expedition the 17th Infantry was accompanied by the 7th Cavalry led by Colonel George A. Custer, and their venture into the Yellowstone area encountered harassing attacks by Sioux under Sitting Bull. Colonel Custer and Sitting Bull's people would meet again three years later.[6]

Captain Marcotte wrote a piece for the *Army and Navy Journal* in which he claimed to have originated a classic Yellowstone fish story: "We crossed the Yellowstone River on our way to Bozeman and founded the Yellowstone army post. Our party was the first that had seen the river since Lewis and Clark discovered it in 1804. I caught the original fish and boiled him in a hot spring not ten feet away, and then wrote the *Chicago Tribune*: 'I can stand in these mountains with my fishing line, catch a fish in a pool of water on one side, and toss it into a pool of water on the other side, where it will boil for dinner.'"[7] Stories such as this would in a few years bring thousands of sojourners, including Henry Flagler, to Yellowstone National Park over the Northern Pacific Railroad.

Following the third Yellowstone expedition the army brought Marcotte back to New Barracks, Kentucky, to serve as the recruiting officer and quartermaster. Upon leaving this assignment he was described as "a battle-scarred officer," "a skilled and competent mechanical engineer," and a "most genial gentleman." In 1878 Marcotte retired from the army "on account of inability incident to service." He and Anna settled in Cincinnati, where he became involved in the activities of the Grand Army of the Republic veterans association and also found employment as a reporter for the *Cincinnati Enquirer*.[8]

In the winter of 1885 Marcotte accompanied a group of northern newspapermen invited to Ocala by Frank Harris, editor of the *Ocala Banner*, for a promotional tour of Florida. Harris and Marcotte struck up a lifetime acquaintance on their first meeting. Both men would later become advocates for Henry Flagler. Harris's intention had been to disseminate favorable press reports about Florida, and it certainly worked with Marcotte. He wrote a long story for the *Enquirer* saying that tales of heat, alligators, and water moccasins had been vastly exaggerated and the charms of Florida underrated. However, Marcotte complained of high prices and poor victuals at Florida's pioneer hotels.[9]

A year later the Marcottes moved to Florida and purchased shares in a land company at Dunnellon, where the spring-fed Wekiva (now Rainbow) River flowed into the Withlacoochee River. They even tried their hand as hotel keepers of what was called the Coochie wayside inn, where guests could feed biscuits to a tame alligator. However, the Marcottes quickly turned operation of the hotel over to another couple. The winter of 1887–88 found them staying as guests at the modest St. George Hotel next to the old Episcopal Church on St. Augustine's Plaza. The following season they rented rooms at the Ocean View on Bay Street overlooking the waters of the Matanzas. They were still identified as being "of Dunnellon," but the Marcottes had decided to make St. Augustine their home.[10]

They took up residence in Dr. Anderson's cottage on Sevilla Street, opposite the west end of the Ponce de Leon's carriage drive. Already Mrs. Marcotte had joined the ladies in the Alicia Hospital Association, and she sponsored a lawn party on Anderson's grounds to raise money.[11] Just after Thanksgiving Captain Marcotte escorted O. D. Seavey and his wife, as well as Martin Johnson Heade and his wife, on a trip to see the natural wonders of Silver Springs and other parts of Florida. Of course, Marcotte took them to Dunnellon, where he still owned land he hoped to sell for development. Heade made some sketches of the waterways that he would afterward turn into paintings. A year later Mrs. Marcotte took the artist Laura Woodward to Dunnellon, and she too would paint a landscape of the area. The Marcottes counted both Woodward and the Heades as friends. Mrs. Heade and Anna Marcotte were stalwarts of the Hospital Association.[12]

One of the first stories Captain Marcotte wrote for the *Times-Union* announced a landmark moment in St. Augustine history. The townspeople celebrated the inauguration of a new era in railroading on January 14, 1890. Ellis Brooks's band kicked off the festivities by marching from the Ponce de Leon to the depot playing triumphal airs. Naturally, a crowd followed the band and packed Union Station. The members of the Alcazar Bicycle Club entertained the throng while they waited for arrival of the train by riding their wheels around and around the ellipse of the park. When the train pulled into the station just at sunset, the boom of a fireworks bomb startled horses lined up in a long row with their carriages ready to receive passengers. More fireworks rent the sky.

The first vestibule train had made the run from Jersey City through to St.

Augustine in a record time of just over thirty-one hours, averaging forty miles per hour over the route. Painted on the sides of the passenger cars was the inscription "New York and Florida Special"—the first of the Florida Specials that would become a proud symbol of state tourism in the coming decades. When everyone was ready, the Brooks band ceremoniously led the parade of carriages and omnibuses from the station back to town.[13]

Nine days earlier another train had arrived unobtrusively at Union Station near midnight in a foggy gloom, carrying 140 black waiters and other workers for Flagler's St. Augustine hotels. These men had been recruited in the North, mostly in New York City, by Frank Thompson. As the train headed south, the men, veteran hotel employees, turned the journey into a celebration. "The party assumed an air of jolly good nature and contentment," wrote one, "which was maintained until a later hour and sleep drove them to the berths in the sleepers which had been provided for them." From the train station they walked down Valencia Street toward town and encountered the massive black outline of the new Presbyterian Church building that had arisen since their previous stay in St. Augustine.[14]

With through rail connections to the North in place and memories of the 1888 yellow fever epidemic fading, both the hotel people and the citizens of St. Augustine looked forward to an excellent season in 1890.

Unfortunately, the San Marco Hotel would not open. Its owner Isaac Cruft had died at his home in Boston on December 30, 1889, and his nephew General George T. Cruft decided not to operate the hotel for the season. Those holding reservations at the San Marco were referred to the Flagler hotels.[15]

The Alcazar had remained open all through the summer and rapidly filled with the arrival of cooler weather. Its popularity and profitability were assured.

On Christmas Eve the Cordova ran up a huge American flag over its ramparts, opened its register book for patrons, and offered them Christmas dinner that evening in its new dining room. During the summer McGuire and McDonald had continued renovations of Franklin Smith's original building. The enlarged dining room glittered with pure white walls, muted gold trim, and windows that opened onto the Sun Parlor. Behind the dining room stood an enlarged, modernized kitchen. The hotel retained its Moorish Alhambra character, but most of the original native Florida pine paneling in the rooms and hallways had been painted over either in white or in some light pastel shade. The coat of paint transformed the dim, gloomy atmosphere of the original building into cheerful brightness. The vegetation in the Sun Parlor had a fresh, more tropical look. One of the hotel's staff had made an expedition to the remote Lake Worth region and returned with barrels containing coconut palms, fish-tail palms, banana plants, air plants, and pineapple shoots. These curiosities added to the Sun Parlor's exoticism and subtly hinted at Flagler's future orientation toward South Florida. The exterior wooden trim, which originally had probably been left in natural wood, received a coat of "reddish brown" paint that contrasted vividly with the gray concrete walls.[16]

The drawing room library held an assortment of leather-bound volumes selected for their snob appeal to please the "artist, book-worm, and connoisseur." These included *Burke's Peerage, Webster's Royal Red Book, Country Families of the United Kingdom, Castles and Abbeys of England, Stately Homes of England,* and *Kelly's Handbook of the Titled, Landed and Official Class.*[17]

Flagler had every intention of turning the Cordova into a first-class accompaniment to the Ponce de Leon. The Cordova contained 228 guest rooms; nearly as many as the Ponce de Leon. Rates for rooms started at just a little less than at the Ponce de Leon: four dollars rather than five. For this, guests received three meals a day and all the amenities of a first-class hotel, including an in-house orchestra. Manager E. N. Wilson and Robert Murray, his steward, were men of long experience in the resort hotel business. The Cordova seemed set for a good season.[18]

Seavey and Flagler planned a novel opening gambit for the Hotel Ponce de Leon: a full-dress ball on the evening of opening day, January 9. Not only were local people permitted to inspect the hotel's public rooms during the day, as usual, but in the evening anyone dressed in formal attire was allowed to enter the Dining Room to join in the festivities. Special trains ran from Palatka and Jacksonville to bring in patrons, since the northern crowd had not yet arrived in full force. Guests danced to the music of the new band headed by Ellis Brooks, hand-picked by Flagler from two prestigious New York City orchestras. Franklin W. Smith, his wife, and his daughter Nina stood out among the early birds that evening.[19]

Henry and Alice Flagler arrived in St. Augustine on February 8, accompanied by Flagler's older half-sister Ann Caroline, always known as "Carrie." She was the daughter of Isaac Flagler's second wife; four years older than Henry, she had been his closest companion. The Flaglers were soon joined by Julia Harkness York, sister of Flagler's deceased wife Mary. She brought her daughter Georgia with her. Twenty-two-year-old Mary Lily Kenan joined this group of ladies at some point during the season. Thus in the winter of 1890 Henry Flagler shared the society of his beloved half-sister, the sister of his dead first wife, his second wife, and his future third wife. These ladies became well known in the halls and salons of the Ponce de Leon.[20]

We do not know when Henry Flagler first met Mary Lily Kenan. By some accounts it happened when he accompanied Henry Walters, president of the Atlantic Coast Line Railroad, on a business trip to Wilmington, North Carolina. Walters's neighbors were Pembroke and Sadie Jones, who circulated in the high society of Newport in the summer and invited friends down to Wilmington during the winters. The vivacious Mrs. Smith famously employed a Russian chef and a black cook to prepare meals for her guests. Mary Lily Kenan and her family also were intimate friends of the Joneses. The story goes that Mary Lily sang to entertain visitors, one of whom happened to be Henry Flagler. However, at this early point it is highly unlikely that they were anything more than passing acquaintances who shared a common friendship with the Joneses and Walters.[21]

On a masculine note, Flagler provided vacationers with another diversion during the new season—a fine baseball stadium where the best professional players in the land could show off their skills. Ponce de Leon Park stood just to the east of the railroad station between Carrera and Saragossa streets on land created by Flagler's fill operations. Everything in the park had been done to first-rate standards. Albert Spalding, the sporting goods magnate and professional baseball executive, had been consulted on the design. The field's covered grandstand seated seven hundred spectators, with a press balcony behind home plate for reporters and two private boxes atop the stadium roof for special guests. The "cheap seats" in the bleachers brought stadium capacity to two thousand. A wooden fence twelve feet high surrounded the field. With an enclosed stadium—rather than

Flagler constructed a first-class baseball field, hoping to attract professional teams to St. Augustine during the winter. *Frank Leslie's Illustrated Newspaper*, March 22, 1890, 164. Courtesy of Kevin Kelshaw.

the makeshift diamond on the fort green—it would be possible to charge admission and attract teams that formerly had refused to play in St. Augustine.[22]

Spalding leased the field from February through early April for his team, the Chicago Colts (later to become the Cubs). He had been one of the leaders in popularizing winter baseball in the South as a way to sharpen players' skills for the summer season and also as a way to add to the team's total yearly income. As early as the 1870s some games had been played in New Orleans, and by the late 1880s professional league ball had become common in Charleston, Savannah, and Jacksonville.

The lease left one day per week open for local games. Seavey hoped that other cities in Florida would field teams to come over to play the St. Augustine boys. Excitement grew as opening day for the stadium approached, although some of the anticipation dipped when it was announced that Spalding himself would not appear as expected. Instead the "Chicagos" were led by Captain Adrian "Cap" Anson and his wife, who served as score keeper. The Ansons stayed in the Alcazar, while the players were put up in the more modest Cleveland House.[23]

On February 14 a large crowd, many of whom came from Jacksonville by special train, filed into the stands under perfect skies to watch the first action on the diamond. Everyone cheered when the Chicago players took to the field in their light gray uniforms, black socks, and black caps. A select team of St. Augustine's finest lost the coin toss and batted first. They put up a good fight, but the game was called at nightfall in the eighth inning with Chicago leading 11 to 5.[24]

The correspondent for the black newspaper the *New York Age* noted that "one of the time honored Southern rules was observed on this auspicious occasion"—black spectators were segregated into one portion of the bleachers. The only black men in the covered grandstand were Frank Thompson and "Walker of New York," who may have been Lee A. Walker, later headwaiter at the Royal Poinciana in Palm Beach. The journalist observed, "Perhaps the official positions of these gentlemen won for them some respect."[25]

A week later the ballpark filled on Washington's Birthday for a game between the Colts and Philadelphia Phillies, who were training in Jacksonville. A writer for the Jacksonville newspaper wrote enviously of the turnout for such games in St. Augustine: "In St. Augustine the townspeople and the tourists turn out by the thousands at these games, and the scene at the baseball park is decidedly a gay and enlivening one. Large equestrian parties are made up for each game and every conceivable kind of rig, from the lordly landau to the diminutive dog cart, is to be seen in the long line of vehicles which is ranged along the high fence. The people there take an interest in the sport. They encourage the managers by their patronage, and they put some style into the thing at the same time."[26]

After nightfall the stadium filled again for a fireworks display. Anyone could enter the field free of charge, but admission to the pavilion was reserved for hotel guests, who had received complementary tickets. High atop the pavilion in the "grand outlook" sat Henry and Alice Flagler with their friends. The pyrotechnic show featured some displays on wooden frames set up in the outfield, while others rocketed into the night sky. The grand finale came when the outline of the new Jacksonville bridge appeared in "lines of crimson fire." Then, a blazing locomotive and train of passenger cars passed over the bridge, accompanied by a crescendo of explosions. As the crowd began to file out of the stadium, lights came on, illuminating the shiny copper dome of the new Presbyterian Church as well as the towers of the Ponce de Leon and Alcazar. Guests at Flagler's hotels hurried to their rooms to renew their makeup and change into formal attire for a grand ball in the Casino.[27]

As the season went on, games at Ponce de Leon Park continued on a more or less regular basis. Fans could buy photographs of their favorite players in souvenir shops around town and could purchase game tickets in hotel lobbies. No photo was more desirable than that of Cap Anson, the first professional player to achieve three thousand career hits and today a member of the Baseball Hall of Fame. When the Brooklyn team came to town, people came out in the morning to watch their workout. Later, a game between Chicago and the Brooklyn Bridegrooms (later the Dodgers) filled the stadium. Henry Flagler and his friends occupied the "lookout" atop the pavilion. The Brooklyn boys looked spiffy in their new white uniforms, but as this was their first outing, they could not match the game-hardened Colts.[28]

Flagler's baseball field received some publicity when *Frank Leslie's Illustrated Newspaper*, one of the most widely read publications in the nation, ran a story on professional teams playing in the South during the cold weather months. W. A. Arkell, owner of *Frank Leslie's* and also of *Punch* magazine, was a guest of the Ponce de Leon, along with his chief illustrator F. H. Taylor. One wonders if Flagler invited them down as his guests to elicit publicity for his new stadium and his resort community. The article pointed out that teams playing in the South seldom made enough money to pay their expenses, but the magazine offered hope that better attendance would bring better results in the future.[29]

By the time the article appeared in *Frank Leslie's*, as if to confirm the story's fears, attendance had dropped off at games. Cap Anson attempted to spark interest by hitting the stadium's first home run in a game on March 17, and the Colts' final game of the season against the Bridegrooms again filled the stadium. After that, the Chicago team departed by train for New Orleans to play some more ball. Captain Marcotte of the *Times-Union* judged the season an overall success for St. Augustine.[30]

A game the people of St. Augustine did not have an opportunity to see was one between the Chicago Colts and the Cuban Giants. Since their founding the Cuban Giants had occasionally played against white teams, but in September 1887 the St. Louis Browns, world champions, had made headlines across the nation when their white players refused to take the field against the Cuban Giants. The white players declared that they were only "doing what's right," but they also added that the game was a bad idea considering "the shape the team is in at present." This incident marked the beginning of a concerted effort by white teams to squeeze the few black players in the major leagues out of baseball. One of the most ardent advocates for the exclusion of black team members was none other than Cap Anson of the all-white Chicago Colts.[31]

The black waiters at Flagler's hotels remained as enthusiastic about baseball as ever, but their games were limited to intramural matches among themselves and contests with visiting black teams.[32] Many white visitors turned out to enjoy these games as well as the minstrel shows and cake walks presented by the black employees. One Sunday evening the usual sacred concert by the hotel band was supplanted by a vocal concert by the "Ponce de Leon Chorus," consisting of black hotel workers, both men and women, led by headwaiter Thompson. The black New York Age declared, "The venture was something of a surprise to the many guests of the hotel and a complete success; in fact a novelty of the first order."[33]

Such recitals by black entertainers posed a dilemma for the performers. Men such as Frank Thompson advised his black waiters that roughness, uncouthness, and illiteracy were weaknesses. Yet white audiences expected blacks to behave in a stereotypical "primitive" way. In his critique of a minstrel performance by waiters from all the town's major hotels, Captain Marcotte wrote in praise, but added: "At the same time they should not become so 'high toned' as to 'put on such style' as to knock the edges off the genuine negro. If they do so, they spoil the negro minstrelsy so far as [the spectators] are concerned."[34]

Away from the critical eyes of the white citizenry, the black population of St. Augustine maintained an independent society. A dynamic, autonomous African American community prospered in the largely black neighborhood of Lincolnville, where Washington Street served as the center of business and civic activity. Black hotel men visiting from the North found a congenial local society with a vigorous middle class that welcomed the strangers and their payroll money. "Among the colored people of St. Augustine," wrote a black correspondent, "interesting events have been quite as plentiful as among their white neighbors; ball, hops, receptions, etc., have been as plentiful as huckleberries on a bush." At a fair to raise money for First Baptist Church, the Cordova's C. C. Randolph was pitted against the Ponce de Leon's Frank P. Thompson in a popularity contest. Thompson's supporters out-contributed Randolph's and won a spectacular cake for their champion.[35]

The opening of Alicia Hospital on February 18 was a landmark occasion for the whole St. Augustine community. In the absence of Alice and Henry Flagler, Dr. Anderson and the trustees presided over the occasion. Anna Marcotte headed the tea committee, and Confederate General Edmund Kirby-Smith's daughter Bessie assisted as one of the young ladies pouring for the guests as they strolled through the facilities. Other ladies of the Hospital Association, most notably president Elizabeth Heade, had been meeting for weeks in the black chapel on Granada Street to sew linen for use in the new hospital. The facility was not yet ready for occupancy, but by March 4 the newspaper reported that one patient was receiving care.[36]

Three weeks later the second annual Hospital Fair occupied the Casino for three evenings. The amusements and booths generally repeated the themes of the previous year's fair. Alice Flagler presided over a booth "laden with quantities of beautiful things, many of them the work of Mrs. Flagler, who paints beautifully on silk, satin and Bolton cloth [a cloth used in quilts]." Anna Street Morton, second lady of the land, was visiting St. Augustine and served as Alice's assistant. Also helping host the table were Mary Lily Kenan and Carrie Flagler. A wooden box with a spinning wax cylinder on top and a brass horn like a trumpet attracted a stream of curious onlookers. It was called a phonograph and when activated produced the words, "I am a cute little thing invented by Thomas Edison in 1877, but not born to perfection until 1888. I can talk, although not having a tongue; can hear without ears, and can think without brains. Ha! Ha!"[37]

Many distinguished guests attended the Alicia Hospital Charity Ball held in the Dining Room of the Ponce de Leon. Alice Flagler, of course, as the benefactor of the hospital, had to be there, but Flagler himself also made a rare appearance. His older half-brother Dan Harkness mingled with the crowd. Forty-six years earlier Flagler, as a clerk in Dan's general store in Republic, Ohio, had slept beneath a counter, using sheets of wrapping paper to ward off the cold. John W. Archbold, who had taken over functional leadership of Standard Oil by this time, also circulated among the throng on the polished oak floor. Among the ladies present was Miss Mary Lily Kenan. At midnight the crowd feasted on a red snapper and quail supper, and then the older guests retired for the night, while the two bands repeated the evening's music program and dancing by the younger set continued until two in the morning.[38]

The fair raised $4,000 and the Charity Ball added almost another $1,000. So, by the end of the season the ladies could brag that the Hospital Association had $10,000 invested drawing 7.5 percent interest. Four local doctors rotated in three-month shifts working at the hospital free of charge, with Dr. Anderson taking the first months. Friends of the hospital made donations from time to time as they saw fit. The office received, by one accounting, two jars of fruit, some old linen, some old muslin, a load of firewood, fifty oranges, and a fifty-cent piece left by a visitor to the facility. The hospital proved its worth on April 27 when the first baby was born there, a little girl who was named Alicia.[39]

During the 1890 season the Hotel Ponce de Leon hosted probably the most extraordinary gathering of notables ever assembled in its long history. Having invited Democratic president Grover Cleveland to be his guest in the previous two years, it is likely that Flagler invited Republican president Benjamin Harrison to come in 1890. There is no document attesting to such an invitation, but some people in St. Augustine anticipated a visit from the president.[40] In any case, during March a host of luminaries from the Harrison family and administration came to the Ponce de Leon as Flagler's guests. The first to arrive was Vice President Levi P. Morton, with his wife Anna, three daughters, and a small group of friends. They came in Flagler's private railroad car and arrived at night on March 4 without any prior announcement of their coming. The Mortons' New York home stood just one house away from Flagler's residence on Fifth Avenue.

The party was ushered into the Rotunda, where Professor Brooks's regular evening concert was in progress. At the sudden appearance of the vice president the orchestra struck up "The Star-Spangled Banner," and everyone rose in respect and to catch a glimpse of their noted visitor. Curious guests came running from other parts of the hotel. At the vice president's request no formal reception was held, but Flagler gave them a hearty welcome and, due to the late hour, bade them go directly to the suites of rooms reserved for them.[41]

Ten days later, first lady Mrs. Caroline Harrison and her son Russell, with his wife and a group of friends, arrived in St. Augustine. They were accompanied by Mrs. Mary Wanamaker, wife of Postmaster General John Wanamaker, who furnished the private railway car for the journey. John Wanamaker had pioneered the modern department store in Philadelphia. Henry, Alice, and Harry Flagler received the travelers in the Rotunda of the Ponce de Leon. Captain Henry Marcotte was on hand in his capacity as correspondent for the *Times-Union*, and he confided to his readers that years earlier in the army he had known Russell Harrison when Russell's father, the future president, was an officer and Russell was a child.[42]

Also in Flagler's hotel at this time could be found George F. Roberts, president of the Pennsylvania Railroad; Frederick Vanderbilt, director of three railroads; and Thomas Bailey Aldrich, poet and editor of the *Atlantic Monthly*. Mrs. Eunice Beecher, widow of the country's most famous clergyman, Henry Ward Beecher (brother of Harriet Beecher Stowe), stayed in the more modest Cordova.[43]

A correspondent to the *Chicago Times* told this story from 1890: "Hamilton

Disston had arranged to introduce me to Claus Spreckles, the millionaire sugar manufacturer and planter. We saw him coming across the rotunda and Mr. Disston presented me. While we three were talking, Henry M. Flagler and Vice-President Morton joined the group, and then in turn, Governor Flower of New York (then in Congress), Chauncey M. Depew of New York and Charles A. Dana of the 'New York Sun,' an eminent group for money, brains, and reputation."[44]

Chauncey Depew, president of the New York Central, had arrived in St. Augustine after having stayed in bed with influenza most of the trip. However, no mere virus could keep the exuberant, loquacious New Yorker down for long, and he declared himself cured by Florida's eighty-degree warmth.[45]

Many of those gathered in St. Augustine had come especially for the dedication of the new Presbyterian Church that Flagler had devoted to the memory of his deceased daughter Jennie Louise. In this church Carrère and Hastings had designed another unique masterpiece of architecture that had no counterpart in the United States.

Sometime during the final stage of the Byzantine building's construction, a reporter for the local *Evening News* walked through the church with Thomas Hastings. The writer explained that the church was built on the plan of a Latin cross and that its architecture reflected the period of the early Renaissance, with aspects that drew from the Venetian style. The two towers on either side of the front entrance were placed to prevent the building from looking top heavy, while the four towers surrounding the central dome acted as buttresses to receive the thrust of the tallest walls. The interior mahogany woodwork had been done by Pottier and Stymus, the same company that had created the interiors of the Ponce de Leon. The walls were pure white, although Hastings hoped to decorate them someday with elaborate frescoes. He particularly pointed out the four triangular sections of the vaulting below the dome that he hoped someday would be painted with portraits of the four evangelists. Although Hastings did not mention it, he hoped to place a row of plaster statues across the bottom of the arched wall at the north end of the nave. Large polished brass chandeliers in the form of a double cross and brass lamp stands at the ends of the pews stood out in shining contrast to the white walls. The cruciform chandeliers copied those in St. Mark's Basilica in Venice. All the lights used gas, not electricity. The windows, which did not hold stained glass, did not attract attention and were probably made of simple crackled glass.[46]

When the building was complete and speakers mounted the pulpit, it immediately became obvious, to everyone's dismay, that words spoken in the cavernous, vaulted room rebounded from the concrete walls, creating echoes that made words almost unintelligible. Later an attempt would be made to baffle the reverberation by stretching piano wire across the opening of the dome at intervals of

Memorial Church was built just north and west of the grounds of the Hotel Ponce de Leon. By permission of Library of Congress.

ten or twelve inches, but this proved ineffective. Only many years later, when the church leaders covered the walls and ceilings with sound-absorbing felt, did the acoustics improve.[47]

Two weeks before the day scheduled for the dedication service, wagons hauling mature palm trees for the church's landscaping arrived on a near-freezing weekend and were hurriedly planted—on Sunday. This violation of the Sabbath (and the town's blue law) elicited criticism of Flagler from various people in town, some of who were probably motivated more by spite than by sincere piety. Captain Marcotte wrote a story for the *Times-Union* absolving Flagler of any blame for the sinful planting, explaining that Flagler surely would have prevented it had he known. Nor did any fault lie with the congregation or pastor. The blame, if any was really merited, belonged to McGuire and McDonald, who were responsible for the building until it was turned over to the Presbyterians. However, Marcotte added, "The people of this city know that Messrs. McGuire and McDonald are law-abiding and Christian gentlemen, and are incapable of purposefully offending the feelings of any one."[48]

Years later Flagler recalled this incident and told writer Edwin Lefevre that he had, in fact, authorized planting the trees on that Sunday, considering the placing of the palms an act of worship. Some had sourly predicted that the "Sabbath-desecrating palmettos" would soon die, he added, but as Flagler observed to a friend while exiting the church one day, "Every one of the wicked things lived!"[49]

Flagler chartered a private railroad car to bring his pastor from West Presbyterian Church and its organist and choir to St. Augustine for the dedication. Rev. John R. Paxton had succeeded Thomas Hastings as West Presbyterian's minister. A dynamic speaker, Paxton attracted huge crowds on Sundays. The choir of the church, unlike those in most churches, consisted only of the organist and four well-paid concert vocalists. It was dubbed "the $6,000 choir."[50]

On the morning of the church's dedication service the streets outside were packed with townspeople and winter guests who turned out for the great moment. The police and ushers allowed only small groups of people to enter at a time. When Mrs. Harrison and her party arrived, the crowd strained to get a look; likewise with the arrival of Vice President and Mrs. Morton. The elders of the church, including Dr. DeWitt Webb, Oscar B. Smith, and Ward G. Foster, occupied the front pews. The trustees, led by Dr. Anderson, came next, followed by the dignitaries from Washington and then in pew 20 the Flagler family. Joining Henry and Alice were Harry H. Flagler and Jennie Louise's husband Fred Benedict. Members of the congregation had affixed a silver plate on pew 20 identifying it as the place reserved for Flagler. Thomas Hastings, Joseph McDonald, and James McGuire also occupied seats near the center of the church. Many of the overflow crowd sat in chairs and campstools placed in the aisles.

The artist George W. Seavey had decorated the front of the church around the pulpit with lilies and garlands of white roses. The elaborate baptismal font of Sienna marble donated by Fred Benedict had not yet arrived to take its place before the pulpit—it would arrive in June. Rev. Edwin Knox Mitchell, pastor of the St. Augustine church, opened with the invocation: "Bless him who had it in his heart to build this house in tender memory of one whom he hath loved long since and lost, and wilt thou sanctify his sorrow and give comfort and consolation unto his heart."[51]

Paxton gave the sermon, saying in regard to Flagler's contributions to St. Au-

Henry Flagler stands on the steps of the south entrance to Memorial Church. © Flagler Museum Archives.

gustine: "It is the catholic mind of the noble man, my friends, who built this church and assisted the bishop of Rome to restore his cathedral, and the followers of John Wesley to rear a beautiful building in this city. And today he gives the Presbyterians a house of prayer for souls, beautiful enough to move a savage's wonder or make the atheist pray." He added that the church also served as a remembrance of the architects, builders, and "humble workmen" whose minds and hands had wrought this wondrous structure. Then he concluded: "And last of all, let it be dedicated with a hearty 'God Bless you, dear man,' to him whose heart is as large as his purse—the generous, modest, brotherly-loving, magnificent man—who built it for your honor, my people, in memory of his sainted and glorified dead. Long may he be spared to us, and whatever he does, may it prosper. Amen."[52]

In the afternoon Mitchell spoke at a memorial service for Jennie Louise, formally ending a year of mourning for Flagler and his family. Once again the church filled to beyond capacity. The pastor delivered a message that touched both on timeless themes and reflected modern religious sentiments. He declared that reason could not detect God but that the tribulations of life forced men toward

God and their fellow men. "The daughter is his father's pride, and the son his constant joy," Mitchell reminded the audience. The mention of Jennie Louise's name brought tears. "Sacred is indeed and holy is the memory of the dead." He concluded with an allusion to the church building and to Jennie Louise: "Thy memorial shall endure from generation to generation, and a grateful people will long revere and bless the father, who had it in his heart to mingle so sacredly the thought and love of thee with the thought and love of God." The service concluded with the singing of "Rock of Ages," the hymn composed by the grandfather of the architect.[53]

On April 4 Flagler and Alice sat down with their lawyer and representatives of the Presbyterian Church to transfer legally the ownership of the new church from Flagler to the trustees of the local congregation. There were two documents. The first simply and freely bestowed the church building, which Flagler noted was being given in memory of his daughter and was to be called "Memorial Church." The second document involved a trade of properties. Flagler gave the Presbyterians the new manse attached to the side of the church in exchange for the old Presbyterian Church building on South St. George Street and the Presbyterian Manse on North St. George Street. Flagler autographed the documents with his usual bold, elegant signature, and Alice signed away her dower rights in her thin, spidery—but steady and equally attractive—signature.[54] The second document was typical of Flagler in that it mixed philanthropy with business.

Many of the illustrious people in town for the church dedication turned out as spectators for the Tropical Tennis Tournament. Mrs. Harrison, Mr. and Mrs. Morton, the Vanderbilts, and Chauncey Depew and his wife all joined Flagler to watch at least some of the action. As in the previous year, young Oliver S. Campbell won the singles title. Later that year he would claim the U.S. Open Tennis Championship, which was then held in Newport, Rhode Island. The Tropical Tournament concluded with a supper and dance in the Alcazar sponsored by the tennis club.[55]

During these weeks St. Augustine enjoyed a banner season. So many visitors arrived that it was rumored some newcomers had to sleep in the railroad station for lack of rooms; in the Cordova, manager Wilson was forced to turn his office into a sleeping chamber for one night to accommodate a couple with reservations.[56]

Guests in the Hotel Ponce de Leon enjoyed the novelty of the Edison Improved Phonograph machine that had proved such a hit in the Casino at the Hospital Fair. George M. Rogers, a Philadelphia merchant who sold Edison's invention, amused people with demonstrations of his cunning device. It could both record and play back messages from wax cylinders. O. D. Seavey recorded a little talk about the wonders to be expected in the upcoming Ponce de Leon landing day celebration. When Professor Brooks was presented with a gold badge near the end of the season for his fine orchestral performances, the phonograph rasped out a little prerecorded speech of congratulation.[57]

One glaring deficiency of St. Augustine as a seaside resort was its lack of easy access to the Atlantic beach. Those wishing to bathe in salt water or just to walk on the seashore were required to hire a boat or ride the steamer *Myth* that ferried passengers to a dock across the bay, where a little steam engine pulled open cars along a tramline that ran down Anastasia Island past the lighthouse to South Beach at the inlet entrance. A new opportunity opened up in early March of 1890 when the St. Augustine and North Beach Railway began picking up passengers at Union Station and carrying them north across the marshes and over North River to North Beach (today's Vilano Beach). The ride cost twenty-five cents and took about fifteen minutes. At the beach visitors found a neat two-story pavilion with a restaurant and dance floor, surrounded by bathhouses for changing clothes and rental cottages for overnight stays. A grid of streets had been cut through the scrub, and those wishing to erect their own beachside cottage could purchase a lot. All this was the work of a group of entrepreneurs from Macon, Georgia.[58]

Henry Flagler had little to do with this North Beach project and, in fact, deliberately kept his distance. Back in early 1886 when he had just begun his St. Augustine developments, he had considered a plan to run a railroad down from Pablo Beach—modern day Jacksonville Beach—to North Beach. He wrote to one of his railroad executives, "Would like to talk with you about the 'North Beach' enterprise when I come South. Am not sure that I want you to run a road there, but my own views in relation to the matter are undecided." He was more negative in another letter: "The Pablo Beach extension would not accommodate citizens of St. Augustine. It would simply build up a beach resort for Jacksonville alone."[59]

The alternative Flagler had in mind was building a spur line from St. Augustine over a bridge across Matanzas Bay to Anastasia Island and South Beach. He envisioned the railroad bridge being built somewhere below St. Francis Barracks on the south side of town. He realized that guests at his hotels desired easy access to the Atlantic shore. Back in the fall of 1885 Flagler had written to Dr. Carver about the idea of building a bridge to Anastasia Island. "I think very favorably of the scheme," he told Carver, "but I have ideas in connection with it, which if carried out, will make it a much more important matter than you have considered it." Possibly Flagler had a beachfront hotel in mind, but if so, he evidently never took steps to advance this idea.[60]

In 1890 he wrote a long letter to James McGuire ruminating on the question of just where a bridge to the island might be built. Flagler felt the bridge should be constructed south of the center of town. "A bridge carried across the river from the Plaza," he opined, "would be something of a nuisance, especially for small sailing craft." As a yachtsman, Flagler hated to see the fine sheet of sailing water in front of the town ruined by running a bridge through the middle of it. Moreover, Flagler would not invest more time and effort in any project relating to Anastasia Island until the legal battles with the Fish heirs over ownership of Anastasia Island had run their course.[61]

Flagler did assist the North Beach Railway by renting space in Union Station to serve as the road's terminal and allowing it to run its train along his rail line up to the Fort Mose area. Here the North Beach road split off, and Flagler permitted it to lay its rails across his gravel pit at Fort Mose. However, during the ensuing months the railway did not operate at a profit, and Flagler showed no interest in putting any money into North Beach projects. When one man suggested that Flagler invest some money, he replied, "While I may have an indirect interest in the prosperity of that North Beach enterprise, there is no question in my mind but that the parties who own the property should be the ones to make the necessary advance of money. I don't want to do so." On another occasion he reminded his railroad superintendent William Crawford, "I think I asked some time since whether the North Beach R. R. had paid their rent, and were doing so promptly."[62]

Flagler's concern about the railroad's finances was well placed, for in the spring of 1891 the North Beach Railway directors made a proposal to the St. Augustine City Council to run its rail line down San Marco Avenue along the bay front to the south end of town and operate as a trolley line to move passengers in town. After this plan came to naught, the road's mortgage was foreclosed, and its property and rolling stock were sold at auction. A hurricane in August 1893 would wash away the railroad bridge; the partly submerged iron pivot span remained visible until the 1970s, when it was removed as a hazard to navigation. A "new" North Beach company purchased the old resort and brought excursionists over by boat during the summer of 1894, but this endeavor also ended badly in February 1895, when the pavilion and four cottages burned to the ground. Finally, in 1900, Frank and Kate Usina settled on North Beach and established a riverfront oyster roast pavilion that evolved into a successful, enduring seaside resort. Today the old roadbed of the North Beach Railway is clearly visible in satellite images of the marshes north of Fort Mose State Park.[63]

Early in the 1890 season a committee of leading citizens including Dr. Anderson, O. D. Seavey, and Joseph McDonald had decided to revive the Ponce de Leon landing Celebration, which had not been held since 1885.[64] For three days at the beginning of April the city enjoyed a break from routine business for a little distraction. Someone had discovered that the extent of the block around the

Hotel Alcazar measured just about exactly a half mile—making it a likely track for staging pedestrian and bicycle races. A large crowd gathered to watch cyclists spin round and round on the new asphalt streets in a three-mile race, a two-mile race, and a one-mile race. The two-mile race featured amateurs riding the normal "safety bicycles" seen on the streets every day. On the bay front people lined the docks and seawall to watch races by oarsmen valiantly rowing single sculls in choppy waters. In the yacht race Mayor W.S.M. Pinkham's celebrated schooner *Cheemaun* enjoyed the brisk wind and added another win to its long list of victories.[65]

During the days before the celebration, various organizations had vied to create the most elaborate archway over streets and intersections. On the eve of Ponce de León's landing, Governor Francis P. Fleming came by train to occupy a room at the Hotel Ponce de Leon. The next morning Juan Ponce de León arrived by rowboat at the seawall just south of the fort, while two batteries of state militia fired cannon salutes from the fort green. Ponce then entered the first carriage in a procession, followed by the governor in the next carriage, the mayor, contingents of soldiers, stalwart citizens dressed as Lafayette's Frenchmen, Continental Army volunteers, and frontiersmen. Several bands supplied music as the parade wended its way through the streets and under the celebratory arches. When the carriages passed in front of the Hotel Ponce de Leon, the boom of its fireworks bomb marked the parade's passing. That night everyone gathered on the bay front for music, fireworks, and a procession of lighted yachts.[66]

The Hotel Cordova received the honor of hosting the final ball of the 1890 season. For the Cordova it had been a good year, but perhaps Flagler staged this ball to add class to the third best of his hotels. Admission was by invitation only, but residents in all the hotels and local townspeople were included on the guest list. The Dining Room and Sun Parlor received fancy decorations, and Professor Brooks's full orchestra provided sprightly music to fit the festive mood. Alice Flagler, Carrie Flagler, and Dr. Anderson joined the crowd who danced in the dining room or lounged and chatted in the spacious halls and courts. The midnight supper table featured a sugar pyramid into which representations of alligators, palmettos, sailboats, the lighthouse, Fort Marion, the City Gates, and the Oldest House had been carved. Atop this pyramid rested a pineapple, which had come to symbolize the Cordova's exotic Sun Parlor.[67]

By the end of March the flow of strangers exiting St. Augustine reached full tide. Making reservations for a sleeping car north became difficult. Yet each train pulling into Union Depot brought more travelers, so the hotels remained near capacity for a little while longer. S. D. Gray, the correspondent for the black newspaper the *New York Age*, wrote: "But we shall not be surprised to awaken some fine morning to find Florida empty as the proverbial barn, for when the traveling public takes a notion to move, amenable to the dictates of fashion, it rises like one man and is off like a flock of quail."[68]

By mid-April the birds had flown. Captain Marcotte made a circuit of the hotels and commented, "To walk through the lobbies of the closing hotels, and to read the registers, is like visiting a cemetery and reading the headstones. Nothing but names and pleasant memories remain of the numbers of delightful people who have gone."[69]

The Cordova closed at noon on April 14 when Miss Georgie Smith of Portland, Maine, who had been there on Christmas Eve when the hotel opened, pulled down the American flag from atop the building. She and several others had spent the entire season in the Cordova. The next day the Hotel Ponce de Leon lowered its front gate, but not before a group of veteran hotel residents made the walk across King Street to the Alcazar, where rooms awaited them. Brooks's band provided a musical welcome in the Alcazar courtyard.[70]

On the day the Ponce de Leon closed, Alice and Carrie Flagler took a train for the North. Mary Lily Kenan may have been with them, since it was said that the party intended to stop in Wilmington, North Carolina, on the way to New York.[71]

Henry Flagler headed in the opposite direction. He and Anderson were accompanied by a group of men associated with Flagler's railroad and with the Florida East Coast Canal Company. At the time the canal company was excavating what would eventually become the Intracoastal Waterway linking Chesapeake Bay with Biscayne Bay. At Daytona, Flagler's party boarded the steamboat *St. Augustine*, which took them along the canal to Jupiter, and after a short railroad ride to Juno the party arrived at the waters of Lake Worth. As far as we know this was the first time Flagler visited the Palm Beach area.[72]

On their return to St. Augustine, the "transportation magnates" met in the Alcazar to discuss the future of rail and water transport along the East Coast of Florida. By this time James E. Ingraham, president of Henry Plant's South Florida Railroad, had joined the group. Nothing resulting from this meeting was announced to the public, but it obviously involved questions of competition and cooperation between the canal and rail lines that ran in parallel along the coast.[73]

Following the meeting Flagler left for Wilmington to rejoin Alice and Carrie on his way to New York.[74]

In New York, on the third day of July, Flagler went down to the pier of the New York Yacht Club at 26th Street on the East River to take possession of a new yacht that had just been built for him. The *Alicia* came from the works of Harlan and Hollingsworth in Wilmington, Delaware, and had been christened, appropriately, by Anne Pyle, wife of the illustrator Howard Pyle, whose pictures

Flagler College professor Tom Rahner built this model of the *Alicia*. An actor, director, and playwright, Rahner is also an occasional impersonator of Henry Flagler. Author's photo.

of knights in armor and pirates on the high seas excited boys reading adventure books and magazines of the day. One can imagine that the romantic side of Henry Flagler would have appreciated that touch. The *Alicia* represented the epitome of engineering and luxury. The vessel's sleek steel hull measured 183 feet, making it one of the largest private yachts in America. W. K. Vanderbilt's 252-foot floating palace *Alva* topped the list, with Flagler's *Alicia* coming in just behind William Astor's *Nourmahal* as the seventh longest yacht. E. C. Benedict's *Oneida* measured just 138 feet.[75]

The *Alicia's* two powerful steam engines were supplemented with schooner-rigged sails, making her one of the fastest vessels afloat. Guests enjoyed running water in their staterooms, private bathrooms, electric lights, and steam heat. Teak woodwork predominated throughout. A crew of twenty-four men served the vessel and its passengers. A steward and cook looked after meals. In the main salon, light entered through a stained glass ceiling. Ever the practical businessman, Flagler fitted up the pilot house as an office, with a desk and typewriter for his secretary.[76]

He immediately sailed the *Alicia* to Larchmont where he could show her off at the annual Fourth of July regatta. Later in the summer Flagler and his friend Anderson could be found anchored at Bar Harbor entertaining guests on board. Thereafter Flagler would sometimes forgo the commuter train ride into Manhattan, steam the *Alicia* from Mamaroneck up the sound to the Yacht Club dock, and from there take a cab to 26 Broadway. His secretary J. C. Salter might accompany him, taking dictation along the way.[77]

Flagler put the *Alicia* to practical use in July 1890, when he invited on board for a meeting his New York colleagues Charles C. Deming, treasurer of Flagler's railroad; Joseph R. Parrot, lawyer for the railroad; and Mason Young, vice president of the Indian River Steamboat Company. At this conference it was decided that Flagler's railroad would be the primary carrier of passengers and freight as far south as Titusville, and that the Indian River Steamboat Company would transport passengers and freight from that point southward. Almost certainly Flagler was laying the groundwork for a move into the Lake Worth region, a fabled land of tropical wonder that at the time had become a hot topic for development speculation.[78]

Following the close of the busy winter season in St. Augustine, McGuire and McDonald demolished the Presbyterian Manse on St. George Street to make way for the new City Building. After their workers knocked off for the day, hopeful people would pick through the rubble searching for Spanish doubloons, which were rumored to be buried under every old building—and which did turn up once during a house renovation. By November the merchants who would occupy stores on the ground floor had moved in, and before the end of the year the city quietly took possession without major ceremony. The building would serve the city down to the year 1973, when it was torn down to make way for the Columbia Restaurant.[79]

In the spring of 1890 a rumor swept the streets of St. Augustine that Flagler had become so frustrated by the opposition and obstacles thrown in his way by some parts of the local community that he had decided to abandon any further undertakings in town. Supposedly the "Minorcans" or "native element" had declared war on the "progressives class of people," led by the Flagler interests. In response, the rumor went, Flagler had halted his gravel trains and laid off two hundred workers, with further drawdowns in the offing for the future.[80]

Without a doubt tensions were simmering between the "old-timers" and the "newcomers." A major part of the trouble came from the simple, undeniable fact that older residents felt they were being overwhelmed by a tidal wave of outsiders, who usually had greater wealth and education than the natives and who unavoidably altered the status quo. A common complaint held that only those who were fortunate enough to tap into the hotel economy—boarding house keepers or hackmen, for example—benefited from the flood of winter visitors. After all, Flagler brought down his hotel workers from the North rather than hiring local people. Yet everyone saw their taxes go up as land speculation and property values increased. This aversion to higher taxes had resulted in a revolt by property owners the year before, and the city council had been forced to roll back taxes for everyone, except Flagler. Complaints about higher property assessments broke out again in the spring of 1890. One person spoke before the city council, saying that higher valuations on land were unrealistic because "the bottom had dropped out of the boom."[81]

Alarmed by this controversy, a group of old-time citizens put together a testimonial praising Flagler for his work in town. He responded in a reassuring letter, saying that he had not particularly felt an "unfriendly spirit" in town and hoped that he would enjoy good times in the future in St. Augustine while promoting it as a pleasure resort for visitors and improving the welfare of its residents.[82]

Captain Marcotte used his *Times-Union* column to lecture the "old fogies," declaring: "The great majority of the people here, and all the common sense ones, know that Mr. Flagler's improvements have pushed the town ahead at least one-hundred years, and that the advantages therefrom are incalculable, and they will accept and do all in their power to further every project of his, knowing that the city will benefit thereby." He declared that the unprogressive "croakers" would just have to learn how to find new ways to earn a livelihood, "living in the meantime on fish at high tide and clams at low tide, and bewailing imaginary misfortunes."[83]

Nevertheless, in reality Flagler's great building projects in St. Augustine had all been completed, save for the City Building and some additions to his railroad facilities. Hundreds of men were no longer needed to fill the marshes and build the hotels, churches, hospital, and railroad. In July Flagler privately wrote, "My building at St. Augustine is rapidly drawing to a close. We have recently dismissed two of our most experienced foremen, and are narrowing down the expense acct. to a minimum." In December he sent McGuire and McDonald a check for $2,000, closing his accompanying letter with a bit of frustration: "I had hoped that we would have reached the end of our big pay roll before this date."[84]

Flagler might have been experiencing some problems balancing his spending and his income in 1890. Several times during that year and the next he mentioned in his letters the need to be conservative in spending. The whole country slid into recession in the fall of 1890, causing the Republican Party to lose control of the House of Representatives in the November elections. To his cousin Thomas H. Hastings Flagler wrote, "We are in the midst of the most severe financial crisis that I have ever known, and the outlook is not at all hopeful. I fear that the stringency will very seriously [affect] travel to Fla. this winter." Flagler was forced to sell some of his Standard Oil stock to Rockefeller. This stock sale, and probably others, would prove unfortunate a decade later when Standard's securities increased dramatically in value with the advent of the automobile and the sudden creation of a huge demand for gasoline.[85]

For all his professed love of St. Augustine, Henry Flagler had indeed now refocused his attention on lands to the south, where he envisioned new challenges to be met and overcome. His wider interest southward was already manifest in the extension of his railroad down to Daytona, but sometime in 1890 or 1891 he added the Ormond Hotel in Ormond Beach to his property interests south of St. Augustine. The owners of the hotel were John Anderson, Joseph D. Price, and New York financier Stephen V. White, who had all come to this distant area in the 1870s to grow oranges. In 1887 they hired S. B. Manse, the contractor for Franklin Smith's Casa Monica, to build a seventy-five-room wooden hotel for them in Ormond on a rise of piney woods between the Halifax River and the Atlantic. It opened in the same month as Flagler's Ponce de Leon, January 1888. At that time the hotel ranked as a first-rate establishment, but it stood in an empty wilderness, which some romantics regarded as an attraction. This remote outpost of a hotel did excellent business.[86]

Flagler bought into the Ormond Hotel by purchasing White's share of the property. Anderson and Price would remain as managers. When the transaction took place is not known—it may not have been completed until 1891—but in August 1890 Flagler wrote to McGuire and McDonald that he would like to see the hotel expanded in time for the 1891 season. John W. Ingle, supervising architect in St. Augustine for Carrère and Hastings, drew up plans for an expansion that would double the Ormond Hotel's size, while McGuire and McDonald acted as builders—all seasoned Flagler men. Flagler cut his railroad's shipping rate for construction materials by 20 percent to lower the cost of building the addition.[87]

If he did not already own a part interest in the hotel by that time, he soon would. In late October he visited St. Augustine and paid Ormond a quick call. A week later he took Anderson with him for another visit. Flagler's Standard Oil associate Benjamin Brewster, who had accompanied him to St. Augustine in May 1885 when Flagler first began buying land there, accompanied Flagler on this trip as well. Brewster may have served as Flagler's expert property appraiser. By mid-November Flagler had returned to New York, and the enlarged Ormond Hotel would be so packed with visitors the following February that it would have to turn some away. All the time Flagler remained silent about his financial interest in the hotel, and the general public continued to think of it as belonging to Anderson and Price.[88]

As mentioned, during the summer of 1890 Flagler gave the Alcazar a second try as a summer resort. The complex had attractions: the Casino pool provided everyone in town with a place to cool off during hot summer days. The shady courtyard, surrounded by tall concrete walls, always remained a few degrees cooler than the surrounding streets. In the evenings visitors could stroll around the loggias and perhaps find a night-blooming cereus adding its fragrance to the atmosphere. A portion of the Brooks orchestra continued to offer serenades through the month of April. Nonetheless, Captain Marcotte could see that the spirit of the place had departed. "Despite the soul inspiring strains from Brooks orchestra, the beautiful sweet scented growths that make delicious the air about court . . . there is a lonesome vacancy here; in fact, an aching void, as it were, that gives the ladies a kind of 'Willie we have missed you' gaze."[89]

In mid-April the desk clerk gave Captain Marcotte a house count of 141 heads, a respectable number, and a month later rentals were running ahead of the previous year; but all was not well at the Alcazar. Every month the hotel lost money. In July Flagler wrote to O. D. Seavey directing him to economize for the rest of the summer by cutting staff. Seavey remained officially the manager of the Alcazar, although he and many of the Ponce de Leon's workforce had gone to upstate New York to open the new Hotel Champlain for the summer season. Reducing the quality of service went against the grain of Flagler's business principles, but so did losing money. Only as fall arrived and November passed its midpoint did Flagler find some financial news to his liking, but by then the increasing patronage at the Alcazar reflected early birds arriving for the 1891 winter season. Flagler's attempt to make the Alcazar a summer resort had failed and would not be repeated. He would later open the Hotel Continental in Jacksonville Beach as a seaside refuge for summer vacationers, but this venture likewise proved unsatisfactory.[90]

During the summer of 1890 Flagler was finally able to make arrangements to remove a nuisance that had plagued his Hotel Ponce de Leon from the beginning. Standing on Cordova Street, across the way from the rear of the hotel, stood the county jail. This decrepit tin-roofed wooden building had long been a blight on the neighborhood. Prisoners locked up in the jail created disturbances and shouted through the windows at passersby; some inmates were insane people held there because the town had no other place to keep them.[91]

In September 1889 a grand jury considered indicting the county commissioners for neglect of duty over this. Instead they issued a scathing report on conditions in the jail. "In this climate, keeping three persons in a space five feet by seven is adding torture to confinement, and is contrary to the whole spirit of our laws, and is a blot on our civilization." The jail had five small cells, in each of which two or three men were confined. Water came in buckets from a shallow well in the yard. Each cell had a pail to serve as a toilet. What little ventilation there was came from small windows. The excuse for this disgrace was the usual one: no tax money available for anything better.[92]

To resolve this problem, in March 1890 the county commissioners met privately with Flagler to hear his proposal for a new jail. The commission referred the proposition to a committee, and by April they had plans in hand for a large brick jail that would be constructed north of town facing San Marco Avenue on part of the old Henry Williams farm. Flagler would purchase the old jail lot for $5,000 and contribute $10,000 toward the cost of the new jail. Some objected to the plan, declaring that Flagler wanted "to possess himself of the whole city." The commissioners, however, were glad to accept the proposal.[93]

From his summer lodgings in the North, Flagler kept track of progress on the new jail. In early October he wrote to ask McGuire and McDonald, "How are the County Commissioners getting along with the new Jail building? Their contract stipulates that they were to remove the old building, and give me possession of the Cordova St. lot on or before Jan. 1st, and I don't want any failure."[94]

Perhaps not surprisingly, it would not be until February 4 that the first prisoners were locked up in the new jail. Captain Marcotte reported, possibly in jest, that two prisoners made an easy escape, and one of them returned to the old jail, where he felt more comfortable than in the new high-toned "Ponce de Leon" jail. The new jail would serve St. Johns County until 1953 and is today a tourist attraction known as the Old Jail.[95]

14

Hotel Life in Paradise, 1891

*The Ponce de Leon had more pretty girls in it than
any hotel I ever saw in my life.*
—Editor Charles A. Dana, quoted in *Times-Union,*
March 24, 1891

The 1891 season began at the Hotel Alcazar with a traditional Thanksgiving Day
dinner. The Alcazar would have the early arrivers all to itself for a week longer
than in previous years because Flagler decided to open the Ponce a week later
than usual. Experience had shown him that the first week's bookings were not
enough to justify welcoming guests; moreover, the New York vestibule trains
did not start running to Florida until mid-January. Although the opening was
scheduled for January 19, some eager "Ponce de Leon regulars" were permitted
to leave the Alcazar on January 17 and go into their rooms in the larger hotel.
Everyone else showed up on the scheduled day for the customary mass rush into
the building by the general community for open house. At three in the afternoon
fireworks went off on the rooftop, the portcullis rose, Brooks's band struck up
"Hail Columbia," and everyone pushed in to be greeted with cheery fires in the
Rotunda fireplaces. That evening trumpets from the towers announced the beginning of a fireworks display for the people gathered in the Alameda.[1]

Joseph White, a patron of many resorts, left a short account of his first registration at Flagler's hotel: "I had heard that one of the most interesting features of
the Ponce de Leon . . . was an elegant cushioned sofa, located just in front of the
office, the object of it being to catch guests who fainted on the presentation of
their bills." He was disappointed to observe no such sofa. He reported that the
cost of the Ponce de Leon was in line with other first-class hotels, five to twenty-
five dollars a day. Mrs. Marcotte turned this observation into a complaint: "It is
a pity that a false impression of the prices charged at this princely hotel should

get abroad through the love of show on the part of some of the guests, who come once and remain a short time; but it is so. In reality, the prices asked here for ordinary rooms are not in advance of those charged at other houses."[2]

Some guests attempted to elevate the grandeur of the hotel by pronouncing every syllable of its name and giving it a Castilian lisp: "Ponth-a-da-lion." But most fell into the habit of calling it "the Ponce."[3]

Across King Street the Hotel Cordova stood on trial. It had been a miserable failure under Franklin Smith's ownership and lagged behind the Alcazar and Ponce de Leon during its first two years under Flagler. He hoped to attract more patrons in the coming year. Flagler wrote to manager E. N. Wilson in December: "This winter will be the test of the question, and it is of the greatest importance that you so administer the Cordova that we shall get the very best results possible. I do not favor the holding of a cent so close to the eye that we lose sight of the dollar beyond, but I do favor the most rigid economy consistent with a proper administration of the house."[4]

The Cordova opened on January 28, but an "advance guard" of about a dozen repeat residents moved in a week earlier. One, a Mrs. J. D. Lyon, came with a lady friend, two manservants, a maid, and a pet poodle. Dogs normally were forbidden, but a very few women received special dispensation for special dogs. At the end of its first week the Cordova had registered one hundred guests—not a great start, but not bad either. To attract visitors inside the building, Flagler scheduled the hotel band to give concerts in both mornings and afternoons in the Sun Parlor. In the evenings many guests socialized over games of whist and euchre in the parlors, suggesting that the hotel appealed to a more sedate clientele.[5]

The Cordova had an excellent opportunity to expand its house count because up North in New York City the talk about "gayeties in Florida" had reached unheard of levels. "Never before has there been so much interest in Southern trips as this year," asserted the *New York Times*. Beginning the last week in February the Florida Specials ran every day rather than three times a week as in the past. By March all Flagler's hotels experienced days when there simply were no rooms left unoccupied. Manager Wilson at the Cordova was again forced to turn his office into temporary sleeping quarters, along with the children's play room and the round tower parlor.[6]

Mixed in among this crowd of upper-class arrivals came an assortment of bunco artists, confidence men, swindlers, and outright thieves who followed the wealthy hotel crowd to Florida with the hope of finding easy pickings amid the relative anonymity of a resort throng. They employed an ingenious variety of dodges to con unsuspecting victims out of their money.

The first step in any swindle is to identify a victim. The newspapers of that day made this easier by publishing the names and hometowns of distinguished visitors at the hotels. An elderly woman or man traveling alone stood out as a likely target. One newspaper story explained how a trio of con men located marks: "They have a pal—a woman—who works the hotels, and here obtains information as to the financial standing of the ladies' husbands, ladies generally being prone to gossip."[7]

Usually the bunco artists worked as a team, and sometimes a member of the gang would be an attractive woman. Always they were well dressed, well mannered, and well spoken. In a typical scam, for example, one partner might act simply as a lookout, the "spotter," surveying the area, perhaps the Plaza, to see if any police or hotel detectives were in sight. A second might approach the mark with a friendly greeting: "Hello! I'm Rodney Hornswaggle from Detroit, where it was ten degrees above zero when I left. Where are you from?" Such a greeting would not be out of place in a society of strangers, where one of the first things to get out of the way in any meeting was where a visitor hailed from. By the end of a short, friendly conversation the confidence man had learned that the mark was named Hubert White, that his home was in Philadelphia, that he owned a wholesale hardware company, that he was staying at the Cordova, and that his wife had recently passed away. A little later the third member of the team would approach Mr. White with the swindle. He might say, "Good morning Mr. White. I'm Reginald Cutpurse. I deal in leather goods. You may recall that we met in Philadelphia last summer at your hardware store. Say, I have a problem, don't you know. My checkbook is in my luggage, and the railroad inadvertently sent it on to Winter Park. I'll have my bag back tomorrow, but until then could I borrow twenty dollars? I'm staying in a room on the third floor of the Cordova."

Mr. White, being a good person and not wanting to admit that he did not remember meeting Mr. Cutpurse the previous summer, would lend his fellow Cordova resident twenty dollars with the expectation of getting his money back the next day, but it never came.

Or perhaps Mr. Cutpurse would explain to Mr. White that he did not have any cash on him because his wallet had been lost, but he did have a hundred-dollar Philadelphia municipal bond that was not negotiable in St. Augustine. Would Mr. White do him the favor of buying it for just fifty dollars?

Or perhaps Mr. Cutpurse had a winning lottery ticket, but he could not claim his prize until tomorrow, and unfortunately he was leaving on the four o'clock train today, but he would be happy to sell his winning lottery ticket to Mr. White.

If one of the bunco team was a beautiful woman, she might easily persuade Mr. White, alone and far away from home, to put himself into a compromising position whereby he could be blackmailed.[8]

To educate their guests, the hotels published a flier reading: "Beware of confidence men. Positively identify anyone who may approach you purporting to be an acquaintance, or the son of an acquaintance, before accompanying him anywhere. You do not care to see their books or care to witness the paying over of lottery money. Strangers approach daily with these games. Further particulars will be given at any of the hotel offices."[9]

To combat these criminals, Flagler and other hotel owners hired house detectives to keep an eye on the multitude of people circulating within the hotels. These private detectives would be sworn in by the town sheriff as deputies with authority on the premises of their hotels. The Ponce de Leon also engaged security guards, one of whom stood at the front gate and another at the rear carriage path, to give those entering the grounds the once over. Although the house detectives maintained a low profile, they were usually well known to the hotel staff.[10]

Mrs. Marcotte once published a tribute to a pair of "accommodating and very affable" Flagler hotel security men. She declared that the people of St. Augustine should thank them "for their cleverness in spotting evil disposed persons as fast as they reached Union Depot. These two modest gentlemen are familiar with most of the thieves who are apt to take a 'winter tour' to our State, consequently their services were invaluable, especially when it might be known that diamonds and other jewels lie about the bureaus of my lady's dressing rooms by the hat full."[11]

Karl Abbott, one-time desk clerk at the Alcazar, told of the day that Smiling Diamond Joe Connor, "a suave, well-set-up man about forty years old," arrived at the registration desk with "a lovely old lady about seventy-five years old with him that he introduced as his mother." Abbott recognized Connor. Not wanting to create a scene, Abbott registered him—then "hot footed it" up to the office of hotel manager William McAuliffe to explain the situation. McAuliffe, an experienced hotel hand, instructed Abbott: "Now go down to Connor and tell him Mr. McAuliffe sent you, and that Mac wants to know whether he is working or on vacation. Connor is the slickest jewel thief in the business, but his word is as good as a government bond, and if he says he is on vacation don't worry about it any more." When Abbott asked Connor this question, Connor thought about it for a minute and then said, "You go back and tell Mac that I'm on vacation." He stayed at the Alcazar for about a month without incident.[12]

Every hotel had a safe where guests could lock up their valuables, but inevitably some thefts occurred, large and small, since a multitude of strangers passed through hallways and guest rooms that were only minimally secure. Bellmen and chambermaids ranked as prime suspects whenever anything went missing. To keep tabs on the bellmen, their captain made a tabulation of every call that came in from any room, the time of the call, and the name of the bellman who went to answer the call.[13]

In defense of the employees who had access to rooms, Captain Marcotte told the story of a young couple who complained that a wallet containing money and railroad tickets had been stolen. The hotel detective questioned the hotel staff, but he suspected that the couple had simply inadvertently packed the wallet into their baggage. This turned out to be the case, and when the couple some days later attempted to use the "stolen" tickets, they were confronted with their mistake. However, the couple refused to apologize to anyone. In particular they were not going to apologize to any bellman or chambermaid.[14]

A large part of simple pilferage from the hotels resulted from guests' incorrigible desire to take home some souvenir from a famous hotel. Most of this need operated on an innocuous level. One woman staying at a boarding house paid a baggage smasher a quarter to purloin a prestigious Alcazar label to place on her satchel. Once a hotel waiter explained how items disappeared from the Dining Room: "The ladies and gentlemen don't steal them—they just kinder slip them into their pockets as mementos of the big hotel and says, 'Mr. Flagler gave it to me!'" The waiter added that the only reason the seasonal strangers didn't abscond with the lighthouse was because the lighthouse kept its lamp on all night.[15]

As might be expected, the local newspapers were reluctant to publish very many stories concerning crime and vice, since they were expected to uphold St. Augustine's reputation as a wholesome place for respectable people to vacation in safety.

Although prostitution must have been an established fixture of society in those hypocritical Victorian times, one would not know it from reading the newspapers. On one rare occasion Captain Marcotte made an oblique reference to it in the *Times-Union*: "Judge Cooper increased the city's fund this morning by collecting fines from three fast drivers and from six (ditto) women."[16]

A clandestine broadsheet calling itself *The Wonderer* (evidently published only once) took a more direct approach. It called Lorillard Villa "Gilbert's Gambling Den" and accused the grand jury of letting gamblers know in advance of impending raids so that they could take care to avoid being caught. It even identified the "Block House" on the "Block Road" as the resort of "soiled doves" and went so far as to name one of the men known to frequent this house.[17]

On the streets of town and along the seawall, small-time operators plied their trade of shell games, dice games, and three-card monte on small, portable tables that could quickly be set up and broken down. The police were criticized for letting these thimble riggers get away with it, but if arrested, the sharpsters simply paid their fines and went right back out onto the streets again. Some gambling enterprises were more elaborate. The former villa of George Lorillard once became home to a casino with a roulette wheel and poker tables. Several saloons maintained gambling rooms on the second floor. In the summer of 1889—when there was no danger of catching a well-heeled northern visitor—the town sheriff raided these gambling dens and arrested several men. The proprietors saw their equipment burned, but they easily paid the fines. Mrs. Marcotte, as guardian of public morals, criticized the city's tolerance of such gambling, but one suspects the more practical-minded men in town realized that a certain amount of this kind of recreation had to be tolerated in a resort devoted to amusements.[18]

Jay Gould enjoyed a reputation as swindler on Wall Street, but in St. Augustine he ranked as an honored celebrity. He returned to St. Augustine in early February with his daughter Helen, his wife having passed away in the time since his previous visit. Gould also brought his personal physician with him. As was expected of noted guests, he reassured the local press that he found the Hotel Ponce de Leon impressive: "It is the finest hotel in this country or in the world; and, in fact, the whole party was charmed with its magnificent beauty." He declared that he wanted to visit Ormond, take a steamer down the Indian River, and then go to Tampa and inspect Henry Plant's big new hotel there.[19]

That night, just after midnight, Gould awakened with stomach cramps. His physician decided that Gould should return to New York, and the next morning he was assisted out of the hotel and into a carriage. "He was extremely pale and haggard, and winced as if with sharp pain, when he was lifted over the hanging steps of the vehicle," reported Captain Marcotte. The press followed his progress northward, while his doctor reassured them that Gould had experienced only an "indisposition" while at the Ponce de Leon and was also troubled with a head cold. In reality Gould may already have been suffering from the effects of the tuberculosis that would kill him two years later. However, the highly publicized illness that struck Gould while he was at the Ponce de Leon may have planted seeds of doubt about the healthfulness of the place in some people's minds.[20]

The Flaglers arrived in St. Augustine on February 20, and, as in the previous year, Mary Lily Kenan came with them. At the Ponce de Leon they joined Mary Lily's oldest and dearest friends, the Wilmington railroad man Pembroke Jones and his wife Sadie. Dr. Anderson hosted a reception at Markland to welcome Mrs. Flagler and her guest Miss Kenan, who entertained the small gathering with a few songs, for she possessed a fine, well-trained voice. While Flagler busied himself with a constant stream of business matters, Alice entertained friends with little dinner dances in the hotel. At the Alicia Hospital Fair she managed one of the choice corner locations in the Casino, selling "valuable things" she had solicited as donations for the fair. Mary Lily and Sadie Jones acted as her smiling assistants, along with some other hotel society ladies. One evening Mary Lily took charge of a candy booth, according to the report of the *Times-Union*. "Miss Kenan, a sweet, pretty young lass, a typical flower of North Carolina (Wilmington), presided over the bon-bons at a little table all by herself." At the Charity

Ball, Mary Lily accompanied Alice, who wore "a gown of white toile with white satin ribbon garniture, and handsome diamond necklace."[21]

The Alcazar, with its appended therapeutic baths and huge Casino, enjoyed an excellent year. The band played in the Casino every evening, with some evenings designated as "dancing nights" for those wanting to waltz across the hardwood mezzanine. Other evenings were given over to water sports such as comic tub races. Frank Greatorex, noted sportsman-about-town, amazed audiences with a one-and-one-half somersault high dive from the second balcony. The water level was only about seven feet at the deep end, so the risk of a broken neck posed a very real hazard. Singing and cake walks by the hotel waiters filled some evenings.[22]

Of course, those so inclined could don bathing suits and test the water themselves. One young lady left this account of her routine while surveying the swimmers at the Casino pool: "About 12 every day, we sit about and watch them, and chat and gossip, and coax the men to do the most ridiculous things. The other day Creighton Webb was induced to make the leap fourteen times. I really felt sorry for him. One girl would say, 'Oh! Amuse us some more.' He would plunge again, and some one would clap their hands and he would fearlessly leap again." People who wished to enter the water but not make an exhibition of themselves could wade into the enclosed semicircular sections of the pool at either end.[23]

A patron of the Turkish bath left this description of the experience:

You plank down your little dollar and give it to the bath man. He gives you a locker in which you deposit your valuables (if you have any). He then escorts you to your dressing room. There you strip and when you emerge he will escort you to the steam room. There you spend about ten minutes walking up and down contemplating your chances for an eternal residence in Hades. The temperature is 110 degrees and in a few minutes every pore in your skin is opened and perspiration streams from your carcass. The good natured man will then come in, give you a good slap on the back and tell you that you have perspired enough.

You are then escorted to a scrub room, which somewhat resembles a section in a morgue. The attendant "lays you out" upon a warm marble slab and the rubbing process begins. He rubs you all over with his naked hands; gives you a good, solid slap every now and then which makes your delicate flesh tingle. Then he turns you over and gives your back a good rubbing from the back of your ears to your heels. He flaps you over on your back again, you are kindly requested to close your eyes, and with a sweet scented soap and good stiff brush he scrubs you energetically all over. Then he grabs you under the arm pits, hoists you to a sitting position, and gives your head a good shampoo. He then lands you on your feet and places you under the shower bath.

From the scrub room you are taken to another shower where all sorts of sprays are fired at you, one in particular is the needle spray. This produces a sensation which you will never forget. The attendant then dries you and encloses you in a Turkish robe. Then you go to the reclining room and lie there on a comfortable lounge, enjoy a cigarette, and when you feel like it you can go to your dressing room and depart.[24]

When it came to outdoor sports, the Tropical Tennis Tournament appeared to be headed for oblivion. Franklin W. Smith's son G. Stuart Smith and L. Harrison Dulles, who had managed the event in the first four years, resigned from the tournament committee. They went beyond this and spoke openly of what they said was lack of support from the St. Augustine community. "We do not feel inclined," said Smith, "to urge tennis men to travel a thousand miles to compete for prizes which contestants in a third-rate tournament would scorn." Dulles added that the lack of worthy prizes "has held us up to ridicule among the tennis men in the North." They said they would support a tennis tournament to be hosted at the Magnolia Springs hotel instead of one in St. Augustine. In response to these complaints, O. D. Seavey said he had donated exactly the amount of money that Smith and Dulles had requested for the previous year's tournament and that after the conclusion of the tournament they had returned part of what he had donated.[25]

A few days later the matter generated a physical confrontation in the Rotunda of the Ponce de Leon after an article appeared in the New York Herald questioning the social pretensions of St. Augustine, the Hotel Ponce de Leon, the Tennis Club, and the Gun Club. Several gentlemen cornered G. Stuart Smith and demanded that he write an apology and retraction for what they declared to be falsehoods. They also warned Smith to "steer clear of the hotel that he was trying to damage, as he was not wanted." The Gun Club took exception to Smith's published remark that the club "has not taken with the upper ten very well, either because of its mixed membership or because the birds are clay." The snobbish mention of "mixed membership" referred to the club's drawing upon local society rather than restricting itself exclusively to the winter season crowd. Captain Marcotte defended the quality of the Gun Club's affiliates by publishing a list of its members, leading off with Dr. Anderson; John Dismukes, the president of the First National Bank in St. Augustine; and Captain Harry R. Anderson, of the Fourth United States Artillery. The list also included winter visitors such as Henry M. Cutting, whose family made Mrs. Astor's list of the Four Hundred in the upper crust. It was indeed a mixed lot—all estimable men, but by the standards of high society certainly not all upper ten level.[26]

O. D. Seavey responded to the desertion of Smith and Dulles by taking charge of the tournament committee himself. At a meeting in the Ponce de Leon the tennis club reorganized and scheduled the Tropical Tournament for the week following the Magnolia Springs contest. More substantial solid silver prizes were offered to players. The tournament came off as planned, except for two days of rain delays. The Alcazar's courts had been converted to red clay, which, while more to the liking of the players, became sodden with rainwater. Oliver S. Campbell won a silver pitcher for his victory and had his name placed on the City Gates trophy for the third time. One more victory and he could take the huge City Gates trophy home with him. Later that year he also repeated gaining the title of U.S. Open Champion at the Newport tournament.[27]

While staying at the Ponce de Leon, some of the tennis players and other young college men put together a baseball team to challenge the best of the black players. Many of these white collegians hailed from the top colleges in America: Harvard, Yale, and Columbia. Captain Marcotte was intrigued, writing, "There are 'events' and 'affairs' of the season recorded as the best, it is seldom that such a one is reported as a game of baseball between the young gentlemen guests of the Ponce de Leon and the 'nine' of that hotel's waiters." After the game Captain Marcotte was chagrined to report: "The Black Boys 'Did Up' the Tennis Men at Baseball. . . . The game of baseball Saturday was as amusing as it was novel, and the lovers of baseball will take great comfort in reading the following scores, especially our 'colored citizens.'" The waiters had blanked the gentlemen 11-Love.[28]

Captain Marcotte's wife Anna reported that a "fashionable" crowd turned out for the game. "If they anticipated a great deal of excitement, they were disappointed, for the handsome young men were no match for their dusky opponents, at least at the bat. In vain their gallant Captain, Mr. Conkling, begged them to make an effort to work harder. It was no go; they did not make a single run, but they did themselves proud in posing." However, she astutely observed that the tennis players practiced to play tennis, while the waiters honed their baseball skills every day.[29]

In 1891 Seavey failed to find a professional baseball team to make Ponce de Leon Park its headquarters for the winter season and thus fell back on the old standby of games between the black hotel waiters. Many white visitors at the hotels turned out for these games, and once a guest put up a hundred-dollar purse "to inspire the boys." Among the players were some Cuban Giants, or as they called themselves in St. Augustine, the "Cuban Brothers."[30]

It would not be until near the end of the winter season that Ponce de Leon

Park saw what Captain Marcotte called the "first real game of baseball" between two professional teams. The Clevelands (pre-Indian "Spiders") played the Pittsburghs (later the Pirates) in a three-game series. Led by genuine superstar Pete Browning, an eccentric power hitter, the Pittsburgh team came in as favorites, and large sums of money changed hands among sporting men in the stands. However, with the series tied 1–1, Cleveland took the final contest on a chilly afternoon. Captain Marcotte noted for the *Times-Union* that there was a "good audience—large enough, it is hoped, to encourage the return very soon of the victors of this 'rubber.'" Anna Marcotte brought the ladies into the picture, writing for the *St. Augustine News* that "a large and fashionable audience witnessed the game, including many of the ladies now in the city who apparently were greatly interested, growing excited when occasion required."[31]

In the absence of a full slate of baseball games, Ponce de Leon Park became the venue for other events. The waiters from the hotels competed in a field day of events, ranging from a dash, a hurdle race, and a tug-of-war to a contest to see which waiter could find and put on his own shoes from a pile in the center of the field. Cash prizes went to the winners as an incentive. Later teams of ex-college men from Jacksonville and Palatka played a game of football, with Palatka winning by a touchdown.[32]

On a higher plateau of culture, Flagler arranged for a concert in the Ponce de Leon by the most eminent vocal prima donna in the country: Emma Thursby. Hailed as the "American Nightingale," Thursby possessed both great physical beauty and a silvery soprano voice. She and her sister Ina, both confirmed spinsters, spent every winter from 1889 through 1892 in Florida, often venturing as far south as Palm Beach but also spending weeks at a time in the Ponce de Leon. After dinner on March 28 the waiters cleared the Dining Room of tables and arranged the chairs in tiers with numbers affixed to their backs, since seating for this special event was by reservation. Professor Brooks warmed up the audience with selections from Wagner, while the waiters acted as ushers for the evening. Thursby was then forty-five years old and in exceptional form. A consummate performer, she charmed the large crowd, offering songs from both America and Germany.[33]

If Thursby gave the men someone to sigh over, statuesque, handsome William Gillette turned ladies' heads. A popular actor, he also wrote plays and then directed them. Today he is credited with making American drama more realistic and less melodramatic. A few years later he would be the first actor to portray Sherlock Holmes wearing a deerstalker cap, smoking a curved briar pipe, and muttering, "Elementary, my dear fellow."[34]

While Gillette brought realism to the stage, Archibald Clavering Gunter kept the tone of his many popular novels and stage plays at a level nearer to farce.

He stayed at the Ponce de Leon for a while and then moved over to the more modestly priced Cordova for the month of March. Born in England but raised in California, Gunter enjoyed wide popularity in his day, but his fame has not lasted to the present. He turned his visit to St. Augustine into the 1891 novel *A Florida Enchantment*, which soon also became a play. The story is a comedy of mistaken identities revolving around the Ponce de Leon's house physician and his lady love. One scene in his novel takes place in the Dining Room during one of the regular dances, when only a few dancers spun around the floor between the three rows of chairs ringed around the walls of the great hall. "It is the usual watering place hop. . . . the dancing ladies many, the dancing men few."[35]

These regular Tuesday and Friday evening dances were a new feature in 1891. Guests had to possess a ticket to be admitted, but all the hotel managers in town were given tickets to distribute. Mrs. Marcotte, who served as both social cheerleader and critic, noted that these dances were well attended but that most people merely sat and socialized, while only thirty or forty couples danced. "Whatever is the matter with the young people?" she asked. "Is the present generation degenerating?" In mid-February when the hotel was full, guests acted on their own to turn one of these regular hops into a full-scale, high-toned ball.[36]

Another noted literary figure, Charles A. Dana, attracted attention when he came to the Ponce de Leon. Dana had garnered both fame and controversy for his outspoken opinions as editor of the *New York Sun* newspaper. Naturally he was asked the standard question: "What do you think of the Hotel Ponce de Leon?" He replied, "Good gracious! It is bewildering; ahead of anything in the world except the Del Monte, in California. One thing you can say, and that is that the Ponce de Leon had more pretty girls in it than any hotel I ever saw in my life." The Hotel Del Monte had been built as a luxury seaside resort at Pebble Beach, near Monterey, in 1880, but it burned in 1887. Later it would be replaced by a modern hotel of the same name.[37]

Dana had arrived in his own private railway car. Behind Union Station ran several lines of tracks where private cars could be parked in rows while their owners tarried in the hotels. Over the 1891 season about sixty such private cars came to the depot.[38]

In St. Augustine trains arrived at Union Station every afternoon full of travelers, making St. Augustine's hotel keepers very happy. The San Marco, which had reopened after being shuttered in 1890, gained its share of the visitors and reclaimed some of its pre-Flagler eminence. However, an interesting new phenomenon became apparent: each morning's departing trains carried large numbers of travelers away from St. Augustine, not to return North but to more southerly destinations in Florida. Captain Marcotte reported, "Over one hundred people, who spent Sunday at the several hotels, left this morning for South Florida, the majority of them going to the Indian River." Fascination with the East Coast had captured the imagination of the northern strangers.[39]

A few of the visitors to St. Augustine actually came from the other direction—up from South Florida. Captain E. E. Vaill, formerly of the St. Augustine Hotel, paid a visit to look up old friends and spin yarns about his recent adventures as captain of his "floating hotel," the old sidewheel single-stack riverboat *Rockledge*, anchored far down the coast at Jupiter Inlet. He said that winter visitors to the Lake Worth area had grown to be quite a large number even though only a few scattered homes, boarding houses, and the modest Cocoanut Grove and Lake Worth hotels had been built along its shores. One Lake Worth resident, Robert R. McCormick, paid a visit to St. Augustine and stayed with his wife at the Cordova. McCormick, a Denver railroad man, had purchased a large tract of land covered with coconut palms on the east bank of Lake Worth, just a stone's throw from the stunning blue waters of the Gulf Stream. He had built a substantial "cottage" with interior woodwork of mahogany salvaged from a shipwreck. McCormick was one of several wealthy northerners who had recently decided to pioneer in this faraway tropical paradise.[40]

Some of the southward-bound travelers undoubtedly stopped at Flagler's newest acquisition, the Ormond Hotel. This novel hotel, standing in a pine forest overlooking the Atlantic, had recently doubled in size from its capacity of previous years and filled up from Friday through Monday every week when both the railroad and steamboats dropped off passengers. When General Russell A. Alger, former governor of Michigan, visited the Ponce de Leon with his family, Flagler took them down to see the Ormond. A few days later Secretary of War Redfield Proctor and Attorney General William H. Miller visited the Ponce de Leon, and Flagler put together a large party of one hundred men, including Charles A. Dana and General John M. Schofield, to visit Ormond. The secretary of war had broad powers that touched upon land developments and river and harbor improvements—things that vitally concerned Flagler.[41]

After Secretary of War Proctor's party visited Ormond, some of the group crossed the peninsula to visit the port city of Tampa, where the Navy's Great White Squadron rode at anchor in the bay. The other attraction at Tampa was a palatial new hotel, the Tampa Bay Hotel, just opened in February by Henry B. Plant. It is not clear whether Flagler traveled with the group to Tampa, but it seems most likely that he simply returned directly to St. Augustine from Ormond.[42]

In Florida lore there is an apocryphal story about Henry Flagler and Henry Plant that goes something like this: "Flagler wired Plant: 'I hear there has been a small hotel built on the west coast. How do I find it?' Plant telegraphed back: 'Just follow the crowd!'"[43]

Flagler and Plant had been business partners since 1882, and they shared a common interest in bringing northerners to Florida. Flagler's railroad was dependent upon Plant's Savannah, Florida, and Western Railroad (on the board of which Flagler served) to deliver southbound travelers to Jacksonville. In Florida they became friendly but wary competitors in developing the state. Plant had been an occasional visitor to the Ponce de Leon since its inception. He purchased land in Tampa for his own hotel just a month after the Ponce de Leon opened; Plant must have had a keen interest in seeing how his friend Flagler managed his hotel properties. Flagler showed reciprocal interest in Plant's project. In September of 1889 Flagler, Anderson, and a few other friends and business associates traveled to Tampa to see how work was progressing on Plant's already famous "huge hotel." A month later Plant and his son Morton were in St. Augustine, stopping for lunch at the Alcazar before proceeding to Tampa. After the Tampa Bay Hotel opened, Plant spent a few days at the Ponce de Leon, it was said, "trying to discover the secret of its great success."[44]

Although the Tampa Bay Hotel represented the kind of more southerly resort that drew patrons away from St. Augustine, it would not supplant Flagler's Ponce de Leon, or his later Palm Beach hotels, as the ultimate destination for the elite of northern society. In fact, the Tampa Bay Hotel proved to be a mammoth, impressive disappointment. It enjoyed only a short life under the Plant system's ownership before being sold to the city of Tampa. Today the grand old hotel building is the center of the University of Tampa's campus.[45]

Following the visit of Secretary of War Proctor and his party to the Tampa Bay Hotel in March 1891, Henry Plant brought Admiral John P. Walker and the captains of two of the White Squadron's battle cruisers up to St. Augustine to visit Flagler's hotels. When they arrived, the towers of the hotels flew strings of the flags of all nations. Flagler took the navy men on a carriage ride around town to see the sights, and in the evening threw an impromptu ball in their honor. Alice and Mary Lily were there. Afterward one of Seavey's now-well-known pyrotechnic displays lit up the heavens.[46]

Some other noted military figures visited St. Augustine that season. General O. O. Howard came to inspect the troops at St. Francis Barracks. At the time Howard commanded army troops in the Southeast, and today he is remembered as the founder of Howard University. Captain Marcotte was pleased to note that he had once met General Howard prior to the Battle of Chancellorsville. General Stephen Vincent Benét, head of army ordinance, also stopped by the Ponce de Leon. He had been born in St. Augustine and had risen from his humble Minorcan origins to a place of prominence. His grandson, also named Stephen Vincent Benét, would become a noted poet and author of the still popular short story "The Devil and Daniel Webster."[47]

The 1891 season turned out to be an excellent one for St. Augustine's hotels, the best since 1888. Although peaked early, about the first week of March, house counts remained healthy into April because miserably cold weather and an influenza epidemic up North persuaded people to remain a while longer in Florida.[48]

Flagler's right-hand man at 26 Broadway, William H. Beardsley, wrote to tell Flagler of the good reviews his hotel was receiving in New York: "Such of the 'Standard' people who have recently returned from the South, are enthusiastic in their expressions of admiration for the Ponce de Leon, and of the excellent service it affords." In his next letter Beardsley commented on the relationship between Flagler's extended work hours and the triumph of his hotel enterprises: "Am gratified indeed to hear of the success of the Hotels, it ought to be a sufficient compensation to you for 'thumping away until ten P.M.,' and I believe it is."[49]

The Flaglers and Mary Lily planned on departing St. Augustine quietly with the morning train in mid-April when the Ponce de Leon closed, but their friends would not allow them to go without some sort of gracious sendoff. On the eve of their departure the Flaglers were lured into the Reading Room, where a small party had gathered to bid them farewell. A chorus of black vocalists offered a few songs, and a table of hors d'oeuvres gave an excuse to stay and talk for a while. The next morning the Flaglers found that the railroad car *Alicia* had been decorated with flowers under the supervision of steward Bush. Professor Brooks and his band were at the station to maintain a stream of music until the train pulled out of sight.[50]

A week before he departed, Flagler had brought Thomas Hastings down from New York to confer with McGuire and McDonald on some major alterations to the Hotel Alcazar. Flagler's second-best hotel enjoyed the happy problem of being too popular. Originally intended to provide extra rooms for the overflow from the Ponce de Leon, the Alcazar had emerged as a full-fledged hotel almost from the start. Now Flagler planned to add more guest bedrooms and a larger dining room and to convert some ground-level stores into a new parlor. "The front of the Alcazar will not be changed this year," Flagler declared, "but if the contemplated changes are made and they meet the requirements of the public, next year, I may have the ellipse (colonnade) built." An elaborate crescent portico in Hastings's original design, the "ellipse" had never been added to the front of the Alcazar, leaving the building with a stark, fortress-like façade overlooking the Alameda gardens.[51]

The Alcazar closed on May 1, 1891, having been open continuously for three years. Two stalwart matrons continued to occupy their rooms until May 20. It seemed strange to many that the familiar hotel should suddenly fall silent.[52]

To expand the number of guest rooms by about forty, workmen labored

Originally the southern wings of the Hotel Alcazar rose only three stories high. By permission of Florida Historical Society.

To increase the capacity of the Hotel Alcazar, a fourth story was added to the southern wings in 1891. By permission of Library of Congress.

during the sweltering summer heat to add a fourth floor around the rear three sides of the building. They did this by cutting windows into the existing concrete parapet, adding a raised, sloping tin roof, and screening the added floor by extending a red brick balustrade between the existing chimneys. Most people looking up at the roofline would never notice the change. The ladies' parlor on the second level of the west side was divided into several bedrooms and bathrooms. Then, four shops on the ground floor below the old parlor were consolidated into one long, new parlor. The white surrounds of the doors and windows and the capitals of the fluted pilasters in the new room were trimmed with cream and gold, while the walls were painted old gold and the ceiling a "delicate" green. Opening off the parlor stood a writing room accented with red carpet and drapes. Today this parlor serves as the City Commission meeting room.[53]

To increase the size of the dining room McGuire and McDonald eliminated a small outdoor garden area behind the existing dining room. They covered this former garden space with iron grillwork and roofed it with glass panels painted pale blue on the inside to cut the sun's glare. Valencia tile in dark gray and red covered the floor. Opening this airy new extension of the dining room brought light into the whole dining area. More than a hundred people could be seated in the dining room extension.[54]

Back in the rear of the Alcazar complex, over the Casino, more sleeping rooms were added, dubbed the "Bachelors' Quarters." To connect the hotel proper more conveniently with the Casino, McGuire and McDonald built a roof over the two formerly open second-story-level walkways connecting the two sections of the building. This enclosure amounted to an admission that the weather in St. Augustine had not turned out to be as conducive to outdoor living as Carrère and Hastings had originally imagined.[55]

The final step in making the Alcazar a fully independent hotel came with the severing of the electrical umbilical cord connecting the Alcazar with the Ponce de Leon. The unsightly power lines and poles running across the Alameda were taken down. Behind the Alcazar workers erected a "dynamo building" to house two generators that would supply electricity to the Alcazar, Baths, and Casino. Altogether this amounted to about three thousand lights. Prior to this time, the Alcazar had been obliged to rely on gas lighting whenever the Ponce de Leon was not in operation.[56]

During the summer of 1891 Flagler moved to remedy an annoying shortcoming in his hotels—their reliance upon water from his artesian wells and the uncertain supply of rainwater collected from rooftops and stored in cisterns. The faint hint of sulfur that wafted from the hotel's taps and toilets indicated a lack of refinement that fell short of the perfection Flagler desired. Years earlier he had asked McGuire to survey the route from Green Cove Springs, across the St. Johns River, to St. Augustine to test the feasibility of piping the spring's water to his hotels. The great distance made this notion impractical.[57]

Flagler therefore set out to build a private waterworks to supply soft water for his hotels. This was not an entirely new enterprise for him since a few years earlier he and some other men in the town of Mamaroneck had incorporated a municipal water company to supply the village. The company bought an old mill and rebuilt its dam to create a reservoir, then piped water to residences and businesses in town. Flagler intended to do the same thing for his hotels.[58]

He hired a surveyor to locate a site where his railroad to Palatka crossed over the headwaters of Moultrie Creek. He sent a sample of the creek water to one of his scientists at Standard Oil, who reported that the only significant impurity was organic matter. Workmen cleared a forty-acre tract of all plants and vegetation to leave a bare white sand bottom, and then they threw a dam across the creek to create an impoundment of about thirty acres. A two-story house was built to hold a boiler and pump to direct water through a masonry vault filled with lime that would remove the brown tint common to Florida streams. Then the water passed through a twenty-ton filter of crushed flint stone to remove particulates. An engineer and his assistants lived upstairs in the pump house. They fed wood into the boiler to generate steam for the pumps and were responsible for ensuring that all the machinery worked properly.[59]

The purified water went into a huge iron storage tank thirty feet high and thirty feet in diameter that fed a ten-inch pipeline carrying the water four and a half miles to the hotels in town. The water tank did not need to be elevated since the level of the land fell twenty-six feet from the water plant on its way to town, and this created enough pressure to push the water through the pipeline. The water line rested in the sand alongside the railroad tracks to Union Station. From there Flagler laid pipes under the sidewalks along Valencia and Cordova Streets to his three hotels.

The system went into operation about the beginning of February 1892 and would remain in use at least until 1915. The only problem came in later years when breaks in the corroded pipeline occasionally caused washouts under the railroad tracks.[60]

Supplying food for those living in his hotels also presented Flagler with logistical challenges. Winter visitors to St. Augustine had long complained of the victuals served in local hotels and boarding houses. Tough, stringy Florida range cattle beef, seafood from the surrounding waters, and tinned vegetables imported from up North appeared on tables as standard fare. A few local farmers grew fruit and fresh vegetables for the winter visitors, but with the building of the great new hotels, their production fell far short of the volume needed. Captain Marcotte used his *Times-Union* column to entreat farmers to grow more, reporting that Flagler's hotels alone spent $35,000 on "garden sass" in a season. Hotel stewards ventured into the countryside to search out farmers and make agreements to purchase their crops. Generally Flagler's hotels fared better than most because they could afford to pay top price.[61]

Part of the problem resulted from the fact that not much farmland had been opened up in the interior. Most of the population still clustered near towns, just as in Spanish colonial days.[62]

The first major pioneer to open up a large new area for cultivation was Utley J. White, whose railroad from Palatka to Dayton Flagler had recently purchased. White had started a farm called Merrifield along Flagler's railroad to Palatka about twenty miles from St. Augustine in a region of flat grasslands, pine trees, and cypress heads that often flooded during rainy periods. People had long thought of it as a useless barren, but White recognized its potential, especially now that Flagler's railroad provided a way to get crops to market. First White dug a drainage ditch to Deep Creek (a tributary of the St. Johns) to remove standing water; then he drilled artesian wells to irrigate his crops when they needed water. By the winter of 1889–90 White offered onions, cabbage, turnips, lettuce, parsley, oats, and carrots for sale in St. Augustine. One of the men to take note was Henry Flagler.[63]

Flagler decided to start a farm of his own to supply fresh fruits and vegetables to his hotels, but he also wished for the farm to be an experimental station to see what crops would grow in Florida's soil and climate. After all, Flagler's railroad needed customers, and a thriving farming population in East Florida would mean shipping business for his road.

The person Flagler had in mind to take charge of his vegetable farm was Thomas Horace Hastings, who was described as "a man of intelligence and refinement" and also as a "city man." A personal relationship existed between Flagler and Hastings, whom he called "Cousin Tom." Flagler's grandfather Solomon Flagler was Hastings's great-grandfather; back another generation Thomas H. Hastings and the architect Thomas Hastings shared a common great-great-grandfather. The relationship may have been more personal than the distant ancestral link suggests because Flagler's father Isaac had performed the marriage ceremony in Lockport, New York, for Cousin Tom Hastings's parents. When the younger Hastings first came to St. Augustine, he served as manager of the Casino during the 1890 season.[64]

Flagler invested about $30,000 in purchasing acreage, drilling wells, and building greenhouses, tenant housing, and a small two-story home for Hastings and his family. He called the farm "Prairie Garden Farm," but when the time came to establish a railroad station there, Flagler suggested a new name to his railroad superintendent Crawford: "How would 'Hastings' do?"[65]

Hastings's first major crop appears to have been rice, suggesting that the historically wet landscape lent itself to this grain, but soon he was selling cucumbers, cabbage, onions, tomatoes, radishes, green peas, parsley, watercress, strawberries, and various other vegetables. He also tried sugar cane. Interestingly, he does not seem to have grown potatoes—which would soon become and remain Hastings's signature crop. Flagler took an interest in the operations, wished him well, and offered advice.[66]

In November 1891 Flagler came to St. Augustine with O. D. Seavey and Seavey's wife in his private railway car so that Seavey could prepare for the opening of the Alcazar and Ponce de Leon. Flagler had to attend to some business. First he paid a visit to Thomas Hastings to see how farming operations were going. Then he proceeded down to Ormond to inspect his railroad and hotel interests there. After that he turned his attention to the little settlement of San Mateo.[67]

Below Palatka, on the east bank of the St. Johns River, a handful of hearty pioneers had established extensive orange groves. They shipped their fruit out by way of steamboats, but they also wanted a link to Flagler's railroad. Back in March a group of San Mateo citizens had called upon Flagler in St. Augustine and invited him to come down to see the extent of their enterprises. Flagler took them up on their offer, and when they petitioned him for a rail extension and offered to give him land for a right-of-way, he agreed to run a four-mile spur to their village.[68]

On November 25 the normally reserved Flagler was evidently in an ebullient mood. His workers had constructed a little temporary station house for San Mateo at Flagler's workshop in West Augustine, and they loaded it on a flatcar to push it along the tracks to the rural settlement. Painters hurried to apply a coat of paint even as the train slowly rolled on its way. Dr. Anderson and Captain Marcotte came along in the *Alicia*, but just before reaching their destination Flagler got out of his private car and positioned himself inside the station house so that he would be the first to receive the welcome of the little crowd that turned out in reception. While laborers muscled the station house off the flatcar and Flagler chatted with local men, the ladies of San Mateo invaded the *Alicia* to decorate it with clusters of oranges.[69]

About this time Flagler purchased two orange groves of twelve and sixteen acres to give himself a stake in the future success of San Mateo. On New Year's Eve he would bring virtually the whole settlement to St. Augustine on a special train, give them carriage rides around town, have Seavey feed them lunch at the Alcazar, and send them home happy in the evening. A man who had been a youngster at the time later recalled that Flagler "was very fond of the little town of San Mateo. He would often sit in the orange packing house."[70]

The day after Flagler delivered the station house to San Mateo was Thanksgiving, and he hosted a private dinner for fifty friends in the Alcazar dining room, where the electric lights now drew their current from the Alcazar's own power house. The next day he departed for New York with a load of San Mateo oranges, and the hotel opened for guests. Flagler had hired the 5th Infantry Band from St. Francis Barracks to provide music in the afternoon and again in the evening for a dance in the Casino. Among the crowd were Captain and Mrs. Marcotte, with their friends Mr. and Mrs. Heade and Rev. and Mrs. Samuel Paine of Memorial Presbyterian Church. Fireworks capped off the evening.[71]

15

The Season in St. Augustine, 1892–1893

Every one in St. Augustine has the same cure for ennui . . .
"Wait till the Ponce opens."

—*New York Times* reporter, 1892

Anna Marcotte had something new for winter sojourners in the 1892 season: a sprightly little society magazine called the *Tatler*. She got the name from a copy of an eighteenth-century London coffee house gossip tabloid in Dr. Anderson's library. Visitors tarrying in St. Augustine could read about themselves and their friends in its pages, while hotel and railroad operators might advertise their services to their most likely customers. In her premier issue she stated her purpose as "recording the movements of the travelers, where they are and what they are doing, and in a pleasant, chatty manner; describe the entertainments and amusements they attend and enjoy." The *Tatler* cost ten cents a copy or one dollar for a season's subscription. Mrs. Marcotte set up her office alongside her husband's desk in the *Florida Times-Union* room on the ground floor of the Alcazar. Here she kept a register of guests at the hotels so that visitors trying to locate friends might find out where they were staying. Prior to formal balls, ladies could have descriptions of their costumes dropped off for use in stories by both the *Tatler* and the *Times-Union*.[1]

Mrs. Marcotte styled herself "editor and proprietor" of the *Tatler* and published it in Jacksonville at a prominent print shop. If Flagler had anything to do with establishing this little magazine, there is no evidence of it. In fact, during the journal's first season no advertisements by Flagler enterprises appeared in its pages, but from 1893 onward Flagler's hotels and railroad purchased full-page advertisements in every issue. As might be expected, Mrs. Marcotte acted as a cheerleader for both Flagler and the St. Augustine community, although she would occasionally scold her readers for some shortcoming she perceived in society. Nevertheless she published only morally uplifting stories in her magazine.

The 1892 season opened auspiciously, with yellow fever scares receding into distant memories and the annual migration southward by Pullman car becoming a matter of comfortable routine. The Ponce de Leon opened on January 18, while the opening of the Cordova was delayed until January 26 since by this time Flagler could reliably calculate that its rooms would not be needed until the season was well advanced. Some regulars returned for their fifth season.

A reporter from the *New York Times* recorded his impressions of January in the Ancient City: "Every one in St. Augustine has the same cure for ennui when he finds a Northerner afflicted with it early in the season. He fills his soul with the joy of anticipation, by saying to him: 'Wait till the Ponce opens; wait till the Ponce opens.' And this is so constantly reiterated in your ears that you begin to imagine that the opening of a hotel in Florida is quite beyond the run of such things. The great event occurred last Monday afternoon, and if Scott had been describing the affair he undoubtedly would have said that 'the gates flew open and the horsemen entered.' When the great iron gates leading to the court of this pet hobby of Henry M. Flagler's were thrown open, the multitudes poured in. To have seen the people one would have thought nothing short of Barnum's circus could have attracted such a crowd. . . . The report of a cannon told the people of St. Augustine and to the rest of the country for several miles around that the Hotel Ponce de Leon had opened for the season."[2]

The social calendar commenced with the nationally publicized Hermitage Ball to raise money for the restoration of President Andrew Jackson's Tennessee home. Just three years earlier the Ladies Hermitage Association had acquired custody of Jackson's long-neglected country plantation house, and they needed money to fix it up. In Florida the leader of the Hermitage cause was Ellen Call Long, "a large woman of commanding presence." Her father, two-time governor Richard Keith Call, had been the only prominent politician in Florida to speak out against secession. After the war Long had written a popular novel called *Florida Breezes* that offered a romanticized fictional history of the state. She had contacted Flagler and recruited his assistance in staging this charity event.[3]

The day of the ball Governor Francis P. Fleming arrived by train from Tallahassee in Flagler's private car, to be welcomed at Union Station by Flagler himself and Captain T. M. Woodruff, commander of St. Francis Barracks, whose troops fired a volley in salute to the governor. That evening the army band played in the loggia of the Ponce de Leon while the crowd gathered for the much-publicized event. Just after ten o'clock Brooks's orchestra struck up "The Star-Spangled Banner," and a line of costumed characters from American history processed from the East Hall through the Rotunda and up the main stairway to the Dining Room. Sprinkled among the formally dressed civilians were military men in uniform. A portrait of Jackson, draped in American flags, hung in the central archway of the lofty room. A four-foot-long model of the Hermitage, molded from white sugar and illuminated by electric lights from within, stood in the center of the supper table.

Henry Flagler received congratulations and thanks from well-wishers for his generosity in providing the accommodations for the evening, while Alice attracted attention with her ensemble: "Mrs. Flagler wore a beautiful gown of white tulle, *en traine*, the front breadth embroidered in mother of pearl and gold, the skirt finished with pearl fringe a half a yard deep, the bodice décolleté, the neck finished with white ostrich, the front embroidered to correspond with the skirt, chiffon sleeves very short and caught up with bows of broad white velvet. Similar ones with long loops finished the back of the corsage; her necklace was many strands of pearls, and a spray of marguerites formed a fillet for the hair."[4]

In a side room guests could inspect artifacts including a sword bestowed on Jackson by the State of Tennessee in honor of his victory at New Orleans, a letter written by Daniel Boone, and a candle captured from the tent of General Cornwallis at Yorktown. While looking over the Jackson relics, patrons could also talk to Alfred Jackson, son of "the faithful Negro woman who prepared the modest food for the hero."[5] Today the Ladies Hermitage Association continues to manage the Hermitage, and Alfred Jackson is prominently buried close to the tomb of Andrew and Rachel Jackson in the home's garden.

Ten days after the ball, Flagler departed in his private car for Tampa to see for himself the completed Tampa Bay Hotel and to talk with Henry Plant. Dr. Anderson went along to keep him company, while Miss Grace Dobson of Boston, one of Alice's companions for the season, accompanied Alice on the trip. A few days later Flagler and Anderson traveled to Charleston for a business meeting with the Plant system's railroad men. As a director of Flagler's railroad, Anderson went as both business partner and friend. The conferees gave no statement to the press, but their meeting certainly centered upon the major railroad building and consolidation projects that both Flagler and Plant would soon embark upon in Florida.[6]

During the rest of the winter season Flagler busied himself with his development projects, making short trips to Ormond and back to New York City, but he found time to entertain the railroad car builder George M. Pullman and his family. Flagler lent Pullman his motor launch for a cruise on the waters of the Matanzas, and at least once he and Alice sat through the Sunday evening sacred concert in the Rotunda with Mrs. Pullman. The Pullmans spent more than a month at the Ponce de Leon.[7]

Mary Lily Kenan did not accompany Alice to St. Augustine in 1892 as she had for the previous two seasons, but a small circle of ladies kept Alice company while at the Ponce de Leon. Alice and her husband appeared at the Washington's Birthday Ball and at the Charity Ball for Alicia Hospital, and Alice presided over a booth during the Hospital Fair in the Casino. She was assisted in her booth by Anne Lamont. Mrs. Marcotte wrote of her: "Miss Lamont, of New York, a bright clever young woman, wore a beautiful and becoming gown, and was one of the belles of the evening."[8]

Anne Lamont came to St. Augustine because young Harry Flagler, with whom she was quietly involved romantically, was also in St. Augustine. Harry had just returned from an extended tour of Europe. Anne could be considered "the girl next door," since her home stood one block south of the Flagler residence on Fifth Avenue. Her father, Charles A. Lamont, had made a fortune in sugar refining and stock speculation before he either committed suicide or accidentally fell from an upper story of his home in 1873. Anne's widowed mother enjoyed a reputation as a sweet, Christian woman and as "one of the queens of society." If her mother was a queen, Anne reigned as a princess. While they stayed at the Ponce de Leon, Alice gave Harry and Anne a reception where their friends could visit the couple, who were not quite yet acknowledged as a couple.[9]

Out of doors the national pastime, baseball, continued to occupy the minds of local citizenry and winter visitors alike. In December 1891 W. R. Harrington, the young manager of the Minneapolis baseball club, came to St. Augustine and, with the backing of O. D. Seavey, managed to organize a five-team semi-professional league for the state of Florida. Tampa, Jacksonville, Orlando, and Ocala joined St. Augustine to form the league. Each team signed visiting professionals from the northern baseball associations to augment the local talent on its roster. Jimmy Ryan, outfielder for the Chicago Colts, and George Kurtz, another northern professional, joined Harrington's team. The season opened with a New Year's Day game in Ponce de Leon Park against a team from Orlando. Nearly a thousand people filled the stands. Captain Marcotte captured the spirit of the occasion: "The game showed a lack of practice, but it was full of redeeming features, the best being the Orlando's right fielder who wore a cowboy hat which alone was worth the price of admission, while to see him 'play ball' was a sight indeed." St. Augustine trounced Orlando 16–7.[10]

A black against white game attracted a large crowd a month later. Harrington's St. Augustine team took on the Hotel Ponce de Leon team, some of whom played for the Cuban Giants in the summer. In fact, the *Times-Union* advertised the game as the Harringtons versus the Cuban Giants. Captain Marcotte wrote that the large crowd in Flagler's stadium "were treated to the finest exhibition of ball playing that has been given in the South in many a day." The Giants led until the bottom of the eighth inning, when St. Augustine's Ryan singled to bring in Kurtz with the winning run.[11]

The black waiters' baseball teams of the Ponce de Leon, Cordova, and Alcazar also played games among themselves, and these assumed more importance for ball fans as the state league fell apart in March.[12]

In the absence of enough baseball action, men who admired horsemanship sponsored equestrian tournaments in Ponce de Leon Park. These contests were popular at many resorts during this time and attracted large crowds. The core event, "heads and rings," was a military cavalry exercise. Horsemen would race past three poles with canvas "heads" fixed to their tops and then pass a pole with a brass ring suspended from it. The riders would slash with a saber at the heads and then attempt to spear the ring with the tip of their saber. Accuracy and speed won the competition. The other events lacked the glamour of the cavalrymen's saber work. There were egg-and-spoon races, contests to gather potatoes and deposit them in a barrel, and even one event in which a rider had to sew a button on a shirt while racing against his fellow competitors.[13]

While festivities occupied guests during the winter of 1892, Flagler became involved in the affairs of the Presbyterian Church. He first took up the pleasant task of completing its interior decoration, and this brought him back into contact with some of the artists who had contributed to the ornamentation of his hotel.

In the years following completion of the Hotel Ponce de Leon, Carrère and Hastings from time to time continued to collaborate with mural artist Herman Schladermundt on various commissions, usually the homes of rich men, including William Rockefeller's country home in Tarrytown, New York, which was constructed in 1888–89.

In January 1892 Schladermundt and George W. Maynard made a proposal to Carrère and Hastings for decorating the interior of Flagler's Memorial Church. The heart of their proposal was that they would "richly ornament" the central dome of the church in embellishments that would be "symbolic or illustrative, and ecclesiastical in character." In the four main quadrants of the dome, they suggested, Maynard would paint images of the four evangelists. They also advanced a plan to cover the large blank arched wall at the north end of the central nave with "a fine biblical figure composition, by Mr. Maynard."[14]

Flagler expressed an interest in going ahead with this proposal and suggested adding white crackled glass to improve the look of the windows. Schladermundt and Maynard responded with a second proposal to place decorative stained glass windows in the church. "We propose to furnish geometric pattern in leaded work for the dome and side windows, the central portion of each window being enriched with appropriate motifs. The rose window, we prefer to elaborate, but mainly in the richness of the color."[15]

For some reason nothing came of these propositions at the time. Schladermundt would supply the stained glass windows a few years later, but it would be only years later, in the 1950s when the church underwent a major renovation, that symbols of the four evangelists took their places in the dome, perhaps inspired by the original Schladermundt-Maynard proposal, which had remained in the church archives.[16]

The probable reason for the failure to follow through with the Memorial Church project may have been that Maynard and Schladermundt received a better offer: a chance to contribute to the World's Columbian Exposition in Chicago in 1893. Instead of returning to St. Augustine in 1892 to resume working for Flagler, Maynard and Schladermundt hastened to Chicago to take part in preparations for the world's fair. Some familiar New Yorkers were also on the scene. Maitland Armstrong, who probably had a hand in creating the Tiffany glass windows in the Hotel Ponce de Leon, held a position on the fair's planning committee. Hastings's former employer and friend Charles F. McKim designed the Agricultural Building, with Maynard and Schladermundt assuming responsibility for the hall's mural embellishments. Maynard created his usual straightforward symbolic female figures, while Schladermundt executed the borders, fine details, and lettering. This description of Schladermundt's part in the murals' creation suggests that he had filled a similar role in the decorations of the Hotel Ponce de Leon.[17]

A few years later, in 1895, another project brought some of Henry Flagler's artists together once again: Boston's Public Library. The firm of McKim, Mead and White served as architects for the building, while Schladermundt painted the decorations in the dome and Virgilio Tojetti, who had done the ceilings in the Ponce de Leon's Grand Parlor, painted the ceiling of the ladies' reading room.[18]

The following year Herman Schladermundt married Anna Gardner of Cleveland, Ohio. Her father George W. Gardner had once been mayor of Cleveland and was one of Henry Flagler's old friends. Flagler first met John D. Rockefeller in George Gardner's office back in the days when they were all involved in the business of trading in grain.[19]

The Schladermundts settled down in a large cottage in the community of Lawrence Park in Bronxville, New York. Their modest house included a large, two-story-high studio where Schladermundt could work on projects. Lawrence Park had been planned as a refuge for creative people seeking to escape the turbulence of New York City yet wanting to be within commuting distance by way of the New York Central Railroad. Among Schladermundt's neighbors were Otto Henry Bacher, who had done some of the etchings for Flagler's promotional book *Florida: The American Riviera*, and Wall Street reporter Edwin Lefevre, who would later write a penetrating magazine feature on Henry Flagler. Schladermundt's friend John Carrère would sometimes bring his family by to socialize. In an 1899 Lawrence Park "lawn fête" to raise money for consumptive working girls, the women who served as hostesses were Anna Schladermundt, Frances Folsom Cleveland, and Caroline Hastings, the wife of Thomas Hastings's brother Frank and a niece of E. C. Benedict.[20]

In 1895–96 Maynard and Schladermundt created their best known works of art when they joined other leading American artists in contributing to the Jefferson Building of the new Library of Congress. Maynard filled one hallway ceiling with allegorical figures, and in one of the main side pavilions he reproduced the symbolic characters he had earlier used in the Hotel Ponce de Leon: Adventure, Conquest, Discovery, and Civilization. A careful look at Discovery reveals to the eye of a seafarer that Maynard had corrected an error in his first attempt at this emblematic female: in the Ponce de Leon version she incorrectly grasps a ship's tiller in her left hand, but in the Library of Congress version she has shifted the tiller to her right or starboard hand: the steering side.

In the Jefferson Building project Schladermundt oversaw execution of the mosaics and stained glass. He personally designed the stained glass windows in the dome above the main reading room. In the semicircular openings he placed the official seals of all the states in the Union; however, he revised each seal to give it more artistic composition and proportion. A correspondent writing to the *New York Times* raved over the effect on the state seals: "In the library they were taken up by the artist and redesigned carefully without changing in the slightest their meaning or historic character."[21] The state emblems in the Library of Congress are reminiscent of the crests of the Spanish kingdoms on the walls and ceilings of the Hotel Ponce de Leon, supporting the theory that these elements of the Ponce's decorations are also from Schladermundt's hand.

Unlike the decoration of the church's interior, Flagler's second involvement with the Presbyterian Church in the winter of 1892 involved much more negative emotions and interactions. A controversy over the pastorate of Rev. Samuel D. Paine dragged Flagler into an unpleasant dispute over church personalities and politics.

Samuel D. Paine had been active in the St. Augustine community as early as 1882, when he arrived to organize Olivet Methodist Church and build its unique chapel on stilts over Maria Sanchez marsh. Born in England, Paine had run away as a boy to join the British Army and had served in the artillery during the Crimean War. Emigrating to America, he went into the Union Army and served as an artillery lieutenant in a Maine field battery, engaging in bloody action at the Battle of Fredericksburg. For the rest of his life, as a veteran military man, he would give lectures on his experiences in these two wars. In St. Augustine, at least for a while, he supplemented his income by serving as part-time manager of the Florida House, a hotel that did not have a bar or serve wine at meals.[22]

In May 1890 Rev. Edwin Mitchell, who had preached at Jennie Louise's memorial service, departed St. Augustine in poor health for travel in Europe, leaving Memorial Presbyterian Church without a pastor. During the summer Flagler corresponded with church board members Dr. Anderson and DeWitt Webb about a replacement. Paine was then serving at a Methodist church in Jacksonville, but he came to preach what must have been a trial sermon at Memorial Presbyterian Church in August. In October the church announced that Paine had accepted a call to become minister, and on November 1 he preached his first sermon before a crowd that included Flagler.

His topic was human violation of God's laws, but his message specifically condemned "the tremendous curse of intemperance." The nation spent billions of dollars on intoxicating drinks each year, he declared, that could be better used to build schools and strengthen homes. Flagler reported to W. G. Warden that "he gave us a good sermon," without commenting on the thrust of the address. However, Flagler may have harbored some reservations; he added that Paine's appointment was for one year only, giving the congregation time to test his fitness. In a show of generosity, Flagler presented Paine with a "very handsome silk gown" to wear in the pulpit.[23]

Flagler was himself a man of temperate drinking habits, and he certainly understood the suffering caused by drunkenness, which truly rose to the level of a national disgrace in those days. Yet he also believed in personal choice and personal responsibility. Flagler knew well that most of the patrons of his hotels wished to be able to share a bottle of good wine at dinner and that some desired stronger drinks. Perhaps as a display of both tolerance and disapproval, Flagler placed the bar of the Hotel Ponce de Leon inconspicuously on the ground level beneath the Dining Room in an alcove that patrons entered from the carriage drive.[24]

At the same time that Paine preached from the pulpit against strong drink, his wife Lizzie was elected president of the local chapter of the Women's Christian Temperance Union, an organization dedicated to the legal prohibition of alcoholic beverages. However, Paine's reformist impulses extended beyond this issue. He became president of the local Humane Society, an organization championed by Mrs. Marcotte, and spoke in favor of strong enforcement of the state's new law against the slaughter of Florida's plume birds to satisfy the vanity of ladies' fashions. The Grand Army of the Republic, the organization of Union veterans, appointed Paine its chaplain at its national convention in Detroit. In his address to the convention he spoke against the move to segregate black veterans from their white compatriots.[25]

Such outspoken convictions got Paine into trouble with some of his parishioners at Memorial Church. The issues and attitudes that spawned opposition can be guessed from an anonymous letter published in the *St. Augustine Evening News* praising one of his sermons, delivered with "great earnestness": "Mr. Paine told us that he was not preaching to please us but to make us realize the great responsibility resting on each of us. . . . It is very rare in this day and generation to hear a minister preach so fearlessly as Mr. Paine. It has become about the universal custom among ministers (especially in rich churches) to sheer around the commonest sins even, and be very careful not to tread on any one's toes, for fear of losing caste and friends in church, but thank the Lord there is one man left that has the courage to state his convictions from the pulpit." The article went on to say that Paine opened communion to everyone, not just Presbyterians.[26]

Later, after he had left Memorial Church, Paine said in an interview with a northern newspaper: "Don't let us spend all our time attacking the saloon and forgetting to attack the club house of the rich man. Let us have the courage to attack the rich man who drinks as well as the poor man."[27]

The difficulties some members of Memorial Church had with Paine can be surmised: he preached too earnestly, he opened communion to non-Presbyterians, and he spoke too strongly and too often on the temperance issue.

Paine hoped to stay on at Memorial Church past his one-year contract. He bypassed the church session and wrote directly to Flagler asking to have his term extended for another year as "simple justice" while he sought a calling from another church. He added that some of his enemies in the church were under the impression that Flagler opposed his remaining. However, if he truly wished for Flagler's help in holding onto his position for a time, he should not have added, "I don't want to be kicked out of this pulpit as every other minister has been."[28]

Flagler replied emphatically that Paine had been hired for one year only, and his contract was extended only until the first Sunday in March. Paine's suggestion that his term be lengthened so that he would have time to search for a position at another church struck Flagler as absurd. "It seems to me very clear, that what you call 'simple justice' is nothing but selfishness."[29]

When Paine preached his farewell sermon on February 21 a huge crowd turned out to hear what he would say. In his habitual intense way, Paine defended his views on temperance and denominational tolerance and said that, to his regret, his pastorate had caused dissention in the church. (A short time later he would blame his leaving on "a small opposition that annoyed me.") Both Paine and some of his many friends in the congregation were moved to tears by the emotion of the moment. He concluded by asking those assembled to rise and sing "My Country 'Tis of Thee." Afterward Paine was surrounded by well-wishers, and he was allowed to take another month to vacate the manse.[30]

While Paine served at Memorial Church, his son Ralph D. Paine studied at Yale, making a reputation as both scholar and athlete. He gained selection to the prestigious secret leadership fraternity Skull and Bones. While visiting his parents in Florida, Ralph anonymously wrote a little promotional pamphlet for Flagler's railroad entitled *The St. Augustine Route*, which Captain Marcotte praised as "just splendid." A few years later young Paine would join with his friend and fellow writer Stephen Crane and future Florida governor Napoleon B. Broward running guns to Cuban rebels in Broward's seagoing tug the *Three Friends*. After that, he covered the Spanish-American War, the Boxer Rebellion, and World War I as a newspaper correspondent. In 1908 he authored an article for *Everybody's Magazine* on the building of Flagler's railroad to Key West. Before his untimely death in 1925, Paine had authored forty books and many magazine articles. His father had passed away in Jacksonville in 1909 as an honored and well-regarded member of the community.[31]

As the 1892 season approached its conclusion, rumors of a typhoid fever epidemic raced about the city and through northern communities as seasonal vacationers returned home from St. Augustine to tell their stories. The same thing had happened on a lesser scale in 1891, when a report surfaced in Boston of "numerous deaths at the Ponce de Leon" due to unhealthy conditions. Captain Marcotte had responded at the time by writing that in four years only one guest had died in the Ponce de Leon and of causes unrelated to his stay at the hotel. He added that in the same years only one person had died in the Cordova—of heart disease—and three visitors had passed away in the Alcazar, and "each of these three people came expecting to die—in fact, they would have been disappointed if they had not."[32]

In 1892 reports of unhealthy conditions had circulated as early as February, but Captain Marcotte assured local readers of the *Times-Union* that John B. Walker, editor of *Cosmopolitan* magazine, had visited the Ponce de Leon and Cordova and had found them perfectly healthy. Then on April 5 Elizabeth Park of New York died while staying at the Hotel Cordova. Dr. Fremont Smith certified that she had died of typhoid fever. This death inspired a spate of articles in northern newspapers describing a typhoid outbreak in St. Augustine and other parts of Florida. Supposedly Mrs. Park's death had caused a dozen people to depart the Cordova hastily.[33]

Soon thereafter a visitor from Newport, Rhode Island, died after returning from St. Augustine, and others were reported ill upon their arrival home in the North. Suspicion centered upon the Cordova, but all the Flagler hotels fell under a cloud. The newspapers explained that the hotels had been built on "recently made ground" or on "sandbars little above the water level." The old idea that digging in the soil released sickness came up again. A "prominent society man" declared authoritatively: "The bad sanitary condition of St. Augustine has frightened a great many people. No less than three deaths this spring from typhoid fever are due to the vile drainage of St. Augustine. There were more people there this season than the hotel could take care of, and unless the hotel accommodations and the drainage is improved these people will simply go to California or Europe, instead of Florida, in the Spring."[34]

That, of course, was the great fear among St. Augustine's hotel keepers. The city Board of Health issued a statement saying rumors that the Cordova had been closed or condemned by the Board of Health were "absolutely false." The *Times-Union* denounced "the senseless rumor that this famous hostelry 'will not be opened next year.'" However, the departure of the Cordova's genial manager E. N. Wilson at the end of the season to take permanent charge of a downtown hotel in New York City was an omen that did not bode well for the future of the Cordova.[35]

Dr. Joseph Porter, state health officer of Florida, made an investigation and issued a preliminary statement: "It is to be regretted that cases of typhoid fever have occurred in St. Augustine during the past few weeks, but whether the producing cause was imported or of local origin has not been definitely settled." Captain Marcotte made a tabulation of deaths in the first four months of the year and found that only one death was attributed to typhoid, while three others were diagnosed as "typho-malarial fever." All these deaths occurred among strangers visiting town, and it was likely that the origin of their disease lay outside St. Augustine, he asserted.[36]

In his typical way, Henry Flagler hired one of the country's leading experts on epidemic diseases to conduct an inquiry into the deaths in St. Augustine and the sanitary conditions of his hotels. The man he picked was John Shaw Billings, who had been the lead physician of the Union's Army of the Potomac during the war. At the time Flagler hired him he was professor of hygiene at the University of Pennsylvania and librarian for the surgeon general's office, in charge of compiling information on every disease known in the United States. (Later Billings would lead the committee that drew up the specifications for the proposed New York Public Library, which would be designed by Carrère and Hastings.)

On June 13 he made his report to doctors Andrew Anderson and Fremont Smith, who were identified as "Physicians of the Hotels Ponce de Leon, Alcazar, and Cordova." He concluded that no cases of typhoid fever could be attributed to anything in Flagler's hotels, nor to locally produced ice, milk, or vegetables examined by him. He said there had been about twenty-five reported cases of typhoid fever and that probably only seven people contracted the disease in St. Augustine. The source of contagion could not be identified and was probably random. The *Times-Union* commented editorially that the number of people with illnesses was remarkably low considering that forty thousand people had passed through St. Augustine during the season. It added that the typhoid had shown up when the winter strangers arrived, and cases ceased with the end of the season.[37]

Again, as was his wont, Flagler did not let the matter go at that. He hired A. C. Abbott, Philadelphia's chief of the Bureau of Health, to inspect the water and sewer utilities of his hotels. Other than some suggestions about improving the water trap barriers in the drains of the refrigerators, he found nothing to criticize in the hotels' systems. Sewage drained through large pipes Flagler had installed beneath Treasury and King streets to empty into Matanzas Bay beyond the low tide mark. Disposing of raw sewage in this way was standard practice across the country at the time.[38]

Still not satisfied, Flagler brought Dr. Billings back to town in October, and he went over the hotels again with Dr. Anderson to make sure of the hygienic conditions. Billings gave his approval. Then Flagler hired Philip Prioleau, engineer for the City of Jacksonville, to oversee the mapping of every pipeline in each of the hotels so that future maintenance would be made more efficient.[39]

During the following season no local person in a public position mentioned the scare of the year before, but menus in Flagler's hotels bore a little note at the bottom reading, "The water used in the Hotel Ponce de Leon for drinking and culinary purposes is distilled, and absolutely pure." However, as had been rumored in the spring, the Hotel Cordova did not open as an independent hotel in 1893.[40]

While Flagler busied himself with his hotel and railroad affairs in northeast Florida, far to the southwest his partner, friend, and rival Henry Plant continued developing plans of his own. On March 15 James E. Ingraham, the tall, handsome president of Plant's South Florida Railroad, set off from Fort Myers with a small expedition of surveyors across the Everglades to Miami. They arrived twenty days later, "dirty and half starved," to be welcomed on the banks of the Miami River by Mrs. Julia Tuttle, who fired a cannon in salute and raised the American flag over her place at old Fort Dallas. Ingraham had made the acquaintance of Mrs. Tuttle two years earlier at her family home in Cleveland. At that time she told him of her plans to relocate to Miami, which she did in 1890, joining her father, who had moved there in 1871. Mrs. Tuttle purchased the 640 acres around the old Seminole War fort and later added more acreage in the vicinity. She told Ingraham, "Someday someone will build a railroad to Miami, and I will give to the Company that does so one-half of my property in Miami, for a town site. Perhaps you will be the man." Ingraham replied, "Miami is a long way off from

Tampa, but stranger things have happened, and I may yet call on you to fulfill this offer."[41]

Plant may have sent Ingraham on his expedition with the idea of running his railroad from Fort Myers to Miami, or he may simply have been considering the prospects of draining the Everglades to create farmland. Plant already owned a spur rail line running from Sanford in the middle of the state to Titusville on the Atlantic coast; it would have been easy for him to turn south and continue in the direction of Miami, although his route to Miami would have been more circuitous than Flagler's. Perhaps Plant and Flagler had already made a gentlemen's agreement that confined Plant to the western half of the peninsula, but at any rate Flagler aimed to run his own railroad directly southward as rapidly as it could be done to preempt as much real estate as possible. As it turned out, Ingraham would make it to Mrs. Tuttle's homestead a few years later but as vice president of Flagler's railroad, not Plant's.

James E. Ingraham joined Flagler's inner circle in October 1892. He was almost twenty years younger than Flagler, having been born in Wisconsin in 1850 and having come to Florida in 1876 as general manager of Henry Sanford's interests. He laid out the town of Sanford and helped President Grant turn the ceremonial first shovelful of dirt for the South Florida Railroad during Grant's 1880 tour of the state. When Henry Plant purchased the railroad a few years later, Ingraham became his right-hand man in Florida and helped develop Tampa. A tall, sandy-haired man with a huge mustache, Ingraham exuded an affable air of competence. Flagler and Ingraham had gotten to know each other because of Flagler's service on the board of directors of Plant's Investment Company. When it became clear to Flagler that his railroad would span the East Coast of Florida, Flagler hired Ingraham away from Plant. At first Flagler put Ingraham in charge of recruiting immigrants to Florida, but soon Ingraham's wide experience put him in the center of most of Flagler's enterprises, other than the hotels. Interestingly, Ingraham was the only man to work for all three of Florida's "Henrys": Sanford, Plant, and Flagler.[42]

At the same time that Flagler hired Ingraham he also took Joseph R. Parrott on board his growing enterprises as his principal legal expert and frequent advisor. Born in Maine in 1859, Parrott had studied law at Yale, where he rowed on the crew. Ralph Paine, the minister's son who had also rowed at Yale, described Parrott as "broad-shouldered, square-jawed." He came to Florida in the mid-1880s as lawyer for the Jacksonville, Tampa and Key West Railway, which he took over as receiver when that road went bankrupt. Flagler appreciated Parrott's railroad experience and his capacity for hard work—although in later years Parrott's prodigious capacity for labor would seriously stress his health.[43]

In March 1893 Flagler put both Ingraham and Parrott on the board of the

Jacksonville, St. Augustine and Indian River Railway along with his son Harry and Dr. Anderson.[44] In hiring Parrott and Ingraham, Flagler had flanked himself with two chief lieutenants who would carry his dreams all the way to Key West and for the remainder of his life.

When business journalist Edwin Lefevre studied Flagler's executive managers during a 1909 visit to Florida, he discovered that Flagler maintained a veil of privacy between himself and them, and yet they all strongly identified with Flagler. As Lefevre found:

> When deciding disputes or settling any manner of business matters, [they] always act, not for "the good of the company" or its profit, but invariably as they think Mr. Flagler would personally act.... The *esprit de corps* is amazingly strong. He gives them a free hand. By putting them on their honor, he also puts them on their mettle, though, after all, their chief motive-force appears to be personal loyalty.... He has had these same men in his employ many years. It may show that his judgment in the first instance was good. But you are surprised to hear that he never once praised them to their faces: never expressed pleasure or gratitude in their wisdom or success or fidelity to duty; never patted them on the back, never called them by their first names. And yet they all love him![45]

At the time that the 1892 season ended in St. Augustine, Flagler's railroad terminated at Daytona, as it had for the past three years. However, he now set off in earnest southward. The first leg of his extension reached only fourteen miles to New Smyrna, but people in Jacksonville and St. Augustine were already thinking big: "On to Biscayne Bay." The goal, or so ran the speculation, was to reach deep water where ships going to and from South America could dock. Real progress could not keep up with speculation, and it would not be until September 25 that Captain Marcotte rode the first passenger train to New Smyrna in order to report the event to the world. The mayor wired the news back to St. Augustine over the telegraph line that ran alongside Flagler's railroad.[46]

While Flagler's railroad builders, mostly black men and Italians, labored on the fifty-eight-mile link from New Smyrna to Rockledge, Flagler added the shallow-draft steamboats *Courtney* and *Santa Lucia* to handle passengers and cargo on the Indian River and Lake Worth. To span the seven-and-a-half-mile land barrier between the Indian River and Lake Worth, an enterprising company had built a narrow-gauge railway called the "Celestial Railroad" because it linked two landings known as Jupiter and Juno. Farther south still, at the lower end of Lake Worth, beginning at the settlement of Lantana, the Dade County commissioners had built a wagon road south to Biscayne Bay.[47]

With the expansion of his rail line, Flagler purchased three big new locomotives from the Schenectady works to supplement the two that had been handling his traffic. They pulled new cars painted metallic yellow—"Flagler Yellow" it would soon be called. Captain Marcotte declared that the fast new locomotives made the trains look like "streaks of yellow lightning." The cars had the words "East Coast Line" and "St. Augustine Route" painted on their sides. However, the new official name of Flagler's railroad became the Jacksonville, St. Augustine and Indian River Railway, to indicate that it now stretched beyond the Halifax River. The new symbol of the railway became a tropical pineapple, that native American fruit symbolizing opulent hospitality. Flagler assigned James McDonald the task of building train stations along the route south. Over the next few years this project would eventually take him away from St. Augustine and carry him to Miami and Nassau.[48]

Flagler decided to abandon the original service and repair shops of his railroad in South Jacksonville and build new facilities in St. Augustine. This required more filling of the San Sebastian marshes north of Union Station to create dry ground for the new buildings. One of the most useful new facilities was a round house with a turntable that allowed the orientation of locomotives and cars to be reversed on the tracks. Union Station gained a forty-foot extension on its west side to accommodate more passengers. To provide housing for the workmen and their families who would be employed in the shops, McGuire and McDonald began building modest cottages in the vicinity of the station. These neat, simple houses rented for twelve dollars a month. Within a few years a neighborhood of cottages lined the streets. Flagler's railroad shops would become the single largest year-round employer in town for most of the next century.[49]

According to Flagler's account books, the total cost of filling the San Sebastian marshes came to $137,238. His wharf on the south side of King Street added another $6,052 in costs.[50]

Flagler came down from New York in November 1892 to inspect the progress on his railroad down along the Indian River, but then he retraced his travel as far as Savannah for a meeting of the board of directors of the Plant system. A few days later Henry Plant and other railroad men came to stay at the Alcazar. While Plant was in St. Augustine Flagler took him to Sunday services at Memorial Presbyterian Church. After the Plant men departed, Flagler and Ingraham went off on another tour of the Indian River region.[51]

It would not be until well into the next winter season that Flagler's railroad finally reached Rockledge. When the first train from Jacksonville to Rockledge arrived at Union Station in St. Augustine in February 1893, Henry and Alice Flagler, accompanied by Henry Plant and New York's Tammany boss Richard Croker, were on the platform to wish it well on its journey. The Ponce de Leon band gave it a musical sendoff, and every steam whistle in the vicinity blew its top. Railway superintendent William Crawford's private car was attached to the train, but he rode in the locomotive cab with the engineer all the way. Back in the passenger cars Captain Marcotte and the other travelers enjoyed a lunch served by the Ponce de Leon waiters. It took seven hours and twenty minutes to make the 177 miles from Jacksonville to Rockledge. That put Flagler's railroad halfway to Miami. At the time a traveler could go from New York to Rockledge by railroad, Rockledge to Jupiter by steamship, Jupiter to Juno by rail, Juno to Lantana by steamboat, and Lantana to Lemon City on Biscayne Bay by stagecoach. A route from New York to Miami, such as it was, had been opened. Flagler himself made the trip to Miami twice, covering the last leg in what he called a "mule cart— fortunately that had lumber springs under the seat."[52]

In 1892–93 all of Florida was presented with a chance to showcase its progress and prosperity at the World's Fair scheduled for Chicago in celebration of the 400th anniversary of Columbus's discovery of America. Unfortunately, Floridians responded to this opportunity with a lackadaisical spirit, almost missing out on the occasion altogether. To the extent that Florida did participate in the World's Columbian Exposition, credit belongs to two men: Arthur C. Jackson and Henry Flagler. Jackson provided the enthusiasm and drive, while Flagler provided the money.

Flagler may first have become interested in the fair in April 1891 when the president of the fair's commission, Michigan's ex-senator Thomas W. Palmer and his wife stayed at the Ponce de Leon. Flagler escorted them on a trip to Ormond to show off his part of the state. In its session that winter the state legislature failed to appropriate any money for planning an exhibit, but in the fall Arthur Jackson took it upon himself to promote Florida's participation in the fair. Jackson had prepared Henry Plant's exhibit for the Universal Exposition in Paris in 1889, and thereafter Jackson had become a freelance promoter of Florida. He announced that the Florida building for the Columbian Exposition should be a half-scale model of St. Augustine's Fort Marion, complete with real Spanish cannon and guards in Spanish uniforms. However, when the legislature met again in January 1892, they once more failed to appropriate any money for the fair, and a convention of county commissioners also came up with no plan for funding. At this time conservative "Bourbon" Democrats maintained a firm hold on state government, and they valued low taxes above all else.[53]

Seemingly undaunted, Jackson pushed ahead. He came up with a new idea to raise $200,000 by publishing a *Gazetteer* featuring stories about the state and its products. Each person, company, city, or county wishing to be included in the volume could purchase a page for $200. Jackson must have consulted with

The Florida Pavilion at the 1893 World's Fair in Chicago reproduced St. Augustine's Fort Marion on a smaller scale. Flagler put up most of the money to make sure Florida would be represented at the fair. Author's collection.

Flagler prior to making this proposal because Flagler immediately pledged to pay $20,000 for a hundred-page historical and descriptive narrative on Florida. However, Flagler made his offer contingent upon others coming up with another $200,000.[54]

During the summer Jackson traveled to Chicago to make arrangements for the Florida pavilion with World's Fair managers, and he also visited Flagler in New York to obtain a fresh pledge of cash if the state could somehow raise just $20,000. At this point it had become evident that the *Gazetteer* idea simply was not gaining traction; instead Jackson now offered to sell space in the Florida building to counties by the square foot. St. Johns County commissioners took the lead by voting to pledge $1,000 to buy space for a county display. The county's association was headed by O. B. Smith, editor of the *Weekly News*, and included Mayor W. S. M. Pinkham, state senator F. B. Genovar, president of the board of trade W. W. Dewhurst, and Captain Marcotte.[55]

With less than four months until the fair's official opening on Columbus Day in October, Flagler simply advanced Jackson $10,000 to build the Florida building. Florida's miniature Fort Marion was made of pine wood, plastered-over with a coquina shell mixture, and it looked quite exotic amid the conventional white-painted state exhibit buildings surrounding it. In the end, according to Jackson's public accounting, Flagler provided $15,000 for the exhibit, Florida counties came up with $7,000, and various other private donors added a little more. The state legislature gave nothing.[56]

Although the official inauguration of the fair came in October 1892, it would not be until May 1893 that the crowds could enter the grounds to ride the Ferris wheel and witness the exotic dancing of Little Egypt. In the spring of that year civic leaders urged Floridians to fill the building with examples of the state's products. Anna Marcotte editorialized in the *Tatler* encouraging greater support of the Florida building, which she wrote might as well be called "Mr. Flagler's Fort." She added that too many citizens "quietly fold their hands and allow others to perform their duties for them . . . in fact, the majority of Floridians want blessings forced down their throats."[57]

Jackson toured the state, going as far south as Lake Worth and Biscayne Bay, to rustle up displays of unique products, such as that region's pineapples. The phosphate miners contributed a large pile of phosphate pebbles that occupied the center of the little fort's courtyard. Flagler's gardener Richard Dale shipped dozens of Spanish bayonet plants to decorate the grounds and then went to Chicago himself to oversee all the plantings in and around the building. Thomas Hastings shipped samples of his rice crop. Ponce de Leon studio artist Marie a' Becket provided a painting, but it went into the Women's Building. Overall, however, the Florida exhibits were embarrassingly skimpy.

"The display is so completely disgraceful," wrote one Florida visitor, "that you feel utterly wilted in the presence of it." He declared that Florida's legislators should be hog-tied and brought to witness the state's shame. At least the Florida display had no rustic Negroes or Seminoles for gawking fairgoers to view, although elsewhere the fair featured assorted "aboriginal" people on exhibit.[58]

In St. Augustine the 1893 season started in grand style with the opening of the Hotel Ponce de Leon. It had become the custom of many local citizens to appear at the hotel on opening night for dinner with the newly arrived guests from the North. One table near the entryway was occupied by members of the press, including Captain and Mrs. Marcotte and Miss Abbie Brooks—Sylvia Sunshine. She had begun spending her winters in St. Augustine around 1888, and at that point everyone learned that the author of *Petals Plucked from Sunny Climes* was actually the modest, retiring Miss Brooks of Atlanta, Georgia. (Only years later would it be discovered that Brooks was also a pseudonym and that she had other secrets to conceal.)[59]

Miss Brooks lived in genteel poverty on the fringe of polite society. However, in 1892 she had somehow managed to finance a nearly year-long trip to Seville, Spain, where she hired a copyist to translate documents from the earliest days of the Spaniards in St. Augustine. In this she followed Buckingham Smith as the second researcher to delve into the Archives of the Indies and begin laying the foundation for a scholarly history of Florida. She hoped to bring out a book of documents but could find no publisher willing to undertake such an esoteric volume. Meanwhile, from time to time Brooks published short articles in the *Florida Times-Union* based on her research.[60]

In 1894 she got into a debate with George R. Fairbanks of Fernandina, the acknowledged authority on Florida history, about the location of the first settlement of St. Augustine. Marcotte had found a letter of Don Thomas Alonzo Las Alas from 1600 that referred to "old St. Augustine" being on Anastasia Island until it was washed away by the sea. Thus, concluded Brooks, Pedro Menéndez must have landed on the island and built his fort and village there. Fairbanks replied that the settlement had to have been on the mainland since the standard Spanish accounts of the founding did not describe the first landing place as an island, and in addition, Menéndez marched overland to attack the French at Fort Caroline, so his home base had to have been on the mainland.[61]

Fairbanks was correct. However, Brooks had been the first to uncover evidence that St. Augustine had at one time been located on Anastasia Island. This fact was subsequently lost to historians until the 1970s, when new documents uncovered in the archives in Spain enabled historians to put the pieces of the puzzle together. Menéndez had indeed established his beachhead on the mainland, but it did not remain there for long. After a few months Indian hostility forced the Spanish to retreat to Anastasia Island, and the settlement remained there until 1572, when the town was reestablished on a site just south of the Plaza. To this day no archaeological remains of a sixteenth-century Spanish colony have been found on the island, and it is probable that it was indeed washed away by the sea.

Unfortunately for Brooks, she was unable to find any patron to support her research or promote dissemination of her findings. She offered her translations to the State of Florida for $2,500, but the state legislature declined to make the purchase.[62] Years later in 1909 she published *The Unwritten History of Old St. Augustine*, but this pioneering book had virtually no impact on the standard histories of Florida.

The hotel community experienced a scare during the night of January 24 when the roof of the Alcazar Casino caught fire, and crowds of people turned out in the streets in whatever clothes they could throw on to witness the excitement. It all started about 2:30 in the morning when a night watchman making his rounds saw an unusual glow coming from the room of a hotel porter in the Bachelors Quarters on the fourth floor above the Casino pool. He woke the sleeping occupant of the room, and they found a small fire around the gas light fixture in the ceiling. When they pulled on the fixture, a whole section of ceiling fell in, revealing an extensive fire that had been smoldering for a while in the crawl space under the roof. Someone called the fire department, and the men living in the Casino came running with buckets of water, but smoke soon drove everyone from the top floor of the Casino.

St. Augustine's two fire engines arrived quickly and began shooting streams of water high up on the roof. The hotel's own steam pumps that normally lifted water up into the water tanks on the roof were attached to fire hoses to augment the firefighters' apparatus. A telephone call to Jacksonville brought one of their fire engines to St. Augustine riding on the back of a flatcar. The train made the run in thirty-seven minutes, the fastest time ever recorded over the thirty-six-mile route.

O. D. Seavey took up a position at the double doors that led from the Casino's mezzanine ballroom into the Baths section of the building. Seavey directed the firefighters' efforts, since he knew in detail all aspects of the building. The crowded warren of small employees' rooms on the fourth floor above the Casino became an inferno, but if the fire could be confined to the Casino wing, the rest of the Alcazar complex could be saved. That was how it turned out. The solid concrete walls proved the building's salvation, limiting fuel for the fire to the pine wood in the roof, ceilings and floors. The firefighters gained the upper hand relatively quickly, and before dawn most of the excitement was over.[63]

During the fire the Alcazar's kitchen had supplied the firemen with coffee and sandwiches, and in the morning the dining room opened for patrons as if nothing had happened. The hotel band played in the courtyard later in the morning. Captain Marcotte informed his readers that his office in the front of the Alcazar remained open for business, and electricity for the lights was operating as usual. Seavey took out a big advertisement in the Times-Union stating that the fire "did no damage whatever" to the hotels or the Turkish and Russian Baths. "Each hotel is accommodating guests without interruption."[64]

McGuire and McDonald's work crews were out the day after the fire cleaning up the debris. For the rest of the season events usually held in the Casino ballroom, such as the Alicia Hospital Fair, were moved over to the Cordova dining room and parlors. This could easily be done because in 1893 the Cordova's kitchen and dining room were not opened to serve meals to guests. In fact, the Cordova did not operate as an independent hotel but served only to provide rooms for the overflow of guests from the Ponce de Leon and Alcazar when the season reached its height in March. Those staying in the Cordova dined in either the Ponce de Leon or the Alcazar.[65]

By March the reconstruction of the Casino had progressed to the point that swimmers were allowed back into the pool. The south side of the pool area had been boarded up because that was where the greatest damage had been done and where reconstruction took the longest. Remarkably, this fire would be the only one of any consequence to occur in any of Flagler's hotels throughout their long history—a tribute to their concrete construction and the quality of their utility systems.[66]

The embers of the Casino fire had hardly cooled when the Flaglers arrived in St. Augustine. Mrs. Marcotte reported that they both appeared to be in good health. "As usual, Mr. Flagler is overwhelmed with business as soon as he arrives." Alice threw herself into the social whirl, going boating on the Matanzas, dancing at a ball in the San Marco for the benefit of the hospital, attending a hop at the Cordova, and later taking charge of a booth at the Trinity Church fair. Her companions at these affairs were usually Julia Marshall Talbot and Eliza Ashley, one of Henry's favorite cousins. Eliza and her husband Eugene Ashley, a lawyer of Lockport, New York, were close friends of Henry Flagler and would play increasingly important roles in his personal life in the next few years.[67]

Mrs. Talbot and Mrs. Ashley were among the circle of ladies who hosted an elegant farewell tea for Alice Flagler in the mezzanine of the Ponce de Leon overlooking the courtyard. The Flaglers were about to leave their suite in the Ponce de Leon and move into their private residence Kirkside. Bowers of ferns and flowers, sprinkled with electric fairy lights, decorated the fireplaces, and musicians from the hotel orchestra provided music as Alice's friends filed past to offer their congratulations upon the completion of her new home. Alice had recently spent much of her time planning the move to Kirkside. Her husband was not there the share the moment since he and Henry Plant were off on an ocean cruise to evaluate the tourist potential of the Bahamas and Jamaica.[68]

Construction of Kirkside had begun months earlier in July 1892 on a lot that encompassed all the land west from Memorial Church to Ribera Street. The far

Flagler's home, Kirkside, stood just west of the Presbyterian Church. The house was demolished in the 1950s. From the collection of the St. Augustine Historical Society Research Library.

end of the grounds preserved the last remnant of wild trees and undergrowth from rustic Lovers' Lane. Some of the coquina stone from the old Presbyterian Church on St. George Street, which was torn down at this time, went into garden walls at Kirkside and into stone pillars erected outside Memorial Church. In a departure from the Mediterranean themes they had employed so far, Carrère and Hastings designed the home in Colonial Revival style, painted all white with green shutters and a huge front portico with a classic Greek pediment supported by four tall fluted Ionic columns. Flagler had chosen this style partly as a matter of practicality: a wooden house could be constructed quickly in time to be occupied in the 1893 season. One can guess that like other wealthy, patriotic Americans of the day, he also wished to identify himself with the spirit of the American Republic. However, Carrère and Hastings incorporated an open-air patio at the rear of the building to take advantage of the mild winter days. Flagler planted delicate Caribbean palms in this atrium. The layout of the house featured large, open ground-floor rooms that would be ideal for entertaining, while upstairs were several bedrooms with adjoining baths and sitting rooms to accommodate long-term guests. Pottier and Stymus supplied the interior hardwood trim and decorations. Captain Marcotte was given a tour of the home and pronounced his approval: "There is nothing in the decorations or the furnishings that is not in keeping with the simple but correct taste of the master and mistress of 'Kirkside.'"[69]

When Flagler returned from his trip to the Bahamas and Jamaica, Mrs. Marcotte welcomed him, saying he was "looking very well and slightly bronzed from the sea voyage." Flagler seemingly weathered the elements better than Anderson, who returned "badly sunburnt, but in his usual happy frame of mind, having captured a great cocoa bean from which cocoa and chocolate are manufactured." Henry Plant had invited railroad and hotel men from all across the country on an eleven-day excursion to Nassau and Jamaica with the intent of showing them the potential for tourism in those places—and drumming up business for Plant's steamship line. Flagler declared himself enthusiastic about the possibilities and would follow up on this voyage of exploration very quickly.[70]

To celebrate St. Patrick's Day Flagler hosted a stag dinner at Kirkside for Catholic Bishop Moore, Father Edward McGlynn, and Reverend Smythe of Memorial Presbyterian Church. Father McGlynn, a controversial and popular advocate of liberal reforms, had been preaching to large audiences in Florida while on tour from New York. Flagler had given McGlynn use of his private railroad car for a trip to Rockledge.[71]

While the men monopolized Kirkside, Alice hosted a spur-of-the-moment dance and dinner in the west alcove of the Ponce de Leon's Dining Room. Even though the invitations to fifty of Alice's friends went out only on the day of the event, the women and their escorts dressed up formally for the occasion. Mrs. Marcotte's *Tatler* put an exclamation point to the evening: "The hostess and many of her guests wore pearls of such unusual size and beauty that the function might, with propriety, be called the pearl dance. There are no ornaments worn by women more beautiful, and their adoption by the ladies on this occasion was a happy thought. Mrs. Flagler's pearls are a number of rows perfectly matched and of beautiful coloring, and were in perfect harmony with her gown, a blue *royale* silk, with a rich luster, the low corsage profusely trimmed with exquisite *pointe* lace, the same material falling over the high puffed sleeves, the skirt, with a demi-train, with a fall of the same lace finishing it. Her *coiffure* was high, with diamond ornaments."[72]

Outdoor amusements during the 1893 season continued some traditions, dropped others, and added new twists.

The Tropical Tennis Tournament was canceled because of competing tournaments in Magnolia Springs and Tampa, both sponsored in conjunction with their winter resort hotels. The date available for St. Augustine's tournament conflicted with other social events in town. However, local tennis aficionados went ahead and organized their own "Free and Easy" handicap tournament and played a full schedule of matches on the Alcazar courts.[73]

Baseball continued to struggle to establish itself. George Gore, who was reaching the end of a fourteen-year career as center fielder for the Chicago White Stockings, New York Giants, and St. Louis Browns, organized a St. Augustine team to play all comers. Local boys made up most of the squad, but a couple of northern professionals were also in the lineup. At least twice they played the Cuban Giants, continuing the tradition of interracial contests. However, the attempt to form a state semi-pro league was not repeated, and Captain Marcotte wrote that their games drew only "fairly well."[74]

As in previous years, equestrian tournaments brought some spectators to Ponce de Leon Park, and several gentlemen attempted to introduce the high-toned sport of polo to St. Augustine. Chief among the organizers of the Polo Club who gathered in the reading room of the Alcazar were several Flagler men: O. D. Seavey, James Ingraham, James McDonald, Dr. Anderson, Louis Colee of the Transfer Company, George Gore of the baseball team, and Captain Marcotte—an old infantryman. Lacking polo clubs anywhere else in Florida to challenge them, the gentlemen divided into Blue and White teams to play contests among themselves.[75]

The event that drew the largest crowd to Ponce de Leon Park was a race between professional bicyclist John S. Prince and a relay team of two horses. In a day when every man was expected to know and appreciate horseflesh, a race with a man mounted on a newfangled mechanical wonder tapped into deep emotional reservoirs. Prince had been born in England and first entered professional races on the Continent before emigrating to the United States in 1884. An impressively tall, lean athlete, he made a good living and became famous touring America and racing against both other professional bicyclists and sometimes horses. In St. Augustine, Jack Alexander, a sportsman of note, challenged Prince to a twenty-mile race against two of his Kentucky thoroughbreds. Prince would ride on a quarter-mile wooden oval laid out in the ballpark, while the horses would run outside the track, giving the human/bicycle tandem a shorter course to run. However, the horses would race alternate miles, affording them a chance to take breathers. Two local Minorcan boys acted as jockeys.

As was the custom of the day, many of the spectators in the stands openly placed bets on the race. The relay team of horses took the lead from the start and led by as many as three laps midway through the race, but in the second half of the race Prince began to wear down the ponies. He caught the horses entering the final mile—at which point more bets were laid down—and in the final half-lap he sprinted away to victory. This result led many in the crowd who had lost money to cry fraud, declaring that Alexander had held his horses back. For his part, Alexander complained that the race referees had misled him by telling him that Prince still lagged a lap behind entering the final mile. Controversy raged.[76]

Three weeks later man and horse got a rematch, and, as might be expected, interest in the race rose to an even higher pitch. Bookmakers did a land office business. Even the ladies got in on the wagers—bestowing their esteem on the horses, it was said, not the man. A huge crowd packed the grandstand and bleachers for the race. This time Prince did not allow the horses to build much of a lead, but he could never draw them back, and they stretched their margin to almost a minute and a half by the end of twenty miles.[77]

This intriguing contest of man versus beast proved the grand finale for Ponce de Leon Park. The baseball stadium had not proven a worthwhile enterprise. Except in its initial season, the park had not been able to attract a professional baseball team for winter training, and games among local teams did not draw large paying crowds. Only a generation later would state league baseball become a big attraction in communities across Florida. The various other exhibitions put on at the stadium were not worthy of the fine facilities. At the beginning of the 1893 season Seavey had written to railroad superintendent Crawford asking for reduced fares to bring in fans from Jacksonville. Seavey explained that he was trying to keep expenses down at the park.[78]

Flagler decided that the ballpark property, with its location next to the railroad station and workshops, could be put to better use. In April workmen dismantled the grandstand and moved it to an empty field south of King Street on the San Sebastian River waterfront. The grandstand would be rebuilt but not the tall board fence that had surrounded the field. Many of the boards from the fence would be used to build an extension to the Transfer Company's stables. Thereafter a simple picket fence circled the outfield, and there would be no attempt to attract professional players to St. Augustine. Flagler used the former grounds of the ballpark to build additional modest cottages for his railroad workers and ran Almeria Street right over the former location of home plate. After 1893 baseball virtually disappeared as a spectator sport during the winter season.[79]

By the winter of 1893 everyone believed that Flagler's railroad would push on to Lake Worth in the very near future. Clearly his interest in the region had been growing for several years. In February 1890 his railroad builder John Maclennan and canal digger George F. Miles stayed at the Hotel Lake Worth in Palm Beach. A month later, E. N. Wilson, manager of the Cordova, stopped by the same hotel. Flagler himself visited Palm Beach in April 1890.[80] His hotel expert O. D. Seavey vacationed on the lake in December 1891 prior to his annual opening of the Ponce de Leon. Mrs. Seavey brought back a coconut blossom stalk as a memento of their trip to the tropics. Thus Flagler had thoroughly familiarized himself with the Lake Worth area by 1893.

However, there was a huge obstacle in the way of Flagler's progress. So far his railroad building had been rewarded by the State of Florida with large grants of land for every mile of track he laid, but south of Rockledge the state had run out of available land. All the state-owned property had been promised to the company digging the coastal canal. But as it turned out, the canal company had run out of cash about this time. Its directors turned to Flagler as the source for an infusion of new capital, and Flagler was only too happy to oblige—at a cost of half the company's land grants. This was a good deal for the canal men because the railroad, although it would compete with the canal in transporting people and cargo, would increase the value of the company's remaining half of the state's land grants. On those terms a new company, the Florida East Coast Canal Company, was organized in St. Augustine in March 1893, with Flagler as president. He would continue as president only until 1896.[81]

With the way cleared, Flagler got busy. In February and early March James Ingraham spent three weeks in South Florida looking over lands for a railroad right of way.[82] After returning to St. Augustine for a brief visit, Ingraham turned around and went south again with Flagler as his traveling companion. They were met at the northern head of Lake Worth by Albert Robert, a recent Yale graduate who had set himself up as a real estate agent. Young Robert took Flagler and Ingraham by naphtha launch to the home of his parents Mr. and Mrs. Frederick Robert, wealthy socialites who spent their summers in Saratoga and had built a substantial winter home on the lake. The next day Flagler met with the leading citizens of Lake Worth at the Palm Beach Yacht Club to make a proposal: if they could raise a subscription of $30,000, he would have his railroad on the shores of the lake by the following January. Emma Gilpin, one of the locals, wrote in a letter, "The Florida Mogul has come at last, is now on the lake about his railroad and hotel property—and everyone is in a fever of excitement."[83]

While Flagler and Ingraham were in Palm Beach the local newspaper, the *Juno Tropical Sun*, reported that the McCormick home and coconut grove had been sold to Arthur C. Jackson, the World's Fair commissioner, who was in the area soliciting exhibits for the Florida pavilion. Jackson was said to be planning on making the McCormick place his home. In reality, the purchaser of the McCormick property was Henry Flagler. Jackson, who owed Flagler a big favor because of Flagler's support for the World's Fair, had evidently made a "straw purchase" of the property to conceal Flagler's interest in the McCormick place. Flagler was at the same time buying up surrounding properties and no doubt wished to disguise what he was doing as far as possible to keep prices from skyrocketing—which they already had. Everything suddenly came into focus when it was announced that Flagler had purchased two hundred acres of land, including McCormick's, with frontage on both Lake Worth and the Atlantic Ocean, and that he would build a hotel on this property. He had also purchased fifty acres on the west side of the lake that would become the heart of the new town of West Palm Beach. Albert Robert, who managed these purchases quietly and astutely, had pulled off a major coup for his client.[84]

To celebrate his triumph, Flagler and Alice gathered up a trainload of friends and business associates in St. Augustine and traveled to Palm Beach to see the site of his newest inspiration. Anderson, of course, came along, as did Ingraham and George F. Miles, whose dredges were digging the Intracoastal Waterway canal. John D. Maclennan, the railroad builder, brought his wife Georgiana, who was the daughter of Flagler's sister-in-law Julia Harkness York. McGuire and McDonald were also in the party; Joseph McDonald would relocate to Palm Beach to supervise construction on site. The party totaled twenty-five or thirty.

They arrived at the Celestial Railroad's landing at Juno with a cold northeaster whipping up whitecaps on the lake, and some must have wondered about South Florida's reputation for balmy weather. After spending the night in Palm Beach's best hotel, the Cocoanut Grove House, they awoke to a fine spring day. That evening the Robert family hosted a moonlight reception at their house and grounds. The reporter for the local newspaper wrote, "The dress suits of the gentlemen and gowns of the ladies foretold the social future of our quondam 'paradise.'" Flagler showed some blueprints of his hotel to the assembled gentry, an indication that his plans were already well advanced. After some singing by a trio of ladies and a few bites of supper, the gathering broke up, with some guests walking home along sandy paths under the coconut palms, while others took to boats on the water to head home. The community newspaper opined: "In the near future Palm Beach will be the garden spot of the world."[85]

Even as the men in their swallowtail coats and women in their gowns celebrated, workmen were already grubbing up palmetto roots and cutting down palms to clear the ground for the five-hundred-room hotel Flagler planned. It would be called the Royal Poinciana, for the trees that bloomed with red canopies during the summer. McDonald brought his wife and children down and took over the Cocoanut Grove House as his headquarters. (That hotel would burn to the ground in October.) In St. Augustine he put out word that four hundred men were needed to construct the hotel, while railroad builder Maclennan advertised for a thousand workmen. Flagler had promised the people of Lake Worth a railroad and a hotel within ten months, so there was no time to waste.[86]

The extension to Lake Worth constituted the largest single increase in his railroad mileage so far attempted. That summer Maclennan had to position more than a thousand men, more than a hundred mules, and dozens of pieces of building equipment along the route. He built temporary commissaries to feed and supply the workmen. It took six weeks for supplies to reach the work sites from the North. Maintaining the numbers in the workforce became a constant battle, since a steady stream of men deserted their jobs on a daily basis. Most of the laborers were black men, but some were Italians, and even a band of Swedes joined the work. One can hardly blame those who gave up on this arduous work. One of Flagler's foremen reported: "It is a fight all day long with the clouds of mosquitoes, and when it clouds and rains is simply torture continually."[87]

Back in St. Augustine, by this time the dramatic transformation in the pattern of winter visitation to Florida had become a major topic of conversation among both visitors and local business and civic leaders. The writer Julian Ralph noted: "An unexpected peculiarity of the great watering place is that it is growing to be more and more the custom for the winter visitors to spend a large part of their time traveling." Anna Marcotte wrote, "We have never had so many guests in one season before, and, it would be safe to add, so few season guests." She advised her northern readers to "stop and rest a bit" in St. Augustine; but her suggestion failed to resonate. The winter "stranger" of days gone by had become the modern "tourist," skipping from place to place on the new rail network in search of another novelty.[88]

The 1893 season closed at the Ponce de Leon with a gala concert by the Brooks orchestra in the Rotunda. A large crowd in buoyant spirits turned out for the event, which was a "request" evening when the musicians played music selected by the hotel guests. The Flaglers arrived late because they had been enjoying dinner at Kirkside with their new friends the Robert family of Palm Beach. At Flagler's request the orchestra repeated their opening number, the soulful intermezzo from Pietro Mascagni's new opera *Cavallera Rusticana*, which was a smash hit at the time and, unlike so much nineteenth-century music, has remained a popular standard down to today. Other requests included an up-tempo xylophone solo and the rousing brass tune "March of the Salvation Army." However, as the evening went on the mood grew melancholy. Everyone joined in singing "My Old Kentucky Home" and the popular ballad "You'll Remember Me," which they repeated three times. Then the crowd started an impromptu chorus of "To Champlain we will go, with Seavey we will go," sung to the tune of "A Hunting We Will Go." Some of the guests intended to follow manager Seavey to the Hotel Champlain in upper New York for the summer. Captain Marcotte ended his account of the evening by saying, "'Auld Lang Syne' brought the audience to its feet and 'Good Bye' was in order, and so closed the season of '93 at the Ponce de Leon.'"[89]

The concert made a fitting conclusion to the Hotel Ponce de Leon's sixth season, for an era was coming to an end in the great hotel's history. Its grandest days were already behind it. The next season the Hotel Royal Poinciana would open in Palm Beach, and the glory of being the ultimate luxury resort of the nation would shift southward. Flagler would never again attempt so magnificent a structure as the Ponce de Leon: the Royal Poinciana would be built of wood, with few artistic pretensions. But the wealthy elite took to it in numbers that would soon dwarf those formerly attracted to St. Augustine. Flagler's first hotels in Florida became victims of his success in opening up South Florida. Yet the Hotel Ponce de Leon would always remain the flagship of the Flagler hotel system and would outlast its newer sister houses to the south.

16

After the Ball Is Over,
1893–1895

Just think what a fruitful field a resort hotel is for drawing
on characters to fill a society play.

—Musical producer Charles H. Hoyt, *Washington Post*, 1894

After the Ponce de Leon closed for the 1893 season the Flaglers remained at Kirkside for another ten days since Henry had some loose ends to tie up before departing north. Most evenings they entertained friends and business associates at dinner. Henry Plant passed through, and Flagler took him down to the end of the rail line, which by then had almost reached Eau Gallie. This settlement on the Indian River would soon become the shipping point at which building materials for the Royal Poinciana would be transferred from trains to barges for transportation south. Then on April 29 the Flaglers boarded their private car *Alicia* to depart for New York. A crowd of well-wishers turned out to bid them goodbye.[1]

O. D. Seavey left St. Augustine a month after the Flaglers, his departure delayed by the illness of his wife Caroline, who had been running a fever for weeks. Shortly after they went north, word came that she was not expected to recover from her illness, but soon she and her husband made it to the Hotel Champlain for the summer, and a second report indicated that Mrs. Seavey was slowly gaining strength. Then in late August while escorting a tour group to Montreal, Canada, O. D. could not be located as the group disembarked at the train station. Mrs. Seavey was whisked off to a hotel without being told the news of her husband's disappearance. Rail yard authorities mounted a search and found Seavey lying unconscious beside the track outside the station. He had evidently fallen from the coach's landing as it approached the station, breaking his right arm and lacerating his head. Flagler telegraphed word to McGuire in St. Augustine, and he gave the news to Captain Marcotte to share with the community. A week later

O. D. Seavey, the Hotel Ponce de Leon's manager, designed a knife for use in eating oranges. It had a curved blade that was sharp on one edge and serrated on the other edge, with a forked tip for extracting seeds. Author's photo. By permission of Beth Rogero Bowen.

Marcotte reported that Seavey was recovering nicely: "'Os' always lands on his feet." Both Seaveys would return to St. Augustine in December for the coming season, but Mrs. Seavey was now described as an "invalid."[2]

The first task for Flagler's workmen during the summer of 1893 would be completion of repairs to the Casino. Six fire hydrants were installed in the corners of both levels of the Casino. These were connected to the artesian well and the powerhouse's steam pumps. In an effort to minimize the risk of future fires, the original gas fixtures in the Casino were removed and a whole new system of electric lights was installed. The entire Alcazar complex received new electrical wiring, with the wires enclosed in brass conduits to eliminate the danger of sparks from "crossed wires."

With almost eight hundred electric lights gleaming off the Casino's pure white walls, the interior took on a much more brilliant aspect than before. The whole Alcazar assembly of buildings totaled two thousand lights. By August the plasterers and painters had finished their work, covering up the damage from the fire and from the placement of electrical conduits. When the roofers had installed new courses of red tile and blue slate atop the Casino, everything emerged better than it had been originally.[3]

The pioneer electrical system of the Ponce de Leon, now seven years old, also received a complete updating, with new switches and circuit breakers and wires enclosed in conduits "to be on the safe side." Altogether this required 150,000 feet of brass tubing, installed by a team of more than eighty workers. The number of individual lights increased to four thousand. Visitors noticed the increased luminosity in the Rotunda and Dining Room, where a row of lights held in plaster lions' heads ringed the rooms. The original wagon wheel chandelier hanging from the center of the Dining Room vault came down. It had been intended as a temporary fixture anyway and had never illuminated the murals on the ceiling satisfactorily.[4]

During the late summer and fall two hurricanes struck St. Augustine. The first hit at sundown on August 27, pushing down trees and taking shingles off roofs. The Flagler buildings escaped relatively unscathed, except for the Presbyterian Church, which lost several windows. The pomegranate atop the eastern pillar of the City Gates toppled off. The second, a lingering four-day storm in early October, flooded the city with ocean water to a depth never seen in modern times. The already high tides of the fall equinox period rose over the seawall, and waves crashed directly against the walls of Fort Marion. Orange Street became a canal connecting Matanzas Bay with the San Sebastian River. The waves lifted boats and docks over the seawall and deposited them on Bay Street, dislodging some of the granite capstones of the seawall. Water pushed into every building along Bay and Charlotte streets. The relentless ocean spray covered plants all over town

The Ponce de Leon's Dining Room was first lighted by a temporary circular chandelier, but this was later removed and lion's head sconces were installed on the walls. By permission of Library of Congress.

with a killing layer of salt. The pomegranate on top of the west pillar of the City Gates came down.[5]

James McGuire was away in New York conferring with Flagler when the storm blew in, so Annie McKay, as next in the chain of command, went into the streets during the gale, directing workers to the various Flagler buildings. Alicia Hospital, with its waterfront location south of town, suffered the worst flooding. Again the hotels experienced only minor harm since floodwaters, not high winds, did most of the damage.[6]

Wreckage from the storm littered the streets—and much of the wreckage consisted of the cypress blocks that had been used to pave the streets five and six years earlier. When water rose over the pavements, the wood simply floated loose. On Bay Street at the foot of the Plaza the blocks washed away in all directions. Boys went around collecting the blocks and stacking them in mounds along the sides of streets. When workmen put the old, worn, and decayed blocks back in place, the resulting surface endangered the ankles of anyone trying to walk over the streets. St. Augustine returned to the old practice of dumping oyster shells into the worst of the potholes.[7]

Harry Harkness Flagler at age twenty-three was already a director of his father's railroad company. By permission of Flagler College.

A week after the hurricane Flagler returned to St. Augustine bringing his son Harry, Dr. Anderson, and a group of his railroad officers with him. As he often did, Anderson had spent the past three months in New York as the guest of the Flaglers. After an overnight stay at Kirkside, Flagler and his associates sped off to Palm Beach to inspect the Royal Poinciana, which had risen from the sand with amazing speed. Although the plaster and paint on the walls were still damp and four hundred workmen were still hammering away, Flagler and his men slept beneath the roof of the mammoth hotel. It would have almost twice as many bedchambers as the Ponce de Leon. From the top of its central tower Flagler had a breathtaking view of the Gulf Stream, which passed just offshore at this point, and, seventeen miles away, the beacon from Jupiter lighthouse. A few days later Flagler was back in St. Augustine examining the rebuilt Casino, the refurbished Cordova, and the new electrical systems in the Ponce de Leon and Alcazar. Then he departed to spend the Christmas season in New York with Alice.[8]

Harry Flagler had detached himself from the inspection party in Palm Beach and returned to St. Augustine. For the first time in his life, twenty-three-year-old Harry was on his own in St. Augustine. He stood on the brink of making some decisions that would alter the rest of his life. A month earlier his engagement to Miss Anne Lamont had been announced in the newspapers. The prospective marriage of one of society's most attractive young ladies and the very handsome heir to a vast fortune made for a great story.[9]

Harry set himself up as a bachelor at Kirkside and would remain through mid-December. We have no record of what he did during this six-week period, but presumably he familiarized himself with the hotels during this time when their staffs were preparing to open for the season. James Ingraham took Harry under his wing and accompanied him on an inspection trip down the railroad line. "I want Mr. Harry Flagler to become better acquainted with the work in hand and especially the traffic," Ingraham explained to one of the railroad managers. Back in March at a meeting in the Ponce de Leon, Henry Flagler had appointed his son a director of the railroad so that he would have access to the inner workings of the company. After this solo observation flight into the practical affairs of business, Harry returned to New York to rejoin his family and fiancée.[10]

In the fall of 1893 prospects for the coming winter season appeared bleak because a nationwide economic depression had descended upon the country that summer. Economists blamed the catastrophic panic on a chain reaction that began when overextended railroads went bankrupt, causing banks that held railroad bonds to fail, and this wiped out the savings of millions of small depositors while making it impossible for businesses to obtain the credit needed to continue in operation. To make things worse, the bottom fell out of the already low prices farmers received for their crops. Millions of men lost their jobs, their homes, and their farms. Jacob Coxey led a protest march of unemployed men from Ohio to Washington. Workers at George Pullman's factory town went on strike, sparking a general railroad workers' strike in the Midwest. President Cleveland sent in the army to break the strike. This unprecedented financial train wreck brought a level of suffering that would not be felt again until the Great Depression of the 1930s. The "Gay Nineties" were hardly gay at the gritty level of everyday life.

East Florida weathered the storm better than the rest of the country because of Henry Flagler's railroad building and the opening up of Palm Beach. More than three thousand men were directly employed on various Flagler building projects reaching from Jacksonville to Lake Worth. When Captain Marcotte spotted two of Flagler's payroll men lugging bags of silver dollars for distribution on payday, he observed, "It doesn't look much like hard times in the Ancient City."[11]

However, when Alfonso Papy, who operated the barber shops in Flagler's hotels, came back from the Hotel Champlain, he reported that business at the resort had fallen short of expectations. When Seavey himself returned he said that at first he had not been hopeful for the coming season, but recently he had come to believe that the usual visitors from the Northeast could be counted on to come down, and new vacationers from the Midwest might decide to visit, since the railroads had lowered their ticket rates.[12]

In a reversal of roles from the previous year, the Cordova was the first Flagler hotel to open in the fall, while the Alcazar remained closed. Flagler offered no explanation for this change, but it may have been made because the Cordova was less expensive to operate. Since the Cordova was lighted by gas, it was not necessary to operate the electric dynamos of the Alcazar powerhouse. The cost of a room and three meals a day ranged from three to four dollars. Young Clarence B. Knott, who had acted as Seavey's cashier since the days of the Magnolia Springs Hotel, became manager. The hotel sponsored a lavish Thanksgiving Day dinner, followed by a hop with music provided by the Fifth Infantry Band, hired from St. Francis Barracks. At Christmas the hotel prepared an even more elaborate dinner. The ninety or so early birds probably felt quite snug and at home.[13]

Seavey staged the grand reopening of the Casino on New Year's Eve with a ball in the upper mezzanine. The new electric lights and fresh paint delighted the crowd, many of whom came from Jacksonville and Palatka for the event. Guests could walk next door to inspect the Turkish and Russian Baths, which also were being reopened for the season. At midnight the electric light message "Feliz Ano Nuevo" in the Casino was transformed as the number "93" faded to black and was replaced by a brilliant "94."[14]

The Alcazar did not open as an independent hotel in the 1894 season but took in the overflow from the Ponce de Leon and Cordova after January 25 when the crowds were larger. Those rooming at the Alcazar ate their meals in either of the other two Flagler hotels or elsewhere in town. The shops and businesses occupying ground floor spaces, such as Greenleaf and Crosby, were open for customers as usual.[15]

The Ponce de Leon opened on January 10, a week earlier than in recent years, with the usual explosive blast and playing of "The Star-Spangled Banner." At the ball that evening Anderson accompanied Flagler's sister-in-law Julia Harkness York and her husband Barney. However, the most intriguing men at the ball were two Englishmen, Billy Thompson and George Converse, managers of the English boxing champion Charles Mitchell, who was in St. Augustine training for the world heavyweight championship boxing match.[16]

Months earlier some enterprising hotel men in Jacksonville had lured Mitchell and the American champion "Gentleman Jim" Corbett to Jacksonville for the contest. Governor Henry Mitchell, Mayor Fletcher, and Duval County Sheriff Napoleon B. Broward threatened to use legal force to prevent the fight, but the promoters eventually got their world championship match. Corbett set up his training camp in Pablo Beach east of Jacksonville, while some local businessmen induced Mitchell to train in St. Augustine. He took over a couple of cottages near the lighthouse, where he would have privacy and miles of beach on which to jog. Mitchell and his entourage came across the bay to town to walk through the Flagler hotels and gardens and swim in the Casino pool.

Excitement over the impending battle ran high and climaxed on the day of the fight. "When Mitchell arrived at the St. Augustine dock this morning," reported a northern newspaperman, "he was greeted by a tremendous crowd, many ladies from the fashionable Cordova and Ponce de Leon hotels being present." Mitchell's men pushed their way through the crowd and into a carriage that took them to the Ponce de Leon, where Mitchell received a rousing send-off from his friends. Then the ordeal was repeated at Union Station, where an even larger mob had assembled.[17]

The fight itself, held in a hastily erected arena in Jacksonville, proved an anticlimax. The larger, heavier Corbett knocked out Mitchell in the third round. The fighters' tribulations did not end with the fight, as both were arrested for assault. This necessitated their staying around for another month until Corbett's trial, during which he was quickly acquitted. Mitchell never went to trial. After this final round of sparring was concluded, Corbett came down to St. Augustine to see the sights. The champion stopped by the Cordova during the evening when a dance was in progress. Mrs. Marcotte wrote, "It was remarkable how many ladies required drinking water and were obliged to leave the room when it was bruited about that Corbett the champion was in the ante-room."[18]

The Flaglers arrived in St. Augustine earlier than was their custom because Henry wished to oversee completion of the railroad to Palm Beach and preparations for opening the Hotel Royal Poinciana. They came on January 10 in the *Alicia* railroad car, accompanied by the retinue of household servants necessary for maintaining Kirkside. While Flagler plunged into his business affairs, Mrs. Marcotte reported that Alice was "busy arranging the many pretty womanly belongings and rare bric-a-brac she delights in." Harry joined the family at Kirkside in mid-January. Mrs. Marcotte assumed that he was "becoming initiated in the care of different interests in the State belonging to his father." Harry also entered into the social scene, escorting his stepmother to a ball at the Ponce de Leon and to a reception at Philip Ammidown's home on St. George Street as well as shepherding the daughters of W. G. Warden to a ball at the San Marco.[19]

The gay dancers at these social events were not as numerous as in years before, but the Marcottes did not lament this fact or even acknowledge it. Captain Marcotte praised the Cordova for its excellent season but failed to point out that the Alcazar was closed except as an ancillary to the Cordova and Ponce de Leon. Mrs. Marcotte broke loose once and scolded readers of the *Tatler* for overreacting to "hard times." She argued, "While there are very few persons who are not experiencing 'a shrinkage in dividends,' or a reduction in salaries, there are very many who have adopted habits of economy not absolutely necessary." She asserted that wearing last year's gowns deprived workers of jobs. Some of the men who had migrated to St. Augustine in years past to find work when Flagler began his activities in town had by this time moved south to labor on new Flagler projects.[20]

In the last week of January Flagler gathered Parrott, Ingraham, and other railroad executives and friends for a quick trip to the end of the rail line, now rapidly approaching its destination in West Palm Beach. Captain Marcotte observed that Flagler always liked to be the first to ride over the new extensions of his railroad. A few days later when the Royal Poinciana opened on February 15, Flagler and his lieutenants again came down for the occasion. He had invited several members of the national press to accompany him on his train in order to publicize his latest business triumph.[21]

Alice did not go with Flagler for this momentous event. She remained behind in St. Augustine with Harry, evidently awaiting the appearance of Harry's fiancée Anne Lamont. Harry and his stepmother attended quiet receptions for society matrons in the winter resort colony until Anne and her mother and brother Lansing arrived on February 20. They took rooms in the Ponce de Leon. The *Tatler* placed its seal of approval on Anne: "Miss Lamont is a bright winning young gentlewoman with a gracious dignified bearing, whose former visit was enjoyed by a wide circle of friends, as this is sure to be."[22]

Just at the time the Lamonts arrived, a seriously ill Henry Flagler returned from Palm Beach. During his travels he had come down with some contagious disease, probably influenza. This turned into a serious affliction for a gray-haired sixty-four-year-old man. He went to bed at Kirkside, and McGuire placed barriers on Valencia Street to divert traffic to and from the rail station away from Flagler's home so that he would not be disturbed by passing horses and carriages clattering on the asphalt. John Maclennan sent a letter to Parrott informing him that Flagler was "quite ill" and that Parrott should keep "detail and worries of the work and general business away from him." Alice canceled the invitations sent out for a tea honoring Anne Lamont. After three days the barriers were removed from Valencia Street, and Captain Marcotte reported that Flagler was recovering, but his recuperation would turn out to be slow.[23]

Flagler's illness prevented him from entering into the social events of the season, but he had seldom attended these affairs in past years anyway. Before the annual Charity Ball for Alicia Hospital, Alice gave a dinner for Harry and Anne in the west alcove of the Ponce de Leon's Dining Room. Roses were the order of the evening. Ferns and roses decorated the tables, which were lit by lamps with pink shades. Each lady was given a bouquet of long-stemmed roses, while the men received a rose boutonnière. Anderson and all the Flaglers' circle of friends enjoyed the reception. Afterward they went to the ball.[24]

Richard Dale, Flagler's gardener, lived in a house Flagler had built for the family on Carrera Street facing the rear of Kirkside. Dale's son Russel, in his words "just a little shaver" at the time, was a "backdoor" friend of Alice Flagler. "I was," he later wrote, "in a small way a pet of Mrs. Flagler's and had the run of the grounds." Since she was unable to have children of her own, Alice may have adopted Russel to some extent. His other friend at Kirkside was Alice's parrot, which would occasionally escape and fly into some nearby tree. Russel would be called upon to coax the parrot from its perch and return it to its home at Kirkside.[25]

In March the Ponce de Leon played host to the most celebrated honeymooners in America: Charles H. Hoyt, fabulously successful Broadway producer of musicals, and his bride Caroline Miskel, the strikingly attractive blonde actress and vocalist. A magazine writer summed it up: "The most successful playwright of his day, happily married to the most beautiful woman of her time." Hoyt's musical comedies, full of physical action and slapstick and lively tunes, made millions of Americans happy and made Hoyt a rich man. In 1891 he had signed a long-term lease on Madison Square Theater, where he staged his plays. In that year he produced *A Trip to Chinatown*, which would continue performances for three years—the longest run of any Broadway production up to that point. The play was not much for narrative plot, but it introduced the popular tunes "Reuben, Reuben, I've Been Thinking," "The Bowery," and "After the Ball Is Over"— the single most popular song of the fin de siècle era. Thomas Edison's first commercial movie featured a scene from *A Trip to Chinatown*.[26]

Two "Ladies' Entrances" allowed women to pass into the hotel without going into the Rotunda, where men engaged in the business of registering and paying bills. Such social niceties were passing away by the nineties. Ralph, "Our Own Riviera," *Harper's New Monthly Magazine*, March 1893, 501.

Naturally the Hoyts attracted notice while at the Ponce de Leon. Hoyt was already famous for always dressing formally in public. His new bride wore a sunburst diamond brooch presented by her husband as a wedding gift. Guests at the hotel went around humming tunes from *A Trip to Chinatown*. At the Hospital Fair so many admirers crowded around Mrs. Hoyt that it caused a distraction, and she departed early to escape the attention.[27]

On his way back to New York, Hoyt spoke to a Washington reporter about his next production. "I got some good ideas for the play from the gathering of people at the Ponce de Leon Hotel in St. Augustine. Just think what a fruitful field a resort hotel is for drawing on characters to fill a society play with lots of humorous situations." Hoyt's next musical, *A Black Sheep*, was indeed set in a hotel, but he located the hotel in wild west Arizona, with no obvious connection to his Florida honeymoon experience, except perhaps that the plot involves inheritance of a family fortune.[28]

The little colony of artists who worked in the Ponce de Leon studios continued to be a feature of the hotel's social order. Martin Johnson Heade ranked as the first among equals. His studio, number 7, occupied the extreme west end of the row. Unlike the other artists, who headed north for the summers, Heade counted his cottage on San Marco Avenue north of town as his year-round home. However, beginning in 1890 he and his wife started taking a few months off during the hottest time of year to visit friends in northern locations. By this time almost all his production consisted of floral still life compositions.[29]

Felix de Crano, an artist with connections in New England and Philadelphia, first came to the Ponce de Leon in the 1893 season. He would eventually become one of the artists most identified with St. Augustine and its landscapes. He would later have his own cottage just west of the hotel. Otto Merkel, W. Staples Drown, George W. Seavey, and Marie a' Becket returned in 1894. Miss a' Becket, who had long suffered from poor health, ended both the '93 and '94 seasons by taking a room at Alicia Hospital to regain her strength.[30]

Another distinguished artist, William Aiken Walker, did not occupy a studio at the Ponce de Leon but spent several winters in St. Augustine in the 1890s and later. Walker was born in Charleston, South Carolina, and made his reputation as a painter of Old South scenes. He is especially noted for his small, realistic paintings of rural Negro life that are not quite realistic in spirit since they idealize poverty by making it appear quaint. Walker stayed away from the formal receptions at the Ponce de Leon and lived in the modest Magnolia Motel on St. George Street, where he enjoyed lingering in the parlor after dinner to play cards. He maintained a studio at the Thomas Tugby house nearby.[31]

Miss Laura Woodward had joined the Ponce de Leon artists' row group in 1890 and exhibited there through the 1893 season. Born in rural New York, Woodward made her way professionally during the 1870s and 1880s as a rare female artist in the Hudson River landscape school. She exhibited, when permitted, in the Northeast, and sometimes her path crossed those of Martin Johnson Heade and Louis C. Tiffany. By the time she reached St. Augustine her technique had evolved into the lighter, more delicate Barbizon style. Henry and Alice Flagler visited her studio during a regular Friday reception and purchased one of her paintings.[32]

Unlike most of the other artists, she remained in Florida during the summer months, seeking out and sketching the wild places and looking for landscapes more exotic. She once said, "I was disappointed in St. Augustine. It wasn't the South as how I imagined." In May 1890, just one month after Flagler's first visit to Palm Beach, Woodward and her sister Libbie checked into the Cocoanut Grove House. She returned to the Lake Worth region to paint in the summer of 1893 (and possibly earlier).[33]

In January 1894 she opened her studio in the Ponce de Leon only long enough to show some of her recent paintings before she packed up her paraphernalia and departed for Palm Beach. Captain Marcotte paid tribute to her pioneering spirit, observing that "her paintings of the Lake Worth and Indian River Country have aided in making those sections so popular." The Flaglers had one of her paintings, of a royal poinciana tree, hanging in Kirkside. Woodward was on hand for the opening of the Hotel Royal Poinciana, and Flagler built a studio for her in the new Yacht Club building. She would spend the rest of her life in a little cottage near the great hotel, painting local scenes for the winter visitors.[34]

On March 20 Flagler made two announcements that created a sensation in the resort community: O. D. Seavey had resigned as manager of the Hotel Ponce de Leon, and Flagler's son Harry would assume overall supervision of the three hotels in St. Augustine.

News of Seavey's departure "came upon the public—especially the guests of these hotels—like a thunderclap out of a clear sky, causing universal regret and surprise," wrote Mrs. Marcotte. Seavey was so thoroughly identified with the Flagler hotels that his leaving seemed beyond the realm of the possible. However, there had been omens for some while. Seavey gave no explanation for his resignation, but it almost certainly had to do with the poor health of his wife. Captain Marcotte said as much, writing that Mrs. Seavey had been reluctant to return for the current season. The Seaveys had abandoned the house at 20 Valencia Street that Flagler had built for them, instead occupying a suite of rooms in the Alcazar. Mrs. Seavey failed to appear at any of the usual social functions and spent most of her time inside their apartment.[35]

Flagler's statement that his son Harry would assume responsibility for overseeing the three hotels and other Flagler properties in St. Augustine came as just as much of a shock as news of Seavey's resignation. It seemed to be an indication of Flagler's intention to relinquish control of his empire in Florida. Henry Adams, vacationing in Tampa, took it that way. He wrote to his friend and next-door neighbor John Hay that the national depression had constricted travel to winter resorts. "Florida is shut up after a disastrous season. . . . So is Flagler himself, I understand, and his son reigns over Eastern Florida."[36]

Of course, anyone familiar with Harry's gradual introduction into the workings of the Flagler railroad and hotel empire knew that Harry was being prepared to take over at least some of his father's executive duties. Assuming supervision of the established hotels in St. Augustine made a natural starting point. Captain Marcotte judged Harry a "most capable and worthy" person to relieve Flagler of the "multiplicity of exacting cares" of making executive decisions involving a railroad, a chain of hotels, a steamship line, a canal company, and a land company. Mrs. Marcotte seconded her husband's judgment, writing of Harry: "He is a pleasant, courteous gentleman, evidently possessing much of his father's business ability."[37]

Having received his commission, Harry left St. Augustine for the North to take part in preparations for his wedding.[38]

His father and mother, along with Dr. Anderson and some other friends, headed the other way to Palm Beach. Flagler wanted to ride his railroad all the way to West Palm Beach. He had missed the pounding of the last spike on the extension on March 19 due to his illness. At that time Mrs. Marcotte had written, "The one alloy in the rejoicing at the culmination of the great enterprise was the absence of Mr. Henry M. Flagler, the projector and builder; excessive weakness resulting from sickness that was aggravated by the cares of his many projects in this State alone prevented his presence at the triumphant completion of his great project." The Flagler party all stayed in the Royal Poinciana. In the bright sun and warmth of Palm Beach, Flagler began to regain his health. Mrs. Marcotte reported a few days later: "He has discarded his cane, joins in out and indoor amusements, and has gained six or seven pounds." Shortly thereafter they were back in St. Augustine and then hurried to New York for Harry's wedding.[39]

In St. Augustine the last big event of the season was the Tropical Tennis Tournament. Seavey had worked out the schedule of Florida's winter circuit of tennis tournaments with the hotel interests in Tampa and Green Cove Springs so that St. Augustine could hold the Tropical Tournament near the end of March, as

The City Gates trophy of the Tropical Tennis Tournament is back in St. Augustine today after being carried away by Oliver Campbell following his fourth victory. Author's photo.

preferred. The tournament became the social event of the week, although brisk windy weather held down the number of spectators to just the serious enthusiasts until the final day. The large City Gates trophy stood on display in the Rotunda of the Ponce de Leon. After an absence of two years, Oliver Campbell had returned to try for a fourth win, which would entitle him to ownership of the City Gates trophy. However, Gregory S. Bryan went into the contest as the favorite, having just won the tournaments in Tampa and Green Cove. Nevertheless, Campbell, who had not played in these earlier contests, won easily and took home the heavy championship trophy.[40]

Campbell would remain a serious sportsman for the remainder of his life in New York, where he made his living on the New York Stock Exchange. Campbell would pass away in 1953. Today his memory is enshrined in the International Tennis Hall of Fame at Newport for his three consecutive wins in the U.S. Open from 1890 to 1892. Sometime around 1960 the City Gates trophy turned up in a pawn shop in New York City and was purchased as a gift for the City of St. Augustine. Today it is in the custody of the St. Augustine Historical Society.[41]

Ironically, Campbell's capture of the City Gates trophy signaled the beginning of an abrupt decline of popular interest in tennis in St. Augustine. Like baseball before it, tennis simply faded away as one of the chief spectator amusements among the winter visitors.

On April 4 one of the hotel staff asked Seavey to come to the Dining Room to attend to some small matter, and there he was surprised by the entire staff, which had gathered to send him off in style. One of the veteran guests of the Hotel Ponce de Leon made a little speech with tears in his eyes and handed Seavey a velvet bag containing an elegant Swiss watch and a card signed by all the staff: McGuire and McDonald's names were prominent (although McDonald was absent in Palm Beach), along with those of Frank Thompson, Annie McKay, and the rest. Many had been with Seavey since the days of the Magnolia Springs Hotel, and a few from before then. Seavey declared that he felt no regret for the times they had spent together. The hotel orchestra struck up "For He's a Jolly Good Fellow" and "Auld Lang Syne." He would soon leave for the Hotel Champlain to spend the summer as usual.[42]

The scheduled date for closing the Ponce de Leon had been announced as April 21, but it was moved up to April 10. No explanation was given for cutting short the season, but simple lack of patronage would be the probable cause. Brooks's orchestra staged its customary end of the season concert in the Rotunda and finished with the usual round of sweet and sad tunes including the new one, "After the Ball Is Over." The house count for the year 1894 came to the lowest total since the disastrous yellow fever season of 1889, but perhaps more ominously, it continued a gradual downward slide that would persist for the rest

Carrère and Hastings furnished the *Architectural Record* with this photograph for an article on their St. Augustine buildings. The two men young men without beards in the photo may be the architects themselves. Carrère and Hastings, "The Illustrations," August 25, 1888, 87.

of the decade. The fundamental causes were easy to identify: the profound recession in the general United States economy that limited vacation travel, combined with the diversion of winter visitors to more southerly places such as Tampa and Palm Beach that could guarantee warmer weather.[43]

After the middle of April only the Cordova remained open, but enough newcomers arrived in town to keep it comfortably full. In fact, manager Knott declared, "If things keep on this way I will not be able to close the hotel." Nevertheless, it did close on the last day of April. To please the community, the Casino swimming pool remained open all summer, beginning an off-and-on tradition that would last well into the next century. Many a St. Augustine youngster in future years would learn to swim in the Casino pool.[44]

In New York the Flaglers had something to celebrate: the wedding of Harry Flagler and Anne Lamont. They made a strikingly handsome and accomplished couple. The two had grown up a block away from each other on Fifth Avenue and had been acquaintances since childhood. The wedding service took place in Madison Avenue Baptist Church on April 25, and only those with cards were admitted. Still, a standing-room-only crowd packed the church. "The gowns worn by the guests were more gorgeous than those seen at any recent event," wrote a society page reporter. The bride dressed in a white satin gown with a necklace made from several rows of pearls. The stepmother of the groom attracted notice in a "pearl-gray satin" gown. Anne's brother Lansing gave the bride away. Afterward a small group of well-wishers repaired to the Lamont home for a reception catered by Delmonico's. John D. and Cettie Rockefeller were there, along with William and Almira Rockefeller and some of the Vanderbilt neighbors.[45]

Harry began his service as overseer of the St. Augustine division of the Flagler empire that spring. His first official act was to announce that Clarence B. Knott, who had managed the Cordova during the season, would take over administration of all three of the St. Augustine hotels. Just as Seavey had reported to Henry Flagler, Knott began informing Harry of current business affairs. In one of his first letters Knott stated that the manager's cottage at 20 Valencia had been leased for a period of five years at $1,000 a year. A kitchen and laundry were added to the rear of the building to make it a self-sufficient home. It would not thereafter be used as the winter home of the Ponce de Leon's manager. Knott added, "I will let the matter of the Studios and other rents rest until I see you, as also the Cutting Cottage [on Carrera Street]." Harry wrote to Ingraham saying, "I hope everything will go on well this summer at the south, and that next winter will bring us a big business." His use of the word "us" suggests that Harry had identified himself with his father's St. Augustine enterprises.[46]

In New York City Henry and Alice closed their Fifth Avenue home with the arrival of the summer's heat and relocated to their rambling country house on the seashore at Mamaroneck. Anderson came up from St. Augustine and spent some time as the Flaglers' houseguest. Another visitor was Dr. George G. Shelton, the handsome, clean-shaven homeopathic physician who had treated Jennie Louise at the time of her death. Shelton would later say it was around this time that he began to become concerned about Alice's increasingly erratic behavior. He probably discussed this with Flagler, who evidently had long been aware of Alice's deteriorating mental condition. In recent months she had become unpredictable and short tempered when around her husband. Flagler seems to have hoped that this conduct still fell within the bounds of normal behavior. However, he would later write that "a few years after our marriage, she developed signs of insanity." Thus Alice's descent into mental illness may have been manifest to Flagler for a long time before the summer of 1894.[47]

Nevertheless, for the moment the Flaglers attempted to carry on a normal life and followed their customary routine of seasonal migrations from New York City to Mamaroneck to St. Augustine and now to Palm Beach.

During the summer of 1894 the biggest project in St. Augustine was the filling in of the boat basin at the foot of the Plaza. When the army built the seawall in the 1830s, they left a gap in the wall and behind it constructed a large rectangular enclosure where small vessels could find shelter. Over the years this basin had filled with silt so that most of it became dry at low tide, and all sorts of flotsam tended to accumulate there, leading to demands to fill in this foul receptacle of refuse. However, the boat basin had also become one of the antique attractions of the town and a favorite subject for artists.

In July the town council voted to fill in the basin, and in August workers began dismantling the coquina stone walls enclosing the basin and reusing the stone to build a continuous wall across the entrance way. When this work was done there remained the problem of filling the huge depression where the boat basin had been—an expensive and tedious proposition if done by mule cart.[48]

Just at this inopportune moment another hurricane overwhelmed St. Augustine. Near sunset on September 25, when winds began picking up from the northeast, most boat owners moved their craft out of the bay and around to the comparative shelter of the San Sebastian River. They had learned their lesson the previous year. By dawn the next day winds had increased to higher speeds than in the prior year's storm, although flood tides did not rise quite as high. One of the first things to go was the recently built section of seawall at the boat basin site. All the docks along the seawall were ruined, save for the South Beach Railway's new pier. "The Yacht Club house," reported Mrs. Marcotte, "went to pieces like a card house." W. W. Dewhurst wrote to Flagler that some chained-together buoys battered the clubhouse apart. Hundreds of sea turtles penned in enclosures under docks and destined to become turtle soup for wealthy Yankees gained their liberty. The high winds smashed windows in Flagler's hotels, drenching the interiors of many rooms. Thomas Hastings's decorative weather vanes atop the Ponce de Leon's towers were bent sideways. A flying board shattered the plate glass window of an Alcazar store. Telegraph lines connecting St. Augustine to the outside world went down. Flagler's railroads to Jacksonville and Palatka were cut by washouts. The intrepid Mrs. Marcotte took the first news from St. Augustine to Jacksonville by commandeering a handcart and having a couple of strong men pump her along the rails to Jacksonville.[49]

Long-term damage to the city was not extensive, although the town council was forced to spend another precious thousand dollars of taxpayers' money rebuilding the caved-in seawall section. Heth Canfield, who was in the process of excavating Maria Sanchez Creek to create what is today Maria Sanchez Lake, offered to rent his dredge to the city to pump sand into the "sinkhole" where the boat basin had been. The city took him up on this offer, and the modern method of pumping up sand from the bay bottom and piping it into an area to be filled completed the work quickly and at relatively low expense. In the end the city gained about one hundred feet more park space at the east end of the Plaza, and

Bay Street now ran straight through beside the seawall without the former detour around the boat basin. But one more historic landmark had fallen to progress.[50]

In early December 1894 Flagler came to Florida with Henry Plant and a group of executives from several other railroads on a grand tour of the tracks within the state. Flagler ended his part of the excursion in Palm Beach. Harry, Anne, and Alice arrived in St. Augustine a few days later, with Harry and Anne taking rooms in the Cordova, while Alice, escorted by James Ingraham, continued to Palm Beach to join Flagler. On December 11 all the Flagler family reunited in St. Augustine for the wedding of Rev. John M. MacGonigle, the new pastor of Memorial Church.[51]

Flagler had been instrumental in bringing MacGonigle to Memorial Presbyterian. His story had a familiar ring in St. Augustine: a northerner in failing health who sought a warmer climate in order to survive. More than a year earlier, in October 1893, the trustees of the church, led by Dr. Anderson, had sat down with Flagler to consult him about offering a call to MacGonigle. The trustees justified this meeting to sound out Flagler by explaining, "Mr. Flagler has a kindly disposition toward and is liberal in aiding these church matters." Flagler was agreeable. MacGonigle had been a pastor in Pittsburgh and came with strong recommendations as a sound, commonsense preacher.[52] MacGonigle's wedding took place in the small Episcopal church on the south side of the Plaza facing the Catholic cathedral. The modest little chapel could not hold many people, so only those with invitations were admitted. The bride, Jennie Ruggles, had lived in town since her childhood and was seen as a fitting mate for the middle-aged widower MacGonigle. Anderson acted as MacGonigle's best man. All the Flaglers were in attendance, along with many of the key employees of the hotels and railroad. After the wedding everyone walked down St. George Street to the bride's home for a reception, and then the newly married couple hastened off to Tampa in Flagler's private rail car on the first leg of a honeymoon trip to Havana.[53]

During the brief time that Flagler was in town a swarm of people descended upon him to present petitions for their particular causes. Mrs. Marcotte encountered him in a dark gray business suit, a handsome, dignified, "well knit" figure. Speaking of his enterprises in St. Augustine, he told Mrs. Marcotte, "Of course every one wants to see the idiot who did it." She saw him as a benign, kindly, intellectual patron of the city. "He listens with patience to hundreds who wish him to assist their schemes, although he can, on occasion, rid himself of a bore by the lifting of an eyebrow." His private secretary, Jasper C. Salter, was at his side almost continuously and did his best to buffer Flagler from the press of humanity. Henry and Alice did have an opportunity to walk over to the Cordova one evening and look in on one of the Wednesday night dances and socialize with some of their friends.[54]

In mid-December the whole Flagler family departed for the North to spend Christmas in New York.

The 1894–95 winter season in St. Augustine opened on a hopeful note. Although the country remained in a deep depression, the economy had turned upward, and laboring men were slowly returning to their workbenches. Interestingly, in St. Augustine seasonal visitors began arriving in unusually large numbers in November, and the hotels responded by opening their doors sooner than in years past. The Cordova started taking in guests on November 5, and a few old-timers had already been camping out in rooms at the Ponce de Leon for some days even before then. Manager Knott, with his wife and son, lived in a suite in the Ponce de Leon, which allowed him to shuttle back and forth across King Street tending to both hotels. The Alcazar remained closed and, as in the previous year, was not expected to open as an independent hotel.[55]

Beginning in December the Cordova hosted Wednesday evening hops for its guests and those from other hotels who had received admission cards. At the first dance only two members of the hotel orchestra had arrived, but the pianist and a violinist produced enough volume to please the audience. Captain and Mrs. Marcotte were among those present and commented favorably on the number of people who actually danced. Anderson put in an appearance in the company of Miss Elizabeth Smethurst. A few weeks later James McGuire reported to Harry Flagler: "The Cordova is having a good run of business and running along very well."[56]

Henry Flagler seconded McGuire's sentiments in a letter he sent his son two weeks later: "The Ponce de Leon is filling up rather slowly; the Cordova has a very fair house count, but the Royal Poinciana is taking the wind out of all the rest. 352 guests there yesterday. With the exception of the Royal Poinciana, I think the Cordova has as many guests as any Hotel in the state. The Tampa Bay Hotel probably stands next." Interestingly, although Flagler addressed his letter to his son "Dear Harry," he still signed his name formally as "H. M. Flagler," as he did with everyone.[57]

Not all the news coming to Harry in New York brought cheer. The state of Florida suffered back-to-back catastrophic freezes in December and early January that wiped out most of the state's citrus and winter vegetable crops. Manager Knott wrote to tell Harry that the young rubber tree planted at the Ponce de Leon had been lost, along with most of the decorative plants, save for the native palm trees. McGuire reported that some pipes in the hotels had burst from freezing.[58]

Although Harry exchanged letters with several of the system's executives in St. Augustine on a variety of matters, he seems to have taken a particular interest in the musicians hired for the hotels. In November 1894 Harry exchanged letters with Knott regarding the orchestras, and after visiting the hotels in December, Harry complained about the band's lack of proper dress and raised his objection to the ensemble's leadership. Alcazar manager Joseph Greaves replied that henceforth the orchestra members would be dressed in black cutaway coats with gray trousers. He added that he would hire "another conductor that will please you." Knott reported that the Hungarian Gypsy Band playing in the Casino won great approval from the guests and that Casino receipts were up.[59]

The Hotel Ponce de Leon opened on January 16 with the usual fanfare and invasion by crowds of townspeople. In a sign of the times, a few of the old reliable "first day" signers of the guest register were away at Palm Beach and would not appear until later.

Henry and Alice enjoyed the opening day dinner in the Dining Room seated at a table with Rev. and Mrs. MacGonigle. Sitting unobtrusively in the southeast corner of the great hall were manager Knott with his wife and O. D. and Mrs. Seavey. Mrs. Seavey had regained her health, and O. D. had been enjoying quail shooting in the fields near Hastings. Seavey would not say what his plans for the future were but explained that they would be spending the winter in a cottage near the Magnolia Springs Hotel where his Florida career had begun.[60]

After dinner, the opening day ball was held, not in the vaulted Dining Room as

The Hotel Granada stood just across the street from the Ponce de Leon. It marked Franklin Smith's reentry into the hotel business on a modest scale. The Villa Zorayda stands on the right. Postcard in author's collection.

The northeast corner of the Hotel Ponce de Leon's grounds featured a shell walk flanked by rows of palms—one row still survives. On the right is the driveway where hotel supplies were delivered to the utility wing of the building. On the left, across Cordova Street, stands the Bacchus Club, with its upstairs bay window. Later Raymond Ponce's funeral home would occupy the building. From the collection of the St. Augustine Historical Society Research Library.

in past years, but in the more intimate Grand Parlor. Knott had covered the floor in the center parlor with linen to make a surface for dancing. Alice and MacGonigle led off the first dance. Henry, as was his custom, never attempted to dance. The eight-piece orchestra played from under the archway to the third parlor. The move of the dance from the Dining Room to the Parlor was an indicator of the declining numbers of patrons attending the balls, as was the shrinkage of the orchestra. During the 1888 opening season the hotel orchestra had numbered twenty-five musicians.[61]

Shortly after the opening of the Ponce de Leon, in February Franklin W. Smith and his son George Stuart Smith opened the Hotel Granada just across King Street from the west wing of the Ponce de Leon and next door to the Smiths' home, the Villa Zorayda. Back in 1889 Franklin Smith, recently returned from a visit to the excavated ruins at Pompeii, had built the Pompeiian Arcade on the site to house shops and a restaurant. To convert the building into a hotel in 1895, Smith added two new stories of rooms. Since Smith's resources had declined over the years, the addition was constructed of wood, over which wire mesh was nailed and then a coat of concrete plaster was added to give the building a more substantial look. The Hotel Granada advertised itself as an upscale establishment with a "social club house" atmosphere.[62]

Along with the Granada, another restaurant and "social club" opened just to the side of the Hotel Ponce de Leon on the northeast corner of Cordova and Treasury streets: the Bacchus Restaurant. It started the year with a complimentary dinner for Mayor W.S.M. Pinkham, state senator Frank Genovar, Judge C. M. Cooper, Judge William MacWilliams, Captain Marcotte, and other influential men in the community. The owners of the Bacchus Restaurant were brothers Edward R. and John R. Bradley, notorious gamblers from Chicago. Everyone knew their trade, but they were also recognized as refined gentlemen. Openly the Baccus Restaurant offered excellent private dinners prepared by an outstanding chef, but upstairs in a private room the Bradleys ran a discreet, well-managed gambling place for gentlemen who wished for something more in entertainment than the hotels provided.[63]

All the men at the complimentary dinner knew they were being solicited to maintain silence about the Bradleys' gambling operation. At some point even Henry Flagler became aware of the situation, but he excused it by saying that St. Augustine was a city, and he could not be expected to police a whole city. The Bradleys held up their end of the bargain by running a first rate restaurant on their ground floor and admitting only respectable men to the upstairs sanctum. A reporter for the *Washington Post* commented on the "high stakes games" of poker and told of one man who paid for his fifty-dollar-a-day vacation out of his winnings.[64]

The Bradleys would continue to operate the Bacchus Restaurant until the end of the season in 1898. That same year they opened the Beach Club in Palm Beach near the Royal Poinciana, having followed Flagler and the millionaires to Palm Beach. One of the Bradleys told a reporter that the Bacchus Club in St. Augustine had been closed because it did not produce a profit, while the Beach Club did. The Beach Club would continue to operate down to Edward Bradley's death in 1946.[65]

Meanwhile Dr. Anderson was busy doing good for the poor people of St. Augustine. The great depression of the 1890s had put a financial restraint on the Buckingham Smith Benevolent Association, on the board of which Anderson served. Many of the railroad securities in which the bulk of the association's endowment was invested were no longer paying dividends. The home for aged and indigent black people had already been vacated by its residents a decade earlier, and the building had recently been used as a school to teach black children vocational skills. In the summer of 1894 Sarah Mather, the last redoubtable member of the original Board of Lady Managers, passed away, and the trustees decided to turn the home into a hotel and use the profits to aid needy black residents by other means. This decision subjected Anderson to some criticism, but the board felt it had done the right thing, and the Benevolent Association carried on its good work in other ways—which it continues to do today.[66]

The result was that St. Augustine gained a new hotel, the Hotel Buckingham. The structure was remodeled to make it into a comfortable, modest winter home for sojourners from the North. (Today the Buckingham is long gone, and the Flagler College gymnasium occupies the site.)[67]

In the realm of his personal life, to the amazement of almost everyone, Dr. Anderson, a confirmed bachelor for many years, decided to get married. For all those long years of singleness he may have been mourning the loss of Nellie Baldwin, the love of his youth; witness his assertion (chapter 1) that "I would never fix my affections upon any-one, for the end thereof is pain and sorrow." Flagler once recalled that Anderson had confided to him, "Living one's misfortunes down is a terribly slow and painful process." Flagler also noted Anderson's "cold blooded" personality and unwillingness to give rein to his emotions.[68]

Anderson had known his bride, Mary Elizabeth Smethurst, since she was a girl. She was twenty-four years younger than her fifty-six-year-old groom, but at age thirty-two she was recognized as a mature woman of substance in local society. Henry and Alice Flagler came up from Palm Beach for the wedding and stayed in Kirkside. A goodly selection of St. Augustine society crowded into Trinity Episcopal Church for the ceremony, notably including some of Anderson's black friends, especially his old family cook Aunt Lettie, who declared that she was happy "to see her boy getting so sweet a young wife." After the wedding the bride's mother held a reception in her home, the Gibbs mansion on Bay Street not far from Fort Marion. The couple went off for a honeymoon at Plant's Tampa Bay Hotel and then Flagler's Royal Poinciana. When they returned to St. Augustine the newlyweds stayed in the Ponce de Leon while workmen fixed up Anderson's old bachelor's quarters, Markland house, to make it suitable for a woman to inhabit. A few years earlier Flagler had commented on the doctor's comfortably threadbare home: "One thousand dollars would furnish a house better than the Doctor's is furnished."[69]

Mrs. Marcotte, having seen the Flaglers at the wedding, noted that they were "looking remarkably well and . . . enjoying their stay at Palm Beach." However, just a few days earlier Flagler had written to Harry, who remained in New York, "Alice is about as usual." This cryptic comment meant Harry was well aware of his stepmother's mental instability. A few days after Anderson's wedding Flagler attended the funeral of Col. Nathan W. Osborn, former commander of St. Augustine's Fifth Infantry, in Memorial Presbyterian Church. Alice was not present but sent a wreath of white roses. Then the Flaglers returned to the McCormick cottage, which had become their home at Palm Beach. Flagler had turned the dining room into an office and installed his secretary J. C. Salter in the kitchen.[70]

In mid-February the Hotel Alcazar opened, a happy surprise for friends of that establishment, for it had been announced earlier that the Alcazar would be used only as housing for those who could not find rooms in the Cordova or Ponce de Leon. However, enough patrons had arrived to justify opening the kitchen and dining room to make the Alcazar a self-sufficient hotel in its own right. The Casino had already been operating as the most popular gathering place in town for residents of the hotels. The Imperial Hungarian Gypsy Band provided colorful music mornings and evenings, and a small restaurant opened at the west end of the upper level to provide light refreshments for those who wished to linger and perhaps dance to the music. For the athletically minded, a trapeze and gymnastic rings had been added, hanging from the rafters above the water, for daring aerialists to perform stunts. One evening a huge crowd of almost a thousand people turned out to be entertained at a cake walk presented by the Ponce de Leon waiters.[71]

The famous, or infamous, public speaker Robert Ingersoll, who had made his reputation advocating rational thought and criticizing organized religion, packed the Casino for a lecture on Shakespeare that met the critical approval of both Marcottes. Other notables also passed by. Mrs. U. S. Grant made a second appearance at the Ponce de Leon. Captain Marcotte organized a reception in the Grand Parlor where she could accept the greetings of veterans of the Union Army, the soldiers of the local Third Artillery, and invited civilians. Mrs. Grant and some lady attendants stood in the center room of the parlor to shake hands with about two thousand people who filed in from the hotel's west wing and exited into the Rotunda. George Pullman and his family, as in previous years, stopped at the Ponce de Leon, which Pullman was quoted as declaring "the most perfect hotel in the world." However, like many others, the Pullmans spent most of their time that season in Palm Beach. Henry Clay Frick, manager of the Carnegie Steel Works in Homestead, Pennsylvania, took a suite at the Ponce de Leon with his wife during the bloody labor dispute of 1892. In the midst of the strike, an attacker shot and stabbed Frick, but he survived. He was a man admired by many Americans and hated by others. Some years later Thomas Hastings would design Frick's extravagant home on Fifth Avenue.[72]

An old wintertime friend of St. Augustine, James Renwick, returned, obviously suffering more than before from his chronic throat troubles—possibly caused by asthma. "He is not so well this season as usual," reported Mrs. Marcotte. In past years the man ladies called "Uncle Jim" had brought his yacht *Jean* to Matanzas Bay and had stayed in various hotels around town. He became a close friend of Bishop Moore, who hired him to design the new high altar, bishop's throne, and Blessed Virgin altar for the church he had redesigned. During the 1894 and 1895 seasons Renwick settled comfortably and quietly into a suite of rooms in the Ponce de Leon. When the Ponce closed in early April, he moved over to McGuire's Valencia Hotel to extend his stay for another month before departing for New York City. He would die there in June.[73]

Harry and Anne Flagler did not arrive in St. Augustine until mid-February, their coming delayed by Anne's illness with the flu. The couple visited Palm Beach for a couple of days to pay their respects to Henry and Alice, and then they returned to occupy a suite in the Ponce de Leon. Dr. and Mrs. Anderson held a reception at Markland to welcome the young Flaglers to town. The new Mrs. Anderson wore her wedding gown, while Anne's "quaint pearl necklace" attracted notice. They received guests in the front parlor, and a buffet table occupied the center of the rear parlor. Although Markland presented an imposing front to King Street, these two large downstairs parlors were the only rooms spacious enough to hold any number of people, and no doubt some guests socialized in the hallway. In the coming weeks other prominent members of the town's winter "cottage" society held similar receptions in their homes for the youthful Flaglers.[74]

Harry and Anne Flagler appeared to be settling into the spheres expected of them. The hotel managers submitted their reports to Harry and consulted with him, while the young couple delved into society bustle. Mrs. Marcotte encountered the Flaglers outside one of the Ponce de Leon's weekly dances, and she left a flattering description of the moment: "In the corner leading to the parlor sits the owner of it all, Mr. Harry Harkness Flagler, and his gentle, attractive young wife, her face more than usually bright and happy over the arrival of Mrs. Lamont, her mother, who sat with her—a stately, dignified lady—greeting with winning cordiality those presented to her: occasionally Mr. Lansing Lamont, the son and brother, would join the group for a moment, agreeable as of yore. Mr. Flagler looks younger than he is, and strangers wonder that so young a man should assume the personal care of such wealth; but Mr. Flagler possesses business ability and discernment, with great decision of character, and will undoubtedly cope successfully with the difficult position."[75]

In March when the crowds in the hotels were larger, the dances returned to the Ponce de Leon Dining Room. One ball was themed as a Louis XIV *bal poudré* affair in which the women applied "beauty patches" to their cheeks and piled their hair up in pompadour styles dusted with white powder. Anne Flagler, who served as one of the four patronesses of the ball, received compliments for her ensemble: "Her gown was from the other side and worn for the first time, a cream *moiré* striped with blue satin with pink roses brocaded over it, the dress was *en traine* the bodice low with dashes of blue chiffon that was carried down the skirt and caught with a cluster of pink roses." A few days later after a regular Monday night concert in the Rotunda, the orchestra relocated to the Grand Parlor for an informal dance. Harry and Anne went in and "seemed to thoroughly enjoy dancing together."[76]

The Alicia Hospital Fair and the Charity Ball for the benefit of the hospital had been highlights of the social season in previous years, but both faced hard times in the 1895 season. The hospital had been forced to close its doors during the summer of 1894 because the securities in its endowment were not paying enough dividends to meet expenses. Anna Marcotte continued as president of the Ladies Hospital Association, and Anderson remained as president of the trustees. They attempted to find ways to economize on expenses. Harry Flagler provided the use of the Casino free of charge, but this year only one side of the mezzanine floor was needed for the booths and tables. Several old reliable lady workers were absent. Alice Flagler, of course, was in Palm Beach, and Anne Flagler, for whatever reason, did not hostess a table. Relatively few guests from the hotels attended. The fair netted a profit of only $1,463, compared to more than $6,000 from the first fair in 1889.[77]

The annual Charity Ball came off a week later, and it displayed all the élan of earlier balls. Two bands played on opposite sides of the vaulted Dining Room, more than a hundred couples danced, including Harry and Anne and Dr. and Mrs. Anderson, and at midnight the guests sat down to supper in the east and west bays off the central hall. The usual colored electric lights sparkled throughout the hotel grounds. The fair and ball must have served their intended purpose, for Anderson reported that Alicia Hospital was back to normal operations, its finances running in the black.[78]

In that winter season of 1895 a new game known as golf made its appearance in St. Augustine. Its arrival was not unexpected since two years earlier Harry Lillywhite, an Englishman who managed the tennis courts at the Alcazar, had described it to Captain Marcotte as the ancient national pastime of Scotland. Lillywhite explained that golf "is every year becoming more universally recognized as one of the most fashionable as well as fascinating of out-door amusements." Mrs. Marcotte seconded the call for golf: "Why does not St. Augustine have a Golf Club? The revival of this old fashioned game is 'the fad' of the moment abroad." It seemed that the game was played on "grounds" resembling the "open downs or heath" near the Scottish seaside. St. Augustine stood near the seaside—why not have a golf course here too? The difficulty lay in the absence of open fields near the town's hotels. The Ponce de Leon's manager Knott began to investigate possible locations, but those outside town would require a paved road to be accessible by carriage. Mrs. Marcotte envisioned a country club with tennis and polo as well as golf.[79]

The solution, such as it was, came when the U.S. Army gave permission to lay out golf links on the green of Fort Marion. Everyone realized that the fort grounds were too confined to meet the requirements of a golf course, but this would have to do until a more spacious place could be secured. Edmund Pendleton, descendent of a Virginia patriot of the same name, took the initiative in organizing the St. Augustine Golf Club. Many familiar names appeared on its membership roll: C. B. Knott, Mr. and Mrs. Harry H. Flagler, Dr. and Mrs. Anderson, G. Stuart Smith and his sister Nina, the artist Felix DeCrano and his wife, and others. The inaugural game was played in late February. The club pitched a large marquee on the north side of the green near the Warden cottage to serve as headquarters and refreshment pavilion. Ladies served tea, and nearby the Third Artillery band played sprightly tunes. A mixed foursome of two gentlemen and two ladies were the first to place their golf balls upon little mounds of earth on the sand "teeing ground." The three links of the course formed a triangle around the fort green, with three rounds of the links making a complete nine-hole match.[80]

Members of the golf club tried their skills every day on the fort green, but only on Tuesdays did the club host receptions under its shelter. Players carried as many as a full complement of seven sticks, but some chose to employ just three. Participants were required to learn new terms such as "mashey niblack," "brassy bulger," and "putter." If your ball fell inside the fort's earthen glacis, a "lofter" was the recommended stick to extricate it. The game became the most intriguing new pastime of the season. "Golf has come to stay," judged Captain Marcotte, "as it takes with many tourists."[81]

Harry Flagler supported the new game. He donated silver toiletry items from Greenleaf and Crosby to be handed out as prizes in the first tournament, and he served as one of the scorekeepers who followed players around the circuit. Anne poured tea for the club ladies. In a later handicap tournament Harry received a duffer's handicap of twenty but still managed to negotiate the nine holes in a miserable ninety-eight strokes. John Maclennan, perhaps showing skills learned by building railroads across broken terrain, won the match with a score of 53. Harry played in the next two tournaments, finishing dead last in both and not improving his scores.[82]

In March 1895 Ohio governor William McKinley, his wife, and his chief advisor Mark Hanna made a swing around the southern states endeavoring to line up support among Republican Party leaders for his selection as the nominee in the next year's Republican convention. Already many presumed he would be the next president. His tour came to a temporary halt in Thomasville, Georgia, when he came down with a severe cold and decided to stay in bed for a few days. This threw off his itinerary, and he canceled a planned visit to Palm Beach, but Flagler had also invited McKinley to be his guest at the Ponce de Leon, and Flagler came up to meet the governor in St. Augustine. McKinley was still not feeling well when he reached Jacksonville and declined to make a public speech, although he conferred with Republican leaders in his hotel. Former St. Augustine mayor John Long met McKinley in Jacksonville to escort him to the Ancient City, where he was to be greeted by Mayor Pinkham and other dignitaries. They departed Jacksonville on the 12:50 train.[83]

At almost the precise moment McKinley's train left the station in Jacksonville, a spark from the forge in Masters' blacksmith shop on north Charlotte Street in St. Augustine set the roof on fire. That part of Charlotte Street had long been the commercial center of town, and its mixture of old Spanish coquina houses, great and small wooden homes, and wooden commercial buildings formed a warren of combustible materials ideal for an urban conflagration. The town's fire engines arrived on the scene within a few minutes, but the flow from the fire hydrants amounted to little more than a trickle of sandy sludge. Mayor Pinkham was conspicuous, directing the firefighters and swearing profusely. Fortunately, a slight breeze came from the west, pushing the main impulse of the spreading flames toward the seawall. Residents and business owners began throwing household goods and other items of value into the streets. Anderson appeared on the roof of his mother-in-law's home, the Gibbs mansion, attempting to beat out flying embers that landed on the roof. When this effort proved futile, he joined others in piling her possessions into Bay Street. The fire would continue burning north until it reached the open ground surrounding Fort Marion, and there it died for lack of fuel.

Meanwhile flames had jumped Charlotte Street farther south and began to consume and threaten buildings on its west side. Residents of the Florida House, Magnolia Hotel, and Lorillard House began to evacuate these big old wooden buildings fronting on St. George Street. If the flames reached them, the whole northern half of the city would surely be lost. James McGuire proved the man of the hour. He attached fire hoses to the powerful pumps in the Hotel Ponce de Leon and unrolled the hoses for some three hundred yards to the scene of the fire. The battle to contain the blaze centered on the two-story wooden Genovar Cigar factory, which ran from Charlotte Street almost to the rear wall of Genovar's Opera House, which opened onto St. George Street. If the cigar factory went, everything else would follow. Great streams of water from McGuire's hoses saved the cigar factory building and prevented an even greater catastrophe.[84]

It was bad enough. About fifty buildings were lost, and hundreds of people were left to camp wherever they could find shelter. Some slept in the old Slave Market, while others found refuge around the fort and even inside its casements. Harry Flagler led the donors to a relief fund, chaired by Anderson, with a hundred-dollar contribution. His father took this opportunity to announce that the Carcaba cigar factory, which had been destroyed in the fire, would be relocated to the old St. Mary's Convent building on the lot east of the Ponce de Leon. He added that Carcaba could occupy some empty rooms in the City Building until the convent building could be renovated as a cigar factory.[85]

When Governor McKinley and his party arrived at Union Station a thick plume of smoke could be seen to the east. The fire on Charlotte Street still raged and threatened to consume most of the city north of the Plaza. Mayor Pinkham was on the other side of town directing efforts to contain the fire, but Henry Flagler greeted the governor and escorted him directly to the Ponce de Leon, where rooms had been reserved for his party. After refreshing themselves the McKinley group boarded carriages for a tour of the historic sites in town and even went to observe the smoldering district of the afternoon's fire. After dinner that evening the governor and his wife and friends greeted leading Republicans and some Democrats in the Grand Parlor. The Flagler men, father and son, were among the crowd of several hundred, as were Hamilton Disston and the ever-present Captain Marcotte, who recorded the event. In future years Henry Flagler would not be personally close to McKinley, but from time to time he would send President McKinley brief notes of approval on some matter or another, and very occasionally he would offer political advice.[86]

The 1895 season closed with better house counts than the previous year—an indication of the slow recovery of the national economy—but Palm Beach continued to drain patrons away from Flagler's hotels in St. Augustine. Ponce de Leon manager C. B. Knott reported to Harry Flagler early in the season that the hotel had had its best January house count since 1891, but at the same time more people were moving on to Palm Beach than ever before. Some people staying in the Cordova, Alcazar, and Ponce de Leon were waiting for a room to become available in the Royal Poinciana, which was almost continually filled to capacity. Mrs. Marcotte tried to put a positive face on matters by saying that the previous year's fear that St. Augustine would become only a "way station" to Palm Beach had not come true. She added that the prospect of another Flagler hotel opening on Biscayne Bay would likewise just increase the total number of winter visitors to Florida and would benefit every town up and down the East Coast.[87] But of course St. Augustine had indeed become a way station en route to South Florida.

Edwin Augustus Moore, a visitor from Connecticut, noted that most tourists experienced St. Augustine "on the one day plan." Sightseers took a carriage ride around town—which the driver circuited as quickly as possible in order to hire another load of fares—and then on the morrow the visitors hustled away to their next Florida venue.[88]

Harry and Anne Flagler left St. Augustine to return to New York on April 3 after what was apparently a successful term as the resident Flagler family in town.

A week later Henry and Alice came up from Palm Beach, where they had spent the season. However, Henry did not remain long at Kirkside. A few days later he and two of his railroad executives returned to Palm Beach, accompanied by an army engineer. The military man's presence was necessary since the War Department's permission was required for building any bridge across a navigable waterway. A few days later Flagler returned to St. Augustine in company with James Ingraham, who had just made an expedition down the Keys to Key West. Flagler made no announcements regarding his movements, but it was easy enough to guess what was going on: Flagler was moving farther south. Some thought he might be headed for Key West right away.[89]

A month later Flagler finally revealed his plans for the immediate future. He traveled down to Palm Beach with some of his lieutenants and Dr. Anderson to announce that he would be building a second large hotel in Palm Beach, across the way from the Royal Poinciana beside the ocean. This new hotel would be called the Palm Beach Inn and would be ready for the 1896 season. Later it would be renamed the Breakers, and, after burning down twice and being rebuilt each time, it remains today one of the great luxury hotels of the world.[90]

The announcement the public had been expecting of Flagler's decision to move on to Biscayne Bay did not come. By this time it was well known that Flagler had paid at least one visit and probably more to the Biscayne Bay area. Out of public sight he had been busy negotiating with Julia Tuttle in Miami and other major landowners in the territory south of Lake Worth to receive grants of land if he extended his railroad to Biscayne Bay. These negotiations took some time to complete. Flagler drove a hard bargain with Mrs. Tuttle, writing to her, "I am incurring great risk, with comparatively little inducement." He explained that dredging a ship channel into Biscayne Bay would take years of political wrangling and expensive work, while it would be easy for him to build a pier for ships to dock at Palm Beach. Flagler also expressed his concerns about working with Tuttle in dividing town lots in Miami, since Flagler was accustomed to working alone, not with a partner. But he assured her that he hoped to close all his land deals by the first of July so that the railroad could be built to Miami by February.[91]

Meanwhile, Flagler and Alice closed up Kirkside and returned to New York City early in May. It was the last time Alice would see St. Augustine.[92]

Flagler still had some work to do in Florida. Near the end of May he and his secretary J. C. Salter returned to St. Augustine to pick up Ingraham and two other railroad men for a quick trip to Palm Beach and back. Then Flagler made the return trek to New York once more. His frequent rapid excursions were facilitated by his fellow railroad presidents, who extended the courtesy of handling his private car at no cost and expedited his passage over their rails. Of course, Flagler reciprocated this consideration on his Florida road.[93]

During that summer of 1895 in New York, Alice's mental state fell apart. Her stepson Harry later recounted two incidents of Alice's strange behavior, though he evidently did not witness them himself. In the first case Alice wrote a check to her manicurist for one million *roses*, and the surprised manicurist showed this check to Henry Flagler. In the second instance Alice reportedly had a miniature portrait of herself set in diamonds by Tiffany's Jewelers and sent to the czar of Russia. Harry did not know whether this gift was intercepted before delivery to the czar.[94]

Dr. Shelton, who served as the Flagler family physician, saw Alice often to treat her various minor complaints, and he became increasingly concerned about her worsening mental condition. During his visits she began to confide in him about all sorts of supposed scandals in society and insisted that her husband had long been unfaithful to her. Later in the summer when the Flaglers were at Mamaroneck, she excitedly showed Shelton three pebbles, claiming that they possessed magical powers, and she declared she would send one of them to the czar of Russia. When Shelton told Flagler of this strange conversation, Flagler agreed to return to their Fifth Avenue home where Shelton could see Alice on a regular basis. Here Mrs. Flagler's delusions became more rampant, evidently facilitated by her fascination with a Ouija board, an innocuous recent invention intended to be used around the parlor table as family entertainment. In October Flagler called in two physicians who were experts in psychotic conditions. When Alice openly made threats of violence against her husband, the doctors, assisted by a female matron, forced Alice into a carriage and took her to an asylum that cared for a handful of wealthy patients in Pleasantville, not far north of New York City.[95]

In the midst of his wife's catastrophic mental collapse, Flagler and his son Harry experienced a fundamental break that led to a permanent estrangement of the two men. Essentially they never spoke to each other again. The violence of this separation cannot be explained, but the causes seem easy to understand. Henry Flagler wanted his son to become the heir to his business empire, but Harry wished to make his own way in an entirely different direction. In his will Flagler would leave Harry only a small portion of his estate, explaining that Harry "has not shown for me the filial regard that would make me inclined to do more for him." Dr. Anderson's daughter Clarissa would later say that the elder Flagler simply could not understand or accept Harry's interest in music. Flagler's biographer Sidney Walter Martin wrote that Henry Flagler was "probably" overbearing in his dealings with his son. Martin gave Harry Flagler a chance to refute this judgment, but Harry kept his peace.[96]

Harry and Anne would not be in St. Augustine for the 1896 season, and when the directors of the Florida East Coast Railway met there in April, Harry was conspicuously absent. Instead Harry remained in New York and became a major patron of classical music. He used the considerable organizational talents he inherited from his father to promote the cultural advancement of the city. Interestingly, John D. Rockefeller's son, John D. Jr., likewise did not follow his father into an executive position with Standard Oil but instead devoted his life to philanthropic causes, taking care to invest for the benefit of humanity the wealth his father had amassed.

The newspapers, which Henry Flagler detested, were unaware of Ida Alice's insanity and institutionalization, and they also did not detect the split between the older and younger Flagler men. Naturally many people close to the Flaglers and key executives in the Flagler system knew the truth. Certainly the Marcottes knew, but neither the *Times-Union* nor the *Tatler* even made mention of Alice's obvious absence from the St. Augustine and Palm Beach social scene. None of the Flagler family troubles found their way into the yellow tabloid journalism of the day—at least not for a few years.

Privately Henry Flagler sank into profound grief. Suddenly he was left almost alone in the world. His daughter was dead, his wife insane, and his son estranged. Anderson attempted to console him, and Flagler acknowledged his gratitude:

> Thank you for your "thoughts" of me and for your "hopes" in my behalf— Not a day passes, but that I call myself to account for what I fear my friends may think is an unmanly weakness—I summon all the philosophy I am capable of. I reason about it, I realize that mine is no exceptional case, but it is no use. You have known me, my dear Friend, in one great sorrow; then it was comparatively easy to think and speak of Heaven. Now it is not so— this is something immeasurably harder to bear than death. It needs God himself. His personal presence and I am devoutly thankful that He has not deserted me. For all this, I am grateful to you for your tender sympathy, for it helps me.
>
> Henry's desertion of me has made my burden much heavier—and I constantly wonder why this additional sorrow was necessary—God knows and I must trust Him.[97]

Shelton advised Flagler to go to Florida, since he could do no good for his wife by remaining; moreover, removing himself from the scene of his anguish would be good for Flagler's own mental health. Shelton wrote to Anderson: "Mr. Flagler starts for Florida next week. I have advised very strongly that he do that because he is almost prostrated with grief and anxiety. I have seen him in deep trouble, but never has anything taken such a hold upon him as this. I hope you will keep him in the South until the edge of his grief wears off. . . . I believe you can cheer him more than anyone."[98]

17

On to Miami, 1896–1897

It strikes me that we have outgrown the Ponce de Leon.
—Henry Flagler to Joseph Parrott, September 9, 1895

With his family life in shambles, Flagler fled from New York to Florida. He and his private secretary J. C. Salter came down in Flagler's personal car, which was no longer referred to as *Alicia* but simply as no. 90. They arrived in St. Augustine on October 30. Flagler would spend five days in town so that he could attend to business and inspect the changes made in his properties.[1]

At the conclusion of the 1895 season Flagler had decided to abandon the practice of the past two years during which the Cordova had served as his number two hotel, while the Alcazar only provided rooms for the overflow from the other hotels. In the 1896 season the Alcazar would revert to its former position as the primary adjunct to the Ponce de Leon, and the Cordova would be used to accommodate any surplus of guests, while its dining room would be utilized for public entertainments when necessary. Shortly after the hotels shut down in the spring, McGuire sent a team of twenty workmen into the Alcazar to make some major alterations in preparation for the hotel's elevated status for the next season.

To make the suites upstairs more attractive, forty-eight new private bathrooms were added. Some bedrooms at the ends of hallways were sacrificed in order to extend the hallways to the exterior walls so that sunlight would shine into the halls' interiors. The second story walkways from the hotel to the Casino were roofed over so that guests could make the walk without being exposed to the elements. However, the most striking alteration was made on the ground floor, where McGuire's workers tore out the wall between the northern portion of the dining room and the lobby. This created an impressively large rectangular entrance hall, giving the Alcazar a grand room nearly on the scale of the Ponce de Leon's public areas. Today visitors to Lightner Museum can experience the impressive ambiance of this room, which has been renovated once again in modern times. In order to draw attention to the new Alcazar, workmen installed four-foot-tall letters spelling "ALCAZAR" across the front of the hotel between the towers. Multicolored electric lights shone from these letters.[2]

When McGuire took Flagler on an inspection tour of the improvements in the Alcazar, Flagler noted that guests wishing to go from the new entrance hall to the ladies' parlor on the west side of the courtyard were required to exit onto the open arched portico and walk the few paces between the rooms. In case of cold, windy weather, ladies in their gowns would be exposed to the elements. Why not, Flagler suggested, enclose the arches of the portico across the front of the new hall and incorporate the portico into the entrance hall, then also enclose the first three arches on the west side to create an interior hallway connecting the two public rooms? Within half an hour McGuire had his workers busy making this change. Large glass windows with lifting sashes in the middle were placed into the arches, with white lace curtains to decorate the new windows. This prosaic treatment was not what Carrère and Hastings had originally had in mind, but then they had underestimated the nasty weather that St. Augustine sometimes experiences during the winter. (The windows in the loggia arches have long since been removed, but the outlines of their frames are still visible on the concrete of the arches. The wall of the foyer has also been restored, and the loggia is open once again, as Carrère and Hastings intended.)[3]

Following his brief stay in St. Augustine, Flagler was off for Palm Beach in private car no. 90, with his railroad and hotel executives attached in car no. 91, a new private car he had acquired in 1893 for use by his railroad officers.

A new bridge had been built across Lake Worth to connect the Royal Poinciana to the mainland so that guests could ride their Pullmans right up to the gate of the hotel. As the *Jacksonville Daily Florida Citizen* explained, "It has been from the start H. M. Flagler's wish to be the first to cross this bridge." Just south of the hotel Flagler set up housekeeping in the old McCormick cottage, now called Sea Gull Cottage. His cousin Eliza Ashley and her husband Eugene came down from Lockport, New York, to share the place with Flagler. Eliza would serve as hostess. Friends and visitors, such as the Andersons and Plants, would drop by from time to time.[4]

Flagler brought his launch *Adelante* down to Lake Worth for use on the local waters. It received the new name *Kathleen* in honor of James Ingraham's young daughter. A new naphtha engine replaced its original steam engine, and when the fuel tank for this engine exploded in August 1895, Ingraham found himself burned, battered, blown overboard, and stranded in mud until a passing boat rescued him. "A man of robust constitution," Ingraham spent only a few days at home in bed before returning to his labors encouraging home seekers to settle in the Lake Worth region.[5]

Flagler maintained a small fleet of watercraft on Lake Worth, but the *Kathleen* seems to have been the most substantial vessel of the lot. Parties used it for cruises around the lake, and later when the coastal canal was opened to Biscayne Bay, the *Kathleen* could be used to explore New River at Ft. Lauderdale and carry guests to Miami.[6]

During the summer and fall of 1895 Flagler's Florida enterprise had taken on a whole new consolidated aspect, extending its scope far beyond St. Augustine and transforming its public image into a "system" spanning the East Coast of the state. The Jacksonville, St. Augustine and Indian River Railway adopted the simple name Florida East Coast Railway, in turn commonly shortened to FEC Railway. This railroad would carry winter visitors to any one of a chain of Flagler hotels operating under the umbrella of the East Coast Hotel System. The Ponce de Leon, Alcazar, and Cordova headed the list, but it now included the Ormond, Royal Poinciana, and Palm Beach Inn. For the first time the public became fully aware that the Ormond was a Flagler property. From the steel pier at Palm Beach vacationers could board the steamer *Northumberland* of the FEC Steamship Line to cruise to Nassau.

True to his Standard Oil philosophy, Flagler applied a systematic approach to supplying his hotels. Young Clarence B. Knott, described as a "born organizer," was put in charge of large warehouses in St. Augustine where supplies for all the hotels could be purchased in bulk and distributed to the various hotels as needed. Linen, silver, china, and glassware—even electrical parts, plumbing fixtures, and tennis balls—would be purchased from specific companies. Knott would obtain samples of goods from several companies to make sure they met Flagler's high quality standards, and then he would negotiate the lowest possible price with one supplier. For example, in 1903 Wanamakers of Philadelphia received the contract for all fabric materials, from table and bed linen to carpets and window draperies.[7]

He would bargain with orange grove owners to purchase the production of their whole grove. Nonperishable food goods would be stocked in large quantities during the fall, while most fresh food items came in during the season to be stored in cold rooms until shipped out. Meat was procured by the ton. Only a few items, such as garden vegetables, eggs, poultry, and fish, would be purchased locally by the various hotel managers as needed. Every other day a train of refrigerator cars would head south carrying supplies for the hotels, then return north on alternate days carrying produce from the farms of the lower East Coast.[8]

The Flagler system owned and operated its own dairy to supply milk, cream, and butter to its hotels. When the Ponce de Leon opened in 1888 most of its

Flagler's dairy cows grazed on filled marshland west of Ribera Street. Later Flagler would build the YMCA on an eastern corner of this property. Postcard in author's collection.

dairy needs had been served by D. B. Usina, a local man whose Oakland Dairy milk wagons made early morning rounds to most of the town's hotels. In 1892 Flagler purchased his first milk cows. Ponce de Leon manager O. D. Seavey said he still expected to purchase most of the hotels' milk from local farmers, but he wanted to have a more certain supply in case Usina and other dairymen in the area could not meet the demands of Flagler's hotels. Actually, Flagler was moving to make himself largely independent of outside suppliers. He joined the American Jersey Cattle Club, the membership of which included John D. Rockefeller, three Vanderbilts, and a number of other gentlemen who wished to breed very high quality stock. The club (today the American Jersey Cattle Association) maintained a registry to document the bloodlines of all the cattle owned by its members. The western portion of what had been Dr. Anderson's orange grove became the cow lot where Flagler's herd grazed.[9]

James McGuire assumed charge of the dairy, taking care to order the cows' feed and look after their health. He hired the men who did the milking and purchased glass bottles labeled "Ponce de Leon Dairy, St. Augustine, Fla." The herd totaled between seventy and one hundred head, with about half of them located in St. Augustine and the rest scattered down the East Coast. McGuire evidently took great pride in the dairy and once told a breeder that Mr. Flagler "is very much interested in his dairy." However, Flagler brushed off a request for information from another breeder by saying of his cattle: "I pay no attention to them and seldom see them." He referred the inquiry to McGuire.[10]

In later years, following Flagler's death, the hotel system abandoned its dairy operations. McGuire wrote to a farmer in Hastings, "We have practically disposed of our dairy." Soon thereafter he wrote to another farmer offering two cows at what he deemed a "bargain price." By that time the YMCA building had been constructed on part of the cow pasture, but the rest of the land would remain largely an open field until after World War II.[11]

As the system expanded, St. Augustine became a smaller and smaller part of the whole. Flagler wrote to Parrott in the early fall of 1895 suggesting that the image of the Hotel Ponce de Leon be deemphasized in the hotel company's advertising. "It strikes me that we have outgrown the Ponce de Leon," he observed. James Ingraham expressed a similar thought about the declining importance of St. Augustine and its hotels when he reported that "the Southern portion of 'our territory' is much more prosperous than the Northern."[12]

St. Augustinians watched the rise of South Florida as a rival resort area and were reluctant to see their chief patron depart for more southerly regions. One letter writer to the *St. Augustine Herald* held out the hope that Flagler and his hotel guests would realize the error of their ways: "St. Augustine will be a lasting monument to a marvelous individual. . . . Wise and wealthy tho Mr. Flagler may be, he will one day admit that St. Augustine was a field more worthy of his promises than Palm Beach, for here is a city, a center and a place of *residence*, while there is a great hotel, with a few degrees higher temperature, *nothing more*."[13]

In order to compete with places such as Palm Beach, the citizens of St. Augustine attempted to make their town more attractive as a resort by building a bridge connecting the city to Anastasia Island and its beach. This idea had long been discussed and now came to fruition—but not without some conflict over the location of the bridge. The easiest way to construct a bridge would be simply to begin at the Plaza and build straight across the bay to the already existing dock and terminal of the South Beach Railway on the island. This location, however, would cut Matanzas Bay squarely in two, eliminating it as a sheet of open water for yacht racing or just for pleasure sailboating. Opponents of this site advocated locating the bridge somewhere south of town, where a utilitarian bridge would not obstruct the sweeping vista from the town and where it would be much less of a barrier to recreational sailing. James McGuire and Dr. Anderson signed a petition gotten up by the Board of Trade favoring the Plaza site, while many boatsmen, including W.S.M. Pinkham and James Renwick, put their names to a counter-petition. Captain Marcotte used his column in the *Times-Union* to advocate the southern location.[14]

Early in the debate it became evident that those favoring the Plaza location for the bridge enjoyed most of the public support. A new group of investors bought out the old South Beach Railway and formed a new company that would operate a toll bridge for carriages, pedestrians, and bicycles in conjunction with the railway on the island. The bridge would consist of palm tree trunk pilings supporting a wooden deck wide enough for two lanes of horse-drawn traffic, with a separate lane for individuals on foot. Boats would pass through a 181-foot-long steel turnstile draw resting on a pivot atop a concrete column sunk into the bay bottom.[15]

The Matanzas River bridge opened on January 1, 1896. Most businesses closed for the day's celebrations. St. Augustine's black citizenry commenced the festivities with a parade in honor of Emancipation Day, commemorating the day in 1863 when Lincoln's Emancipation Proclamation went into effect. The black fraternal lodges, decked out in their regalia, marched in procession along with two brass bands, ladies in colorful dresses, fifty carriages, and a float bearing the Goddess of Liberty. Then at noon the bridge's steel draw pivoted into place, the American flag rose over the tollhouse at the foot of the bridge, and the Fifth Infantry Band struck up patriotic airs. Carriages rolled across the bridge, the St. Augustine Light Infantry marched over to take target practice at the army's island rifle range, and squads of bicyclists wheeled over the water. That evening hotels threw fancy dinners in celebration.[16]

Henry Flagler was in Palm Beach when the bridge opened, for he was focused on developments farther south down the peninsula. Early in January the dredges working on the Florida coastline canal broke a passageway through from Lake Worth to Biscayne Bay. As was his prerogative, being president of the canal company, Flagler and his lieutenants boarded the steamer *Biscayne* in Palm Beach to make the first passage through the new waterway. One of the men on board the ship left this recollection of the moment when the vessel entered Biscayne Bay: "Mr. Flagler was on the upper deck of the steamer and looking eastward he saw a large tramp steamer near the shore. He requested the captain blow a salute, which was promptly answered by the liner." Along the west shore of the bay Flagler's work train was laying track on its way to Miami. "Mr. Flagler remarked, 'Gentlemen, how wonderful! See ocean traffic on one side, the canal in the center and the railroad on the other side, and all within hailing distance of each other.'" That night Flagler and his men slept in Mrs. Tuttle's hotel.[17]

With both canal and rail connections to Miami assured, Flagler decided the time had come to begin work on his next big hotel in Miami. He called John Sewell into his office in Palm Beach to provide marching orders. Sewell commanded a workforce of two hundred black men who were kept busy clearing land and filling marshes to make Palm Beach an attractive resort rather than a tangled wilderness. Sewell noted that Flagler personally tended to much of the detail work involved in his developments. Flagler instructed Sewell to take only a few of his crew with him at first because finding lodging and food would be difficult. A couple of days later Flagler walked down to the dock in front of the

Royal Poinciana to see his land clearing expedition off, giving Sewell a letter of introduction to Mrs. Tuttle.[18]

When Sewell arrived in Miami he was surprised to find that Captain Vaill and his floating hotel *Rockledge* (a sign board above the pilot house read "Floating Hotel") had preceded him to Miami by one day. He would spend his first few nights as the captain's guest.

Vaill's Florida voyages, which had begun in St. Augustine, came to an end in Miami. He had long been plagued by gout, and now the doctors diagnosed him with Bright's disease. He would soon be forced to retire to the Sailors' Snug Harbor home on Staten Island, New York. His floating hotel *Rockledge* was dismantled in the Miami River, and its hull sank to the bottom, where it rested for many years. Vaill returned to Florida in 1903 to revisit old friends and places, and he passed away on October 19, 1904, at Snug Harbor. Some of his descendents live in St. Augustine today.[19]

Sewell found shelter for his workmen as best he could and went to deliver his letter of introduction to Mrs. Tuttle. Then he began leveling out a space on the north bank of the Miami River for the Hotel Royal Palm. This included flattening an Indian burial mound where Sewell uncovered a number of human bones—which he considerately reburied in an unmarked grave. When the hotel site had been prepared, Sewell turned his attention to dynamiting pathways through the local coral rock so that a grid of streets could be opened through the town that Flagler and Tuttle had planned. In later years Sewell and his brother Everett would serve multiple terms as mayor of the town they helped to build from the ground up.[20]

In St. Augustine the 1896 winter season started on a tentative note. During the fall the future of the San Marco Hotel became a subject of discussion for men hanging around the post office and courthouse, since it seemed likely that the hotel might not open for the season. In November the speculations acquired some substance when it was announced that the Cruft heirs had sold the building to Albert Geiger of Boston, who declared his intent to lease the hotel for a season or two and then demolish it to erect a more modern hotel in its place. In mid-December news came that the hotel would be open after all. The San Marco would be managed by John W. Spitler, a well-known local businessman who operated a wholesale meat market, and William Burton, an established northern hotel man. Thus the city's second largest hotel would assume its usual place as a center of social activity.[21]

As in the previous year, the Alcazar opened first among the Flagler hotels, on November 3, with the Cordova held in reserve for the overflow crowds expected when the season peaked in late February and March. The Ponce de Leon would not open until January 20, continuing the practice of shortening its season. There was a shake-up in management of the Ponce de Leon after Clarence Knott was promoted to overall command of the Flagler hotel system. Romer Gillis, head desk clerk of the Ponce de Leon, moved up to be manager. However, he shared duties with Robert Murray, former steward of the Cordova, who would continue to oversee affairs at the back of the house while Gillis supervised the front office.[22]

This dual management would continue for two seasons, and then Murray took over for the next thirty-three years. He was a lifelong bachelor, and his sister Mrs. George M. Fletcher served as hostess for the hotel.

The day before the Ponce de Leon opened people passing by the west side of the hotel on King and Valencia streets were startled to see "For Sale" signs on the west lawn. Was the grand hotel for sale? As was quickly ascertained, only a fifty-three-foot-wide strip of land along Sevilla Street was for sale. All this time everyone had assumed that this parcel of land belonged to Flagler since it fell within the hotel's concrete border wall, but the property was actually part of the Anderson family estate. The signs were just the latest evidence of the continuing legal battle with Anderson and Flagler on one side and the Northrop heirs on the other.[23]

By this time Flagler had purchased Anderson's interest in the Markland estate, except for the grounds around Markland House itself, and he owned the adjoining land on the San Sebastian River that he had filled for the railroad and Union Station. The Northrops claimed not only a three-fifths interest in the Anderson property but also the filled land since, they argued, the owner of a property adjoining swamp land also owned any extension of land made by filling the swamp. In January 1895 *Northrop v. Flagler* went to court, naturally attracting much attention. Ex-governor Fleming served as lawyer for the Northrops, while C. M. Cooper, a future congressman, acted on Flagler's behalf. The proceedings went on for more than a week and ended in a mistrial. However, the Northrops' claim to the filled land was upheld.[24]

Before the case went to court Flagler had been negotiating with young Claudian B. Northrop, grandson of Dr. Anderson's deceased half-sister Emily, to give some of the disputed land to the Northrops in settlement of their claims. However, the land they wanted was the strip of property closest to the Hotel Ponce de Leon. Everyone realized that taking this land from the hotel's grounds would spoil the appearance of the hotel's landscape, but the Northrops held this land hostage, and Flagler was too stubborn to be intimidated. Thus in November 1895 Flagler settled the Northrop claim on their terms. Flagler gained control of all of the former Anderson estate except the strip of land between the Hotel Ponce de Leon and Valencia Street, which became the Northrops' property.[25]

Thus the Northrops put up "For Sale" signs on the west side of the Ponce de

Robert Murray served as manager
of the Hotel Ponce de Leon from
1896 to 1929. From the collection of
the St. Augustine Historical Society
Research Library.

Leon lawn in January 1896. The signs remained in place for almost three months, but no buyer came forward. Near the end of March Flagler brought this convoluted and extended litigation to a conclusion after nearly ten years of wrangling by purchasing the strip of land.[26]

Thanks in part to the generosity of Henry Flagler, in early February St. Augustine gained another church. The town's Baptists had organized a congregation in the 1880s, but it did not prosper for lack of a building of its own. Flagler came to the aid of the church in 1890 by donating a lot on Saragossa Street; however, the Baptists had trouble raising the money needed to construct a suitable building. Thus construction would not begin until the summer of 1894, and by then Flagler and the Baptists had traded his original lot for one on the northwest corner of Sevilla and Carrera streets, across the way from the Barcelona Hotel. At the last moment Flagler suggesting moving the church site once again to the lot across from Grace Methodist on Cordova Street, but the Baptists deemed the location unsuitable since it might seem disrespectful to their "Methodist brethren." At last the yellow brick, Norman-style church began to rise in August 1894—but only after Baptist leaders had shown Flagler the plans to make sure they had his approval. Although the church had stood in a state of near-completion since 1895, the dedication of Ancient City Baptist Church came on February 2, 1896. The service was held in the afternoon so that all the churchgoers of the town might attend. Rev. John MacGonigle of Memorial Presbyterian read the scripture, and

The Riding Academy took over the tennis courts of the Alcazar for several years. Author's collection.

Rev. S. Hamilton Day of Grace Methodist offered a prayer before Rev. J. B. Hawthorne of First Baptist Church of Atlanta preached the dedication sermon.[27]

The bicycle revolution that had taken hold back in 1892 entered a more radical phase in 1896. "Early in the season," wrote Mrs. Marcotte, "cycling was a fad; it seems to be growing into a craze, a disease not confined to any class, age, sect or color." A half dozen or so "bicycle emporiums" opened in town for the sale and rental of wheels. The premier bicycle venture was the Riding Academy established at the Hotel Alcazar. The nets were taken down at the recently re-asphalted tennis courts behind the Casino, and instructors gave personal coaching to novices wishing to join the adventure on wheels. The academy was sponsored by the Columbia Cycle Company, which furnished fifty bicycles of various sizes and styles for the enjoyment of customers. Flagler's asphalt streets around his hotels served as an ideal surface for riders, and the city fathers came under increased pressure to improve the paving on the rest of the town's streets, although adding a layer of oyster shell here and there was about all they were able to accomplish. Cyclists who ventured as far as the beach discovered a wonderfully smooth, firm surface on which to roll.[28]

The mix of horses, people on foot, and others mounted on bicycles created potentially dangerous conditions on the town's streets. "There is considerable complaint about the carelessness of bicycle riders here," wrote Captain Marcotte. "There have been several slight accidents, and several times more serious ones would have occurred but for the agility of the pedestrians, who managed to get out of the way. Some one suggests that the pedestrians wear bells to warn the riders of their presence." Instead the town council passed an ordinance requiring bicycles to be equipped with bells and also with lights during the dark winter months.[29]

The captain's wife used the pages of the *Tatler* to prognosticate about the impact of the wheel on larger society: "The advent of the bicycle and its very general adoption for the purpose of facilitating business as well as for pleasure will revolutionize the streets and roads of the country within a very few years—has already done more to effect dress reform for women than all the lectures ever delivered or editorials written against long dresses, heavy skirts and tight lacing." She observed that some women went about town in their cycling costumes all day long.[30]

The Golf Club opened its new season with a reception the week before Christmas in its new clubhouse on the northern edge of the fort green. Lucy Abbott, who originally owned the whole tract of land north of the fort, was guest of honor at the reception. She had rented one of her cottages to serve as the golfers' headquarters—although she complained of golfers entering the grounds of her home in search of errant balls. Ladies of the club used the large parlor to serve tea and punch, while gentlemen who wished to play cards took over another room. Men could change clothes in a separate room equipped with lockers, although some members arrived on bicycles already dressed in their knickerbockers. Two new holes were added, named "Little Misery" and "Demi-lune," giving the course a total of five holes. The first of these new links required golfers to pitch their balls down into the covered way, the area behind the fort's earthen outer ramparts. The second entailed a tee shot over the northwestern corner of the covered way, offering the possibility of falling into this deep obstacle. The club added a new provision to its rulebook, admonishing: "Players are earnestly cautioned to refrain from playing as long as pedestrians are in the line of play." The numerous sightseers passing to and from the fort, the town's leading curiosity for tourists, created a hazard for both golfers and innocent passersby.[31]

One local cottage resident who must have had some golf balls bounce into his yard was William Deering, who owned the large shingled home just north of the fort green on the bay front. Deering manufactured farming equipment in his factory near Chicago. His company would soon combine with several rival companies to form International Harvester. Deering had first wintered in St. Augustine in 1891 because of his failing health. A modest, retiring man, Deering and his family remained largely outside the whirl of society and enjoyed sailing on the bay. Deering would later move to Coconut Grove near Miami, where he would build a house in 1910. He passed away there in 1913. His son James would build the winter home "Vizcaya" on Biscayne Bay in 1914. Today Vizcaya is one of Miami's monuments to the age of great private homes.[32]

Noted personalities continued to stop by Flagler's St. Augustine hotels. Henry

Clay Frick returned for another visit, as did William Rockefeller—who went on to Palm Beach in the private car Flagler sent to meet him. The president of the Illinois Central railroad, Stuyvesant Fish, who lived in a New York townhouse designed by Stanford White, came by the Ponce de Leon. His wife Marion, who set trends in New York and Newport society, brought a party of gay young people with her, along with a squad of servants. Andrew Carnegie and his wife spent several days at the Ponce de Leon during two visits in February and March. Their family owned a winter home, "Dungeness," on Cumberland Island in Georgia. Joseph Pulitzer, who had a cottage on Jekyll Island, Georgia, also came down the coast to spend time at the Ponce de Leon. Cornelius Vanderbilt brought a huge retinue of friends and servants who occupied nearly twenty rooms in the Ponce de Leon. Mrs. Marcotte explained, "Mr. Vanderbilt is very unassuming, the ladies and gentlemen going about in most democratic fashion while here." Yet she added that the Vanderbilts usually dined upstairs in a private room set up for them, with their own headwaiter to bring up dishes from the main kitchen below. The country's leading banker J. P. Morgan stopped in St. Augustine for only two hours on his way to Palm Beach.[33]

Not all the notable personalities who visited were wealthy. Dr. Henry M. Field, editor of the Presbyterian publication the *Evangelist*, counted Henry Flagler as a longtime acquaintance. Flagler came up from Palm Beach to greet Field and show him the Ponce de Leon personally. "I have found the men who say the least do the most," was Field's tribute to Flagler. The American public knew Field as the author of several popular books on world travel and as the brother of trans-Atlantic telegraph cable layer Cyrus Field. Another religious leader, Frances E. Willard, the president of the Women's Christian Temperance Union, made an address in Grace Methodist Church. In addition to her stand against drunkenness, Willard championed all sorts of liberal causes, including votes for women. Appropriately for a champion of the common people, she stayed at the modest Barcelona, but some ladies held a reception for her in the parlor of the Alcazar. True to her modern bent, she took lessons in bicycling at the Alcazar's Riding Academy.[34]

Dwight L. Moody, the leading evangelical preacher of the day, also gave a lecture at Grace Methodist Church one afternoon. He and his wife stayed at the Ponce de Leon. Flagler had first met Moody back in the fall of 1885 when Moody came knocking at the door of Flagler's home at Mamaroneck. "I was at first very much vexed that he should have presented himself at my house," Flagler wrote to Rockefeller, "but I shortly became greatly interested in this man and listened with much attention to all he had to say of his work." Moody had established in his hometown of Northfield a school for destitute girls from the mills and rural farms of Massachusetts. Flagler asked Rockefeller if he had investigated whether

Moody's work was worthy of support, and when Rockefeller replied yes, Flagler wrote that he would contribute a modest sum to Moody's cause.[35]

In March Flagler brought Sir William Haynes-Smith, the governor-general of the Bahamas, and his family to the Ponce de Leon to show off the best of his hotels. The governor-general reciprocated by inviting Flagler to Nassau as his guest. Some local citizens thought Flagler might be smoothing the way for construction of a new Flagler hotel in the Bahamas, but Joseph McDonald denied this. He told the *Tatler*, "In regard to the rumor that Mr. Flagler would build a hotel there, that story has no foundation in fact. The trip was purely a pleasure trip. Oh yes, I saw plenty of hotel sites, some very fine ones, of my own selection, but I have not yet been ordered to make plans for any hotel upon any one of them." While McDonald may have been telling the strict truth about not having orders to plan a new hotel, it can be assumed that the trip was not all pleasure—as future developments would soon bear out.[36]

On April 13, 1896, Flagler's special train rolled into Miami. Anderson and many of Flagler's railroad and hotel executives were on board this inaugural run. Flagler had arrived at Biscayne Bay, and there was no place left to go in Florida, except Key West. Perhaps Nassau presented a more attainable next goal.[37]

Meanwhile life in Flagler's original resort center, St. Augustine, had settled into an almost dowdy routine. What had once been an enchanting adventure now became simply a stay in a resort hotel community. Mrs. Marcotte noted that patrons of the hotels questioned the gaiety of the season. "The season now drawing to a close has been regarded as a quiet one," she admitted. It had also been short, with a peak during the last two weeks of February and the first two weeks of March. Although the Casino held numerous entertainments, and while the Ponce de Leon hosted weekly dances in the parlor, few really grand events aroused enthusiasm. The ladies of the Hospital Association abandoned their annual fair in the Casino, and although the elaborate Charity Ball came off in the Dining Room of the Ponce de Leon as usual, in earlier years the hotel had presented two or three grand balls.[38]

The winter season came to an ignominious conclusion at the Hotel San Marco. It had not been a good year for the huge, well-loved, but increasingly worn hotel. Managers Spitler and Burton had fallen behind in settlement of their bills and were paying out cash as quickly as it came in. Then on a Wednesday near the end of March, just days before the hotel's scheduled closing, the owners of a bicycle shop that had rented wheels through the San Marco entered the lobby in the company of a lawyer and the police to issue an arrest warrant against the managers for embezzlement. The bike shop men were followed quickly by other lawmen and lawyers from other firms who placed claims against the hotel's assets for unpaid bills. These creditors feared that the hotel would close without settling its outstanding accounts. Unfortunately for everyone, when the police showed up, many of the guests hastily checked out, reducing the flow of income and making it more difficult to pay the hotel's obligations.[39]

The next day a judge dismissed the charges of embezzlement, and the managers tried to pull things together at the hotel to keep it open for one more week, but about half their guests had departed already because of the hubbub. The hotel remained open only a few more days with a handful of guests before shutting its doors. Captain Marcotte doubted that all the creditors would be paid but suggested that it was their own fault for "knocking the props" from under the hotel managers.[40]

The 1896 season closed quietly when the Alcazar shut its gates on May 1. Altogether it had not been a very happy season. The whole United States still labored under the pall of the greatest economic depression in its history, while Florida suffered the additional burden of having lost its income from the orange groves because of the 1895 freeze. One dependable source of income for St. Augustine had long been the army base at St. Francis Barracks, but even that fell under a shadow.

During the summer of 1896 the people of St. Augustine began to realize that it was likely only a matter of time until the War Department pulled the army garrison out of St. Augustine and closed St. Francis Barracks. Built around the remains of the old Spanish Franciscan convent, the Barracks did not meet the requirements of a modern military base. Its five-and-a-half-acre grounds, surrounded by private residences on three sides, were simply too small. However, the army's post contributed a great deal to St. Augustine's year-round economy, and losing it would cause a significant injury to the community's financial health.

Beginning back in 1891 Henry Flagler had set in motion efforts to preserve St. Augustine's post by acquiring additional property on which to locate the garrison. W. W. Dewhurst, who was handling Flagler's land claims on Anastasia Island, proposed a site at the south end of town on the east side of the Maria Sanchez marshes, where the government already owned a five-acre site known as the Powder House Lot (not to be confused with the Old Powder House Lot to the north, off Cordova Street). Dewhurst owned some land himself that might become a portion of a new base, and he sounded out other property owners in the area about selling their land to the government. When Flagler received Dewhurst's report, he replied, "I must confess that I am greatly surprised at the prices put upon these lots."[41]

The next step in this process came in December, when Florida senators Call and Pasco introduced a bill in the U.S. Senate (with a companion bill being introduced in the House) to sell St. Francis Barracks at auction and purchase the tract of land at the south end of St. Augustine between the bay and the Maria Sanchez marshes. The Senate passed the bill, but in the House the bill remained pigeon-holed in a military subcommittee. To encourage action, the St. Augustine Board of Trade sent Dewhurst to Washington as a lobbyist. As he later acknowledged, he was handicapped in these negotiations because he owned some of the lots that would be purchased for the new base, and this made him a self-interested party in the transaction. When the holdup appeared to be the $30,000 price tag for purchase of the new property, Flagler let it be known that he would be willing to pay $40,000 for the St. Francis Barracks site. Upon his return from Washington in May 1892, Dewhurst admitted that the House was unlikely to pass the bill—and this proved to be a correct forecast.[42]

St. Augustinians' next efforts to keep the army in town centered on proposals that did not require congressional action. Secretary of War Daniel S. Lamont, a personal acquaintance of Flagler's, established a military reservation on an 860-acre tract of land owned by the government south of the lighthouse on Anastasia Island. The garrison might be relocated to this site, which had the added advantage that a fort to protect the harbor entrance might also be erected there. The army did set up a rifle range on the site; however, nothing further happened to advance this idea.[43]

Dewhurst continued to pursue the plan of moving the army base to the Powder House Lot site. He wrote to Flagler with the idea that instead of purchasing land to the north of the lot, new land should be created by filling the marshes to the south, as Flagler had already demonstrated could be done. At the same time, Dewhurst suggested another plan: Flagler himself could purchase the lots north of the Powder House Lot and then trade that property to the government in exchange for a government-owned lot next to the Plaza on which the Vaill block of buildings had been built. Vaill's lease on this lot would soon expire, and Flagler already owned a mortgage on the concrete buildings on the Vaill property. Trading the two parcels of land would not require any expenditure of taxpayers' money. Flagler responded that he would be willing to follow Dewhurst's lead in attempting to acquire the properties adjacent to the Powder House Lot, but he added, "I am getting *awfully tired* of spending my time and money in trying to secure a larger Post."[44]

Once again bills were introduced in the U.S. Senate and House embodying the proposition to trade land adjacent to the Powder House Lot for the government's lot on which the northern part of the Vaill buildings stood. At the request of Congress, the War Department made a thorough review and several army officers issued reports. They were all negative. In the first place, the new reservation at the Powder House Lot, even with the added land, would encompass only fourteen acres: too little for a military base. Half the proposed ground was subject to flooding during spring tides and would have to be filled. Even then the base would be surrounded by marshes on three sides. Also, the land adjoined Alicia Hospital, which stood on the shore of Matanzas Bay to the east, and this hospital housed patients with infectious diseases. Colonel E. C. Bainbridge of the 3rd Artillery stationed at St. Francis Barracks concluded his recommendation with the observation that the lands proposed for the new base "do not contain a single element of suitability for a military post." In his judgment, their acquisition would be "inadvisable and hurtful to the service."[45]

To cap the argument against the exchange of property, some of the army reports pointed out that the Vaill lot was more valuable than the land offered in trade. Major Thomas Handbury of the army engineers felt that the government should keep the Vaill lot since it would be a suitable future location for a new customs house or post office. He pointed out that the present building on the Plaza holding the post office and other government offices was "one of the ancient structures of the town, and could, to the advantage of the beauty of the place, be vacated and torn down." This latter advice was not taken, and the building, today known as Government House, continued to be used as a post office until the 1960s.[46]

Flagler's lobbyist in Washington, John H. Flagg, reported the bad news to Flagler: "Every one of these officers 'sets down' on the whole thing and sets down all over it. I do not see any way to extricate either bill from the debris occasioned by the downfall." Flagg felt that the army officers had simply made up their minds to abandon the post, even though some politicians favored keeping it. Perhaps, Flagg suggested, St. Augustine's leaders should unite around the idea of turning the twenty-acre reservation around Fort Marion, partly occupied by the golf course, into the location of a new post.[47] At that point Flagler gave up his efforts to preserve an army post in St. Augustine.

He traveled from Florida to New York in the spring of 1896 and received encouraging reports from one of Alice's physicians. It had been seven months since Flagler had last seen her. The doctor said she seemed to be gaining some control over her delusions and could even talk about them in an objective way. Dr. Choate was even more encouraging and went so far as to say, "I regard Mrs. Flagler as entirely cured." Choate decided to allow Alice to return home and accompanied her as far as White Plains, where Flagler came up to meet her on June 5, the thirteenth anniversary of their marriage. One of the nurses from the Pleasantville asylum accompanied Alice to the Flaglers' home at Mamaroneck. Once at home Henry found, to his great pleasure, that Alice seemed to be restored to her old self. To Anderson he wrote, "I am surprised and need not say delighted at the outcome—it seems too good to be true."[48]

A month later Flagler reported to Anderson that he and Alice had hired an instructor to teach them how to ride bicycles and that they were taking rides of as many as ten miles each day. However, ominously, Flagler mentioned that Alice was knitting an Afghan for Dr. Anderson's new baby Clarissa. "It seems an irony of fate," wrote Flagler, "that Alice, who is so fond of babies, can't have one of her own." Many of Alice's delusions appeared to spring from her failure to provide Flagler with children. Eugene and Eliza Ashley, who had spent most of the winter with Flagler in Palm Beach, came to stay with the Flaglers at Satanstoe, their Mamaroneck home. Soon after their arrival Eliza took Henry aside to inform him that Alice, when out of his presence, was conversing with her about bizarre things, just as she had a year previously. Soon Flagler too realized that Alice could be completely lucid one day, while the next day she would wander off into a dream world of delusions.[49]

Flagler wrote to Anderson telling him of Alice's relapse: "It almost breaks my heart to write this sad news. Please do not mention it to anyone." Just at this time Dr. Choate died, and Dr. Carlos F. MacDonald took his place at Pleasantville. MacDonald was one of the best known physicians in New York. He had chaired the state commission on lunacy and had been the medical supervisor for New York's first executions of criminals by the electric chair. A few years earlier MacDonald had stayed briefly at the Hotel Alcazar, but it is unlikely that he knew Flagler before seeing Alice as a patient at Pleasantville. MacDonald advised Flagler to be on guard for his safety since Alice had repeatedly made threats against him while in confinement. MacDonald still held out hope that Alice might recover her right mind with the passage of time—though she might be incurably insane. He advised Flagler to sleep in a separate bedroom, but this Flagler refused to do. Finally, in early October Alice managed to get her hands on a Ouija board and retreated into her bedroom, where she obsessed over the board, going completely out of her mind.[50]

Rather than return Alice to Pleasantville, Flagler hired a doctor and nurses to come and live at Satanstoe with Alice in the hope that somehow she could be restored to her senses. Flagler himself went to New York City, where he took up residence at the Langham Hotel on Fifth Avenue near his home. The doctors instructed him to stay away from Alice as his presence increased her agitation. Flagler's secretary Jasper Salter explained the situation to Anderson: "The strain upon him was great indeed. However, now that the shock has come, he looks more composed. The feeling that he can now sleep without any apprehension must afford his mind some relief. It is indeed a sad case." Flagler followed this with a letter of his own to Anderson. "I often feel that I should break down if it were not for the messages of love and comfort you so generously send me. I receive similar ones from others but none touch my heart as yours do."[51]

As during the previous winter, Flagler went away to Florida and threw himself into his enterprises with the same vigor as in the preceding twelve years. He and the Ashleys rode private car no. 90 into St. Augustine on January 8 and went to stay at Kirkside, which Miss McKay had put in order for his arrival. During his stay in St. Augustine, Flagler arranged to pay his state and county taxes, amounting to $7,355, although they were not due for several more months. He did this because the chronically cash-strapped county had run out of money at the end of the year and was on the verge of paying its bills with IOUs. Captain Marcotte thanked Flagler through his *Times-Union* column, writing that Flagler, "having the spare change, came to St. John's County's relief."[52]

After two weeks at Kirkside Flagler and the Ashleys invited Dr. Anderson and Joseph Parrott to join them for a journey down to Miami for the grand opening of Flagler's newest hotel, the Royal Palm. This large wooden structure continued the style and dimensions of the Royal Poinciana. It stood amid coconut palms on the north bank of the Miami River where it emptied into Biscayne Bay. Nearby was old Fort Dallas, and across the way stood the Brickell home, relics from Miami's pioneer days. Flagler signed his name on the first line of the register book.[53]

They did not remain long in Miami but departed for Tampa, where the South Atlantic and Gulf States Harbor Defense and Improvement Convention was set to convene. With the rebellion in Cuba heating up and calls for United States intervention growing, civic leaders in those states nearest Cuba wanted protection in case war broke out with Spain. Henry Plant greeted Flagler at the Tampa Bay Hotel, which served as the headquarters for the convention. Governor William D. Bloxham welcomed the delegates and called for building forts at the South's seaports. A spokesman for the Plant system also extended his welcome, but the assembly shouted for Henry Plant himself to speak. Thereupon Plant, who was in declining health, stood up to show himself, saying, "As you want a practical demonstration of 'Plant,' I am willing to gratify you." Then the crowd began to chant "Flagler, Flagler." Henry Flagler stood, made a deep bow, and declared, "I know nothing which will interest you, but I do know something that interests me and that is Florida." In the evening Plant and Flagler hosted a reception for the visitors. General Schofield also served as a host, representing St. Augustine and, unofficially, showing the U.S. Army's interest in national defense.[54]

A few days after the convention, in the first week in February, Flagler picked up General Schofield in St. Augustine along with a group of railroad executives and their wives for a pleasure tour down the East Coast. They visited the orange groves and the ruins of the old sugar mills at Ormond before continuing to Palm Beach, where they put up for the night in the Royal Poinciana. The next day they went out to inspect a pineapple field (in those days the primary crop of the Lake Worth region) before heading to Miami for a boat trip up the Miami River to the falls, where water from the Everglades spilled over the limestone formations west of town. By nightfall they were back at the Royal Poinciana, and the next day found them once again in St. Augustine. Altogether it amounted to a breathtaking display of the speed with which visitors could span the entire East Coast on Flagler's railway. A few years earlier this trip would have taken arduous days by rail, riverboat, and stagecoach.[55]

Following this whirlwind trip Flagler set up housekeeping at the McCormick's Sea Gull Cottage in Palm Beach with the Ashleys, yet he continued to maintain an active pace of travel from one point to another along the coast, attending to his multiple ventures. His private railroad car became almost a second home and office. For a man who professed to hate travel, Flagler certainly did a lot of it. One wonders if his movements were intended to take his mind off the tragedy of his wife's illness; yet even before Alice's insanity, Flagler had shown the same relentless dedication to his business affairs.

Earlier in St. Augustine, as the summer of 1896 turned to autumn, speculation had once more centered on whether the Hotel San Marco would open after the debacle of the previous spring's raid by creditors. In 1896, however, there was no last minute reprieve for the great wooden hotel, and it would stand a dark hulk all winter. About the only life around the building consisted of golfers, who walked across San Marco Avenue to play the four new holes of golf that had been added on the grounds at the rear of the hotel. Now the golfers could play a standard nine holes on the Fort Marion course.[56]

The Alcazar and Ponce de Leon opened on their regular schedules and received their usual quota of patronage—except, as Mrs. Marcotte noted, that the veteran coterie of "first day signers" at the Ponce de Leon had shrunk to just Mrs. Deborah Shedd. She returned for the ninth year in a row, maintaining the same room each year, having furnished it to her own liking. Alone among the guests of the hotel, she was allowed to keep a pet animal, a well-behaved old dog named Dolly. Most of her former associates had either passed away or chosen to winter elsewhere. During the season visitors at the Ponce de Leon could attend a dance in the Grand Parlor each week, but not a single high formal ball brought life to the Dining Room. Instead the Charity Ball moved to the Casino, where the swimming pool was drained of water and decorated as a sunken garden with supper tables set amid potted palms. Dancing and entertainments occupied all three levels of the Casino. Three bands played music continuously, and a tenor soloist on the upper balcony sang popular arias from well-known operas. It amounted to a novel experience, but it was not the same as a grand ball in the Dining Room of the Ponce de Leon. Perhaps realizing that the event had lost some of its luster, the management cut the usual admission price from five dollars to three.[57]

Once again the ladies' Hospital Association did not attempt to hold a fair in the Casino, settling instead for a lawn fete on the tennis courts behind the Casino. The new Hospital Auxiliary held a competing lawn party on the grounds of Markland. The dueling fundraisers demonstrated that the feud between the ladies of the original association and the trustees of the hospital continued to simmer. The new Hospital Auxiliary's affair raised $992, while the old association's event netted just $322. However, led by Anna Marcotte and "appreciating the good intentions of the Auxiliary," the ladies of the association voted to turn over their proceeds to the Hospital Auxiliary.[58]

Although the ladies' association continued to operate for many years more, the heyday of its importance had passed. There would be no more Hospital Fairs in the Casino, and by 1901 the annual Charity Ball for the hospital had become simply the Ponce de Leon Ball. Nevertheless, Alicia Hospital continued to serve the community just as before.

The Alcazar had surpassed the Ponce de Leon as the center of action around Flagler's Alameda plaza. Sixty rooms in the Cordova opened in February to take the guests who could not find accommodations in the Alcazar, and in a reversal of what Flagler had originally envisioned, some patrons turned away at the Alcazar desk went across King Street to the Ponce de Leon. C. B. Knott told Flagler, "The Alcazar will have to have an additional story in a couple of years if business keeps like this." Expanding the Alcazar seemed unlikely, particularly since it had already received an extra story just five years earlier, but sending guests to the Cordova required keeping an extra set of books and hiring another crew of desk clerks.[59]

Over in the Ponce de Leon, the solarium or "400 Rotunda" became an increasingly popular location for receptions and card parties. This room stood in the center of the fourth floor, under the central dome, duplicating the larger dome just below it. A large hole in the center of its floor, surrounded by a railing, permitted light from the solarium to filter down to the oculus of the lower domed Rotunda below. Sometimes the hotel orchestra played music on the third floor, with the music floating upward through this opening in the floor. The wall on the south side of the 400 Rotunda consisted of tall glass doors that could be slid open to admit the breezes from outside. The panoramic view of the Alcazar and the rooftops of the city could not be matched—unless one walked out onto the rooftop and climbed the stairs into one of the two towers.[60]

Downtown in St. Augustine one of the ancient landmarks disappeared: the deep white sand of St. George Street. The street had been paved with cypress blocks in recent years, but these wooden blocks had been fighting a losing battle with rot and wear. Captain Marcotte reported, "A lady visiting here received a bad fall while trying to ride her wheel over the wretched cypress block pavement." This echoed a complaint that had been heard for centuries, and now, finally, something was done to change its condition: a pavement of vitrified brick was laid down, extending all the way from the City Gates to the Plaza. The absurdity,

The "400 Rotunda" filled the space under the dome of the Ponce de Leon. In the center of its floor was a circular opening that allowed light to enter the oculus of the main Rotunda dome below. By permission of Library of Congress.

of course, was that on the brink of the twentieth century the rest of St. Augustine's streets remained sand or shell, except for those places where Henry Flagler had already laid his hand. (Today St. George Street is a pedestrian mall paved with a coarse shell concrete intended to evoke the days of sand.)[61]

By this time the large tract of land formerly made up of the Ball estate, the Powder House Lot, and the land lying north to Orange Street was filling up with houses. They were mostly modest cottages, not the Newport mansions Flagler had once envisioned. Near the east end of Carrera Street McGuire and McDonald had erected a pair of neat two-story cottages at numbers 7 and 9, across the street from Grace Methodist Church. During the 1897 season Lieutenant General John M. Schofield and his family occupied one of these cottages. When he was not socializing, Schofield was putting the finishing touches on his memoir, *Forty-Six Years in the Army*. He had retired in 1895 while serving as the commanding general of the army. Anderson's daughter Clarissa remembered him as a large bald man who rode a tricycle around town and was "spoiled to death" by the deference shown him at social gatherings.[62]

In South Florida Flagler continued as active as ever in new enterprises. The Bahamas exerted a powerful pull on him, and by this time he clearly was deeply involved in making preparations for a leap across the Gulf Stream. In 1897 the shallow-draft sidewheel steamer *Monticello* regularly sailed from Miami to Nassau. Flagler had largely abandoned the steel pier at Palm Beach as impractical, since it jutted right out from the beach into the open waves of the Atlantic. Besides, Miami stood a good deal closer to Nassau, making a water voyage much shorter. Flagler and Mrs. Ashley took a quick trip to Nassau in late February and brought the daughter of Governor-General Sir William Haynes-Smith back with them to the Royal Poinciana. Two of the other passengers on the *Monticello* were a "Mr. and Mrs. Stranahan," possibly Frank and Ivy Stranahan, who operated a trading post on New River at Fort Lauderdale, where James Ingraham had just laid out a new town site.[63]

In March 1897 Henry Flagler gathered up a party of friends and business associates and took a steamer to Key West, where he officially opened the newest hotel in the Florida East Coast hotel system, the Hotel Key West. It was also the oldest hotel in his system, having been remodeled from the antebellum Merrill House, where former President U.S. Grant had stayed during his 1880 tour of Florida. Flagler had leased the hotel from Jefferson B. Browne, a relentless Key West promoter who would later claim that in 1891 he had discussed with Flagler the idea of extending his railroad all the way to Key West. As a state legislator Browne became a key Flagler ally in clearing legal obstacles standing in the way of Flagler's railroad to Key West. However, in 1897 Flagler expected guests to take passage on his steamship *City of Key West* to reach his latest hotel. The three-story wood-frame building had been refurbished by Flagler, but it maintained the look of an ordinary Florida hotel, with porches on all three stories of its front. It wasn't much, but it gave Flagler a toehold in Key West and signaled that he might someday do more.[64] He would not operate this hotel as part of his system for long; by 1901 it dropped from the advertisements listing Flagler's hotels.

In mid-March Governor-General Haynes-Smith came to the Royal Palm in Miami on the *Monticello* to retrieve his daughter. Flagler made him feel at home by flying the Union Jack from the roof of the hotel and having the band play "God Save the Queen" when Haynes-Smith paid a visit to the Royal Palm's casino. Then Flagler took him to sample life at Palm Beach. A few days later Flagler entertained twenty-five members of the Bahamian legislature and their wives at a banquet in the Royal Poinciana. Amid many toasts to the queen and to Henry Flagler, the British colonials made it clear that they wanted Flagler to extend his reach to their territory.[65]

In the course of this British invasion, Henry Plant, with his wife and son Morton, came to pay their first visit to Miami. Naturally Plant was curious about Flagler's new hotel, and surely Flagler was proud to show it off. Now the joke circulating had Plant following the crowd to find Flagler's hotel.[66]

The Florida season was drawing to a close by then, and Flagler had one more thing he desired to do. For the past few weeks the FEC Railway had run a shuttle train between Palm Beach and Miami, going and returning the same day. Flagler wanted to ride the last of these trains. On its return run over the sixty-eight miles between the two cities, the train clocked just sixty-seven minutes—a record speed of more than a mile a minute.[67]

Mr. and Mrs. Pembroke Jones of Wilmington, North Carolina, came to Palm Beach at this time. Although the *Tatler* did not mention it, Mary Lily Kenan probably came along with her friends the Joneses. Flagler took the whole group to Key West and back, and then they all moved up to St. Augustine to wind up the season. The Joneses stayed at the Ponce de Leon, while the Ashleys and Mary Lily—now clearly named as part of the group—resided with Flagler at Kirkside.[68]

They would remain only a few days in St. Augustine. Flagler attended the season finale concert by the hotel orchestra in the Rotunda of the Ponce de Leon. At his suggestion the Sunday evening concerts always ended with the playing of the doxology, and it became customary for everyone to stand and join in singing. Some bowed their heads. Afterward the crowd discovered that Flagler had quietly slipped away without giving them the opportunity to express their appreciation and say goodbye. His train left for the North that night.[69]

Five days after Flagler's departure William Jennings Bryan arrived at Union Station in St. Augustine to be welcomed by a crowd of several hundred people. Just a few months earlier he had lost the race for the presidency of the United States to William McKinley, but he remained one of the most popular and influential politicians in the country.

Flagler's departure probably had nothing to do with Bryan's arrival, but Flagler most likely would not have gone out of his way to meet Bryan, whom he considered something of a crank as well as a threat to men of capital and the economic well-being of the country. Bryan's populist political philosophy rankled against Flagler's orthodox conservative principles.[70]

Florida's populistic ex-senator Wilkinson Call also felt and reciprocated Flagler's political hostility. Writing to Bryan, Call said, "I have incurred the enmity and opposition in every form, both in public and private life of Henry M. Flagler of the Standard Oil Company, and the band of millionaires and multi-millionaires who are secretly confederated to strike down by the use of money and by fraud and perjury any man who is *sincere* in his support of the Democratic principles."[71] Years later, after Bryan had run for president twice more, Flagler would sigh, "I doubt very much if we shall ever be rid of Bryan until his death occurs."[72]

Bryan's death might have occurred during his visit to St. Augustine in 1897. Following his reception at Union Station, this champion of the common people was escorted on a tour of the palatial Hotel Ponce de Leon and then to a suite of rooms on the second floor of the Alcazar, in the southwest corner that had previously been occupied by John Jacob Astor IV. After dinner the local reception committee took him to the Hotel San Marco, where he would speak from the front steps since no hall in town could hold the crowd of about two thousand who turned out to hear the greatest orator of the age.[73]

Two flights of steps led up to the broad porch of the San Marco, and between them a platform measuring about twenty by twenty feet extended out toward the driveway and front lawn, creating a stage for the speaker. The atmosphere of a political rally prevailed, with numerous lanterns lighting the scene and the First Artillery Band filling the night with lively tunes. Bryan gave a standard speech on good government and called for free coinage of silver to end the nation's economic depression. As he spoke, he noticed that the deck below him moved as he shifted his stance. At the conclusion of his speech, he turned to one of his hosts and asked, "Do you deem this platform safe?" Just then the crowd pressed in to congratulate him, and with a loud crack, a whole section abruptly collapsed, falling about fifteen feet to the ground. Two dozen people tumbled into a heap. An exploding lantern set one woman's clothing on fire, and the man who extinguished the flames suffered severe burns. Many people fractured arms and legs and suffered various contusions from the fall.

Fortunately for Bryan, Dr. S. G. Worley, chief surgeon for the FEC Railway, was standing next to him when the stage collapsed. The doctor dislocated his thumb as he fell but helped Bryan into a carriage and took the visitor to his office. There he sewed four stitches over Bryan's right eye, applied a plaster to his bruised forehead, and treated his injured right leg. The next morning Bryan issued a statement saying he felt "all right, but I was considerably shaken up. My chest and legs are very painful." Then he was off to Tallahassee to meet Governor Bloxham. Bryan's cousin, William S. Jennings, who had been on the stage the night before, would be elected Florida's governor a few years later.[74]

The Hotel San Marco would make news one last time before the year was out. Standing in his home at a little past three in the morning on November 8, 1897, Jake Masters could see a fire burning in the boiler room at the rear of the Hotel San Marco. He ran toward the hotel, firing his pistol in the air to attract attention, and awakened the caretaker who lived in the huge, empty building. When a couple of policemen arrived, they too began firing their pistols. Someone ran to the firehouse in the City Building to ring the fire bell—but found that the rope to the bell had been cut. When the fire engine finally made it to the hotel, the firemen discovered that holes had been punched in the water pipes where the hoses were attached. Clearly an arsonist had been at work.

Everyone knew what was likely to come next in this huge pine-wood structure, and dozens of men rushed into the ground floor and began carrying out furniture. As the fire spread throughout the five-story building, it lit up the whole town, and people in the country for miles around could see the flames. One eyewitness declared, "It was a grand sight. . . . most sparks flew east on to fort grounds."

A group of local businessmen offered a five-hundred-dollar reward for anyone who helped apprehend the perpetrator, and Flagler reportedly added another five hundred dollars to that sum. James McGuire lit a boiler in the Ponce de Leon to keep up steam for the hotel's pumps—just to be prepared, in case the arsonist struck again.[75]

The San Marco's career had lasted only a dozen years. It had pioneered the grand upscale resort hotel in St. Augustine and inspired Henry Flagler to build his even grander hotels. It would be easy to suppose that the owner himself had arranged the hotel's destruction, given that declining patronage had made the large hotel unprofitable.

Just a week before Henry Flagler returned to New York in the spring of 1897, on March 23, Ida Alice Flagler had been returned to the sanitarium at Pleasantville. The previous winter in Mamaroneck had been awful, as she descended more profoundly into insanity. Alice's delusions progressed to verbal threats and even physical violence. Once she managed to find a pair of scissors and stabbed one of her doctors in the hand. Finally Dr. MacDonald recommitted her to Pleasantville, where she resided with six other wealthy women. There she calmed down but remained totally out of touch with reality. Her brother Charles Shourds came from Boston to see her from time to time, but she exhibited the same symptoms in his presence as at other times. Her husband did not visit her but sent flowers twice a week. Henry Flagler never saw her face again.[76]

With Alice now out of his life, that summer in New York City Flagler developed a relationship with Helen Long, who was described as a very beautiful young woman of modest family circumstances. Six years earlier she had married Clarence Foote, a man with equally modest career prospects. As the narrative of her story later unfolded in the newspapers, Helen regretted her hasty decision to marry Foote. She abandoned him and moved to New York City, where she lived with her parents and resumed using her maiden name, Long. Supposedly Flagler first noticed her while attending a performance at the Metropolitan Opera and obtained an introduction. She would afterward say that Flagler became her financial advisor; however, the relationship was evidently more than that. Her estranged husband, Foote, would subsequently claim in a divorce suit that Flagler paid for Helen's apartment, took her cruising on his yacht, gave her large sums of money, and finally gave her a house at 27 East 57th Street.[77]

While the testimony of a scorned husband, given in a divorce suit, should be weighed with skepticism, two specifics of Clarence Foote's charges can be independently verified. In August 1897, Flagler's yacht *Alicia* anchored at Shelter Island, New York, with Mrs. Hiram H. Long, Helen, and Helen's younger sister Irene aboard as Flagler's guests. Her father's business partner J. H. Clary and his wife were also on board. The presence of such a large party of guests on the *Alicia* throws an entirely different perspective on Mr. Foote's allegation that Flagler and Helen had "cruised together" on his yacht. Bringing Helen's family into the picture suggests that perhaps, having lost both his wife and son, Flagler was already looking to rebuild his life with a third Mrs. Flagler.[78]

The charge that Flagler gave Helen a house at 27 East 57th Street also seems to be true. A published record of real estate transactions shows that on October 20 Jasper C. Salter, Flagler's confidential secretary, transferred to Helen Long a four-story, stone-front dwelling at 27 East 57th Street. The house stood just three blocks north of Flagler's home on Fifth Avenue.[79]

However, for the moment few outside the small circle of Flagler's staff and Helen Long's family seem to have known about their relationship. In January 1898 Flagler would depart for Florida, and the trail of documentary evidence for any connection between Flagler and Long ends. However, it is important to note that Mary Lily Kenan would not pay Flagler a visit in Florida during the winter season, perhaps indicating that Flagler's connection with the other potentially significant woman in his life had, for the moment, fallen into abeyance.

18

Into Caribbean Waters,
1897–1899

I have come to the conclusion that the best way to help
others is to help them help themselves.

—Henry Flagler, in Lefevre, "Flagler and Florida," 1910

On October 23, 1897, Flagler, his secretary Jasper Salter, and James McGuire stood in the shipyards of the William Cramp Ship and Engine Company in Philadelphia to enjoy festivities surrounding the launching of the SS *Miami*, a steamer commissioned by Flagler specially for carrying passengers from the port of Miami to Nassau in the Bahamas. Flags flew from every available vantage, with Flagler's personal burgee of blue and white diamonds floating from both the bow and stern staffs. The steel-hulled *Miami* had been constructed with a flat bottom and drew only ten feet of water so that it could pass through the channel Flagler was then dredging in shallow Biscayne Bay to reach docks near the mouth of the Miami River and the Hotel Royal Palm. The *Miami*'s powerful twin engines could propel the vessel through the seas at fifteen knots, allowing it to make an overnight run between Miami and Nassau in just over ten hours. It accommodated 120 passengers in elegantly decorated white and gold staterooms, each equipped with electric lights and—important for cruising in the tropics—an electric fan.[1]

The *Miami* sailed for Florida in January, and at the same time Flagler, accompanied by the Ashleys and their friend Alice Pomroy, took a parallel course south by train for St. Augustine. Miss Pomroy lived near the Ashleys in Lakeport, New York, and became Eliza Ashley's wintertime traveling companion. The Flagler party stayed briefly at Kirkside. Then they were off for Miami. Flagler signed his name on the first line of the house register when the Royal Palm opened.

Meanwhile, the SS *Miami* paid a visit to Jacksonville, where citizens went on board to inspect Flagler's latest marvel. As the *Miami* passed St. Augustine, people stood on rooftops and on the beach at Anastasia to cheer and signal their good wishes. At Palm Beach calm seas allowed the *Miami* to tie up at the steel pier to pick up hotel managers Fred Sterry and C. B. Knott. In Miami Flagler took a small steamer out to the entrance of Biscayne Bay to await the arrival of his ship. During his wait he inspected the dredges, which were having a difficult time cutting a channel through the limestone bottom. Everyone enjoyed lunch and kept an eye on passing storm clouds. However, as if on signal, just as the *Miami* came into sight a rainbow spanned the sky. Flagler boarded the *Miami* to see if he might ride her into the harbor, but the captain evaluated the situation and decided to anchor just outside the bay rather than chance grounding in the unfinished channel.[2]

On January 17 Flagler and a boatload of passengers took a steamer from the docks near the Royal Palm out to board the *Miami,* and she made the passage to Nassau without incident, although headwinds all the way slowed the voyage to thirteen hours. A large crowd turned out at the dock in Nassau to celebrate this landmark event in Bahamian history. Flagler did not disappoint them. He announced that he had made an agreement with the government to provide "fast and frequent" steamship communication with the mainland (for which he would be paid an annual subsidy of almost $17,000). He also revealed that he had purchased the landmark Royal Victoria Hotel, which stood on a hillside overlooking the bay. This storied inn had been the scene of cat-and-mouse games among Confederate blockade runners and Union agents during the Civil War, but now it was slated to be demolished and replaced with a modern Flagler system hotel. As it turned out, at the request of local businessmen Flagler would in fact keep the Royal Victoria open and build a new hotel, the Colonial, on a site near the waterfront. After three days in Nassau the *Miami* returned to Florida, and this time it steamed through the new channel and almost up to the docks before anchoring. The turning basin alongside the docks had not yet been excavated. Altogether it had been a most satisfactory excursion.[3]

Flagler would spend most of the season in Palm Beach with the Ashleys and Alice Pomroy. Occasional visitors such as the Andersons and other friends dropped down for extended visits. Flagler went boating with actor Joe Jefferson on Lake Worth and ate dinner with Governor William Bloxham at the Royal Poinciana. He took a party of friends to St. Augustine in mid-February to watch the water sports exhibitions in the Casino pool. Near the end of March he accompanied a party of railroad men and important persons from Nassau, including Spencer Churchill (cousin of Winston) and his wife, to celebrate the *Miami*'s first docking at the wharf in Miami. Flagler's railroad track ran out onto the dock so that his guests could step right from their Pullmans onto the gangplanks of Flagler's steamships.[4]

In 1897 he became part owner of a different enterprise: a newspaper. Although outright ownership of a paper was new to him, he had already been deeply enmeshed in newspaper business for a long time prior to this. Several years earlier he had replied to a letter inquiring about a report that he intended to launch a newspaper by writing: "There is not a particle of truth in the rumor that I am about to start a newspaper. If I had to take my choice between a den of rattlesnakes and a newspaper, I think I would prefer the snakes." Flagler was disingenuous in this answer. He truly did not like newspapers, which among other things had published an avalanche of stories critical of Standard Oil over the years, and he may not have intended starting a newspaper of his own at the time he answered the letter, but he was at that very moment actively engaged in efforts to manipulate newspapers and the men who owned and edited them.[5]

As earlier noted, from his years at Standard Oil Flagler had learned the value of controlling as much of the environment impinging on his business interests as possible. That included the flow of information and opinion that newspapers furnished to the reading public. For his hotel and land companies his major concern centered on inserting promotional advertising in newspapers. This advertising served the straightforward purpose of marketing Florida as a desirable place for tourists and settlers, and it also indirectly bought the favor of newspaper owners by providing them with a flow of revenues from his purchases of advertising space.

However, when it came to his railroad, Flagler's interest in newspapers took quite a different turn, since the nation's railroads were objects of furious debate in the newspapers. Taken as a whole, railroads constituted the largest investment of capital in the country at the time and aroused the greatest political controversies of the day. Railroads wielded great power in the economic well-being of states and in the politics of every state. Reformers demanded government controls over railroads to eliminate such things as the infamous "rebates" on shipping rates that Flagler himself had extracted from railroads on behalf of Standard Oil in earlier years. These calls for reform resulted in Congress's passage of the Interstate Commerce Act in 1887 and the Florida legislature's establishment of a state railroad commission in 1888. Charges that the railroads or the corporations corrupted the Florida government through bribery and chicanery became standard fare in newspapers. Flagler desired to stifle this criticism and replace it with positive stories and editorials favorable to the railroads. In politics he wished to promote the election of conservative politicians and the defeat of "reformers." It is no wonder that in the ledger books of his empire, Flagler debited expenses related to newspapers to the account of the FEC Railway.[6]

During the early days of the Hotel Ponce de Leon Flagler exchanged letters with O. D. Seavey on the value of advertising for the hotels in national and local newspapers. Flagler thought advertising, beyond a strict minimum necessary to inform the public of his hotels' openings, resulted in very little increase in patronage. "This matter of advertising is one of the most perplexing ones connected with the business," Flagler admitted. He felt that if you placed advertisements with one newspaper, you made enemies of all the other newspapers in which you did not advertise. "I confess my inability to deal with this subject, except upon the broad principle of advertising with none."[7]

In St. Augustine Flagler purchased the support of the *St. Augustine Evening News* by lending its owner, Oscar B. Smith, $2,000 and then forgiving repayment of the loan. "This course would enable you to keep the ownership and control absolutely in your own hands," Flagler wrote in his letter canceling the debt. Flagler courted Smith's favor since he not only ran the town's leading newspaper but also owned the Lyon Building and served in the state legislature.[8] Flagler would send Smith pamphlets and copies of speeches favorable to business interests, with the suggestion that he hand them on to other members of the state legislature. Sometimes he had real news for Smith. Flagler used his position on the board of directors of Western Union to have the company run a new copper wire from New York to St. Augustine that would make service better and cheaper. He sent word of the change to Smith with the admonition: "This is due to my influence, although I do not want it so stated in your paper, neither do I want you to publish the fact that the information comes from me."[9]

Flagler's relationship with St. Augustine's metropolitan newspaper, the *Florida Times-Union* in Jacksonville, evolved into a long, complex saga. In the 1880s the *Times-Union* was owned and edited by a dapper, hyperactive little fellow named Charles H. Jones, who sported a luxuriant beard and an oversized ego. Jones had built his newspaper into the most influential journal in the state. He vigorously promoted Florida's economic development and his own influence as a player in state politics. He had editorially supported creation of the state railroad commission, criticized Standard Oil for receiving favorable freight rates from the railroads, and leaned in the direction of the "populist" wing of the Democratic Party. In 1887 a syndicate of conservative banking and business interests in Jacksonville incorporated the Florida Publishing Company to bring out the *Jacksonville News-Herald* as an alternative to Jones's *Times-Union*.[10]

Flagler threw his support to the *News-Herald*. Prior to the opening of the Hotel Ponce de Leon, Flagler favored the *News-Herald* by giving its reporter a rare short personal interview, and his men fed it inside information on construction of the hotel. He allowed bundles of the *News-Herald* to be shipped to St. Augustine on an earlier, predawn train, rather than the train carrying the *Times-Union*, so that the *News-Herald* would reach the breakfast tables of readers in St. Augustine before the *Times-Union*. Jones filed a complaint with the railroad commission protesting this favoritism, but the commission refused to intervene. However, a short time later Flagler's Jacksonville, St. Augustine, and Halifax River Railway dropped the practice of discriminating against the *Times-Union*.[11]

The conflict between the two newspapers terminated in April when Jones left Jacksonville and moved on to St. Louis to take control of a larger newspaper. He sold the *Times-Union* to the Florida Publishing Company, which closed the *News-Herald* in favor of the much better established *Times-Union*. By this time the brothers John N. C. Stockton and Telfair Stockton had emerged as the prime movers in the Florida Publishing Company. Beginning in the fall of 1888 Flagler made a series of bond purchases and loans to the Stocktons that eventually totaled $30,000. Presumably he hoped that this infusion of money would sway the editorial policies of the *Times-Union* in a more conservative direction. When the newspaper published an editorial to which Flagler objected, John Stockton wrote him an apology, saying, "We hope soon to complete the financial agreement entered into with you last March, and trust in the future you will have no cause to complain of our management." However, the Stocktons entertained political ambitions, and as populist sentiment grew in strength during the 1890s, the *Times-Union* moved toward a more anti-corporation philosophical position.[12]

By 1893 Flagler and the Stocktons were at war. Stockton wrote to U.S. Senator Wilkinson Call, a leader of the populist Democrats, telling him that the Flagler interests were "hovering over us like buzzards do over dead animals." Shortly thereafter Flagler wrote to his railroad vice president J. R. Parrott, who made his home in Jacksonville, to call upon John Stockton and pressure him about the *Times-Union*'s debts. "What I want is to exert an influence upon him that will bring him to time." When John Stockton sought the position of collector of internal revenue in Jacksonville, Flagler wrote to President Cleveland's secretary of war Daniel Lamont, a personal friend of Flagler's, declaring that he and Henry Plant and fellow railroad man H. Reiman Duval opposed the appointment. Flagler told Lamont that the Stocktons "have been doing untold harm by backing up a set of miserable demagogues who are not only discouraging Capital from coming into the State but would be glad to drive out much of the Capital already here."[13]

In August 1893 Flagler wrote to Parrott advising him to "watch the Savannah Morning News for an item, a few days hence, relative to a new paper at Waterdog."[14] In Flagler's secret code book "Waterdog" stood for Jacksonville.

This new paper appeared on newsstands in December to challenge the *Times-Union*. The masthead of the *Daily Florida Citizen* listed Lorettus S. Metcalf, the distinguished former editor of the *North American Review* and *Forum* magazines, as "editor and proprietor." However, the actual proprietors of the *Daily Florida Citizen* were Henry Flagler, Henry Plant, and H. Reiman Duval—all representing railroad interests. The *Citizen* pursued a moderate editorial policy but clearly sympathized with the conservative Bourbon Democrats whenever an issue such as the railroad commission came up. The *Times-Union* continued to be more openly and firmly anti-Bourbon, styling itself the champion of the common people against the wealthy special interests.[15]

In the spring of 1894 Flagler, Plant, and Duval pulled all advertising for their hotels and railroads from the *Times-Union*. Not only did the Stocktons lose the advertising revenues, but readers would have been deprived of the practical information contained in the railroad schedules had not the *Times-Union* printed its own versions of the trains' arrival and departure times. In retaliation, the *Times-Union* imposed a virtual blackout on stories relating to Flagler's hotels. A reader scanning the *Times-Union* in the winter season of 1895 might think that the San Marco Hotel was the only big hotel in St. Augustine—the Ponce de Leon and Alcazar merited only the merest glancing mention from time to time. This standoff of reciprocated boycotts lasted through 1896 and into 1897. Flagler, Plant, and Duval finally put an end to the matter in September of 1897 by purchasing the Florida Publishing Company and consolidating the two papers into the *Florida Times-Union and Citizen*.[16]

After the takeover of the *Times-Union* Flagler would, from time to time, send letters to its editor, George W. Wilson, suggesting material for editorials. Often he included a clipping from another newspaper that he found expressed his sentiments. Almost always Flagler's letters related to matters of politics, but in 1901, following his controversial divorce and remarriage, Flagler wrote to Wilson: "I trust you will not think I am churlish in this matter, but I am very much in hopes that I can live a winter at least in Whitehall without having anything said of it in the newspapers." One wonders how many stories relating to Flagler did *not* appear in the newspapers because of Flagler's ownership or influence over the press in several Florida cities.[17]

During the summer of 1899 Flagler established the St. Augustine Printing and Publishing Company to bring out the *St. Augustine Evening Record*. Davis E. Thompson, a newspaperman from Jacksonville, was listed as the editor and proprietor of the *Record*, and Flagler's name did not appear among the gentlemen listed in the articles of incorporation. The absence of any reference to Flagler was deliberate. In a letter to J. R. Parrott, Flagler explained, "I note what you say regarding the newspaper situation in St. Augustine and Key West. . . . I trust you appreciate the absolute necessity of having our relation to these enterprises kept a profound secret. If it leaks out that we are interested, somebody will surely start an opposition paper in the expectation that we will buy them out." As it was, Flagler purchased and closed down all three of St. Augustine's other papers: Smith's *St. Augustine News*, the *St. Augustine Daily Herald*, and the *St. Augustine*

Morning Journal. In the fashion of Standard Oil, Flagler eliminated three competing, financially struggling newspapers and replaced them with one sound paper.[18]

Although Flagler was a Republican, his newspapers—like virtually all the papers in Florida—of necessity supported the Democratic Party since the Republican Party had shrunk to almost nothing once black citizens were eliminated as voters. The *Record's* initial declaration of principles stated: "Politically the Evening Record will be an untiring worker in the ranks of the Great Democratic Party, National, State, County, and municipal. At all times and under all conditions espousing the cause of the plain people—the toilers, and zealously supporting the Party's Platform and Candidates." This was standard boilerplate Democratic Party rhetoric, but in fact, when the *Record* took an editorial stand it usually sided with business and capital. In 1900 the *Record* dutifully supported populist Democrat William Jennings Bryan for president, but on the state level the *Record* promoted the conservative, pro-business Bourbon faction of the Democratic Party. During the 1904 election the conservative leanings of the *Times-Union* and the *Record* became a campaign issue as the populist Democratic candidate for governor, Napoleon Bonaparte Broward, made "corporation" control of the state's newspapers a major theme of his campaign. John N. C. Stockton, a disappointed candidate for Congress who knew the financial history of the *Times-Union*, loudly proclaimed that the *Times-Union* spoke for Standard Oil. When Flagler's ownership of the *Record* became known, its editor Davis Thompson declared that it did not matter that "Mr. Flagler furnished the money to establish it" because the *Record* always promoted St. Augustine and St. Johns County.[19]

Flagler used his financial power to influence other newspapers in the state. He lent money to the owners of the *Gainesville Sun* and the *Pensacola News*. In Miami he gave financial help to the *Miami Metropolis,* and when new owners took over the paper and adopted an anti-corporation editorial policy, Flagler bought the *Metropolis* and renamed it the *Miami Herald.*[20]

Taken together, Flagler's initiatives to exert influence over the state's press are impressive, although he himself probably thought of his dealings with the press as an irritating distraction from his main concern with running his railroad, land, and hotel businesses. It is little wonder that he placed newspapers in the same category with rattlesnakes.

In St. Augustine the new year of 1897 began for the town's black citizenry with the annual Emancipation Day celebrations on January 1, but on the following day America's most noted black citizen, Booker T. Washington, president of Tuskegee Institute, slipped quietly into town for apparently the same reason most visitors came—just to see the sights and visit friends. He left the same day on the afternoon train for Jacksonville, where he was scheduled to speak at the

Park Theater. His train arrived late, delaying the event. James Weldon Johnson, principal of Jacksonville's Stanton School, made an extended introductory address. The twenty-seven-year-old Johnson had been chosen to introduce Washington because of Johnson's recognized eloquence as an orator. He also agreed with Washington's assessment that in the face of increasing discrimination, black Americans would have to depend upon themselves to improve the circumstances of their daily lives.[21]

Later on in the season Johnson's younger brother J. Rosamond Johnson would appear at the Alcazar Casino as the leader of the Florida Baptist Academy jubilee singers. The Johnson brothers were familiar with hotel life since their father had been the headwaiter at Jacksonville's St. James Hotel. (The elder Johnson may have welcomed Henry Flagler into the St. James dining room in 1878.) The concert in the Casino raised money for the black school that would evolve into today's Florida Memorial College of Miami. Johnson had already studied at the New England Conservatory of Music and bore the title Professor Johnson, as head of his school's music department. He impressed the crowd with a baritone solo and his piano rendition of the "Royal Poinciana March," one of his own compositions.[22]

Early in January the Casino served as the venue for the first showing of a moving picture in St. Augustine. A large audience turned out to watch the landmark film *The Corbett-Fitzsimmons Fight*, which was the longest movie made up to that time, recording in documentary style all fourteen rounds of the world championship bout in which Bob Fitzsimmons knocked out Jim Corbett, who had won the title a few years earlier in Jacksonville. The film had been shown in northern cities since May of the previous year, and a representative of the Veriscope company came to the Alcazar to introduce it locally. The movie men stretched a large white canvas across the west end of the Casino pool and seated the audience on both sides of the pool. The cameraman experienced a bit of a tussle with the projector but soon got it going. The *Times-Union* deemed it a good show.[23]

Three weeks later another early moving picture company, Biograph, showed off its wares in the Casino to an audience that included Mrs. Marcotte. The movie stunned the veteran newswoman, who had never experienced such a "wonder of this electronic age." The audience's "enthusiasm was boundless.... The reproductions of living, moving men and women, life size, of galloping horses, dashing trains, gave very general satisfaction. While the audience was a good one, had the people of St. Augustine had the least idea of what the show would be, the great hall would have been crowded." Mrs. Marcotte may have substituted for her husband in writing the *Times-Union*'s account of the show, for it used some of the same language as her *Tatler* story: "The pictures are as realistic as in life, some of a thrilling character, but all are instructive and strictly moral."[24]

Early in the season sportsmen at Flagler's hotels were pleased to learn that a golf course would be built at the south end of town for use by guests of the hotels. A sixty-acre tract at the extreme south end of the peninsula on which the town of St. Augustine rests was leased from the Bicycle Club, which had already constructed a one-third-mile-long bicycle track at the northern end of the property. The bike track would remain, but the rest of the land would be devoted to a nine-hole golf course. Joseph Greaves of the Alcazar surveyed the ground and found the land very low and covered with marsh grass and seacoast scrub, with a sprinkling of cedar trees. A crew of workmen got busy clearing, leveling, and rolling the ground, and after the absurdly brief period of just two weeks duffers began hitting balls around the newly fashioned course. On February 11 the hotel managers, who constituted the club's executive board, hosted a gala opening reception under a big blue and white tent at what was grandly deemed the "Country Club." Hundreds of people rode their bicycles down oyster-shell-paved Central Avenue (today's Martin Luther King Avenue) to the event, while others took more conventional carriages. Ladies in their afternoon gowns served punch, and the First Artillery Band supplied the music. General Schofield, the Andersons, William Deering and his family, and many of the usual hotel and cottage community showed up to give the new venture their blessing.[25]

A little booklet published by the hotel system two years later attempted to present the course in a flattering light, but the primitive conditions it describes are likely to make modern golfers smile: "A short velvety turf covers almost the entire course; the teeing grounds are made of hard muck, and the putting greens, of the regulation size, are built of the same material, well tamped, and sprinkled daily with a layer of sharp beach sand." Sand tees and sand greens (and they were nevertheless called "greens") were standard in Florida at the time, although within a few years the Plant system hotels began to advertise genuine grass putting greens.[26]

The "Tower Tee" stood in the marshes at the edge of the Country Club operated by Flagler's hotel company for a few years at the turn of the twentieth century. Author's collection.

Flagler usually did things in a first-class way, and this extended to his venture into golf. He hired one of the top professional golfers in America to serve as the resident advisor and instructor for his hotel chain. Alexander Findlay, like almost all top players of the day, had immigrated to America from Scotland. He ended up on the rolling plains of Nebraska in the mid-1880s, and in this unlikely spot he began constructing golf courses and teaching Americans how to play the game. By the time Flagler hired him Findlay had made Boston his headquarters and was making and selling golf equipment. His work for Flagler required him to travel from Palm Beach to Miami to Ormond and to St. Augustine promoting the game and offering suggestions to refine the layouts of the courses.[27]

A month after inauguration of the golf course, the Country Club became the venue for two weeks of races featuring a half dozen of the best bicyclists in the world. At the time, bicycle races of all kinds, from short sprints on indoor wooden velodromes to six-day races, drew huge crowds. This phenomenon was widespread; the Tour de France would first be contested in 1903. Professional racers toured the United States, and several cities in sunny Florida hosted the bicyclists in the winter of 1898. Big crowds turned out in St. Augustine to watch the competitors spin around the hard-packed coquina shell track. Earl Kiser of Dayton, Ohio, attracted a lot of attention because he held the world's records over the half-mile and the mile distances and because he was the American favorite racing against Europeans.[28]

In January 1898 Flagler received a new private railroad car built for him by Jackson and Sharp. It stretched to more than seventy-eight feet in length, compared to the sixty-four feet of his original *Alicia*. Flagler had not used that name for several years, and the FEC called the car simply no. 90. When Flagler received his luxurious new palace on wheels, it inherited the number 90, and his older car became no. 91. The older car and another car numbered 92 would be used by Parrott and other executives of the railroad while on their rounds. Flagler felt so at home in no. 90 that his personal stationery contained two addresses: "26 Broadway" and "Private Car 90."[29] Today no. 91 is preserved at the Henry Morrison Flagler Museum in Palm Beach, and no. 90 is on exhibition at the Indiana Transportation Museum.

The usual round of resort community activities played out in 1898 against the backdrop of impending war with Spain because of the revolutionary turmoil in Cuba. In December of the previous year a flotilla of four U.S. Navy torpedo boats had anchored in Matanzas Bay. The officers and crew received the full treatment: an oyster roast on the beach, two banquets in the Alcazar dining room, a dance in the Casino, and a reception for the officers by Dr. Anderson at Markland. The visit of the flotilla to Florida waters was intended as a display of military might for the benefit of the Spanish.[30]

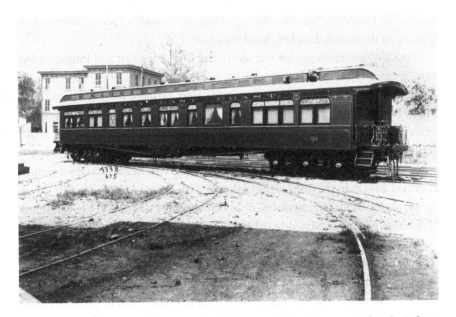

Private car no. 90 replaced Flagler's original car in 1898. Today it is preserved in the Indiana Transportation Museum. By permission of Delaware Public Archives.

In February the U.S.S. *Maine* paid a visit to Havana harbor as another demonstration of American power. When the *Maine* exploded and sank to the bottom of the bay, tensions soared in the United States. Mrs. Marcotte used the pages of the *Tatler* to advise calm and suggest that peaceful diplomacy should be the first approach to settling the conflict. However, she also declared that Americans could not turn their eyes away from the suffering of the people of Cuba, nor forgive a Spanish government that starved women and children. Mrs. Marcotte organized a Benefit Concert in the Casino to raise money for the widows and orphans created by the *Maine* disaster. The concert by the First Artillery Band ended with the playing of "The Star-Spangled Banner." Mrs. Marcotte noted that "the entire audience rose during the performance of it." This solemn moment had its awkward aspect in that no one seemed to know the words to the song; she published the text of all four verses in next issue of the *Tatler*. The practice of standing and removing hats for the playing of "The Star-Spangled Banner" had been started recently, and Mrs. Marcotte noted that the music had become the "national anthem." Cleveland's secretary of war Daniel Lamont had issued orders a few years earlier that "The Star-Spangled Banner" should be played at every raising and lowering of the flag on a military base. When Lamont visited the Ponce de Leon in March 1897 Captain Marcotte spoke with him and was proud to point out that many visitors witnessed this ceremony at St. Francis Barracks twice a day. However, "The Star-Spangled Banner" would not receive official designation as the national anthem until the 1930s.[31]

Ironically, preparations for war led to the long-expected and long-dreaded downgrading of St. Francis Barracks as a military post. Out of the blue, in mid-March, St. Augustine received news that the First Artillery Regiment was being withdrawn and sent to Charleston, where it would be consolidated with other artillery units. This struck a severe blow to both the economy and social order of the town. The officers and their wives had long been a presence in St. Augustine's society. Officers in their dress blue uniforms had been a standard feature of formal dances in the hotels. The regimental band—and its predecessors over the years—had regularly performed concerts on the Plaza and in the ballrooms of the hotels. Captain Marcotte sighed, "The band, too, will be sadly missed."[32]

Within a few days word came that an infantry company would replace the artillery regiment, but that meant fewer soldiers—and no band. James Ingraham hurried to Washington to visit the War Department to plead St. Augustine's case. On the way home he stopped in Atlanta to confer with Brigadier General William Graham, commander of the Department of the South. Ingraham sent reassuring (but ultimately inaccurate) news that the army expected to increase the size of the garrison at St. Francis Barracks over time.[33]

On March 23 the sixty-five men of Company B, Fifth U.S. Infantry, arrived at Union Depot early in the morning and marched through town to the barracks. Two days later they retraced their steps to the station escorting the First Artillery. The army made a grand display of its exit. The band played martial airs as the troops marched by. When they passed along King Street between the Ponce de Leon and Alcazar, the musicians offered a salute to the grand hotels. A large crowd assembled at the depot to bid the First Artillery and their band farewell. The possibility that they were going off to war lent added gravity to the moment.[34]

A few days later General Graham and two members of his staff checked in to the Hotel Ponce de Leon to meet Ingraham and continue down to Palm Beach to confer with Flagler. The party traveled in Flagler's private car to Miami. The newspapers reported that they discussed defense of the East Coast of Florida, for Flagler's railroad provided the most rapid means of transportation from the North to South Florida. Some worried that a raiding party landed from Spanish ships could cut that railroad link. However, most likely Flagler wanted to know how his railroad and docking facilities in Miami might fit into the military's plans should Cuba be invaded. Flagler's Hotel Key West was already being used as headquarters for the officers conducting the Court of Inquiry into the sinking of the *Maine*.[35]

All this martial activity fed fears of various sorts. One evening about sunset an unidentified ship appeared off the harbor entrance, and as Captain Marcotte declared, "it did not take long for the report to circulate that a Spanish man-of-war was anchored off the bar with guns trained on the Ancient City." The next morning hotel system supervisor Knott explained that the vessel was just the yacht of a Yankee tourist who had come up from Miami.[36]

In 1898 the Ponce de Leon began holding garden parties on the west lawn, a tradition that would continue for the rest of the hotel's operation. Thomas Hastings had planned this open space as an area for outdoor activities, but only slowly over the years had it been landscaped into an area hospitable for leisure interests. A storm in the mid-1890s had flattened much of the shrubbery, and McGuire renewed the setting by planting dozens of sabal palms. Dr. Anderson did the same on the Markland grounds, creating a palm-lined path from his home to the hotel. Years later when the trees matured, the replanted section of the hotel grounds would justly be called the Palm Garden, but for the moment the ladies in their gowns and the orchestra in their uniforms held their entertainments amid somewhat straggly young palm trees.[37]

O. D. Seavey showed up for the annual Charity Ball at the Ponce de Leon. His friends welcomed him with a dinner in the Dining Room before it was cleared for dancing. Seavey was enjoying his first season as proprietor of his own hotel. He had organized a company and purchased the Magnolia Springs Hotel, where his Florida ventures had begun almost two decades earlier. The hotel had been closed for two years, but Seavey fixed it up with amenities required at a modern hotel: a nine-hole golf course, concrete tennis courts, two swimming pools, a bowling alley, and even a dark room where amateur photographers could develop film from their Kodaks. Tucked away off the beaten path and on the St. Johns River, the Magnolia Springs seems to have matched Seavey's interests, which had evolved toward rustic outdoor pursuits such as quail shooting. He also owned the Hotel Aspinwall in the Berkshire Mountains at Lenox, Massachusetts, where he spent the summers. For many years he and his wife would live in a cottage on the grounds of the Magnolia Springs Hotel, and he would pass away there in 1923.[38]

Near the end of March 1898 guests assembled in the courtyard of the Alcazar for its version of an outdoor party. To their surprise, at the stroke of nine o'clock a fireworks explosion on the roof sent a shower of golden confetti down from above, and thousands of electric lights flashed on among the garden's plants and trees. Those at the party could enjoy the novelty of walking over a rustic wooden bridge that had been constructed to span the center of the court's fountain. This simple arched bridge would become one of the signature elements of the Alcazar building, and its concrete successor remains so today.[39]

A quiet, slender young man may have mingled among the guests at the party.

He had checked into the Ponce de Leon under the name "Lieutenant Albert" of Philadelphia. In actuality he was Prince Albert Leopold, heir apparent to the throne of Belgium, who was touring America incognito to further his education. He and his small entourage walked around town like any other tourists and enjoyed a sail on the bay. Captain Marcotte disclosed his identity in a *Times-Union* story as the prince departed town for New Orleans. In 1909, as Albert I, he would succeed to the crown of Belgium, and he would later win praise for his stalwart stand against the German invasion of his country during the opening days of World War I.[40]

With the threat of war against Spain overshadowing the occasion, the Ponce de Leon closed on April 6. The concert in the Rotunda on the evening before concluded with a patriotic crowd of guests and townspeople singing "My Country 'Tis of Thee."

Flagler, the Ashleys, and Alice Pomroy arrived in St. Augustine in time to witness the closing of the Ponce de Leon. On the evening of their arrival the Alcazar turned on all the electric lights in its garden in welcome. The party took up residence in Kirkside, but a few days later, following his usual routine, Flagler gathered up Knott and McDonald for one last tour of his railroad and hotel chain as far south as Miami. Then on April 13 the Flagler party took a train for the North, concluding the resort season. Flagler's involvement in Florida would assume a whole new cast twelve days later when Congress declared war on Spain.[41]

Henry Flagler's new Bahamas ventures were part of a continuing close involvement of Florida with the islands of the Caribbean. Juan Ponce de León had, after all, been governor of Puerto Rico before attempting to become governor of Florida. Cuban soldiers had often walked the streets of St. Augustine in the days when the Castillo de San Marcos stood as the northernmost outpost of Spain's empire in the Americas. In the 1890s St. Augustine housed three cigar factories that employed Cuban workers and imported leaf tobacco from Havana. When the long-simmering revolution for Cuban independence flared up in the 1890s, St. Augustine was unavoidably drawn into the conflict.

Several years earlier in 1892 José Martí, the exile leader of Cuban patriots, had come down from New York to St. Augustine and met with other Cuban rebel leaders. They walked to Tolomato Cemetery and paid their respects to Father Felix Varela, an earlier generation's spokesman for Cuban independence who had died in exile in St. Augustine. They formed an organization known as the Club Padre Varela, and while in St. Augustine Martí's group issued a statement outlining their goals. Some took this as Cuba's declaration of independence.[42]

In October 1895 the City Council of St. Augustine had adopted a resolution endorsing "the struggles of the people of Cuba for liberty, independence, and self-government" and calling for the United States government to recognize the Cuban rebels legally as the potential new government of Cuba. Supporters of the Cuban Relief Fund had held a program in the Alcazar Casino in February 1896 to raise money for Cuban exiles living in the United States and to buy guns for rebels inside Cuba. Noted New York dance instructor Maude Madison appeared in dramatic tableaus, first bound in chains and then reappearing later as the symbol of Liberty, waving the new red, white, and blue striped flag of "Free Cuba." (The name Cuba Libre would soon be applied to a mixed drink composed of the new beverage Coca-Cola and the old beverage rum.) The following year, as revolutionary turmoil in Cuba increased, the War Department closed Fort Marion to all civilian visitors but relented a week later when the local army colonel protested that the fort was more a tourist attraction of historical interest than a real military base.[43]

After the sinking of the *Maine* in 1898, concerns about security intensified. A week before the declaration of war a group of citizens headed by Bartolo Genovar, owner of the opera house and chairman of the county commissioners, sent a petition to Secretary of War Russell Alger requesting protection. Flagler did not sign the petition but informed Ingraham that the effort had his support. The petition read: "In the event of hostilities between the United States and Spain, Saint Augustine is in greater peril from attack by hostile force than any city in the country." It explained that St. Augustine lay in clear view of ships at sea, it was the largest city south of Charleston located directly on the coast, and, moreover, the Spanish would remember St. Augustine as an important military outpost. Perhaps in response to this request, the army moved one of the big, eight-inch Civil War vintage howitzers from the water battery of Fort Marion to a sand bluff south of the lighthouse overlooking the harbor entrance.[44]

St. Augustine's two state militia units, the Rifles and the Light Infantry, stepped up their training as the threat of war increased. They sometimes performed their drills on King Street so that the public could admire their preparations. When the declaration of war came, Governor Bloxham refused to designate which of the state's local militia units should report—probably for fear of offending those communities whose volunteers he left out. Hence in May both of St. Augustine's companies marched to the fort green to be photographed before embarking on a train for Tampa to join the army gathering there. Upon their arrival in Tampa the Light Infantry were turned around and sent home, as Florida had exceeded its quota of volunteers. The Rifles suffered perhaps a worse fate. The expeditionary force sailed for Cuba without them, leaving the St. Augustine boys to spend the war months in Fernandina and later Huntsville, Alabama, before being mustered out.[45]

One St. Augustinian who did manage to get into the fighting in Cuba was fifty-eight-year-old Captain Henry Marcotte. As special correspondent for the *Army and Navy Journal*, he wrangled a spot with the Gatling gun battery that engaged in the major land battle of the war, the Siege of Santiago. The commander of the three-gun battery, Lieutenant John H. Parker, later expressed his gratitude to the War Department for allowing Marcotte to accompany them. Not only was Marcotte a veteran of the Civil War and Indian wars but he also had years of experience living in a tropical environment. Parker thanked him for "the valuable advice and assistance which he has given continually. His large experience of war, his clear head and good judgment have always been at hand to aid, his cool example to myself and my men under fire did much to steady us and keep us up to our work when we were first called on to face that ordeal."

Parker later wrote that unlike some so-called war correspondents, Marcotte stayed right at the front and even accompanied the scouts sent ahead to locate a firing position for Parker's primitive machine guns. "When the battery went under fire, Marcotte was with it. It was the first time most of the members had passed through this ordeal, but who could run, or even feel nervous, with this gray-haired man skipping about from point to point and taking notes of the engagement as coolly as though he were sitting in the shade of a tree sipping lime-juice cocktails, a mile from danger."

Parker, with Marcotte's backing, suggested to General Joe Wheeler (the same man who, as a Confederate officer, had fled from Lieutenant Amos B. Rhodes's cavalry charge many years earlier; see chapter 13) that the Americans advance more quickly to seize high ground nearer the city. The former Confederate, however, chose a more cautious approach. During the Battle of San Juan Hill, Parker's Gatling guns proved to be deadly effective in clearing the field of Spanish soldiers menacing the flank of Colonel Teddy Roosevelt's Rough Riders.[46]

One hundred miles to the west of Captain Marcotte's position, Henry Flagler's yacht *Alicia* also managed to get into the action in the waters off Cuba—except that she was no longer the *Alicia* but the USS *Hornet*. Flagler had sold his vessel to the navy on April 8, 1898, for use as an auxiliary cruiser with what was called the "Mosquito Fleet." The navy took her to the New York Naval Yard, removed her rear mast and sails, added a belt of armor plating to her sides, and painted her flat lead gray. The newly configured *Hornet* received armament of three small-caliber swivel cannon, two even smaller cannon, and four machine guns. In the navy's eyes the *Hornet*'s primary asset would be her ability to move fast, since she was expected to catch Spanish supply ships bringing provisions from neutral British Jamaica to the Spanish troops in Cuba.[47]

After a very quick refitting, the *Hornet* sailed for Key West on April 18 and arrived off Havana on April 24 to join the American fleet. She first went to blockade the port city of Matanzas about sixty miles east of Havana. While cruising along the beach she shelled some Spanish workers putting up a telegraph line. Then the navy sent the *Hornet* around to the south coast of Cuba to blockade the port of Manzanillo, where ships were resupplying the besieged Spanish troops in Santiago. Showing a good deal of initiative, the *Hornet* and two other lightly armed auxiliary ships sailed into the harbor in an attempt to sink Spanish warships and merchantmen anchored under the guns of the local fort. For two hours the American sailors blasted away and received fire in return from the antiquated Spanish shore batteries. Then a lucky shot tore into the *Hornet* and smashed her main steam line, scalding one man to death and severely burning two others. One of the *Hornet*'s companions pulled her to safety outside the harbor, and she soon returned to blockade duty, capturing the small schooner *Salve Maria* just days before the end of the war.[48]

With the end of the fighting the *Hornet* returned to Norfolk, Virginia, and continued an uneventful career until being sold by the navy in 1910 to a gentleman from New Orleans. The buyer was Samuel Zemurray, the owner of vast banana plantations in Honduras, who used the *Hornet* to transport ex-Honduran president Manuel Bonilla and a band of mercenary soldiers to Honduras where they staged a successful revolution. The U.S. Navy seized the *Hornet* and returned her to New Orleans, where the ship drops from sight.[49]

St. Augustine played only a peripheral role in the war. Tampa had been chosen as the port of embarkation for the expeditionary invasion force bound for Cuba, but the passage of the army through Florida spilled over to the East Coast. In June, C. B. Knott and Annie McKay went down to Miami to open up the Hotel Royal Palm to accommodate army and navy officers stationed there, as well as their families. The FEC Railway's yellow coaches rolled past St. Augustine carrying thousands of soldiers bound for camp amid the palmettos outside Miami. The only direct role St. Augustine played for the military was as a prison. Fort Marion, which in earlier years had incarcerated American Indians, became the home for soldiers convicted by courts martial of various offenses ranging from petty to more serious.[50]

Soldiers training in camps around Jacksonville and Fernandina visited town for relaxation and recreation. Local merchants greeted them and their money as welcome relief during the normally dull summer season, but the presence of hundreds of young men on holiday raised the potential of difficulties as well. The ladies of the Women's Christian Temperance Union attempted to head off trouble by offering free ice water from a barrel on the Plaza, and another group of women distributed sandwiches and lemonade at the Worth House. Many of the boys took off for healthy recreation at the beach, but one afternoon a crowd of rowdy soldiers mobbed the sheriff and a deputy when they tried to arrest a soldier. Worse, some broke into Tolomato Cemetery and pried open graves looking for valuables or simply souvenirs. They succeeded in carrying away bones and ornaments from the vaults, leaving behind names scrawled on the plaster of a chapel. They chipped so much coquina from the City Gates that some suggested placing piles of loose coquina near the Gates to prevent further vandalism.[51]

As soon as the fighting stopped in Cuba the War Department ordered most of the troops home as rapidly as possible, knowing that in the tropics yellow fever and malaria posed a much graver danger than Spanish rifles. The first two weeks of August saw the same yellow FEC coaches carrying soldiers north. The local brass band celebrated with lively tunes when the trains stopped at Union Station. Teddy Roosevelt and some of his Rough Riders evacuated Santiago on Flagler's SS *Miami*, which had also ferried troops to Cuba at the start of the invasion. The *Miami* took Roosevelt all the way home to New York.[52]

What John Hay called the "Splendid Little War" had an important impact on the state of Florida. Most important, Dr. Walter Reed's discovery while in Cuba of the microbe that caused yellow fever, and that its carrier was a mosquito, finally made year-round living in Florida a realistic prospect for potential home seekers from the North. More immediately, thousands of young men from all over the country passed through Tampa, Jacksonville, and Miami. Across the country citizens read about Florida in their daily newspapers. The *Times-Union* noted that many of the soldiers visiting St. Augustine took Kodak photos of the ancient relics of the town and its new palatial hotels. "Thousands after thousands of pictures of the hotels have been taken, and these are being sent to friends all over the country. It will prove a great advertisement for St. Augustine and Mr. Flagler's hotels."[53]

The increase in Florida tourism created one of the country's first modern travel agencies. By 1898 Ward Foster's El Unico souvenir shop in St. Augustine had evolved into the Standard Guide Information Bureau, dispensing "definite and accurate" information on hotels, railroads, and steamship lines for travelers moving about Florida. As the story went, people wanting to know anything about sojourning in the state would be directed to "ask Mr. Foster." Thus the company became known as "Ask Mr. Foster." It moved from under the arch on King Street to the square tower of the Cordova at the corner of King and Cordova streets. Foster made his business conspicuous by erecting a large sign above the entrance.[54]

Foster offered his services to the public for free, charging transportation and accommodations companies a small fee for disseminating their rates, schedules, and availability. James McGuire, who managed Flagler's properties in St. Augustine, considered Foster an "objectionable tenant" because he blocked the sidewalk outside his office with a clutter of racks displaying tourist brochures. Nevertheless, Foster's aggressive approach worked so well that he soon opened branch offices in various towns across the state and eventually across the nation. Today Ask Mr. Foster continues to do business worldwide under the name Carlson Wagonlit Travel.[55]

In 1899 Flagler returned to Florida a bit later than had been his recent custom, traveling down in mid-January directly to Palm Beach, skipping his usual brief stopover in St. Augustine. He brought Eugene and Eliza Ashley and their Lakeport friend Alice Pomroy with him to share Sea Gull Cottage. During the winter Flagler rode his private car no. 90 up and down the line attending to his various businesses. He went to Jacksonville to escort former secretary of state William Day and his wife to Palm Beach; then he went off to Nassau to see how work was progressing on the Colonial Hotel.[56]

However, during these winter months Flagler was deeply involved in shaping the affairs of his personal life. Ever since the unexplained disappearance of Alice Flagler from the scene, gossips among the resort crowd had wondered if Flagler would find a new wife. Given Alice Pomroy's long visits to Flagler's cottage in Palm Beach, many presumed that she was the object of his attentions, but the gossips would be obliged to continue their speculations for more than another year while Flagler worked quietly to advance his plans. By the winter of 1899 he had decided upon Mary Lily Kenan and had begun negotiations with the Kenan family to pave the way for his union with their daughter.[57]

In early February Flagler took a train to visit Mary Lily's parents, Mr. and Mrs. William R. Kenan Sr., in Macon, Georgia. Mary Lily's younger sister Jessie lived in Macon with her daughter Louise. Jessie had married Clisby Wise some years earlier, and he had abandoned her shortly after Louise's birth in 1895. Flagler agreed to construct a new house for the unfortunate Jessie in Macon. Then the elder Kenans and their youngest daughter Sarah accompanied Flagler to Palm Beach. Mr. Kenan would soon return home, but Sarah and her mother stayed for the rest of the season.[58]

On his trip to Nassau, Flagler took the Kenans with him to enjoy the exotic scene while he inspected progress on construction of the Colonial. When he returned to Palm Beach, Governor-General Sir Gilbert Carter, with his wife and daughter, followed. Flagler took the governor and his whole party up to St. Augustine for a few days to enjoy the town where Flagler's enterprises had their origins. The British flag flew outside the main gate of the Hotel Ponce de Leon in welcome. Mrs. Marcotte held a brief interview with Flagler, writing, "Mr. Flagler is looking unusually well and seems pleased with the condition of his vast possessions here. In speaking of the Ponce de Leon he said it was true the house was more beautiful than before, that age had darkened the wood and harmonized its coloring." Governor Carter obliged by adding, "It is the most magnificent hotel I ever saw or could have imagined." Dr. and Mrs. Anderson hosted a dinner for

Flagler and his friends at Markland. In her story of the dinner Mrs. Marcotte explained that Sarah was the younger sister of Mary Lily, the "Miss Kenan" people were accustomed to seeing in St. Augustine.[59]

St. Augustine was experiencing a relatively quiet season, with the guest count at the Ponce de Leon failing to match even the mediocre numbers of the mid-decade depression years. Still, the season had its moments. John Philip Sousa, the "March King," came to town at the end of January to perform a Sunday afternoon concert in Genovar's Opera House on St. George Street. He received an enthusiastic reception from the standing-room-only crowd. Afterward Sousa and a few of his band checked in at the Hotel Alcazar. Sousa and the Alcazar's manager Joseph Greaves had known each other for years since they both had long-standing connections in Manhattan Beach, New York, where Sousa's career had started and where Greaves managed the Oriental Hotel in the summertime. This winter Sousa and his band were touring the South, so he was on his way the next day. He would make a repeat appearance at Genovar's in February 1906.[60]

In February playwright Charles Hoyt returned to the Ponce de Leon a broken man. His celebrated wife, the stunning actress Caroline Miskel, had died the previous October, leaving Hoyt desolate. He had long been known for his prodigious work habits, which included locking himself in a hotel room with a bottle of whiskey and a box of cigars until he had completed his next play. He came accompanied by his personal physician and the mother of his deceased wife. He also went to visit Palm Beach for a few days, and the stay in Florida seemed to improve his condition. Anna Marcotte wrote that he could be seen lounging about the hotel and enjoying the sunshine on carriage rides. He appeared to be in good spirits. A friend wrote back to New York that rumors of Hoyt's mental and physical breakdown were exaggerated. It was reported that he had simply become exhausted from overwork and the emotional strain of losing his wife, but in Florida he had regained his vigor. However, in reality Hoyt never did recover his equilibrium and would die in Charleston, New Hampshire, on October 20, 1900.[61]

Henry Flagler broke away from his St. Augustine visit in March and went north on an errand. He returned, according to the *Tatler*'s account, "bringing old friends with him." They all went with Flagler to stay in the Royal Victoria Hotel in Nassau. Mary Lily was among this group, joining her mother and sister Sarah. By this time April had come around, and the moment had arrived for Flagler to make his annual finale tour of his empire. He gathered Dr. Anderson and some of his hotel and railroad executives for a visit to Nassau and Key West and then a return up the rail line from Miami. At the end of April Flagler and his party closed up Kirkside and departed for the North, ending another seasonal cycle in Florida.[62]

Mary Lily Kenan caught Flagler's interest after Alice was institutionalized. By permission of Flagler College.

During his weeks in Florida, Flagler completed negotiations with the Kenan family to seal his relationship with Mary Lily. He gave Mary Lily some valuable engagement gifts. On April 3 his confidential secretary William Beardsley at the Standard Building on Broadway wrote a letter to William R. Kenan Sr. informing him that one thousand shares of Standard Oil stock, recorded in the name of Mary Lily Kenan, had been placed on deposit with the company. Flagler had evidently presented the stock certificates to Mary Lily a few days earlier. According to Kenan family tradition, he also gave Mary Lily a long strand of Oriental pearls, held together with a diamond-studded clasp, and a diamond bracelet. The stock, which was probably worth about half a million dollars, and the jewels made Mary Lily a very wealthy woman. Of course, all of this was done in absolute secrecy.[63]

Flagler probably picked Mary Lily to be the wife of his old age because he thought she would make a good companion. He had known her for many years. She came from a respectable family, had a refined education for a woman of her times and class, and possessed an agreeable personality. Elizabeth Lehr, one of Newport's grand dames, thought of Mary Lily Kenan of Wilmington, North Carolina, as a sort of country mouse. Lehr wrote of her: "She was not beautiful. . . . Mary Lily was small and frail. Her little oval face was covered with freckles, her big wistful dark eyes were always rather tired. Her smile was sudden and very sweet. No one ever dreamt of calling her anything but plain in those days when feminine charm was supposed to be opulent and highly coloured." Having just passed the age of thirty-two, she might have been rescued from spinsterhood by Flagler's proposal.[64]

To clear the way for his possible marriage to Mary Lily, Flagler took steps to have his wife Ida Alice declared legally insane. He had not been in Alice's presence for more than two years. It had been four years since the people of Florida had last seen her, and all this time her absence had remained a riddle. No stories of her insanity had reached the newspapers.

Flagler went through the formality of sending a lawyer to inform Alice that he was petitioning to have her declared insane. She probably had no idea what was happening. According to her caregiver, Dr. Carlos MacDonald, she believed Henry Flagler was dead. Afterward, when told of Alice's reaction, Flagler wrote to MacDonald, "I am glad to know that Mrs. Flagler took the petition as she did." Evidently Alice's hold on reality was completely gone.[65]

When Flagler filed his legal papers with the New York courts, the newspapers finally got wind of the story. They published accounts—based on Dr. Shelton's and Dr. MacDonald's testimonies concerning Alice's delusions—about her impending marriage to the czar of Russia. She was said to collect pebbles and keep them in silken bags, thinking they were valuable and possessed magical properties. The stories focused on aspects of Alice's insanity and made no judgments on the propriety of Flagler's legal maneuvers.[66]

We have little documentation of Flagler's life during the summer of 1899. He reportedly spent his time living at a resort hotel in Mount Arlington, New Jersey, and stayed in the Langham apartment house on Fifth Avenue when he visited New York City. Since he was away from Standard's offices during the winter months, Flagler felt bound to stay close to New York during the summer months when his associates took their vacations. On June 26 he was an honorary pallbearer at the funeral of Henry B. Plant at Plant's home near the Flagler residence on Fifth Avenue. Mary Lily's movements are likewise unrecorded until December, when she served as maid of honor at the wedding of a friend in Wilmington. Flagler sent his private car to take the bridal couple on their honeymoon, but he evidently did not attend the wedding and was probably in Florida at the time.[67]

Like other very rich men of his day, such as Andrew Carnegie and John D. Rockefeller, Flagler found himself obliged to give a great deal of time and attention to the issue of philanthropy. His Christian upbringing had instilled in him a profound sense of obligation to humanity, yet exactly how to give help was problematic. Certainly he experienced no shortage of suggestions for how he should dispose of his money. Requests for money for charitable purposes besieged him every day. He complained to his Palm Beach minister George Ward that nearly every day's mail brought letters asking for a donation of one kind or another. At the same time that he was expected to help charitable causes, Flagler's business enterprises in Florida required huge infusions of capital. "The calls made upon me for money are simply overwhelming," he moaned to his lawyer Parrott, "and I am feeling poorer than Lazarus."[68]

Flagler hoped to minimize petitions for bequests by maintaining a low public profile and avoiding publicity for the gifts that he did make. This came naturally to a man of his retiring demeanor, but it also became a deliberate strategy for creating space where he could carefully consider how he might dispose of his wealth for good causes. To give one example, when James Ingraham solicited a donation for an addition to Trinity Episcopal Church, Flagler offered a contribution smaller than Ingraham had hoped for and added that he would give it "upon the *express condition* that the amount be placed on your list as 'from a friend.'"[69]

As a man who had risen from poverty by his own initiative and hard work, Flagler had long pondered the role that giving should play in his personal life. To one man who complained of having lost his orange grove to a freeze, Flagler replied, "I think I appreciate your feelings, for in my earlier days I had some pretty severe struggles with poverty."[70] To Edwin Lefevre he explained that his convictions about disposal of his money went back to his early days as a store clerk: "I realized that the vice of avarice is only kept in check by the cultivation of a cheerful and helpful spirit. So I carried sandwiches in my pocket, and as an offset gave as much to others as I could afford. Thus I got discipline in two ways."[71]

For a consummate businessman like Flagler, it is hardly surprising that his fundamental philanthropic impulse carried him down commercial avenues. Basically he felt that the best way he could help humanity was by being a successful businessman. His friend Frank Harris of the *Ocala Banner* explained that although Flagler built no libraries and founded no great charitable organization, he quietly contributed to many good causes without drawing attention to himself. However, Harris declared that Flagler's primary inclination was to help people by being a good businessman. "He believed that to give employment to the un-employed was the most commendable and best system of charity."[72]

Flagler told Lefevre, the Wall Street writer, "The hardest problem a man has is how to help people. This desire to help others comes when a man has more than enough for his own needs. I have come to the conclusion that the best way to help others is to help them help themselves." Thus his Florida enterprise. Flagler added, "If it wasn't for Florida, I'd be quite a rich man today."[73]

It did not contradict Flagler's basic premise to add that in helping others, he also helped his business ventures. He explained, "Mr. J. R. Parrott, Vice President [of the FEC Railway], is thoroughly saturated with my idea, and that is that it is not only our duty, but to our interest to help people doing business along the line of the Road to make every dollar they can."[74] Helping farmers after the Great Freeze of 1895 also helped preserve the shipping business of the railroad.

Flagler's most extensive attempt to explain his core beliefs about philanthropy is contained in a letter to a minister in which Flagler declined to contribute to the pastor's cause:

I am trying to conscientiously recognize the responsibilities of wealth. . . . If it were not for the misery and wretchedness of mankind, I think I might lead a happy life, in spite of all my own sorrows. Aside from my regular contributions to various public channels (Christian and benevolent), I have a domain in Florida peculiarly my own. I am the sole owner now of a Railroad in Florida 462 miles in length. 300 miles of this Road traverses a country which was entirely unoccupied when I built the Road. My Land Commissioner, through my instructions, has exercised a great deal more care as to the character of the colonists who go in, than the numbers. Con-sequently we have a class of people whose first need is a school-house, next a church. Acting upon the principle that we appreciate that which costs us something, I have in all these cases required the colonists to raise all the money they would for such purposes, and then in some way they get the remainder, without knowing exactly how. I feel that these people are wards of mine and have a special claim upon me. It may seem egotistical, but it is never-the-less a fact, that I am doing this work in Florida wholly by myself, without making any appeal to others to assist me, and in doing so am pay-ing out a great many thousands of dollars every year.[75]

James Ingraham must have heard Flagler express similar sentiments many times, for he later wrote, "Mr. Flagler had come to feel that the owed certain duties to the people of the State of Florida. He told me that he felt that his great fortune had been given to him "to help his fellow men help themselves" and that he could follow out this idea better in Florida than anywhere else. He stated that he knew of no use for his money that would do as much good as he was doing by building up a great country out of a wilderness. He said he preferred to do that than to remain in New York where he might have become one of the richest men in the world."[76]

Flagler's paternalistic instincts extended particularly to the people directly employed in his companies. In a policy that mixed benevolence with self-help, Flagler asked his employees to contribute to designated funds that would provide medical services for them at Alicia Hospital. The Hotel Cordova employees agreed to pay 1 percent of their salaries into a sick fund. The Ponce de Leon employees pooled their contributions and donated them to the Hospital Association. Beginning in 1892 workers on Flagler's railroad were assessed six dollars a year for medical care. Six beds at Alicia Hospital were reserved for railroad employees, and Dr. S. G. Worley, who maintained an office in St. Augustine, agreed to serve as the railroad's doctor.[77]

In the case of one particular worker who suffered from a drinking problem, Flagler asked that special action be taken to help him, rather than simply discharging him. "If Mr. Chambers is on a spree, I suggest that you take him (by force if necessary) to the Keeley cure at Jacksonville, and have him kept there until he sobers up." Three days later Flagler wrote again, saying, "I sincerely hope that the difficulty he has been laboring under has been overcome. Before taking any summary steps in this matter, we must make another effort to save him."[78]

The life and death of artist Robert German afford another example of Flagler's benevolence. German occupied a studio at the Ponce de Leon from 1888 to 1891. A "tall, pale young man" from Germany who painted small portraits and then landscapes of regional scenes, he had endured ill health during the entire time he stayed in St. Augustine. He remained in town over the summers rather than traveling north, and by the winter season of 1891 he was too ill to occupy his studio, sending a friend to represent him during the week.[79] That summer he ventured to the Catskills, but his health deteriorated further, and Flagler took him to Mamaroneck, where he passed away. Captain Marcotte wrote in his obituary, "At the time of his death the deceased was the guest of Mr. and Mrs. Henry M. Flagler, at both their lovely home on the shore and on the yacht Alicia, and enjoyed every care which even loving parents could bestow, at the hands of these generous people, who admired the patience and ability of the sufferer." In St. Augustine Dr. Anderson closed German's studio in the Ponce de Leon and auctioned off the remains of his art and personal effects.[80]

On another occasion Mrs. Flagler took an interest in the health of the doorman in their home, an "intelligent, polite, faithful, sober, honest and industrious colored man" named James Nichols. The Flaglers sent him to a specialist in New York City, who recommended a summer of light work in a cool environment. This moved Flagler to write to his friends Anderson and Price, who managed the Mount Washington Hotel in the White Mountains during the summer, asking if Nichols might find a place in their hotel even though they employed a white staff. Flagler offered to pay part of his salary.[81]

Sometimes his dealings with employees were of a highly gratifying nature. One Thanksgiving morning Flagler paid a visit to the home of his railroad manager William Crawford on Carrera Street and invited him to dinner, but he found that Crawford had plans to eat at home with his family and relatives. Flagler departed after placing an envelope in Crawford's hands. Only later in the day did Crawford open the envelope and find inside the deed to the house. It was a token of recognition for Crawford's years of service as superintendent of the railroad. Interestingly, eight years earlier when Flagler had first contemplated buying the railroad, he had wondered whether he should employ Crawford, who was reputed to have a problem with alcohol. In another example of generosity, his housekeeper Annie McKay received a fine shingled cottage at 18 Valencia Street as her home (although she would rent it out and live in the Ponce de Leon).[82]

Faced with requests for help that came from all over, Flagler tempered his generosity with a firm dose of skepticism. His sympathy for others was tinged by a profound feeling that individuals were responsible for their own welfare. His longtime employee and senior gardener William Fremd wrote, "I loved Mr. Flagler. For he was a real man, full of ambition and generous to a fault. He always thought of the other fellow and was ever ready to extend a helping hand to any deserving one in distress." The key word was "deserving." Flagler once wrote to his pastor Ward about a widow in Orlando who admitted to being addicted to morphine: "Hers is a pitiful case if true." He asked Ward to investigate the situation. "I am trying to recognize the responsibility of wealth, but I am a firm believer in the doctrine of doing the Lord's business on business principles, and as it is not possible to relieve the wants of all who come to me, I am compelled to discriminate carefully."[83]

William Crafts, who had secured a place with Carrère and Hastings on Flagler's recommendation, wrote to Flagler many years later complaining of his inability to earn a successful living. Flagler wrote back, probably exasperated by Crafts's repeated pleas for help: "The world is full of men who are unsuccessful. I cannot explain it. I have sometimes, however, thought that perhaps the fault was inherent in the individual."[84]

Interestingly, considering Flagler's expressed desire to see people improve themselves, he often declared his doubts about the value of higher education. He once wrote to a parent: "I can say with positive knowledge that a very large percentage of the successful men in our country, with whom I am acquainted, had no more education than was acquired in our common schools. If your boy has got the right kind of *STUFF* in him, he can get on in life with very little of the education which is obtained from books."[85]

Flagler's skepticism about the value of "book learning" was no doubt shaped by an early experience in Ohio when he supported four young men in college— all of whom entered professions and ended up failures. To a man who had asked him to assist his school, Flagler replied, "Today the garrets of this great City [New York] are full of just such men, and like all men who are failures, they have failed to [blame themselves] and have looked around to lay blame upon somebody else,—so within the last quarter century, the cry of the Plutocrat and Gold Bug has been heard." Flagler declared that the four young men he had helped send to college would have been better off to learn a trade. "All that I learned from books was obtained before I was fourteen years of age," he explained. Yet, in the end, he offered this petitioner a grant of four hundred dollars for his school.[86]

At least twice Flagler rejected requests for aid from gentlemen at Western Reserve University in Ohio, suggesting that perhaps the four men he had helped earlier may have attended that institution. To the first petitioner he simply wrote that he had deep-seated reservations about giving that particular help, although he added: "I trust you will not infer that I am wholly insensible to the demands of all that is good and beneficial to mankind. I am trying in a small way to meet these questions fully realizing that the Vice of avarice can be best checked by cultivating the grace of benevolence."[87] To the second he wrote, "Not a day passes that I do not receive half a dozen similar appeals, and I am already so heavily obligated in behalf of objects of Christian benevolence, I do not feel I can add to a burden which is already too great for me to bear."[88]

Flagler seems to have taken a modest interest in the Florida School for the Deaf and Blind, which had opened in St. Augustine in 1885 on a five-acre tract of land donated by Captain E. E. Vaill. In 1889 he allowed the school's teacher to use the children's playroom of the Ponce de Leon to stage a demonstration of what the children were learning. Each fall he provided the children at the school with Thanksgiving dinner.[89]

However, in 1906, when a proposal for expansion of the school came under discussion, Flagler bridled at requests that he step forward to underwrite a portion of the cost. In private letters to his St. Augustine lieutenants he displayed a pettiness untypical of his normally more generous spirit. However, he was provoked. First, he declared that the State of Florida had responsibility for the financial support of its educational institutions. Then he observed that the town's businessmen seemed more greedily interested in the school for the money that it brought into the local economy than in terms of genuine sympathy for the children. "Viewed from this selfish standpoint, I cannot understand why it should be any advantage to me. The teachers won't board at the Ponce de Leon or Alcazar, nor have we any dry goods and groceries to sell." Last, he commented bitterly that the community of St. Augustine had not done its part in maintaining the public improvements he had contributed to the town over the years. "I would rather give money to communities that show a little more public spirit than St. Augustine has done." Yet Flagler wrote that he wanted to do the right thing, and his lawyer Parrott offered his opinion that the school was a worthy object of charity.[90]

In spite of his reservations about the value of higher education, Flagler gave generously to a wide variety of educational institutions over the years. The Carlisle Indian School in Pennsylvania received a small sum of money from Flagler to educate western Indians. He was familiar with the work of Captain Richard Pratt in St. Augustine among the Indians held captive in the old Spanish fort, work that ultimately led Pratt to found the Carlisle School.[91]

When the Sisters of St. Joseph were adding to their school buildings in St. Augustine, Flagler rejected a request for an interest-free loan because it "does not commend itself to my business judgment," but he suggested that they instead request an outright contribution.[92]

An Episcopal minister who had been educated at Kenyon College in Ohio later wrote that when he thanked his bishop for paying his expenses, the bishop replied that the thanks should more properly be directed to Henry Flagler.[93]

Flagler's friend and Palm Beach minister George Ward received annual gifts of $1,000 for Rollins College, where he was president.[94] When Flagler made his highly publicized grant of $20,000 to the Florida Agricultural College in Lake City for a new gymnasium, he wrote to the president of that institution to say that the gym should not be referred to as the "Flagler Gymnasium." Thus much of his benevolence went unrecognized.[95]

19

Modern Times, 1900–1902

You see, we were in the background. We were
more or less the mechanical force.

—Joseph McAloon, interview, 1974

The modern era arrived in St. Augustine in 1900. It came rolling down Ribera Street in an automobile driven by John Bell of Yonkers, New York, who rented the Flagler-owned Swayne cottage on that street for the season. Like most new things in St. Augustine, this first motor-carriage immediately elicited some alarm and consternation. Fritchieff Monson, an old-timer who had once operated the ferry over the San Sebastian, stood up before the city council to speak on "the evolutions of a motor cycle or automobile which is daily seen on the streets." He asserted that it traveled at an illegal rate of speed, posing a threat to the safety of pedestrians and horse-drawn vehicles. The town elders pondered the question for a few minutes before deciding that existing ordinances covered the new conveyance. Flagler wrote to Ingraham with the observation, "Automobiles seem to have come to stay, and I presume the opposition to them at St. Augustine has got to run its usual course."[1]

A letter writer to the *St. Augustine Evening Record* who signed himself "Progress" agreed: "Our level streets are well adapted to the use of the automobile; every consideration of health, cleanliness, and comfort argue in favor of their use, but the first one that appears is greeted with determined opposition." The new autos, he argued, were better than horse-drawn carriages since they were "less expensive, noiseless, clean and rapid, do not wear the pavement, and they are sure to come."[2]

The prediction proved correct. A year later Mrs. Marcotte reported that autos were "flitting hither and thither filled with delighted people." She noted approvingly that Anastasia's hard sand beach made a fine avenue for "automobiling," and, as an original member of the humane society, she looked forward to the day when horses could be turned out to pasture and their work taken over by machines.[3]

John Plumber, a traveling salesman for the Locomobile Company, set up headquarters in the Alcazar for a week to demonstrate how safely the new vehicles could be operated. The *St. Augustine Record* observed that automobiles for hire could now be seen in line outside the hotels along with the horse-drawn conveyances to take guests for a spin around town. Progress did not come without some setbacks. A car making its way along north Charlotte Street near the fort became bogged down in deep sand, and bystanders had to help push it out of its predicament.[4]

There were other signs of the arrival of modern times. Over the direct rail line from New York to St. Augustine travel time on the "specials" had been reduced over the past ten years from thirty-six hours to just twenty-six hours. By 1902 three direct trains arrived daily from Chicago and one from Cleveland, signaling the rising popularity of Florida among midwesterners. Flagler's locomotives began a switch to burning coal rather than wood, partly because fewer pioneers living along the tracks were able to supply the railroad with firewood. West of town, at the start of the new year, workmen began removing the wooden ties from the old Tocoi railway—the iron rails had been salvaged a few years earlier—to convert the road bed into a wagon road. The last remnants of the railroad that had first brought Flagler to St. Augustine disappeared. Today County Road 214 follows the path originally set by the Tocoi railroad.[5]

By 1902 people in St. Augustine could make long distance telephone calls to New York, Chicago, and other places over the wires of the new Southern Bell Telephone Company. Delivery of mail to individual homes had begun a few years earlier in the summer of 1898, so citizens no longer needed to walk or ride to the post office on the Plaza to pick up their mail. Red U.S. Mail boxes were also placed in strategic locations around town for deposit of outgoing mail. However, once again, little in town ever happened without controversy, and one city councilman protested the post office's requirement that houses be numbered: "The city could not force any man to number his house," he argued, "any more than to force him to paint his fence yellow."[6]

The Hotel Ponce de Leon kept pace with modern times by undergoing another round of renovations to its heating, electrical, and plumbing systems in 1900–1901. Some 160 semi-private bathrooms were added by placing them between two adjoining sleeping rooms, so that the bath could be accessed from both rooms. (Private baths in every room did not become standard until Ellsworth Statler built his Statler Hotel in Buffalo in 1908.) One conspicuous improvement appeared in the Grand Parlor. For several years dances had been held in the center salon, but the floor's carpeting, even when covered with smooth, heavy linen fabric, wore out the dancers' legs. A highly polished oak floor went into that central area.[7]

At the Hotel Ponce de Leon balls men began to appear in tuxedo and black tie, rather than traditional white tie and tails. Mrs. Marcotte, usually an advocate of all things modern, considered this a fashion embarrassment for the men.[8]

Mrs. Marcotte also found it necessary to lecture the ladies. She wrote that if a member of society from fifty years ago returned to America, he would be dismayed to see "women by the hundreds, in every walk of life, on the streets, in public halls and private parlors chewing gum, their jaws going as though endeavoring to satisfy a hunger that had consumed many hours. He might see them coolly remove the masticated compound when 'tired nature' refused longer to perform the work, and affix it to the most convenient piece of furniture from a caryatid in the rotunda of the Ponce de Leon to the pew in church." Two visitors at Flagler's hotels, Thomas Adams of Tutti Frutti fame and Edward Beeman, the maker of Beeman's Pepsin Gum, must have appreciated the rampant popularity of chewing gum.[9]

In billiard rooms around town some of the billiard tables were replaced with ping-pong tables to feed that latest craze. Outdoors the tennis players took back the Alcazar courts from the bicyclists as the bicycle fad settled down to a routine.

Over in the Casino black entertainers at the cake walks, and sometimes white singers, their faces blackened with burnt cork, were performing a new kind of music called ragtime. These lively, energetic tunes inaugurated the modern era of popular music, but they did not bring joy to everyone. A writer for the *St. Augustine Record* remembered times when the "hotel help" sang "the old plantation melodies and sang them in a way often to bring tears to the eyes of their hearers." The writer suggested "cutting out the rag-time horrors" and returning to "genuine negro melodies" such as "Swing Low, Sweet Chariot."[10]

The catchy tune "Under the Bamboo Tree," which told of the love of an African prince and princess, swept the country and echoed from the rafters of the Alcazar Casino.[11] The music had been arranged by Bob Cole and the lyrics were written by J. Rosamond Johnson, who had performed in the Casino five years earlier. By this time he and his older brother James Weldon Johnson had departed Jacksonville for the far greater opportunities of New York City. They made a living writing popular melodies, and one of their conventional songs, "Lift Every Voice and Sing," would soon became renowned as the "Negro National Anthem." James Weldon Johnson would serve as the first black executive of the National Association for the Advancement of Colored People and become a recognized voice among the writers of the Harlem Renaissance of the 1920s.

In another sign of the times, the Villa Zorayda ceased to be a private home and became a tourist attraction. Franklin W. Smith, who had preceded Flagler to St. Augustine and encouraged Flagler's earliest hotel plans, had stopped coming to St. Augustine for the winters a few years earlier in order to concentrate on his grand project of a national gallery of architecture and art in Washington. He tried to interest Flagler in this undertaking, but Flagler declined, saying his Florida ventures were absorbing all his income. Early in the 1900 season Mrs. Smith and Nina, now Mrs. Duryea, spent a few last months in the Villa Zorayda before emptying the house of their personal possessions.[12]

The Smiths had tried to sell the home in 1899 but, finding no buyers, turned it over to Ward Foster to manage as a tourist attraction. Curiosity seekers could pay fifty cents to walk through the building and admire the oriental ornamentation. In 1902 the Villa Zorayda became a social club and restaurant.[13]

Flagler had been up and down the East Coast in the fall of 1899 tending to affairs in his realm, but in early January he departed St. Augustine for the North. He returned two weeks later bringing his secretary J. C. Salter and his usual coterie of friends: the Ashleys, Alice Pomroy, and Mary Lily Kenan.

They went right to Miami to be on hand for the seasonal opening of the Hotel Royal Palm before returning to Palm Beach, where Flagler stayed in Sea Gull Cottage. The Flagler party took their meals at the Royal Poinciana. Then they were all off for a quick visit to Key West and after that to Nassau in the Bahamas. Flagler wanted to be on hand for the opening of his new hotel, the Colonial, which stood on the bay front overlooking the harbor's amazingly clear water, where black boys would dive for coins tossed in by the tourists. The Colonial, like Flagler's hotels in South Florida, had been built by McDonald in the same utilitarian wood-frame colonial style. That first evening everyone celebrated with a grand ball. The governor of the islands Sir Gilbert Carter attended, as did an assortment of seafaring guests from their yachts anchored offshore.[14]

Dr. and Mrs. Anderson and their two young children joined Flagler's party from time to time during these weeks. They had turned Markland over to builders who were enlarging and modernizing the antebellum house. Besides that, Anderson was suffering from poor health and appreciated basking in the warmer climate. They spent most of their time at the Palm Beach Inn right on the beach but took brief trips with Flagler to Nassau and Miami.[15]

Flagler kept up a brisk pace between Palm Beach, Miami, Nassau, and Key West. At Nassau he and his friends took a motor launch to the beach across the harbor for a "wash party" and later enjoyed a cake walk by the hotel's black employees. Everyone was immensely pleased when Mary Lily's maid and her partner took the cake. Twice the colonial governor invited Flagler and his associates to Government House for dinner. By this time the Ashleys and Alice Pomroy had left the group, although Flagler always had some other ladies around so that he was not conspicuously alone in the company of Mary Lily.[16]

In St. Augustine Mrs. Marcotte proclaimed, "Golf is surely king!" "Should you doubt it," she explained, "happen into the Alcazar about ten in the morning, when golfers in red coats and green, gather there to await the trap that carries them to the field. It is a pretty picture, especially when some of the golfers are women. They gather in groups to discuss the scores of yesterday, and speculate on those of tomorrow." Golf enthusiasts adopted the Hotel Alcazar as their headquarters. Bulletin boards recorded the standings of individuals in the golf world's pecking order of scores and handicaps. The hotel company's Country Club at the south end of the city had a fine new clubhouse just opened for the season. The *St. Augustine Record* seconded Mrs. Marcotte's enthusiasm for golf: "The game is destined to become the national sport of America."[17]

In February some of the world's greatest golfers played the Country Club course. Willie Smith, a transplanted Scotsman and winner of the previous year's U.S. Open, started the action by shooting a record 34 for the course's nine holes. A few days later Smith played George Low, another Scot, who had finished second to Smith in the U.S. Open. This rematch over thirty-six holes proved, in Mrs. Marcotte's words, "the most exciting game ever played here, scores of spectators following the players over the course." Smith edged Low 150 to 152. However, this was just a warmup for the main event of the year.[18]

In 1900 Harry Vardon, the world's greatest golfer, came to St. Augustine. Vardon had been born on the English Channel island of Jersey into a family of modest circumstances. He made his way to Scotland, where he learned the game of golf by caddying for the gentlemen who played. By 1899 he had won the British Open three times. In that year the Spalding brothers offered Vardon a huge sum of money to come to America and play a series of golf matches to promote the new Spalding golf ball called the "Vardon Flyer." Flagler's golf professional Alex Findlay had spent the summer of 1899 in Britain, winning several tournaments but losing to Vardon. While there Findlay negotiated appearances by Vardon at Flagler's chain of hotels during his stay in America.[19]

Thus Vardon appeared at the Hotel Ponce de Leon in February to match his skills with the best in America. One lady at the hotel commented, "He looks just like other men." Mrs. Marcotte elaborated: "He is a quiet, unassuming fellow, wears a green golf suit, smokes a brierwood pipe." Some of the hotel guests offered him the helpful advice that in playing Florida's courses he should be careful of alligators lurking in the rough.[20]

As luck would have it, the day of the big match dawned with blustery winds pushing gray clouds across the sky. This did not deter a large gallery from turning out, and Flagler's course managers stationed lines of men holding ropes along

This group of golfers posed to have a picture taken in Palm Beach. Harry Vardon, reputed to be the best player in the world, stands second from the left. George Merritt, second from right, would later design the famous course in Ormond Beach. From the collection of the St. Augustine Historical Society Research Library.

the fairways to hold back the crowd. Vardon drove his ball from the first tee into the marsh bordering the fairway, but under course rules he was allowed to lift his ball without penalty. After that shaky opening, the game went Vardon's way. Twice Smith's putts rimmed the cup without falling, and by the end of eighteen holes he trailed by eight strokes. Vardon shot an amazing 71, tying Smith's course record of 34 on the second go-round of the nine holes. After a break for lunch, the gallery returned wearing heavier clothing, and the golfers went at it again. The reporter for the *New York Times* wrote, "The wind was blowing a gale when the men reached the tower for the thirteenth hole." The crowd cheered for the American champion Smith, and he closed the gap but still lost by six strokes.[21]

Vardon continued his Florida tour as far south as Miami and remained in the United States long enough to win the U.S. Open. He would later win the British Open three more times for a total of six, a record never equaled. Vardon is remembered today as the man who popularized the "Vardon Grip," in which the fingers of the hands are overlapped on the club handle. He also proffered an oft-quoted piece of advice to golfers: "Don't play too much golf. Two rounds a day is plenty."

Thomas Edison stopped by the Alcazar at the end of February 1900. He had last been in St. Augustine in 1886 when he stayed at the San Marco on his honeymoon, so this would be his first encounter with Flagler's palatial hotels. Since he left no record of his visit, we can only guess why he chose to stay at the Alcazar rather than the Ponce de Leon. Perhaps the typically rumpled inventor did not wish to don formal dress for dinner. He and his family were passing through just as tourists, and they departed to take Flagler's railroad for Palatka and from there a steamer up the Ocklawaha to Silver Springs, with a trip to Tampa and Plant's hotels finishing up their vacation. A year later he would begin making annual visits to Fort Meyers, where he located his winter home.[22]

Edison's interest might have been drawn to a new electrical wonder in town: four sleek Daimler electric-powered launches that cruised Matanzas Bay for the entertainment of winter visitors. Two additional dynamos, driven by Westinghouse gasoline engines, had been added to the engine room behind the Alcazar, which allowed for more lights in the Alcazar complex and provided current to charge the batteries of the power launches. Electric wires were strung from the powerhouse to the foot of the bridge where the launches were moored. An electric sign that lit up at night advertised their availability at a rate of fifty cents an hour. On moonlit evenings the launches would go out for excursions on the water, their searchlights illuminating places of interest. The storage batteries allowed for voyages of up to six hours.[23]

Alas, the electric boats would enjoy only one year of use in St. Augustine before being sent to Lake Worth for service with Flagler's hotels there.[24]

Electricity entered into the Baths of the Alcazar in the form of new therapeutic treatments that added a novel element to the old features of the standard Turkish and Russian baths. The *Tatler* touted their benefits: "Hot and cold saline and hydro-electric baths for rheumatism, gout, and all nervous disorders. Complete electrical baths, static, sensoral, galvano-faradic currents with hydro-electrical douche, the Schott system for heart disease, and the Nauheim baths. Massage in all its branches by graduates." If the treatments did not cure you, you got your money's worth in attention from the staff and their innovative equipment.[25]

St. Augustine gained a distinguished winter season family in 1900: Major General John R. Brooke and his wife. Brooke had served as an officer in the Union army during the Civil War, fighting in the thick of the action at Gettysburg and Cold Harbor. During the Spanish-American War he led the occupation of Puerto Rico and then served as governor-general of Cuba. He and his wife made the Hotel Alcazar their home during the winters and lived in Philadelphia the rest of the year. The Brookes became an integral part of the inner circle of St. Augustine society and frequently found themselves in the company of Henry Flagler.[26]

Brooke may have gained a measure of prominence from the Spanish-American

War, but the hero of that conflict was Admiral George Dewey, the victor in the Battle of Manila Bay. When he visited St. Augustine that season some people envisioned him as the future president of the United States. In the wake of victory in the Spanish-American War, Americans reveled in unalloyed expressions of patriotism, and Admiral Dewey's presence gave St. Augustinians reason to join the celebration. Flagler had invited Dewey to come to Florida as his guest, and Dewey was likely pleased to get away from all the mandatory celebrations in the North, although he was obliged to run a gauntlet of receptions at southern cities as his train made its way to Florida. He arrived quietly at Union Station with only a handful of local notables to welcome him and just a small crowd of citizens on hand because his train arrived earlier than expected. At the front gate of the Hotel Ponce de Leon, manager Robert Murray greeted the admiral, and a seventeen-gun salute boomed forth from the roof of the hotel. The admiral's four-star flag flew from the staff beside the entrance. General Schofield escorted Mrs. Dewey through the gardens into the hotel, with Mrs. Schofield following behind on the admiral's arm. The admiral and his party stayed in the same wing of the hotel occupied earlier by President Cleveland.[27]

A few days later the honored couple found themselves in the Grand Parlor shaking hands with about a thousand people who were fortunate enough to receive elegant little pasteboard invitations to a reception. Again General Schofield presided over the affair, with a committee of hotel and military officers (including the ubiquitous Captain Marcotte) escorting small groups of citizens into the parlor to be personally introduced by name. In the Rotunda the hotel orchestra played patriotic music to entertain those lined up waiting to be presented. Dr. and Mrs. Anderson had their turn.[28]

Flagler was conspicuously absent, but he was on his way up from Palm Beach. He and Mary Lily and their friends had stopped at the Hotel Ormond for a couple of days to do some sightseeing. Annie McKay and the Andersons went down from St. Augustine to join them. They all went on an excursion by boat one mile up the Tomoka River to have lunch at a rustic log cabin built for hotel guests venturing on exploring expeditions into the Florida "jungles." Later they stopped by a hop at the hotel's casino.[29]

The next evening in St. Augustine they had dinner with Admiral and Mrs. Dewey in one of the intimate private dining rooms just off the entrance to the Ponce de Leon's Dining Room. Eighteen people joined Flagler around a large round table. Mary Lily, wearing a white gown, was escorted for the evening by a young lieutenant from St. Francis Barracks. General and Mrs. Schofield led the local representatives, as they had throughout Dewey's visit. They were joined by Dr. and Mrs. Anderson, Rev. and Mrs. MacGonigle, James Ingraham and his wife, and three army couples.[30]

After dinner the admiral's party walked through the lavishly decorated court-yard of the Ponce de Leon and front garden of the Alcazar to join an outdoor party already in progress in the center court of the Alcazar. Here the decorations reached extraordinary heights. Thousands of electric lights had been added to those usually in the garden. Strings of multicolored lights wound up the palm trees, while others created outlines of a star, an American insignia shield, and an admiral's flag on the walls of the building. The house orchestra played under a palm-thatched pavilion in one corner of the square. Small tables for supper were scattered about. White ducks floated in the center pond and a large stuffed alliga-tor rested near the entrance to the Alcazar lobby. "The log cabin in the southeast corner of the quadrangle," reported the *Evening Record*, "contained a trio of cos-tumed darkies who accompanied by banjo and guitar, sang sweet negro planta-tion melodies which moved everyone—save the stuffed alligator just outside the door." Altogether the tableau formed a complete period piece of Floridiana from the heady age of imperialism, militarism, and racism.

Flagler and Dewey strolled through the gay crowd to absorb the atmosphere and then ascended to the second story to get a view down into the courtyard. Af-ter this the guests of honor returned to their rooms in the Ponce de Leon, while the younger set moved into the Alcazar lobby to dance until the morning hours.[31]

The Deweys were eventually allowed some peace and quiet to enjoy their stay, although whenever they ventured out in public people's eyes turned toward them. The admiral and his wife called on Flagler at Kirkside, and he took them on a tour of the Presbyterian Church and manse. Twice they made excursions on the hotel's electric launches, and they attended a garden party on the west lawn of the Ponce de Leon before they departed for the North.[32]

Flagler may have been late in coming up to meet Admiral Dewey because his old friend John D. Rockefeller had been visiting in Palm Beach and Miami. Flag-ler had long before invited his partner to come down and see how things had changed in Florida since his visit of 1884. When his railroad reached Daytona, Flagler had written to Rockefeller, "I believe this country would be a revelation to you, if you would take a week to look into it." However, for years Rockefeller apparently went no farther south in the wintertime than Georgia, but in 1898 he wrote to a friend, "It is marvelous what Mr. Flagler has wrought in that southern country, and I regret not to have paid him a visit long ago." On this visit to Florida in 1900 and again in 1901 Rockefeller seems to have bypassed St. Augustine and headed straight for warmer parts of the peninsula.[33]

Flagler's minister at the Royal Poinciana Chapel next to the hotel, George Ward, later told of a conversation in which Rockefeller said, "About ten or fifteen years ago this man (pointing to Mr. Flagler) said, 'I am going to invest about $30,000 in an orange grove in Florida. Don't you want to join me?' I told him

'I guessed I wouldn't.'" Rockefeller then looked about the great hotel and landscaped grounds and mused, "I think he's got at least $30,000 in here now. It looks like it."[34]

Following their arrival in St. Augustine Flagler and Mary Lily received a warm welcome from their friends. James Ingraham and his wife took them and a large party on a carriage caravan ride across the new Matanzas bridge and several miles down the hard-packed sand of the beach. A few days later Mrs. M. H. Spades opened her new house across Sevilla Street from the Ingrahams' house for a reception. The usual crowd appeared: the Andersons, Schofields, Albert Lewises, and Marcottes, among others. Soon thereafter Eliza Ashley and Alice Pomroy came up from Palm Beach to join Flagler at Kirkside. Mrs. Marcotte explained that Mrs. Ashley played the role of hostess at Flagler's Palm Beach cottage during the season. Flagler was planning a new home there, one in the Cuban style built around a central courtyard. Since Flagler had become accustomed to warm weather, Mrs. Marcotte went on, he would make Palm Beach his winter home, with only brief visits to St. Augustine at the beginning and conclusion of each season.[35]

No allusions to any kind of connection between Flagler and Miss Kenan ever appeared in print. Nor was there any reference to the absence of Ida Alice Flagler, at least in Florida publications. As might be expected, an undercurrent of speculation swirled in society gossip about Flagler's intentions and the objectives of the women around him.

Flagler and all his chief lieutenants, plus MacGonigle, made one last tour of the system by rail as far south as Miami, and then on April 28 Flagler and his lady friends—Ashley, Pomroy, and Kenan—left for the North.[36]

In 1900 the last U.S. Army troopers quietly moved out of St. Francis Barracks. On the books the post remained open but unoccupied. Sergeant Brown, who oversaw Fort Marion, also watched over the barracks. A reporter for the *St. Augustine Record* wrote, "It is impossible to restrain the feeling of regret as well as the flow of pleasant memories as one walks about the now quiet and lonely precinct of St. Francis Barracks. For the first time in its history St. Augustine is without a military garrison."

In 1907 Governor Broward would go to Washington and obtain a lease on the property for the State of Florida, and the headquarters of the state militia were relocated there. However, this did not bring any troops or even any significant number of state employees. It would not be until 1921 that St. Francis Barracks would become state property and headquarters of the Florida National Guard.[37]

During the summer of 1900 Flagler received some unwanted public notice when a man named John H. Malden sued him for almost $19,000, alleging that Flagler had paid him less than the true value for seventy-five shares of Standard

Oil stock Malden sold to him. The case hit the newspapers because it involved a prominent Standard Oil executive, money, and Flagler's private life. At the time Malden filed his suit he was in the awkward position of serving time in a Manhattan jail popularly known as "The Tombs," on a charge of passing bad checks.

The instigator of the lawsuit may have been Malden's lawyer W. L. Flagg, who declared that the case had been brought to "show up the Standard Oil Company and its methods of transacting business." Flagg had been involved in legal proceedings against Standard Oil by the State of Ohio two years earlier, becoming embroiled in a heated shouting match with Standard's John Archbold in court.[38] Flagg seems to have made pursuit of Standard a personal vendetta.

The aspect of the case that raised eyebrows involved Malden's charge that a woman named Helen Long lived in an apartment paid for with money provided to her by Flagler and that Flagler had first given her the stock certificates. Unfortunately for Malden's case, it appeared that he had taken the stock certificates from Long, sold them for his own benefit, and had then proceeded to spend wildly until he ran out of money and wound up in jail.

When Flagg was unable to produce Malden for the court trial, the judge summarily dismissed the case. However, Flagg had succeeded in getting Helen Long's name on the public record and placing Flagler's private life and financial dealings in doubt. As it later turned out, efforts to use the Helen Long case against Flagler had not gone away even though the Malden case was dismissed.[39]

During the summer of 1900 Flagler made another long railroad tour of the Great West. He had undertaken his first such trip west in 1887, covering, he said, 5,408 miles. He reported back to Anderson, "It is an amazing country." Then he had made a second journey in 1889, when he and Anderson discovered Flagler, Colorado. In 1900 he went again as part of a tour sponsored by the Yellowstone Park Transportation Company, which delivered tourists to Yellowstone via the Great Northern Railroad and then took them around to the sights and hotels on stagecoaches. The railroad owned the tour company, and Flagler evidently hoped to learn something that might be of use to his own railroad and hotel enterprises. He spent some time looking through the hotel registers and wrote to his railroad operations manager that most of the guests came from the Midwest, not the East.[40]

When Flagler returned to Florida for the 1901 season, he had yet another hotel project in the works: the Hotel Continental on the ocean at Atlantic Beach east of Jacksonville. He had prepared the way for this venture by purchasing the Pablo Beach Railroad in the summer of 1899, thus connecting the FEC main line with Atlantic Beach and, after Flagler built an extension, with the deepwater docking facilities farther to the north at Mayport. During the winter of 1900–1901, while the hotel was being built, Flagler made several trips from Palm Beach to the construction site to see how things were progressing. Since the hotel was located in the northern portion of Flagler's domain, James McGuire, not Joseph McDonald, oversaw construction of the hotel. In later years the Continental would prove a failure among Flagler's endeavors in Florida. It was intended to be a breezy beachside summer resort for southerners to visit during the hot summer months, but the concept simply did not engage travelers as expected, and Flagler eventually leased out the hotel to put it out of his way.[41]

Returning from one of his visits to Atlantic Beach in January 1901, Flagler stopped by St. Augustine to pick up the Anderson and Schofield families and take them to Palm Beach. There Dr. Anderson was reunited with his old friend Dr. Fremont Smith and his family, who hosted a dinner for Flagler, the Andersons, and the Schofields. The party enjoyed a week or so of socializing in Palm Beach before Flagler took off for a visit to Nassau to look into how his hotels were doing there.[42]

On his voyage to the Bahamas Flagler was accompanied by several of his lieutenants and by a newcomer, William R. Kenan Jr., the twenty-nine-year-old younger brother of Mary Lily. Flagler had become intrigued with the abilities of Mary Lily's brother and wanted to show him around the East Coast system. Perhaps he saw young Kenan as the possible heir to his empire, for that would be how things eventually turned out, at least in part. Kenan had graduated from the University of North Carolina in 1894 with a degree in science and had subsequently worked for General Electric and Union Carbide. He had been introduced to Flagler in New York in 1899, and his first business dealings with Flagler had come in May 1900, when he proposed selling chemically treated railroad crossties to the FEC Railway. That summer Flagler sent him to Palm Beach to make estimates for installing an electric power plant in the Breakers. Clearly impressed with Kenan's skill in negotiating and overseeing this assignment to completion, a few months later Flagler instructed McGuire to consult Kenan on the proposed electric plant for the Hotel Continental, adding that if Kenan disagreed with the man McGuire had already contacted for the job, Kenan should be given the contract. "There are very few men of his age who have had as much experience and who are as competent as he," Flagler wrote to McGuire.[43]

Kenan reciprocated the respect. He would later write: "Mr. Flagler had the most remarkable memory of any person I have ever met. He read everything, talked to everybody on any subject, and always recalled what he read or heard. Should you discuss some subject, be it engineering or scientific, with him, and a year or more later you related the same thing, be sure to have it the exact wording, because he surely would say: 'Now let me see, on such and such occasion you told me so and so and this is different. Now which is correct?'"[44]

Dr. Anderson enlarged Markland to make it more than ever an ideal showplace home. The Greek colonnades radically changed the simple exterior of the house. Author's photo.

Kenan's older sister Mary Lily did not appear in Florida, probably because her presence would have thrown additional fuel on speculation about Flagler's intentions toward her. In November 1900 a newspaper story had reported that Miss Kenan and Flagler would be married the next May. When approached by reporters about this story, Mary Lily's father William R. Kenan Sr. declared that he knew nothing about the matter. The *Richmond Times* editorialized that an official announcement would surprise no one: "It is currently rumored that she has been the recipient of marked attention from Mr. Flagler." However, one major obstacle stood in the way. Henry Flagler remained a married man.[45]

In early February Eugene and Eliza Ashley came down to Palm Beach accompanied by their Lockport neighbor Alice Pomroy. As had become the norm during the past few years, Eliza acted as the hostess of Flagler's household at Sea Gull Cottage.[46]

In St. Augustine the Andersons finally moved back into their enlarged and renovated Markland home after twenty months of renovations. It had been transformed from a simple antebellum home into a Greek Revival mansion with large Corinthian columns on the front and east side. A whole new western half of the house had been added, bringing it to the dimensions originally envisioned by the first Dr. Anderson back in the 1830s. The new section contained a library in the

Henry Flagler gave this portrait of Dr. Anderson to Mrs. Anderson as a Christmas present in 1900. It hangs in Markland house today. By permission of Flagler College.

front, furnished in dark oak paneling, and a dining room at the rear with equally elaborate wood ornamentation and a turquoise ceiling. In the rear a modern kitchen had been put in, with more bedrooms and baths upstairs.[47]

Flagler gave the Andersons housewarming gifts for Christmas: an oil portrait of himself for them both and one of Dr. Anderson as a present for Mrs. Anderson. He sent the paintings down to McGuire in November with instructions to keep the portrait of Dr. Anderson stored in the FEC office so that Mrs. Anderson could be surprised at Christmas. Flagler's gift to young Andrew that Christmas was a choo-choo train purchased from F.A.O. Schwarz in New York. He mailed McGuire a catalogue describing the toy. He wanted a five-by-seven-foot table built, standing at a height that would allow the doctor's son to observe the action. "The cars run by mechanical power," Flagler explained, "which is wound up by a key fitting in the locomotive or the tender. The train can be stopped by moving one of the switches. If you do not get on to the matter readily, call in one of our men from the railroad shops and perhaps they can help out." Such meticulous attention to detail had built Standard Oil and the Florida East Coast Railway.[48]

Mrs. Anderson had another railroad matter to take up with Flagler. During the evening hours, just about bedtime, a switch engine in the railroad yard would routinely begin its convolutions, moving cars around. The noise disturbed the tranquility of the Anderson residence. On one occasion when Flagler stayed as a houseguest, Mrs. Anderson took care to see that he occupied a bedroom on the west side of the house, nearest the tracks. Flagler got the message, and in days thereafter the Andersons' rest was not disturbed.

The renovated Markland became the showplace of St. Augustine, and Mrs. Anderson made the most of it, opening the house to receive guests for an "at home" every Wednesday. The Andersons became more socially active than ever. They were frequently joined by General and Mrs. Schofield, who by this time had moved into the Seavey cottage behind the Ponce de Leon at 20 Valencia Street. This house would also be enlarged in 1902 to make it more welcoming for gatherings. Down the way at 6 Valencia stood the "Casa Amarilla," the home of the Albert Lewis family. Lewis was a lumber baron from Bear Creek, Pennsylvania. Flagler had originally built the home in 1899 for his house physician Dr. Fremont Smith, but Smith and his family lived in it for only one season before moving to Palm Beach, where he became Flagler's hotel physician at the Royal Poinciana and Breakers. The Andersons, Schofields, and Lewises all had young children: Clarissa and Andrew Anderson, Georgina Schofield, and Hugh Lewis and his brother and sister. These children went to parties together and sometimes shared tutors.[49]

Elizabeth Anderson engaged in so many activities that Dr. Anderson joked, "I only catch her at meal times." She served as president of the Women's Exchange, which occupied a room in the northwest corner of the Alcazar. Anderson explained that the Women's Exchange was "a sort of club where they meet to exchange gossip, I think, and sell things at larger prices." He observed that the ladies seemed to be doing a "land office business" raising funds for charitable causes.[50]

In late February and early March Flagler enjoyed another long visit by John D. and William Rockefeller and their wives. They all took a trip to Miami that included a venture up the Miami River to the falls, and they attended a grand ball at the Royal Poinciana, but for John D. Rockefeller the most intriguing aspect of the stay may have been visits to the golf links. He followed a foursome of players around the course during a tournament and on at least one occasion, following Vardon's advice, played two rounds himself in one day. Soon he would become the most famous duffer in the country, but he applied the same intensity to golf that he had employed in the oil refining business and eventually became a competent player. For the rest of his long life he would incorporate golf into his regular routine.[51]

In early March Flagler went to St. Augustine to stay as Anderson's guest at

Markland. Herman Schladermundt arrived from New York at the same time and attended the Sunday evening concert in the Ponce de Leon's Rotunda beneath the murals he had helped to create. A day or so later Flagler, Anderson, Schladermundt, and Rev. John MacGonigle enjoyed a private organ concert in Memorial Church to cultivate a frame of mind for thinking about a dramatic improvement to the church building. They took up the proposal Schladermundt and Maynard had made back in 1892 to place artistic stained glass in the windows of the church. There is no record of what glazing originally filled the church's window openings, but crackled glass seems likely, and some of this kind of glass is still present in a side door today.[52]

Later that summer MacGonigle would travel to New York to confer again with Schladermundt and with Carrère and Hastings as preliminaries on the windows progressed. MacGonigle received credit for suggesting the Apostles' Creed as the theme of the windows, but Flagler himself may have taken a part in the selection. In a December 1901 letter to his friend Dr. George M. Ward, minister of the Royal Poinciana Chapel in Palm Beach, a chapel still operating today, Flagler objected to Ward's proposal that the Apostles' Creed be dropped from the order of service during the next winter season's services. Flagler declared that "not one person in five hundred who ever attended church" would not have the Apostles' Creed on the tip of his tongue and expect to recite it during services. Although he had written, "I haven't a drop of denominational blood in my veins," evidently Flagler felt strongly on this subject, for he usually followed a policy of keeping his hands off such matters of church liturgy. (Flagler's friend John D. Rockefeller could have told him that there were plenty of Baptists who never recited the Apostles' Creed, or any other creed, in church.)[53]

Schladermundt completed the drawings of the window designs during the summer of 1901, and MacGonigle traveled north again to visit Schladermundt's studio in Lawrence Park to give advice and approval. With the exceptions of two large windows above the east entrance and two rose windows, the Memorial Church's tall, narrow lancet windows did not lend themselves to expansive compositions. Thus it was decided that the lower portion of each window would contain a symbolic emblem to accompany each element of the Apostles' Creed. The approach replicated the one Schladermunt had used in the state seals in the Library of Congress. Under each symbol a phrase of the creed was written in opalescent glass. The resulting windows were bright, colorful, crystalline, and wholly impressive. Before shipping the windows off to Florida, Schladermundt exhibited five of them at the National Arts Club gallery on West 34th Street.[54]

Actual fabrication of the windows was done by Decorative Stained Glass Company, which operated out of a workshop at 46 South Washington Square. The company had been founded in 1883 by two of John LaFarge's former partners,

Herman Schladermundt created the magnificent decorative glass windows for Memorial Church. The windows echo some of the design features Schladermundt had used in the murals of the Ponce de Leon. Author's photo.

HE ASCENDED INTO HEAVEN

Thomas Wright and John Calvin. They handcrafted windows for many of the country's stained glass artists, most prominently John LaFarge and D. Maitland Armstrong—but not for Louis C. Tiffany, who of course had his own much larger factory. Calvin came to St. Augustine to install the windows in Memorial Church in January 1902, although the largest windows were not put in until the summer.[55]

Flagler made one more major alteration to the church the following year. At the time he was building his new home, Whitehall, in Palm Beach, and the firm of Batterson and Eisele was placing decorative marble work for him there. The company had done the marble in the Hotel Ponce de Leon years earlier. Flagler engaged them also to position marble borders around the east and south doors of Memorial Church. The large marble tablet over the south entrance bears the inscription: "1889 In Memoriam." When put in place, the slab covered a small round window above the door depicting a dove of peace. Flagler ordered McGuire to remove a large lantern hanging outside the door so that it would not obstruct the view of the inscription.[56]

Flagler sometimes wondered if he had burdened the St. Augustine church by presenting them with such a monumental building, for its maintenance required more than the members of the small year-round congregation could afford. He privately told a minister in Miami that "the Memorial Church at St. Augustine is a pretty heavy burden upon me—upwards of $3,000 per annum for several years." However, he may have had a personal motive for sinking still more money into the church for stained glass and marble: he was thinking of building a mausoleum next to the church as his final resting place. Still, for the moment, he also considered the alternative of erecting a new church and tomb in Palm Beach.[57]

Nevertheless, in the winter of 1901 Flagler was thinking about gaining a new lease on life and not about dying. He had finally completed preparations for obtaining a divorce from Ida Alice so that he could marry Mary Lily Kenan.

His first step had been to establish himself as a citizen of Florida. In April 1900 he sold his home at 685 Fifth Avenue to Charles W. Harkness of Philadelphia for $325,000. Charles was the son of Stephen V. Harkness, the older relative who had originally bankrolled Flagler's entry into a partnership with Rockefeller to form Standard Oil. Keeping the house within the family may have been a way for Flagler to reserve the option of regaining the property sometime in the future. At some earlier point he had transferred ownership of his country home at Mamaroneck to the Florida East Coast Railway.[58]

Next he declared Florida to be his place of residence and registered to vote in Palm Beach. He swore that he owned no businesses in New York, only stock investments. His construction of Whitehall provided ample evidence of his intent to make Florida his home.[59]

The next step required obtaining a change in Florida's law regarding divorce. At the time, following biblical teaching, only adultery qualified as grounds for divorce. The state legislature meeting in Tallahassee heard Flagler's name mentioned only in regard to his offer to donate $10,000 to the state Agricultural College (later the University of Florida). This generous offer was accepted by unanimous resolutions of both the Senate and House. The divorce bill, innocuously described in the House as "An act to amend the laws of Florida regarding the mode of procedure in cases of insanity," received little scrutiny and passed with large majorities in both houses a few days later. Governor William S. Jennings, who had narrowly missed falling with his cousin William Jennings Bryan at the Hotel San Marco three years earlier, knew that Flagler was behind the bill, and he received some advice to veto it. As a populist-leaning politician, Jennings realized that he could win support among the common people by standing up to a man who embodied the rich special interests; but former governor Duncan U. Fletcher, who was acting as Flagler's lobbyist on the bill, urged Jennings to sign the bill—which he did.[60]

All the publicity surrounding the Flagler divorce led to the discovery of Ida Alice's long-lost nephews who had been given up for adoption back in the 1870s, the sons of her sister Mary and Edward W. Taylor (see chapter 3). After his marriage to Alice, Flagler had contacted the New York Juvenile Asylum in an attempt to find out what had happened to the boys, but state officials had no record of their whereabouts. Then in 1901, when stories of the Flagler divorce reached newspapers in the Midwest, one of the boys' adopted aunts recognized the relationship and put them in contact with Flagler. Two of the Taylor men still lived in Iowa, where they had been raised, while the third had become a railroad engineer in the state of Washington. Each would receive a $189,000 legacy from Ida Alice's estate.[61]

While the Flagler divorce was making headlines in Florida, the embarrassing Helen Long case materialized in the New York and other northern newspapers once again. A story was put out by an unknown source alleging that Clarence W. Foote had named Flagler as a co-respondent in a divorce suit for "alienation of the affections" of his wife. According to the story, Foote was suing Flagler, John Malden, and John W. O'Bannon. The newspaper accounts rehashed the previous year's tale of Helen Long, John Malden, and the Standard Oil stock certificates, adding that in recent months Long had moved to South Dakota and had there obtained a divorce from Foote. Subsequently she had married O'Bannon, a handsome, wealthy manufacturer of book binding materials. Foote alleged that the divorce was illegal and wanted $100,000 in damages.

When a reporter for the *New York Times* interviewed John M. Mitchell, Flagler's lawyer, Mitchell declared that as far as he knew no such suit had been filed, and he implied that the story had been planted by a lawyer retained by the Vigilance League, an organization dedicated to cleansing New York City of vice. Mitchell said in his opinion this issue resulted from a criminal conspiracy by "some people who have posed in the community as extra good" to blackmail Flagler. He threatened to bring suit against the organizers of this conspiracy if they proceeded—and evidently they did not. Nothing was ever heard of the case after that.[62]

Helen Long O'Bannon would die just two years later from blood poisoning following surgery. Her new husband John O'Bannon became very wealthy when Henry Ford adopted his artificial leather for the upholstery of Ford cars for a number of years. However, O'Bannon lost his sanity and died a pauper in 1923.[63]

Flagler, who seems to have remained in Florida all spring, wasted no time following passage of the divorce law and began legal proceedings on June 3. He brought the presiding judge Minor S. Jones and his own attorney George P. Raney to West Palm Beach in his private car to publish legal notices of the case at the county courthouse. By this time Raney, a legislator from Leon County, was recognized as the man who had guided the divorce law through the legislative process. The case was heard in Judge Jones's chambers in Miami on August 12, 1901. Flagler was represented by a New York lawyer and by Raney. Ex-governor Fleming acted as guardian *ad litem* for Alice Flagler, and he posed no objection to the divorce. Flagler's New York lawyer testified that Mrs. Flagler had been adjudged a lunatic by a court in New York more than four years earlier. Dr. Mac-Donald and Dr. Shelton gave learned opinions that there was no hope for her cure. Flagler himself spoke, saying he had not seen his wife for more than four years and did not expect to see her ever again. He explained that he had provided a fund of more than two million dollars to ensure that she received proper care. The court appointed Eugene Ashley as Mrs. Flagler's financial custodian, a role that he also assumed under the laws of New York. The next day Judge Jones granted the divorce.[64]

A little over two months later Flagler married Mary Lily at the old Kenan homestead in Kenansville, North Carolina, near Wilmington, on August 23, 1901. He traveled to the ceremony accompanied only by Eugene Ashley, and just the Kenan family and a few friends attended the ceremony in the Kenan home, which overflowed with flowers sent by well-wishers. An orchestra from Wilmington provided music for the occasion. Afterward Laura Rockefeller offered a typical reaction to the wedding: "We have the announcement of Mr. Flagler's marriage to a Miss Kenan, of N. Carolina. She is thirty-six, he, seventy-two." Actually Mary Lily had just turned thirty-four.[65]

The newlyweds took a train for Flagler's Mamaroneck home Satanstoe, now owned by the FEC Railway, and arrived quietly to be greeted by a few friends at the country rail station. Flagler had recently remodeled the home, adding a music room with a ceiling imported from Europe for Mary Lily and a smoking den for himself; the change in ownership was needed to change his legal residence to Florida. They spent a few days answering letters and telegrams and sending cards of thanks for wedding gifts. Then they were off for Newport to visit Mary Lily's friends the Pembroke Joneses. In January 1902 the Florida East Coast Railway board of directors would deed Satanstoe over to Mary Lily. Flagler also gave Whitehall in Palm Beach to his bride, possibly as a wedding day gift.[66]

Only after Flagler's marriage did most Floridians become aware of the "Flagler Divorce Law," and it thereafter became a major political controversy. Flagler's ability to secure passage of a law that suited his specific needs clearly illustrated the way in which wealthy special interests could control the government. It meshed perfectly into the critique of conservative establishment politics being propounded by reformist critics. Some of Florida's newspapers charged that Flagler's gift of money to the state college for a gymnasium amounted to a thinly veiled bribe and that other monetary inducements had been employed to secure votes for passage of the divorce bill. However, Flagler also had his defenders. Frank Harris of the *Ocala Banner*, who was a trustee of the state college, said the donation to the college set a good example for others to follow and that Flagler had not wanted the gift to be publicized. Harris declared, "Our state has never had a better friend." He also argued that most states already recognized insanity as grounds for divorce. Harris would soon become one of Flagler's personal acquaintances. The "Flagler Divorce Law" remained in political dispute until the legislature repealed it in 1905 as a symbolic rebuke to the political power of the state's wealthy elite.[67]

Did Flagler bribe the legislature? No one ever offered solid proof of it, and no member of the legislature ever admitted to having received any special consideration from him. However, he did pay Fleming $15,000 and Raney $14,500 for their services as his divorce lawyers, and this has raised speculation that these generous payments represented reimbursement for expenses they had incurred in obtaining passage of the divorce legislation. A letter Flagler wrote to his lieutenant Joseph Parrott two years later shows Flagler recognized that spending money could influence legislation. He advised Parrott that he would be willing to "chip in" money to see that an anti-monopoly bill recently introduced in the legislature could be killed "if it can be done at a moderate expense."[68]

Flagler continued to come in for criticism on a national level, too. Muckraking journalist Ida M. Tarbell, through the intercession of Standard executive Henry H. Rogers, managed to obtain an interview with Flagler during this time. She noted that he was not, for the moment, a popular man around the Standard offices at 26 Broadway. "There were scandals of his private life," she wrote, "which, true or not, his fellow financiers did not like. Bad for business." She found her interview with Flagler frustrating, for he refused to answer any of her specific questions about the way Standard conducted its business. Instead Flagler told her about his impoverished childhood, leaving home at the age of fourteen, and how the Lord had permitted him to prosper in years since, but he refused to comment on how railroad rebates might have contributed to his prospering. She was surprised, according to her account, that "he did not conceal his distrust of John Rockefeller. 'He would do me out of a dollar today,' he cried, off his guard and with an excited smash of his fist on the table; and then, catching himself and with a remarkable change of tone: 'That is, if he could do it honestly, Miss Tarbell, if he could do it honestly.'"

"I was never happier to leave a room," she wrote of her interview, "but I was no happier than Mr. Flagler was to have me go."[69]

If the Tarbell account of Flagler's comments on Rockefeller can be trusted, it would be the only recorded instance of either Rockefeller or Flagler saying anything negative about the other. By this time the two men, who had been such inseparable business partners, saw less and less of each other. They had lived as neighbors for more than thirty years from their Euclid Avenue days in Cleveland down to the point when Flagler sold his Fifth Avenue house. After that Flagler lived at Mamaroneck when he was in New York, although he continued to come in to his office at 26 Broadway regularly. Rockefeller did not frequent the Standard Oil Building and lived most of the time at his country home on the Hudson River north of town, enjoying the life of a country gentleman—including a daily round of golf. In the winters he sometimes went no farther south than New Jersey, although he also visited Augusta, Georgia, where there was a nice golf course.

After spending the summer of 1901 in the North, the Flaglers returned to Florida in time to have Thanksgiving dinner at Markland with the Andersons. James Ingraham and Joseph Parrott, with their wives, joined General and Mrs. Schofield and a few others in the new, dark-paneled dining room. Mary Lily established a link to St. Augustine society by becoming a member of the board of the Ladies Exchange, almost certainly at the behest of Mrs. Anderson. After that the Flaglers went down to Palm Beach, where they stayed in one of the beachside cottages because their new mansion Whitehall was not quite finished. Mary Lily's parents and sisters joined the family group. Her cousin Dr. Owen Kenan came down to help Dr. Freemont Smith care for the guests at the Breakers and Royal Poinciana.[70]

Flagler's grand new home Whitehall was the main attraction of the season in Palm Beach. Carrère and Hastings had designed a house that blended the tropical elements of a Cuban home—tile floors and roof and an enclosed courtyard—with classical and American colonial elements. Pottier and Stymus had complete control of Whitehall's interior, unlike at the Hotel Ponce de Leon, where Hastings had maintained direction. The interior decorators went all out with elaborate European ornamentation from various periods of French and Italian history. Flagler did ask Carrère and Hastings to lower the ceiling of the grand entrance foyer so that it would look more like a home and less like a palace. Still, Whitehall emerged as a fantastic palatial edifice.[71]

The Flaglers showed off their new home for the first time late in January with a reception and dinner, though the decorators were still putting finishing touches on the place. Clarence Eddy of Chicago, possibly the best known organist in the world, played on the great organ Flagler had installed in the music room, and then the guests crossed the atrium for a meal in the dining hall. Admiral and Mrs. Dewey, who were Flagler's guests for the season in Palm Beach, joined Mr. and Mrs. Frederick Vanderbilt, Dr. Anderson, Mr. and Mrs. Samuel Andrews, and a few others at the long table. Many years earlier Andrews had been John D. Rockefeller's first partner in oil refining before Flagler joined the company.[72]

Over the next two months Mary Lily played hostess to a series of receptions that allowed a stream of the curious to admire Whitehall's interiors. An assortment of her relatives and friends stayed as guests in the upstairs bedrooms. Flagler brought Anderson and his family down for a while, and they all took a trip to Nassau together. The stage actor and humorist Joseph Jefferson, well known locally as an avid fisherman, often turned up as the Flaglers' companion at various social events. One evening a group of friends gathered in a private room of the Royal Poinciana to play the highly competitive new card game called bridge, and afterward the wealthy white folks staged a cake walk for their own entertainment. Mary Lily strolled with John Jacob Astor as her partner, while her sister Jessie was paired with Frederick Townsend Martin.[73]

Frederick Martin was noted as one of the leading members of Mrs. Astor's list of the New York Four Hundred and a member of the Bradley-Martin family, whose fantastically expensive costume ball at the Waldorf Hotel in 1897 had attracted widespread condemnation for its wasteful display of wealth. Martin, while continuing to live the life of a wealthy socialite, became famous for his trips to the Bowery, where he would hobnob with the poor and provide them with elaborate dinners at Christmas time. In his book *The Passing of the Idle Rich* he condemned the very life he lived.

Martin admired Flagler, writing, "When I first met Henry Flagler he was a white-haired old man whose every gesture and every word spoke of tremendous will power and force of character. . . . I think I owe an enormous debt of gratitude to Henry Flagler, for his example has enabled me to support life's troubles with more patience than is my nature, and he has done much to help me to fight the hard battle of self-control." He also respected the way Flagler did good for his fellows by creating successful businesses that employed thousands of laborers.[74]

Although Flagler attended many social occasions with his wife, he hardly played the role of the idle rich man. He was sometimes seen being propelled along by a servant in one of the distinctive bicycle chair rickshaw contraptions characteristic of Palm Beach, where no horse-drawn or motor-powered vehicles were allowed. This way he could enjoy the air as he inspected various parts of his local domain. He was never so happy as when engaged in some new enterprise.[75]

The 1902 season in St. Augustine produced no great sensations as almost everyone seemed to be just passing through on their way to Palm Beach. One party of overnight guests at the Ponce de Leon was led by Henry H. Rogers, vice president of Standard Oil. Included in his group were Thomas B. "Czar" Reed, the former speaker of the House of Representatives, the author Mark Twain, and Laurence Hutton, former literary editor of *Harper's Magazine*. Rogers had become Twain's close friend after rescuing him from financial ruin a decade earlier when a publishing house Twain had founded went bankrupt.

Writing home to his wife, Twain explained, "We came to the hotel to dine and wait for the evening train; but concluded to stay all night, for which I was glad, as I was very tired. I was in bed and asleep by 8 o'clock, but the others went to some kind of a show, and Hutton did not get to bed till after midnight and the show wasn't worth it." Twain was up in the morning before everyone else and took the opportunity to write his letter. "After breakfast we leave for Palm Beach, where there is another of these vast hotels—vaster than this one, I believe. It is a 9 or 10 hour journey. We shall stay all night there—take the ship at Miami, if she is there." The vessel they met in Miami was Rogers's yacht *Kanawha*, which would take them to Cuba and then the Bahamas before returning to New York. A reporter caught Twain before he left St. Augustine, and he said only that this was his first visit to Florida and he was delighted with St. Augustine.[76]

The Flaglers visited from Palm Beach the second week in April and stayed in rooms in the Ponce de Leon, although the hotel had recently closed for the season. They took their meals in the Alcazar. Mary Lily's brother William and cousin Owen joined her sisters Sarah Kenan and Jessie Wise and Jessie's daughter Louise. Flagler and Parrott went up to inspect the new Hotel Continental in Atlantic Beach, and then Flagler brought the whole family up to see the place.[77]

While he was in St. Augustine Flagler discussed major changes in the Alcazar with James McGuire. For several years the Alcazar had filled to overflowing during the height of the season. The Cordova had been taking the excess patronage, but this put a strain on the staff of the Alcazar, handling two hotels. Someone hit upon the novel idea of building a connecting bridge at the second story level between the Alcazar and Cordova. This would eliminate the need for a second front desk at the Cordova. Flagler seems to have been skeptical of the proposal; a week after leaving St. Augustine he wrote to remind McGuire that no final decision had been made on the changes. Later that fall, after McGuire had built the bridge, Flagler wrote to him saying, "I feel you are to be congratulated upon the success with which you have accomplished the changes in the Alcazar and Cordova. I only hope that the future patronage of the houses will justify the expenditure."[78]

The bridge was not a perfect solution, for guests staying in the Cordova were far removed from the heart of the Alcazar—the staff referred to the Cordova as

An overhead hallway connected the Alcazar to the Cordova so that the two hotels could be operated by the same staff. From the collection of the St. Augustine Historical Society Research Library.

"Siberia"—but it worked reasonably well. Guests walking down the bridge's long hallway over Cordova Street would scarcely realize they were leaving one building and entering another. Desk clerk Karl Abbott noted that the rooms in the top story of the Alcazar, known as the "North Pole," were also difficult to rent, so he would try to induce customers to take a room there for a few days on the promise of being moved to a lower level later.[79]

The Alcazar's dining room had long been a problem since the hotel had originally been built with only a small café, and its later expansion could accommodate only a limited number of diners. When the hotel filled to capacity, sometimes guests had to wait to be seated. To expand the dining room McGuire demolished a portion of the arched portico on the east side of the Alcazar that led from the hotel to the Casino and built an addition all the way out to the sidewalk on Cordova Street. This expansion proved a permanent solution to the hotel's need for more dining space.[80]

Flagler and McGuire discussed another project in the spring of 1902: construction of a new building for the Florida East Coast Railway Hospital. The hospital had been operating since 1898. Injured and ill workers from as far away as Miami would come to St. Augustine for treatment, but as the number of railroad employees increased, the old building became overcrowded. The new three-story hospital, standing on King Street near the depot, was completed by July. It could accommodate 150 patients and included such modern services as an X-ray room.[81]

Henry and Mary Lily left St. Augustine on April 22 for Hot Springs, Virginia, where the Royal Poinciana's manager Fred Sterry had just opened a new hotel called the Homestead. They spent some time there before proceeding to Mamaroneck, where they invited guests over for house parties. August found them in Newport for the height of that summer resort's season.[82]

A little later that year Flagler wrote to Sterry about a conversation he had had after the board of directors' meeting of Western Union. Jacob H. Schiff, who also served on the board with Flagler, had complained of the inferior rooms afforded to him at the Royal Poinciana by Sterry. He felt that he and his family had been slighted because they were Jewish. Flagler apologized to Schiff for the treatment he had received and then wrote to Sterry about Schiff: "He is a very modest retiring man, and if he didn't belong to the race he does, would be a social acquisition." Flagler continued, "This Hebrew question is a difficult one, and if Mr. S. is encouraged to come, I don't know but what it will result in others, although he is of the very highest rank. . . . I don't want to influence your judgment in this matter one particle. Do just as you think best."[83]

What Flagler called the "Hebrew question" had been percolating for years and had first burst into the open back in 1877, when Henry Hilton denied rooms in the Grand Union Hotel at Saratoga to Joseph Seligman, although Seligman seems to have invited the confrontation to expose anti-Jewish discrimination. At the time Flagler entered the hotel business the question of inclusion or exclusion remained unsettled. Clearly at least a few Jewish guests had long visited Flagler's hotels. Baron Alphonse de Rothschild, the head of the French branch of the great Jewish banking consortium, attended the Tropical Tennis Tournament at the Hotel Alcazar in 1890. Charles H. Schwab and his wife were seen at the Royal Poinciana and during a later season at the Charity Ball in St. Augustine. Oscar Straus, owner of Macy's Department Store and the first Jewish member of the president's cabinet, stayed at the Ponce de Leon. Three years after Flagler wrote his letter to Sterry, Meyer Guggenheimer occupied rooms at the Ponce de Leon.[84]

Discrimination against Jews increased with the advent of the twentieth century and the arrival of millions of East European Jewish immigrants in the United States. Even then, communities seem not to have adopted uniform practices on the acceptance of Jewish clientele in hotels, although it is difficult to gauge the extent of discrimination because presumably much of it was not overt but was rather handled by "gentlemen's agreement." Clearly resort locales catering to Jewish-only guests proliferated in places such as the mountains northwest of New York City and on the New Jersey seashore. Aside from the single letter to Sterry quoted here, the Flagler archives are silent on the question.[85]

In Florida's resort hotel society individuals danced an intricate minuet scored to the complexities of religion, race, and social class. At the end of each season some of the female employees living upstairs in the laundry building could be seen waving handkerchiefs from the windows in farewell to sister workers as their train pulled out of Union Station for the North. In the *Tatler* Anna Marcotte also bade goodbye to the men and women who worked in the hotels, wishing them well until they returned again in the following winter. Mrs. Marcotte mused, "Now the question to ask ourselves is, who gets the most real happiness out of this merry-go-round, the butterflies of fashion or those who toil to give them pleasure?"

Karl Abbott, desk clerk of the Alcazar, was pretty sure it was the workers: "A peculiar psychology governs the actions of the typical resort employees. They are a gypsy lot who live more like circus people than any other I know—here today, gone tomorrow. New England in the summertime—Florida or California in the winter. Following the sun and tourist trade." The workers rode in the second-class railroad cars, thus evading the need to maintain decorum in the first-class coaches. They would sing and play as if going to a picnic. He added that some of the workers, at least the men, played poker on the train all the way from St. Augustine to New York, and some lost a season's wages during the trip.[86]

When fall arrived the process would be repeated in the other direction. Some employees would have continued in a group with their band of fellow workers to some northern resort, perhaps managed by someone who also directed one of Flagler's Florida hotels. In this case the return to Florida would almost be predetermined. To fill vacancies Flagler's hotel executives opened offices in New York in the fall, sometimes in the Standard Oil building, where prospective workers could walk in to apply for positions. Flagler also used employment services that specialized in seasonal hotel workers. He paid for one-way fares south to Florida. Often the Clyde Steamship Line, which operated a passenger service between New York City and Jacksonville, would carry employees on the first leg of their journey. At Jacksonville the workers would find tickets to St. Augustine on Flagler's railroad awaiting them.[87]

Some workers were expected to supply their own uniforms. Railroad manager R. T. Goff wrote to one newly hired porter, "Equip yourself with one blue suit. We will furnish cap, buttons and badge."[88]

Flagler provided living quarters for several hundred workers at his hotels. Their quarters virtually amounted to a second-tier hotel with its own staff of workers to serve the other employees. Workers bunked two or three to a room. White male employees of the Ponce de Leon lived on the upper floors of the utility wing of the hotel above the kitchen, while the Alcazar had its bachelor quarters above the Casino. Two narrow stairways accessed the area. The rooms were cramped, but at least each had a window, a closet, and a sink. The men shared two common toilets at the end of halls. After the 1893 fire, long ropes attached to metal rings were coiled at the ends of the halls below windows to serve as a means of escape in case of another fire. Women employees lived upstairs in the laundry building on Valencia Street, while black men lived in the barracks on south Cordova Street.[89]

Where and what an employee ate depended upon his or her standing in the hotel establishment's rigid hierarchy. The Ponce de Leon and Alcazar managers lived in their own suites in the hotels and entered the dining room on an equal standing with the guests, much like the captain of an ocean liner. They would sit modestly to one side but order food from the same menus as the guests. The first officers—that is, the heads of departments: assistant manager, room clerk, auditor, housekeeper, and a few others—entered the dining room from the kitchen and sat by themselves in the rear. The second officers, one level down, ate in a separate dining room off the kitchen and ate from the hotel menu, except that the expensive entrées were marked off. "The balance of the 'help,'" according to Abbott, "ate in a cafeteria which adjoined the kitchen and which they called the 'zoo.'" These workers ate food prepared for them from a separate kitchen. One year the Alcazar faced a near rebellion from the men who tended the boiler room. James McGuire advised the manager, "What these men need is plain substantial food; pie or cake does not cut any figure with them." He suggested that the cook ought to be able to alter the offerings and pacify the workmen.[90]

Abbott noted that employees were strictly segregated by rank at all times. First officers and second officers did not socialize after working hours, even though their relations might be cordial. Abbott approved of this military discipline, feeling that it made the whole system work efficiently.[91]

Black employees were served in separate dining rooms: one for black officers, one for black male workers, and another for black female workers.

The maids, valets, and nurses who came with the guests from the north were assigned sleeping rooms in the same, more modest areas of the hotels as the employees. They also ate in separate dining rooms near the kitchen.[92]

Above all, the hotel employees were required to keep entirely separate from the guests unless their work required close interaction. For example, employees could not enter the Dining Room, Rotunda, or Grand Parlor of the Ponce de Leon unless their work required their presence in one of these rooms. Joe McAloon, who worked on the maintenance staff, explained, "You see, we were in the background. We were more or less the mechanical force." However, he added that "we would slip in when we could" to catch a glimpse of whatever the rich people were doing. One of the female employees who bunked in the laundry building said she was directed to walk straight from the laundry, along Valencia Street, to the back door of the hotel without wandering about the grounds. She also said the women were expected to be in their rooms after the evening curfew, but that being young and lithe, they would sometimes climb through a window to go and socialize in town.[93]

Abbott explained that although the hotel workers supposedly lived in a separate sphere, they constantly shared tidbits of information about the goings on in the upper echelons of resort society. "To show you how the hotel grapevine works," he wrote, "when Flagler walked from his residence to the hotel, the doorman, the instant he came in sight, told the bellboys, and the boys told the clerk, the clerk phoned the housekeeper. Three hundred people passed the word, 'The old man's coming' before he was in the door."[94]

Flagler tended to regard the legions of men and women working in his Florida enterprises as his private employees who worked for him personally. He considered his Florida ventures, however large they might be, as his own private businesses that he could run as he pleased. He may have co-founded the world's first modern giant corporation, but Flagler tended to think like a small business owner in his fundamental ideas about economics and business. In most ways he was a typical conservative Republican, with little appreciation for "modern" economic ideas. For example, he once wrote to George Wilson, editor of the Times-Union, that the rights of the individual were paramount in business. He noted approvingly that so far labor unions had not penetrated Florida to any great extent, but that the previous year in Palm Beach he had been "forced" to make terms with a labor union in order to get work done. "My workmen at Palm Beach were dictated to by a labor organization," he fumed. The term "my workmen" apparently came naturally to him.[95]

When locomotive engineers complained about their pay, Flagler's lieutenant Joseph Parrott wrote, "If any of the engineers in the employ of this Company are not satisfied with the pay which they are receiving I sincerely hope that they will look elsewhere for employment." Parrott added that costs for operating the railroad were going up, but the state railroad commission prohibited the road from raising rates. However, sometimes Flagler and his executives were obliged to acquiesce to limitations on the free employment of workers. Eventually some of the St. Augustine hotel staff were unionized, and James McGuire learned to live with this constraint. For example, in writing to one man to offer him a job maintaining the physical plant, McGuire added: "This is a union job and hence it will be necessary for you to be a Union man and in good standing."[96]

Flagler mixed his authoritarianism with paternalism. Business writer Edwin Lefevre put a favorable spin on Flagler's businesses by explaining that unlike other corporations, Flagler's had a heart because they were owned by just one man, and that man had a conscience. "Mr. Flagler always decides in favor of what is just and fair and kind. I cannot say as much of any other 'big man,' though it must be remembered that while other corporations have no souls, this one has, and it belongs to Henry M. Flagler."[97]

By all accounts Flagler treated his employees with dignity and respect, within the bounds, as he saw it, of sound business principles. Richard Edmonds shared a telling anecdote about riding in a railroad car with Flagler when it was required to make frequent stops: "Repeatedly during the day after the train had been stopped, when the flagman was called in, I saw Mr. Flagler quietly get up and go to the platform to open the gate to enable the flagman to step into the car without difficulty, doing this as naturally and quietly as though it were a matter of course that he should do it."[98]

Flagler's personal household staff both gave loyalty to Flagler and received it in return. He would remember some of them in his will. When he built his palatial home Whitehall in Palm Beach, it became necessary to increase the size of his household retinue. He solicited the assistance of Royal Poinciana manager Fred Sterry in securing new help, explaining that they would live comfortably, with running water in their living quarters. "My servants have been with me a good many years and have had no one really over them," he explained, concerned that hiring someone to be in overall charge of Whitehall might upset some of his old retainers. He suggested that he would need one or two more "colored men" and perhaps three "capable intelligent colored girls" to act as parlor- and housemaids.[99]

In his racial attitudes, Flagler seems to have held beliefs typical of white Americans of the day. During the thirty years following the end of Reconstruction in 1876 a pervasive movement swept the South to deny black Americans their political rights and to impose racial segregation on civil society. A profound belief in the innate inferiority of black people undergirded this development. Flagler's behavior seems to have been in accord with the trends of the day. Although he was a Republican, belonging to the party of Abraham Lincoln and Emancipation, Flagler declared himself "opposed to indiscriminate negro suffrage." He aligned himself with the faction of the Republican Party that felt Republicans could never emerge as a legitimate second party in the South unless they jettisoned the black wing of their party. Flagler advised Presidents McKinley and Roosevelt to appoint only white men to government patronage positions in the South.[100]

As an owner of a railroad, Flagler was forced to confront the issue of racial segregation in passenger cars and train stations. In 1887 the Florida legislature passed a law requiring separate cars for black and white passengers. This law met with some resistance. For example, a black woman refused to leave the first-class car on a train to Palatka. When the conductor attempted to remove her, she bit him on the hand, and finally she had to be wrestled out by a couple of black porters. Conversely, one white "Florida Cracker" wanted to sit in the second-class car where black passengers rode because he would be allowed to smoke his pipe there but not in the white passengers' first-class car. He was also carried from the car by the train's crew.[101]

Flagler's railroad complied with the state's segregation law, but evidently Flagler wished for the separation of the races to be done with as little overt coercion as possible. On one occasion he instructed his FEC passenger manager and the station boss in Daytona to avoid placing "White" and "Colored" signs in the depot's two waiting rooms if at all possible. "We had thought the people at Daytona would soon learn which waiting room was set aside for white people and which for colored and it would not be necessary to have signs painted over the doors.... I think if you will use a little discretion and handle the people as easily as possible, until they get used to the two waiting rooms, we will have no difficulty."[102]

In theory cars and facilities provided for black passengers were supposed to be equal in quality to those provided to whites, but this was seldom the case. A black leader once wrote to the FEC asking for better accommodations for black passengers. He did not request integration of cars, just equal quality cars. The railroad replied that the numbers of black passengers riding on the trains did not justify the expense of adding a separate first-class car to seat them. Thus black travelers, no matter how well dressed or well behaved, continued to ride in the second-class cars. However, eventually some of the day coaches were converted into "combination cars" with a partition in the middle to separate first-class black passengers from the smoking section.[103]

When the venerable black leader Frederick Douglass dropped down from Jacksonville for an afternoon visit, Flagler's railroad provided him with a private car for the trip. We do not know what motivated the railroad to give Douglass use of a private car, but it may have been to avoid the dilemma of either insulting a distinguished guest by asking him to ride in the second-class passenger car or allowing him to travel in a first-class car normally reserved for white people. Douglass gave a speech at Genovar's Opera House to a mixed-race audience, who responded to his remarks by rising to sing the national anthem.[104]

Likewise, when Edward Wilmot Blyden, the black Liberian diplomat and writer who is today known as the "father of Pan-Africanism," visited St. Augustine, Flagler's own private railroad car carried him to Jacksonville.[105]

Dr. Anderson, who was well known as a friend of St. Augustine's black community, sent Flagler a book for his consideration containing an extended examination of the "race question." The book, *Ham and Dixie*, had been written in 1895 by Joseph B. Sevelli Capponi, the principal of Lincolnville's public school no. 2. Capponi claimed to have been born in Florida, educated at Biddle University in North Carolina, and licensed to practice law in Texas and Florida.[106]

Capponi's book came out just before Booker T. Washington gave his "accommodation" speech at the Atlanta Cotton States Exposition, and, like Washington, Capponi advised black Americans to accept segregation and political disfranchisement for the time being. Both men exhorted black men and women to lift themselves up by concentrating their energies on moral living, education for trades and careers that would advance the race economically, and cooperation with well-meaning whites. Capponi admitted that the present degraded position of black Americans had resulted from slavery and continuing repression by whites, but he counseled blacks to endure the persecution and stand together to help themselves improve their own lot. Beyond this, he declared that his personal experiences had shown that some white men were willing to help black people advance. Here he probably had people such as William G. Warden, the patron of his school, and Dr. Anderson in mind.

Capponi's book seems not to have received much attention. His call for greater black-white dialogue and cooperation went no further than the limited white philanthropy that supported black colleges such as Washington's Tuskegee Institute. Racial segregation and the elimination of black political rights actually accelerated as the United States entered the twentieth century.

For his part, Henry Flagler was not averse to supporting the efforts of his black employees to help themselves. He would give the Casino over to the hotel waiters and bellmen to hold fund-raising balls, jubilee concerts, and cake walks to raise money for the black ward at Alicia Hospital. Nor were black performers excluded from his halls. The renowned classical tenor Sidney Woodward from Boston sang concerts on at least two occasions in the Alcazar Casino.[107]

20

The Challenge of Key West,
1903–1906

Build one concrete arch and then another, and pretty soon
you will find yourself in Key West.

—Henry Flagler to Dr. Andrew Anderson, 1904

The Flaglers returned to Florida during the second week of December 1902.
Flagler wrote ahead to his chief lieutenant Joseph Parrott with specific instructions about his travel itinerary: he wanted to visit the freight docks at Mayport
on the St. Johns River while passing through Jacksonville. Then, after spending
time in St. Augustine, he desired to look over his orange grove at San Mateo.
He also wanted to visit Stetson College to see what sort of building had been
constructed with the money he had donated for a science hall, "but I don't want
anyone at Deland except Professor Forbes [the president] to know of my visit."
He instructed Parrott, when arranging for a carriage to Deland, to "try and fix it
so that the telegraph operator won't know who is making the trip."[1]

Flagler and Mary Lily arrived in St. Augustine and checked in at the Alcazar
for a two-week visit. He used his time to catch up on his business enterprises in
town. They celebrated Christmas in St. Augustine, and the Andersons hosted a
dinner party for them and some of their friends. The Flaglers were developing a
routine of spending some time in St. Augustine while on their way to and returning from Palm Beach.[2]

They reached Palm Beach in time to stage a formal New Year's dinner at
Whitehall. Then they hurried off for visits to Miami and Nassau, where Flagler
could check on those regions of his empire and renew acquaintances with the
local civic and political leaders. Then they settled down in Whitehall to enjoy
the company of Mary Lily's parents and most of her siblings, save for her brother

William, who was busy with his own career. The Andersons came down for two weeks to stay as houseguests with the Flaglers. Before the Washington's Birthday Ball at the Royal Poinciana, the Flaglers enjoyed dinner in the banquet hall, with Henry and Mrs. Anderson at one end of the table and Mary Lily and Dr. Anderson at the other end.

A few days later Anderson returned to St. Augustine, but Elizabeth Anderson stayed to help Mary Lily prepare for a grand *bal poudré* at Whitehall. Not only did the guests arrive in Louis XIV costumes, but the Flaglers had real European royalty on hand in the form of the duke and duchess of Manchester (although she was an American girl). Mary Lily wore a powdered wig and "a superb gown of pink *panne* velvet trimmed with bands of silver." The ball spilled out into the atrium under the stars, where Neapolitan mandolin players and singers filled the darkness with melodies. The ball's souvenirs—gold cufflinks and scarf pins for the men, brooches and pins for the ladies—arrived in a rickshaw drawn by five "pickaninnies." Altogether it amounted to a display of wealth that might have left the Sun King in the shade.[3]

Henry Flagler probably got more enjoyment from amusements such as a visit to the Boat House, a rustic floating restaurant on Lake Worth where visitors were served fried chicken and cornbread with their wine. Two of his most frequent companions in Palm Beach were Joseph Jefferson and Frederick Townsend Martin, both of whom seem to have lived more casual lifestyles, although Martin was "the acknowledged leader of the very 'smart set.'" The infamous Harry Lehr made an appearance at Whitehall one evening and livened up the gathering by playing the piano to accompany Flagler's house organist Russell Joy. Lehr, a newcomer to the upper social order, aspired to become the arbiter of who belonged in high society, but his flippant demeanor and comic antics failed to amuse many among the old establishment.[4]

Flagler's close companion Joseph Jefferson was perhaps the most famous comic actor in America at the time, having made his reputation portraying Rip Van Winkle in a stage play he wrote himself. His perpetually ebullient spirit made him a natural comic performer. Grover Cleveland counted Jefferson as a personal friend, and following Cleveland's secret cancer surgery in 1893 he spent some time recuperating in Jefferson's home. Jefferson had visited Florida as Flagler's guest in 1895 and would thereafter become a fixture of the winter season in Palm Beach. People most often encountered him indulging in his favorite passion, fishing.[5]

In St. Augustine the depression years of the 1890s were becoming a distant memory. Flagler's hotels, as well as the rest of the town, entertained more visitors than had appeared in many seasons. The Alcazar, with its Cordova "annex" and the Casino, led the festivities. "The addition of the Cordova to the Alcazar

A rare photograph of a smiling Henry Flagler (*right*) standing outside Sea Gull Cottage with actor Joseph Jefferson (*left*) and builder Joseph McDonald. By permission of Historical Society of Palm Beach County.

was made none too soon," declared the *New York Tribune*, "as the East Wing, as it is now called, is filled with guests, who are delighted with the new furnishings, large rooms, and commodious baths." About 150 of the upper story rooms in the Cordova had been refurbished, giving the Alcazar/Cordova a capacity for 450 patrons—a number that it reached on several days during the height of the season. The newly renovated rooms in the Cordova hardly rose to the grand heights first imagined by Franklin W. Smith and Henry Flagler. Their walls and ceilings were covered with garish wallpaper, and they had wall-to-wall carpeting, mundane brass beds, and other ordinary hotel-room furnishings. Yet they met a need.[6]

During the first week of March desk clerks throughout the town unexpectedly found themselves confronted with crowds of people disembarking from trains in search of lodgings for the night. A flood of tourists heading south collided in St. Augustine with a wave of those returning north from Palm Beach. Mrs. Marcotte walked from hotel to hotel to witness the spectacle: "Private parlors are used as bedrooms, ends of corridors are now fitted up for sleeping rooms with portieres separating them from the rest of the corridor, and eagerly sought for, reception rooms, reading and writing rooms are all utilized as sleeping rooms." After a few days the unusual tide ebbed to more manageable levels, and the hotel men could heave a sigh of relief while counting up their profits from an excellent season.[7]

Although the numbers of tourists had increased to match the halcyon days before Palm Beach opened up, something had been lost in the ambiance of St. Augustine as the epitome of winter resorts. No longer did the Ponce de Leon host a Washington's Birthday ball or the annual charity ball or the fair in the Casino for the benefit of Alicia Hospital. In fact, as Mrs. Marcotte lamented, dancing had vanished from the St. Augustine social world. "Think of it! Not a ball or even a hop at the Ponce de Leon or Alcazar." She yearned for winter residents to return to those elegant balls of yesteryear that gave "ladies such fine opportunities to display their handsome gowns, but even this does not tempt them."[8]

The Flagler hotels also gave up their marsh-front golf course at the Country Club. The annual FEC golf tournament would be held on the Golf Club's Fort Marion course. Plenty of golfers still walked this course, but playing the game had become just another part of the routine of resort life.[9]

The antique city of St. Augustine and its fantasy castle hotels remained an essential place to see for any Florida vacationer, but for most visitors it was no longer a place to stay for the season. The Ponce de Leon continued to attract some interesting passersby during the 1903 season. One who stopped in was L. Frank Baum, the prolific author of *The Wizard of Oz* and many other children's books and plays. Across the way in Alcazar Finley Peter Dunne and his bride spent several days of their honeymoon enjoying golf and seeing the sights. They were accompanied by a valet and a lady's maid, but to the public Dunne appeared as his newspaper alter ego, the humble Irishman "Mr. Dooley," who offered up homespun observations, in mock-Irish dialect, on the events and personalities of the passing scene. In St. Augustine, as everywhere, strangers greeted him as "Mr. Dooley."[10]

Mr. Dooley expounded on hotel life: "No, sir, hotel life is not f'r th' likes iv us Hinnissy. It's f'r thim that loves mad gayety, th' merry rattle iv the tillyphone bell, th' electric light that ebbs an' flows, th' long an invigoratin' walk to th' bath, th' ilivator that shoots ye up an' down or passes ye by, th' clink iv th' dark ice in th' pitcher, an' th' mad swirl iv th' food in th' restaurant where th' moist waiter rubs y're plate affectionately with th' other man's napkin an' has an attractive ear f'r ivry wurrd iv ye're private conversation. All this is f'r th' rich. Gawd bless thim an' keep thim out iv our detached or semi-detached hovels or homes, th' only possessions th' poor have left."[11]

One day former president Grover Cleveland quietly slipped into the Rotunda of the Ponce de Leon dressed in his traveling clothes and a slouch hat. Some people recognized him and hurried over to offer him their greetings. After dinner in the Dining Room, Cleveland sat in hotel manager Robert Murray's office in the east hallway behind the registration desk and smoked a cigar. General Schofield joined the small group assembled in the office. Cleveland was on his way down to Stuart on the lower East Coast, where he planned to do a little fishing. Some political leaders wanted Cleveland to run for president again, but he had not the slightest inclination in that direction, having found an occupation much more to his liking. No president, before or since, has spent so much time on hunting and fishing expeditions in the wilds of Florida.[12]

In the spirit of the times St. Augustine gained a new tourist attraction with appeal to the general run of Yankee tourists venturing to Florida on vacation—an alligator farm. Everett C. Whitney took over management of his father's Ponce de Leon Spring in West Augustine on the banks of the San Sebastian and came up with the idea of putting Florida's iconic reptiles on display. A lone alligator had long made the spring its home, and in March 1902 Whitney hired an alligator hunter to haul the 'gator, now grown to almost eight feet long, from its den in an embankment. The alligator planted its teeth deeply into the hand of its captor antagonist as it was extracted from its lair, but this 'gator nevertheless became the first specimen to go into Whitney's fenced compound. He quickly added another dozen alligators to his collection and then began purchasing bears, wildcats, snakes, and other Florida animals to put on exhibition. By November Whitney was ready to open his attraction to the public, and he invited everyone to come in free of charge for the first two weeks to see what he had done.[13]

In January when paying customers from the North arrived, Whitney staged a spectacular stunt to drum up interest in his alligator farm. He promised to ride an alligator across his pond and then to turn the animal on its back and put it to sleep—feats that would later become standard fare in alligator-wrassling shows. "Quite a large crowd of strangers" turned out to witness the exhibition, reported the *Record*; they may have come away a touch disappointed that "no mishaps marred the performance."[14]

That spring Whitney moved some of his alligators to the pavilion at the terminus of the South Beach Railway on Anastasia Island. Soon Felix Fire and George Reddington assumed control of the South Beach pavilion and its alligators, and in the spring of 1904 they placed more than two dozen additional 'gators in the collection at the beach.[15]

At this time the number of year-round residents in St. Augustine, which had declined during the 1890s, began to swell. Vacant lots around town that had stood empty for years gained neat new cottages. The dream of a high-toned winter Newport was gone, and in its place rose a modern middle-class twentieth-century American city.

In Palm Beach the Flaglers abruptly ended their stay near the conclusion of

March and hurried northward to Baltimore, where Mary Lily's father, William R. Kenan Sr., was under care at Johns Hopkins University hospital. Anna Marcotte expressed disappointment that the Flaglers would not be able to spend April in St. Augustine as they had planned. However, the Flaglers must have found the elder Kenan doing well, for they quickly turned around and came back to St. Augustine. Leaving Mary Lily there, Flagler gathered up his railroad executives and headed down to the end of the rail line below Miami.[16]

Flagler was now seriously involved in the search for a place to build a deep-water port for trade with the Caribbean. Some months earlier he had sent engineer William J. Krome to Cape Sable at the extreme southern tip of the Florida peninsula to discover if a port could be established there. Krome and his expedition returned to Miami exhausted, mosquito bitten, and convinced that a rail line could not be laid across the Everglades to Cape Sable. That left only one alternative place to go: Key West.[17]

When Flagler reached East Palatka on his return to St. Augustine he found a telegram waiting for him saying that Mr. Kenan's condition had taken a turn for the worse. At St. Augustine he received another telegram reporting that Kenan had passed away. The Flaglers left immediately for Wilmington to attend the funeral.[18]

However, at the end of April Flagler once more returned to St. Augustine, by himself, for another inspection tour down the Florida East Coast line. He and his railroad men, plus Anderson, watched the potato harvest at Hastings before proceeding down the railway. On May 7 Flagler finally bade farewell to Florida for the season and headed north to rejoin Mary Lily.[19]

The Flaglers spent a quiet summer at Mamaroneck; Mary Lily had entered an extended period of mourning to honor her father's memory. Later during the summer the St. Augustine Record reported that she experienced an extended "nervous illness." Nor was Flagler's health good. In his letters to McGuire, he complained of a lingering cold and then a severe toothache, and the St. Augustine Record reported that he suffered from "a serious attack of lumbago."[20]

Early December found the Flaglers back in Florida and ensconced in the familiar confines of the Hotel Alcazar, where they could enjoy the hospitality of the Andersons and other old friends in St. Augustine. However, Flagler was anxious to see how the extension of his railroad south of Miami had progressed in his absence, so he assembled Anderson and the rest of his railroad department chiefs and headed to Miami. There they picked up John Sewell, who had advanced from land clearer to mayor, and traveled more than twelve miles south to No Man's Prairie, where the rails stopped. The immediate objective of the railroad builders was the potentially rich farmland of the Perrine land grant. Returning from this expedition, Flagler and Mary Lily went to Jacksonville to meet Mrs. Kenan,

Henry and Mary Lily Flagler. The marriage of seventy-two-year-old Henry Flagler to thirty-four-year-old Mary Lily Kenan drew critical comment from society. By permission of Flagler College.

Mary Lily's two sisters, and her young niece Louise Wise, who would all spend the early part of the season with them at Whitehall.[21]

The season opened auspiciously in St. Augustine. Nationwide prosperity and confidence brought an increasing flood of winter visitors, although clearly most were just passing through on their way south. The number of local shuttle trains departing from Union Station each day for Palm Beach had increased from one to four.[22]

The Hotel Ponce de Leon lost one of its distinguishing features in 1904 when its most famous artist, Martin Johnson Heade, abandoned his studio at the rear of the hotel. Moreover, the artists' receptions that had been regular social events in earlier years no longer enlivened Friday nights. Only Heade and Felix De-Crano had occupied spaces during the 1903 season, and, as mentioned, Heade's poor health had prevented him from attending to his studio most of the time and a friend had manned his space to sell his paintings. In 1904 DeCrano moved into Heade's studio, no. 7, while Heade spent his time at home on San Marco Avenue near the old Nombre de Dios mission amid his flower gardens and vials of sugar water hanging from the porch eaves to attract hummingbirds. In March he was well enough to attend a reception at the Andersons' home. The doctor's daughter Clarissa remembered Heade as a dour old man, and she assumed he was disappointed at not receiving greater acclaim as an artist. However, when his editor from *Forest and Stream* magazine called on him in his sunny cottage, the editor found a still bright and engaging friend and enjoyed a pleasant time reliving memories of past adventures into the wilds.[23]

Heade would pass away on September 4, 1904, at the age of eighty-five. His widow Elizabeth continued to live in St. Augustine in the winters until 1912 and used DeCrano's old studio no. 1 in the Ponce de Leon as a place to exhibit and sell her husband's works. During his lifetime Heade's Hudson River School realism had already fallen out of favor as other, more modern styles came into vogue. For many years the art world almost forgot him, but then after World War II his work gained wide attention and acclaim. Today art museums count themselves lucky to have a Heade in their collection.[24]

The St. Augustine Yacht Club underwent a transformation in the winter of 1904. The venerable club had been in decline for years. Anna Marcotte observed that its members showed "little interest in yachting and none in society." Many of the founders had passed away. Anderson and only about a half dozen other old-timers survived. To infuse new blood into the club, it took in a large class of new members. Some were wealthy men such as William Deering, a noted sailor on Matanzas Bay, and Albert Lewis, but others were simply respectable gentlemen such as James Ingraham, Rev. J. Coffin Stout of the Presbyterian Church, banker John T. Dismukes, canal engineer George F. Miles, artist Felix DeCrano, Captain

Marcotte, and the hotel managers Robert Murray and Joseph Greaves. The following year the club took the even more radical step of admitting its first woman member, Miss Barbara Warden.[25]

To liven things up, the club ordered five same-design sailboats and held a series of races through the season. Anderson named his little sloop the *Clarissa*. A reporter for the *New York Tribune* thought the contests made a fine spectacle: "The race last Saturday was a 'dandy,' to quote one of the skipper owners. There was a fine wind, and the boats fairly flew along. Then came a squall that made things lively for a moment, each boat showing her centerboard." Anderson crossed the finish first in this race and ultimately won the cup for accumulating the best score over the series. However, he had to overcome an early lead in the series by the newcomer Miss Warden.[26]

Henry Flagler's yachting days were over, but about this time he found a new pursuit that rejuvenated his spirits. In late January the Flaglers and a few friends traveled to Ormond to watch the automobile races being held on the beach. Automobiles and their potential for the future had become Flagler's latest fascination. A year earlier he and August Belmont Jr., heir to his father's banking empire, had proposed building a hard-surface road from Palm Beach to Miami. In St. Augustine Albert Lewis, James Ingraham, Robert Murray, Joseph Greaves, and some of the town's other leading men formed the East Coast Good Roads Association to promote the idea of constructing a highway from Jacksonville to Miami. Flagler's *Florida Times-Union* got behind the idea. Down the way Anderson and Price of the Ormond Hotel threw in their support for the coastal highway.[27]

Anderson and Price promoted automobile racing on the hard sand of the beach at Ormond. Ransom E. Olds, founder of both the REO and Oldsmobile companies, had brought a car down in 1903 to race against one built by Alexander Winton, another early car maker. The wide, smooth white sand beach at Ormond was a revelation to auto enthusiasts, who pronounced it the best racecourse in the world. While stopping in St. Augustine, Olds told a *Record* reporter that constructing good roads for automobiles would cause people to build winter homes in Florida and remain all season.[28]

The January 1904 races attended by Flagler attracted a large crowd, including Governor Jennings and guests from St. Augustine who came down on a special train chartered by Flagler. Some of the most noted automobilists in the country entered the competition. In a day when cars were toys of the rich, William K. Vanderbilt Jr. personified the gentleman enthusiast. He drove his own cars. So did Carl Graham Fisher, a youthful inventor from Indianapolis who would soon become wealthy manufacturing auto headlights. Fisher would later invest his fortune in building the Indianapolis Speedway and in developing Miami Beach. Barney Oldfield, who emerged as America's first great racecar driver, guided Winton's Bullet-2 in a world record time of forty-three seconds for a measured mile during an elimination heat. (That amounted to eighty-four miles per hour.) In the one-mile final race held the next day spectators seated in bleachers erected on the dunes above the beach could not see Oldfield's and Vanderbilt's cars until they neared the finish line because of a haze hanging over the beach. Oldfield emerged from the fog to win by a large margin in this highly publicized match-up, but Vanderbilt enjoyed the consolation of winning a five-mile race later in the day.[29]

During the races a reporter for the *Daytona Gazette-News* claimed to have encountered Flagler calmly smoking on the veranda of the Ormond Hotel. When informed of the new world record, Flagler supposedly replied, "Is that so? Now if he had only a sail on that machine, he might have gone a little faster." To the reporter Flagler seemed disinterested in cars, but—if this conversation ever happened—Flagler may simply have been employing his habitual practice of hiding his thoughts behind a screen of indifference.[30]

The three days of races wound up with an elaborate dinner at the Ormond Hotel. Flagler and Vanderbilt each donated $500 to support the next year's event, while eight others chipped in $250 each. Although delays and disorder had often frustrated spectators and racers alike, everyone looked forward in anticipation to larger and more exciting events in the future.[31]

Social activities at Whitehall took on a subdued tone for the season to honor the memory of Mary Lily's father. She did not hold regular weekly "at homes," although she hosted teas on the south veranda for a few friends. The Flaglers did not attend any of the balls at the Royal Poinciana. After Mary Lily's family departed, Flagler's sister-in-law Julia Harkness York and her daughter Georgiana, who was married to Flagler's railroad builder John Maclennan, came to Whitehall for a stay.[32]

On occasions when Henry Flagler was obliged to host formal dinners for visiting dignitaries, he made them stag affairs so that Mary Lily would not have to break her time of mourning. When Nassau's governor-general Sir Gilbert Carter paid a return visit to Palm Beach, Flagler filled the banquet hall with a distinguished assembly of gentlemen and businessmen—and the actor Joseph Jefferson, who could be counted on to leaven any gathering. On Flagler's left sat Attorney General Philander C. Knox. The steel magnate and fine art collector Henry Clay Frick joined Roland F. Knoedler, the New York art dealer who supplied Flagler with paintings for the Hotel Ponce de Leon and Whitehall. Some of Flagler's usual Palm Beach friends such as Samuel Andrews and Frederick T. Martin also sat at the table. After dinner and cigars, Flagler rose and offered a toast to King Edward VII and—although it must have pained him to do so—to trust-busting President Theodore Roosevelt. Sir Gilbert replied that he hoped relations between the United States and Great Britain would grow closer. Flagler, who had just turned seventy-four, then toasted Joseph Jefferson on his seventy-fifth birthday. Jefferson responded by saying an actor always appreciated an excuse to speak.[33]

A week later Secretary of War Elihu Root sat in the place of honor with a different group of men, save for Frederick T. Martin, who seemed to be near Flagler's side much of the time. Flagler's youthful brother-in-law William R. Kenan Jr. joined the assembly. Two of America's most famous financiers also sat at the table. One was John Jacob Astor IV, who had honeymooned at the Ponce de Leon in 1891 before he constructed his Astoria Hotel in New York. He was a familiar face in Flagler's Florida hotels. (Astor would go down with the *Titanic* in 1912.) August Belmont Jr. was also there. Although he talked with Flagler about building roads for automobiles, his main enthusiasm was for horse racing, which he had supported by building Belmont Park race track.[34]

Another of the men at the dinner, H. Reiman Duval, Flagler's partner in railroading and ownership of the *Florida Times-Union*, may have been in Palm Beach on business. Afterward he and Flagler would go to Miami to observe the progress in laying the FEC's track southward.[35]

William R. Kenan Jr. would marry Alice Pomroy a month after the dinner at Whitehall. Kenan was just thirty-two, and she was forty. Both lived in Lockport, New York. They had known each other since about 1900 because their common association with Flagler sometimes brought them together. The Flaglers attended the wedding, and it was believed at the time that Flagler had encouraged the match, which would prove to be a long and apparently happy union.[36]

In March the seasonal flow of tourist traffic turned north, filling St. Augustine's hotels with guests who wished to take a respite from the tedium of riding in the confines of a railroad car by spending a day or two in the Oldest City. Among those stopping over at the Ponce de Leon were Mrs. Sara Roosevelt and her twenty-two-year-old son Franklin D. Roosevelt, who was then engaged in graduate studies at Harvard. They were returning from an ocean liner cruise around the Caribbean. In Nassau they had stayed at the Colonial, dined with Governor-General Carter, and gone swimming with the governor's daughters in the "wonderful blue water." However, Mrs. Roosevelt found the hotel food "very bad." Returning by way of Miami, they lunched at the Royal Palm and sat on the veranda to keep cool while awaiting their train for Palm Beach. At the Royal Poinciana, Mrs. Roosevelt noted in her diary, "Crowds of overdressed vulgar people throng the hotel. Food a *little* less bad than at Nassau. We enjoyed a ride in bicycle chairs to the Jungle, Ostrich Farm and Alligator Farm and later I watched Franklin in the surf and was glad when he came out."

Then they took an overnight train to St. Augustine. "Cooler here and I find it more interesting than Palm Beach," she recorded. "Drove out to Point Moultrie thro' woods. All quite pretty and enjoyed the fort and the town. The Hotel is Moorish in style. Sent a trunk home." The next day they took another "nice walk" in town and then departed for the North. Along the way they stopped in Washington to have dinner with their "most charming" cousin, President Theodore Roosevelt.[37]

Franklin Roosevelt would not return to Florida until 1924, after he had been stricken by polio, when he vacationed in the southern part of the peninsula to immerse his crippled legs in warm ocean waters.

The Flaglers followed the migration up to St. Augustine at the conclusion of the season in Palm Beach. They took Frederick T. Martin and Flagler's Harkness relations with them to stay in the Ponce de Leon and, when it closed, at the Alcazar. Flagler closeted himself with his hotel men Parrott and McDonald to discuss improvements to the Royal Poinciana and Breakers in Palm Beach. Then the Flaglers assembled their St. Augustine friends—the Andersons, Schofields, MacGonigles, and a couple of railroad men—for a pleasure trip south on the railroad.[38]

No sooner did they return than Flagler turned around and set off southward again with Anderson and a larger group of his railroad men. In Miami they picked up engineer William Krome and boarded the steamer *Martinique* for a surveying trip along the Keys. As was his custom, Flagler made no announcements regarding his activities, but it was at this point that he made the decision to go to Key West. Anderson later recalled that in gazing across the open water at the white string of islands, "I was astounded at the temerity and vastness of the proposition." Flagler reassured him, "It is perfectly simple. All you have to do is build one concrete arch and then another, and pretty soon you will find yourself in Key West."[39]

It would not be until May 4, 1904, that the Flaglers left St. Augustine for the North. Their stay in town had been the longest in a while, and locals hoped Flagler would return for even longer visits in the future.[40]

On their way north they stopped for a while at the Homestead Hotel in Hot Springs, Virginia, which was managed by Flagler's Royal Poinciana manager Fred Sterry, and then in the late summer they went farther north to Bretton Woods, New Hampshire, to stay with the Ormond's Anderson and Price at their Mount Washington Hotel. In between Flagler made a flying trip all the way to Miami by himself to satisfy his concerns over the extension of the railway. Then he returned to rejoin Mary Lily at Mamaroneck. While in New York, Flagler still visited his office at 26 Broadway tending to business.[41]

That summer in the White Mountains at the Mount Washington Hotel, Flagler went automobiling with his Standard Oil partner Henry H. Rogers. Flagler jokingly gave Rogers a hard time over the difficulties his car encountered climbing the steep, unpaved mountain roads. But Flagler also approached his friend John Anderson about purchasing an automobile himself—one that would beat Rogers' car. Anderson knew J. S. Hathaway of Boston, who represented the White Motor Car Company, a subsidiary of White Sewing Machine. At Flagler's summons, Hathaway took a train to the Mount Washington and met Flagler. According to Hathaway, Flagler said, "Young man, Anderson here tells me you sell a machine that will beat out Rogers. What do you say?" Hathaway replied, "I do. The White Steamers will beat anything, especially on hills." Flagler responded, "That's a pretty big order." "Well it's right," said Hathaway. Flagler asked, "Got any of them on hand?" "They're coming and going every few days," concluded Hathaway.

At this point, according to Hathaway, Flagler pulled out his checkbook to put down a five-hundred-dollar deposit, but failed in three attempts to fill out a check properly. Thereupon "Mr. Flagler slapped a table gong and called a bell-hop. 'Would you mind going up to my room and asking Salter, my secretary, to come down here?' The bell-hop brought the secretary back and Flagler said, 'Salter, I'm trying to write a check for $500 for this young man, and I don't seem to get it right. You do it.' Flagler turned to me and said, 'I haven't written a check myself for ten years.'"

Flagler also asked Hathaway to find him a chauffeur, and Hathaway sent him William M. Frisbie, who delivered the car by driving it to the Mount Washington Hotel. Frisbie would remain in Flagler's employ for several years.[42]

Flagler's new limousine-body steamer had seats for the driver and four passengers. A newspaper reporter gave it a rave review: "The car is a beauty, snow white, noiseless, and smooth running." Its eighteen-horsepower engine rated among

Henry Flagler and friends depart in his White steamer for a pleasure tour from a resort hotel, probably the Mount Washington in Bretton Woods, New Hampshire. From the collection of the St. Augustine Historical Society Research Library.

the most powerful passenger car motors of the day. White was gaining a reputation for making rugged automobiles and actually produced more steamers than the famous Stanley company. Eventually White would concentrate on building trucks for businesses that needed heavy-duty vehicles.[43]

Soon Flagler and his friends were motoring from hotel to hotel and from one scenic view to another. A newspaperman encountered them and reported: "The party was all dressed in the latest automobile costumes, and I doubt if Henry M. Flagler ever enjoyed anything more than those same automobile trips in the White Mountains." The *New York Times* declared, "Mr. Flagler has taken the automobile fever."[44]

When he was not out on the roads, Flagler investigated the garage at the Mount Washington where guests sheltered their cars during their stays. The autos fascinated Flagler, but he also carefully examined the garage building itself. He and Anderson and Hathaway measured the dimensions of the stalls in which cars and their equipment were stored. Flagler noted that cars were growing larger with each passing year and required more room. He had a specific purpose in this study because he intended to erect a similar garage at the Ormond Hotel. During the 1904 races large tents had been temporarily set up to shelter the cars. Flagler and James McGuire exchanged a series of letters in September 1904 in which Flagler gave very specific instructions on the features to be incorporated into the proposed facility at Ormond. Perhaps Flagler himself had as much to do with the design of what would become the famous Ormond Garage—known as Gasoline Alley—as anyone. It would remain a landmark in Ormond until its demise by fire in 1976.[45]

The Flaglers returned to St. Augustine on December 16, 1904, in car no. 90, accompanied by James Ingraham's daughter Kathleen, whom they had picked up in Washington, D.C., where she was attending school. Their Whitehall organist Russell Joy also shared the car. Mrs. Marcotte greeted the party and found the Flaglers "in excellent health and spirits." They spent only a few days in St. Augustine before heading off to Miami with Dr. and Mrs. Anderson, and then returned to Palm Beach, where the Flaglers would spend the winter at Whitehall as usual.[46]

They erected a huge Christmas tree at Whitehall and celebrated the holiday with all Mary Lily's circle of close relatives. On January 2 Joseph Parrott, his wife, and a few other guests joined the family to mark Henry Flagler's seventy-fifth birthday with a dinner in the banquet hall. Although Flagler had now spent twenty years in Florida elaborating his dreams, he was in no mood to slow down. A month later found him in Key West, where he stood up amid an assembly of leading citizens to ask if they wanted him to extend his railway to their island. The crowd enthusiastically declared that they did and would offer him inducements to come. Then, for the first time, Flagler made a public announcement that he would build his railroad across the Keys, no matter what the cost.[47]

Mary Lily spent the Palm Beach season giving and going to receptions. Sometimes she would sing as part of the entertainment. Flagler stuck to business and attended the occasional dinner. His most unusual expedition of the season came in the form of a trip to Cuba with Sir William Van Horn, builder of the Canadian Pacific Railroad and now the prospective sponsor of a railroad across the length of Cuba. He asked Flagler to build a resort hotel in Cuba, but Flagler demurred, saying he had plans for a railroad car ferry from Key West to Havana. Someone else could build the hotel.[48]

Early in the season the Flaglers went to Ormond to look over the large automobile garage and two-story dormitory for drivers and mechanics that McGuire had erected near the hotel. The hotel itself had added a hundred new rooms to accommodate the race crowd. As Flagler prepared to leave for Palm Beach, his new friend J. S. Hathaway of the White Motor Company arranged for an impromptu race between the FEC train and Hathaway's steamer over the distance from Ormond to Daytona. Flagler took a seat in the auto, and as the train left the station, they raced off down the beach. Hathaway's car beat the train by two minutes. Afterward Flagler said he enjoyed "the most delightful ride of my life. Now I understand why automobilists are so enthusiastic over the beach."[49]

Two weeks later the whole Flagler-Kenan family assemblage at Whitehall traveled to Ormond for the opening of the automobile races. When they arrived at the station—in a sign of the times—three touring cars belonging to the hotel were on hand to carry them to their accommodations, where they were greeted with a little ceremony by the hotel staff. Flagler walked through the huge, brick-paved garage to savor the sights, sounds, and smells of the autos. His own White steamer and chauffeur William Frisbie had just arrived by train from the North, and before long he took Mary Lily out for a spin in his own auto down the beach to Daytona and back.[50]

The 1905 races were marred by strong winds, weather cold enough to freeze radiators, and unexpectedly high tides; someone on the local arrangements committee had failed to take into account the full moon. Before the racing started, disaster struck a car manned by a driver and Frank Coker, son of the Tammany boss Richard Coker. They swerved to avoid a wave on the beach, flipped over, and were both killed. On the first day of the races, when Mrs. Marcotte and a crowd from St. Augustine arrived at the Ormond Hotel, they were disappointed to find that all the action had been moved ten miles south to Daytona. Spectators were obliged to take carriages and cars down the beach to a place in the dunes where a grandstand had been erected. Flagler used his own car and the cars of the Ormond Hotel to shuttle Dr. Anderson and his St. Augustine friends around.

Part of the trouble with arrangements for the spectators came from the rivalry between Ormond and Daytona business interests for primacy as headquarters for the races. Despite all the difficulties, world speed records continued to fall. Henry Ford attracted some attention by bringing a small car with a big motor to compete against the European machines, but his entry broke its crankshaft before the races even started.[51]

In January Dr. Woodrow Wilson, president of Princeton University, came down to Florida to recuperate from surgery. He and his wife stopped over in St. Augustine to have lunch with the novelist Edwin Asa Dix, who had been part of the winter cottage community since 1901. Dix had graduated from Princeton in 1881 as one of its most accomplished students. Traveling on to Palm Beach, the Wilsons took rooms at the Breakers and enjoyed the sunshine and Gulf Stream breezes. During their two-week stay Mary Lily Flagler entertained Ellen Wilson at a reception in the Grill Room of the Royal Poinciana, while Henry Flagler made Dr. Wilson part of a gentlemen's dinner at Whitehall honoring the governor of the Bahamas, Sir William Grey-Wilson.[52]

Shortly thereafter the expatriate American novelist Henry James visited Flagler's hotels in Palm Beach and St. Augustine. James was then living in England but paid a visit to his home country to call on relatives, earn money by delivering lectures, and survey the "American Scene." He went to Palm Beach in February and stayed right on the ocean at the Breakers, one of the most scenic venues in America. James did enjoy the "velvet air"; however, for the most part, the phlegmatic author turned a jaundiced eye on Florida, where he said a sliver of civilization followed Flagler's railroad along the east coast while the rest remained pine barrens, palmettos, and swamps. The people in the resorts, as well, failed to measure up. They were "decent, gregarious and moneyed," he wrote, "but overwhelmingly monotonous and on the whole pretty ugly." Leaving Palm Beach he went to St. Augustine to stay at the Ponce de Leon for a few days.[53]

As a close friend of Constance Fenimore Woolson, who had died tragically a decade earlier, Henry James must have been curious to see for himself this "Ancient City" she had described in her 1875 *Harper's Magazine* articles. Alas, he discovered that the intervening thirty years had not been kind to the town's claim to romantic atmosphere. Little remained of the old Spanish town, save for the cathedral façade (of "yellow ancestry"), City Gates, and Castillo de San Marcos—but even this fort was surrounded by "horrible modernisms." He may have had in mind the hulking, wooden St. Augustine Museum that had been erected on St. George Street to satisfy the public's appetite for what James deemed "humbuggery." He did, however, find the locals' desire to please "irresistible."[54]

James judged Flagler's buildings, touched by the European-trained hands of Carrère and Hastings, more to his liking. Writing to his brother, the philosopher

William James, he said, "On the other hand this huge modern hotel (Ponce de Leon) is in the style of the Alhambra, and the principal church ("Presbyterian") is that of the mosque of Cordova."[55]

Within the walls of Flagler's fabled inn James found the romance that he sought. He declared: "The Ponce de Leon . . . comes as near producing, all by itself, the illusion of romance as a highly modern, a most cleverly-constructed and smoothly-administered great modern caravansary can come; it is largely 'in the Moorish style' (as the cities of Spain preserve the record of that manner); it breaks out, on every pretext, into circular arches and embroidered screens, into courts and cloisters, arcades and fountains, fantastic projections and lordly towers, and is, in all sorts of ways and in the highest sense of the word, the most 'amusing' of hotels. It did for me, at St. Augustine, I was well aware, everything that an hotel could do."[56]

Late in March Grover Cleveland stopped over to spend the night in the Ponce de Leon on his way south to Vero Beach to renew his battles with the fishes. He was accompanied by his friend and physician Dr. Joseph D. Bryant. Many old-time residents of the hotel took the opportunity to exchange greetings with him, and Mrs. Marcotte noted, "He was looking well, but is aging."[57]

On April 5 Edith Roosevelt, wife of the current president, paid an afternoon visit to St. Augustine with three of her teenage children, Kermit, Ethel, and Archie. Mrs. Roosevelt and her children were traveling the South while her husband was off on a camping expedition in the West. Their arrival had not been announced and nobody recognized them, so they were able to visit the fort (the boys explored the dungeon) and walk down St. George Street gathering up armloads of curios without attracting attention. Although the Ponce de Leon had closed for the season, they were shown through all the elaborate public rooms of the hotel. Then they caught the evening train to return north.[58]

As warmer weather arrived in South Florida, vacationers retreated northward to enjoy the more temperate breezes in St. Augustine. The Flaglers went to St. Augustine as soon as the Royal Poinciana closed near the end of March. Frederick Townsend Martin had already relocated to the Ponce de Leon, joining Flagler's relatives Mrs. York, Mrs. S. V. Harkness, and Mrs. Maclennan. Mary Lily brought a couple of North Carolina friends with her, the Kenan clan having already departed Florida for their homes. While Mary Lily enjoyed the social life of town, her husband set off for South Florida with his railroad men and Senators James Taliaferro of Florida and William Frye of Maine. Flagler's survey team had just returned from another expedition down the Keys preliminary to launching construction of the tracks in earnest. Flagler could not resist taking a break in the journey on the way down to give his party a ride down the beach in his hotel's automobiles on the leg from Ormond to Daytona.[59]

Upon his return to St. Augustine from South Florida, Flagler went out on the bay and south down the river with Dr. Anderson and George Miles to watch the dredge working on the cut that would connect the Matanzas River with the Halifax River to the south. This section of the coastal canal had proven to be the most difficult to excavate of the whole route because of the huge volume of sand and rock to be displaced. However, work seemed to be progressing, and the engineers expressed optimism about achieving a breakthrough soon.[60]

While Flagler was in town he and Dr. Anderson drew up a new charter of incorporation for the general hospital. Without any public notice, the name of the hospital changed from Alicia Hospital to Flagler Hospital. Workmen quietly took down the large marble slab with the name "Alicia" engraved upon it and placed it into storage, removing an awkward reminder of Flagler's vanished second wife. In the 1960s the plaque would be discovered, and a second inscription with the new words "Flagler Hospital" would be carved on the reverse side of the marble. Today it stands outside the entrance of the modern Flagler Hospital.

The hospital facilities had been modernized and expanded in recent years, causing the hospital to incur a debt of several thousand dollars. In 1906 Mrs. Anderson and the ladies' association would stage the first Hospital Fair in the Casino held in more than a decade to raise money that would retire the debt. The formal affair revived the spirit of bygone days in St. Augustine society.[61]

In the spring of 1905 the moment arrived for Flagler to say goodbye to one of his closest companions, Joseph Jefferson. The normally high-spirited actor had arrived in Palm Beach in December 1904 suffering from acute stomach pains. His wife and youngest son Frank kept him company in his beachside cottage, "The Reef." On sunny days his body servant Carl would take him out on rides in a bicycle chair, and when he felt up to it Jefferson assumed his usual routine of fishing. At the end of March he went up the coastal waterway a short distance to Hobe Sound, where his son Charles maintained a winter home. Here he rendezvoused with his long-time fishing companion Grover Cleveland, and they spent a few days angling. Unfortunately his physical condition deteriorated so much that he was compelled to return to his cottage and rest in bed.[62]

Flagler came down from St. Augustine to visit Jefferson, whose son Joseph Jr. later related that when Flagler entered the bedroom, he said, "Joe, I want to embrace you." The son continued, "The two old men kissed each other several times, and then his father remarked: 'I don't think that I will see you alive again.'" His phrasing was awkward, but Jefferson's prediction proved correct. On Easter Sunday, April 23, he passed away while gazing out from his second-story bedroom window over the Atlantic Ocean. Flagler sent his private car no. 90 and a baggage car down to Palm Beach to carry the family and casket north to New York. When the train stopped on its way through St. Augustine, Flagler went to

Henry Flagler with his dog Delos, driven by George Conway, Palm Beach, ca. 1910. The human-powered rickshaws of Palm Beach, known as bicycle chairs or wheel chairs, came into service because horse-drawn and motor-powered vehicles were not allowed. © Flagler Museum Archives.

Union Station to pay his respects to his friend and offer sympathy to Jefferson's family.[63]

Another man to whom Flagler bade farewell for the last time was Frank P. Thompson. The 1905 season had been Thompson's seventeenth as headwaiter of the Ponce de Leon. Over the years he had been a conspicuous fixture at the hotel, standing at his station beside the entrance to the grand Dining Room and welcoming guests, many of who had become old acquaintances. As Flagler's hotel empire had grown, so had Thompson's responsibilities. He was styled "Headwaiter in Chief" for all the Flagler hotels, with responsibility each fall for recruiting some six hundred waiters in the North and ensuring their safe passage to Florida. As each man was hired, he would be given a circular badge allowing him to board the special trains hired to transport Flagler's troops to Florida. Upon arrival at Jacksonville they were met by the headwaiters from the several hotels, who would take charge of the crews. Before departing for points south, including Nassau, everyone would celebrate with a festive ball in Jacksonville to get into a proper spirit for the coming season.[64]

At the same time that Thompson assumed a larger role in the Flagler system, he also became a leader in the national black hotel waiters' union. Organized in Chicago in 1899, the Head and Second Waiters National Benefit Association started as a traditional mutual aid society charged with "caring for the sick and burying its dead," but it also aimed to improve the education of black waiters and, like a traditional trade union, to protect and promote the employment of its members. Thompson was appointed to the Board of Managers in 1901, and in 1902 the members elected him president. Prior to his election, he addressed the convention on "Why We Should Organize," declaring, "There are no organizations for the benefit of the colored race that amount to anything."[65]

In a move to strengthen the association, Thompson led the board to open the union to rank and file waiters, known as "side waiters." However, in the face of what Thompson called "the trend of the times" toward discrimination in American society by both law and social convention, he had little more to offer than Booker T. Washington's accommodationist approach. He counseled his fellow waiters to practice Christian patience. "Let us restrain our passions and practice courtesy. Keep before our eyes the highest ideals, be kind, tender hearted and forbearing if you would reap the finest harvest of practical success. Courtesy has a commercial value for it will promote success and good feelings among those with who we come in contact." He predicted a change of heart in America: "Nothing lasts for eternity." He foresaw a time as society evolved when people would be judged on their worth, not by accidents of birth, and he stressed that his fellow waiters could advance the pace of progress by maintaining a strong organization.[66]

When the Ponce de Leon closed the year before, in April 1904, Thompson had left the hotel suffering from severe abdominal pains. He had been troubled by a stomach disorder for some weeks, but this time his wife and young son accompanied him home to Brooklyn and put him to bed, where he would remain through the spring and into the summer.

Having been reelected president of the Waiters Association in 1903, Thompson felt obliged to attend its convention in Atlantic City in the summer of 1904. He was too weak to stand, so a friend read his president's address for him. He recovered enough to return to the Ponce de Leon for the 1905 season, and when he appeared again for the annual meeting of the union that summer, he was well enough to deliver his presidential address himself, saying he thanked God "that we are permitted to continue our union of fellowship on this side of the great divide."

He was again reelected president, although some in the audience, seeing his haggard appearance, believed the speech to be his farewell message. This proved to be true. He would die in Brooklyn in December, and memorial services were held both there and in Philadelphia. He was just fifty years old, and he missed witnessing the founding of the NAACP by four years. Mrs. Marcotte wrote a brief epitaph in the *Tatler*: "Regular visitors will miss his kindly greeting."[67]

The Flaglers left for the North early in May 1905. Automobiles continued to receive a good deal of attention from Flagler. During the summer he tried out a large, heavy touring car powered by a gasoline engine, purchased from the F. B. Stearns Company of Cleveland, but it proved less reliable than his White steamer. Mary Lily suffered a mishap in Mamaroneck with this car when a twelve-year-old girl dashed out in front of it and was run over. Mary Lily sent the girl to a doctor, and it turned out she was no more than bruised. Flagler enjoyed more luck with his White steamer. They went up to Mount Washington early in August. From there he wrote to Oscar Smith in St. Augustine, "We are having delightful weather in the mountains, and I am enjoying my automobile very much." To Roy York in Cleveland he declared: "My White car is working admirably." He explained that on a touring trip his driver took a wrong turn, and, although burdened with five people, the steamer went right up "Breakneck Hill." Flagler's partner in promoting the races at Ormond, W. J. Morgan, visited him at Mount Washington and wrote, "The automobile may add years to the life of Mr. Flagler, as its health-giving qualities are already appreciated." He noted that Flagler seldom went out in a horse-drawn coach anymore.[68]

A few weeks later Frank Harris, editor of the *Ocala Banner*, stopped in to see Flagler in his office at the Standard Building after the Flaglers had returned to Mamaroneck in the fall. Like Morgan, he found Flagler full of vitality. "He is in splendid health," Harris wrote, "as straight as an arrow, and although [almost] seventy-six years of age, would easily pass for sixty. He attributes his remarkable vigor to his simplicity of living.... He eats three simple meals a day, and, except on extraordinary occasions, retires at 9:30 and enjoys sound slumber." However, Flagler did some darker foreshadowing in the interview, as Harris noted: "His greatest ambition is to complete his marine railroad to Key West and live until the accomplishment of the great undertaking."[69]

As the Florida East Coast Railway grew in mileage and in volume of traffic, the size of the complex of buildings around Union Station increased. Just east of the station, across Malaga Street and south of Valencia, stood the three-story headquarters building that housed the business offices. Behind the station, on the banks of the San Sebastian, the workshops increased in size and sophistication to handle the growing needs of the railroad. The car shed grew into a mammoth structure 430 feet long and 60 feet wide. The carpenter shop expanded to 150 feet long. Inside these buildings the company added all sorts of modern apparatus needed to repair locomotives and cars. To power this equipment an electrical plant with a 2,000-kilowatt dynamo went into another large building. Skilled workmen would completely overhaul passenger cars, renewing the steel rolling chassis, reupholstering the seats, and repainting the exteriors. During the fall one locomotive per week was being completely disassembled, refurbished, and reassembled for use in the coming season. The passenger and freight depot building itself gained a sixty-foot wing on its south side.[70]

In the fall President Theodore Roosevelt followed his wife's visit to St. Augustine with one of his own. Mrs. Roosevelt and the children had surely told him about their trip to the Ancient City in the spring, and perhaps this aroused his curiosity.

Henry Flagler seems to have had a greater antipathy to Theodore Roosevelt than to any other person. Doubtless a large part of this hostility sprang from Flagler's disgust with Roosevelt's frequent rhetorical flourishes against "malefactors of great wealth," with Standard Oil serving as the prime example of a malevolent corporate predator. Flagler once wrote to Oscar B. Smith, "I note what you say about the brutal attack on Mr. Rockefeller. I have no command of the English language that enables me to express my feelings regarding Mr. Roosevelt. He is _____."[71]

The employment of a dash shows Flagler's deep-seated unwillingness to employ profane words. The writer Lefevre noted: "He never swears. I think 'Thunder!' is his strongest expletive. And I have yet to hear him call any one a 'd—d fool.' The nearest he comes to it is: 'Now, wouldn't you think a man would have more sense than that?'"[72]

On a later occasion Flagler wrote to another friend, "I am glad that Teddy is going to Africa soon, for I want to spare him the humiliation of knowing that he has been 'all wrong' in his persecution of the Standard. I would like to keep him swelled up as much as possible, so that when a lion swallows him, he won't be able to disgorge him."[73]

Roosevelt's actions did not match his red hot rhetoric. He was not strictly a trust buster, preferring government intervention in the economy to promote old-fashioned ideas of honesty. When the government's antitrust suit against

Standard Oil finally reached resolution in the Supreme Court in 1911, it broke up the single great corporation into smaller component parts without changing the value of the company, except perhaps to make its successor companies more valuable.

Early in Roosevelt's presidency Flagler's chief lieutenant Joseph Parrott had made a call upon President Roosevelt in Washington, and he subsequently wrote to Flagler about his interview. When Parrott suggested that Flagler himself might visit the president, Flagler replied, "I don't believe there is a man in America who dreads such a thing as much as I do. I am glad you saw him, for I am sure I don't want to do it."[74]

In the fall of 1905 President Roosevelt decided to pay a visit to Henry Flagler's home territory by extending his tour of the southern states to include a visit to St. Augustine. The Board of Trade assumed charge of local arrangements for the visit, taking into consideration the president's request that there be minimal ceremony on his arrival and nothing at all planned for the second day of his visit, a Sunday. Rev. J. Coffin Stout of Memorial Presbyterian Church, while passing through Washington, called on the president and invited him to attend worship services at his church, and Flagler extended an invitation for him to spend the night in the Hotel Ponce de Leon. Since the opening of the winter tourist season lay still a month away, St. Augustine would be required to take special steps to shake off its summertime somnolence.[75]

Roosevelt arrived at Union Station from Jacksonville on a train pulled by a freshly painted black FEC locomotive with a framed portrait of the president on the front. Two huge arches shaped from cedar limbs and palm fronds framed the landing platform, with a stuffed eagle perched atop the primary arch. Several carloads of tropical palms and colorful shrubs had been brought up from South Florida. The new electric dynamo at the depot lit up the scene, and everything sparkled with tiny red, white, and blue lights. The Board of Trade's welcoming committee met the president and walked with him across a Brussels carpet to an awaiting carriage. As the President had requested, no band played a welcome, there was no hand shaking, and no one made a speech of greeting. On the ride through town almost every house shone with lights and crowds cheered, while the president tipped his hat and occasionally stood up to acknowledge the applause. At the City Gates a girl presented him with a large floral key, temporary doors formed from bowers of blooming branches swung open, and, as he rode through, two young maidens atop the columns showered petals down on his head. The president seemed to enjoy himself immensely. At the front gate of the Hotel Ponce de Leon Annie McKay greeted him and expressed Flagler's regrets at not being there to extend a welcome himself.[76]

The Ponce de Leon's courtyard had been prepared with its usual array of electric lights to impress the president as he walked to the front door. Ingraham, McGuire, McDonald, and William R. Kenan Jr. were on hand to represent Flagler. McGuire put the hotel's boilers into commission so that the electric lights would work, and the elevator also went into service to carry the president's party to the third floor. He was given the suite that Flagler had become accustomed to using in recent years on the southwest corner of the building. The rooms overlooked the Palm Garden on the west side, had a view of King Street to the south, and opened onto the balcony overlooking the courtyard. The president's bedroom, furnished in "subdued gold," expressed the "quiet elegance" preferred by its owner. One floor below, secret service men and newspaper reporters occupied only slightly less grand accommodations.[77]

After taking a half hour to change from their traveling clothes, the president's party emerged for another ride through town, going to Fort Marion under lighted arches and past trees and porches festooned with Chinese lanterns. Again, as the president wished, no brass band played, and since custom precluded the firing of a twenty-one-gun salute after sunset, Roosevelt entered accompanied only by the cheering of the large crowd who had squeezed into the fort's quadrangle. The gas company had laid temporary pipes into the fort to illuminate the area, and two large locomotive headlights shone on the speaker's podium so that the citizenry could clearly see their president.

Standing under a canopy formed from large American flags, Roosevelt gave a speech rich in platitudes about "good citizenship," but he decried the division of the country into the rich who looked down upon the poor and the poor who envied the rich. Then he pointedly condemned the "unhealthy" growth of "a spirit which is warped." He declared, "The crooked man who has got a good deal more than the average amount of sense will cause a lot of trouble. It is not the scoundrel who fails, but the scoundrel who succeeds who interests us." The allusion could not have been lost on the Flagler men in the audience.[78]

After the speech Roosevelt and his party rode down to the south end of town to the Valencia Hotel for a seafood dinner presented by the Board of Trade. James McGuire had built the hotel years earlier as his own business venture. Governor Broward sat at the table, and James Ingraham and four others gave little speeches. After the dinner adjourned at eleven, the president returned to his rooms at the Ponce de Leon. Walking out onto the balcony to observe the lighted courtyard below, he was heard to remark, "Say, isn't that a beautiful sight!" Then he retired to Henry Flagler's subdued gold bedroom and went to sleep in Henry Flagler's bed.[79]

The next morning Roosevelt attended the eleven o'clock service at Memorial Presbyterian, where a packed crowd had come out to catch a glimpse of the popular chief of state. Roosevelt sat in Henry Flagler's pew and sang the hymns lustily. Stout made no mention of the president in his sermon. Then the president was off for lunch in the west alcove of the Ponce de Leon's immense empty Dining Room before taking an early afternoon nap. At three the party made a brief ride around town, past the shuttered and empty St. Francis Barracks to Corbett's Dock, where the visitors boarded a launch for North Beach. After landing and hiking over the sand dunes "they proceeded to divest themselves of their clothing" and plunged into heavy surf. By this time of year the water temperature had reached chilly levels and a brisk October wind blew, but the president reveled in exposing himself to nature. He had been warned of the undertow and of "man eating sharks," but Roosevelt had swum with sharks in Cuban waters and counted the rigorous life a tonic to the system. That evening he departed to resume his tour of southern states.[80]

William R. Kenan Jr., no fan of the president, later wrote: "Every possible thing was done for the comfort and pleasure of the President and he seemed to enjoy his stay, but I am sure that he did not express his thanks to any one, either personally there, or to Mr. Flagler at a later date by letter." For his part, Flagler wrote to McGuire, "Miss MacKay telegraphed me the 'greetings' she gave the president. Please express to her and accept for yourself my thanks for the pains taken to provide the President so fine a reception."[81]

When the Flaglers arrived in St. Augustine by special train on December 9, 1905, Flagler's White steamer limousine picked them up at Union Station to carry them to the Ponce de Leon, where they would stay along with the Kenans—everyone taking meals at the Alcazar. On Sunday after they attended services at Memorial Church a crowd of well-wishers surrounded them and declared their pleasure at seeing everyone looking so well. Then Flagler got right down to business with a tour of inspection down his railroad. He took Anderson and his lieutenants to Miami, where they boarded the hard-working steamer *St. Lucie* for a cruise along the islands to Key West, where contract laborers were building northward, aiming to link up with crews working south from Miami.[82]

Rather than heading on to Palm Beach, the Flaglers celebrated Christmas at the Ponce de Leon. McGuire and McKay erected a huge evergreen tree in the center of the Rotunda and decorated it with electric lights and elaborate trimmings. Families from town answered invitations to attend. Everyone received gifts. Young Louise Wise distributed gifts to a small crowd of children that included Hugh Lewis. Clarissa Anderson later recalled that one year all the girls received parasols. Mary Lily had the pastry chef bake a cake from her old family recipe, and this was washed down with apple punch. In the middle of the afternoon the Flaglers and Kenans enjoyed a family dinner in the west alcove of the Dining Room, with holly and evergreen table decorations and red paper Christmas bells swaying from the chandeliers.[83]

In the succeeding days Mary Lily threw a coming out party for James Ingraham's daughter Kathleen and five other local young ladies in the Ponce de Leon's Dining Room. A few days later Mary Lily and Elizabeth Anderson hosted a dance in the same room. Although the sparse gathering only partly filled the large room, Anna Marcotte judged the event "one of the most charming functions ever given in the beautiful dining-room where so many famous balls were held before dancing became a lost art." Mary Lily led off the dancing with James Ingraham as her partner. She wore a black lace dress and the long strand of pearls Flagler had given her as an engagement present. The single strand of pearls hung down below her waist, serving to accentuate her diminutive size. Generals Schofield and Brooke lent military heft to the gathering, and Captain Marcotte now bore the imposing title "Commander, Department of Florida" of the Grand Army of the Republic veterans organization.[84]

After a Sunday evening concert in the Alcazar, Professor Gaston Mercadante, leader of the four-piece orchestra, received a request to play "You Alone," one of his own compositions. Mercadante had spent ten seasons at the Alcazar as pianist, and when the Flaglers had arrived in December he had presented Mary Lily with an autographed copy of the published sheet music to "You Alone," which read, "Respectfully dedicated to Mrs. H. M. Flagler." The syrupy lyrics, written by M. E. Wooster, told of a lover who crooned to his lady, "You are mine for ever more, I live sweetheart for you alone."[85]

Other social events followed in rapid succession: a birthday party for Flagler in the Alcazar grill room, a dance in the Casino, and a reception at the Yacht Club. Mary Lily took time during the day to receive treatments at the Alcazar Baths. For the first time since 1888 Flagler was on hand for the day when the Ponce de Leon lifted its iron gate. He watched the annual opening day stream of townspeople crowd into the hotel for a few hours of gaping at the splendors of the rich people's resort palace. Mr. and Mrs. William Ford created a sensation when they rolled up to the gate in a sulky pulled by one of their pet ostriches. Ford had leased the old Country Club golf course and turned it into an ostrich farm as an attraction for the tourists.[86]

Three days after the opening of the Ponce de Leon the Flagler-Kenan party departed for Palm Beach. Mary Lily expressed her pleasure at the reception they had received in St. Augustine and said they would return in April.[87]

In Palm Beach the Flaglers settled into their customary routine at Whitehall, giving and attending receptions for their friends. Mary Lily's relatives occupied their usual rooms upstairs, and Frederick Townsend Martin stayed as a houseguest for some time. The Pembroke Joneses and their Wilmington friend Henry Walters, president of the Atlantic Coast Line railroad, came down for a visit and trip to Miami. Flagler's sister-in-law Julia Harkness York and her daughter

Georgiana Maclennan represented Flagler's side of the family. General and Mrs. Schofield lived in Whitehall as guests, with the general accompanying Flagler to Key West to inspect locations for docks and a hotel shown to them by officers from the local navy station. However, this year Flagler did not host any great dinners for men of wealth and power at Whitehall. Quite possibly he was too involved in work on the Key West Extension to spare the time and energy for social events. He went back and forth along the Keys inspecting work on the railroad and the living conditions of the men employed on this most unusual project.[88]

Motor cars continued to assume a larger role in resort life. Flagler may have attended the annual New York Automobile Show the previous December; his purchase of several more White steamers for use at his hotels made news at the show. The Royal Poinciana gained its own large garage for autos, and the bridge to West Palm Beach was widened so that cars could drive over to the mainland and back. Flagler cooperated with Dade County to build a seventy-mile-long lime rock road from West Palm Beach to Miami. He and Mary Lily, in their "large White machine," drove the distance in about four hours. In Volusia County he likewise contributed funds for the construction of a hard-surfaced road from Ormond to New Smyrna. On at least one occasion Flagler took advantage of the new roads around Ormond for an automobile party excursion to Bulow Ruins, Buckhead Bluff on the Tomoka River, and New Smyrna. Several motors made up the pleasure caravan.[89]

The races on the beach at Ormond-Daytona attracted more contestants than ever. Francis E. Stanley showed up with several of his steamer cars, one of which cut the mile record to 32⅕ seconds (almost 112 miles per hour). Henry Ford also came with several cars, drivers, and mechanics. Flagler joined the spectators, along with his brother-in-law William R. Kenan Jr., William's wife Alice Pomroy Kenan, and Sarah Kenan. Mary Lily and her mother stayed home at Whitehall. As in previous years, Flagler's *Florida Times-Union* publicized the races and the FEC Railway ran special trains from Jacksonville and St. Augustine to bring spectators.[90]

St. Augustine attempted to join the excitement by staging races on its own broad, hard beach. Flagler's hotels put up a small purse to purchase prizes. Failing to attract any of the nationally famous drivers or manufacturers who competed at Ormond, local auto enthusiasts settled for races among themselves, driving their standard street machines. A northeaster blew in, causing postponement of the races for a few days, but finally the small crowd of people who rode the South Beach Railway out to the beach could observe a three-day series of races that tested both machines' and drivers' skills. Charles Wheeler, driving a thirty-two-horsepower Peerless, won the five-mile out-and-back race over four other entries in eight minutes and thirty seconds. Other races verged on the comical.

A slalom race sent drivers weaving through a row of barrels. Another required drivers to avoid running over eggs, while yet another asked the drivers to get out of their cars, take off their coats, crank their engines, put their coats back on, and race one mile. Several handicap races gave the lower horsepower cars a chance to win.[91]

At the height of the season Flagler and Mary Lily made an appearance at the Dade County Fair in Miami. As luck would have it, overcast skies and rain soaked the fairgrounds all week. At the fair's conclusion Mary Lily handed out prizes from the steps of the Royal Palm to those winning awards in various categories. When the crowd began chanting for Flagler to say something, the habitually taciturn businessman stood up to offer a "brief and pointed" speech. He took the need for cooperation as the theme of his talk, saying that we all need the help of others. He even made a joke: "How often we hear the boast 'I am a self-made man.' It must be a comfort sometimes to God to be relieved of the responsibilities of some of these products." He continued by saying that the railroad would be nothing without the people who made use of it. Then he praised the people of Dade County for having the hope and optimism to become pioneers in this frontier region. Finally he condemned those who sowed discord by spreading divisive, misleading arguments, and he called for working together toward the common good.[92]

When the Schofields returned to St. Augustine from their visit with the Flaglers in Palm Beach, the general resumed his normal quiet rounds about town. He appeared to be in good health. Then on Friday, March 2, he suffered a stroke that sent him to bed in his home at 20 Valencia Street, and two days later he passed away. Flags in town were lowered to half-mast, while in Palm Beach Flagler canceled a gala musical event out of respect. The funeral was held at the home of the Episcopal minister, and afterward Captain Marcotte and the Chatfield post of the Grand Army of the Republic escorted the hearse to Union Station. Elizabeth Anderson accompanied the general's widow Mary and daughter Georgina to Washington with the coffin in Parrott's private car (probably no. 91, the old *Alicia*). Schofield would be interred at Arlington National Cemetery. Clarissa Anderson later recalled that her father attempted to obtain a widow's pension for Mary since the general had not been a wealthy man.[93]

Former president Cleveland stopped by St. Augustine in early March. He and some friends slipped through Union Station by way of the baggage department to avoid creating a scene on the passenger platform. In the afternoon he took his party on a carriage ride around town to show them the sights, and then they enjoyed dinner at the Ponce de Leon. The *Record*'s reporter observed, "Although not exactly ill he is not feeling quite as well as usual and is off in weight." He and his friends were going to Stuart for some fishing and duck shooting. Cleveland said he missed Joe Jefferson and would regret not seeing him on their usual fishing grounds. That evening he took a night train south.[94]

This would be Cleveland's final trip to Florida. In March 1907 he and his old friend Elias C. Benedict would go duck hunting on the Santee River in South Carolina rather than venturing farther southward.[95] In June of the next year Cleveland would pass away of heart failure at his home in Princeton, New Jersey, where he had been living modestly for the past decade. Among those sending flowers or condolences were Helen and Thomas Hastings, Joseph Jefferson's widow, and E. C. Benedict. Hastings designed a modest monument to stand over Cleveland's grave in Princeton Cemetery. Frank Hastings, Thomas Hastings's brother and Benedict's secretary, served as co-executor of Cleveland's estate and later as business manager for his widow Frances Cleveland.[96]

The Flaglers moved from Whitehall at the end of March when the Royal Poinciana closed and relocated themselves and some friends to the Ponce de Leon. This followed their usual pattern, but something was different this year. They would remain in St. Augustine for a full six weeks, and as Mrs. Marcotte noted, they enjoyed their stay "with increasing pleasure." Although he said nothing, Flagler was pondering returning to St. Augustine and investing more of himself in the town where his Florida venture had begun.[97]

At the conclusion of a Wednesday evening concert in the Alcazar, with the Flaglers probably in attendance, Professor Mercadante played Mary Lily's song "You Alone," and the audience refused to stop applauding until he and the small orchestra had performed an encore. Clearly people in St. Augustine wished to demonstrate their affection for the Flaglers.[98]

One thing is certain: Flagler had decided that his earthly remains would be interred in St. Augustine. He had been thinking about this for some time. As far back as the fall of 1902 he had corresponded with John Carrère about the cost of a mausoleum, and at that time he confided to Joseph McDonald that he had at first thought of placing it near the chapel in Palm Beach, but in the spring he had decided to add a mausoleum to Memorial Church in St. Augustine. In mid-March 1906, just before going to St. Augustine, he wrote to James McGuire to inquire about obtaining the sand and bricks that would be needed to build the foundation and inner fabric of the mausoleum. Carrère and Hastings would design the tomb, while Batterson and Eisele, who had handled the marble work at Whitehall, would execute the marble facings of the mausoleum.[99]

Flagler said nothing in public about this very private decision. When McGuire started work on the tomb in early April, the St. Augustine Record stated only that it would be circular in design, would cost $100,000, and would be finished in marble. "Further details could not be obtained." Flagler's name never appeared in stories relating to the mausoleum. By November it had been completed, but still nothing was published regarding its purpose.[100]

Flagler had another, more visible building project under way during 1906. The *St. Augustine Record* had been published in a rented workshop on Hospital Street (today's Aviles Street), with its editorial office across the street downstairs in the Library Building, today the Historical Society Research Library. In January work began on a new brick building for the newspaper's home that would stand on Cordova Street just south of the Alcazar tennis courts. On March 1 workmen placed a metal cylinder filled with memorabilia of the day under the cornerstone of the building. By August the newspaper had completed the move into its fine new headquarters, although it would not be until October that the public was invited in for a tour of the facility. The Record Building would serve the newspaper until 2001, when it moved into a new state-of-the-art facility outside town. Today the old Record Building remains a prominent downtown landmark and has been converted into apartments.[101]

One of the cub reporters for the *Record* was Russel Dale, son of Flagler's gardener Richard Dale, who had passed away in 1899. The younger Dale's beat took him from place to place gathering information about goings-on in town. One day Dale was standing at the registration desk of the Hotel Ponce de Leon carefully copying the names and hometowns of guests who had recently arrived. After a while the desk clerk started to fidget, and Dale looked around to see what was bothering him. There behind him stood Henry Flagler, patiently waiting for his turn with the clerk.

Dale related this story to show the "gentle, dignified, soft spoken, and considerate" side of the man townspeople respectfully called "Uncle Henry." He explained, "We had an affectionate regard for him on whose wisdom and bounty so many of us were more or less dependent." Dale grew up in a home Flagler had built for his family.[102]

In April Flagler convened with the directors of the FEC Railway and the FEC Hotel Company in St. Augustine for their annual corporation meetings. Since he owned almost all the stock in both companies, the meetings were scheduled to last only half an hour. Later in the month Flagler took his usual end-of-season inspection tour of the railroad down to the end of the line. Then on May 15 the Flaglers left for the North.[103]

Before departing Flagler gave a statement to the *Record* saying he would move his legal residence from Palm Beach to St. Augustine. He explained that he was making the change to be closer to the headquarters of the FEC Railway so that it would be easier for him to keep abreast of developments in construction of the Key West Extension. He added that he still intended to spend two or three months at Whitehall in Palm Beach each winter. Interestingly, he did not use Kirkside as his residence while in St. Augustine. Perhaps he simply did not want to go through all the rigmarole of opening the house and installing a household staff; or perhaps the house held too many memories of his earlier life with Ida Alice.[104]

Although he had made his announcement, Flagler still harbored reservations about making St. Augustine his official hometown. He complained to Ingraham: "The condition of our asphalt streets (made originally by me and given to the City) excites my disgust every time I go to and from the R.R. Depot. I have realized from the beginning that St. Augustine was a dull place, but it does seem as though twenty years would stir up some little measure of public spirit; enough to at least keep the only street we have to the Railroad in decent condition."[105]

Flagler had a point. Since the western portion of King Street remained unpaved, most traffic from the west side of town chose to follow the route down Valencia Street, and after nearly twenty years of wear and tear it began to fall apart all at once. As if to insult Flagler personally, a huge pothole developed in the street right in front of Kirkside. Someone—probably McGuire—placed a barrel in the depression, with a lighted lantern at night, as a warning to those traveling along the street.[106]

Ingraham replied to Flagler's letter by saying that the city's streets were in poor shape because of the local government's aversion to taxes. He added that Flagler benefited from the town's low tax policy since he owned extensive property in town. Ingraham concluded by saying that he was glad Flagler had decided to return to St. Augustine since many people felt that he had "soured" on the place long ago.[107]

Joseph Parrott heard similar complaints from Flagler. Parrott explained St. Augustine's lack of progressive spirit as the failure of local businessmen to work together for their common good. He added that he did not think Flagler was poorly regarded in St. Augustine by the local citizenry, although he warned Flagler against trying to run the town once he established himself there. Parrott advised simply asking that the streets be kept clean.[108]

21

Returning to St. Augustine,
1906–1911

I have never changed my feelings
of affection for St. Augustine.

—Henry Flagler to civic leaders, 1907

During 1906 St. Augustine took two important steps in becoming a modern city: it acquired a municipal electric power plant and started laying track for a streetcar system.

Up to this time only Flagler's Ponce de Leon, Alcazar, and railway depot had enjoyed the benefits of electricity. In the spring of 1905 the gas company, originally established by W. G. Warden and Dr. Anderson twenty years earlier, purchased a dynamo capable of furnishing electric power both to the city government for street lighting and to private homes and businesses. However, the gas company's contract with the city expired in April 1905, and the city council negotiated a new agreement with an outside company called the St. Johns Light and Power Company. It promised to build a much larger electric power plant and develop an electric trolley line through the town's streets and all the way across the bay out to South Beach. It began construction of a big facility on South Ribera Street and, in the meantime, purchased the gas company's generator to supply electricity until its own much larger plant was completed. In February 1906 some businesses tapped into the new electric lines, and in March electric arc lights began to appear along city streets. Since the old gaslights still served some areas of town for a while longer, citizens could see how much more brightly the new electric lights illuminated the night.[1]

Proposals to build a streetcar line had long been a point of friction between Henry Flagler and many people in St. Augustine. An effort to establish a trolley system had first been made in 1886, only to founder, at least in part, because of Flagler's opposition. He envisioned King Street as the Fifth Avenue of St. Augustine, an attractive boulevard lined with stately homes and fine establishments like his hotels. Flagler and his neighbors in New York City had managed to prohibit streetcars on Fifth Avenue. He desired to keep the clatter and clanging of trolley cars away from his resort hotels in St. Augustine. However, King Street had long served as the main east-west transportation axis of the town, and local interests saw a modern streetcar line both as a practical and beneficial improvement to the old town and as more convenient transport to South Beach.[2]

In the summer of 1886 a number of business and professional men, including some close to Flagler, wrote him a letter declaring that the street railway was a *"public necessity"* and that they felt "the sentiments of a majority have been thwarted" by Flagler's opposition. In replying to this letter Flagler skirted the issue, saying he desired only the "highest good of the City" and had no personal interest in the matter, especially of a financial nature. "I think it must be evident to every person that a desire for gain was not the motive that has prompted my investments in St. Augustine. I can make more money in this city [New York] in a month than I can in St. Augustine in a life time. The improvement of the place has been, and will be, a source of great gratification." The latter comment was a gentle reminder that the community stood to gain a great deal by not antagonizing Flagler.[3]

This first streetcar proposal quickly went away, but similar propositions by other investors continued to arise over the following years. When another prospective builder came forward in 1890, Flagler asked a lawyer to investigate whether he had the legal right to block a trolley track on King Street. After all, Flagler maintained, he and Anderson had donated land to the city so that the street could be widened. The lawyer replied that Flagler could reclaim the land he had given to the city, but he could not block construction of track on the original line of the street. In 1894 Flagler discouraged yet another proposal to build a trolley line on King Street by refusing to allow the line to extend up Malaga Street to the depot. However, the issue never came to a confrontation because the company advocating the line eventually walked away from the venture. Building a streetcar system that could pay its way in a small town was a difficult proposition even under the best of circumstances.[4]

The St. Johns Light and Power Company's effort in 1906 finally prevailed, perhaps because Flagler realized that his vision of King Street as a splendidly landscaped Fifth Avenue had failed to materialize. In October the company purchased the South Beach Railway since the line to the ocean beach offered the promise of good revenues. By that time work was progressing on King Street. To make way for the tracks, Clarissa Anderson's magnificent oaks trees in the center

Trolleys roll in front of the Hotel Ponce de Leon, overcoming years of resistance by Henry Flagler. From the collection of the St. Augustine Historical Society Research Library.

of the street were cut down, turning what had been a shaded canopy avenue into a starkly open vista. Soon workers were busy laying trolley tracks down the center of the street with poorly placed brick pavement on either side. By December the tracks ran on King Street from the San Sebastian to Matanzas Bay, and six months later St. Augustine's citizens could ride this first segment of the line from one side of the town to the other.[5]

In 1907 Anderson attempted to compensate somewhat for the loss of his mother's oak trees by planting a row of sabal palms on either side of King Street from Sevilla Street to Ribera Street. These palms survive today, although few people pay them any heed.[6]

When the Flaglers went north for the summer in the spring of 1906, they swung westward to the mountains of North Carolina to pay a visit to Mr. and Mrs. George Vanderbilt at their wooded estate and home Biltmore. George's father had spent some time at the Ponce de Leon a few years earlier, and George himself might have been part of his father's party on that occasion. A carriage ride around the landscaped grounds and gardens added interest to the visit. Then the Flaglers sampled other resorts of the Blue Ridge Mountains.[7]

The rest of the summer followed a familiar routine: Mamaroneck in the early summer, followed by the Mount Washington Hotel at Bretton Woods in late August. Here Flagler and H. H. Rogers continued their love affair with automobiles. The New York Times reported that Flagler "has had a new White Steamer especially constructed for his use here." A story in the *New York Tribune* added, "Mr. Flagler and Henry H. Rogers both have their automobiles at the Bretton Woods garage, and are having a fine time speeding over the mountain roads. The distances between the best mountain resorts makes it delightful to run about." Thirty other guests at the Mount Washington maintained autos, and they ranged on day trips over a circuit of about thirty miles in all directions.[8]

Friends who had spent the previous winter in Florida came to visit. Mrs. Schofield and her daughter Georgina arrived with a party of Kenans. Louise Wise demonstrated for her elders her proficiency at swimming underwater in the hotel pool. Parrott came by with another of the FEC executives. General Brooke and Reverend Stout, with their wives, dropped in. The more relaxed, rustic White Mountains suited Flagler's temperament more than the socially pretentious atmosphere of Newport or Bar Harbor. As soon as the colorful fall foliage dropped from the trees, the Flaglers went home to Mamaroneck.[9]

When Flagler returned to New York he received some "serious" photographs at 26 Broadway from Mark Twain, who evidently had been introduced to him by their mutual friend Rogers. Flagler thanked Twain for autographing the portraits and could not help adding a bit of humor: "I showed them to one of our trusted men who has had a severe nervous breakdown. You will be glad to know that he left my office completely recovered."[10]

Flagler suffered an illness of some sort while at Mamaroneck. He wrote a letter to Ingraham on November 19 in an uncharacteristically shaky hand saying, "I am still confined to the home but am better, and hope to go out tomorrow and to town Wednesday." He informed Ingraham that he and Mary Lily expected to start for Florida on November 26 and spend a few days in Richmond and Raleigh on the way down. Flagler's illness may have been nothing serious, but it may also have foreshadowed health problems to come.[11]

When the Flaglers arrived in St. Augustine in early December the *Record* declared, "Mr. Flagler is in unusually good health and is quite as strong and vigorous as of yore." They stayed in a suite in the Ponce de Leon, where Mary Lily received guests and Flagler set up an office for himself and J. C. Salter. When the Alcazar opened, they joined the crowd that gathered for the first dinner and thereafter took their meals in the Alcazar dining room.[12]

Two weeks later he and Mary Lily gathered up Anderson, the FEC railroad chiefs, and a few other friends to inspect conditions along the Key West Extension. A hurricane had swept over the Keys in October, drowning dozens of workmen, including some whose barracks barge was washed away into the Gulf. Flagler went to every work camp along the route to satisfy himself that steps were being taken to prepare for future storms.[13]

At this time, very quietly, without any public notice, the remains of Mary

The Flagler mausoleum designed by Carrère and Hastings stands next to Memorial Church. Author's photo.

Harkness Flagler, Jennie Louise Flagler Benedict, and her daughter Margery were brought down from Woodlawn Cemetery in New York and interred in the mausoleum beside Memorial Church. Twin sarcophagi in the center of the tomb received the bodies of Mary and Jennie Louise. Undertaker Raymond A. Ponce, whose funeral home occupied the former Bacchus Club, placed the little body of Jennie Louise's infant in her arms. Henry Flagler wrote to his son Harry to tell him about the arrangement of the mausoleum containing "your dear mother" and "Jennie and her baby." He explained that two separate sarcophagi rested to either side, reserved for himself and "Mrs. Flagler." Flagler's second wife Ida Alice was left completely out of the picture.[14]

That December the Kenans came down to visit. Mary Lily's aging mother headed the group, although she seldom went out to social events. Jessie Wise and her daughter Louise stayed until the first of the new year, when they left to put Louise in school. Mary Lily's other sister Sarah, William R. Kenan Jr., and Alice Pomroy Kenan completed the tribe. As in the year before, the Flaglers celebrated Christmas around a huge tree in the Rotunda of the Ponce de Leon. Santa Claus himself arrived to distribute gifts. In the afternoon about seventy guests joined the Flagler and Kenan families for dinner in the Dining Room. A few days later the Flaglers stood in the Rotunda to welcome some five hundred teachers of the Florida Education Association to a reception around the Christmas tree.[15]

Acting on Parrott's observation that St. Augustine's business and civic leaders failed to work in harmony, Flagler decided to bring all the town's leading men together to begin the process of developing a more cohesive community spirit. At four in the afternoon on January 1 a crowd of perhaps as many as four hundred men congregated around the post office and then walked to the Ponce de Leon, where they entered through the King Street gate and courtyard. At the front door Dr. Anderson and James Ingraham greeted every man personally, and other members of the reception committee introduced each man by name to Mr. and Mrs. Flagler, who stood in the center of the Rotunda.

Afterward everyone proceeded to the west alcove of the Dining Room, where sandwiches, punch, and cake awaited them. William MacWilliams, long-time lawyer and politician, acted as master of ceremonies for the occasion. The men formed a circle around the perimeter of the room. Mayor E. E. Boyce was called upon to wish everyone a happy new year and to express the city's best wishes to the town's new citizens, the Flaglers. Bartolo Genovar, chairman of the county commission, recounted the day in January 1888 when he, as representative of the "native element" of St. Augustine, had presented Flagler with an engraved medallion extending their welcome to the city. Flagler's friend O. B. Smith offered greetings from the Business Men's League, while Antonio Entenza spoke for the workingmen, saying "every soul among this army of toilers loves you."

MacWilliams, as president of the Board of Trade, declared: "There was a time when this city held attractions for you more dear than any other place in Florida, but of late years we were prone to think you had left us and wandered off to worship at strange shrines, and today we are grateful to learn that you are still true to the old city."[16]

Flagler responded by saying he had been denied "the gift of tongue. This I learned early in life and I resolved to try to be a doer of things rather than a talker about them." He informed Commissioner Genovar that the framed medallion hung on his office wall and was one of his treasured mementoes. Flagler concluded with an announcement: "I have never changed my feelings of affection for St. Augustine and have made provision that when my life ends my body shall remain here." However, he said no more about the new mausoleum that now stood beside Memorial Church.

After that others stepped forward to offer congratulations and toasts. Ingraham spoke on behalf of Mary Lily, mentioning that she had recently become a landowner in St. Augustine. Ingraham did not say it, but Flagler had transferred ownership of Kirkside to Mary Lily.[17] The diminutive Mary Lily seemed distinctly out of place amid this sea of masculinity. Ingraham asked the Alcazar band to strike up "Dixie" in honor of this southern belle from North Carolina.[18]

Interestingly, Flagler waited a full year before officially changing his residence from Palm Beach to St. Augustine, and even then, he listed his home as the Hotel Ponce de Leon. He and Mary Lily did not use Kirkside. Perhaps it just was more convenient to set up a simpler household in the hotel.[19]

A few days later the Hotel Ponce de Leon opened with the usual pomp and ceremony and crush of curious townspeople invading the public rooms. Manager Robert Murray stood near the front desk to welcome guests, while Henry Flagler "sat quietly by" observing the commotion. In the following days the Flaglers stayed busy with dinners and receptions given by the Andersons, the Albert Lewises, and other leading families in town. They went to Jacksonville for the wedding of U.S. Senator James Taliaferro's daughter and stayed to visit with the Parrotts, who lived next door to the senator. Then on January 18 they were off for Palm Beach.[20]

The Flaglers had employed a new organist at Whitehall, young Arthur Spalding, to replace Russell T. Joy. On his way down from the North, Spalding stopped in St. Augustine to inspect the organ at Memorial Church with Anderson ("one of Mr. Flagler's chums"), Stout, and the church's organist. A fancy "vox humana" had been added to the organ, and the locals did not quite know what to make of it, saying it sounded like a "nannie-goat." Spalding assured Anderson that the instrument was working properly, and Anderson paid the bill for the addition.

Flagler was out of town when Spalding passed through, but the young man enjoyed staying for free at the Alcazar and charging his meals to "Flagler."[21]

Spalding preceded the Flaglers to Palm Beach, and one afternoon he spotted a private railway car detached on a siding and presumed that the Flaglers had arrived. He decided, with some trepidation, to make his presence known to his employers. "I walked up the front walk and could see through the open work front door Mr. Flagler seated in one of the big gold arm chairs like a king on his throne. I immediately aimed for Mr. Flagler, at which moment he started towards me, shaking hands very cordially, and taking me over to introduce me to his wife—an unaffected, cordial, homelike and charming woman."[22]

One of Spalding's next letters home continued in the same vein: "He is certainly a fine old man, one of the gentlest and kindest I ever met. As we came out of church this noon, a little girl ran up and kissed him, then walked along part way with us, holding on to his hand. He is just that grandfatherly sort of man, and he and his wife seem devoted to each other."[23]

Spalding's other letters contain intimate details of the Flagler household that did not find their way into print in the society columns. He tells of one evening when the family and a houseguest gathered around the organ to sing some old hymns out of two hymnals that they shared. "Mrs. Flagler used to sing considerably before she was married but has given it up since. Her voice now shows lack of practice, but I should judge it was pretty good in its day. After we had sung a while, Mr. Flagler suggested that I play one or two 'great big things' as he expressed it (he is so deaf that he can't hear the soft things that other people are always calling for) so I played the March from Tannhauser and the March of the Priests from Athalia, and he began to clap before I got through either piece. He likes a lot of noise and one of his favorites is the Anvil Chorus from Il Trovatore, which unfortunately I haven't arranged for organ."[24]

At age seventy-seven Flagler's eyes and ears had begun to fail him, and he was becoming more susceptible to illnesses, yet he continued to hurry on with his building projects while holding back the hands of the clock. His newspaper friend Frank Harris of the Ocala Banner offered this description of Flagler two years later: "His vision is not as clear as it once was and he is somewhat deaf, particularly in one ear, which causes him some embarrassment. Except for these infirmities he is suffering from no physical ailments. Tall and erect, he presents a perfect type of manhood. He prefers a straight-back chair, and never occupies a rocker unless there is nothing else to be had."[25]

The Flaglers spent a quiet season in Palm Beach, entertaining a few close friends and relatives who came down for stays of a week or more. Elizabeth Anderson and the Parrotts escorted Mary Lily to the Washington's Birthday Ball in the Royal Poinciana, where Mary Lily attracted attention wearing a white gown and her "magnificent pearls." The Andersons and Frederick Townsend Martin stopped in as houseguests at Whitehall. William Rockefeller and Chauncey Depew, now a U.S. senator, stayed at the Royal Poinciana, but Flagler took them for excursions in his launch and overland in his White steamer. All the while Flagler went back and forth on his rail line to Ormond for the auto races and to Miami, the Keys, and Key West to keep tabs on construction of the railroad.[26]

On February 9, 1907, Flagler hooked up his private car to a locomotive and went across the bridge connecting the causeway from the mainland to Key Largo. This milestone crossing put the FEC Railway onto the chain of islands heading toward Key West. Work on the Key West Extension—"Flagler's Folly"—had already consumed two years and had cost dozens of lives, but now it was visibly on its way.[27]

In St. Augustine the season progressed about as usual, with plenty of visitors but most of them just passing through. However, Montgomery Ward, his wife, and their daughter spent five weeks at the Alcazar. Ward, a Chicago businessman, was famous as the originator of mail order mass merchandising. Mary Custis Lee, daughter of Robert E. Lee and granddaughter of George and Martha Washington, honored the Washington's Birthday formal ball in the Casino with her presence.[28]

The grand event of the 1907 season was the Ponce de Leon Celebration. The last observance of this kind had been held in 1902 on a very modest scale, but the Business Men's League had decided a year in advance to revive this festive commemoration of St. Augustine's storied history. Joseph Parrott told the town's citizens that the FEC Railway would pay one-quarter of the costs of the celebration, up to $1,250, and that the railroad would transport units of the state militia to town for free. The dates for the activities were set for early April in the hope of encouraging tourists to delay their departure from Florida for a little while longer.[29]

All season long the town buzzed in anticipation. Townsmen formed little companies of Indians, Frenchmen, Englishmen, and Spaniards to train for their parts in the pageant. When the costumes arrived from up North, they were distributed accordingly: red coats and white breeches to the English, white coats with red facings to the French, and "plush, velvet, silk and satin" garments for the lucky Spanish grandees. The savage Indians wore feathers, war paint, and—to simulate nudity—long john underwear. Decorative archways were erected at several intersections around town by various organizations: the FEC Railway at the depot, the Knights of Columbus in front of the cathedral, the labor unions at the corner of King and Cordova, Albert Lewis at the east end of Valencia, and the town's black citizens at the corner of Bridge and Washington—the entrance to the black business block. A tent was set up on the Plaza to direct visitors to private homes where people had agreed to rent rooms for the overflow of visitors.[30]

As luck would have it, a northeaster blew in on the appointed day, causing a twenty-four-hour delay, but on April 3 the caravel bearing Juan Ponce de León and his conquistadors bore down from North River and landed between Corbett's Dock and the Matanzas Bridge. They were met at the seawall by scarlet-robed Catholic priests from the cathedral who raised a cross. Ponce knelt to receive their blessing. Mayor E. E. Boyce delivered a brief address declaring that Ponce had landed on March 27, 1512—the incorrect date still in most of the era's history books—and Congressman Frank Clark declared his support for another celebration in 1908. Then horses appeared to carry the Spaniards away for a parade around town. The city's mounted police led the way, followed by the First Regimental band from Jacksonville, the Catholic contingent, the Spaniards, and finally the Indians bringing up the rear. The parade concluded on the fort green, where T.S.L. Brown opined that St. Augustine had been blessed by two landings: one by Ponce and a more recent one by Henry M. Flagler. Thousands turned out to witness the spectacle. Richard L. Parks, a piano tuner and teacher at the school for the deaf and blind, who was himself blind, wrote and published the "Ponce de Leon" march for the occasion.[31]

The next day Dr. DeWitt Webb, president of the Historical Society, portrayed Don Pedro Menéndez de Avilés, and the previous day's theatricals and parade were repeated. In a particularly intriguing highlight of the procession, the marchers walked up from the fort green to a vacant lot at the north end of Water Street, where tradition held that Menéndez had celebrated the first mass. This folklore had been handed down from ancient Spanish times, and it proved to give a remarkably accurate approximation of the Menéndez landing site. Today the Great Cross of Nombre de Dios Mission, commemorating the first mass, stands on the site, and just to the north of it, at Fountain of Youth Park, archaeologists have excavated relics of the nation's oldest successful European settlement.[32]

That evening "Oglethorpe's Bombardment of the Fort" took the form of a fireworks show. Four U.S. Navy torpedo boats maneuvered close to the seawall and played their searchlights over the upturned faces of the throng crowded onto the fort green. The finale of the fireworks ignited a fiery bust of Ponce de León on the ramparts of the fort, followed by a blazing portrait of Henry Flagler. Afterward those who wished to dance the night away repaired to the fort's gun deck, where an orchestra awaited them, playing under swaying Japanese lanterns.[33]

On the third day military units marched on the Plaza, coming south from San Marco Avenue, north up Bay Street, and from the west on King Street. Three decorated horse-drawn wagons served as floats for lovely young ladies. The band played the Spanish national anthem and raised the Spanish flag on one staff, followed by the "Marseillaise" and the raising of the French flag, then "Rule Britannia" and the British flag, and finally the American flag and "The Star-Spangled Banner." The band then struck up "America the Beautiful" and "Dixie"—the celebration's only slight reference to Florida's brief moment under the Confederate flag.[34]

Flagler wrote a letter to the editor of the *St. Augustine Record* saying, "Will you permit me to use the columns of *The Evening Record* to express to the good people of St. Augustine my appreciation of the compliment paid me in the fireworks last evening, and to say, further, that I am much gratified with the success of their Ponce de Leon entertainment, which I have greatly enjoyed."[35]

The festivities continued for a while longer. Albert Lewis hosted a dinner in the Alcazar for the officers of the torpedo boat flotilla; Mary Lily attended, along with the Flaglers' usual St. Augustine circle. Two days later the Flaglers invited their friends to an informal dance in the parlor of the Alcazar. Flagler finished off the season by taking Anderson and General Brooke with him on the traditional inspection trip down the railroad. This time they could go all the way to the far tip of Key Largo. Then in mid-May the Flaglers were off for Fred Sterry's Homestead Hotel in Hot Springs, Virginia, on their way home to Mamaroneck.[36]

Two days after the Flaglers' departure the dredges excavating the coastal canal finally broke through the last barrier of limestone rock separating the Matanzas River from the Halifax River. It had taken twenty-five years of digging, and the route of the canal northward to Jacksonville Beach still remained to be opened. A few days later a small boat arrived in St. Augustine, having wended its way up from Miami. James Ingraham, the intrepid explorer who had once waded across the Everglades to Miami, took the *Kathleen* (formerly Flagler's *Adelante*) down to Miami, making him the first to traverse the canal from north to south. In many places the channel wandered along a makeshift path, requiring further deepening and straightening in the next few years, but another milestone in the development of Florida had been reached.[37]

During the summer Flagler suffered a lingering illness that evidently persisted for months. The first hint that something was wrong appeared in an early August *New York Times* article saying, "Mr. Flagler has been kept indoors for a time by a slight illness." Then on September 27 the *Washington Post* ran the story: "Henry M. Flagler, vice president of the Standard Oil Company, is seriously ill in the Mount Washington Hotel, Bretton Woods, N.H. His condition is such as to cause the gravest alarm to his friends." The article went on to say that Dr. Owen Kenan was on hand to treat him and that Flagler had contracted influenza while in Florida in April. Supposedly the illness had been brought on by overwork and worry about the Key West Extension.[38]

The *New York Times* telephoned the Mount Washington Hotel and got the night clerk, who said Flagler had left the hotel a week earlier and seemed to be in good health when he departed. The next day the *Washington Post* ran a brief retraction, saying Flagler was in his office in New York City and had issued a statement saying he was not ill. Since the story had raised alarm in St. Augustine, the *Record* published an account telegraphed by a local man who said he had seen Flagler in New York and found him in good health.[39]

Despite the denials, Flagler clearly had been sick. When he returned to Florida in the fall, he was described as "recently recovered" from his illness. Years later James Ingraham would refer to "Mr. Flagler's long illness in 1907."[40]

Flagler had good reason to be overwrought in 1907. The American economy, which had been doing well since the late 1890s, began to slow down, and securities prices on the New York Stock Exchange started an agonizing slide. Then in the autumn what has been called the "Panic of 1907" sent frightened citizens across America rushing to their local banks to withdraw their deposits. Banks in many regions failed, and some of the large central banks in New York City also seemed on the verge of collapse. According to James Ingraham, Flagler once said that his New York business manager William H. Beardsley had "saved his life" by his astute handling of Flagler's finances during this crisis.[41]

The effects of the recession hit St. Augustine hard. On July 31 the Florida East Coast Railway announced the layoff of three hundred skilled mechanics and the closing of the railroad shops. This followed earlier firings of carpenters, boilermakers, blacksmiths, and other tradesmen as the railroad gradually cut back on its activities. The payroll of the FEC's skilled workers made up the largest single source of income for St. Augustine, especially during the summer months when the hotels were closed. This came on top of the Garcia-Vega cigar factory's move from town to Tampa earlier in the year. The steam whistle at the railroad shops, which called men to work in the mornings, fell silent. In these modern times, that whistle had come to replace the bells in the Catholic cathedral as the signal of the start of a new day.[42]

Joseph Parrott gave the *St. Augustine Record* an interview in which he said the railroad was forced to make retrenchments due to rising costs of materials and wages combined with stagnant income. He explained that the railroad had invested three million dollars in Florida and could not expect to recover that investment anytime in the near future. He also blamed increased government regulations and lawsuits for increasing the railroad's expenses. Finally, he said he did not know when things would get better.[43]

Henry Flagler was quoted in the *Washington Post* and *Atlanta Constitution* as saying that work on construction of the Key West Extension would stop on January 1 and would not resume until the financial markets recovered. He was also said to have declared that he had seen "the present stringency coming for a long time. It was foreshadowed by the popular feeling against railroads and corporations, as reflected in the state and national legislatures."[44]

Whether Flagler actually said this or not, Parrott issued a declaration denouncing the stories as "yellow journalism" and saying that work on the extension would continue. He estimated that the line would reach Knights Key in mid-January, and from that point the railroad would be able to establish a harbor for ships going to and coming from Cuba. Furthermore, he emphatically avowed that Flagler's financial resources were fully adequate for the task at hand in the Keys. In truth, however, costs of the extension had overreached even Flagler's capability to keep going. In a way, it was remarkable that Flagler had managed to get as far as he had without borrowing money. A year later he would ask J. P. Morgan to manage the sale of ten million dollars' worth of bonds to fund completion of the road to Key West.[45]

By November the FEC resorted to paying its employees in script—paper IOUs—saying there was no currency available from the banks because of the panic. Railroad representatives declared that the paper "checks" were worth their face value in gold, and the local First National Bank said it would accept the paper at its full value. It amounted to more bad news on top of everything that had gone before. The winter tourist season was at hand, and if the only railroad down the East Coast could not get its operations in order, the outlook for Palm Beach, Miami, and every smaller city along the road looked bleak.[46]

However, in New York City the financial titans, including J. P. Morgan and John D. Rockefeller, pooled their capital and bailed the banks out of immediate danger. With remarkable speed the money markets righted themselves, and the economy resumed its upward march. In St. Augustine the FEC started rehiring laborers in mid-November, and on November 25, the day before Thanksgiving, the morning whistle sounded once again, signaling the reopening of the shops. Perhaps everything would be right with the world after all.[47]

The Flaglers, nomads that they had become, arrived in St. Augustine on December 11, but Flagler wasted no time in heading south on the railroad in company with Anderson, Parrott, R. T. Goff, and a few others to satisfy his curiosity about progress on the Key West Extension. A few days later Flagler journeyed the other way to Jacksonville to pick up Mrs. Kenan, Sarah Kenan, Jessie Kenan Wise, and her daughter Louise. A little later they would be joined by William R. Kenan Jr. and Alice Pomroy Kenan. The Flaglers and Kenans embarked on the usual round of daytime receptions and evening dinners. During the unusually warm sunny days the men wore white flannels and the women white dresses.[48]

Mary Lily particularly seems to have enjoyed herself. She attended a card party in the drawing room of the Alcazar and won a prize for her skill at bridge.

On a 1908 expedition down the Keys during the construction of the overseas extension are (*left to right*) Captain Marcotte, Senator James P. Taliaferro, Thomas V. Porter, and Flagler. Flagler took important state and national men with him, and Marcotte came to record the trip. By permission of Flagler College.

She resumed practicing her music, playing the piano to accompany herself. Perhaps she sat at the ornate Steinway in the Grand Parlor. Mrs. Marcotte flattered her by writing, "Her voice is very sweet and well trained." Mary Lily oversaw decorating of the Christmas tree in the Ponce de Leon Rotunda, and on Christmas Day, wearing a red dress, she played the role of Santa, distributing gifts to everyone. Later on in January she would sing a solo at the Wednesday evening prayer service in Memorial Church.[49]

Her husband had more serious work at hand. Near the end of the year Flagler headed out once again for the Key West Extension. He carried General Brooke and Senator Taliaferro with him, along with Captain Marcotte, who would write a story about the "railroad that went to sea" for publication in newspapers across the country. Flagler may have offered his guests one of his favorite observations:

Flagler rode the first train across Long Key Viaduct. His private cars no. 90 and no. 91 are attached, carrying Flagler, his friends, and his railroad executives. By permission of Library of Congress.

"Well, there is one thing for which travelers will bless me when they travel by rail over the keys—they will never be troubled with dust."[50]

The first truly monumental engineering feat of the project, the Long Key Viaduct, was nearing completion. This bridge spanned more than two miles of open water. Flagler and his men would come back again at the end of January to take the first train across the viaduct. Flagler attached a boxcar and his two personal cars, no. 90 and no. 91, to a locomotive for the exhilarating ride. He placed a photographer alongside the concrete arches of the bridge to capture the picture of this first train on its passage. Images like this of a train steaming over the Long Key Viaduct's row of arches would become the signature view of the Overseas Railway.[51]

The railroad had already been completed on the other side of the viaduct so that when the bridge opened, trains could continue a few more miles to Knights Key. On February 5 regular trains began once-a-day service from Miami to Knights Key. Here Flagler had constructed a pier into deep water. Passengers arriving by train would embark on one of Flagler's steamers for a four-hour trip to Key West or a ten-hour voyage to Havana. Flagler's idea of rapid communication with the Caribbean had been achieved—even if he never arrived in Key West. On April 22, 1909, the first train of twenty-seven refrigerator cars filled with Cuban pineapples headed north from Knights Key. This represented the kind of perishable farm produce that Flagler hoped would make the extension a profitable enterprise.

However, connection with Cuba had its downsides. Florida pineapple growers complained that they were now in competition with foreign producers. Also, the tourist trade going to Cuba threatened to siphon off winter visitors who might have stopped in Flagler's Florida resorts—particularly "Spanish" St. Augustine. Flagler admitted as much in a letter to his traffic manager: "While I have but little doubt that the through train service to Knights Key (or Key West) has had and will have an unfavorable influence upon our St. Augustine hotel business, I am still of the opinion that we had better try it one Winter more."[52]

The roadway now reached more than halfway to Key West, but beyond Knights Key lay a seven-mile stretch of blue water to the next island, and that must have daunted even the most confident of engineers.

The Flaglers attended the opening dinner at the Ponce de Leon with Mary Lily's family. Sarah Kenan hosted fifteen teenage girls at a table in the west alcove of the Dining Room next to the Flagler-Kenan family table. After dinner came the traditional concert in the Rotunda, followed by "old time" dancing in the ballroom, concluding with the Virginia reel. A week later the women sponsored a "Leap Year Dance," in which the ladies got to choose their partners for the dances. The ball began in the hallway outside the Grand Parlor, where the invited guests gathered. Anderson, "with true courtly grace," approached Mary Lily, knelt, and presented her with a magnificent bouquet of American Beauty roses. When the doors to the parlor opened and the orchestra struck up a march, Mary Lily went in on the arm of General Brooke, followed by Flagler, who escorted Mrs. Brooke. It was like old times at the Ponce de Leon, except that balls no longer required the much larger space of the Dining Room.[53]

The Alcazar operated under new management during the 1908 season. Joseph Greaves had gone off with most of his staff to direct the Royal Palm in Miami. John Anderson, for twenty years the co-manager of the Ormond Hotel, came up to replace him. Anderson enjoyed major improvements to the Alcazar and its Cordova "annex." During the previous summer the bathrooms had been modernized with new fixtures and bathtubs, while the electrical system underwent an upgrade. Anderson encountered one problem: how to pronounce "Alcazar." He submitted the question to John Carrère in New York. Carrère sent a long, complex reply in which he said the question was clouded by the fact that Alcazar was an Arabic word. He favored the snobby Castilian lisp in pronouncing it "Alcah-thar." However, he noted that Americans "shied" at this articulation, so he admitted that he "vulgarized" the last syllable by saying "-zar," adding, "Perhaps this is a safe middle course for all good Americans to pursue." Carrère concluded his letter: "I envy you the blue sky, the sun and the yellow sand. As I look out of the window it is all gray and slushy."[54]

John Anderson had been one of the original promoters of the automobile races on Ormond Beach, and he had long supported road building in the region around his Ormond Hotel. He brought his enthusiasm for good roads to St. Augustine. Anderson found kindred spirits in Albert Lewis and O. B. Smith. On one occasion they went on an expedition over the road to Jacksonville, locating the bad spots and recommending improvements to the county commissioners. Flagler's *St. Augustine Record* editorialized that the county should spend money building a hard-surfaced road. With the completion of such a road "automobiles will come in droves, bringing tourists and money."[55]

The days when St. Augustine could hope to become the winter Newport had vanished long before. When the *Record* published a special edition that winter, it depicted the town as a typical modern American city with attractions for year-round residents: "Pictured as the winter playground of the wealthy and fashionable, this city has not been portrayed as a resort with accommodations easily within the reach of people of moderate means." James McGuire used more pointed language in private when he wrote to the manager of the Royal Poinciana, telling him that the town was full of "cheap people." Although Mrs. Marcotte often wrote fondly of earlier days at Flagler's hotels, she philosophized that the replacement of formal balls with informal dinners, followed by card playing, gave people greater pleasure.[56]

Just in time for the 1908 season the electric trolley line reached South Beach, making the journey from town more convenient than ever. Visitors could eat lunch at the pavilion and take a stroll on the beach or change into bathing suits for a plunge into the surf. In the evenings the pavilion hosted parties and dances under electric lights. The Burning Spring, a museum of Florida curiosities, and the pen of alligators maintained by George Reddington and Felix Fire proved irresistible attractions for Yankee tourists. The alligators competed with Everett C. Whitney's "alligator farm" west of town at Ponce de Leon Spring. Whitney's advertisements touted his attraction as not just a "pen" but a true "farm," where baby alligators were hatched from eggs and attendants wrestled the 'gators. Reddington and Fire replied that they had "the largest 'gator farm in the world" with the biggest specimens. "No visit to Florida is complete without a visit to this place." Whenever a horse died in town, Reddington and Fire would buy the carcass and toss it into their pen.[57]

Ultimately Whitney would lose the battle and close his farm. This enterprising promoter of St. Augustine attractions died tragically in a house fire in 1912. The lone surviving alligator farm, and the whole seaside pavilion area at South Beach, would succumb to erosion by 1920. The alligator farm moved to its current location farther from the Atlantic shoreline and has remained the most popular privately owned attraction in town ever since. Evidently tourists from the North believe no visit to Florida is complete without getting a good look at an alligator. The iron artesian well pipe that once supplied water to the Burning Spring and

The YMCA Building was Flagler's last major construction project in St. Augustine. This post-card shows the front of the building on Valencia Street. From the collection of the St. Augustine Historical Society Research Library.

the original alligator pens continued to be visible at low tide off the southern end of Anastasia State Park until the early years of the twenty-first century.[58]

In 1908, like a ghost from the past, Franklin W. Smith appeared in town, saying he had come to see if he could sell the Granada Hotel and Villa Zorayda. Three years later in 1911 Smith would die in Boston, where he had spent his last years in retirement. Two years after that Abraham S. Mussallem purchased the Villa Zorayda, which continues to be owned by his family down to the present.[59]

Smith had been one of the original founders of the YMCA back in the days before the Civil War, but St. Augustine had not established a YMCA branch until 1905, when national leaders came to town and organized a chapter. Flagler endorsed the program and offered to construct a building on land west of Ribera Street that had been used as the Ponce de Leon Dairy pasture. For some reason progress in bringing the local YMCA to reality took a long time. Surveyors did not get onto the site until January 1906. The architect of the building, John W. Ingle, arrived only in the fall of that year.[60]

Ingle had a long history with Flagler's enterprises. He had been the supervising architect in St. Augustine for Carrère and Hastings when the hotels and churches were built. He worked on the enlargement of the Ormond Hotel, designed the chapel at the Hotel Royal Poinciana and the Presbyterian Church in Miami, helped plan the Hotel Colonial in Nassau, and designed the Fort Dallas Bank in Miami.[61]

The YMCA building seemed to be nearing completion in January 1907, but it would not be until the summer that young men began using the facilities. At first the Y had been intended only for the employees of the FEC Railway, but membership quickly opened to young men from town.[62]

Finally the building was ready for a formal dedication on January 10, 1908. The portion of well-worn Valencia Street outside the YMCA had been paved with cement to provide a respectable-looking setting. During the afternoon curious visitors walked through the building to inspect the reading room, bowling alley, gymnasium, sleeping rooms, and various other facilities. The Ponce de Leon orchestra played tunes to provide ambiance.

At 7:00 in the evening the Alcazar band came in to play, while in the reception hall visitors sipped punch served by Mrs. Flagler, Mrs. Ingraham, and Mrs. Stout. J. D. Rahner of the FEC Railway presided over the formal ceremonies. James Ingraham told stories of the good works of the YMCA. Then Henry Flagler was called upon to make some remarks. "His appearance called forth a great ovation," wrote Mrs. Marcotte, "one that must have stirred his heart." Flagler began by saying that he felt like the man who went to a pond just to fish but ended up falling in. He recalled that in his Presbyterian youth, ten pins and playing cards were regarded as "inventions of the Devil" but said the YMCA's "more liberal spirit" was showing that amusements could keep young men from going astray. He concluded, "You now have the proper means to enjoy yourselves in the right way. The more you enjoy yourselves the better pleased I will be."[63]

The YMCA building would serve the community over the next seventy years, but in 1982 the aging property was sold to Flagler College, which demolished it and established a tennis complex on the site.

Following the dedication of the Y, the Flaglers departed for Palm Beach. Their two-month stay followed the normal pattern of receptions and dinners, with Flagler heading off for Miami and the Keys from time to time, showing off his work to visitors and watching over developments. Mary Lily had her family to keep her company, while Frederick Townsend Martin, the Andersons, the Brookes, and a few other guests occupied upstairs bedrooms in Whitehall for a couple of weeks at a time. Mary Lily kept up her singing, performing for the Fortnightly Club—a cluster of fashionable ladies—and once sang the offertory hymn at the Royal Poinciana Chapel.[64]

The Flaglers returned to St. Augustine just in time to be on hand for the repeat of the Ponce de Leon Celebration. This year's edition followed the general lines of the previous year, although the historical vignettes offered more action: the Indians ambushed Ponce de León, and his swordsmen had to fight to claim the land; U.S. troops fired their muskets in defense of the fort during the fireworks display, and Indians burned down and "massacred" pioneer settlers on the fort green. Governor Napoleon B. Broward, whose ancestry went far back into Florida's past, made a speech inside the fort urging further development of the state. Powerboats raced on Matanzas Bay, baseball players wielded their bats and balls, and cowmen showed their bravery by taunting a bull into repeated charges. The hotel men credited the show with keeping visitors in town for an extra week.[65]

As St. Augustine celebrated its storied history, another of its landmarks from Spanish times was obliterated. The moat running west from the fort to the San Sebastian River dated back to the early 1700s, when the Spanish built the Cubo Line to defend the city against the British to the North. This strip of land, with its earthen wall and ditch, constituted "The Lines"—in modern times federal government property. Anyone wanting rights to cross it had to obtain permission from the War Department. Flagler had run afoul of this restriction when he tried to extend his rail line during construction of the Hotel Ponce de Leon. For this reason, and the fact that the ditch served no purpose other than to collect refuse and breed mosquitoes, townspeople saw it as a nuisance and had long wished to eliminate it.

In 1907, at the request of Florida's congressmen, the War Department conveyed the property to the School Board of St. Johns County with the stipulation that the land be used only for educational purposes. To fill the moat the city began carting away sand from what was left of the Santo Domingo Redoubt, a strong point in the Cubo Line. Some history-minded people delayed the destruction for a moment, but then the sand went into what was left of the moat. Today a low spot in the earth at the west end of Orange Street is all that remains of the old moat. On top of the newly created land the county built a three-story brick public school that would serve the community for many years and is today the headquarters of the school board. Just to the east of this building the Santo Domingo Redoubt has been reconstructed in facsimile, although it is placed on the wrong side of Orange Street.[66]

After Flagler had taken his annual end-of-the-season inspection tour to the Keys, the Flaglers spent the month of May in Fred Sterry's cottage next to the Homestead Hotel in Hot Springs, Virginia, before returning to Mamaroneck. Flagler wrote to his friend George Ward that he had suffered a "bilious attack" due to his frequent changes of residence, but a month later he and Mary Lily were at Mount Washington and apparently in good health. Dr. Owen Kenan joined them, as did Jessie and Louise Wise and Flagler's old friend H. H. Rogers.[67]

In June 1908 Flagler resigned as a vice president of Standard Oil Company, although he continued to maintain a chair on the board of directors. The New York Times did not consider the move unusual. "He is getting to be a pretty old man and desires to have fewer duties to perform." Flagler had not taken an active role in administration of the company for many years prior to this. A year after his resignation, he would write to John Archbold, the effective leader of Standard, to confirm that he had in fact been reappointed to the board. Flagler added: "If I was reelected as a Director, and the time should ever come when you want an active man in my place, do not for one moment hesitate to make the change. Notwithstanding my long connection and large pecuniary interest in the Company, I feel that my years and absence each year from New York, render me unfit to take any active part in the management of the Company."[68]

The federal government's latest investigation of Standard Oil did turn up one surprise. Under questioning by the Justice Department's Frank B. Kellogg about the origin of the Standard Oil Trust, Rockefeller testified: "I should say that H. M. Flagler and C. T. Dodd [the company lawyer] should have the credit for that. I am sure it was not I. I did not know enough about legal matters for so progressive a step as that was." A year later the leading stockholders of the company were revealed. Rockefeller stood far ahead of any others. The Harkness Estate ranked second and Flagler fifth. At the time Standard securities were rapidly increasing in value as the demand for gasoline increased with the growing popularity of automobiles.[69]

The Flaglers spent October and November at Mamaroneck. Henry wrote to Dr. Shelton to say that the first snow of the winter had fallen, and that both he and Mary Lily were feeling well. Mary Lily (and probably Henry too, although he was not mentioned in the newspaper account) went into the city to attend a huge reception at the Plaza Hotel thrown by Frederick Townsend Martin. He explained that the gathering was an attempt to bring society people and theater people closer together. Ethel Barrymore, America's reigning queen of the stage, shared the spotlight with Mary Lily Flagler, Chauncey Depew, August Belmont, and a glittering crowd.[70]

The Flaglers arrived in St. Augustine in early December but hardly paused before heading south. They stopped over in Titusville, where Flagler talked with a local newspaper reporter, who wrote, "He is in better health than he has been for a number of years without an ache or pain, contented and happy, and the extension work does not seem to worry him in the least." Flagler was probably feeling cheerful because he had firmly decided to carry on with the work building the railroad to Key West. Construction of what would come to be called the "Seven Mile Bridge" was just about ready to commence, and Flagler wanted to be on hand at Knights Key to witness the first concrete being poured into the piers of the bridge.[71]

Returning to St. Augustine, the Flaglers joined the Kenan clan at the Ponce de Leon, where the usual Christmas party in the Rotunda and a Japanese-themed party for young people highlighted their activities. Mary Lily's uncle Thomas S. Kenan and his wife, who lived in Raleigh, came for an unusual visit. The Ponce de Leon opened a little earlier than usual, on January 5. Flagler wrote to Shelton, "The 'Season' opens today with the opening of the Ponce de Leon, the Royal Poinciana and the Ormond Hotel. Business thus far has been very good; more people in the South than have been in former years at this time."[72]

Flagler's attention was naturally focused on the Key West Extension. He and Parrott paid a visit to the Port of Tampa to see how the Atlantic Coast Line (which had absorbed Plant's rail system) handled their rail terminal and docks. Then he put together an expedition to go to Key West. Riding in Flagler's private car was Henry Watterson, the influential editor of the *Louisville Courier-Journal*. Perhaps to keep the noted newspaperman company, Frank Harris of the *Ocala Banner* also came along. Harris returned to sing Flagler's praises for his perseverance in overcoming obstacles to the extension.[73]

The Flaglers went to Palm Beach with the declared intention of living quietly, but they seem to have been as active as in recent years, although their favorite entertainment had come to be sunset receptions for a few friends on the south veranda of Whitehall. They went out to dinner at the hotels occasionally, and Mary Lily socialized with her lady friends, sometimes offering a song for the occasion. Flagler's growing deafness probably encouraged his already retiring lifestyle. When the writer Edwin Lefevre visited for several days while researching his article for *Everybody's Magazine*, he sat on the couch next to Flagler's good ear. "It is none too good at that," he added. Yet Flagler would not be repressed, and he and Mary Lily went off to visit the Long Key Fishing Camp, former workmen's quarters that Flagler had converted into a lodge for sportsmen.[74]

The 1909 season opened in St. Augustine without being chronicled in the pages of the familiar *Tatler* magazine. After seventeen years of celebrating the happenings of winter society, Anna Marcotte's paper simply failed to appear, with no explanation being offered for its demise. Presumably the *Tatler* went the way of the grand formal balls that had once graced Flagler's elegant hotels. Captain and Mrs. Marcotte continued to be prominent figures in the town's social order. The captain remained active in the Grand Army of the Republic, while his wife served as an officer of the Humane Society. For several summers they rented Flagler's cottage at 9 Carrera Street, across from Grace Methodist Church. During the winter season they would occupy a suite in the Cordova so that Flagler could rent the cottage to northern visitors. Then in 1907 the Marcottes purchased the house at 9 Carrera.[75]

The venue of the 1909 Ponce de Leon Celebration moved from the Plaza to the north green of Fort Marion to provide a broader stage for theatricals. On the south side of the field spectators occupied places on the fort's ramparts and earthen glacis, while on the north side the celebration committee erected a temporary reviewing stand to accommodate additional onlookers. The committee had built a box for Flagler in the stand, but he proposed to sit in the bleachers with the rest of the crowd until the marshals forced him to take the place prepared for him.[76]

Ponce de León landed majestically from his caravel, the Indians left their palm-frond teepees to greet him peacefully, and then the players all took their places in line for a parade around the streets of town. The next day the action became more violent, with mounted Indians and Spaniards fighting it out. (Neither the Spanish nor the Indians possessed horses at the landings of Ponce and Menéndez, but historical accuracy counted for little in the drama of the moment.) By the third day the crowd had been treated to flaming log cabins, fireworks, and a colorful array of military units. To the east on the bay powerboats raced, and on the west side of town the local baseball team played games with the teams from Rollins and Stetson.[77]

Flagler wrote to Dr. Anderson to describe the action: "We are in the midst of a Ponce de Leon celebration, which is most creditable to St. Augustine. Would do credit to a City of 100,000 inhabitants." Flagler was most impressed with the marching units from the U.S. Army and visiting militias, saying they made "quite a display."[78]

Flagler had to write because Anderson and his wife were not in St. Augustine for the season, having gone to Santa Barbara, California, to spend the winter. This unusual absence from home went unexplained, but their failure to appear amid town society may have been a sign that Elizabeth Anderson's health had begun to deteriorate. In the spring they traveled to New York City, where she underwent "a very serious operation" that was deemed "entirely successful." After that they withdrew to Chester, Nova Scotia, to their usual summer retreat.[79]

During the Ponce de Leon festivities moving picture cameramen busily recorded the exploits. The Kalem Company of New York turned the footage into a movie called *Ponce de Leon Fete*. A month following the live action, two versions of the movie appeared in Genovar's Opera House and the Plaza Theater. People from town packed the houses to see themselves on the screen and kept up a running commentary from their seats as the drama progressed.[80]

The Kalem Company would soon establish a studio in Jacksonville, as would a number of other early movie production troupes. During the winter months Florida provided a much better location for outdoor shooting than did New York. The first movie filmed in St. Augustine appears to have been a travelogue short entitled *A Trip to St. Augustine*, made in 1906. In March 1910 *A Honeymoon through Snow to Sunshine* debuted in town just a few weeks after the filmmakers appeared to shoot scenes. During succeeding years the Ancient City, with its many quaint settings, would prove an attractive locale for the movie makers.[81]

The town gained a new venue for stage productions with the opening of the

Jefferson Theater in February 1909. The four-story brick building stood on the site of the St. Augustine Transfer Company office at the corner of Cordova Street and Cathedral Place, next to the Ponce de Leon. Abram M. Taylor, the long-time manager of the Alcazar Casino, was the moving force in originating the theater and would become its first manager. Taylor had gone to Jacksonville earlier to see Joe and Will Jefferson when they performed there, and he asked their permission to name the new theater in honor of their father Joseph Jefferson. They were agreeable and would bring their comedy *Henrietta* to the Jefferson in the fall to open the theater's second season. The theater soon began screening silent movies and would remain a popular location for plays and school graduations until its demolition in 1955 to make way for the bank building that presently occupies the site.[82]

The annual meeting of the Florida East Coast Railway Board of Directors brought a significant change in the management of the railroad. Flagler officially stepped down as president of the railroad and turned over the reins to Joseph Parrott. Henceforth all operational department heads would report directly to Parrott, although as chairman of the board, Flagler still maintained immediate contact with William Beardsley, the treasurer. The following year Flagler would similarly reorganize the Florida East Coast Hotel Company, again making Parrott president, with Anderson serving as vice president—and perhaps as Flagler's personal representative. Just as Flagler had already surrendered power in his first career, Standard Oil, to the next generation of managers, he now began relinquishing daily control over his second empire to younger men.[83]

Nevertheless, Flagler remained actively involved in oversight of the Key West Extension. In April and again in May, he went on expeditions down the railroad into the Keys to look over progress on the bridges personally. Even as he traveled, he wrote to Beardsley to say he had been sick and felt "quite weak." On his second trip south Flagler took Mary Lily with him, but the rest of the time she remained behind at the Ponce de Leon. She had one opportunity for a public event when the United Daughters of the Confederacy held a convention in St. Augustine. Mary Lily welcomed the ladies to the Rotunda of the Ponce de Leon and showed them around to the various public areas of the hotel.[84]

When the Flaglers returned to St. Augustine from their final jaunt into the Keys, they read in the newspaper that their good friend Henry H. Rogers had died suddenly of a stroke while at home in New York City. Their social life in the North would be profoundly diminished by his passing. Still, the Flaglers managed to get around. From Mamaroneck they would sometimes drive in their automobile up to Briarcliff Manor overlooking the Hudson River to socialize with other New Yorkers who went there to escape the city. August found the Flaglers back in their usual haunts in the White Mountains. When the weather turned rainy, Flagler and the Mount Washington Hotel's male guests would entertain themselves by repairing to the cellar to watch the stock returns come in on the ticker. Flagler's continued love of motoring around the mountain roads on sunny days testified to his good health. James Ingraham visited and wrote home about plans for an automobile ride and picnic. By October the Flaglers were back in New York. They and a party of friends went to the Plaza Hotel to watch the grand parade of New York's Hudson-Fulton Celebration pass by below their hotel windows.[85]

The Flaglers escaped New York in early December, riding a cold wave south. A little while later William R. Kenan Jr., Alice Pomroy Kenan, Sarah Kenan, Jessie Wise, and her daughter Louise came down to join them; Mary Lily's mother did not come with the party. After the usual Christmas celebration in the Rotunda of the Ponce de Leon and the opening of the hotel, the Kenans returned to their homes in North Carolina. From St. Augustine Flagler and Parrott took at least two trips down the line—once stopping in Ormond to drive an auto on the beach—and then Mary Lily joined them for a venture all the way to Key West. When they departed St. Augustine for Palm Beach they were accompanied only by Flagler's secretary J. C. Salter and Mrs. Janet N. Mitchell, a woman hired to be Mary Lily's friend and companion.[86]

In some respects the Flaglers' season of 1910 in Palm Beach seems to have unfolded according to the usual routine: informal luncheons, the Washington's Birthday Ball in the Royal Poinciana, a moonlight fete in the coconut grove under electric lights, and a trip to Miami for the Dade County agricultural fair, where Mary Lily annually handed out prizes. However, there were no formal dinners or balls at Whitehall, although Mary Lily's frequent teas on the south portico for friends brought visitors to their home.[87]

The Flaglers do not seem to have entertained houseguests at Whitehall during the 1910 season. The Andersons apparently did not come down, and Frederick Townsend Martin stayed in a suite at the Royal Poinciana. Of Mary Lily's relations only Owen Kenan, the hotel's house physician, spent the season in Palm Beach.[88]

The Flaglers' growing isolation from society can be attributed partly to Henry Flagler's increasing physical ailments. Although his mind remained clear and he still stood erect, often displaying hearty vigor, from time to time he would remain at home nursing various illnesses. Beyond this, his hearing continued to worsen and his eyesight began to dim. Dr. Anderson wrote to one of his relatives: "I am sorry to say that Mr. Flagler is not at all well.... His failing sight and hearing make him very blue." An anonymous writer for the *Washington Post* explained that "curtains have been forming over his eyes for several years and now cover them almost completely." Although Flagler still got around by himself, he sometimes failed to distinguish people he encountered. He apologized to a friend, "My sight has become so bad I did not recognize you until I heard you speak." Some photographs of Flagler from this period show him wearing sunglasses, a common way of reducing the glare that cataracts produce in bright light. Given Flagler's pride and retiring sensibility, it is hardly surprising that he should have attempted to minimize the occasions when his deficiencies in sight and hearing would be exposed.[89]

In interviews given many years later Anderson's daughter Clarissa offered another reason for the Flaglers' increasing remoteness from society. Clarissa Anderson Gibbs's testimony is open to doubt since she was just in her mid-teens in those days, and she spent most of her time at boarding school in New York. Yet her father was one of Flagler's closest friends, and she knew all the principal actors in the Flagler circle. Briefly, her narrative ran: Henry Flagler was deeply absorbed in his railroad enterprises and neglected the needs of his wife. In Palm Beach "people would come and visit in the early days, and they dropped off, and they were more or less by themselves with a companion nurse. She had nothing to do, and that's when she started drinking a little bit. . . . You can't blame her— married to an old man who didn't pay any attention to her. He wasn't interested particularly in what she did. Made her go to bed with him at eight o'clock. She was a young woman."[90]

The "companion nurse" she mentioned was Mrs. Janet Mitchell, who accompanied the Flaglers most of the time.

Clarissa Anderson Gibbs recalled visiting Whitehall one day to find Flagler stretched out on a fancy couch in the entrance hall, taking a nap with a handkerchief over his eyes. She thought Mary Lily objected to this, but Flagler did as he pleased. One suggestion as to Mrs. Flagler's attitude toward her role in her husband's life came from Frank Harris of the *Ocala Banner*. He told of a "favorite poem" that Mary Lily gave him titled "The Rights of Women," in which the author holds that the primary "right" of women is to serve their families from birth to death. "Murmur not that women's mission is thy lot," it advised, for women will receive a reward for their devotion in Heaven.[91]

Whether Mary Lily developed a dependence on alcohol, and perhaps even drugs, can be neither proven nor discounted on the basis of existing evidence. Her unexpected death at the relatively young age of fifty is a suggestion that she suffered from substance abuse. Although lacking in a firm foundation, the insinuation about Mary Lily's drinking has become a permanent part of the Flagler story.

Following the end of the tourist season, the Flaglers spent all of April and May and the first week of June in St. Augustine. James McGuire wrote to O. D. Seavey to bring him up to date on affairs in town. Of Flagler, he reported, "Occasionally he has had a poor spell, but otherwise has been feeling fine and in good spirits."

His mood surely would have been buoyed by what he saw on his inspection trips along the Keys. Work was progressing so well that the engineers expected to be able to run the first train to Key West in January 1911.[92]

Before leaving St. Augustine Flagler instructed McGuire to make some major repairs in the Dining Room of the Hotel Ponce de Leon over the summer. Many of the large bulls-eye glass sash windows in the east and west sections of the Dining Room required glass replacement and re-leading. More important, large portions of the paint in the ceiling murals of these east and west wings had scaled off. This had been a chronic problem from the hotel's earliest years because the murals were painted on dry plaster, making it difficult for paint to adhere to the chalky surface. In addition, water had leaked into the ceilings through damage to the roof, causing stains and discoloration.

McGuire hired Herman Schladermundt to do the renovations. Beginning in August McGuire shipped crates of windows, six at a time, to Schladermundt's home studio in Bronxville, New York. Then Schladermundt and an assistant came down to St. Augustine and repainted the murals. McGuire erected the staging to elevate the painters to the level of the murals, and he also furnished the sheets of gold leaf needed to revive the glow of the art. Flagler College, the current custodian of the Hotel Ponce de Leon building, would undertake a major restoration of the murals for the building's hundredth anniversary in 1988.[93]

During the summer McGuire also made major renovations to the ground floor foyer and eighty-five rooms in the Cordova building. This included putting in place thirty-five bathrooms with modern plumbing fixtures. Steam radiators replaced the original gas space heaters. Installation of an elevator made passage from floor to floor more convenient. Making these changes posed something of a challenge. On the Fourth of July McGuire wrote to Flagler, "This work has become very interesting to me and I am giving it all my attention." This investment in the Alcazar "annex" showed that the Alcazar continued to enjoy a large patronage each year.[94]

Another change McGuire made became one of the lasting mementoes of the Flagler era in St. Augustine. Up to this time, except for a few concrete or brick sidewalks, most of the walkways around Flagler's hotels—and in the rest of town—were made of wooden planks. McGuire contracted with Southern Clay Manufacturing Company of Chattanooga, Tennessee, to supply tens of thousands of ceramic clay paving tiles with a double-bulls-eye pattern molded into their surface. McGuire first used these on the sidewalks running along the east and west sides of the Alcazar complex, but later he laid them in various locations around town. McGuire continued to use these tiles until 1914, when Southern Clay stopped making them. Many of the vitrified bricks used in paving streets at this time came from the same company. The names "Reynolds Block," "Robbins," and "Southern Clay Mfg. Co." can still be read on these bricks today, and the City of St. Augustine continues to reuse these "Flagler" paving materials as it resurfaces streets and sidewalks.[95]

By this time traffic had just about worn out Flagler's twenty-year-old asphalt streets. This had happened partly because of the city's chronic lack of money but also because the city lacked the equipment and skilled laborers to do the work. Finally in the fall of 1909 the city purchased a steam roller and an asphalt processing machine mounted on a wheeled wagon. The seller of the equipment sent a man to show local contractors how to use the apparatus so that henceforth the town had the option of using either brick or asphalt on its streets. All the makeshift concrete and brick patches that had been put into the asphalt streets over the years were pulled out and replaced with a uniform coat of asphalt that made the streets as good as new. During this period of street surfacing the last of the old wooden block pavements vanished into oblivion.[96]

The Flaglers do not seem to have ventured to the White Mountains that summer, instead spending all their time at Mamaroneck. Still, Flagler continued going into New York to the Standard Building once or twice a week. One day the hydraulic elevators in the building malfunctioned, and Flagler, one month short of his eightieth birthday, struck out up the stairs for his office. His secretary Warren Smith wrote: "We tried to stop him, even sent a chair to one of the landings, where he could rest, but he persisted in coming the rest of the way immediately by foot, and arrived none the worse for wear apparently, at our 18th floor office!" Such determination would serve him well when disaster struck the Key West Extension in the fall.[97]

As September turned to October Floridians heaved a sigh of relief that the most dangerous period of hurricane season had passed. The Key West Extension had been hit by storms in 1906 and 1909, and it seemed contrary to the law of probability that yet another hurricane could strike—but it did. In St. Augustine the telegraph warned that a storm was heading for the Keys. Then the telegraph line from the extension went dead, and soon hurricane force winds arrived in northern Florida. The damage to St. Augustine proved superficial, but at the lower end of the extension the storm undermined recent work on both the track bed and the massive concrete bridge piers, forcing engineers to go back and build again with even more robust foundations. Completion of the road to Key West would be set back a year.[98]

The Flaglers came back to St. Augustine in the first week of December, but this time only Owen Kenan joined them. As Flagler's health slipped, Kenan's presence became more important than ever. Mary Lily also greatly enjoyed the

Flagler and Delos enjoy a quiet moment on the loggia of the Hotel Ponce de Leon with the Alcazar in the background. By permission of Flagler College.

company of her favorite cousin. They attended the opening dinner at the Hotel Alcazar with a throng of early arriving hotel guests and some invited townspeople, including Dr. and Mrs. Anderson.

For some undisclosed reason the Flaglers did not hold their traditional Christmas Day reception in the Rotunda of the Hotel Ponce de Leon. Instead they went to Palm Beach for the day, taking Dr. Kenan with them. They ate Christmas dinner in the privacy of the dining room in car no. 90, which had been decorated with red ribbons and holly wreaths. Flagler took walks and drives around Palm Beach to see what changes had been made in a year's time, and then, after spending just the day, they returned to St. Augustine.[99]

January went by without the Flaglers attracting public notice. Mary Lily's brother William R. Kenan Jr. stopped for a day while passing through on his way to Palm Beach on business. They did attend the wedding of Elizabeth Anderson's sister Alice at the Episcopal Church and the reception afterward at Markland. A few days later Albert Lewis and his wife gave a dinner for Mary Lily at the Ponce de Leon, but that was the only time her name appeared in the newspaper. Then J. C. Salter came down from New York, and they departed for Palm Beach.[100]

The Flaglers seemed to have enjoyed a fairly active social life in Palm Beach, although placid afternoon teas on Whitehall's south loggia and rides in the resort community's distinctive bicycle–wheel chair hybrid vehicles were the order of the day. Flagler could often be seen riding in one of the bicycle chairs holding a fluffy white dog in his lap. Virginia Sterry, the daughter of Flagler's manager of the Breakers, had decided that Mr. Flagler needed a pet; Delos appeared and became Flagler's constant companion. Flagler wrote a friend, "I don't know what we would do if not for the dog Mr. Sterry sent us. He is a beauty, and no words of mine can portray his good sense."[101]

One day the Flaglers went on a "wheel chair party" to Alligator Joe's menagerie along with Mr. and Mrs. Chauncey Depew and the novelist Thomas Nelson Page and his wife. Another time, on one of his rail expeditions down the Key West Extension, Flagler took his friend Frederick Townsend Martin, his organist Arthur Spalding, Mary Lily and her companion Mrs. Mitchell, and Henry Walters, president of the Atlantic Coast Line.[102]

Ex-senator Depew, a noted raconteur, was credited with a joke involving a young lady who went to a newsstand and asked for a joke book. When told that the stand had no joke books, Depew was said to have suggested: "Give the young woman the latest edition of the Florida East Coast timetable." Many Floridians and visiting northerners must have found the humor strained because traffic on Flagler's railroad had become snarled as tourists wishing to return north competed with trains of cars carrying perishable farm produce.[103]

Flagler was acutely aware that the FEC's single track had become clogged with too many railroad cars, but for the moment there was little he could do about it. In an interview with the *Manufacturers' Record* he explained that he would build a parallel line immediately to double-track the FEC's rails, were it not for the current expenses of building the Key West Extension and the construction of a new line to bring winter vegetables out of the recently drained Everglades region around Lake Okeechobee. "I have never wavered in my faith in the ultimate very great development of the section into which I was putting my millions of dollars," he stated. "I have always looked for great things, but the development now taking place far exceeds my anticipations."

He went on to predict that growth in the South would outpace the development of the rest of the country in the future because of the South's tremendous natural assets. "In the year in which I was born," he said, "the United States had only 24 miles of railroad. Today it has nearly 240,000 miles." Flagler's figures may not have been exact, but he correctly recognized that he had lived through and played a large role in the most revolutionary era in American history.[104]

As growth shifted Florida's center of population down the peninsula, cries went up to move the state's antebellum capital from Tallahassee to a more centrally positioned city. St. Augustine offered itself as the best location for the new capital, pointing out that Flagler's railroad made it accessible from any point up and down the state. St. Augustine's state representative William MacWilliams introduced a bill in the House providing for a popular referendum on moving the capital east of the Suwannee River.

Flagler had already made his views known to James Ingraham a decade earlier when the question had arisen. "My interests in Fla. are so general, I cannot afford to let the impression go abroad that I favor any particular locality," he wrote privately. "I mean to be absolutely neutral in respect of this matter, and it is my desire that those who represent me in Fla. should maintain the same attitude toward the question." As it developed, the MacWilliams bill went nowhere. The entrenched politicians of northern Florida had no interest in losing power to newcomers downstate.[105]

St. Augustine's business and civic leaders decided not to put on a Ponce de Leon Celebration in 1911. The effort had proven too much to be sustained. However, the Southern Championship powerboat races came off in spectacular fashion. The St. Augustine Power Boat Club had taken over the old Capo's Bath House off the seawall and turned it into their headquarters. During the races the town's new brass band played from the club's dock. Thousands of spectators lined the seawall, fort ramparts, and bridge to watch the inboards speed around the water north of the bridge and circle out almost into the inlet. Yachts anchored in Matanzas Bay flew their signal flags in profusion. On the second day of the championship the crowd got a huge bonus: a biplane appeared from the east and circled over the bay before landing on a sandbar off the fort. Then the airplane took off and flew over one of the speedboats, paralleling its course, but the race proved no contest, as the airplane easily outdistanced the boat.[106]

The airplane was the *Shooting Star*, a Curtiss pusher with the engine in the rear, piloted by James J. Ward, one of the pioneers of American aviation. Ward and fellow pilot J. A. McCurdy were barnstorming through Florida trying to make a living but also promoting aircraft manufactured by Glenn Curtiss, who had raced motorcycles at Ormond Beach just a few years earlier. Two days before James Ward's appearance over the speedboat races he and McCurdy had put on an exhibition of stunt flying at South Beach. Spectators were supposed to pay a dollar admission to witness the flights, but few bothered to pay since the beach was public property. The Hotel Ponce de Leon, which had accommodated millionaires and presidents, hosted its first twentieth-century aeronaut.[107]

A decade into the twentieth century some notable deaths altered the established order in St. Augustine. Mrs. Deborah Shedd, the last of the first-day register signers at the Ponce de Leon, failed to return for the 1908 season. She had been coming to town without fail each winter since 1880. In December 1910 she died quietly at home in Stamford, Connecticut.[108]

John Anderson died suddenly in Ormond in February 1911, and his long-time partner in the hotel business, J. D. Price, passed away at his Hotel Bretton Hall in New York City that November. They had pioneered the settlement of Ormond and co-managed the hotel there until their deaths; Anderson had also managed the Mount Washington in New Hampshire, where Flagler spent the summers, and for a season Anderson ran the Alcazar. Today the river highway in Ormond Beach is named John Anderson Drive.[109]

In May William Howland Pell passed away in the Xavier Lopez house on King Street, a Queen Anne cottage that still survives today. Pell was descended from one of the first Pilgrim families of Massachusetts and had been wintering in St. Augustine since the 1850s, save for the years of the Civil War. He had been a robust favorite in society and was famous for taking bevies of young ladies and children for swims at the beach. Pell, who always wore a flower in his lapel, loved birds and all animals. He helped found the Humane Society and, at his own expense, erected a concrete fountain on King Street in 1887 in front of the post office, where horses knew they could reliably find a drink of fresh water. Horses also recognized Pell as the man who always carried cubes of sugar in his pockets. A year after Pell's death, his son Howland presented a bronze bas-relief to the city. Dr. Anderson made a speech as the plaque was unveiled on the back of the water fountain.[110]

In New York City John Carrère spent Sunday, February 12, 1911, visiting friends in preparation for embarking on a ship to join his wife and daughter in Paris. He called on Thomas Hastings in the morning at the home of Hastings's father-in-law in Greenwich, Connecticut, where Hastings was convalescing from typhoid. Carrère dined that evening with his architect friend Donn Barber on 74th Street in Manhattan. After dinner, at ten o'clock at night he took a motor taxi for home, but as the cab passed through the dark intersection with Madison Avenue, an onrushing trolley car crashed broadside into the taxi, demolishing the cab and ejecting Carrère into the street. An ambulance rushed him to Presbyterian Hospital, but he never regained consciousness and died there March 1. Two days later the still unfinished New York Public Library was draped with black crepe and opened its doors for the first time so that mourners could pay their respects to Carrère as his coffin rested in state in the rotunda of the building he helped design.[111]

When the Flaglers returned from Palm Beach they found a "Welcome Home" greeting waiting for them, signed by a host of their friends in St. Augustine. Flagler's secretaries Salter and Warren Smith were with him, while Mary Lily was accompanied by Janet Mitchell. The season concluded with the usual tour of inspection down along the railway line and the annual meetings of the directors of the railroad and hotel companies.[112]

Henry Flagler sits in a straight-back chair on the dock at Knights Key. By permission of Flagler College.

The *St. Augustine Record* published a letter in May from a farmer to Flagler that revealed, perhaps inadvertently, the extent of Flagler's loss of eyesight. The writer's purpose was to promote Florida agriculture, but almost as an aside he wrote: "I am extremely sorry to learn of the failing of your eyesight, and to such an extent that it is a strain to even sign your name." It may have been this letter that prompted Captain Marcotte to propose churches setting aside a day of prayers for Flagler to "thank God and pray that he may be spared in better health to us." Marcotte, who had served as chronicler of Flagler's enterprises over a quarter century, declared that in these modern times many newcomers to Florida simply were not aware of the tremendous changes Flagler had wrought in the region. The captain did not ask that any monuments be erected to Flagler; his works already stood as his monuments. But Marcotte did think a day of prayer would be a fitting acknowledgment of the debt Floridians owed their greatest benefactor.[113]

The Flaglers spent the summer and fall at Satanstoe in Mamaroneck rather than going up to the Mount Washington. Flagler still kept up the habit of visiting his office in the Standard Building every week or so, to have a stenographer send out replies to his mail. He composed a letter to a friend that explained succinctly why he had become so reclusive in recent years: "I too, regret that I am not going to be in the mountains this summer, but my eyesight has become so indistinct and my hearing so impaired, I do not get any satisfaction in being where there is any crowd of people, and for this reason we are spending the summer at our home on Long Island Sound."[114]

The Andersons dropped by in the fall on their way home to St. Augustine from their summer home in Chester, Nova Scotia. Anderson provided the kind of comfortable companionship Flagler desired. Anderson's daughter Clarissa later recalled that the two old men would often sit together for hours without doing much talking, just enjoying each other's company.[115]

When the Flaglers went to St. Augustine at the beginning of December they took with them Warren Smith, Mrs. Mitchell, and Dr. Owen Kenan. The customary trip down the rail line took on heightened meaning since the extension had almost been completed to Key West. Their train took them to the dock at Knights Key, and from there a boat carried them just fourteen miles to Spanish Harbor, where they boarded another train for the remainder of the trip to Key West. Only this short gap, which included the Seven Mile Bridge, remained unfinished.[116]

Just before Christmas Mary Lily's uncle Thomas Kenan died at home in Raleigh, North Carolina. Mary Lily hurried north to attend the funeral, but Flagler remained in St. Augustine. When she returned just before New Year, she was dressed in black mourning clothes. At Christmas in 1911 there was no gathering of the Kenan family in St. Augustine and no celebration around a Christmas tree in the Rotunda.[117]

22

Final Days, 1912–1913

Well, Fred, I guess I'll have no use for Heaven
unless there are railways to be constructed there!
—Henry Flagler to Frederick Martin,
Things I Remember, 1913

Henry Flagler marked his eighty-second birthday very quietly in the Hotel Ponce de Leon. No party or dinner highlighted the day. A few close friends dropped by to wish him well, and a pile of letters and telegrams poured in to express good wishes. The next day he and his party went off to Daytona to spend a few hours. At this point only Dr. Kenan kept him company, and Mary Lily traveled with just Mrs. Mitchell. As Flagler's empire had grown larger, the compass of his world had grown smaller. However, a week later they joined the throng at the opening dinner of the Hotel Ponce de Leon to experience the excitement of another season's arrival. Then they were off for Palm Beach.[1]

January 22 had long been set as the date for the first train to enter Key West, and the president of the United States had agreed to be present for the occasion. Flagler was no great admirer of the new chief executive, once writing, "I wish I could say something encouraging about President Taft, but his attitude towards the business interests of the country is not what most business men had hoped for." The breakup of Standard Oil would occur under Taft, not Roosevelt. Nevertheless, the president's presence in Key West would add the stamp of historical significance to the occasion. Then, just days before the opening ceremonies, Taft backed out, citing concerns with Congress. A lowly assistant secretary of war would represent the president. On the other hand, a large group of congressmen would make the trip to Key West.[2]

The wheels of Flagler's train to Key West started rolling in St. Augustine on January 21 when FEC president Parrott, in private car no. 91, left Union Station

The mayor of Key West guides Henry Flagler through a path of flowers, while Mary Lily Flagler follows behind. From the collection of the St. Augustine Historical Society Research Library.

with private car no. 92 attached. The second car carried Mary Lily's old friend Henry Walters, president of the Atlantic Coast Line. Both presidents brought their ranking lieutenants with them. In Palm Beach the train rendezvoused with Flagler and attached his private car no. 90. Back at Union Station, a little while after the railroad men's train departed, the train carrying Florida governor Albert Gilchrist passed through. Then the train of the congressional delegation pulled into the station. Mayor DeWitt Webb, along with past mayors including Dr. Anderson, welcomed the congressmen to St. Augustine and quickly bade them farewell on their journey south.[3]

After stopping over for the night in Miami, the caravan of what would eventually reach seven trains set off for Key West. Flagler's train arrived at 10:43 in the morning. Bleachers had been built to hold some of the crowd. A brass band played, while steam whistles of all sorts blasted from all parts of the town. The cigar factories had closed for the day; many in the crowd spoke excitedly in Spanish. Lines of state militia and army coastal artillery soldiers formed ranks to hold back the mob. Mayor J. N. Fogerty kept a firm grip on Flagler's arm to steady him as they waded through an ankle deep carpet of flowers. Mary Lily followed behind, still dressed in mourning black and carrying a huge bouquet of flowers that almost swallowed her up. School children waving American flags sang. "I can hear the children," Flagler said, "but I cannot see them."[4]

At the welcoming ceremony Parrott made one of the several speeches and presented Flagler with a mahogany case containing a solid gold replica of a telegram congratulating him upon the completion of the railroad. It came as a gift from the employees of the FEC Railway. For the rest of the day the city of Key West showed off its best assets to the visiting dignitaries. Later in the afternoon the first regularly scheduled "New York to Havana Special" arrived and delivered its passengers to the docks, where they boarded a ship for Cuba.

That evening, before a crowd of three hundred, Flagler was induced to make a few remarks. His short speech would turn out to be his valedictory. He began:

> Perhaps in justice to myself I ought to say that speaking in public is not my best hold, but thank God, I came to the conclusion that you would all recognize that fact before I sat down.
>
> Someone has very properly, very wisely, I think, divided life into two parts—one climbing up the front stairs of youth—the other creeping down the back stairs of old age. Well now, I have crept pretty nearly to the bottom so far as years are concerned, but I thank God that from the summit I can look back over twenty-five or six years since I became interested in Florida with intense satisfaction at the results that have followed my pioneer work.

He concluded by saying he hoped to live ten more years to watch Key West grow.[5]

The citizens of St. Augustine got a chance to share in the excitement of the moment some weeks later when a newsreel brought moving pictures of the Key West celebration home to the Orpheum Theater on the Plaza. When the camera showed a closeup of Flagler, the audience broke out into applause. A month later, when Flagler returned to St. Augustine, he took the opportunity to convey his thanks in person to the FEC employees who had given him the golden telegram gift, and the Record published a letter from him expressing his gratitude in a more formal way.[6]

Prior to coming up from Palm Beach, Flagler took the precaution of writing to James McGuire to inquire about the width of the door in the Ponce de Leon's portcullis. "When I go up to St. Augustine, I want to bring my wheel chair, and I am wondering whether the opening (gate) in the portcullis is wide enough to admit its passage." The allusion to "my wheel chair" indicates that by this time Flagler sometimes found this an easier way of getting around than walking, and the fact that he anticipated a possible difficulty shows that his mind remained attentive to details. He indicated to McGuire that the wheelchair was thirty-four and a half inches wide. The gate measures thirty-eight inches.[7]

On May 19 the Flaglers departed St. Augustine for New York City. Flagler had with him Warren Smith and Dr. Kenan as well as his Palm Beach friend Dr. Ward. Mary Lily had only Mrs. Mitchell. Later that summer while at Satanstoe, Flagler dictated a letter to Smith intended for Mrs. George W. Gibbs, an old St. Augustine friend of the family. "My health is about as usual," he reassured her. "I still belong to the 'stay-at-homes,' and am living a very placid, uneventful life."[8]

Frederick Townsend Martin would write in his memoirs about these days: "One Sunday last Autumn I spent an interesting day with Mr. Flagler, Mr. Archbold, and Mr. John Rockefeller." He did not say anything else about that "interesting day," but it may have been a rare moment when the old friends Flagler and Rockefeller got together. For many years they had been going their separate ways, busying themselves with matters that had nothing to do with Standard Oil. This may have been the last time they saw each other.[9]

In mid-September Flagler received a telegram from Dr. Anderson bearing some not unexpected news: Elizabeth Anderson had died at the Andersons' summer home in Chester, Nova Scotia. She had been ill for several years and in serious decline all through the summer. Flagler shared his thoughts with James McGuire in a letter: "Mrs. Anderson was a very great sufferer and death must have been a relief to her, as also the family." Anderson shipped her remains to St. Augustine, where an Episcopal service was conducted at the graveside in Evergreen Cemetery.[10]

Anderson did not accompany his wife's body to Florida and delayed setting out for home until November. On his way he stopped by to visit the Flaglers at Mamaroneck, finding Flagler "looking quite well and in good spirits." Anderson arrived in St. Augustine just a few days before the Flaglers, and in early December they all set off on a trip to Key West. The party returned just in time for the opening dinner at the Hotel Alcazar. Flagler's long-time hotel housekeeper Annie McKay joined them, along with a familiar crowd of winter visitors and invited townspeople. Anderson, soon joined by his children, would spend the season at the Alcazar rather than opening his Markland home.[11]

Flagler's season of good health ended when he came down with a severe case of influenza, made worse by what Dr. Kenan would later describe simply as "complications." Mary Lily went to bed with the flu as well. The Flaglers had planned on going to Wilmington for the marriage of Sarah Kenan to Graham Kenan, brother of Dr. Owen Kenan, but illnesses prevented the trip. Mary Lily's other sister Jessie Wise went to St. Augustine in January to offer what comfort she could. As late as the end of January, Flagler remained convalescent. Anderson wrote to tell his daughter Clarissa, "I have been sitting with Mr. Flagler all the morning." Word of his illness did not leak to the newspapers for weeks, and then a story went out that Flagler was critically ill and not expected to recover. The

Carriages entered the Union Station grounds by one entrance, lined up next to the covered platform to pick up passengers, and departed from the other end of the driveway. The smokestack in the background belongs to the electric company. Postcard in author's collection.

St. Augustine Record waited until late February, when Flagler had gotten better, to respond to the story and brand it false, but clearly Flagler had been in serious condition.[12]

In late December, in the midst of the Flaglers' sickness, President Taft belatedly made his visit to Key West while on his way to inspect the Panama Canal. Taft had just finished third in the 1912 presidential race behind Woodrow Wilson and Teddy Roosevelt and must have been relieved to get out of Washington for a while. On his return trip he stopped in St. Augustine. Mayor DeWitt Webb greeted the president at Union Station, and then, in a sign of modern times, the president and his entourage climbed into automobiles for a drive around town. Taft rode in C. F. Hamblin's Pierce-Arrow, the first lady occupied an Oldsmobile, and the rest of the assembly followed in an array of borrowed, flag-draped vehicles, including Flagler's White steamer. After a tour that included a trip down St. George Street and around the Plaza, the motorcade arrived at the Alcazar. Henry and Mary Lily Flagler managed a brief appearance to greet the president, and Taft was overheard to remark, "I regard the Panama Canal and your railroad as two of the greatest achievements of these times."

Manager William McAuliffe escorted the president to breakfast. Because of his illness Flagler took no further part in affairs. After breakfast Parrott took the president's party on a tour of the not-yet-opened Hotel Ponce de Leon. Then they embarked in the auto cavalcade again for a sightseeing trip down to St.

Francis Barracks, up the bay front past the fort, out to Garnett's orange grove, and back to Union Station. The president declared himself very pleased with his whirlwind visit.[13]

The Hotel Ponce de Leon began the season without the customary pomp and festivities because on the eve of its opening Annie McKay died in her apartment in the hotel. She had been in excellent health until about the time the Flaglers became ill, and then she failed rapidly. Since she was well known both to the winter guests of the hotel and to townspeople, her death threw a pall over what ordinarily would have been a happy occasion. The *St. Augustine Record* paid tribute to her, saying she was "possessed of keen intellect, sound judgment, and was remarkable for her executive ability." Following a high mass at the cathedral Joseph McDonald took her remains to Miami with him in Flagler's private car. At the funeral many employees, both white and black, filled the church to show their respect. She was buried in the McDonald family plot since she had no family of her own, save the people of the Flagler hotel system.[14]

Flagler did not feel well enough to leave for Palm Beach until nearly the middle of February, a month later than his usual timetable, but when he arrived at Whitehall he told friends he was feeling fine. The next day he tended to business in his office in the morning, took a stroll around his hotels, and went for an automobile ride in the afternoon. A few days later he and Chauncey Depew and some friends went to tea under the coconut palms, and he and Mary Lily even made an appearance among the crowd at the extravagant Washington's Birthday Ball in the Royal Poinciana.[15]

At the same time in San Juan, Puerto Rico, high-ranking prelates of the Roman Catholic Church and thousands of Puerto Ricans gathered in the town's central square to observe the solemn procession and reburial of the remains of Juan Ponce de León from a small church into a magnificent crypt inside the cathedral. The bishops performed a requiem mass over the ashes of the man who had discovered Florida and entered mythology as the seeker of the Fountain of Youth.

The city fathers of St. Augustine had once hoped for an international exposition to celebrate the four-hundredth anniversary of the discovery of Florida, similar to the one that had just taken place at Jamestown in 1906. However, evidently Spanish Catholic settlers did not arouse as much interest in America as did Protestant English pioneers, and nothing came of requests for financing from either the national or state government. In fact, as late as January 1913 it seemed that even the usual Ponce de Leon Celebration would not be held that year. But failing to note Ponce's arrival in any significant way would have been a travesty, so the customary landing, parades, and pageantry came off as in some past seasons.[16]

In recent years Flagler's thoughts had increasingly turned toward death. For a man who longed for permanence, death was something to be resisted. He once told his friend and minister George Ward, "I am going to live to be 100 years old. I have a purpose and work to do and I cannot go sooner." Ward replied that no one could control the allotted days of his life. Although Flagler did not respond, Ward felt he silently rejected that belief.[17]

Still, Flagler began settling his thoughts about death. He read the Bible and underlined passages containing God's promises of everlasting life. A few years earlier he had purchased a pineapple field in West Palm Beach and turned it into Woodlawn Cemetery, and at the gate he placed the words: "That which is so universal as Death must be a blessing." The writer Lefevre told of standing on the south lawn of Whitehall with Flagler and the "old, old man" saying, "Sometimes, at the close of the day, when I am fortunate enough to be alone, I come here. I look at the water and at the trees yonder and at the sunset. I wonder if there is anything in the other world so beautiful as this." Flagler's friend Frederick T. Martin recalled sharing a sunset view over Lake Worth with him, when Flagler commented, "Well, Fred, I guess I'll have no use for Heaven unless there are railways to be constructed there!"[18]

On March 5 a dispatch came through to the *St. Augustine Record* office saying Flagler had taken a fall in his home at Palm Beach and broken his hip. Officials in the FEC office denied the story, saying they would have been informed immediately had anything happened to Mr. Flagler. The next day, however, Owen Kenan confirmed that on March 4 Flagler had slipped on a rug covering a marble floor and had fallen heavily, bruising his hip. He added that Flagler was "a man of remarkable vitality" and that were it not for his advanced age the fall would have been nothing. Flagler had been alone at the time of the fall; servants found him and carried him to his room. Later reports said he fell on marble stairs.[19]

A New York joint specialist who happened to be vacationing in Palm Beach examined Flagler and diagnosed a hip fracture that would heal with rest. He stabilized Flagler's body with sand bags and left him in bed. Dr. Anderson, Parrott, and a few other close friends and business associates came in to visit. James Ingraham was allowed a long visit because he brought news from the Flagler empire. He found Flagler stretched out in bed "pale and suffering, but thinking of the people and things of the East Coast of Florida." Ingraham showed Flagler some photos taken on the new line being run into Okeechobee. "Well, I hope it will be a great success. I want to see it very much, that lake and that great country, but I am afraid I never will, but I hope to do so."[20]

A little more than two weeks after the fall J. C. Salter made a statement to the press saying an "erroneous impression of Mr. Flagler's condition has gone out." He explained that Flagler could move the injured leg, that he felt well, and that he hoped to get into a wheelchair in a few days. He added that Flagler felt frustrated at his confinement. "I left him sitting up, smoking a cigar, and discussing his day's business precisely as he always has done." A few days later Flagler had improved to the point that a stretcher was brought in and he was wheeled to Nautilus Cottage, which overlooked the beach just to the north of the Breakers, where he could enjoy the cool ocean breezes. Nautilus Cottage stood next to The Reef, the cottage where Joseph Jefferson had died a few years earlier.[21]

Perhaps because of the stress of the move, Flagler suffered a relapse on April 1, and Anderson, Parrott, Ingraham, Beckwith, and Salter all rushed to Palm Beach to be at his side. According to statements given many years later by Clarissa Anderson Gibbs, Mary Lily was beside herself at this point—perhaps understandably from anxiety and exhaustion, although Gibbs attributed her state to alcohol and drugs. At first Mary Lily refused to allow anyone into Flagler's bedroom, according to Gibbs, but eventually the men did go in.[22]

Although periodic newspaper accounts reported that he was "holding his own," his death seemed imminent. Anderson wrote to his daughter, "Mr. Flagler still lingers. He may do so for some time longer but no one has any hope that he will recover. . . . I am feeling very low in my mind all the time on account of Mr. Flagler. He has been a good friend to me—the best—and now he is going. He has always dreaded going but now he does not know it for his mind wanders. Most of the time he thinks he is in a rail-road car."[23]

Seemingly through sheer willpower Flagler held on. Near the end of April Anderson sent Clarissa the latest report: "Mr. Ingraham called this morning—but had no news. Mr. Flagler remains about the same—He may live months in this pitiable condition. It is very sad and very hard for Mrs. Flagler." The Standard Oil and Florida East Coast systems had always used coded messages for anything of importance sent over the telegraph, and the codebook was used when posting updates on Flagler's condition. His cipher was "suspenders."[24]

At last it became obvious that Flagler was failing. Parrott issued a press release admitting that his death was expected soon. Learning the news, Harry Harkness Flagler telegraphed Palm Beach offering to come down if he was wanted. When Harry and Anne arrived in Palm Beach, Harry found that he was not allowed to go into the Nautilus. He later wrote, "I was not allowed to do so while there was a chance of his recognizing me. He was kept constantly under drugs and was practically in a coma the three or four days after my arrival until his death."[25]

Flagler died at ten in the morning on May 20, 1913. Rockefeller telegraphed Mary Lily that day, saying, "I have just learned with great sorrow of the death of Mr. Flagler, my lifelong business associate and friend." He went on to praise Flagler for his loyalty and his service to the company. An undertaker was brought up from Miami to prepare the body, and the next day Dr. Ward presided over a

Mourners lined King Street as Flagler's casket was carried out through the gate of the Hotel Ponce de Leon. From the collection of the St. Augustine Historical Society Research Library.

memorial service in the Royal Poinciana Chapel. Then James Ingraham led the family to a special train that carried Flagler's remains and a group of those wishing to attend the funeral to St. Augustine. At Mary Lily's request, the train was not draped in black. When it arrived in St. Augustine, a huge crowd met the train at Union Station.[26]

That afternoon Flagler's open casket rested in state in the center of the Rotunda of the Ponce de Leon while thousands of townspeople filed in through the front door and out through the carriage entrance. FEC employees acted as ushers. Flagler's dog Delos was seen in a corridor of the hotel, and Mary Lily would keep him as her lifetime companion.[27]

The next afternoon, May 23, at three in the afternoon, the portcullis of the Ponce de Leon was raised so that the coffin could be carried from the hotel. A long train of sixteen carriages followed Flagler's hearse. Up and down the East Coast of Florida from Key West to Jacksonville all trains on the railway stopped for ten minutes, bells tolled, and business and government offices closed their doors. "The gloom inspired by the loss of Florida's foremost citizen," reported the *St. Augustine Record*, "was intensified by gathering clouds and the splashing of heavy raindrops, as if nature had joined in the funeral mourning and was shedding tears. The silent crowds, with heads bared, heeded not the falling rain, but followed the hearse as it moved slowly away on King Street, thence along Sevilla Street to Memorial Presbyterian Church."[28]

Admission to the church was by card only, but even then the aisles were packed with standing people. A mound of flowers filled the Flagler family pew. As Flagler had requested, the service proceeded along simple, traditional lines. A quartet sang three of his favorite hymns: "Lead Kindly Light," "Abide with Me," and "Nearer My God to Thee." The church's former pastor John MacGonigle, who had moved to Miami, read the scripture; George Ward of the Royal Poinciana Chapel offered a prayer; and Alfred Badger, Memorial Church's current pastor, gave the benediction. Then the church emptied except for the immediate family, and in a brief ceremony Flagler's remains were placed in the mausoleum alongside those of his first wife Mary and daughter Jennie Louise and her baby.[29]

The leading men of Standard Oil sent flowers but were conspicuous by their absence, although nothing was said publicly of this at the time. Perhaps it was simply too far to come from New York. Most of the other principal figures from Flagler's life were there, except for his half sister Carrie. His sister-in-law Julia Harkness York and her husband Barney attended, along with cousins Horace and Thorne Flagler. All the Kenans, including Mary Lily's invalid mother, joined the mourners. The Florida East Coast Railway and Hotel Company executives turned out, as did Flagler's longest-lived employee, William Fremd. John Sewell, who had carved Miami's streets out of limestone rock years earlier, was present. Friends from Flagler's past such as Dr. George Shelton, Henry Walters of the Atlantic Coast Line, and Rev. Peyton Hoge, who had performed the marriage ceremony for Henry and Mary Lily, were there.[30]

Clarissa Anderson was at school in New York, but her father later told her that the atmosphere in the church had been somewhat strained, as the Flaglers sat on one side and the Kenans on the other, and they had little to do with one another. Harry and Anne had stayed with Dr. Anderson at Markland at the time of the funeral, while the Kenans occupied rooms in the Ponce de Leon. Two days after the service the Kenans departed in Flagler's private car, accompanied by Flagler's two secretaries, Salter and Smith; his financial manager William Beardsley; and Leland Sterry, son of the Breakers manager Fred Sterry. Harry and Anne Flagler took a different train the same day for the return trip to New York.[31]

The contents of Flagler's will were made public almost immediately. The people of St. Augustine were relieved to learn that the FEC Railway and Hotel companies were placed in a trust to be administered by William R. Kenan Jr., Beardsley, and Parrott, with Parrott remaining as president of both companies. Flagler clearly wanted to make sure his Florida railroad projects were seen through to completion. St. Augustinians had feared that the FEC Railway would be swallowed up by Henry Walters's Atlantic Coast Line, as had happened to Henry Plant's system. This might have meant the end of the FEC headquarters and workshops in St. Augustine.

The will did not give Harry Flagler any part in the continuing business affairs of the Flagler system. Clearly Henry Flagler had seen young William R. Kenan Jr. as the heir to his Florida empire. However, Harry was hardly left out completely. Flagler left him five thousand shares of Standard Oil stock, and another eight thousand shares of Standard stock were divided equally among Harry's three daughters; the estranged son had also already received generous gifts from his father years earlier. Still, the bulk of Flagler's estate would go to Mary Lily after the trust expired in five years.[32]

On Christmas Day 1915 Abbie M. Brooks, Sylvia Sunshine, passed away in the home of Charles Hopkins on Water Street, just a few paces away from the old Spanish castillo, the history of which she had researched in the Seville archives. She died in near anonymity, and her body was buried in an unmarked grave in Evergreen Cemetery. She left behind a diary in which she was found to have written, "I was a child of strong impulses with a restless disposition. I had no one to check my turbulent inclinations and guide my erring steps, until I made an unfortunate step which I cannot remove with tears of blood."

Although her *Petals Plucked from Sunny Climes* remained a well-known book and was reprinted in 1976, its author continued to be an enigma. Then in the 1980s amateur historians Dick and Yvonne Punnett stumbled upon the trail of Abbie Brooks and, through arduous research aided by some good luck, managed to unravel the mystery of Sylvia Sunshine. Her real name turned out to be Abbie Lindley, and she had been born in Meadville, Pennsylvania, in 1830 to a strict Presbyterian family. In 1856 she bore an illegitimate child who was given the name Hortense and adopted by a family who took in foundlings and orphans. Rejected by her own family, Abbie went out into the world to make a living as a tutor, book seller, and writer, a profession that eventually took her to St. Augustine. Once her identity was known, the Punnetts were able to track down the descendents of Abbie Lindley, and in 2000 they gathered in Evergreen Cemetery to place a stone marker in her memory, although the exact spot of her final resting place remains unknown.[33]

"St. Augustine has fallen into a gentle and wholly delightful shabbiness since the passing of its climax of prosperity," observed a popular guidebook in the years following Henry Flagler's death. Although the town continued to grow and take on more modern aspects, its golden aura as the most fashionable and engaging resort city in the South had faded long before. The writer Lefevre noted, "In all the hotels you see more gray heads than black, or brown, or blonde. They tell you, on the slightest provocation, how many years they have been coming down here for the winter." One aging gentleman who found the atmosphere of St. Augustine congenial was William Dean Howells, the elder laureate of American letters. He spent three winters in town beginning in 1915. He had known Constance Fenimore Woolson and had published some of her writing in the *Atlantic* many years earlier when he edited that magazine—and so had known St. Augustine, at least by reputation, for a long time. His wife Elinor, who passed away in 1910, had been the sister of the architect William R. Mead, Thomas Hastings's friend.[34]

Howells judged Carrère and Hastings's grand hotels "a little archaic. . . . People now do not want that series of drawing and dining rooms which open from the inner patio of the Ponce de Leon; and if they did, they would not have the form fitly to inhabit them; their short skirts and their lounge coats are not for such gracious interiors, but rather for the golf links." He found evidence of modernity in the movie companies that set up their cameras and acted out their pantomimes at various scenic points around town. "No week passed without the encounter of these genial fellow-creatures dismounting from motors at this picturesque point or that, or delaying in them to darken an eye, or redden a lip or cheek, or pull a bodice into shape, before alighting to take part in the drama."[35]

One of these companies, Vitagraph, approached James McGuire in the spring of 1914 with a request to shoot a movie inside the Hotel Ponce de Leon. McGuire sent the proposal to Beardsley in the New York office, and evidently he turned down the request. Vitagraph was making a movie version of Archibald Clavering Gunter's *A Florida Enchantment*, and when the film debuted later that year, with its unlikely tale of the Hotel Ponce de Leon's house doctor and his lady love, the authentic hotel scenes were limited to exterior shots, while the hotel interiors were filmed indoors in Brooklyn before a nondescript painted backdrop.[36]

The following year, when James McGuire's health began to fail, he would retire from the East Coast Hotel Company, which he had served for thirty years. The old bachelor went to Brooklyn to live with his sister and passed away there in 1918. Later that year his long-time partner Joseph A. McDonald died at his home in Miami. After completing Flagler's Hotel Royal Palm, McDonald had gone into business for himself. Always a better politician than his gruff partner McGuire, he served for three years on the first elected town council and today is honored as one of the founding fathers of the city of Miami.[37]

The old New York railroad man and U.S. senator Chauncey Depew made St. Augustine his regular winter home from 1915 onward. Dr. DeWitt Webb persuaded him to become president of the St. Augustine Historical Society in 1919, a mostly honorary position for him but one that he took seriously. He found

James Ingraham spoke at the 1916 dedication of the statue of Henry Flagler at Union Station. Mary Lily had commissioned the statue years earlier, but Flagler refused to have it displayed during his lifetime. By permission of P. K. Yonge Library, University of Florida.

several "treasures" of various and sundry sorts—none related to Florida—to add to the society's museum curiosities. In town he assumed his usual role as dispenser of humorous aphorisms. He would pass away in New York City in 1928.[38]

During February and March 1913, when Henry Flagler was confined to bed after his fall, John D. Rockefeller spent a month at the Hotel Clarendon in Seabreeze, Florida, a little more than two hours away from Palm Beach. We do not know if he visited Flagler; at the time Rockefeller was in Florida the seriousness of Flagler's fall was being downplayed. Rockefeller had discovered that Florida's weather and golf courses made an irresistible combination. He would spend the next winter also in Seabreeze, although he went to Ormond to play the course there. The Ormond Hotel's golf pro George S. Merritt and James McGuire had designed and installed an eighteen-hole course in 1911 and 1912. It incorporated modern Bermuda grass and an irrigation system to keep it green. Enticed by this playing surface, Rockefeller went to the Hotel Ormond in the next two years and in 1917 purchased a home called "The Casements" across the street from the hotel. Rockefeller would spend each succeeding winter there, and he died in the house in 1937. Like Flagler, he had vowed to live to one hundred, but he missed the mark by a little over two years.[39]

Following her husband's death, Mary Lily Flagler lived in a New York City townhouse near her old friends the Pembroke Joneses. She would return to Palm Beach for the winters but did not open up Whitehall until the 1916 season. Then in 1917 she returned to Whitehall with a new husband, Robert Worth Bingham. He was an old college friend of her brother William R. Kenan Jr., someone whom she had seen socially in the early 1890s before Bingham married. He had gone on to be mayor of Louisville, Kentucky, and had become a judge. Mary Lily and Judge Bingham met again after Henry Flagler's death, and since Bingham's wife had also died, both were single. They married in the Joneses' New York townhouse on November 15, 1916. The new couple spent the winter season of 1917 at Whitehall, where Mary Lily entertained her brother, her two sisters, and her cousin Owen Kenan—just as in days of old, save for the huge fact of Henry Flagler's absence and Robert Bingham's presence. But Mary Lily's health began to deteriorate that summer, and she died on July 27, 1917. Just days before her death she had added a codicil to her will giving her husband five million dollars. This led to a nasty controversy between the Binghams and Kenans over the circumstances of Mary Lily's passing, including an unsubstantiated charge that Bingham had deliberately hastened her death.[40]

Mary Lily's will divided most of the Flagler estate equally among her siblings William, Jessie, and Sarah. Mary Lily's young niece Louise Wise, Jessie's daughter, also received a large inheritance. Years earlier she had entertained her elders by swimming underwater at the pools in St. Augustine, Palm Beach, and Bretton Woods. As the sole offspring of the Kenan family's current generation, she seemed to represent the future. The financial securities she inherited were held in a trust fund, from which she obtained a large income each year. Louise was also given Mary Lily's jewels, including the long strand of pearls Flagler had given her before their marriage. In addition, she inherited Mary Lily's properties: Satanstoe, Kirkside, and Whitehall. Almost immediately Louise sold Satanstoe to silent film producer D. W. Griffith, who shot some movie scenes in the old Flagler residence. Since she preferred living in St. Augustine to Palm Beach, in 1924 she also sold Whitehall.

Louise proved unlucky in her marriages. On May 3, 1917, she married Lawrence Lewis in her mother's home in Wilmington, surrounded by her Kenan aunts and Uncle William. From this marriage came two children, Lawrence Lewis Jr. and Mary Lily "Mollie" Lewis. Then, two years following her divorce in 1925, Louise married Hugh Lewis. Hugh was the son of Albert Lewis, and he had grown up during the winters at their home on Valencia Street behind the Hotel Ponce de Leon. Young Louise and Hugh had sometimes played together in children's groups during St. Augustine's social season. This marriage also ended in divorce, and in 1931 she married Frederick Francis, an outstanding athlete in St. Augustine who had formerly served as the tennis professional at the Alcazar.

Louise Wise Francis died at the age of forty-one, leaving her inheritance to her two teenage children.[41]

Henry Flagler's older half sister Carrie—Ann Caroline—had been one of the people closest to him in his youth. She never married and lived the rest of her life in an apartment in New York City. When she passed away in 1917 she left her estate to the nephew she had helped to raise, Harry Harkness Flagler. The legacy amounted to almost two million dollars in Standard Oil stock.[42]

Harry Harkness Flagler, after his break with his father, remained in New York City with his wife Anne. A writer for the *Wall Street Journal* said of him: "He resembles his father in that he is quiet, reserved and even diffident, taking very few people into his confidence and living very much by himself." Harry became a patron of music, serving as a major financial supporter and eventually president of the New York Symphony Orchestra, the younger rival to the New York Philharmonic Orchestra. When the two symphonies merged in 1921, Harry soon became president of the unified society and remained one of the musical society's major financial underwriters. He was known for his business acumen, which naturally was presumed to have come from his father. However, in 1934, when the Great Depression put a stress on all charities, Harry was forced to resign as president due to a break in his health.[43]

Anne Flagler died of heart failure near the end of 1939, and Harry passed away in 1952 at the age of eighty-two. They left behind three daughters: Mary, who would endow the Mary Flagler Cary Music Collection at the Morgan Library in New York; Elizabeth Flagler Harris, who married a Philadelphia aviation executive; and Jean Flagler Matthews. As a middle-aged woman Jean Flagler Matthews would come to appreciate the grandfather she never knew, and she purchased Whitehall, which had been turned into a hotel, in order to restore it as today's Henry Morrison Flagler Museum.[44]

Captain and Mrs. Marcotte, who had played such conspicuous public roles during the Flagler era in St. Augustine, lived comparatively quiet lives after Flagler's death. Captain Marcotte passed away on January 21, 1923, at the age of eighty-three, in his home at 9 Carrera Street. The man who had fought to save the Union and then had served the veterans in Grand Army of the Republic was buried in Arlington National Cemetery. After her husband's death Anna Marcotte went to New York City to live with her daughter. During her years in St. Augustine she had celebrated the luxury of high society, scolded malefactors for their bad manners, worked to beautify the Plaza, helped William Howland Pell protect defenseless animals, and supported Flagler Hospital. She would live to the great age of ninety-three, passing away in New York in the fall of 1935. Their home on Carrera Street survives as Thompson Hall, part of the campus of Flagler College.[45]

Dr. Anderson continued to play a role as one of St. Augustine's leading citizens, although he now assumed the part of elder statesman as a younger generation of boosters rose to the fore. Anderson's primary charges continued to be Flagler Hospital and Memorial Church, where he maintained his position as chairman on both boards. He lived the quiet life of an elderly man, having a driver take him for rides in his Hupmobile, playing pool with "the boys" in the little cottage behind Markland, and in the evenings reading and playing cards with Mary Smethurst, the sister of his deceased wife.

He turned his attention to adding monuments to adorn St. Augustine's public places and enhance appreciation of its historical traditions. He helped finance and oversaw construction of a concrete wall around two sides of the Huguenot Cemetery. Armistice Day, November 11, 1921, had been selected by President Warren G. Harding for interment of the Unknown Soldier in a marble tomb at Arlington National Cemetery, and Anderson saw to it that St. Augustine marked the day with its own noteworthy memorial service. He hired local sculptor Adrian Pillars to design a commemorative base for a flagpole that would stand in a circular park near the east end of the Plaza. The ornate base of the flagpole contained relief images of Ponce de León, Menéndez, Andrew Jackson, and Henry M. Flagler.

In his speech at the unveiling, Anderson declared of Flagler: "I am glad an opportunity has occurred to write his name upon enduring bronze in the center of the city for which he did so much. . . . His conferees at 26 Broadway told him he was building a road which led nowhere; it ran through sand and ended in a swamp, and now some of them play golf in the garden which he made in the desert. . . . He advanced the development of the East Coast a hundred years or more. His courage—his tenacity—his foresight—his will to overcome difficulties made him a Prince among men, a super-man. . . . All hail to the name of Henry M. Flagler. His work is imperishable and its value to the nation inestimable."[46]

Two years later Anderson appeared again at an Armistice Day ceremony at the east side of the Plaza to speak at the unveiling of a statue of Juan Ponce de León. Anderson had obtained permission from President Harding to have a copy made of the statue that stands in San Juan near the explorer's last resting place.

During the 1920s exuberant Americans were erecting skyscrapers in their cities to rejoice in the prosperity of the day. St. Augustinians raised the eight-story First National Bank Building next to the cathedral in a monument to modern enthusiasm, but the town also decided to build a bridge of monumental scale to replace the old wooden bridge that had spanned Matanzas Bay since the 1890s. When Anderson saw the grand proportions of the bridge's design, he made a gift to the people of St. Augustine in the form of two monumental lions sculpted in Carrara marble to stand at the foot of the bridge. He contracted with the firm of F. Romanelli of Florence to produce the statues. The Romanelli company specialized in making copies of classical statues.

Anderson would not live to see the lions unveiled at the opening of the bridge during the Ponce de Leon Celebration in 1927. Late in November 1924 he fell ill, and his son Andrew and daughter Clarissa were called to his side at Markland. Just before dawn on December 2, he passed away. His funeral brought out the largest outpouring of public sympathy since the death of Henry Flagler. Flags flew at half staff around town, including on what was now called Anderson Memorial Flagpole. Memorial Church filled to overflowing. The black residents were very much in evidence in tribute to Anderson's many philanthropic activities devoted to the town's black residents. The students of Florida Normal and Industrial Institute, located on the west side of town, stood in a line on Sevilla Street to show their respect. Young black students and friends of his family bore Anderson's coffin from the church and placed it in the same horse-drawn hearse that had borne the remains of Henry Flagler a decade earlier. Anderson's body went to Evergreen Cemetery to join that of his wife and other noted and humble people who had once made St. Augustine their home.[47]

In January 1924 Thomas Hastings returned to St. Augustine, feeling, he said, like Rip Van Winkle waking up to see all the changes that had taken place since his first visit nearly forty years earlier. He told a reporter for the *St. Augustine Record* that when he first walked to the site of the Hotel Ponce de Leon, it was all swampland. When asked if he would do anything differently today if he were designing Flagler's buildings, he said he regretted that the colonnade he had planned for the front of the Alcazar had never been built. As for the Ponce de Leon, he said he would make few if any changes to the exterior and only some slight alterations to the interior. "The dining room, however, I would leave just as it is. In fact, I find that the entire structure finds favor in the minds of architects not only in this country but abroad."[48]

After the death of his colleague Carrère, Hastings's firm had continued as one of the leading architectural practices in the country. Hastings took special pride in the Memorial Amphitheater at Arlington Cemetery, which was completed in 1920 to receive the Tomb of the Unknown Soldier. Hastings had become an outspoken critic of the new skyscrapers rising in Manhattan, yet he designed the new thirty-four-story headquarters building for Standard Oil at 26 Broadway that swallowed up the earlier building on the site where John D. Rockefeller and Henry Flagler had once directed the petroleum industry of America.[49]

In an essay written in the 1920s Hastings bemoaned the transformation he was witnessing in New York: "The general character of New York has completely changed, and Fifth Avenue, which in my time, as an architect, was our principal residential street, is now lined with commercial structures, many of them 'skyscrapers'; and the most elaborate houses are rapidly being destroyed to make way for business and apartment buildings. It would seem that an earthquake could scarcely have produced greater waste and destruction than has obtained in the last few years. We architects have spent millions of our clients' money on this avenue, where the house-wrecker at the call of the greedy speculator has followed closely after."[50]

With little advance warning, Thomas Hastings died on October 22, 1929, following an emergency operation for appendicitis. He had been staying in his country house at Westbury on Long Island. His funeral service took place two days later in the chapel at Union Theological Seminary, where his father had once been president and where Henry Flagler had held a chair on the board of trustees. The service was largely secular, since Hastings had been skeptical of religion, but the choir sang "Rock of Ages," his grandfather's composition. Hastings's body was buried in Putnam Cemetery near Greenwich, Connecticut, alongside that of his wife and the rest of the Benedicts.

Two obituaries appeared in the New York Times on successive days, both recognizing Hastings's Florida endeavors: "The death of Mr. Hastings is a serious loss to American architecture. Members of his profession have this advantage, that their work lives after them: the good is not so often 'interred with their bones.' Those who, in generations to come, rest in the gardens of the Ponce de Leon at St. Augustine, or pause in front of the Library in this city, or stand, hat in hand, in the Arlington Memorial Amphitheatre above the Potomac, will be able to appreciate Mr. Hastings's talent, and perhaps catch something of the spirit animating him."[51]

The sentiments, of course, were true, but the men who first dreamed of these buildings, Thomas Hastings and John Carrère, disappeared from national consciousness soon after their deaths. American architecture moved onward into Prairie School, art deco, European internationalism, and a myriad of other innovative styles, consigning French Renaissance style, if not some of its fundamental teachings, to the dusty pages of academic volumes on the history of architecture. Only near the end of the twentieth century and into the twenty-first did McKim, Mead and White, along with Carrère and Hastings, enjoy a revival of interest, from both the architectural profession and the wider public.

All the while Alice Shourds Flagler had been living quietly under the care of Dr. Carlos MacDonald and, after his death, in the care of Dr. Charles W. Pilgrim. Most of the time she stayed with other women patients at an asylum in Central Valley, New York, but for a while she lived in a private home. Although she was totally out of touch with reality, her condition was such that she could take automobile rides in the country and could even go to the theater in the company of her attendants. The fund Flagler had set aside for her care continued to increase rapidly in value over the years, and her three nephews and various other family friends received annual distributions from her trust fund. On July 12, 1930, at the

The Hotel Ponce de Leon celebrated its fiftieth anniversary in 1937. Headwaiter Adolph Bittner (*left*) and waiter William Huber fashioned this model for display in the hotel and in New York City. © Flagler Museum Archives.

age of eighty, she passed away following a stroke at the sanitarium in Central Valley. She was buried in Cypress Hills cemetery in Brooklyn. Her two surviving nephews and the widow of the third divided an inheritance of almost fifteen million dollars.[52]

Flagler's stately hotels continued to enjoy reasonably good seasons in the years following his death, but in 1924 the Hotel Ponce de Leon showed a financial deficit for the first time. It would continue to operate in the red thereafter. The hurricane of September 1926 severely damaged the Hotel Royal Palm in Miami, and in 1930 it was demolished. Another killer hurricane in 1928 hit Palm Beach and damaged the Royal Poinciana. The hotel was repaired, but as the Great Depression took hold, it no longer made sense to keep the enormous hotel open, and in 1935 it too was torn down. The Breakers had burned down for a second time in 1925, and the next year a modern steel and concrete Breakers became the center of Palm Beach winter society, as it remains today. The Ormond would continue in operation for decades, although it became a retirement home in its final years. In 1992 it was torn down to make way for condominiums.

In St. Augustine the Alcazar closed permanently at the conclusion of the 1931 season, leaving the Cordova empty as well, except for the stores on its ground floor. With the outbreak of World War II the tourist industry in Florida almost came to a standstill. The Coast Guard took over the Hotel Ponce de Leon in September 1942 as a training center and continued to occupy it until June 1945.

Over the years William R. Kenan Jr., his wife Alice Pomroy Kenan, and his sisters Jessie Kenan Wise and Sarah Kenan had continued to make the Hotel Ponce de Leon their winter home, occupying the same wing of suites once used by Henry and Mary Lily Flagler. During the war they stayed at the Buckingham, but with the Ponce de Leon's reopening in 1946 they returned to their accustomed quarters. Alice Pomroy Kenan would die in the Ponce de Leon on February 12, 1947, in her eighty-second year. Jessie Wise died in January 1968 at home in Wilmington, while her sister Sarah passed away two months later in a Wilmington nursing home. William R. Kenan Jr. lived at his home in Lockport, New York, until his death on July 23, 1965. More than half of William's legacy went to establish a trust, headquartered at the University of North Carolina, dedicated to the betterment of higher education.[53]

Although the Hotel Alcazar had been closed since 1931, a local newspaper reporter observed when he walked through the building during World War II, "Everything seems so solid and permanent that it was impossible to think of the Alcazar as in anything but a state of hibernation. All that seemed necessary was a gentle prod to bring the sleeping giant back to life." Chicago resident Otto C. Lightner, editor of *Hobbies* magazine and collector of Victorian miscellanies, discovered the slumbering Alcazar in 1946, and a year later an agreement was worked out with the City of St. Augustine whereby the city would operate the hotel complex under a perpetual trust, and Lightner would bring his museum collection from Chicago for display in the building. However, Lightner did little to refurbish the building; he would pass away in 1950, and his museum languished due to lack of proper maintenance. In 1968 the city decided to use the front part of the building, the hotel proper, as its city hall. In 1971 the City of St. Augustine proudly moved its offices into this distinguished building. A completely modernized Lightner Museum opened in the Baths area in 1974, while the Casino, with its large swimming pool, now empty of water, became an area of antique shops and a restaurant. Meanwhile, St. Johns County had turned the Cordova building into its courthouse in 1968. When rapid growth in the county forced the government to seek a larger space, hotel magnate Richard Kessler purchased the building and converted it into a luxury resort hotel, restoring its original name Casa Monica. Ironically, the building that had never been a financial success as a hotel is the only Flagler building in St. Augustine now operating as a hotel.[54]

In the 1960s with the passing of the generation who had known Henry Flagler, custody of his legacy fell to his great-nephew Lawrence Lewis Jr., Louise Wise

By the 1950s the garden in front of the Hotel Alcazar had been turned into a parking lot, but today it has been restored as a garden. By permission of Library of Congress.

Lewis's son. Although Lewis made his home in Richmond, he maintained great affection for St. Augustine, where he had lived in the winters with his mother in Flagler's old home Kirkside.

At this point only the Breakers Hotel in Palm Beach continued the tradition of an elite winter resort, while the Ponce de Leon had become a faded anachronism. Without air conditioning, a parking lot for cars, or a nearby golf course, it simply did not meet the requirements of a modern hotel. "I had a large white elephant right in the heart of St. Augustine on my hands," Lewis recalled later. He could not simply shutter the building and walk away, leaving the town with a "dead relic" in its midst. Thus, after several years of deliberations, Lewis announced in January 1967 that the hotel would close and be turned into a private four-year college. The board of Flagler College would be charged with the preservation of one of the nation's architectural treasures, while at the same time providing a top-quality education for new generations of young people. Although the 1960s hardly seemed an auspicious time to be launching a small new private school, Flagler College has proven a remarkable success. Henry Flagler's legacy remains a vibrant part of St. Augustine today.[55]

The statue of Henry Flagler has been moved from its original location in Railroad Park to the front of Flagler College. Author's photo.

Acknowledgments

For the better part of three years I spent many pleasant days reading blurry microfilm and scanning small type in old publications in the Research Library of the St. Augustine Historical Society. My constant companions and guides have been the very competent and knowledgeable staff of the library: Senior Research Librarian Charles Tingley, Chief Librarian Robert Nawrocki, and Assistant Librarian Debra Willis. Dr. Susan Parker, executive director of the St. Augustine Historical Society, has also been of invaluable help.

At Flagler College Peggy Dyess, interlibrary loan specialist, obtained many rare research materials, while archivist Christine Wysocki led me through the Henry Flagler materials preserved at the college. Larry Weeks, director of business services, gave me access to the McGuire Letterbooks. Plant Superintendent Vic Cheney helped with college property.

Susan Swiatosz, archivist at the Henry Morrison Flagler Museum in Palm Beach, led me to important materials preserved there. Tracy Kamerer, chief curator, also made me welcome there. While in Palm Beach I was helped at the archives of the Historical Society of Palm Beach County by Debi Murray, chief curator.

At the George A. Smathers Libraries, University of Florida, curator James Cusick directed me to materials in their holdings, and Laurie N. Taylor of the Digital Library Center supplied me with images. Illustrations credited to the Library of Congress are drawn from the online catalog of the Prints and Photographs Division.

Sister Catherine Bitzer introduced me to the Historical Archives of the Diocese of St. Augustine at St. Joseph's Convent. Ben DiBiase did the same at the Florida Historical Society Library in Cocoa.

Dawn Hugh, archives manager at the HistoryMiami Archives and Research Center, sent me valuable Flagler material from their collection. James A. Ponce Jr. supplied me with some previously unavailable Flagler letters.

Others to whom I owe debts of gratitude are Richard Backlund, Beth Rogero Bowen, Seth Bramson, Karen Harvey, Kevin Kelshaw, John Nelson, Craig Presler, Tom Rahner, Jay Smith, and Joe Woods.

Gail Akin, widow of Dr. Ed Akin, provided me with some of the research materials gathered by her late husband in preparation for his scholarly biography *Flagler: Rockefeller Partner and Florida Baron.* These research notes were simply indispensable in the writing of my book.

Finally, I am most deeply indebted to my wife Susan who is my constant companion and support as well as a critic with years of experience.

The Historic St. Augustine Research Institute provided a grant to assist my research. A generous grant from the St. Augustine Foundation facilitated the publication of this book.

Notes

Abbreviations

AP   Andrew Anderson Papers, St. Augustine Historical Society
FC   Flagler College Archives
FEC   Florida East Coast Railway
HMFM Henry Morrison Flagler Museum, Palm Beach
HMFP Henry Morrison Flagler Papers, Henry Morrison Flagler Museum, Palm Beach
SAHS St. Augustine Historical Society Library
UFL   University of Florida Smathers Libraries

Preface

1. "Henry Clews," *San Francisco Call*, October 24, 1901; the five men ahead of Flagler were J. D. Rockefeller, W. W. Astor, J. J. Astor, W. K. Vanderbilt, and Russell Sage. "Estimate of Fortunes," *Washington Post*, February 15, 1905; in the *Post*'s list, the individuals ahead of Flagler were Rockefeller, Andrew Carnegie, Vanderbilt, J. J. Astor, William Rockefeller, George J. Gould, Marshall Field, William A. Clark, J. P. Morgan, Darius O. Mills, and Henry C. Frick.

2. Lefevre, "Flagler," 180.

3. William Mayo Venable to Carlton J. Corless, January 17, 1952, Henry Morrison Flagler Papers (hereafter cited as HMFP), Henry Morrison Flagler Museum, Palm Beach. Much of Flagler's correspondence is preserved as copies bound in large letterbooks. Some Flagler letters and other materials are conserved individually in file boxes.

4. George Morgan Ward, *In Memoriam*, 18.

Chapter 1. Dr. Anderson of St. Augustine, 1839–1880

1. Graham, *Awakening*.

2. Andrew Anderson to Caroline Fairbanks, March 13, 1839, Andrew Anderson Papers, St. Augustine Historical Society (hereafter cited as AP).

3. Andrew Anderson to Smith Anderson, September 17, 1834, AP.

4. Andrew Anderson to Clarissa Anderson, March 20, 29, 1859, AP.

5. H. B. Jenckes to Mary Reid, May 26, 1862, St. Augustine Historical Society Library (hereafter cited as SAHS).

6. *St. Augustine Examiner*, February 13, August 21, September 25, 1869.

7. Agreements, June 1, 1870; October 14, 1873; April 13, 1875, all in AP, box 1, file 49.

8. Andrew Anderson to Clarissa Anderson, December 28, 1863, AP.

9. Stowe, *Palmetto-Leaves*, 207.

10. Anderson, Memorial Flagpole dedication speech, November 11, 1921, AP.

11. Ibid.

Chapter 2. Visions of the Ancient City, 1869–1880

1. Nolan, *Fifty Feet*, 57–59; "News from St. Augustine," *News-Herald*, February 28, 1888, 2; "John F. Whitney Dead," *New York Times*, April 20, 1902.

2. Woolson, "Ancient City," pt. 1, 1.

3. Moore, *Woolson*, 37.

4. "Hotel Ponce de Leon," *Charlotte Chronicle*, April 5, 1888, 5.

5. Brooks, *Petals*, 206.

6. Ibid., 161.

7. Ibid., 211.

8. Ibid., 183.

9. Ibid., 199.

10. Ibid., 264.

11. Ibid., 166.

12. Ibid., 169.

13. "George Lorillard's Death," *New York Times*, February 5, 1886, 8; "H. E. Hernandez Tells of Former Tourist Years," unidentified newspaper clipping, Marsh Scrapbook, A1, 155, SAHS.

14. St. Johns County Deed Book U, 332–34; "Former Resident Recalls Ferry Service to Island," *St. Augustine Record*, October 21, 1934, 8.

15. "The Great Short-Horn Sale," *St. Augustine Examiner*, October 4, 1873, 2.

16. "William Astor Dead," *New York Times*, April 27, 1892, 1.

17. "St. Augustine Locals," *Florida Times-Union*, December 13, 1886, 1 (hereafter shortened to *Times-Union*).

18. "William Astor Is Dead," *Times-Union*, April 27, 1892, 3.

19. Brooks, *Petals*, 170.

20. Ibid., 163–64.

21. Ibid., 168.

22. *New York Daily Times*, April 5, 1873.

23. Brooks, *Petals*, 170.

24. Lady Duffus Hardy, *Down South*, 1880, qtd. in Carrère and Hastings, *Florida: The American Riviera*, n.p.

25. Brooks, *Petals*, 221–22.

26. Ibid., 207.

27. Barnes and Fairbanks, *Newberry's Diary*, 52, 56.

Chapter 3. The Private Henry Morrison Flagler, 1830–1883

1. Flagler to J. F. Forbes, May 18, 1903, Flagler Letterbook, Henry Morrison Flagler Museum, Palm Beach (hereafter cited as HMFM).

2. Lefevre, "Flagler," 179.

3. Morrow, "Henry M. Flagler," A9.

4. Flagler to Mrs. J. W. Lugenbeel, July 3, 1890, Flagler Letterbook, HMFM.

5. Akin, *Flagler: Rockefeller Partner*, 2–3.

6. George Morgan Ward, *In Memoriam*, 7.

7. Winkler, *Rockefeller*, 75.

8. Flagler to E. N. Wilson, December 8, 1890, Flagler Letterbook, HMFM.

9. "J. C. Salter Talks of Former Chief," *St. Augustine Evening Record*, January 16, 1925, 2.

10. Qtd. in Chandler, *Henry Flagler*, 17.

11. *Bellevue Evening Gazette*, May 26, 1881, qtd. in Chandler, *Henry Flagler*, 299.

12. Chandler, *Henry Flagler*, 17.

13. Morrow, "Henry M. Flagler," A9.

14. Lefevre, "Flagler," 181; Akin, *Flagler: Rockefeller Partner*, 11–12.

15. Lefevre, "Flagler," 180.

16. Morrow, "Henry M. Flagler," A9.

17. Ibid.

18. "Rockefeller's Money," *Wall Street Journal*, October 31, 1908, 6.

19. Nevins, *John D. Rockefeller*, 1:233–36, 627.

20. "Mr. Rockefeller's Splendid Tribute," *Ocala Banner*, November 3, 1908, 2.

21. Lefevre, "Flagler," 183.

22. Morrow, "Henry M. Flagler," A9.

23. Dennett, *John Hay*, 104.

24. "Mr. Rockefeller's Splendid Tribute," *Ocala Banner*, November 3, 1908, 2.

25. Fosdick, *Rockefeller*, 5.

26. Nevins, *John D. Rockefeller*, 1:627–47.

27. Lefevre, "Flagler," 184.

28. Ibid.

29. "Henry M. Flagler," *St. Augustine Evening Record*, May 30, 1913, 7.

30. George Morgan Ward, *In Memoriam*, 16–17.

31. Flagler to W. P. Williams, October 23, 1902; Flagler to T. D. Myers, October 31, 1902, HMFP.

32. Lefevre, "Flagler," 184.

33. George Morgan Ward, *In Memoriam*, 16–17; Certificate of Membership, Florida Historical Society, January 8, 1903, Florida Historical Society Library.

34. "Mr. Rockefeller's Splendid Tribute," *Ocala Banner*, November 13, 1908, 2.

35. Akin, *Flagler: Rockefeller Partner*, 71.

36. "Inheritance Tax Reveals Little Known Facts," *New York Times*, June 2, 1912, 5MI.

37. Braden, *Architecture*, 30.

38. Sidney Walter Martin, *Flagler: Visionary*, 78; Akin, *Flagler: Rockefeller Partner*, 71–72.

39. "Wall Street Breathed a Sigh of Relief," *New York Daily Tribune*, April 3, 1892, 3; "Flagler's Equine Palace," *Times-Union*, May 22, 1892, 3; Harry Flagler, "Misstatements in Martin," HMFM.

40. Gregory, *Families of Fortune*, 187; "The Only Four Hundred," *New York Times*, February 16, 1892, 5.

41. *King's Handbook of New York City*, 1892, 138.

42. "Beautification of the Old Town," *Times-Union*, December 28, 1888, 2; "Facts and Fancies," *St. Augustine News*, March 8, 1891, 7.

43. James Ingraham, "A Man's Work," unpublished manuscript, James E. Ingraham Papers, George A. Smathers Libraries, University of Florida, Gainesville (hereafter cited as Ingraham Papers, UFL).

44. Sidney Walter Martin, *Flagler: Visionary*, 77–78; Akin, *Flagler: Rockefeller Partner*, 72–73.

45. "Mr. Flagler Talks," *Jacksonville News-Herald*, June 20, 1887, 6.

46. *Bellevue Evening Gazette*, May 26, 1881, qtd. in Chandler, *Henry Flagler*, 299.

47. Akin, *Flagler: Rockefeller Partner*, 107; Sidney Walter Martin, *Flagler: Visionary*, 78.

48. Sidney Walter Martin, *Flagler: Visionary*, 79; Akin, *Flagler: Rockefeller Partner*, 107.

49. Hanks, "Pottier," 87; Akin, *Flagler: Rockefeller Partner*, 108; "Lachmont and Orienta," *Munsey's Magazine* 7, no. 5 (August 1892): 524–25; "Satan's Toe in the Pictures," *New York Times*, February 10, 1924, SM10; Harry Flagler, "Misstatements in Martin," HMFM.

50. "With Little or No Wind," *New York Times*, June 7, 1885, 2; Anderson to Harriett, December 29, 1903, AP.

51. "A Resort for Clergymen," *New York Times*, August 2, 1885, 3; Flagler to Anderson, July 6, 1887, HMFP.

52. "Queries Yet Unanswered," *New York Sun*, December 28, 1882, 4.

53. George Morgan Ward, *In Memoriam*, 14.

54. *New York Times*, April 5, June 6, November 19, 1883.

55. "Insanity of Mrs. Flagler," *New York Times*, August 6, 1899, 12; "Mad Old Queen," *Palm Beach Times*, September 26, 1927, Flagler biographical file, SAHS.

56. Sidney Walter Martin, *Flagler: Visionary*, 90.

57. Martin to Thomas R. Hazzard, December 22, 1949, and Martin to W. Howard Lee, September 29, 1949, Sidney Walter Martin Papers, UFL.

58. Martin to W. Howard Lee, September 29, 1949, Martin Papers, UFL.

59. "Half Century on Job Is Celebrated," unidentified newspaper clipping, Fremd file; Anna Fremd Hadley oral history interview, 1962, both at Historical Society of Palm Beach County.

60. Sidney Walter Martin, *Flagler: Visionary*, 89–90.

61. W. Howard Lee to Martin, September 26, 1949, Martin Papers, UFL.

62. Martin to Lee, September 29, 1949, Martin Papers, UFL.

63. Harry Flagler, "Misstatements in Martin," HMFM.

64. Sidney Walter Martin, *Flagler: Visionary*, 91; Harry Flagler, "Misstatements in Martin," HMFM.

65. See Harry Flagler's comments in the margins of Sidney Walter Martin, *Flagler: Visionary*, 91, 92, 113, 170, 251, HMFM.

66. Harry Flagler, "Misstatements in Martin," HMFM.

67. Ibid.; Sidney Walter Martin, *Flagler: Visionary*, 90; Chandler, *Henry Flagler*, 299.

68. "Three Foundlings," *New York Sun*, August 2, 1902, 7; Flagler to W. W. Taylor, November 6, 1901, Flagler Letterbook, HMFM.

Chapter 4. Coming to Florida, 1883–1885

1. Flagler to William Crafts, October 12, 1888, AP.

2. Flagler to J. N. Camden, January 29, 1886, Flagler Letterbook, HMFM; "Hon. J. E. Ingraham Pays Tribute," *St. Augustine Record*, November 11, 1921, 1.

3. Nevins, *John D. Rockefeller*, 2:178; Sidney Walter Martin, *Flagler: Visionary*, 93–95.

4. "Holland's Letter," *Wall Street Journal*, May 15, 1919, 2.

5. "Mr. Flagler Talks," *Jacksonville News-Herald*, June 20, 1887, 6.

6. Lefevre, "Flagler," 184.

7. Sidney Walter Martin, *Flagler: Visionary*, 103–4; Flagler to Rockefeller, February 26, 1885, Rockefeller Papers, part 3, Rockefeller Archive Center, Tarrytown, New York.

8. Advertisement, *Times-Union*, February 6, 1885, 2; "San Marco," *Tatler*, January 23, 1892; "Mid the Orange Groves," *New York Times*, February 14, 1892, 10.

9. "Mr. Flagler Talks," *Jacksonville News-Herald*, June 20, 1887, 6.

10. H. H. Smith, "A Magnificent Hotel," *Washington Post*, April 19, 1891, 3.

11. Rockefeller, *Random*, 10.

12. Winkler, *Rockefeller*, 241.

13. Sworn Deposition of J. E. Ingraham, February 1923, Ingraham Papers, UFL.

14. "Henry M. Flagler," *St. Augustine Evening Record*, May 30, 1913, 7.

15. Lefevre, "Flagler," 184.

16. Ibid., 179.

17. "Howard on Human Nature," *Daily Graphic*, December 17, 1887, qtd. in Castleden, *Early Years*, 26.

18. "Mr. Flagler Talks," *Jacksonville News-Herald*, June 20, 1887, 6.

19. Flagler to S. Thompson, December 7, 1901, HMFP.

20. Clark, "Smith," 35.

21. Flagler to J. N. Camden, January 29, 1886, Flagler Letterbook, HMFM.

22. Nina Duryea, "Franklin W. Smith," *St. Augustine Record*, April 7, 1937, 6.

23. Dahl, "Lincoln Saves a Reformer," 74.

24. Nina Duryea, "Franklin W. Smith," *St. Augustine Record*, April 7, 1937, 6; Last Will and Testament, Smith file, SAHS; *Jacksonville Florida Daily Times*, January 17, 1883, clipping, Smith file, SAHS.

25. Resolution adopted January 11, 1888, Yacht Club Minutes Book, SAHS.

26. Yacht Club file, SAHS; "St. Augustine Yacht Club," *Tatler*, February 3, 1894, 3.

27. Yacht Club Minutes Book, January 2, 1885, SAHS; "St. Augustine Celebration," *Times-Union*, March 28, 1885, 4.

28. *St. Augustine Yacht Club*, members' handbook (New York: Knickerbocker Press, n.d.), 61; Flagler to J. N. Camden, January 29, 1886, Flagler Letterbook, HMFM.

29. "St. Augustine Locals," *Times-Union*, February 26, 1885, 4.

30. Flagler to Rockefeller, February 26, 1885, Rockefeller Papers, part 3, Rockefeller Archive Center, Tarrytown, New York.

31. City Council minutes, February 2, April 13, 27, 1885; Letterbook of Frederick W. Bruce, February 17, 1885, SAHS.

32. Anderson to Harriet, July 31, 1885, AP.

33. Flagler to F. W. Smith, October 16, 1885, Flagler Letterbook, HMFM.

34. For example, Flagler to Anderson, November 7, 18, 1885, Flagler Letterbook, HMFM.

35. St. Johns County Deed Book EE, 16–19, 136–39.

36. Ibid., 116–17.

37. Lease, Hulett, and Burgess to Orange Howes, AP.

38. Akin, *Flagler: Rockefeller Partner*, 119.

39. *St. Johns Weekly*, May 23, 1885, clipping, Hotel Ponce de Leon file, SAHS; "Biggest Hotel Yet," *Times-Union*, May 20, 1885, 4.

40. "Ponce de Leon Hotel," *Jacksonville News-Herald*, August 7, 1887, 12.

41. "Gossip," *Tatler*, March 23, 1901, 2.

42. "Ponce de Leon Hotel," *Jacksonville News-Herald*, August 7, 1887, 12.

43. Robert E. McGuire, "My Family," typed manuscript, McGuire file, SAHS.

44. Sidney Walter Martin, *Flagler: Visionary*, 77–78; "Two Builders of Palaces," *Times-Union*, December 22, 1889, 2; "Joseph McDonald Dies," *Miami Herald*, November 6, 1918, 1.

45. McDonald photo, Historical Society of Palm Beach County; H. E. Lagergren to A. L. Marsh, February 17, 1935, Marsh Scrapbook 5, SAHS.

46. McGuire, "My Family."

47. *Tatler*, January 30, 1892, 12; February 17, 1894, 6.

48. Albion, *Edison*, 3, 20.

49. Theodore H. Whitney to Edison, June 29, 1886, Thomas A. Edison Papers, Rutgers University; Coghlan, "Whitney," 104.

Chapter 5. Architects Carrère and Hastings, 1885

1. Akin, *Flagler: Rockefeller Partner*, 118.

2. Hewitt et al., *Carrère*, 1:38–39.

3. Harry Harkness Flagler to Nina Duryea, April 27, 1949, Smith file, SAHS.

4. Akin, *Flagler: Rockefeller Partner*, 208.

5. Gray, *Hastings*, 19.

6. Ibid., quoting G. Howard Walker.

7. Ibid., 20–12.

8. Hastings, "Relations," 960.

9. Hewitt et al., *Carrère*, 1:39; Gray, *Hastings*, 24.

10. Cardwell, *Maybeck*, 16–18; Woodbridge, *Bernard Maybeck*, 16–18.

11. Hastings, "Letter," 3; Hastings, "Carrère," 65.

12. Hewitt et al., *Carrère*, 1:43.

13. Mead, "Carrère," 45; Cardwell, *Maybeck*, 21; Ossman and Ewing, *Carrère & Hastings: Masterworks*, 10.

14. Hewitt et al., *Carrère*, 1:19.

15. Ibid., 1:18.

16. "Thomas Hastings," *Dictionary of American Biography*, 1932 edition.

17. Gray, *Hastings*, 4.

18. Ibid., 42.

19. Hastings, "Carrère," 71.

20. Hewitt et al., *Carrère*, 1:61.

21. "Monument to be Erected at Woodlawn Cemetery," *American Architect and Building News* 12, no. 361 (November 25, 1882): 255–56; unidentified clipping from Belleview, Ohio, newspaper, Hotel Ponce de Leon file, SAHS.

22. *King's Handbook of New York City*, 1893, 516.

23. Hastings, "Letter," 3; Ossman and Ewing, *Carrère & Hastings: Masterworks*, 10.

24. Gray, *Hastings*, 161.

25. James H. Bridge, quoted in Hewitt et al., *Carrère*, 1:380–81.

26. Crespo, "Florida's First," 117; Mead, "Carrère," 45.

27. Gray, *Hastings*, 32.

28. Flagler to Carrère, January 4, 1910, Flagler Letterbook, HMFM.

29. "Thomas Hastings," *St. Augustine Record*, January 21, 1924, 1.

30. "How the Ponce Was Built," *St. Augustine Record*, December 20, 1906, 1.

31. "Thomas Hastings," *St. Augustine Record*, January 21, 1924, 1.

32. Carrère and Hastings, *Florida: The American Riviera*, 22.

33. Lefevre, "Flagler," 170.

34. Carrère and Hastings, *Florida: The American Riviera*, 24.

35. Lefevre, "Flagler," 182.

36. "How the Ponce Was Built," *St. Augustine Record*, December 20, 1906, 1.

37. "A Magnificent Hotel," *Washington Post*, April 19, 1891, 13.

38. "Entrance Gates for M. E. Church," Carrère and Hastings Digital Collection, University of Florida.

39. Gray, *Hastings*, 29, 221.

40. Hastings, "Carrère," 66.

41. John M. Carrère, "Referred to Our Readers," *American Architect* 17, no. 493 (June 6, 1885): 274.

42. "How the Ponce Was Built," *St. Augustine Record*, December 20, 1906, 1.

43. "Ponce de Leon," *Jacksonville News-Herald*, August 7, 1887, 12.

44. Gray, *Hastings*, 160.

45. Ibid. 151, 193.

46. Hewitt et al., *Carrère*, 2:82.

47. Ibid. 144.

48. Ibid. 160–61.

49. Carrère and Hastings, *Florida: The American Riviera*, 22.

50. "A Magnificent Hotel," *Washington Post*, April 19, 1891, 13.

Chapter 6. Remaking the Oldest City, 1885

1. Anderson to Harriett, July 31, 1885, AP.
2. William Crafts, undated statement, AP; C. M. Cooper to Anderson, August 28, 1885, AP; Flagler to F. W. Smith, September 5, 1885, Flagler Letterbook, HMFM.
3. Flagler to Seavey, September 1, 1885; Flagler to Crafts, September 1, 1885, Flagler Letterbook, HMFM.
4. Flagler to Cooper, September 1, 2, 3, 1885, Flagler Letterbook, HMFM.
5. Flagler to McGuire, September 22, 1885; Flagler to Anderson, September 25, 1885, Flagler Letterbook, HMFM.
6. Judgment 4th Circuit Court, AP.
7. Treasurer's Book, Grace M. E. Church, entries for August 2, September 21, October 2, 1885; March 13, 1886.
8. Boyer, "Flagler at Law," 50–53.
9. Ellen V. Ryall to Flagler, September 12, 1885, St. Johns County Deed Book EE, 521–23.
10. Flagler to C. B. Carver, September 10, 1885; Flagler to Smith, November 10, 12, 17, 1885, Flagler Letterbook, HMFM; "St. Augustine Notes," *Florida Weekly Times*, November 19, 1885, 3.
11. Flagler to Smith, October 16, 1885, Flagler Letterbook, HMFM.
12. Flagler to George Vail, January 2, 1886; Flagler to Smith, December 28, 1885, and January 2, April 24, 28, 1886, Flagler Letterbook, HMFM; St. Johns County Deed Book FF, 596–97; St. Johns County Deed Book JJ, 424–27.
13. Flagler to George I. Vail, May 6, 1886, Flagler Letterbook, HMFM.
14. St. Johns County Deed Book FF, 35.
15. Flagler to Long, September 1, 29, 1885; Flagler to F. W. Smith, September 8, 1885, Flagler Letterbook, HMFM.
16. St. Johns County Deed Book FF, 430–31; Flagler to Anderson, December 28, 1885, Flagler Letterbook, HMFM; Minute Book, Buckingham Smith Benevolent Association, March 19, 1886, SAHS.
17. Flagler to Anderson, November 7, 1885, Flagler Letterbook, HMFM.
18. Flagler to Smith, November 27, 1885, Flagler Letterbook, HMFM.
19. Flagler to W. G. Warden, September 1, 1885, Flagler Letterbook, HMFM.
20. *St. Augustine Evening News*, March 22, 1886, clipping in Alcazar file, SAHS.
21. Bruce to Smith, May 8, June 5, 1885; Bruce to Flagler, June 5, 1885, Bruce Letterbook, SAHS.
22. City Council minutes, June 29, July 20, 1885, SAHS.
23. Flagler to W. W. Dewhurst, September 11, 1885, Flagler Letterbook, HMFM; Bruce to Flagler, July 21, 1885, Bruce Letterbook, SAHS.
24. "Agreement: Jacksonville, St. Augustine and Halifax River Railroad and W. C. Endicott, Secretary of War, December 13, 1885, Railroad Papers, SAHS.
25. Bruce to W. T. Russell, June 23, 1885; Bruce to Flagler, July 6, 10, 20, August 24, 1885, Bruce Letterbook, SAHS.
26. Bruce to Russell, September 20, 1885, Bruce Letterbook, SAHS; Flagler to McGuire, October 5, 1885, Flagler Letterbook, HMFM.
27. Flagler to George Vail, October 15, 1885, Flagler Letterbook, HMFM.
28. "Veteran Hotel Editor Here," *St. Augustine Record*, May 12, 1941, 8.

Chapter 7. First, Buy the Railroad, 1885–1886

1. Directors Minutes, June 8, 16, 1883, Florida East Coast Railway file (hereafter cited as FEC file), SAHS; *Florida Weekly Times*, May 24, 1883, 1; *Times-Union*, April 17, 1885, 4, and June 19, 1885, 4.

2. Flagler to John C. Blair, November 2, 1903, Flagler Letterbook, HMFM.

3. Flagler to W. G. Warden, September 30, 1885, Flagler Letterbook, HMFM.

4. Flagler to McGuire and McDonald, November 28, 1885, Flagler Letterbook, HMFM.

5. Flagler to Green, September 1, 8, October 13, 1885, Flagler Letterbook, HMFM.

6. Flagler to McGuire, September 30, 1885, Flagler Letterbook, HMFM.

7. Flagler to Green, November 6, 16, December 26, 30, 1885; Minutes of JSAHR Railway Board Meeting, January 1, 1886, SAHS.

8. Directors Minutes, FEC file, SAHS.

9. Flagler to J. B. Higbee, February 6, 1886, Flagler Letterbook, HMFM.

10. Flagler to Anderson, January 15, 1886, Flagler Letterbook, HMFM.

11. Flagler to Bentley, January 6, 19, 1886; Flagler to Crawford, January 25, 1886, Flagler Letterbook, HMFM.

12. H. E. Lagergren to A. L. Marsh, February 17, 1935, Marsh Scrapbook 5, SAHS.

13. St. Johns County Deed Book FF, 66–72, 74–79.

14. Bruce to Flagler, September 2, 10, 12, November 11, 1885; Flagler to Bruce, September 5, 1885, Flagler Letterbook, HMFM; "St. Augustine Locals," *Times-Union*, January 17, 1886, 3; March 24, 1886, 3.

15. Flagler to C. M. Cooper, August 28, 1886, FEC file, SAHS; Flagler to R. McLaughlin, April 28, 1886, Flagler Letterbook, HMFM.

16. Flagler to McLaughlin, September 5, 1885, Flagler Letterbook, HMFM.

17. "Old Wharf Being Destroyed," *St. Augustine Record*, January 6, 1903, 1.

18. St. Johns County Deed Book EE, 326–28, 517–19.

19. Flagler to Richard McLaughlin, January 22, 1886, Flagler Letterbook, HMFM.

20. Flagler to Anderson, January 2, 9, 1886, Flagler Letterbook, HMFM.

21. Flagler to Flagg, February 1, 1886, Flagler Letterbook, HMFM; "Ancient City Locals," *Times-Union*, August 20, 1886.

22. Flagler to C. M. Cooper, August 28, 1886, FEC file, SAHS; "Ancient City Locals," *Times-Union*, August 31, 1886, 4.

23. Flagler to McGuire and McDonald, November 2, 1885; Flagler to Crawford, January 19, 1886, Flagler Letterbook, HMFM.

24. "Ancient City Locals," *Times-Union*, August 11, 21, 1886, 4.

25. Flagler to Anderson, December 23, 1885, Flagler Letterbook, HMFM.

Chapter 8. Construction of the Ponce de Leon, 1885–1887

1. Flagler to William Crafts, September 1, 1885, Flagler Letterbook, HMFM.

2. Flagler to Anderson, November 7, 1885, Flagler Letterbook, HMFM; "St. Augustine Locals," *Florida Weekly Times*, November 19, 1885, 3.

3. Flagler to Anderson, November 27, 1885, Flagler Letterbook, HMFM; Hastings, "Letter," 3.

4. "Mr. Flagler's Fine Address," *St. Lucie County Tribune*, February 9, 1912, 1.

5. Bruce to Flagler, June 12, 1885, Bruce Letterbook, SAHS; "Ponce de Leon," *Florida Weekly Times*, January 19, 1888, 1.

6. Flagler to Smith, August 27, 1885, Flagler Letterbook, HMFM.

7. Flagler to Anderson, September 25, 1885, Flagler Letterbook, HMFM.

8. Flagler to McGuire, October 8, 1885, Flagler Letterbook, HMFM.

9. Flagler to Anderson, November 5, 12, 16, 1885, Flagler Letterbook, HMFM.

10. St. Johns County Deed Book EE, 566–69; St. Johns County Deed Book FF, 122–24.

11. Flagler to Anderson, November 16, 1885, Flagler Letterbook, HMFM; St. Johns County Deed Book FF, 357–59; Albert Manucy and C. Raymond Vinton, "The Coquina Quarries," Castillo de San Marcos, 1945, copy of typed manuscript, SAHS.

12. "St. Augustine News," *Jacksonville News-Herald*, October 17, 1887, 1.

13. "St. Augustine," *Times-Union*, April 3, 1898, 2.

14. "Aladdin's Art Outdone," *Harrisburg Telegram*, June 1886, clipping, HMFP; Flagler to Smith, September 1, 1885, Flagler Letterbook, HMFM; Flagler to McGuire and McDonald, September 29, 1885, Flagler Letterbook, HMFM.

15. Flagler to John Flagg, September 12, 1885; Flagler to W. W. Dewhurst, November 27, 1885; Flagler to John Flagg, January 18, April 7, 1886; J. C. Salter to John N. Austin, August 27, 1901, Flagler Letterbook, HMFM; Knetsch, "One of Flagler's Men," 21–22; "Anastasia Land Titles," *St. Augustine Record*, April 9, 1901, 2–3.

16. "Will Make Lots of Wine," *Times-Union*, January 31, 1893, 6; Robert Oliver, "Reminiscences," typed manuscript, SAHS.

17. City Council minutes, October 16, December 14, December 28, 1885; Flagler to F. W. Smith, December 19, 1885, Flagler Letterbook, HMFM.

18. "Coquina and Concrete," *Jacksonville News-Herald*, September 25, 1887, 2; Flagler to Smith, August 27, 1885, Flagler Letterbook, HMFM; Flagler to McGuire, February 6, 1905, HMFP.

19. Flagler to McGuire and McDonald, November 14, 1885, HMFP.

20. Flagler to Smith, September 11, 1885, Flagler Letterbook, HMFM.

21. "Ponce de Leon," *St. Augustine Evening News*, March 22, 1886; Flagler to McGuire and McDonald, December 26, 1885, Flagler Letterbook, HMFM.

22. Flagler to McGuire and McDonald, January 26, 1886, Flagler Letterbook, HMFM; "Ponce de Leon," *St. Augustine Evening News*, March 22, 1886; McGuire to Carrère and Hastings, July 15, 1910, McGuire Letterbook, Flagler College Archives (hereafter cited as FC); "Hackmen Humbug Tourists," *Times-Union*, March 15, 1897, 7.

23. "News from St. Augustine," *Jacksonville News-Herald*, January 1888, 2.

24. James McGuire to Carrère and Hastings, June 15, 25, 1910, McGuire Letterbook, FC.

25. Flagler to McGuire and McDonald, December 28, 1885, Flagler Letterbook, HMFM.

26. City Council minutes, November 15, December 10, 1886.

27. Flagler to J. A. McGuire, January 7, 1886; Flagler to Anderson, February 3, 1886, Flagler Letterbook, HMFM.

28. Flagler to Smith, January 21, 27, 1885; Flagler to Anderson, January 26, 1885; Flagler to Carrère, January 28, 1885, Flagler Letterbook, HMFM.

29. Flagler to Smith, January 15, 21, 1886, Flagler Letterbook, HMFM.

30. Flagler to Seavey, January 20, 1886; Flagler to Anderson, January 26, 1886; Flagler to E. T. Postlethwaite, February 4, 1886, Flagler Letterbook, HMFM.

31. "St. Augustine Dots," *Times-Union*, January 11, 1886, 1.

32. "St. Augustine Locals," *Times-Union*, February 18, 1886, 3; "Ponce de Leon," *St. Augustine Evening News*, March 22, 1886; "Diagram Showing Proposed Enlargement of Grounds," HMFP.

33. Ossman and Ewing, *Carrère & Hastings: Masterworks*, 10.

34. "St. Augustine Locals," *Times-Union*, March 1, 1886, 1; "Construction Department," *Baltimore Manufacturers' Record*, July 3, 1886.

35. Flagler to McGuire and McDonald, November 2, 1885, Flagler Letterbook, HMFM.

36. Flagler to McGuire and McDonald, January 21, 1886, Flagler Letterbook, HMFM; "Ancient City Locals," *Times-Union*, March 18, 24, 1886, 3; "St. Augustine News," *Jacksonville Morning News*, July 22, 1886, 1.

37. "Finest in the World" (quoting a *Times-Union* article), *St. Johns Weekly*, April 24, 1886, 3; Flagler to John T. Devine, April 22, 1886, Flagler Letterbook, HMFM.

38. "Ancient City Locals," *Times-Union*, June 25, 1886, 4.

39. *Jacksonville Morning News*, June 5, July 22, August 10, 1886; *Times-Union*, August 17, 25, December 24, 1886; McGuire to C. D. Boice, April 15, 1914, McGuire Letterbook, FC.

40. "St. Augustine Locals," *Times-Union*, November 2, 19, 1886.

41. "St. Augustine Notes," *Times-Union*, January 18, March 13, 1887.

42. George Morgan Ward, *In Memoriam*, 14.

43. McGuire to "To whom it may concern," April 30, 1915, McGuire Letterbook, FC.

44. McGuire, "My Family."

45. "To Whom It May Concern," January 7, 1937, William Dewhurst Papers, SAHS.

Chapter 9. Transforming St. Augustine, 1887

1. "Ancient City Locals," *Times-Union*, April 24, May 13, October 30, 1886; "St. Augustine Notes," *Times-Union*, February 9, 1887, 2; "City News," *St. Augustine Press*, November 27, 1886, 1.

2. *Leaflet from the Casa Monica*, Cordova Hotel file, SAHS; "St. Augustine Notes," *Times-Union*, December 24, 1886; January 9, February 15, 1887, 2.

3. Smith, *Design and Prospectus*, 38, 45; McAloon, interview with author.

4. "City News," *St. Augustine News*, April 16, 1887, 3; "St. Augustine Notes," *Times-Union*, April 4, 9, 20, 1887; "St. Augustine Notes," *Times-Union*, June 19, 21, 1887.

5. Crespo, "Florida's First," 213–14, 217.

6. "Matters in St. Augustine," *Times-Union*, March 27, July 7, 1888, 2; McGuire, "My Family," 7.

7. "St. Augustine," *Jacksonville Morning News*, August 24, 1886, 3; "St. Augustine Notes," *Times-Union*, January 10, 1887, 8.

8. "Remembrances of John Leffler," typed manuscript, SAHS; "Swept by Flames," *Times-Union*, April 13, 1887, 1; "City Jottings," *St. Johns County Weekly*, April 16, 1887, 3.

9. "The Great Fire," *St. Augustine Press*, April 16, 1887, 1.

10. City Council minutes, May 18, 1887; "St. Augustine Notes," *Times-Union*, July 25, 1887, 1; "St. Augustine News," *Jacksonville News-Herald*, November 23, 1887, 1.

11. Moore to Edward Pace, July 28, 1887, Moore correspondence file, Historical Archives of the Diocese of St. Augustine; "Work of Henry M. Flagler," *Tatler*, February 9, 1907, 1.

12. Moore to Edward Pace, August 27, 1887, Diocesan Archives; "News from St. Augustine," *Jacksonville News-Herald*, December 27, 1887, 2; "Kress Company Buys Valuable Property," *St. Augustine Record*, January 21, 1911, 1.

13. "After the Fire," *Times-Union*, April 18, 1887, 8; "Death of James Renwick," *New York Times*, June 25, 1895, 9.

14. "The Ancient City," *Times-Union*, January 26, 1888, 2.

15. "Tuesday's Holocaust," *St. Johns County Weekly*, April 16, 1887, 3; City Council minutes, June 6, 1887; "The Ancient City," *Times-Union*, March 11, 1888, 1; "Capt Vail Dead," *Miami Metropolis*, November 11, 1904, 1.

16. "St. Augustine Notes," *Times-Union*, September 2, 1887, 2.

17. "St. Augustine," *Florida Weekly Times*, January 19, 1888, 4.

18. Payne, "Cultural Resources"; "St. Augustine Notes," *Times-Union*, January 6, February 1, 1887, 2.

19. "Extensive Improvements," *Jacksonville News-Herald*, August 17, 1887, 1; "St. Augustine Budget," *Jacksonville News-Herald*, October 17, 1887, 4; "St. Augustine Notes," *Jacksonville News-Herald*, September 11, 1887, 2.

20. "St. Augustine Notes," *Florida Weekly Times*, August 25, 1887, 5.

21. "St. Augustine Notes," *Times-Union*, April 3, 1887, 3; "St. Augustine Notes," *Florida Weekly Times*, April 7, 1887, 6; "St. Augustine Notes," *Times-Union*, May 30, August 17, 1887.

22. "St. Augustine Notes," *Times-Union*, July 19, 1887, 2; "Live St. Augustine News," *Jacksonville News-Herald*, August 28, 1887, 5; "Florida News and Views," *Times-Union*, November 17, 1887, 2.

23. "St. Augustine Notes," *Times-Union*, July 12, September 14, 1887, 2.

24. "A Colored Cab Company," *Washington Colored American*, October 10, 1903, 6.

25. Crespo, "Florida's First," 175–76.

26. "Nearly a Block in Ruins," *New York Times*, March 2, 1888, 1.

27. Cardwell, *Maybeck*, 13–16, 22.

28. "Pottier and Stymus Manufacturing Co.," in *King's Handbook of New York City*, 854.

29. Cardwell, *Maybeck*, 21–25.

30. Nichols, "Visit with Maybeck," 30–31.

31. Woodbridge, *Bernard Maybeck*, 15–16; Crespo, "Florida's First," 244.

32. Travel Diary of Julia Mary Weeks de Forest, copy, SAHS.

33. Duncan, *Tiffany Windows*, 200, 210.

34. "Art Notes," *New York Times*, January 25, 1886, 3.

35. Jones, *Maitland Armstrong*, 68–94.

36. "St. Augustine," Jacksonville *News-Herald*, July 23, 1887, 2; "St. Augustine Notes," *Times-Union*, September 20, 1887, 2.

37. "Younger Artists Recognized," *New York Times*, May 14, 1885, 2; Mary Gay Humphries, "Home of Bachelors," *Pittsburgh Dispatch*, June 23, 1889, 10; "New York City," *New York Daily Tribune*, February 23, 1890, 5.

38. Van Hook, "Lyrical," 63–80.

39. "The Day in St. Augustine," *Times-Union*, February 19, 1893, 1; "Artists and Their Work," *Tatler*, March 6, 1897, 2; "Architects of Ponce de Leon," *Tatler*, February 5, 1898, 16.

40. "Symposium of Color," *Jacksonville News-Herald*, November 20, 1887, 2.

41. City Council minutes, December 28, 1886, February 14, 1887; "Sunday in St. Augustine," *Times-Union*, January 7, 1889, 2.

42. City Council minutes, July 3, 1890; Post Office Park file, SAHS.

43. Gray, *Hastings*, 184.

44. Carrère and Hastings, *Florida: The American Riviera*, 30–32.

45. W. A. MacWilliams, "Recollections," MC 63, box 9, file 31, SAHS; Dale, *St. Augustine Boy*, 16, 55.

46. Hewitt et al., *Carrère*, 1:163.

47. Gray, *Hastings*, 184.

48. "Ponce de Leon," *Jacksonville News-Herald*, August 7, 1887, 12.

49. "Hastings," *St. Augustine Record*, January 21, 1924.

50. Carl Rust Parker, *Transactions*, 90–92.

51. Ibid., 91.

52. Barrett, "Fifty Years," 182.

53. "Mr. Flagler Talks," *Jacksonville News-Herald*, June 20, 1887, H. M. Flagler Memorial file, SAHS.

54. Barrett, "Fifty Years," 184.

55. "Sculpture Society," *New York Times*, May 7, 1895, 5.

56. Carl Rust Parker, *Transactions*, 92; "Obituary," *New York Times*, October 18, 1919, 11.

57. Carl Rust Parker, *Transactions*, 92.

58. Barrett, "Fifty Years," 184.

59. Carrère and Hastings, *Florida: The American Riviera*, 24.

60. See for example, McGuire to L. C. Haines, August 22, 1910, January 20, 1910, McGuire Orderbook, 218, FC.

61. McGuire to Fred H. Lemon and Co., November 22, 1919, McGuire April 13, 1912, McGuire Orderbook, 319, FC.

Chapter 10. Electricity, Water, and Final Touches, 1887

1. Richard A. Martin, *City Makers*, 154–55; *List of Edison Plants, May 1st, 1888* (booklet), 3, Edison Papers.

2. *Points of Interest for Hotel Proprietors* (booklet), 3, Edison Papers.

3. Ossman and Ewing, *Carrère & Hastings: Masterworks*, 28.

4. "Machinery—Ponce de Leon," October 12, 1914, McGuire Letterbook, FC; McAloon, interview with author.

5. *William J. Hammer*, 4–8.

6. *List of Edison Plants, May 1st, 1888* (booklet), 3, Edison Papers.

7. McGuire to Parrott, January 6, 1908; McGuire to C. H. Lauther, October 26, 1907, and March 14, 1908; McGuire to L. C. Harris, October 20, 1910, all in McGuire Letterbook, FC.

8. "St. Augustine Notes," *Times-Union*, January 28, 1887.

9. Clough to Flagler, November 7, 15, 25, 1887, FEC Hotel file, HMFP; William M. Jewell to Flagler, February 3, 1888, Correspondence, 1885–91 file, HMFP.

10. "Artesian Water," *St. Augustine St. Johns Weekly*, April 2, 1887, 3; "Artesian Well Engineering," *Scientific American*, 1.

11. "Artesian Well Engineering," Scientific American, 1.

12. A. C. Abbott, "Notes on work done in St. Augustine, June 2 to June 11, 1892," box 8, HMFP; McGuire to L. C. Harris, November 4, 1910, McGuire Letterbook, FC.

13. "Bustle at the Barracks," *Times-Union*, October 9, 1894, 3; "Café of the Ponce," *Tatler*, February 29, 1908, 7.

14. *Times-Union*, June 5, 7, 17, 1887.

15. Flagler to Anderson, June 23, 30, 1887, HMFP.

16. "St. Augustine Notes," *Times-Union*, July 2, 13, 1887; City Council minutes, October 8, 1887.

17. Flagler to Anderson, June 30, 1887, HMFP; *St. Augustine Press*, July 30, 1887, 3; "St. Augustine Notes," *Times-Union*, August 6, 1887, 2.; "St. Augustine Budget," *Jacksonville News-Herald*, October 12, 1887, 1; "St. Augustine Notes," *Florida Weekly Times*, October 13, 1887, 5.

18. *Jacksonville News-Herald*, October 8, 9, 10, 1887.

19. "St. Augustine Budget," *Jacksonville News-Herald*, October 12, 1887, 1; "Yellow Fever in Palatka," *Jacksonville News-Herald*, October 14, 1887, 1; "Ancient City Budget," *Jacksonville News-Herald*, October 27, November 13, 1887, 2.

20. "The Ancient City," *Times-Union*, December 26, 1887, 1.

21. Carrère and Hastings, *Florida: The American Riviera*, 6.

22. Barghini, *Society*, 8.

23. St. Augustine Notes," *Times-Union*, September 28, 1887, 2; "News from St. Augustine," *Jacksonville News-Herald*, December 30, 1887, 2; "Ancient City," *Times-Union*, December 13, 1887, 2; "St. Augustine," *Jacksonville Weekly News-Herald*, December 22, 1887, 2.

24. "News from St. Augustine," *Jacksonville News-Herald*, December 23, 1887, 2; "Ancient City News," *Jacksonville Weekly News-Herald*, November 24, 1887, 1.

25. "News from St. Augustine," *Jacksonville News-Herald*, December 11, 25, 1887, January 10, 1888, 2.

26. "St. Augustine Notes," *Times-Union*, November 13, 1887, 1.

27. "The Ancient City," *Times-Union*, December 30, 1887, 2.

28. "St. Augustine Budget," *Jacksonville News-Herald*, December 11, 1887, 2; "Ancient City," *Times-Union*, December 11, 1887, 1; Hastings, "Letter," 4.

29. "News from St. Augustine," *Jacksonville News-Herald*, December 29, 1887, 2.

30. "Ancient City," *Times-Union*, December 8, 1887, 2; "Ancient City," *Times-Union*, 2.

31. "News from St. Augustine," *Jacksonville News-Herald*, December 29, 1887, 2.

32. MacWilliams, "Recollections."

33. "Happenings in St. Augustine," *Jacksonville News-Herald*, September 14, 1887, 1.

34. Allan Forman, "Hotel Ponce de Leon," *New York Evening Post*, January 17, 1888, 8; Flagler to H. Walters, December 1, 1890, Flagler Letterbook, HMFM.

35. "The Ancient City," *Times-Union*, December 7, 1887, 2; "The Ancient City," *Times-Union*, December 26, 1887, 1; "News from St. Augustine," *Jacksonville News-Herald*, December 28, 1887, 2.

36. "Chit Chat," *Tatler*, January 21, 1893, 2.

37. "Winter in St. Augustine," *Jacksonville News-Herald*, December 18, 1887, 3.

38. "Howard on Human Nature," *New York Daily Graphic*, December 17, 1887.

39. "Ancient City," *Times-Union*, December 25, 1887, 1.

40. "News from St. Augustine," *Jacksonville News-Herald*, December 30, 1887, 2.

41. "Romantic Marriage," *Jacksonville News-Herald*, September 26, 1887; "St. Augustine Notes," *Florida Weekly Times*, September 29, 1887, 5; "St. Augustine Notes," *Times-Union*, November 15, 18, 1887.

42. "St. Augustine Notes," *Times-Union*, November 5, 1887, 2.

43. "St. Augustine Budget," *Jacksonville News-Herald*, December 9, 1887, 1; "The Ancient City," *Times-Union*, December 13, 16, 1887, 2.

44. "About the Alcazar," *Jacksonville News-Herald*, October 30, 1887, 2.

45. "St. Augustine Notes," *Florida Weekly Times*, February 24, 1887, 5; "St. Augustine Notes," *Times-Union*, March 1, 12, 1887, 2.

46. "St. Augustine Notes," *Times-Union*, March 11, 30, 1887, 2; "St. Augustine Jottings," *Jacksonville News-Herald*, October 25, 1887, 2.

47. "St. Augustine Notes," *Times-Union*, May 28, 1887, 2.

48. "St. Augustine," *Jacksonville News-Herald*, June 7, 1887, 2; "St. Augustine Notes," *Times-Union*, June 9, 1887, 2.

49. "City News," *St. Augustine Press*, July 30, 1887, 3.

50. "Ponce de Leon Hotel," *Jacksonville News-Herald*, August 7, 1887, 12; "Ancient City Jottings," *Jacksonville News-Herald*, October 18, 1887, 1; "St. Augustine Budget," *Jacksonville News-Herald*, October 21, 1887, 1.

51. "Ancient City Jottings," *Jacksonville News-Herald*, October 1, 2, 1887; "St. Augustine Notes," *Times-Union*, November 5, 1887, 2.

52. "News from St. Augustine," *Jacksonville News-Herald*, December 23, 24, 1887, 2.

53. Flagler to Anderson, June 18, 1887, HMFP.

54. "St. Augustine," *Jacksonville News-Herald*, July 23, 1887, 2; "Ancient City News," *Jacksonville News-Herald*, January 1, 1888, 3; "The Ancient City," *Times-Union*, January 17, 1888, 2.

Chapter 11. Opening Day, 1888

1. "News from St. Augustine," *Jacksonville News-Herald*, January 4, 1888, 2.

2. "News from St. Augustine," *Jacksonville News-Herald*, January 3, 1888, 2.

3. "Mr. Flagler's Army," *Jacksonville News-Herald*, January 9, 1888, 1.

4. "Pullman Palace Vestibule Trains," *Times-Union*, October 30, 1887, 1.

5. "The Palace on Wheels," *Jacksonville News-Herald*, January 11, 1888, 1

6. "Special," *Jacksonville News-Herald*, January 11, 1888, 1.

7. Ibid.

8. "In Hotel Ponce de Leon," *Jacksonville News-Herald*, January 12, 1888, 19.

9. "Opening," *Tatler*, January 21, 1893, 1.

10. Ibid.

11. Ibid.

12. "Affairs in St. Augustine," *Times-Union*, January 25, 1893, 5.

13. Menu, Ponce de Leon file, SAHS.

14. "Mr. Flagler's Army," *Jacksonville News-Herald*, January 9, 1888, 1; "Special," *Jacksonville News-Herald*, January 11, 1888, 1.

15. "New York to St. Augustine," *New York Age*, January 18, 1890, 4.

16. The medal is preserved in the Flagler Museum in Palm Beach; "A Surprise," unidentified clipping in Castleden, *Early Years*, 23.

17. "Ready for Guests," *Jacksonville News-Herald*, January 13, 1888, 1; "Ponce de Leon," *Times-Union*, January 12, 1888, 1.

18. "News from St. Augustine," *Jacksonville News-Herald*, January 4, 1888, 2.

19. "The Ancient City," *Times-Union*, January 18, 31, 1888.

20. "Casa Monica," *Times-Union*, February 10, 12, 1888, 8.

21. Smith, *Design and Prospectus*, 45.

22. Plimpton, "Florida, 1889," 8; "The Ancient City," *Times-Union*, January 31, 1888, 2.

23. "Ancient City," *Times-Union*, February 18, 1888, 2.

24. Gunter, *Enchantment*, 242.

25. "The Ancient City," *Times-Union*, January 23, 1888, 1; "Wintering in Florida," *New York Times*, January 30, 1888, 8.

26. "News from St. Augustine," *Jacksonville News-Herald*, February 8, 12, 18, 1888, 2.

27. Louise Randolph, "In Old St. Augustine," *Washington Post*, January 21, 1894, 16.

28. "St. Augustine," *Jacksonville News-Herald*, January 11, 1888, 1.

29. "News from St. Augustine," *Jacksonville News-Herald*, March 31, 1888, 2; "Day in St. Augustine," *Times-Union*, May 9, 1891, 2; "Legendary Carriage Driver Dead at 96," *St. Augustine Record*, December 22, 1984.

30. "Pratt of the Palatka Herald Visits the Ponce," *St. Augustine Press*, March 3, 1888, 4; "St. Augustine in Winter," *New York Times*, January 31, 1892, 2.

31. R. T. Goff to J. R. Parrott, January 13, 1896, FEC file, SAHS; L. A. Colee to R. T. Goff, May 13, 1903, St. Augustine Transfer Co. file, SAHS.

32. "News from St. Augustine," *Jacksonville News-Herald*, September 15, 1887, 7; "Ponce de Leon Stables," *Jacksonville News-Herald*, October 9, 1887, 2; "News from St. Augustine," *Jacksonville News-Herald*, February 18, 1888, 2.

33. "Ponce de Leon Stables," *Jacksonville News-Herald*, October 9, 1887, 2; "Gossip," *Tatler*, January 20, 1894, 4.

34. "Gay Gossip from the Spa," *Times-Union*, January 10, 1889, 2; "Thieves in St. Augustine," *Times-Union*, January 15, 1889, 2; "St. Augustine Notes," *Times-Union*, September 24, 1889, 2; "Day in St. Augustine," *Times-Union*, December 26, 1891, 5; "Affairs in St. Augustine," *Times-Union*, January 12, 1894, 2.

35. Drysdale, "Florida Hotels," 11; "Slick of the Slickest," *Times-Union*, March 17, 1894, 2.

36. Plimpton, "Florida, 1889," 6.

37. Drysdale, "Florida Hotels," 2.

38. Quoted in Akin, "Cleveland Connection," 59.

39. "Ponce de Leon Staff," *Tatler*, January 20, 1894, 3.

40. "Ponce de Leon," *Tatler*, January 14, 1893, 12; "Ponce de Leon Opening," *Tatler*, January 23, 1897, 2.

41. Flagler to McGuire, December 18, 1902, box 40, HMFP; McGuire to Sidney M. Cole, September 1, 1908, McGuire Letterbook, FC.

42. *Tatler*, January 21, 1899, 2.

43. Abbott, *Open*, 14.

44. Blouet, *Jonathan*, 276–79.

45. Ralph, "Riviera," 496–97.

46. "News from St. Augustine," *Jacksonville News-Herald*, March 24, 1888, 2; "General George Flynn," *Jacksonville News-Herald*, March 25, 1888, 2.

47. "For Newspaper Readers," *Jacksonville News-Herald*, January 17, 1888, 2.

48. "News from St. Augustine, *Jacksonville News-Herald*, January 20, 1888, 2.

49. "In Hotel Ponce de Leon," *Jacksonville News-Herald*, January 12, 1888, 12.

50. "Virgilio Tojetti," obituary, *New York Times*, March 28, 1901, 1; "An Artist Reception," *New*

York Times, February 25, 1881, 5; "Academy of Music," *New York Times*, August 25, 1885, 5; "Art Ceilings," *Tatler*, February 3, 1894, 10.

51. "Ball at the Ponce," *Times-Union*, January 5, 1890, 1; Barghini, *Flagler's Painting Collection*, 26; Torchia, *Florida Legacy*, 5.

52. Phillips, *Practical Hints*, 181.

53. "The Ponce de Leon," in Castleden, *Early Years*, 36; "News from St. Augustine," *Jacksonville News-Herald*, February 20, 1888, 2.

54. Hanks, "Pottier," 88.

55. Carrère and Hastings, *Florida: The American Riviera*, appendix.

56. "Ponce de Leon," *Tatler*, February 4, 1905, 3.

57. *Hotel Register*, qtd. in Castleden, *Early Years*, 21; "Auction Sales," *New York Times*, January 17, 1892, 14.

58. Mortgage Agreement, R. C. Rathbone and Son, April 17, 1888, HMFP.

59. "Ancient City," *Times-Union*, January 24, 1888, 2; "Ancient City," *Times-Union*, February 1, 1888, 2; "Ancient City," *Times-Union*, February 18, 21, 1888, 2.

60. "News from St. Augustine," *Jacksonville News-Herald*, February 1–2, 1888, 1.

61. "Ancient City," *Times-Union*, March 4, 1888, 1.

62. Gregory, *Families of Fortune*, 205.

63. "Mr. Flagler's Army," *Jacksonville News-Herald*, January 9, 1888, 1.

64. "The Ponce de Leon Ball," *Times-Union*, February 11, 1888, 2; "Ponce de Leon Hop," *Jacksonville News-Herald*, February 11, 1888, 2.

65. "The President's Visit," *Jacksonville Weekly News-Herald*, February 9, 1888, 7; "The President Accepts," *Jacksonville Weekly News-Herald*, February 9, 1888, 7.

66. "The Ancient City," *Times-Union*, February 19, 1888, 1.

67. "The Ancient City," *Times-Union*, February 19, 1888, 1; "News from St. Augustine," *Jacksonville News-Herald*, February 19, 22, 1888, 2.

68. "The Ancient City," *Times-Union*, February 17, 1888; "President," *Times-Union*, February 24, 1888, 1; "Our Guests," *Jacksonville News-Herald*, February 24, 1888, 1.

69. Levenson, *Letters of Henry Adams*, 3:106; "St. Augustine Is Ready," *Jacksonville News-Herald*, February 23, 1888, 8.

70. "Our Guests," *Times-Union*, February 24, 1888, 1.

71. *William J. Hammer*, 6; "Our Guests," *Jacksonville News-Herald*, February 24, 1888, 1.

72. "In St. Augustine," *Times-Union*, February 24, 1888, 1; "News from St. Augustine, *Jacksonville News-Herald*, February 26, 1888, 2.

73. "Died," *New York Times*, September 2, 1910, 9; "Inheritance Tax Reveals Little Known Facts," *New York Times*, June 1, 1912, 5MI.

74. Sidney Walter Martin, *Flagler: Visionary*, 127; Summers, "Benedict," 265.

75. "News From St. Augustine," *Jacksonville News-Herald*, February 27, 1888, 2.

76. "A Brilliant Affair," *Times-Union*, March 2, 1888, 1; "Ponce de Leon Ball," *St. Augustine Press*, March 3, 1888, 1; *St. Augustine News*, March 4, 1888.

77. "The Ancient City," *Times-Union*, January 30, February 10, 16, 1889, 2.

78. "The Ancient City," *Times-Union*, January 27, 30; February 2, 1889, 2.

79. "Nearly a Block in Ruins," *New York Times*, March 2, 1888, 1; "The Ancient City," *Times-Union*, March 2, 4, 1888.

80. "News from St. Augustine," *Jacksonville News-Herald*, February 18, March 3, 1888, 2; "The Ancient City," *Times-Union*, March 5, 1888, 1.

81. "Matters in St. Augustine," *Times-Union*, March 30, 1888, 2.

82. Lefevre, "Flagler," 182.

83. "Ponce de Leon Ball," *Tatler*, March 23, 1901, 5.

84. Paul, *Tiffany*, 40; Deforest, "Travel Diary."

85. Favis, *Heade*, 32–35.

86. Heade, "Notes of Florida," 324.

87. Ibid.

88. Favis, *Heade*, 47.

89. "St. Augustine Locals," *Times-Union*, March 25, 1886, 3; "Ancient City Locals," *Times-Union*, March 31, 1886, 3.

90. "News from St. Augustine," *Jacksonville News-Herald*, February 28, 1888, 2; "Matters in St. Augustine," *Times-Union*, March 26, 1888, 1.

91. "Ponce de Leon Studios," *Jacksonville News-Herald*, February 26, 1888, 6.

92. "Art Studio Reception," *St. Augustine News*, March 22, 1891, 12.

93. Robbins, "Reminiscences," 539.

94. "News from St. Augustine," *Jacksonville News-Herald*, March 11, 1888, 2.

95. "News from St. Augustine," *Jacksonville News-Herald*, March 8, 1888, 2; "Manager Seavey's Ball," *Jacksonville News-Herald*, March 9, 1888, 1; "St. Augustine Carnival," *Times-Union*, March 9, 1888, 1; "News from St. Augustine," *Jacksonville News-Herald*, March 10, 1888, 2.

96. "Jay Gould in Florida," *Jacksonville News-Herald*, March 19, 1888, 1; "The Ancient City," *Times-Union*, March 20, 1888, 2.

97. Morrow, "Henry M. Flagler," A9.

98. "Introduced into Society," *New York Times*, December 27, 1891, 3.

99. "News from St. Augustine," *Jacksonville News-Herald*, March 29, 1888, 2; "News from St. Augustine," *Jacksonville News-Herald*, April 8, 1888, 3; "Matters in St. Augustine," *Times-Union*, April 13, 1888, 2.

100. "Mrs. Grant and the Veterans," *New York Times*, March 14, 1888, 4.

101. "News from St. Augustine," *Jacksonville News-Herald*, March 15, 1888, 2.

102. "News from St. Augustine," *Jacksonville News-Herald*, March 1, 1888, 2.

103. "The Ancient City," *Times-Union*, March 15, 20, 21, 1889, 2; "St. Augustine Lawn Tennis Tournament," *Outing Magazine* 16 (June 1890), 180–82.

104. "News from St. Augustine," *Jacksonville News-Herald*, April 5, 1888, 2.

105. Louise Randolph, "In Old St. Augustine," *Washington Post*, January 21, 1894, 16.

106. "Matters in St. Augustine," *Times-Union*, March 29, 1888, 2; "News from St. Augustine," *Jacksonville News-Herald*, March 29, 1888, 2.

107. "St. Augustine Locals," *Times-Union*, April 24, 1885, 3; "Cuban Giants to the Front," *Cleveland Gazette*, January 21, 1888, 3.

108. Maccanon, *Commanders*, 21–22.

109. *New York Age*, October 15, 1887, quoted in Malloy, "Birth," 3; "Of Race Interest," *Cleveland Gazette*, August 4, 1888, 1.

110. "Casa Monica Hop," *Jacksonville News-Herald*, March 12, 1888, 1.

111. "News from St. Augustine," *Jacksonville News-Herald*, January 11, 1888, 2; "Matters in St. Augustine," *Times-Union*, March 23, 1888, 2.

112. "The Opening," in Castleden, *Early Years*, 48; "He Worked the Waiters," *Times-Union*, April 29, 1889, 2; "Bear Racket at Yale," *New York World*, December 20, 1889, 4.

113. "The Ancient City," *Times-Union*, January 29, February 1, 14, 1888.

114. "The Ancient City," *Times-Union*, February 12, 14, 1888; "News from St. Augustine," *Jacksonville News-Herald*, February 14, 1888, 2.

115. "News from St. Augustine," *Jacksonville News-Herald*, March 18, 1888, 2.

116. "He Worked the Waiters," *Times-Union*, April 29, 1889, 2.

117. "News from St. Augustine," *Jacksonville News-Herald*, March 30–31, 1888, 2.

118. "News from St. Augustine," *Jacksonville News-Herald*, March 16, 1888, 2; "Matters in St. Augustine," *Times-Union*, March 30, 1888, 2.

119. Garratt, "Elements," 401; "News from St. Augustine," *Jacksonville News-Herald*, January 8, 1888, 2; "News from St. Augustine," *Jacksonville News-Herald*, March 31, 1888, 2; Flagler to W. J. Krome, August 23, 1909, HMFP.

120. "Matters in St. Augustine," *Times-Union*, April 2, 1888, 1.

121. "Electricity in Florida," *Times-Union*, April 6, 1888, 2; "News from St. Augustine," *Jacksonville News-Herald*, April 14, 1888, 2; "St. Johns Young Democracy," *Times-Union*, May 16, 1888, 2.

122. "News from St. Augustine," *Jacksonville News-Herald*, February 28, 1888, 2; Blouet, *Jonathan*, 280.

123. "News from St. Augustine," *Jacksonville News-Herald*, March 3, 12, 20, 23, 1888.

124. "News from St. Augustine," *Jacksonville News-Herald*, March 27, 1888, 2; "Matters in St. Augustine," *Times-Union*, March 28, April 11, 1888, 2.

125. "News from St. Augustine," *Jacksonville News-Herald*, April 14, 1888, 2; "Matters in St. Augustine," *Times-Union*, April 16, 1888, 1; Smith to Flagler, St. Johns County Deed Book LL, 658–61; Clark, "Smith," 55.

126. MacWilliams, "Recollections."

127. "Matters in St. Augustine," *Times-Union*, April 5, 1888, 2; "News from St. Augustine," *Jacksonville News-Herald*, April 5, 1888, 2.

128. "Matters in St. Augustine," *Times-Union*, April 11, 1888, 2; "News from St. Augustine," *Jacksonville News-Herald*, April 11, 1888, 2.

129. "News from St. Augustine," *Times-Union*, May 2, 1888, 1.

130. "Matters in St. Augustine," *Times-Union*, April 20, 1888; "Pursuing an Oily Subject," *Times-Union*, April 28, 1888, 1.

131. "Personals," *St. Augustine Press*, March 3, 1888, 1; "Ancient City," *Times-Union*, March 4, 1888, 1; "Cattle Ranches in Florida," *New York Times*, March 11, 1888, 6.

132. "The Day in St. Augustine," *Times-Union*, March 9, 1889, 2.

133. "The State University Again," *Times-Union*, July 16, 1886, 1.

134. "Going Unwhipt of Justice," *Times-Union*, June 30, 1888, 2; "City by the Sea," *Times-Union*, July 21, 1888, 2.

135. "News from St. Augustine," *Jacksonville News-Herald*, April 15, 27, 1888, 2; "Matters in St. Augustine," *Times-Union*, April 22, 1888, 5; "Hotel Cordova," undated booklet in Cordova file, SAHS.

Chapter 12. Upstairs and Downstairs, 1888–1890

1. "A Yellow Fever Canard," *Jacksonville News-Herald*, January 17, 1888, 1.

2. "As to Yellow Fever," *Times-Union*, April 29, 1888, 1; "The Governor's Duty," *Times-Union*, April 30, 1888, 4.

3. "From Ye Ancient City," *Times-Union*, July 2, 1888, 1; "Over in St. Augustine," *Times-Union*, August 10, 1888, 2; "From the Ancient City," *Times-Union*, August 11, 1888, 2; "The Cordon Grows," *Times-Union*, August 13, 1888, 2; "Life in St. Augustine," *Times-Union*, September 9, 1888, 5.

4. "The Delespine Case," *Times-Union*, September 15, 1889, 4.

5. "Life in St. Augustine," *Times-Union*, September 9, 1888, 5; "Ponce de Leon Opened," *Times-Union*, January 11, 1889, 2; "Politics in St. Augustine," *Times-Union*, January 16, 1889, 2.

6. City Council minutes, September 10, October 1, 1888.

7. "Welcome to the Times-Union," *Times-Union*, December 5, 1888, 5.

8. "Life in St. Augustine," *Times-Union*, September 9, 1888, 5.

9. "Ancient City Progress," *Times-Union*, December 6, 1888, 5.

10. City Council minutes, August 25, 1888.

11. Crespo, "Florida's First," 387; "Matters in St. Augustine," *Times-Union*, April 22, 1888, 2; "Welcome to the Times-Union," *Times-Union*, December 5, 1888, 5; "Ancient City Progress,"

Times-Union, December 6, 1888, 5; "Inspiration of the Menus," *Times-Union*, January 12, 1890, 1; "Sunday in St. Augustine," *Times-Union*, January 20, 1890, 2.

12. "St. Augustine News," *Times-Union*, August 18, 1888, 1; "Busy St. Augustine," *Times-Union*, December 9, 1888, 1; "We Will Welcome You, Boys," *Times-Union*, December 18, 1888, 2.

13. O. B. Smith to W. W. Dewhurst, December 8, 1888, chronological file, SAHS.

14. "We Will Welcome You, Boys," *Times-Union*, December 18, 1888, 2; "Cathedral Revisions," *Times-Union*, December 22, 1888, 2.

15. Richard A. Martin, *City Makers*, 239.

16. City Council minutes, June 28, 1886.

17. "Ancient City," *Times-Union*, January 25, February 2, 1888, 2; "Mrs. Flagler's Generosity," *Times-Union*, May 22, 1888, 2.

18. "Sunday in St. Augustine," *Times-Union*, January 13, 1889, 2; Gunter, *Enchantment*, 95.

19. "New Augustine Dumping Ground," *St. Augustine Evening News*, April 25, 1889, 4; untitled clipping, *New York Herald*, March 7, 1893, qtd. in Castleden, *Early Years*, 80.

20. City Council minutes, April 9, 1888; "News from St. Augustine," *Times-Union*, April 29, 1888, 2; "An Ancient City Character," *Times-Union*, April 6, 1889, 2; "Sportsman's Catachism," *Times-Union*, July 23, 1890, 2.

21. "City Notes," *St. Augustine Evening News*, September 21, 1889, 4.

22. "Paving in St. Augustine," *Times-Union*, March 1, 1892, 1.

23. City Council minutes, December 13, 1888; "Who Owns It," *Times-Union*, October 25, 1892, 5; "Day in St. Augustine," *Times-Union*, October 29, 1892, 5.

24. "Day in St. Augustine," *Times-Union*, December 6, 1891, 2; "Sunday in St. Augustine," *Times-Union*, January 4, February 27, 1892, 1; "Entertaining Lecture," *Times-Union*, February 28, 1892, 5.

25. Flagler to Cooper, August 28, 1886, Flagler Letterbook, HMFM; "We Will Welcome You, Boys," *Times-Union*, December 18, 1888, 2; Flagler to McGuire and McDonald, July 19, 1890, Flagler Letterbook, HMFM.

26. "Work of Council," *St. Augustine Evening News*, July 19, 1889, 4; "Council in Caucus," *St. Augustine Evening News*, July 24, 1889, 4; "Mr. Flagler's Proposition," *St. Augustine Evening News*, July 25, 1889, 1.

27. "Ancient City News Notes," *Times-Union*, July 27, 1889, 2.

28. "The Wrangle," *St. Augustine Evening News*, July 26, 1889, 2; "They Accept the Streets," *St. Augustine Evening News*, July 26, 1889, 4.

29. "Work of the Council," *St. Augustine Evening News*, August 9, 1889, 4; St. Johns County Deed Book OO, 525.

30. Crespo, "Florida's First," 164–65; McGuire and McDonald to Carrère and Hastings, June 25, July 15, 1910, McGuire Letterbook, FC.

31. McGuire and McDonald, "Cutting Concrete Pool in Turkish Bath," McGuire file, SAHS.

32. "Ancient City Notes," *Times-Union*, December 7, 1888, 1; "Looking to South Florida," *Times-Union*, December 21, 1888, 2.

33. "We Will Welcome You, Boys," *Times-Union*, December 18, 1888, 2; "Bright Business Prospects," *Times-Union*, December 20, 1888, 2.

34. "Advice to the Butterflies," *Times-Union*, December 29, 1888, 2.

35. "Dots from St. Augustine," *Times-Union*, December 27, 1888, 2; "Wonders of the Alcazar," *Times-Union*, January 4, 1889, 2; "St. Augustine By-the-Sea," *Times-Union*, February 9, 1889, 2; "Resort for the Summer, Too," *Times-Union*, March 22, 1889, 2.

36. "Hotel Cordova," pamphlet, 1889, Cordova file, SAHS.

37. "The Opening Yesterday," *St. Augustine Weekly News*, January 17, 1889, 1; "Ponce de Leon Opened," *Times-Union*, January 11, 1889, 2.

38. "Elegant Rolling Stock," *St. Augustine Weekly News*, January 10, 1889, 8; "The Change," *St. Augustine Weekly News*, January 31, 1889, 8.

39. "Sumptuous Private Cars," *Times-Union*, April 1, 1891, 2.

40. "An Alphabetical Quarrel," *Times-Union*, February 25, 1889, 2.

41. "City Items," *St. Augustine Weekly News*, February 14, 21, 28, 1889, 8; "Opening of the Casino," *Times-Union*, February 23, 1889, 2.

42. "Opening of the Casino," *Times-Union*, February 23, 1889, 2; "Life among the Artists," *Times-Union*, February 24, 1889, 1; "Items of Interest," *St. Augustine Weekly News*, December 12, 1889, 8.

43. "Letter from Mr. Frank P. Thompson," *New York Globe*, April 21, 1883, 2.

44. Malloy, "Truth," 18.

45. Maccanon, *Commanders*, 21.

46. "The Land of Flowers," *Colored American* (Washington, D.C.), February 8, 1902, 7.

47. "Waiters Day," *St. Augustine Weekly News*, February 14, 1889, 1; "An Alphabetical Quarrel," *Times-Union*, February 25, 1889, 2; "Burglars in St. Augustine," *Times-Union*, February 28, 1889, 2; Malloy, "Truth," 5; "Colored Ball," *St. Augustine News*, April 5, 1891, 15; "St. Augustine," *Richmond Planet*, February 2, 1895, 4.

48. "From Philadelphia," *Indianapolis Freeman*, January 10, 1903, 3; "Letter from Mr. Frank P. Thompson," *New York Globe*, April 21, 1883, 2.

49. Malloy, "Truth," 15.

50. Maccanon, *Commanders*, 22.

51. "Ponce Closed," *Times-Union*, April 16, 1892, 1.

52. Blouet, *Jonathan*, 281.

53. "Cutlets from Ancient City," *Times-Union*, February 26, 1894, 2.

54. Maccanon, *Commanders*, 45–46.

55. "The Day in St. Augustine," *Times-Union*, February 7, 1890, 2; Maccanon, *Commanders*, 48; Phillips, *Practical Hints*, 184.

56. Ralph, "Riviera," 498.

57. "Gayeties of Gala Week," *Times-Union*, March 12, 1889, 2; "Amid the Orange Groves," *New York Tribune*, March 22, 1889, 4.

58. "Gayeties of Gala Week," *Times-Union*, March 12, 1889, 2.

59. "Mr. Flagler Received Credit," FEC file, folder 28, SAHS; "Ancient City News Notes," *Times-Union*, December 7, 1888, 1; W. L. Crawford to Flagler, November 29, 1888, Flagler Letterbook, HMFM.

60. "Mr. Flagler Received Credit," FEC file, folder 28, SAHS; "Day in St. Augustine," *Times-Union*, April 4, 1889, 2; "U. J. White Died Last Night," *St. Augustine Record*, February 23, 1917, 1.

61. "Gayeties of St. Augustine," *Times-Union*, February 17, 1889, 2; "Under Summer Skies," *New York Tribune*, March 11, 1889, 2.

62. "Florida Travel Waking Up," *Times-Union*, March 20, 1889, 7; "Will Society Keep Lent?" *New York Times*, February 21, 1915.

63. "St. Augustine Notes, *Times-Union*, February 14, 1887, 5; "St. Augustine Notes," *Times-Union*, July 29, 1887, 2.

64. "The Ancient City," *Times-Union*, January 11, 1888, 2; "Mrs. Flagler's Generosity," *Times-Union*, May 22, 1888, 2; "Honoring the Patriot Dead," *Times-Union*, May 28, 1888, 1.

65. "He Has No Use for French," *Times-Union*, February 27, 1889, 2; "The Great Hospital Fair," *Times-Union*, March 10, 1889, 7; "Gayeties of the Gala Week," March 12, 1889, 2.

66. "All Ablaze with Beauty," *Times-Union*, March 14, 1889, 2; "End of the Hospital Fair," *Times-Union*, March 16, 1889, 2.

67. "Ball of the Hospital Fair," *Times-Union*, March 15, 1889, 1.

68. "A Pointer for Police," *Times-Union*, February 20, 1889, 2; "Lawn Tennis," *Times-Union*, March 13, 1889, 1–2; "Campbell Wins the Trophy," *Times-Union*, March 19, 1889, 2; "St. Augustine Lawn Tennis Tournament," *Outing Magazine*, 16 (June 1890), 182.

69. *St. Augustine Weekly News*, January 17, 1889.

70. "Ejected from the Train," *Times-Union*, January 21, 1889, 2; "Champions Royal Regatta," *Times-Union*, February 14, 1889, 2; "Cuban Giants Play Ball," *St. Augustine Weekly News*, February 14, 1889, 1.

71. Flagler to Harrison, November 8, 1888, Benjamin Harrison Papers, Library of Congress.

72. *Times-Union*, March 21, 22, 1889; "Mr. Cleveland in Florida," *Washington Post*, March 21, 1889, 4.

73. Birth certificate, copy, Memorial Presbyterian Church; "St. Johns County Jail," *Times-Union*, March 23, 1889, 2; "Death of Mrs. Benedict," *Times-Union*, March 27, 1889, 1; "Died on Yacht," *New York Times*, March 27, 1889, 5; Sidney Walter Martin, *Flagler: Visionary*, 127.

74. "State Press Association," *St. Augustine Weekly News*, March 28, 1889, 8; "Two Architects of Fame," *Times-Union*, April 17, 1889, 2; Annual Report of the Florida East Coast Hotel Company, 1889, HMFP.

75. "Ancient City Monster," *Times-Union*, April 25, 1889, 2; "No Chance for a Race," *Times-Union*, April 26, 1889, 2.

76. Flagler to Anderson, December 22, 1885; April 30, 1886, Flagler Letterbook, HMFM.

77. Flagler to Anderson, July 13, 1887, HMFP.

78. "At the City by the Sea," *Times-Union*, August 2, 1888, 2; "News from St. Augustine," *Times-Union*, December 23, 1888, 2; "Two Architects of Fame," *Times-Union*, April 16, 1889, 2.

79. Flagler to McGuire, March 18, 1906, box 40, HMFP.

80. "City Notes," *St. Augustine Evening News*, April 18, 1889, 4; "Progress on the New Church," *St. Augustine Evening News*, May 13, 1889, 3; "Ancient City News Notes," *Times-Union*, May 22, 1889, 2.

81. "Wedded Half a Century," *Times-Union*, May 26, 1889, 2; "City Notes," *St. Augustine Evening News*, July 23, 1889, 4; "Crash at Midnight," *St. Augustine Evening News*, July 27, 1889, 4.

82. "Ancient City Baseball," *Times-Union*, November 8, 1889, 2; "Summer's Work," *St. Augustine Weekly News*, December 5, 1889, 8; "Ancient City Notes," *Times-Union*, December 7, 1889, 2.

83. Flagler to Anderson, June 30, 1887, box 40, HMFP; "Ball Mansion to Be Moved," *St. Augustine Evening News*, May 27, 1889, 4; "Ancient City Improvements," *Times-Union*, October 25, 1889, 3.

84. "Ancient City Improvements," *Times-Union*, October 25, 1889, 3.

85. "Ponce's Season Record," *Times-Union*, April 17, 1889, 2; "The Day in St. Augustine," *Times-Union*, April 28, 1889, 2.

86. "Who Changed the Charter," *Times-Union*, May 19, 1889, 2; "Amid Ancient City Sights," *Times-Union*, September 29, 1889, 1.

87. "Ancient City News Notes," *Times-Union*, May 22, 1889, 2.

88. Unidentified newspaper clipping, Marcotte scrapbook, SAHS; "Alicia Hospital," *St. Augustine Evening News*, May 3, 1889, 3; "For Sweet Charities Sake," *St. Augustine Evening News*, July 12, 1889, 4; *Tatler*, January 16, 1897, February 3, 1900.

89. "St. Augustine Locals," *Times-Union*, November 19, 1886, 1.

90. "Ancient City News," *Times-Union*, May 29, 1889, 2; "Sunday in St. Augustine," *Times-Union*, July 15, 1889, 1.

91. "City Notes," *St. Augustine Evening News*, May 27, 1888, 4; *St. Paul Daily Globe*, June 9, 10, 11, 1889.

92. "City Notes," *St. Augustine Evening News*, July 3, 1889, 4.

93. "About the Firemen's Fund," *Times-Union*, September 20, 1889, 2.

94. "St. Augustine Notes," *Times-Union*, September 24, 25, 1889; Akin, *Flagler: Rockefeller Partner*, 138.

95. "City News," *St. Augustine Evening News*, September 28, 1889, 4; "Cat-Fishing Extraordinary," *Times-Union*, October 4, 1889, 2.

96. "With Little or No Breeze," *New York Times*, June 7, 1885, 2; "St. Augustine Yacht Club, Season of 1893–1894," booklet, SAHS; *Tatler*, January 30, 1892, 8; "Gossip," *Tatler*, February 25, 1897, 6; "Gossip," *Tatler*, March 11, 1893, 5; "Gun Club Notes," *Tatler*, April 1, 1893, 11; "Over in St. Augustine," *Times-Union*, January 7, 1892, 1; "From St. Augustine," *Times-Union*, November 15, 1892, 5.

97. "To Have a City Market," *St. Augustine Evening News*, July 8, 1889, 4; "Our City Market," *St. Augustine Evening News*, July 17, 1889, 2.

98. "Petition of Henry M. Flagler," September 26, 1889, HMFP.

99. "Work of the Council," *Times-Union*, September 27, 1889, 1–2; "St. Augustine's Great Luck," *Times-Union*, September 28, 1889, 5.

100. "Amid Ancient City Sights," *Times-Union*, September 29, 1889, 1; "The Proposal Accepted," *St. Augustine Evening News*, October 1, 1889, 4; "The Offer Accepted," *Times-Union*, October 2, 1889, 2.

101. "New Market Plans," *St. Augustine Evening News*, October 8, 1889, 4; "Another Story Wanted," *St. Augustine Evening News*, October 9, 1889, 2, 4; "Look at This Array," *St. Augustine Evening News*, October 10, 1889, 4; "Work of the Council," *St. Augustine Evening News*, October 11, 1889, 4.

102. "That Ancient Parsonage," *Times-Union*, October 9, 1889, 2; "Ancient City News Notes," *Times-Union*, December 13, 1889, 2.

103. "Augustine's New Market," *Times-Union*, October 14, 1889, 2; "The Day in St. Augustine," *Times-Union*, January 30, 1890, 2; "Washington's Birthday," *Times-Union*, February 16, 1890, 2.

104. "A Great Scheme," *St. Augustine Evening News*, July 20, 1889, 4; "Give Us the Drive," *St. Augustine Evening News*, October 2, 1889, 2; "Ancient City Improvements," *Times-Union*, October 25, 1889, 3; Crawford to Flagler, November 27, 1889, box 14, F.1, HMFP.

105. "Ancient City News Notes," *Times-Union*, December 20, 1889, 2; "Two Builders of Palaces," *Times-Union*, December 22, 1889, 2; "Over the New Bridge," *St. Augustine Weekly News*, December 26, 1.

106. "Death at His Own Hands," *Times-Union*, December 26, 1889, 3; "Daytona Dots," *Times-Union*, January 1, 1890, 2; "Ancient City Excited," *Times-Union*, January 4, 1890, 2; "Saturday, the Fete Day," *Times-Union*, February 21, 1890, 2.

107. H. H. Smith, "A Magnificent Hotel," *Washington Post*, April 19, 1891, 13.

Chapter 13. Memorial Church, 1890

1. "Captain Marcotte Died Yesterday," *St. Augustine Record*, January 22, 1923, 1; "Wore the Gray in Union Army," *Gazette-Bulletin* (Williamsport, Pennsylvania), August 19, 1911, 5.

2. "2nd Regiment, New York Volunteers," New York State Military Museum: Unit History Project, online resource; "Service Record of Captain Marcotte," *St. Augustine Record*, February 8, 1923.

3. John H. Parker, *Gatlings*, n.p.; "Marcotte, Henry," in Henry, *Military Record*, 2:137.

4. "Anna M. Hughes Marcotte," *St. Augustine Herald*, January 18, 1896, clipping in Marcotte file, SAHS.

5. "Met Lincoln at Bed of a Dying Soldier," *New York Times*, February 13, 1927, 2.

6. "An Honest Indian," *Times-Union*, August 10, 1893, 1.

7. "Capt. Marcotte's Fish Story," *Savannah Tribune*, October 29, 1904, 3.

8. "Captain Marcotte," *Daily Inquirer*, February 21, 1875, clipping in Marcotte scrapbook, SAHS; "Barracks Matters," unidentified clipping, Marcotte scrapbook; "Queen City Veterans," *Washington National Tribune*, December 27, 1883, 3; "A Thrilling Edict," *Washington Post*, July 3, 1878, 1.

9. "The Land of Flowers," *Cincinnati Enquirer*, May 31, 1885, clipping, Marcotte scrapbook, SAHS.

10. "City of Ocala and Its Enterprising Businessmen," unidentified clipping, Marcotte scrapbook; unidentified clippings, Marcotte scrapbook; "St. George," *St. Augustine News-Herald*, December 20, 1887, 2; "Beautifying the Old Town," *Times-Union*, December 28, 1888, 2; "Ocean View," *St. Augustine Weekly News*, February 14, 1889, 8.

11. "A Grand Lawn Fete," *St. Augustine Evening News*, July 10, 1889, 4; "Day in St. Augustine," *Times-Union*, May 3, 1890, 2.

12. "Off for Pleasure," *St. Augustine Weekly News*, November 28, 1889, 1; "Day in St. Augustine," *Times-Union*, November 13, 1890, December 2, 1890, 2.

13. "On a Run of 30 Hours," *Times-Union*, January 15, 1890, 8; "Florida Special," *St. Augustine Evening News*, January 15, 1890, clipping in FEC file, SAHS.

14. "New York to St. Augustine," *New York Age*, January 18, 1890, 4.

15. "Ancient City News Notes," *Times-Union*, January 1, 1890, 3; "Ancient City News Notes," *Times-Union*, January 16, 1890, 2.

16. "Opening of the Cordova," *Times-Union*, December 22, 1889, 7; "About the Hotels," *St. Augustine Weekly News*, December 26, 1889, 1; "Ancient City News," *Times-Union*, December 12, 1889, 2; Phillips, *Practical Hints*, 182.

17. Phillips, *Practical Hints*, 183.

18. "Opening of the Cordova," *Times-Union*, December 22, 1889, 7.

19. "Glories of the Ponce," *Times-Union*, December 29, 1889, 7; "St. Augustine Affairs," *Times-Union*, January 3, 1890, 3; "Ancient City Notes," *Times-Union*, January 8, 1890, 2; "Ponce's Opening Ball," *Times-Union*, January 10, 1890, 2.

20. "Sunday in St. Augustine," *Times-Union*, February 10, 1890, 5; "The Port-Cullis Falls," *Times-Union*, April 16, 1890, 2.

21. "Flagler's New Mate," *New York Evening Graphic*, n.d., clipping in Marsh scrapbook, SAHS; Campbell, *Across Fortune's Tracks*, 41–43; Lehr, "King Lehr," 67.

22. "The Baseball Park," *St. Augustine Evening News*, May 30, 1889, 4; "Our Baseball Park," *St. Augustine Evening News*, August 20, 1889, 1; "Base Ball Park," *St. Augustine Weekly News*, August 22, 1889, 1; "New Industries Needed," *Times-Union*, February 9, 1890, 3.

23. "St. Augustine Notes, *Times-Union*, November 23, 1889, 2; "Spalding and the Chicagos," *Times-Union*, February 1, 1890, 7; "Anson and His Batters," *Times-Union*, February 15, 1890, 2.

24. "Anson and His Batters," *Times-Union*, February 15, 1890, 2.

25. "Life at St. Augustine," *New York Age*, February 22, 1890, 4; "The Winter in St. Augustine," *New York Age*, March 15, 1890, 4.

26. "Won by a Close Shave," *Times-Union*, March 14, 1890, 5.

27. "The Inman Party," *Times-Union*, February 21, 1890, 1; "The Ancient City's 22nd," *Times-Union*, February 23, 1890, 2.

28. "Ten to Five," *Times-Union*, March 11, 1890, 8; "Anson's Men Win," *Times-Union*, March 12, 1890, 8.

29. "A Great Game Thursday," *Times-Union*, February 25, 1890, 2; "Professionals," *Frank Leslie's Illustrated Newspaper*, March 22, 1890, 164.

30. "Anson's Home Run," *Times-Union*, March 18, 1890, 5; "Brooklyn Drops Another Game," *Times-Union*, March 19, 1890, 8; "Anson's Parting Triumph," *Times-Union*, March 23, 1890, 5; "Brooklyns Start North," *Times-Union*, March 27, 1890, 8.

31. "A Color Line in Baseball," *New York Times*, September 12, 1887, 1.

32. "From St. Augustine, Fla.," *New York Age*, February 1, 8, 15, March 1, 1890.

33. "Life in St. Augustine," *New York Age*, March 1, 1890, 4; "Artists Reception," *Times-Union*, March 16, 1890, 2.

34. "Annual Address of President," *Indianapolis Freeman*, November 25, 1905, 3; "Day in St. Augustine," *Times-Union*, March 21, 1891, 2.

35. "Winter in Florida," *New York Age*, March 15, 1890, 4.

36. "Sunday in St. Augustine," *Times-Union*, February 17, 1890, 1; "Alicia Hospital," *Times-Union*, February 19, 1890, 1; "The Day in St. Augustine," *Times-Union*, March 4, 1890, 2.

37. "The Hospital Fair," *Times-Union*, March 11, 1890, 1.

38. "For Charity," *Times-Union*, March 14, 1890, 1.

39. "Easter in St. Augustine," *Times-Union*, April 6, 1890, 2; "Sunday in St. Augustine," *Times-Union*, April 14, 1890, 2; "Out of the Old House," *Times-Union*, April 28, 1890; "Fair Next Year Sure," *Times-Union*, May 23, 1890, 2.

40. "The Winter in Florida," *New York Age*, March 15, 1890, 4.

41. "A Live Vice-President," *Times-Union*, March 5, 1890, 5; "Vice President Morton Party," *Washington Post*, March 6, 1890, 1; "Winter in Florida," *New York Age*, March 15, 1890, 4.

42. "Society in the Capital," *New York Times*, March 12, 1890, 3; "In the Ponce de Leon," *Times-Union*, March 16, 1890, 5.

43. "Will Have a New Jail," *Times-Union*, March 6, 1890, 5; "Still They Come," *Times-Union*, March 18, 1890, 1.

44. Article from *Chicago Times*, February 4, 1893, qtd. in Castleden, *Early Years*, 69.

45. "Depew an Athlete," *New York Times*, April 6, 1890, 1; "Here Is Mr. Depew Again," *Times-Union*, April 10, 1890, 1.

46. "The Beautiful Memorial," *Times-Union*, March 16, 1890, 2; undated clipping from the *St. Augustine Evening News*, MC 48.1, SAHS; "Carrère and Hastings," University of Florida Digital Collections, http://ufdc.ufl.edu/caha.

47. H.R.C. Hawkins to Hastings, May 6, 1924, Presbyterian Church file, SAHS.

48. "The Day in St. Augustine," *Times-Union*, March 4, 1890, 2.

49. Lefevre, "Flagler," 178.

50. "A $6000 Choir," *Fort Worth Daily Gazette*, March 12, 1890, 5.

51. "Florida Breathes Easy," *Times-Union*, June 4, 1890, 2.

52. Various unidentified newspaper clippings, Memorial Church records, SAHS; "Dedication of the Church," *Times-Union*, March 17, 1890, 5.

53. Unidentified clipping, Memorial Church records, SAHS.

54. Presbyterian Church records, SAHS.

55. "Tennis Tournament," *Times-Union*, March 18, 19, 20, 21, 22, 1890.

56. "For a President's Wife," *Times-Union*, March 18, 1890, 2.

57. "Street Car or Omnibus," *Times-Union*, March 22, 1890, 2; "The Day in St. Augustine," *Times-Union*, March 27, 1890, 2.

58. "North Beach Road," *St. Augustine Evening News*, July 16, 1889, 4; "North Beach," *St. Augustine Weekly News*, December 19, 1889, 1; "North Beach Opened," *Times-Union*, March 5, 1890, 2; "St. Augustine and North Beach Railway," *St. Augustine Evening News*, June 12, 1890, 1.

59. Flagler to R. McLaughlin, January 28, 1886; Flagler to G. W. Bentley, January 16, 1886, Flagler Letterbook, HMFM.

60. Flagler to C. B. Carver, September 10, 1885, Flagler Letterbook, HMFM.

61. Flagler to McGuire, August 6, 1890, Flagler Letterbook, HMFM.

62. Flagler to Albert Verkouteren, July 30, 1890; Flagler to Crawford, July 9, 1890, Flagler Letterbook, HMFM.

63. "Day in St. Augustine," *Times-Union*, April 11, 1891, 2; "Circuit Court," *Times-Union*, November 3, 1891, 2; "Day in St. Augustine," August 31, 1893, 2; "Ashes Covering an Acre," *Times-Union*, February 5, 1895, 2; Bowen, "North Beach," 98–99.

64. "Ponce de Leon Studios," *Times-Union*, January 19, 1890, 7.

65. "Arches of the Nations," *Times-Union*, March 23, 1890, 2; "Everything Now Ready," *Times-Union*, March 30, 1890, 2; "Bad Weather for Fun," *Times-Union*, April 3, 1890, 2.

66. "Ponce de Leon Arrives," *Times-Union*, April 2, 1890, 2.

67. "Making Ready for Ponce," *Times-Union*, March 26, 1890, 2; "The Cordova's Turn Now," *Times-Union*, March 27, 1890, 5.

68. "Distinguished Visitors at St. Augustine," *New York Age*, March 29, 1890, 1.

69. "Making Room for Ponce," *Times-Union*, March 26, 1890, 2; "Season Fast Waning," *Times-Union*, April 10, 1890, 2.

70. "Season Closing Out," *Times-Union*, April 15, 1890, 2; "The Port-Cullis Falls," *Times-Union*, April 16, 1890, 2.

71. "The Port-Cullis Falls," *Times-Union*, April 16, 1890, 2.

72. "Old Iron on Anastasia," *Times-Union*, April 17, 1890, 2; "Will Extend the Street," *Times-Union*, April 23, 1890, 2.

73. "Ancient City Doings," *Times-Union*, April 25, 1890, 2.

74. Ibid.

75. "Mr. Flagler's New Yacht," *New York World*, April 21, 1890, 1; "Steam Yachting," *New York Times*, September 25, 1890, 9.

76. "Mr. Flagler's New Yacht," *Times-Union*, July 7, 1890, 1.

77. "At St. Augustine," *Times-Union*, September 3, 1890, 2; "A Crash in the Fog," *New York World*, September 5, 1894, 1.

78. Flagler to Mason Young, July 26, 1890; Flagler to W. J. Jarvis, July 31, 1890, Flagler Letterbook, HMFM.

79. "Counterfeit Money," *Times-Union*, April 29, 1890, 2; "Resuming Her Splendor," *Times-Union*, October 22, 1890, 2; "St. Johns Clean Sweep," *Times-Union*, November 8, 1890, 2.

80. "Many Buildings Going Up," *Times-Union*, May 16, 1890, 3; "Our Old Residents," *St. Augustine Evening News*, June 6, 1890, 2.

81. City Council minutes, March 27, 1889; "Lecture to Croakers," *Times-Union*, June 1, 1890, 2.

82. "Mr. Flagler's Reply," *St. Augustine Evening News*, June 3, 1890, 4; "Florida Breathes Easy," *Times-Union*, June 4, 1890, 2.

83. "A Testimonial," *Times-Union*, May 25, 1890, 1; "Lecture to Croakers," *Times-Union*, June 1, 1890, 2.

84. Flagler to C. C. McLean, July 12, 1890; Flagler to S. W. Chrichlow, December 4, 1890, Flagler Letterbook, HMFM.

85. Flagler to Hastings, December 11, 1890; Flagler to O. D. Seavey, Dec 9, 1890, Flagler Letterbook, HMFM; Flagler to McGuire, December 11, 1890, HMFP; Flagler to Rockefeller, December 18, 1890, HMFP, qtd. in Chandler, *Henry Flagler*, 300.

86. "St. Augustine Notes," *Times-Union*, September 8, 1887, 2; "St. Augustine News," *Jacksonville News-Herald*, October 7, 1887, 1; clipping, *Daytona Beach Winter Resorter*, December 31, 1937, HMFP.

87. "Ormond-on-Halifax," *Times-Union*, August 30, 1890, 2; "St. Augustine Notes," *Times-Union*, September 13, 1890, 2; Flagler to W. J. Jarvis, August 25, 1890, HMFP; Flagler to McGuire and McDonald, August 29, 1890, Flagler Letterbook, HMFM; Flagler to C. C. Deming, April 20, 1891, Flagler Letterbook, HMFM; "Reminiscences of W. L. Singleton," HMFP.

88. "Wedding at Moultrie," *Times-Union*, October 31, 1890, 3; "The Day in St. Augustine," *Times-Union*, November 9, 11, 1890, 2.

89. "Ancient City Doings," *Times-Union*, April 25, 1892, 2; "Summer Season On," *Times-Union*, May 1, 1890, 2; "City Notes," *St. Augustine Evening News*, June 23, 1890, 4.

90. "Alcazar Speaks," *Times-Union*, April 19, 1890, 2; "Citizens Organized," *Times-Union*, May 27, 1890, 2; Flagler to Seavey, July 8, 1890, HMFP; Flagler to S. W. Crichlow, November 17, 1890, HMFP; Flagler to Seavey, December 5, 1890, HMFP.

91. "Ancient City Happenings," *Times-Union*, December 13, 1888, 2.

92. "Disgrace to the County," *Times-Union*, September 1, 1889, 2; "Just Escaped Indictment," *Times-Union*, September 22, 1889, 2.

93. "Will Have a New Jail," *Times-Union*, March 6, 1890, 5; "St. Johns County Jail," *Times-Union*, April 18, 1890, 2; "St. Johns Co. Jail," *Times-Union*, June 5, 1890, 2; "Our County Jail," *St. Augustine Evening News*, June 5, 1890, 2.

94. Flagler to McGuire, October 3, 1890, HMFP.

95. "Day in St. Augustine," *Times-Union*, February 5, 6, 1891, 2.

Chapter 14. Hotel Life in Paradise, 1891

1. "Our Hotels," *St. Augustine News*, April 5, 1891, 9; "Day in St. Augustine," *Times-Union*, January 16, 1891, 3; "Ponce de Leon Opening," *Times-Union*, January 19, 1891, 1; "Ponce de Leon Open," *Times-Union*, January 20, 1891, 2.

2. White, *Reminiscences*, 245; "About Our Hotels," *St. Augustine News*, January 18, 1891, 11.

3. Louise Randolph, "In Old St. Augustine," *Washington Post*, January 21, 1894, 16.

4. Flagler to Wilson, December 8, 1890, HMFP.

5. "Day in St. Augustine," *Times-Union*, January 25, 1891, 6; "Day in St. Augustine," *Times-Union*, January 29, 1891, 2; "Day in St. Augustine," *Times-Union*, February 27, 1891, 2.

6. "Society Topics of the Week," *New York Times*, February 22, 1891, 12; "Notes," *St. Augustine News*, March 15, 1891, 12.

7. "The Ancient City," *Times-Union*, February 15, 1888, 2.

8. "Ways of Sharpers," *St. Augustine Weekly News*, December 26, 1889, 2; "Another Bunko Gang," *Times-Union*, March 7, 1885, 4.

9. "News from St. Augustine," *Jacksonville News-Herald*, February 6, 1888, 2.

10. City Council minutes, August 15, 1887; McGuire to Robert Murray, December 20, 1907, McGuire Letterbook, FC; "City Notes," *St. Augustine Weekly News*, February 7, 1889, 1.

11. "About People," *Tatler*, April 1, 1893, 15.

12. Abbott, *Open*, 97.

13. "Affairs at St. Augustine," *Times-Union*, April 6, 1894, 3.

14. "Young Couple's Dilemma," *Times-Union*, February 10, 1891, 2.

15. "Day in St. Augustine," *Times-Union*, March 3, 21, 1891, 2.

16. "St. Augustine News Notes," *Times-Union*, January 15, 1890, 2.

17. *The Wonderer*, MC 63, SAHS.

18. "St. Augustine Locals," *Times-Union*, February 5, 1886, 1; "News from St. Augustine," *Jacksonville News-Herald*, March 4, 1888; "Baseball at the Ponce," *Times-Union*, January 13, 1889, 2; "He Surprised the Sports," *Times-Union*, May 2, 1889, 2; "Bunco," *Tatler*, January 20, 1894, 1.

19. "Day in St. Augustine," *Times-Union*, February 12, 1891, 2; "Looks Like Unification," *Times-Union*, February 12, 1891, 3.

20. "Jay Gould Sick Man," *Times-Union*, February 13, 1891, 1; "Jay Gould's Health," *Times-Union*, February 15, 1891, 5.

21. "Tea at Dr. Anderson's," *St. Augustine News*, March 8, 1891, 8; "At St. Augustine," *Times-Union*, February 22, 1891, 6; "Day in St. Augustine," *Times-Union*, March 11, 1891, 3; "At Alicia

Hospital Fair," *Times-Union*, March 12, 1891, 3; "In Sweet Charity's Name," *Times-Union*, March 18, 1891, 1; "In St. Augustine," *Times-Union*, April 3, 1891, 5.

22. "Day in St. Augustine," *Times-Union*, January 30, 1891, 2; "Opening of the Casino," *St. Augustine News*, February 8, 1891; "Day in St. Augustine," *Times-Union*, February 25, 1891, 2.

23. "In the Loggias," *St. Augustine News*, March 22, 1891, 10.

24. "A Turkish Bath," clipping, Alcazar file, SAHS.

25. "Day in St. Augustine," *Times-Union*, February 14, 1891, 2.

26. "Forced to Retract," *Times-Union*, February 26, 1891, 1; "Gun Club Men Incensed," *Times-Union*, February 26, 1891, 2.

27. "Tennis Club Election," *Times-Union*, February 28, 1891, 1; "Day in St. Augustine," *Times-Union*, March 1, 1891, 2; "Tennis Tournament," *Times-Union*, March 4, 1891, 6; "Day in St. Augustine," *Times-Union*, March 15, 1891; "In the Loggias," *St. Augustine News*, March 22, 1891, 10.

28. "Swell Young Tennis Men," *Times-Union*, March 13, 1891, 2; "Waiters Winners," *Times-Union*, March 17, 1891, 6.

29. "Amusements," *St. Augustine News*, March 22, 1891, 13.

30. "Day in St. Augustine," *Times-Union*, February 11, 20, 27, 28, 1891.

31. "Day in St. Augustine," *Times-Union*, April 2, 1891, 3; "Cleveland Wins," *Times-Union*, April 3, 1891, 1; "Pittsburgh Wins," *Times-Union*, April 4, 1891, 1; "Cleveland Won," *Times-Union*, April 5, 1891, 1; "Baseball at Ponce de Leon Park," *St. Augustine News*, April 5, 1891, 15.

32. "Day in St. Augustine," *Times-Union*, February 11, 23, 1891, 2.

33. Gipson, *Thursby*, 410–12; "Day in St. Augustine," *Times-Union*, March 31, 1891, 2; "Emma Thursby Concert," *St. Augustine News*, April 5, 1891, 14.

34. "Day in St. Augustine," *Times-Union*, January 22, 1891, 2.

35. "Day in St. Augustine," *Times-Union*, February 28, 1891, 2; "Facts and Fancies," *St. Augustine News*, March 8, 1891, 7; Gunter, *Enchantment*, 102, 183.

36. "Notes about Town," *St. Augustine News*, February 1, 1891, 8; "A Pretty Dance at Ponce de Leon," *St. Augustine News*, February 8, 1891, 13; "Beauty and Gallantry," *Times-Union*, February 18, 1891, 1; "Ball at the Ponce de Leon," *St. Augustine News*, February 15, 1891, 13.

37. "Talk with C. A. Dana," *Times-Union*, March 24, 1891, 5.

38. "Sumptuous Private Cars," *Times-Union*, April 1, 1891, 2.

39. "Day in St. Augustine," *Times-Union*, January 27, 1891, 2.

40. "Day in St. Augustine," *Times-Union*, March 2, 1891, 2.

41. "All at Ormond," *Times-Union*, March 13, 1891, 2; "Day in St. Augustine," *Times-Union*, March 13, 1891, 2; "Proctor in St. Augustine," *Times-Union*, March 15, 1891, 6.

42. "Personals," *St. Augustine News*, March 22, 1891, 13.

43. Abbott, *Open*, 81.

44. "A Big Hotel for Tampa," *Florida Weekly Times*, February 9, 1888, 5; "City Notes," *St. Augustine Evening News*, September 23, 24, 1889, 4; "City Notes," *St. Augustine Weekly News*, November 14, 1889, 8; "Facts and Fancies," *St. Augustine News*, March 29, 1891, 7.

45. Covington, *Plant's Palace*, 65, 68, 79.

46. "Personals," *St. Augustine News*, March 22, 1891, 13; "Day in St. Augustine," *Times-Union*, March 27, 1891, 2.

47. "Day in St. Augustine," *Times-Union*, January 10, 1891, 2; "Ablaze with Color," *Times-Union*, February 25, 1891, 1.

48. "Day in St. Augustine," *Times-Union*, April 11, 1891, 2; "A Magnificent Hotel," *Washington Post*, April 19, 1891, 13; "In Hotel Lobbies," *Washington Post*, May 12, 1891, 4.

49. Beardsley to Flagler, March 10, 1891; Beardsley to Flagler, March 14, 1891, HMFP.

50. "Day in St. Augustine," *Times-Union*, April 19, 1891, 2.

51. "Sunday in St. Augustine," *Times-Union*, April 13, 1891, 2.

52. "Closing Up," *Times-Union*, April 20, 1891, 1; "Day in St. Augustine," *Times-Union*, May 21, 1891, 2.

53. "Day in St. Augustine," *Times-Union*, August 12, 1891, 2; "Alcazar," *Tatler*, January 9, 1892, 4.

54. "Our Hotels," *Tatler*, February 6, 1892, 10; "Tavern Tattle," *Tatler*, February 20, 1892, 8.

55. "Day in St. Augustine," *Times-Union*, July 13, 1891, 3; "Alcazar," *Tatler*, January 9, 1892, 4.

56. "Day in St. Augustine," *Times-Union*, July 13, 1891, 3; "At St. Augustine," *Times-Union*, July 21, 1891, 2; "Tennis Courts," *Tatler*, January 9, 1892, 5.

57. "Gossip," *Tatler*, March 23, 1901, 2.

58. Flagler to W. L. Crawford, November 22, 1890, HMFP; "Backing Out," *Times-Union*, September 26, 1891, 2; Scharf, *Westchester*, 870.

59. J. N. Alexander to Flagler, July 8, 1891, HMFP; "Judge Young's Rebuke," *Times-Union*, November 7, 1891, 2; "Sunday in St. Augustine," *Times-Union*, January 11, 1892, 1.

60. "The Alcazar," *Tatler*, January 23, 1892, 10; McGuire to J. R. Parrott, February 24, September 21, 1908, McGuire Letterbook, FC.

61. "Day in St. Augustine," *Times-Union*, March 6, 1891, 2.

62. "Over in St. Augustine," *Times-Union*, January 13, 1892, 1.

63. "A Remarkable Feat," *St. Augustine Weekly News*, November 28, 1889, 1.

64. "Doctor Writes about Founding of Hastings," *Tampa Tribune*, December 12, 1933, clipping, Hastings file, SAHS; Alfred B. Hastings to Leslie Wilson, January 22, 2000, and Betsy Hastings to Leslie Wilson, February 10, 2000, Hastings file, SAHS; "Ancient City Happenings," *Times-Union*, January 25, 1890, 2.

65. Ingraham to Crichlow, August 15, 1894, HMFP; Flagler to Crawford, September 11, 1890, HMFP; "East Coast Farm Lands," *Times-Union*, November 23, 1891, 1; "Real Estate Bargains," *St. Augustine News*, February 4, 1899, 4.

66. Flagler to Hastings, August 19, 1890, HMFP; "An Antiquarian Arrival," *Times-Union*, January 23, 1891, 2; "In St. Augustine," *Times-Union*, November 8, 1891, 2; "Day in St. Augustine," *Times-Union*, January 28, 1892, 1.

67. "Accidentally Shot," *Times-Union*, November 15, 1891, 2; "Dr. Newton's Death," *Times-Union*, November 17, 1891, 2.

68. "Another Road," *Times-Union*, April 15, 1891, 2.

69. "Day in St. Augustine," *Times-Union*, November 26, 1891, 2.

70. "Sunday in St. Augustine," *Times-Union*, December 7, 1891, 2; "Day in St. Augustine," *Times-Union*, January 1, 1892, 2; William T. Sheppard to S. W. Martin, May 2, 1949, Martin Papers, UFL.

71. "Day in St. Augustine," *Times-Union*, November 27, 1891, 2; "Our Hotels," *Tatler*, January 14, 1892, 3.

Chapter 15. The Season in St. Augustine, 1892–1893

1. "Aims and Objects of 'The Tatler,'" *Tatler*, January 9, 1892, 1.

2. "St. Augustine in Winter," *New York Times*, January 31, 1892, 2.

3. "Hermitage Ball," *Tatler*, February 6, 1892, 5.

4. "Hermitage Ball," *Tatler*, February 6, 1892, 3.

5. "Those Giants Defeated," *Times-Union*, February 6, 1892, 1; "Hermitage Ball," *Washington Post*, February 5, 1892, 1; "Eclipsed 'Em All," *Times-Union*, February 5, 1892, 1.

6. "Cow-Boy in Prison," *Times-Union*, February 15, 1892, 2; "Gossip of the Hotels," *Tatler*, February 20, 1892, 3; "Sunday in St. Augustine," *Times-Union*, February 29, 1892, 1.

7. "Day in St. Augustine," *Times-Union*, February 10, 14, 16, March 5, 1892, 1; "Another Big Yacht Race," *Times-Union*, March 18, 1892, 1; "Pullman," *Tatler*, March 26, 1892, 3.

8. "Military Ball," *Tatler*, February 27, 1892, 2; "Charity Ball," *Tatler*, March 19, 1892, 5; "Fair," *Tatler*, March 19, 1892, 2.

9. "Gossip from Hotels," *Tatler*, March 19, 1892, 4; White, *Reminiscences*, 243; "Cotillion," *Tatler*, March 26, 1892, 4.

10. "Winter Baseball," *Times-Union*, December 1, 1891, 2; "Baseball Season," *Times-Union*, January 2, 1892, 2.

11. "Day in St. Augustine," *Times-Union*, February 2, 1892, 1; "Those Giants Defeated," *Times-Union*, February 6, 1892, 1.

12. "Day in St. Augustine," *Times-Union*, February 27, 1892, 1; "Another Big Yacht Race," *Times-Union*, March 18, 1892, 1.

13. "Sunday in St. Augustine," *Times-Union*, March 7, 1892, 1; "The Tournament," *Tatler*, March 12, 1892, 2; "Day in St. Augustine," *Times-Union*, March 20, 1892, 1.

14. Schladermundt and Maynard to Carrère and Hastings, January 26, 1892, Presbyterian Church file, SAHS.

15. Schladermundt and Maynard to Flagler, February 27, 1892, HMFP.

16. Flagler to Carrère and Hastings, February 6, 1892, Presbyterian Church file, SAHS.

17. King, *American Mural*, 83.

18. Shand-Tucci, *Built in Boston*, n.p.

19. Lefevre, "Flagler," 183.

20. "Incidents in Society," *New York Tribune*, May 13, 1899, 7.

21. H. L. Bridwell, "Seals of All the States," *New York Times*, April 16, 1898, RBA258.

22. Paine, *Roads*, 66, 325; untitled clipping, Ammidown Scrapbook, SAHS; "Anglo-American Dispute," unidentified clipping, Bevin Scrapbook, SAHS; "Rev. S. D. Paine Expired," *St. Augustine Record*, February 1, 1909, 1.

23. Flagler to Webb, July 21, 1890, Flagler Letterbook, HMFM; "From the Ancient City," *Times-Union*, August 5, 1890, 2; "At Memorial Church," *St. Augustine Evening News*, November 2, 1890; Flagler to Warden, November 17, 1890, Flagler Letterbook, HMFM; "Day in St. Augustine," *Times-Union*, December 23, 1890, 2.

24. "Hotel Ponce de Leon," *Tatler*, January 23, 1892, 2; "Flagler," *Times-Union*, January 21, 1897, 1.

25. "St. Augustine's Budget," *Times-Union*, August 22, 1891, 3; "Day in St. Augustine," *Times-Union*, December 9, 1891, 2; "We Must Stand Together," *Cincinnati Daily Times*, August 10, 1891, clipping in Bevin Scrapbook, SAHS; "Day in St. Augustine," *Times-Union*, December 2, 1890, February 12, 1891, 2.

26. "Communicated," *St. Augustine Evening News*, November 21, 1891, clipping, Bevin Scrapbook, SAHS.

27. "Dr. S. D. Paine on Patriotism," *Ocean Grove Record*, July 9, 1892, clipping, Bevin Scrapbook, SAHS.

28. Paine to Flagler, February 19, 1892, HMFP.

29. Flagler to Paine, February 21, 1892, HMFP.

30. "Rev. S. D. Paine Resigns," *St. Augustine Evening News*, February 22, 1892, clipping, Bevin Scrapbook, SAHS; "Sunday in St. Augustine," *Times-Union*, February, 22, 1892, 1; "Day in St. Augustine," *Times-Union*, March 17, 1892, 1.

31. "Day in St. Augustine," *Times-Union*, February 5, 1891, 7; "In St. Augustine," *Times-Union*, December 25, 1891, 2; Paine, "Over the Florida Keys," 147–56.

32. "Few Phosphate Kings," *Times-Union*, April 26, 1891, 2.

33. "Day in St. Augustine," *Times-Union*, March 4, 1892, 1; "Died," *New York Times*, April 11, 1892, 5; "Typhoid from Florida," *New York Sun*, April 19, 1892, 1.

34. "Society Topics of the Week," *New York Times*, April 10, 1892, 12; "Two Fashionable

Resorts," *New York Times*, April 17, 1892, 17; "Typhoid from Florida," *New York Sun*, April 19, 1892, 1; "Typhoid's Florida Victims," *New York Times*, April 26, 1892, 5.

35. "Day in St. Augustine," *Times-Union*, April 24, May 3, 1892, 2; "Hotel King," *Times-Union*, May 31, 1892, 1.

36. "Card from Dr. Porter," *Times-Union*, May 2, 1892, 2; "Day in St. Augustine," *Times-Union*, May 3, 1892, 2; "Day in St. Augustine," *Times-Union*, May 15, 1892, 7.

37. "Did Not Originate Here," *Times-Union*, June 29, 1892, 4; "Complete Refutation," *Times-Union*, June 29, 1892, 4.

38. A. C. Abbott, "Notes on Work Done in St. Augustine, June 2 to June 11, 1892," box 8, HMFP.

39. "Day in St. Augustine," *Times-Union*, October 15, November 1, 1892, 3.

40. Dinner Menu, March 28, 1893, Ponce de Leon file, SAHS.

41. Ingraham, Speech to Miami Women's Club, November 1920, Ingraham Papers, UFL.

42. Sworn Deposition of J. E. Ingraham, February 1923, Ingraham Papers, UFL; "Keep Your Head above the Financial Waters and Bet on the Growth of the Country," *Manufacturers Record*, January 26, 1922, 6–62, copy, Ingraham Papers, UFL.

43. Paine, "Florida Keys," 150; "President J. R. Parrott Is Dead," *St. Augustine Record*, October 14, 1913, 1.

44. "Day in St. Augustine," *Times-Union*, March 22, 1893, 1.

45. Lefevre, "Flagler," 177.

46. "On to Deep Water," *Times-Union*, July 1, 1892, 5; "Down the Coast," *Times-Union*, September 26, 1892, 4.

47. "Sunday in St. Augustine," *Times-Union*, December 5, 1892, 4; "New South Florida Route," *Times-Union*, November 16, 1892, 4.

48. "Day in St. Augustine," *Times-Union*, December 6, 1892, 5; "Day in St. Augustine," *Times-Union*, October 4, 1892, 8; "Judge McWilliams Case," *Times-Union*, December 17, 1892, 2; "Tourist Topics," *Tatler*, February 4, 1893, 11; "Big Engines," *Times-Union*, February 12, 1893, 4.

49. "Over in St. Augustine," *Times-Union*, April 15, 1892, 1; "In St. Augustine," *Times-Union*, July 26, 1892, 1; "Day in St. Augustine," *Times-Union*, October 3, 1892, 1; "New Position," *Times-Union*, October 17, 1892, 5; "Day in St. Augustine," *Times-Union*, August 11, 1892, 3; "In St. Augustine," *Times-Union*, October 24, 1892, 5.

50. Flagler to Parrott, September 30, 1903, HMFP.

51. "Day in St. Augustine," *Times-Union*, November 24, 1892, 1; "Firemen of Florida," *Times-Union*, November 29, 1892, 2; "Day in St. Augustine," December 4, 1892, 2; "Day in St. Augustine," *Times-Union*, December 15, 1892, 3.

52. "Gossip," *Tatler*, February 4, 1893, 8; "Through to Rockledge," *Times-Union*, February 7, 1893, 1; "Inauguration of the Extension," *Tatler*, February 11, 1893, 11; "Mr. Flagler's Address," *St. Augustine Record*, January 31, 1912, 8.

53. "Sunday in St. Augustine," *Times-Union*, April 13, 1891, 1; Kerber, "Florida and the Columbian Exposition," 33; "Ft. Marion at the Fair," *Times-Union*, October 19, 1891, 1; "Still There Is a Hope," *Times-Union*, February 23, 1892, 3.

54. "Friend of Florida," *Times-Union*, April 7, 1892, 3.

55. "Now for the Gazetteer," *Times-Union*, April 28, 1892, 8; "Only $20,000 to Raise," *Times-Union*, July 3, 1892, 5; "St. Johns to the Front," *Times-Union*, July 15, 1892, 2; "Paid the Money," *Times-Union*, December 7, 1892, 1.

56. Kerber, "Florida and the Columbian Exposition," 45.

57. "Fair," *Tatler*, April 1, 1893, 9.

58. "Gen. Howard Saluted," *Times-Union*, April 9, 1893, 1; "Talk with Gen. Howard," *Times-Union*, April 11, 1893, 1; "Wonderful Exhibition," *Times-Union*, July 4, 1893, 2.

59. "Ponce de Leon," *Tatler*, January 21, 1893, 4; "Day in St. Augustine," *Times-Union*, May 23, 1893, 3; "Tales from Florida Towns," *Times-Union*, December 15, 1893, 2.

60. "News," unidentified clipping, January 30, 1892, chronological file, SAHS; "In St. Augustine," *Times-Union*, October 22, 1892, 5; "Day in St. Augustine," *Times-Union*, December 21, 1892, 2.

61. "Affairs at St. Augustine," *Times-Union*, March 25, 1894, 11; "Affairs at St. Augustine," *Times-Union*, May 27, 1894, 7; "More about Menendez," *Times-Union*, May 20, 1894, 7.

62. "Only Authentic History," *Times-Union*, April 16, 1895, 2; "Chronicles of Ancient City," *Times-Union*, November 13, 1895, 3.

63. "Big Casino Ablaze," *Times-Union*, January 25, 1893, 3; "Day in St. Augustine," *Times-Union*, January 26, 1893, 6; "Fire," *Tatler*, January 28, 1893, 1.

64. Advertisement, *Times-Union*, January 26, 1893, 8.

65. "Day in St. Augustine," *Times-Union*, March 4, 1893, 1.

66. "Day in St. Augustine," *Times-Union*, March 1, 1893, 1; "Casino," *Tatler*, March 4, 1893, 8.

67. "Gossip," *Tatler*, January 28, 1893, 8; "Gossip," *Tatler*, February 4, 1893, 8; "San Marco Ball," *Tatler*, February 11, 1893, 4; "Cordova Ball," *Tatler*, February 11, 1893, 9; "The Fair," *Tatler*, February 18, 1893, 7; "Washington Birthday Ball," *Tatler*, February 25, 1893, 2; "Gossip," *Tatler*, April 1, 1893, 3.

68. "A Farewell Tea," *Tatler*, February 25, 1893, 3; "Day in St. Augustine," *Times-Union*, February 25, 1893, 1.

69. "Mr. Flagler's New Home," *Times-Union*, July 11, 1892, 1; "Day in St. Augustine," *Times-Union*, November 19, 1892, 1; "In St. Augustine," *Times-Union*, September 19, 1892, 5; "Day in St. Augustine," *Times-Union*, March 3, 1893, 1.

70. "Day in St. Augustine," *Times-Union*, February 16, 1893, 1; "Ideal Winter Voyage," *Times-Union*, March 1, 1893, 5; "Gossip," *Tatler*, March 4, 1893, 7.

71. "Sunday in St. Augustine," *Times-Union*, March 20, 1893, 1; "Day in St. Augustine," *Times-Union*, March 7, 1893, 1.

72. "Private Dance at Ponce de Leon," *Tatler*, March 25, 1893, 8.

73. "Day in St. Augustine," *Times-Union*, March 1, 9, 21, 1893, 1.

74. "Day in St. Augustine," *Times-Union*, January 19, 1893, 3; "Sunday in St. Augustine," *Times-Union*, January 30, 1893, 5; "Day in St. Augustine," *Times-Union*, March 9, 1893, 1.

75. "Equestrian Sports," *Times-Union*, January 31, 1893, 1; "Day in St. Augustine," *Times-Union*, February 16, 23, 1893, 1; "Day in St. Augustine," *Times-Union*, January 20, 1893, 7; "No Tidings of Lander," *Times-Union*, January 24, 1893, 3; "Passenger Agents," *Times-Union*, March 11, 1893, 1.

76. "Prince Beat the Horses," *Times-Union*, February 18, 1893, 1; "Day in St. Augustine," *Times-Union*, February 19, 1893, 1.

77. "Jack Prince and Horses," *Times-Union*, March 12, 1893, 1; "Horses Best Prince," *Times-Union*, March 14, 1893, 1.

78. Seavey to Crawford, January 25, 1893, FEC file, SAHS.

79. McGuire to Flagler, July 23, 1894, HMFP; "Great East Coast Canal," *Times-Union*, April 27, 1893, 1.

80. House register, Hotel Lake Worth, Historical Society of Palm Beach County. Unfortunately, the page on which Flagler's name might have appeared in the register is missing.

81. Crawford, *Big Dig*, 54.

82. "River Ripples," *Juno Tropical Sun*, February 23, 1893, 1; "Day in St. Augustine," *Times-Union*, March 7, 1893, 1.

83. "Welcome to Mr. Flagler," *Juno Tropical Sun*, March 9, 1893, 10; "Palm Beach Breezes," *Juno Tropical Sun*, March 16, 1893, 1; "Railroad Meeting," *Juno Tropical Sun*, March 16, 1893, 8; Emma Gilpin to Sue, March 9, 1893, Historical Society of Palm Beach.

84. "Here and There," *Juno Tropical Sun*, March 9, 1893, 1; "Round About Us," *Juno Tropical Sun*, March 9, 10; "Real Estate Rustics," *Juno Tropical Sun*, March 23, 1893, 8; "Story of Lake Worth," *Juno Tropical Sun*, March 30, 1893, 3; "Albert W. Robert," in Bradley, *Class of '83*, 60–61.

85. "All Off for Lake Worth," *Times-Union*, March 27, 1893, 1; "On to Lake Worth," *Times-Union*, April 3, 1893, 1; "Palm Beach Breezes," *Juno Tropical Sun*, March 30, 1893, 1; "Reception," *Tatler*, April 1, 1893, 2, "Palm Beach Breezes," *Juno Tropical Sun*, April 6, 1893, 1.

86. "Day in St. Augustine," *Times-Union*, March 28, 1893, 1; "Cocoanut Grove House," *Juno Tropical Sun*, May 4, 1893, 1: "After the Blow," *Times-Union*, October 15, 1893, 2.

87. Maclennan to Parrott, August 22, 1893; Alfred Rodd to C. O. Haines, October 26, 1893; Charles Noble to C. O. Haines, June 12, 1893, HMFP.

88. Ralph, "Riviera," 496; "Guests," *Tatler*, March 11, 1893, 1.

89. "Day in St. Augustine," *Times-Union*, April 18, 1893, 8; "Day in St. Augustine," *Times-Union*, April 19, 1893, 1; "Palm Beach Breezes," *Juno Tropical Sun*, April 13, 1893, 1.

Chapter 16. After the Ball Is Over, 1893–1895

1. "Great East Coast Canal," *Times-Union*, April 27, 1893, 1; "Last of the Season," *Times-Union*, April 29, 1893, 1; "Encouraging Outlook," *Times-Union*, April 30, 1893, 7.

2. "Day in St. Augustine," *Times-Union*, May 21, 1893, 1; "Two Ancient City Brides," *Times-Union*, June 1, 1893, 1; "Day in St. Augustine," *Times-Union*, June 8, 1893, 1; "In St. Augustine," *Times-Union*, September 2, 1893, 2; "He Fell from the Train," *Times-Union*, September 6, 1893, 2; "Cleaned Out Playing Keno," *Times-Union*, December 13, 1893, 2.

3. "Day in St. Augustine," *Times-Union*, May 21, 1893, 1; "Day in St. Augustine," *Times-Union*, August 8, 1893, 1.

4. "Social in St. Augustine," *Times-Union*, March 10, 1889, 2; "Day in St. Augustine," *Times-Union*, June 24, 1893, 8; "Electronic System," *Tatler*, January 13, 1894, 5.

5. "St. Augustine Hit Hard," *Times-Union*, August 29, 1893, 1; "Day in St. Augustine," *Times-Union*, October 24, 1893, 2; "City Swept by the Sea," *Times-Union*, October 14, 1893, 1.

6. "City Swept by the Sea," *Times-Union*, October 14, 1893, 2.

7. "Ankles in Great Danger," *Times-Union*, November 28, 1893, 2; "Turkeys Gave No Thanks," *Times-Union*, December 1, 1893, 4; "Bound to Have Bonds," *Times-Union*, December 16, 1893, 2; "Will Make Lots of Wine," *Times-Union*, January 31, 1894, 6.

8. "Need Better Roads," *Times-Union*, July 7, 1893, 2; "Day in St. Augustine," *Times-Union*, October 19, 1893, 3; "Back from Lake Worth," *Times-Union*, October 27, 1893, 2; "Day in St. Augustine," *Times-Union*, October 29, 1893, 6.

9. "Day in St. Augustine," *Times-Union*, October 30, 1893, 7; "An Important Engagement," *New York Times*, September 24, 1893, 19.

10. Ingraham to C. O. Haines, October 31, 1893, HMFP; "Bound to Have Bonds," *Times-Union*, December 16, 1893, 2; Minutes of Stockholders Meetings, March 21, 1893, FEC file, SAHS.

11. "Day in St. Augustine," *Times-Union*, August 22, 1893, 7.

12. "Day in St. Augustine," *Times-Union*, September 28, 1893, 2; "Cleaned Out by Keno," *Times-Union*, December 13, 1893, 3.

13. "Day in St. Augustine," *Times-Union*, August 21, 1893, 1; "Cordova Opens," *Times-Union*, November 15, 1893, 2; "Turkeys Gave No Thanks," *Times-Union*, December 1, 1893, 4; "Ate Turkey," *Times-Union*, December 26, 1893, 2.

14. "Cutlets from Ancient City," *Times-Union*, January 2, 1894, 2.

15. "Alcazar," *Tatler*, January 27, 1894, 4.

16. "Ponce de Leon," *Times-Union*, January 11, 1894, 1; "Ponce de Leon," *Tatler*, January 13, 1894, 2.

17. "All Ready for Battle," *Wichita Daily Eagle*, January 21, 1894, 3.

18. "Cordova Dance," *Tatler*, March 3, 1894, 3.

19. "Hotel Personals," *Tatler*, January 13, 1894, 11; "Chit Chat," *Tatler*, January 20, 1894, 5;

"Gossip," *Tatler*, January 20, 1894, 5; "Ball at San Marco," *Tatler*, February 3, 1894, 2; "Art Notes," *Tatler*, February 3, 1894, 10; "Ponce de Leon Ball," *Tatler*, February 10, 1894, 2.

20. "Hard Times," *Tatler*, February 17, 1894, 1.

21. "Cutlets from Ancient City," *Times-Union*, January 24, 1893, 6; "Cutlets from Ancient City," *Times-Union*, February 14, 1894, 2; "Affairs in St. Augustine," *Times-Union*, February 20, 1894, 2.

22. "Cutlets from Ancient City," *Times-Union*, February 14, 1894, 2; "That Tower Must Topple," *Times-Union*, February 21, 1894, 2; "Gossip," *Tatler*, February 24, 1894, 4.

23. "Chronicles of Old City," *Times-Union*, February 22, 1894, 2; Maclennan to Parrott, February 21, 1894, March Scrapbook 14, 3953, SAHS; "Gossip," *Tatler*, February 24, 1894, 5; "Affairs in St. Augustine," *Times-Union*, February 25, 1894, 8.

24. "Follow Charity," *Times-Union*, March 15, 1894, 1; "Elegant Dinner," *Tatler*, March 17, 1894, 15.

25. Dale, *St. Augustine Boy*, 11, 55.

26. Pearson, "Hoyt," 152; Hunt, *Hoyt*, 7–17.

27. "Playwright Hoyt Married," *New York Times*, March 2, 1894, 3; "Hoyt," *Tatler*, March 10, 1894, 5; "St. Augustine's Story," *Times-Union*, March 10, 1894, 2.

28. "In Hotel Lobbies," *Washington Post*, March 12, 1894, 4; "'A Black Sheep' in Buffalo," *New York Times*, September 11, 1894, S1.

29. "From the Ancient City," *Times-Union*, August 5, 1890, 2; "Day in St. Augustine," *Times-Union*, October 11, 1893, 2.

30. "Among the Artists," *Times-Union*, January 14, 1893, 9; "Affairs in St. Augustine," *Times-Union*, December 22, 1893, 2; "Croker in Old City," *Times-Union*, February 10, 1894, 2; "Day in St. Augustine," *Times-Union*, May 23, 1893, 1; "Affairs in St. Augustine," *Times-Union*, April 11, 1894, 3.

31. Trovaioli and Toledano, *Walker*, 40–42; "Scheme That Failed," *Times-Union*, April 20, 1890, 2; "About Artists," *Times-Union*, February 17, 1894, 7.

32. Pollack, *Woodward*, 32; "At the Artists Studios," *Times-Union*, March 9, 1890, 2.

33. Qtd. in Pollack, *Woodward*, 111; "Sunday in St. Augustine," *Times-Union*, May 5, 1890, 5; "People vs Citizens," *Times-Union*, June 14, 1893, 1.

34. "Cutlets from Ancient City," *Times-Union*, January 15, 1894, 2; Pollack, *Woodward*, 140; "Cyclone Cut the Channel," *Times-Union*, February 1, 1894, 2; "St. Augustine," *Jacksonville Daily Florida Citizen*, October 30, 1895, 2.

35. "Seavey," *Tatler*, March 24, 1894, 2; "Affairs at St. Augustine," *Times-Union*, March 22, 1894, 7; "Seavey," *Tatler*, January 13, 1894, 12.

36. Adams to Hay, April 11, 1894, qtd. in Levenson, *Adams*, 4:180.

37. "And Flagler Abdicates," *Times-Union*, March 21, 1894, 2; "Gossip," *Tatler*, April 7, 1894, 13.

38. "Augustine," *Times-Union*, March 26, 1894, 2.

39. "West Palm Beach," *Tatler*, March 24, 1894, 1; "Affairs at St. Augustine," *Times-Union*, March 29, 1894, 2; "Gossip," *Tatler*, April 7, 1894, 13; "Affairs at St. Augustine," *Times-Union*, April 11, 1894, 3.

40. "Affairs in St. Augustine," *Times-Union*, March 30, 1894, 2; "St. Augustine Tennis Tournament," *Tatler*, March 31, 1894, 8.

41. "Old Tennis Trophy Returns to City," *St. Augustine Record*, April 23, 1961, A6.

42. "Affairs at St. Augustine," *Times-Union*, April 5, 1894, 2; "Testimonial to Mr. Osborn Dunlap Seavey," *Times-Union*, April 7, 1894, 9.

43. "Ponce de Leon," *Tatler*, March 24, 1894, 10; "Affairs at St. Augustine," *Times-Union*, April 9, 1894, 3; Annual Report of the Florida East Coast Hotel Co., various years, HMFP.

44. "Affairs at St. Augustine," *Times-Union*, April 19, 1894, 3; "Affairs in St. Augustine," *Times-Union*, May 2, 1894, 2.

45. "Flagler-Lamont," *New York Times*, April 26, 1894, 4; unidentified clipping, box 2, file 24, AP.

46. "Mr. Clarence B. Knott," *Tatler*, April 7, 1894, 6; Harry Flagler to Knott, April 23, 1894, HMFP; Harry Flagler to Ingraham, May 17, 1894, HMFP; "Affairs at St. Augustine," *Times-Union*, October 15, 1894, 3.

47. "Admitted as a Novitiate," *Jacksonville Daily Florida Citizen*, June 30, 1894, 2; "Caring for the Colonists," *Times-Union*, July 12, 1894, 3; "Affairs at St. Augustine," *Times-Union*, October 14, 1894, 2; Sidney Walter Martin, *Flagler: Visionary*, 169–71; Flagler to W. W. Taylor, November 6, 1901, HMFP.

48. City Council minutes, July 11, 1889; "Will Fill the Basin," *Jacksonville Daily Florida Citizen*, July 27, 1894, 2; "Affairs at St. Augustine," *Times-Union*, August 4, 1894, 2.

49. Dewhurst to Flagler, September 29, 1894, HMFP; "On the East Coast," *Times-Union*, September 28, 1894, 5; "State Cruelly Swept," *Times-Union*, September 29, 1894, 1; "In the Storm's Track," *Washington Post*, September 29, 1894, 1.

50. "Robbers Raid Her Room," *Times-Union*, December 5, 1894, 3; "Affairs at St. Augustine," *Times-Union*, October 12, 1894, 3; "St. Augustine News Notes," *Jacksonville Daily Florida Citizen*, December 28, 1894, 2.

51. "Many Railway Magnates," *Times-Union*, December 3, 1894, 3; "St. Augustine News Notes," *Jacksonville Daily Florida Citizen*, December 7, 1894, 2; "Smith Has a Great Scheme," *Times-Union*, December 8, 1894, 3; "Mrs. Flagler at St. Augustine," *Jacksonville Daily Florida Citizen*, December 8, 1894, 2.

52. "Day in St. Augustine," *Times-Union*, October 20, 1893, 2.

53. "Ancient City Notes," *Times-Union*, December 12, 1894; "Affairs in St. Augustine," *Times-Union*, December 14, 1894, 3; "Beautiful Wedding," *Tatler*, December 15, 1894, 12.

54. "Mr. and Mrs. Flagler," *Tatler*, December 15, 1894, 14; "Cordova Dances," *Tatler*, December 15, 1894, 16.

55. "Hotels," *Tatler*, January 26, 1895, 16.

56. "St. Augustine News Notes," *Jacksonville Daily Florida Citizen*, December 7, 1894, 2; McGuire to Harry Flagler, January 14, 1895, HMFP.

57. Henry M. Flagler to Harry H. Flagler, January 30, 1895, HMFP.

58. Knott to Harry Flagler, January 7, 1895; McGuire to Harry Flagler, December 30, 1894, HMFP.

59. Knott to Harry Flagler, November 22, 27, 1894, and January 7, 1895; Greaves to Harry Flagler, January 4, 5, 1895, HMFP.

60. "Opening Day," *Tatler*, January 19, 1895, 2; "Gossip," *Tatler*, January 19, 1895, 8; "Hotel Personals," *Tatler*, January 12, 1895, 2.

61. Harry Flagler, "Misstatements in Martin," HMFM; "Opening Dance," *Tatler*, January 19, 1895, 2.

62. "A Pompeiian Arcade," *St. Augustine Weekly News*, January 10, 1889, 1; "New Granada Opens," *Times-Union*, February 4, 1895, 2.

63. "Affairs at St. Augustine," *Times-Union*, January 18, 1895, 3.

64. Flagler to E. N. Dimick, June 9, 1899, Flagler Letterbook, HMFM; "In Hotel Lobbies," *Washington Post*, March 29, 1895, 6.

65. "Day in St. Augustine," *Times-Union*, January 19, 1893, 3; "Gambling Results Analyzed," *St. Augustine Record*, March 12, 1900, 1.

66. Upchurch, "Special Gifts," 71–92; "Affairs in St. Augustine," *Times-Union*, October 7, 1894, 6.

67. "Affairs in St. Augustine," *Times-Union*, September 11, 1894, 2.

68. Andrew Anderson to Clarissa Anderson, March 20, 29, 1859, AP; Flagler to Anderson, November 3, 1896; Flagler to DeWitt Webb, July 21, 1890, HMFP.

69. "Personals," *Tatler*, February 2, 1895, 8; "Notable Their Nuptials," *Times-Union*, January 30, 1895, 2; "Notable Wedding," *Tatler*, February 2, 1895, 2; "Personals," *Tatler*, February 16, 1895, 14; Flagler to William Crafts, October 12, 1888, AP.

70. Flagler to Harry Flagler, January 16, 1895, HMFP; "He Goes to His Long Home," *Times-Union*, February 1, 1895, 2; "Arrivals at the Hotels," *Times-Union*, February 3, 1895, 2.

71. "Every Hotel," *Tatler*, February 16, 1895, 1; "Alcazar," *Tatler*, February 23, 1895, 12; "Casino Opening," *Tatler*, January 19, 1895, 11; "Casino," *Tatler*, February 9, 1895, 14; "They Kept Clean," *Times-Union*, April 26, 1895, 3.

72. "Ingersoll Lecture," *Times-Union*, February 11, 1895, 2; "Colonel Robert Ingersoll," *Tatler*, February 16, 1895, 2; "Affairs at St. Augustine," *Times-Union*, February 2, 1895, 2; "Reception at Ponce de Leon," *Tatler*, February 9, 1895, 2; "Chit-Chat," *Tatler*, March 9, 1895, 2; "Gossip," *Tatler*, March 2, 1895, 7; "Personals," *Tatler*, March 23, 1895, 18.

73. "Gossip," *Tatler*, February 23, 1895, 8; "Day in St. Augustine," *Times-Union*, April 5, 1891, 7; "Affairs at St. Augustine," *Times-Union*, October 12, 1894, 3; "Affairs at St. Augustine," *Times-Union*, May 12, 1895, 7; "Mourn for Mr. Renwick," *Times-Union*, June 28, 1895, 6.

74. "Personals," *Tatler*, February 16, 1895, 14; "Hotel Royal Poinciana," *Tatler*, March 2, 1895, 12; "Beautiful Reception," *Tatler*, March 2, 1895, 15; "For the Hospital Fund," *Times-Union*, March 10, 1895, 7; "Grand Lawn Fete," *Times-Union*, March 12, 1895, 2.

75. "Chit-Chat," *Tatler*, March 9, 1895, 2.

76. "Second Assembly," *Tatler*, March 16, 1895, 14; "Chit-Chat," *Tatler*, March 23, 1895, 2.

77. "Gave a Scare to the Girls," *Times-Union*, November 13, 1894, 2; "Fair for Alicia Hospital," *Tatler*, March 16, 1895, 2; "Affairs in St. Augustine," *Times-Union*, March 24, 1895, 2.

78. "For the Hospital Fund," *Times-Union*, March 21, 1895, 2; "Annual Charity Ball," March 23, 1895, 3; "Affairs at St. Augustine," *Times-Union*, April 13, 1895, 3.

79. "Game of Golf," *Times-Union*, January 20, 1893, 2; "Why Does," *Tatler*, February 4, 1893, 2; "St. Augustine Siftings," *Times-Union*, January 17, 1894, 2; "Robbers Raid Her Room," *Times-Union*, December 5, 1894, 3; "Chit-Chat," *Tatler*, February 9, 1895, 3.

80. "Chit-Chat," *Tatler*, February 2, 1895, 6; "First Game of Golf," *Times-Union*, February 21, 1895, 2; "Golf on Fort Marion Grounds," *Tatler*, February 23, 1895, 2.

81. "Golf Club," *Tatler*, March 2, 1895, 2; "Golf," *Times-Union*, February 27, 1895, 2.

82. "Golf Tournament," *Tatler*, March 9, 1895, 12; "Affairs at St. Augustine," *Times-Union*, March 11, 1895, 2; "Golf Tournament," *Times-Union*, March 27, 1895, 2; "Golf," *Tatler*, March 23, 1895, 8; "Golf," *Tatler*, March 30, 1895, 10.

83. "Would Leave the Party," *Princeton Union*, March 28, 1895, 2; "Gov. McKinley in Florida," *Washington Post*, March 29, 1895, 2.

84. "Ancient City in Ashes," *Times-Union*, March 29, 1895, 1; "Two-Hundred Thousand," *Times-Union*, March 30, 1895, 1; "Fire in St. Augustine," *Tatler*, March 30, 1895, 5.

85. "Fire in St. Augustine," *Tatler*, March 30, 1895, 5; "No More Ancient City Now," *Times-Union*, March 31, 1895.

86. "McKinley at St. Augustine," *Times-Union*, March 29, 1895, 2; "Gossip," *Tatler*, March 30, 1895, 15; Flagler to McKinley, *passim*, McKinley Papers, Library of Congress.

87. Knott to Harry Flagler, January 31, 1895, HMFP; "Phenomenal Success," *Tatler*, February 16, 1895, 1; "Hotel Royal Poinciana," *Tatler*, March 23, 1895, 1.

88. Edwin Augustus Moore to Sister, March 17, 1895, photocopy, SAHS.

89. Parrott to C. C. Haines, July 11, 1893, HMFP; "Affairs in St. Augustine," *Times-Union*, April 4, 10, 1895, 3; "Ancient City Notes," *Times-Union*, April 15, 1895, 2; "Won't Extend to Key West," *Times-Union*, April 20, 1895, 6; "Affairs at St. Augustine," *Times-Union*, April 30, 1895, 6.

90. "Thirty-five Acres of Pines," *Jacksonville Daily Florida Citizen*, May 2, 1895, 2.

91. Akin, *Flagler: Rockefeller Partner*, 160–62; "There are Rumors," *Tatler*, March 16, 1895, 1; "Hotel Personals," *Tatler*, March 16, 1895, 12; "To Connect the Islands," *Jacksonville Daily Florida Citizen*, May 4, 1895, 2; Flagler to Tuttle, April 22, 1895, HMFP.

92. "St. Augustine News Notes," *Jacksonville Daily Florida Citizen*, May 3, 1895, 3.

93. "Affairs at St. Augustine," *Times-Union*, May 29, 1895, 3; "St. Augustine," *Times-Union*, May 31, 1895, 2; Flagler to Ingraham, November 19, 1903, HMFP.

94. Harry Flagler, "Misstatements in Martin," HMFM.

95. Sidney Walter Martin, *Flagler: Visionary*, 173–75.

96. Gibbs, interviews with author; Sidney Walter Martin, *Flagler: Visionary*, 126–27.

97. Flagler to Anderson, December 31, 1895, AP.

98. Shelton to Anderson, October 25, 1895, qtd. in Sidney Walter Martin, *Flagler: Visionary*, 175.

Chapter 17. On to Miami, 1896–1897

1. "St. Augustine," *Jacksonville Daily Florida Citizen*, October 31, 1895, 2.

2. "Changes in Alcazar," *Jacksonville Daily Florida Citizen*, May 18, 1895, 2; "Alcazar," *Jacksonville Daily Florida Citizen*, October 28, 1895, 2; "Alcazar," *Jacksonville Daily Florida Citizen*, November 13, 1895, 3; "Alcazar," *Tatler*, January 18, 1896, 5; "Princeton at Augustine," *Jacksonville Daily Florida Citizen*, December 19, 1895, 2.

3. "Alcazar Opened," *Jacksonville Daily Florida Citizen*, November 5, 1895, 2; "St. Augustine," *Jacksonville Daily Florida Citizen*, November 9, 1895, 2.

4. "Tales from the Old Town," *Times-Union*, November 16, 1895, 3; "St. Augustine," *Jacksonville Daily Florida Citizen*, November 16, 1895, 2; "Lake Worth Bridge," *Jacksonville Daily Florida Citizen*, November 17, 1895, 2; "Palm Beach Notes," *Tatler*, February 15, 1896, 8; "Palm Beach," *Tatler*, March 7, 1896, 13.

5. "Changes about the Plaza," *Jacksonville Daily Florida Citizen*, August 29, 1894, 2; "Hotel Royal Poinciana," *Tatler*, January 12, 1895, 6; "Affairs at St. Augustine," *Florida Times-Union*, August 30, 1895, 3.

6. "Palm Beach," *Tatler*, April 7, 1900, 6; "Palm Beach," *Tatler*, February 23, 1901, 9; "Palm Beach," *St. Augustine Record*, February 19, 1903, 6.

7. "Warehouses," *Tatler*, January 27, 1898, 3; "Mainly about People," *Tatler*, January 31, 1903, 7.

8. "Florida East Coast Hotel Company," *Tatler*, March 10, 1900, 30.

9. "Ancient City News," *Times-Union*, January 1, 1888, 3; "St. Augustine Notes," *Times-Union*, November 3, 1889, 9; "In St. Augustine," *Times-Union*, September 19, 1892, 5; "World's Fair Notes," *Dodge City Globe-Republican*, March 31, 1893, 3.

10. McGuire to L. C. Haines, June 18, 1909, McGuire Letterbook, FC; McGuire to Miller and Sibley, June 13, 1910, McGuire Letterbook, FC; Flagler to A. O. Auten, November 6, 1908, HMFP.

11. McGuire to W. R. Sellers, February 23, 1915; McGuire to N. D. Benedict, April 22, 1915, McGuire Letterbook, FC.

12. Parrott to Flagler, July 29, 1895, HMFP; Flagler to Parrott, September 9, 1895; Ingraham to Flagler, June 22, 1895, FEC file, SAHS.

13. "Editor Herald," January 6, 1895, clipping in Bevin scrapbook, SAHS.

14. "Battle over a Bridge," *Times-Union*, April 26, 1895, 3; "Affairs at St. Augustine," *Times-Union*, May 9, 1895, 3; "For the Matanzas Bridge," *Jacksonville Daily Florida Citizen*, May 8, 1895, 2.

15. "South Beach Railway Sold," *Times-Union*, April 23, 1895, 7; "Permit for Matanzas Bridge," *Jacksonville Daily Florida Citizen*, June 21, 1895, 2.

16. "Chronicles of Ancient City," *Times-Union*, January 2, 1896, 6.

17. "Florida Coast Line Canal," *Tatler*, January 18, 1896, 21; "Remembrances of W. L. Singleton," HMFP.

18. Sewell, *Miami*, 17–18.

19. "Capt. Vail [*sic*] Dead, a Miami Pioneer," *Miami Metropolis*, November 11, 1904, 1.

20. Sewell, *Miami*, ix–xiv, 20.

21. "Staggered Out Senseless," *Times-Union*, November 17, 1895, 6; "San Marco to Be Opened," *Jacksonville Daily Florida Citizen*, December 17, 1895, 2.

22. "Promotion for Mr. Knott," *Times-Union*, June 29, 1895, 3.

23. "Signs Give Folks a Start," *Times-Union*, January 20, 1896, 2; "Tales from the Old Town," *Times-Union*, January 29, 1896, 3.

24. "End of Northrop Case," *Jacksonville Daily Florida Citizen*, December 11, 1894, 2; "Northrop vs Flagler," *Times-Union*, January 20, 1895, 3; "An Important Ruling," *Times-Union*, January 24, 1895, 5.

25. C. B. Northrop to Flagler, October 1, 1894; Flagler to Northrop, October 8, 1894; Northrop to Flagler, October 10, 1894, HMFP; "Beginning to Talk Bonds," *Times-Union*, November 26, 1895, 3; St. Johns County Deed Book FF, 234–35.

26. "Tales from the Old Town," *Times-Union*, March 29, 1896, 6.

27. "Day in St. Augustine," *Times-Union*, March 27, 1890, 2; "Affairs in St. Augustine," *Times-Union*, May 21, 1894, 3; "Church to Cost $10,000," *Jacksonville Daily Florida Citizen*, August 11, 1894, 2; G. J. Johnson to Flagler, June 6, 8, 20, 1894, HMFP; "Plans for New Church," *Jacksonville Daily Florida Citizen*, June 20, 1894, 2; "Baptist Church Dedicated," *Times-Union*, February 3, 1896, 7.

28. "Bicycling," *Tatler*, February 29, 1896, 12; "Attractive Island," *Jacksonville Daily Florida Citizen*, December 9, 1895, 7; "Riding Academy," advertisement, *Tatler*, February 22, 1896, 6.

29. "Tales from the Old Town," *Times-Union*, December 12, 1895, 6; "Bicyclists Must Beware," *Times-Union*, December 13, 1895, 6.

30. "The Advent," *Tatler*, March 14, 1896, 1.

31. "Chronicles of Ancient City," *Times-Union*, December 19, 1895, 3; "Golf," *Tatler*, February 1, 1896, 12; "Golf," *Tatler*, February 15, 1896, 10.

32. "At St. Augustine," *Times-Union*, November 22, 1891, 7; "William Deering," *Tatler*, March 21, 1896, 5.

33. "Gossip," *Tatler*, March 7, 1896, 3, 5; "Gossip," *Tatler*, February 15, 1896, 19; "Gossip," *Tatler*, March 7, 1895, 5; "Personals," *Tatler*, February 22, 1896, 9; "Gossip," *Tatler*, March 14, 1896, 7; "Tales from Old Town," *Times-Union*, March 12, 1896, 6.

34. "Personals," *Tatler*, January 25, 1896, 10; "Rev. Doctor Henry M. Field," *Tatler*, February 22, 1896, 2; "Woman's Wisdom," *Tatler*, January 25, 1896, 3; "Bicycling," *Tatler*, February 8, 1896, 6; "Entertainments," *Tatler*, February 8, 1896, 7; "Miss Willard's Lecture," *Times-Union*, February 10, 1896, 7; "Woman's Wisdom," *Tatler*, February 15, 1896, 2.

35. "Dwight L. Moody," *Tatler*, March 28, 1896, 6; Flagler to Rockefeller, October 13, 17, 1885, Flagler Letterbook, HMFM.

36. "Gossip," *Tatler*, March 7, 1896, 3; "Henry M. Flagler," *Tatler*, March 21, 1896, 9; "Palm Beach," *Tatler*, March 28, 1896, 8.

37. Wiggins, "Birth," 21.

38. "Gaity of the Season," *Tatler*, February 29, 1896, 1; "Annual Charity Ball," *Tatler*, March 14, 1896, 2; "Season on the Wane," *Tatler*, March 28, 1896, 1.

39. "Tales from the Old Town," *Times-Union*, March 26, 1896, 6; "San Marco Closes," *Tatler*, April 4, 1896, 13.

40. "San Marco Still Open," *Times-Union*, March 27, 1896, 3; "Tales from the Old Town," *Times-Union*, March 29, 1896, 6.

41. Dewhurst to Flagler, July 16, 1891; Flagler to Dewhurst, August 18, 1891, HMFP.

42. Copies of S. 754 and HR 4436, HMFP; "Mr. Flagler's Offer for the Barracks Site," *Times-Union*, April 26, 1892, 3; "Day in St. Augustine," *Times-Union*, May 24, 1892, 3.

43. "Will Fortify Anastasia," *Times-Union*, September 5, 1893, 2.

44. Dewhurst to Flagler, September 21, 29, 1894; Flagler to Dewhurst, October 9, 1894, HMFP.

45. Major Thomas H. Handbury to William P. Craighill, Chief of Engineers, December 30, 1895; Bainbridge to Adjutant General, no date, HMFP.

46. Major Thomas H. Handbury to William P. Craighill, Chief of Engineers, December 30, 1895, HMFP.

47. Flagg to Flagler, November 18, 19, 1895, HMFP.

48. Flagler to Anderson, May 20, June 8, 1896 qtd. in Sidney Walter Martin, *Flagler: Visionary*, 176–77.

49. Flagler to Anderson, July 5, 1896, qtd. in Sidney Walter Martin, *Flagler: Visionary*, 178.

50. Flagler to Anderson, July 9, 1896, qtd. in Sidney Walter Martin, *Flagler: Visionary*, 179; "In St. Augustine," *Times-Union*, December 19, 1892, 4.

51. "Mrs. Ida A. Flagler Insane," *Washington Times*, July 17, 1899, 5; Salter to Anderson, October 24, 1896, qtd. in Sidney Walter Martin, *Flagler: Visionary*, 182; Flagler to Anderson, November 3, 1896, AP.

52. "Chronicles of Ancient City," *Times-Union*, January 9, 1897, 3; "Flagler Taxes Paid," *Times-Union*, January 22, 1897, 3.

53. "Royal Palm Hotel," *Tatler*, January 23, 1897, 17.

54. "Care for Dixie's Lengthy Coasts," *Times-Union*, January 21, 1897, 1; "Mr. Flagler Returns from Tampa," *Times-Union*, January 24, 1897, 14.

55. "Charming Journey," *Tatler*, February 6, 1897, 12.

56. "Deventery Has Disappeared," *Times-Union*, February 7, 1897, 7.

57. "Southern Railway," *Tatler*, January 23, 1897, 10; "Charity Ball," *Tatler*, March 20, 1897, 2.

58. "Fete for Saturday," *Times-Union*, March 5, 1897, 6; "Ladies to Hospital Aid," *Times-Union*, March 7, 1897, 2; "Hospital Fund Increased," *Times-Union*, March 17, 1897, 7; "Money for Alicia Hospital," *Times-Union*, March 21, 1897, 7.

59. "Cordova," *Tatler*, February 27, 1897, 6; "News of the Ancient City," *Times-Union*, April 4, 1897, 7.

60. "Elegant Tea," *Tatler*, February 27, 1897, 7; "Ponce de Leon Reception," *Tatler*, March 5, 1898, 3.

61. "Accidents to Cyclists," *Times-Union*, February 1, 1896, 6; "St. Augustine Gay," *Times-Union*, January 26, 1897, 3; "City Is Threatened," *Times-Union*, February 5, 1897, 6.

62. "Gossip," *Tatler*, January 16, 1897, 11; Gibbs, interviews with author.

63. "Hotel Royal Palm," *Tatler*, February 20, 1897, 8; "Hotel Royal Palm," *Tatler*, February 27, 1897, 9.

64. "Hotel Key West," *Tatler*, March 6, 1897, 9; "Belle Glade Men Buy Historic Hotel," *Palm Beach Post*, February 5, 1941, 13.

65. "Hotel Royal Palm," *Tatler*, March 13, 1897, 9; "English Jack Still Floats," *Times-Union*, March 20, 1897, 3; "Nassau," *Tatler*, March 27, 1897, 3.

66. "Mr. Plant Visits Miami," *Times-Union*, March 14, 1897, 7; "Flagler's Directions to Plant," *St. Augustine Evening Record*, April 6, 1900, 1.

67. "Fine Palm Beach Weather," *Times-Union*, March 28, 1897, 7.

68. "Royal Palm," *Tatler*, March 20, 1897, 9; "Personals," *Tatler*, March 27, 1897, 19; "Gossip," *Tatler*, April 3, 1897, 7.

69. "St. Augustine's Gay Whirl," *Times-Union*, March 23, 1897, 7; "Gen. Schofield's Daughter," *Times-Union*, April 5, 1897, 3.

70. Flagler to John Flagg, August 29, 1899, HMFP.

71. Call to Bryan, July 13, 1899, William Jennings Bryan Papers, Library of Congress.

72. Flagler to George Shelton, November 18, 1908, HMFP.

73. "William Jennings Bryan in St. Augustine," *Roanoke Times*, April 10, 1897, 1.

74. "W. J. Bryan at St. Augustine," *Times-Union*, April 8, 1897, 3; "Death Was Near Bryan Last

Night," *Times-Union*, April 9, 1897, 1; "St. Augustine's Accident," *Times-Union*, April 10, 1897, 3; "Cozy New $5,000 Cottage," *Times-Union*, April 14, 1897, 3.

75. Unsigned letter to George W. C. Jones, December 13, 1897, San Marco file, SAHS; "Florida Hotel Burned," *New York Times*, November 8, 1897, 1; "Hotel Burned by Firebugs," *Washington Post*, November 8, 1897, 1.

76. Sidney Walter Martin, *Flagler: Visionary,*, 183–84; Flagler to Mary Middleton, October 4, 1899, HMFP.

77. "Wealthy Lover's Money," *St. Louis Republic*, May 10, 1901, 3.

78. "At Prospect House," *New York Tribune*, August 8, 1897, 12.

79. "Jasper C. Salter to Helen M. Long," *Real Estate Record and Builder's Guide*, 60, no. 1553 (December 18, 1897): 961.

Chapter 18. Into Caribbean Waters, 1897–1899

1. "Launching of the Miami," *New York Times*, October 24, 1897, 17; "S S Miami," *Tatler*, January 15, 1898, 2.

2. "East Coast Yachting," *Times-Union*, January 13, 1898, 2; "Personals," *Tatler*, January 15, 1898, 18; "Ancient City," *Times-Union*, January 16, 1898, 2; "Royal Palm," *Tatler*, January 22, 1898, 7.

3. "Her Maiden Voyage," *Times-Union*, January 18, 1898, 2; "Miami's Initial Trip," *Tatler*, January 22, 1898, 10; "New Hotel for Nassau," *Times-Union*, January 22, 1898, 1; "Mr. Flagler in Nassau," *Times-Union*, January 28, 1898, 6; "Henry Flagler's Bahamas Projects," *New York Times*, February 16, 1898, 2.

4. "Palm Beach," *Times-Union*, January 28, 1898, 2; "The Casino," *Tatler*, February 26, 1898, 7; "The Inn," *Tatler*, March 12, 1898, 10; "Palm Beach," *Times-Union*, March 12, 1898, 2; "Miami," *Tatler*, March 26, 1898, 9.

5. Flagler to James Johans, July 30, 1890, Flagler Letterbook, HMFM.

6. Flagler to J. R. Parrott, September 30, 1903, HMFP.

7. Flagler to O. D. Seavey, December 2, 1890, Flagler Letterbook, HMFM.

8. Flagler to O. B. Smith, September 24, 1890, Flagler Letterbook, HMFM; "County Legislators," *St. Augustine Weekly News*, February 7, 1889, 1.

9. Flagler to O. B. Smith, January 26, 1889; Flagler to O. B. Smith, January 4, 1889, Flagler file, SAHS.

10. "Editorial Comment," *Times-Union*, July 25, 1887, 4; Richard A. Martin, *City Makers*, 206–7.

11. "News-Herald's Train," *Jacksonville News-Herald*, January 11, 1888, 1; "Ancient City," *Times-Union*, February 26, 1888, 1.

12. "Here Is That Letter," *Ocala Banner*, February 21, 1908, 4; W. H. Beardsley to J. R. Parrott, September 30, 1903, HMFP.

13. Stockton to Call, June 17, 1893, Cleveland Papers; Flagler to Parrott, August 29, 1893, Flagler Letterbook, HMFM; Flagler to Lamont, November 9, 1893, Cleveland Papers, Library of Congress.

14. Flagler to Parrott, August 29, 1893, Flagler Letterbook, HMFM.

15. W. H. Beardsly to Waldo Newcomer, January 20, 1903, HMFP.

16. "What a Shock," *Times-Union*, May 11, 1894, 4; "All Its Doors are Ajar," *Times-Union*, January 17, 1895, 3.

17. For examples see Flagler to G. W. Wilson, August 4, 1899; Flagler to Wilson, November 25, 1902, Flagler Letterbook, HMFM.

18. "Notice," *St. Augustine Record*, September 7, 1899, 4; Flagler to Parrott, August 4, 1899, Flagler Letterbook, HMFM; "Record Enters upon Tenth Year," *St. Augustine Record*, August 31, 1908, 1.

19. "Politics of the Record," *St. Augustine Record*, September 2, 1899, 2; "Barr's Futile Attack," *St. Augustine Record*, October 27, 1903, 4.

20. W. H. Beardsley to J. R. Parrott, April 14, 1902, Flagler Letterbook, HMFM; Akin, *Flagler: Rockefeller Partner*, 166–67.

21. "St. Augustine," *Times-Union*, January 3, 1898, 2; "The Negro Problem," *Times-Union*, January 3, 1898, 6; Levy, *Johnson*, 66.

22. "St. Augustine," *Times-Union*, March 14, 1898, 2; "St. Augustine," *Times-Union*, March 16, 1898, 2.

23. "News Notes," *Times-Union*, January 5, 1898, 2.

24. "Casino Opening," *Tatler*, January 22, 1898, 15; "At the Casino," *Times-Union*, January 22, 1898, 2.

25. "DuPont Park Leased," *Times-Union*, January 17, 1898, 2; "Golf," *Tatler*, January 22, 1898, 9; "Gay Old City," *Times-Union*, February 12, 1898, 2; "Entertainments," *Tatler*, February 12, 1898, 7.

26. *The Golf Links Located in Florida and Nassau*, booklet, East Coast Golf Club, 1900–1901, SAHS.

27. "Palm Beach," *Times-Union*, January 24, 1898, 2; "Champion Golfer Reaches Florida," *Global Golflore*, Summer 1993, 8, copy, SAHS.

28. "Country Club," *Tatler*, February 26, 1898, 7; "St. Augustine," *Times-Union*, March 6, 12, 1898, 2.

29. "Millionaire's Palace on Wheels," *Washington Evening Times*, January 11, 1898, 4; "Palm Beach," *Times-Union*, January 19, 1899, 2; "St. Augustine," *Times-Union*, January 6, 1899, 2.

30. "Visit of the Atlantic Torpedo Boat Flotilla," *Tatler*, January 15, 1898, 5.

31. "St. Augustine's Gay Whirl," *Times-Union*, March 23, 1897, 7; "Terrible Calamity," *Tatler*, February 19, 1898, 1; "Maine," *Tatler*, February 26, 1898, 2; "St. Augustine," *Times-Union*, February 26, 1898, 2; "Benefit Concert," *Tatler*, February 26, 1898, 2; "Star Spangled Banner," *Tatler*, April 2, 1898, 16.

32. "Gossip," *Tatler*, March 12, 1898, 15; "St. Augustine Surprised," *Times-Union*, March 13, 1898, 2; "St. Augustine," *Times-Union*, March 20, 1898, 14.

33. "Transfer of Troops," *Times-Union*, March 20, 1898, 2; "Post Remains," *Times-Union*, March 21, 1898, 2.

34. "Troops Depart," *Times-Union*, March 26, 1898, 2; "St. Francis Barracks," *Tatler*, March 28, 1898, 15.

35. "Hotel Key West," *Tatler*, March 5, 1898, 11; "Post Remains," *Times-Union*, March 21, 1898, 2; "Preparations Unabated," *Washington Evening Times*, March 26, 1898, 2; "Gossip," *Tatler*, April 2, 1898, 12; "Royal Palm," *Tatler*, April 2, 1898, 8; Robert W. Davis to Flagler, May 3, 1898, chronological file, SAHS.

36. "St. Augustine Surprised," *Times-Union*, March 13, 1898, 2.

37. "Gossip," *Tatler*, February 5, 1898, 6; "Mr. Robert Murray," *Tatler*, March 5, 1898, 15.

38. "Gossip," *Tatler*, March 26, 1898, 14; "Seavey Buys Magnolia Springs Hotel," *Tatler*, January 15, 1898, 7; "First Manager of Ponce de Leon Passed Away," *St. Augustine Record*, April 18, 1923, 6.

39. "Fairy Scene," *Times-Union*, March 29, 1898, 2; "Alcazar Garden Party," *Times-Union*, March 31, 1898, 2.

40. "Prince in Disguise," *Times-Union*, April 2, 1898, 2.

41. "St. Augustine," *Times-Union*, April 4, 11, 13, 1898, 2.

42. "To Organize the Cubans," *Times-Union*, July 25, 1892, 1.

43. "Affairs at St. Augustine," *Times-Union*, October 24, 1895, 3; "Entertainment," *Tatler*, February 8, 1896, 1; "To Cuba's Cause Are True," *Times-Union*, February 11, 1896, 6; "Old Fort Closed Up," *Times-Union*, March 9, 1897, 7; "Can Visit Fort Marion," *Times-Union*, March 15, 1897, 7.

44. "Petition, April 8, 1898," HMFP; "Building Batteries," *Times-Union*, April 15, 1898, 2; "Strange Death," *Times-Union*, April 16, 1898, 2; "Building the Battery," *Times-Union*, April 17, 1898, 2.

45. "Hay Foot, Straw Foot," *Times-Union*, April 21, 1898, 2.

46. John H. Parker, *Gatlings*, 32.

47. "Hard Coal for the Texas," *New York Sun*, April 12, 1898, 2.

48. "Three War Vessels Sail," *New York Times*, April 19, 1898, 4; "Hornet Sails for Key West," *Washington Times*, April 19, 1898, 2; "Coastal Defenses of Cuba," *New York Times*, May 11, 1898, 3; "Hornet Gets a Prize," *New York Times*, August 11, 1898, 4.

49. "Amazing Story of *Alicia*," 8–9.

50. "St. Augustine," *Times-Union*, June 24, 1898, 2; "Troops for Miami," *Times-Union*, June 25, 1898, 2; "St. Augustine," *Times-Union*, July 26, 1898, 2; "St. Augustine," *Times-Union*, January 14, 1899, 2.

51. "A Thousand Soldiers," *Times-Union*, June 20, 1898, 2; "St. Augustine," *Times-Union*, June 21, 1898, 2; "St. Augustine," *Times-Union*, July 19, 1898, 2; "St. Augustine," *Times-Union*, July 21, 1898, 3.

52. "St. Augustine," *Times-Union*, August 4, 14, 1898, 2; "They Leave Santiago," *Times-Union*, August 8, 1898, 1; Mueller, *Steamships*, 34–35.

53. "The Camera Fiend," *Times-Union*, August 24, 1898, 2.

54. "Standard Guide Information Bureau," *Tatler*, March 12, 1898, 16; "Ask Mr. Foster," *St. Augustine Record*, January 20, 1900, 4.

55. McGuire to William McAuliffe, April 25, 1914, McGuire Letterbook, FC.

56. "Palm Beach," *Times-Union*, January 19, 1899, 2; "Royal Poinciana," *Tatler*, January 28, 1899, 6; "Miami," *Times-Union*, February 22, 1899, 2; "Gala Day at Palm Beach," *Times-Union*, February 23, 1899, 1.

57. Gibbs, interviews with author.

58. "Gift of a House by Henry M. Flagler," *New York Sun*, March 15, 1899, 15; "Royal Poinciana," *Tatler*, February 11, 1899, 4; "Palm Beach," *Times-Union*, February 11, 15, 1899, 2.

59. "Ponce de Leon," *Tatler*, March 4, 1899, 3; "Gossip," *Tatler*, March 4, 1899, 11.

60. "St. Augustine," *Times-Union*, January 30, 1899, 2; "Gossip," *Tatler*, February 4, 1899, 13; "Sousa Always a Popular Idol," *St. Augustine Record*, February 5, 1906, 5.

61. Hunt, *Hoyt*, 23; "Hoyt," *Tatler*, February 18, 1899, 7; "C. H. Hoyt's Mind Is Sound," *New York Times*, February 23, 1899; "Hoyt," *Tatler*, February 25, 1899, 14; "Ponce de Leon," *Tatler*, March 11, 1899, 2.

62. "Ponce de Leon," *Tatler*, March 11, 1899, 2; "Royal Poinciana," *Tatler*, March 18, 1899, 7; "Miami," *Times-Union*, April 18, 1899, 2; "St. Augustine," *Times-Union*, April 29, 1899, 2.

63. W. W. Beardsley to W. R. Kenan, April 3, 1899, Flagler Letterbook, HMFM; Akin, *Flagler: Rockefeller Partner*, 149.

64. Lehr, "*King Lehr*," 158.

65. Flagler to Carlos MacDonald, July 5, 1899, Flagler Letterbook, HMFM.

66. "Mrs. Ida A. Flagler Insane," *Washington Times*, July 17, 1899, 5; "Insanity of Mrs. Flagler," *New York Times*, August 6, 1899, 12.

67. Flagler to Alfred Bishop, May 22, 1899, Flagler Letterbook, HMFM; "Funeral of Henry B. Plant," *New York Times*, June 27, 1899, 14; "Brilliant Wedding," *Norfolk Virginian-Pilot*, December 7, 1899, 2.

68. Flagler to Ward, January 12, 1901; Flagler to Parrott, July 27, 1899, HMFP.

69. Flagler to Ingraham, June 20, 1902, Flagler Letterbook, HMFM.

70. Flagler to George Lucas, August 21, 1899, HMFP.

71. Lefevre, "Flagler," 181.

72. "Henry M. Flagler," *St. Augustine Evening Record*, May 30, 1913, 7.

73. Lefevre, "Flagler," 181.

74. Flagler to C. H. Williams, September 17, 1900, HMFP.

75. Flagler to Charles Stevens, September 4, 1901, HMFP.

76. Sworn Deposition of J. E. Ingraham, February 1923, Ingraham Papers, UFL.

77. "Day in St. Augustine," *Times-Union*, January 29, February 2, 1892, 1; "Day in St. Augustine," *Times-Union*, January 29, 1892, 1.

78. Flagler to J. P. Beckwith, August 27, August 30, 1909, Flagler Letterbook, HMFM.

79. "Ponce de Leon Studios," *Jacksonville News-Herald*, February 26, 1888, 6; "Day in St. Augustine," *Times-Union*, March 19, 1891, 2.

80. "Death of Well Known Artist," *Times-Union*, September 7, 1891, 2; "Art Notes," *Tatler*, March 19, 1892, 9.

81. Flagler to Anderson and Price, May 14, 1902, HMFP.

82. "Among the Cottages," *Tatler*, January 14, 1893, 7; "Gossip," *Tatler*, March 30, 1901, 7.

83. William Fremd, "The Flagler Development," *History of Beautiful Palm Beach*, clipping in author's file; Flagler to Ward, January 12, 1901, HMFP.

84. Flagler to Crafts, July 11, 1904, HMFP.

85. Flagler to Mrs. J. W. Whitman, August 28, 1901, Flagler Letterbook, HMFM.

86. Flagler to A. E. Spencer, October 15, 1902, HMFP.

87. Flagler to Mr. Lee, February 16, 1883, HMFP.

88. Flagler to Charles F. Towering, April 14, 1893, Miscellaneous Documents 93–94, Florida Historical Society.

89. "Day in St. Augustine," *Times-Union*, March 9, 1889, 2; Flagler to Ingraham, November 10, 1902, November 19, 1906, HMFP; "Thanksgiving at the Deaf and Dumb Asylum," *Ocala Banner*, December 11, 1908, 2.

90. Flagler to Ingraham, April 24, 1906, July 3, 1906; Flagler to Parrott, July 3, 1906; Parrott to Flagler July 6, 1906, HMFP, copies SAHS.

91. Crocker, *Mrs. Sage*, 368.

92. Flagler to Sister M. Sazarus, April 27, 1886, Flagler Letterbook, HMFM.

93. Thomas Hazzard to S. W. Martin, December 19, 1949, Martin Papers, UFL.

94. Flagler to Ward, November 9, 1899, November 12, 1903, HMFP.

95. Beardsley to Flagler, January 15, 1902; Flagler to George Wilson, June 20, 1902, HMFP.

Chapter 19. Modern Times, 1900–1902

1. Flagler to Ingraham, September 15, 1900, HMFP.

2. "First Automobile," *Tatler*, February 3, 1900, 18; "Council Proceedings," *St. Augustine Evening Record*, February 1, 1900, 1; "Believes in Progress," *St. Augustine Evening Record*, February 22, 1900, 1.

3. *Tatler*, March 2, 9, 30, 1901, 1.

4. "Gossip," *Tatler*, January 19, 1901, 6; "Eleventh House," *St. Augustine Evening Record*, January 24, 1901, 4; "Auto Got Cranky," *St. Augustine Evening Record*, March 11, 1901, 1.

5. "Travel," *Tatler*, January 18, 1902, 6; R. T. Goff to G. A. Miller, August 2, 1898, HMFP; "Oldest City's Newest News," *St. Augustine Evening Record*, January 9, 1901, 3; "Travel," *Tatler*, January 20, 1900, 8.

6. "Within a Few Days," *St. Augustine Evening Record*, September 8, 1902, 4; "Free Delivery," *Times-Union*, July 28, 1898, 2; "Farewell to the Fifth," *Times-Union*, October 19, 1894, 3.

7. "Going South in the Winter," *New York Tribune*, January 13, 1901, sec. 3, 1; Braden, *Architecture*, 312; "Florida East Coast Hotel Co.," *Tatler*, December 24, 1899, 2.

8. "12th Annual Charity Ball," *Tatler*, March 24, 1900, 13; "Eleventh Hour," *St. Augustine Evening Record*, January 2, 1900, 4.

9. "Old Time American Institutions," *Tatler*, March 26, 1898, 1; "St. Augustine," *Times-Union*, February 9, 1897, 3; "Entertainments," *Tatler*, February 12, 1898, 7; "Gossip," *Tatler*, April 5, 1902, 2.

10. "Gossip," *Tatler*, March 17, 1900, 21; "Old Times Songs," *St. Augustine Evening Record*, March 12, 1902, 4.

11. "Casino," *Tatler*, March 7, 1903, 15.

12. Flagler to Smith, August 29, 1901, HMFP; "Mrs. Franklin W. Smith," *Tatler*, February 10, 1900, 14.

13. "Chapin's Farm Agency," *St. Augustine Evening Record*, March 18, 1899, 4; Clark, "Smith," 36; "Villa Zorayda," *St. Augustine Evening Record*, February 9, 1900.

14. "Mr. Flagler's Guests Go North," *St. Augustine Evening Record*, December 4, 1899, 4; "Palm Beach Inn," *Tatler*, January 6, 1900, 3; "Royal Poinciana Opening," *Tatler*, January 20, 1900, 7; "Hotel Royal Palm," *Tatler*, January 27, 1900, 5; "Royal Palm," *Tatler*, February 17, 1900, 5; "Colonial," *Tatler*, February 8, 1900, 8.

15. "Dr. and Mrs. Anderson," *Tatler*, December 24, 1899, 7; "Palm Beach," *Tatler*, January 27, 1900, 4, 11; "Gossip," *Tatler*, March 3, 1900, 20.

16. "Hotel Colonial," *Tatler*, March 3, 1900, 9; "The Colonial," *Tatler*, March 10, 1900, 7; "Nassau," *Tatler*, March 17, 1900, 6.

17. "Hotel Alcazar," *Tatler*, March 3, 1900, 7; "Golf Notes," *St. Augustine Evening Record*, January 17, 1900, 3.

18. "Smith's Good Score," *St. Augustine Evening Record*, February 13, 1900, 1; "Golf Notes," *Tatler*, February 17, 1900, 10.

19. "Golf Notes," *St. Augustine Evening Record*, January 17, 1900, 3.

20. "Golf Notes," *Tatler*, February 17, 1900, 10.

21. "Golf Playing," *St. Augustine Evening Record*, February 17, 1900, 1; "Vardon Defeats Smith," *New York Times*, February 18, 1900, 6.

22. Albion, *Edison*, 20, 52; "Personal Mention," *St. Augustine Evening Record*, February 23, 1900, 1; "Hotel Alcazar," *Tatler*, March 3, 1900, 7.

23. "Alcazar," *Tatler*, January 13, 1900, 2; "Water Living," *St. Augustine Evening Record*, January 20, 1900, 3; "Street Jottings," *St. Augustine Evening Record*, February 23, 1900, 1; "Modern Illumination," *Tatler*, April 7, 1900, 22.

24. "Oldest City's Newest News," *St. Augustine Evening Record*, January 12, 1901, 3.

25. "Alcazar," *Tatler*, January 12, 1901, 9.

26. "Major General Brooke," *Tatler*, January 13, 1900, 8.

27. "Admiral Dewey Comes for a Rest," *St. Augustine Evening Record*, March 23, 1900, 1; "Ponce de Leon," *Tatler*, March 31, 1900, 21.

28. "Dewey Reception," *Tatler*, March 31, 1900, 7; "Dewey Reception," *St. Augustine Evening Record*, March 27, 1900, 1.

29. "Ormond Notes," *Tatler*, March 31, 1900, 11; "Hotel Ormond," *Tatler*, April 7, 1900, 5.

30. "Alcazar Garden Party," *St. Augustine Evening Record*, March 29, 1900, 1.

31. "Alcazar Garden Party," *St. Augustine Evening Record*, March 29, 1900, 1; "Alcazar Garden Party," *Tatler*, March 31, 1900, 12.

32. "Distinguished Guests," *Tatler*, March 31, 1900, 20.

33. Flagler to Rockefeller, March 8, 1889; Rockefeller to William R. Harper, February 28, 1898, both qtd. in Chernow, *Titan*, 345; "Palm Beach," *Tatler*, March 24, 1900, 2.

34. George Morgan Ward, *In Memoriam*, 19.

35. "Delightful Tea," *Tatler*, April 7, 1900, 9; "Mr. Henry M. Flagler," *Tatler*, April 7, 1900, 11.

36. "Personal Mention," *St. Augustine Evening Record*, April 24, 26, 28, 1900, 1.

37. "St. Francis Barracks," *St. Augustine Record*, October 28, 1901, 2.

38. Chernow, *Titan*, 428.

39. "Suit against H. M. Flagler," *New York Tribune*, June 5, 1900, 6; "Flagler's Counter Charge," *New York Tribune*, June 21, 1900, 9; "Mr. Flagler Denies Prisoner's Claim," *New York Times*, June 21, 1900, 7; "Costs to Henry M. Flagler," *New York Times*, June 26, 1900, 10.

40. Flagler to Anderson, June 18, 1887, HMFP; Flagler to J. P. Beckwith, February 11, 1901, Flagler Letterbook, HMFM.

41. "Pablo Road Sold," *St. Augustine Evening Record*, September 6, 1899, 1; "Pablo Beach," *St. Augustine Evening Record*, March 9, 1900, 1; Braden, *Architecture*, 243–46.

42. "Gossip," *Tatler*, January 12, 1901, 6; "Royal Poinciana," *Tatler*, January 19, 1901, 4; "Miami," *Tatler*, January 26, 1901, 4.

43. Kenan, *Incidents: Lifetime Recollections*, 28, 51; Kenan to Parrott, May 18, 1900, FEC file, SAHS; Flagler to McGuire, January 30, 1901, HMFP.

44. Kenan, *Incidents: Lifetime Recollections*, 53.

45. "Raleigh's Budget," *Richmond Dispatch*, November 28, 1900, 3; "Flagler to Marry," *Richmond Times*, November 28, 1900, 8.

46. "Palm Beach," *Tatler*, February 9, 1901, 10.

47. Waterbury, *Markland*, 59–62.

48. Flagler to McGuire, November 27, 1900; Flagler to McGuire, December 4, 1900, HMFP.

49. "Mainly about People," *Tatler*, January 11, 1902, 2; "Birthday Party," *St. Augustine Evening Record*, March 18, 1901, 1; Gibbs, interviews with author.

50. Anderson to Harriett, December 29, 1903, AP.

51. "Winter Resort News," *St. Augustine Evening Record*, February 26, 1901, 1; "Miami," *Tatler*, March 2, 1901, 9; "Charity Ball," *Tatler*, March 16, 1901, 7.

52. "Gossip," *The Tatler*, March 9, 1901, 6.

53. Flagler to George M. Ward, December 16, 1901; Flagler to N. T. Laine, September 16, 1899, Flagler Letterbook, HMFM.

54. "Buffalo Exhibit at the Arts Club," *New York Tribune*, December 15, 1901, 3.

55. *The Tatler*, January 18, 1902; unidentified clipping, Memorial Church Records, MC 24, box 3, file 49, SAHS.

56. Flagler to McGuire, December 18, 1903, Presbyterian Church Records, SAHS.

57. Flagler to W. W. Faris, November 16, 1899; Flagler to J. A. McDonald, November 17, 1902, Flagler Letterbook, HMFM.

58. "Sale of Mr. H. M. Flagler's Home?" *New York Times*, April 14, 1900, 8; S. Osgood Pell to Flagler, June 12, 1900, HMFP.

59. "Henry M. Flagler a Citizen of Florida," *New York Times*, October 9, 1900, 1; undated affidavit by Flagler swearing that he is a citizen of Florida, Flagler Letterbook, HMFM.

60. "Mr. Flagler's Gift," *St. Augustine Evening Record*, April 12, 1901, 1; "Senate and House," *St. Augustine Evening Record*, April 18, 1901, 1; Akin, *Flagler: Rockefeller Partner*, 150–51.

61. "Fortunate for the Taylors," *Minneapolis Journal*, November 25, 1901, 9; "Wealth for Poor Young Men," *New York Sun*, April 16, 1902, 7; "Three Foundlings, $189,000 Each," *New York Sun*, August 2, 1902, 7.

62. "Mr. Flagler Said to Be Co-Respondent," *New York Tribune*, May 10, 1901, 10; "Henry M. Flagler Sued," *New York Times*, May 10, 1901, 16.

63. "Mrs. Mary Helen O'Bannon," *New York Tribune*, September 13, 1903, 9; "Once Millionaire," *New York Times*, July 15, 1923, 6.

64. "Flagler Sues for Divorce," *Ocala Evening Star*, June 11, 1901, 1; "Seeks to Divorce," *St. Louis Republic*, June 14, 1901, 2; Sidney Walter Martin, *Flagler: Visionary*, 188–89.

65. "Bride Becomes Multi-Millionaire," *Washington Post*, August 25, 1901, 3; Laura Rockefeller to John D. Rockefeller Jr., August 28, 1901, qtd. in Chernow, *Titan*, 346.

66. "Flaglers at Mamaroneck," *Washington Times*, August 26, 1901, 5; "H. M. Flagler Reaches Home," *New York Tribune*, August 26, 1901, 9; "News of Newport," *New York Times*, August 31, 1901, 7; Flagler to J. R. Parrott, December 21, 1901, HMFP; Akin, *Flagler: Rockefeller Partner*, 151.

67. "Continuation of the Story," *Ocala Banner*, August 23, 1901, 2; "Henry M. Flagler," *Ocala Banner*, January 17, 1902, 1.

68. Akin, *Flagler: Rockefeller Partner*, 151; Flagler to Parrott, May 19, 1903, HMFP.

69. Tarbell, *Day's Work*, 219.

70. "Gossip," *Tatler*, January 11, 1902, 12; "Women's Exchange," *Tatler*, January 11, 1902, 5; "Palm Beach," *Tatler*, January 11, 1902, 11.

71. Hewitt et al., *Carrère*, 2:75; Ossman and Ewing, *Carrère & Hastings: Masterworks*, 156–64.

72. "Palm Beach," *Tatler*, February 1, 1902, 7.

73. "Palm Beach Notes," *Tatler*, March 1, 1902, 10; "Gossip," *Tatler*, February 8, 1902, 17; "Society," *Tatler*, March 8, 1902, 2; "Palm Beach," *Tatler*, March 8, 1902, 6.

74. Frederick Townsend Martin, *Things*, 273–76.

75. "Palm Beach," *Tatler*, February 1, 1902, 8.

76. Samuel Clemens to Olivia Clemens, March 15, 1902, Mark Twain Papers, University of California, Berkeley; "St. Augustine Hotels," *St. Augustine Evening Record*, March 15, 1902, 5; "H. H. Rogers," *Tatler*, March 15, 1902, 14; "Mark Twain is in Florida," *St. Louis Republic*, March 16, 1902, sec. 3, 1.

77. "St. Augustine Hotels," *St. Augustine Evening Record*, April 11, 1902, 5; "Personal," *St. Augustine Evening Record*, April 12, 1902, 1; "About Our Own People," *St. Augustine Evening Record*, April 15, 1890, 2.

78. Flagler to McGuire, April 28, October 27, 1902, HMFP.

79. Abbott, *Open*, 93.

80. "Alcazar," *St. Augustine Evening Record*, July 28, 1902, 1.

81. "In the New Hospital," *St. Augustine Evening Record*, July 25, 1902, 1.

82. "Personal," *St. Augustine Evening Record*, April 22, 1902, 1; "Personal," *St. Augustine Evening Record*, May 13, 1902, 1; Flagler to Parrott, June 25, 1902, HMFP; "Westchester Clambake," *New York Tribune*, July 30, 1902, 8; "Gay Day in Newport Society," *New York Sun*, August 9, 1902, 10.

83. Flagler to Fred Sterry, October 16, 1902, HMFP.

84. Birmingham, *Our Crowd*, 143–47; "Tennis Tournament," *Times-Union*, March 19, 1890, 8; "Palm Beach," *Times-Union*, March 1, 1890, 2; "Charity Ball," *Tatler*, March 17, 1894, 4; "Mainly about People," *Tatler*, March 1, 1902, 16; "Gossip," *Tatler*, February 8, 1902; "At the Hotels," *St. Augustine Evening Record*, February 23, 1905, 6.

85. Dinnerstein, *Antisemitism*, 42–43, 92; Birmingham, *Our Crowd*, 289, 345.

86. "Picture of Old Pompeii," *Times-Union*, April 12, 1889, 2; "Last Room," *St. Augustine News*, March 22, 1891, 12; Abbott, *Open*, 36, 103.

87. Abbott, *Open*, 33; McGuire to William Michaud, November 22, 1907, McGuire Letterbook, FC.

88. Goff to M. I. Boger, December 6, 1898, Flagler Letterbook, HMFM.

89. Crespo, "Florida's First," 319; "Accommodations," *Tatler*, December 15, 1894, 3; McAloon, interview with author.

90. Abbott, *Open*, 92–93; McGuire to John Anderson, October 26, 1907, McGuire Letterbook, FC.

91. Abbott, *Open*, 93.

92. "Opening of Ponce de Leon," *Times-Union*, January 18, 1892, 1; "Accommodations," *Tatler*, December 15, 1894, 3.

93. McAloon, interview with author; Carroll, interview with author.

94. Abbott, *Open*, 80.

95. Flagler to Wilson, November 18, 1902, HMFP.

96. Parrott to R. T. Goff, September 14, 1900, Flagler Letterbook, HMFM; McGuire to Fred S. Keeler, September 14, 1910, McGuire Letterbook, FC.

97. Lefevre, "Flagler," 177.

98. Richard Edmonds, "What Henry M. Flagler Did for Florida," *St. Augustine Evening Record*, May 30, 1913, 3.

99. Flagler to Sterry, October 16, 1901, HMFP.

100. Akin, *Flagler: Rockefeller Partner*, 205; Flagler to A. C. Haskell, October 1, 1890, Flagler Letterbook, HMFM; Flagler to Parrott, November 7, 1901, Flagler Letterbook, HMFM; Flagler to F. B. Squires, January 7, 1901, Flagler Letterbook, HMFM.

101. "Negroes Getting Their Rides," *Jacksonville News-Herald*, July 18, 1887, 4; "Amenities of Railroad Travel," *Times-Union*, December 26, 1889, 1; "Ancient City Happenings," *Times-Union*, January 22, 1889, 2.

102. Flagler to R. T. Goff and F. J. Niver, December 7, 1896, HMFP.

103. T. LeRoy Jefferson to J. P. Beckwith, July 18, 1904; Vice President to Jefferson (unsigned), July 22, 1904, FEC file, SAHS; "Colored People," *St. Augustine Evening Record*, November 23, 1905, 2; "Adding to Equipment," *St. Augustine Evening Record*, February 2, 1906, 1.

104. "Fred Douglass Once More," *Times-Union*, April 9, 1889, 2.

105. "Sumptuous Private Cars," *Times-Union*, April 1, 1891, 2; "St. Augustine News," *New York Age*, January 4, 1890, 4.

106. Sidney Walter Martin, *Flagler: Visionary*, 178; "Ham and Dixie," *Times-Union*, October 8, 1895, 3.

107. "Musicale," *St. Augustine News*, March 29, 1891, 12; "Colored Ball," *Tatler*, March 5, 1892, 12; "Chronicles of Ancient City," *Times-Union*, February 22, 1894, 2; "Casino," *Tatler*, March 28, 1903, 10; "St. Augustine Hotels," *St. Augustine Evening Record*, February 18, 1904, 6.

Chapter 20. The Challenge of Key West, 1903–1906

1. Flagler to Parrott, December 8, 1902, HMFP.

2. "At the Hotels," *St. Augustine Record*, December 13, 1902, 5; "Alcazar Opens," *Tatler*, January 10, 1903, 4; "Mainly about People," *Tatler*, January 10, 1903, 5.

3. "Mainly about People," *Tatler*, January 10, 1903, 5; "Palm Beach," *Tatler*, January 10, 1903, 17; "Nassau," *Tatler*, January 24, 1903, 19; "Palm Beach," *St. Augustine Record*, February 18, 1903, 6; "Palm Beach," *St. Augustine Record*, March 2, 1903, 6; "Palm Beach," *St. Augustine Record*, March 5, 1903, 6; "Palm Beach," *Tatler*, March 7, 1903, 7.

4. "Palm Beach," *St. Augustine Record*, March 4, 1903, 6; "Ponce de Leon," *Tatler*, February 21, 1903, 3; "Palm Beach," *Tatler*, March 14, 1903, 7.

5. Dunlap, *Frank*, 72; "Affairs in St. Augustine," *Times-Union*, January 16, 1895, 3.

6. "St. Augustine Entertainments," *New York Tribune*, February 22, 1903, 8; "Alcazar," *Tatler*, April 4, 1903, 8; "Alcazar," *Tatler*, January 10, 1903, 2.

7. "Ponce de Leon," *Tatler*, March 7, 1903, 2; "Plenty of Room for Tourists," *St. Augustine Record*, March 14, 1903, 1.

8. "Golf," *Tatler*, March 21, 1903, 1.

9. "Country Club," *St. Augustine Record*, December 16, 1902, 4; "Golf," *Tatler*, February 14, 1903, 20.

10. "Ponce de Leon," *Tatler*, March 14, 1903, 4; "Versatile Mr. Dunne," *St. Augustine Record*, December 16, 1902, 4; "Alcazar Opens," *Tatler*, January 10, 1903, 4; "Ponce de Leon Concert," *Tatler*, January 23, 1904, 4.

11. Dunne, *Dissertations*, 243.

12. "Grover," *St. Augustine Record*, February 9, 1903, 1; "Ponce de Leon," *Tatler*, February 14, 1903, 2.

13. "Alligator Hunt," *St. Augustine Record*, March 26, 1902, 1; "About Our Own People," *St. Augustine Record*, September 19, 1902; "About Our Own People," *St. Augustine Record*, November 15, 1902.

14. "Will Ride Gator Tomorrow," *St. Augustine Record*, January 24, 1903, 1; "Unique Ride," *St. Augustine Record*, January 25, 1903, 1.

15. "Whitney's New Enterprise," *St. Augustine Record*, March 2, 1903, 5; "Bitten by an Alligator," *St. Augustine Record*, May 23, 1903, 1; "Improvements to be Made," *St. Augustine Record*, May 30, 1903, 1; "Captured More," *St. Augustine Record*, May 27, 1904, 1.

16. "Gossip," *Tatler*, April 4, 1903, 19; "Local Happenings," *St. Augustine Record*, April 7, 1903, 3.

17. "Harris on the East Coast," *St. Augustine Record*, March 9, 1903, 4; "Miami," *Tatler*, March 28, 1903, 7; Chandler, *Henry Flagler*, 216.

18. "Local Happenings," *St. Augustine Record*, April 7, 1903, 3; "Mr. Kenan's Illness," *St. Augustine Record*, April 14, 1903, 8.

19. "Mr. Flagler Here," *St. Augustine Record*, April 28, 1903, 8; "Inspection Trip," *St. Augustine Record*, April 30, 1903, 1; "Personal," *St. Augustine Record*, May 7, 1903, 8.

20. Flagler to McGuire, June 15, July 27, 1903, HMFP; "Mrs. Flagler Convalescent," *St. Augustine Record*, August 24, 1903, 1.

21. "About Our Own People," *St. Augustine Record*, December 15, 1903, 2; "Extension Inspected," *St. Augustine Record*, December 22, 1903, 3; "Local Items," *St. Augustine Record*, December 28, 1903, 5; "Palm Beach," *Tatler*, January 9, 1904, 11.

22. "Palm Beach," *Tatler*, February 20, 1904, 11.

23. "Reception at Studios," *Tatler*, February 7, 1903, 1; "Gossip," *Tatler*, January 23, 1904; "Elegant Reception," *Tatler*, March 12, 1904, 11; Gibbs, interviews with author; Favis, *Heade*, 104–5.

24. Favis, *Heade*, 105–7.

25. "St. Augustine Yacht Club," *Tatler*, February 20, 1904, 25; "Yacht Club," Tatler, March 4, 1905, 25.

26. "Fleet," *St. Augustine Record*, November 20, 1903, 1; "On Florida East Coast," *New York Tribune*, January 24, 1904, 7; "Gossip," *Tatler*, March 25, 1905, 3; "Clarissa the Winner," *St. Augustine Record*, April 5, 1904, 1.

27. "League," *St. Augustine Record*, February 18, 1903, 1; "East Coast Resort Notes," *St. Augustine Record*, March 12, 1903, 6; "Good Roads Enthusiasts," *St. Augustine Record*, April 7, 1903, 1.

28. "Ormond," *Tatler*, March 21, 1903, 16; "Mr. Olds on Good Roads," *St. Augustine Record*, March 31, 1903, 1.

29. "Ormond Races," *Tatler*, January 23, 1904, 23; "Mr. Flagler at Ormond," *St. Augustine Record*, January 30, 1904, 5; "Vanderbilt Beaten in Automobile Race," *New York Times*, January 29, 1904, 1.

30. "Automobile Chat," *Daytona Gazette-News*, October 8, 1904, 2.

31. "Florida East Coast," *New York Tribune*, January 31, 1904, 7; "Vanderbilt Beaten in Automobile Race," *New York Times*, January 29, 1904, 1.

32. "Palm Beach," *Tatler*, January 30, 1904, 7; "Palm Beach," *Tatler*, March 5, 1904, 5; "Palm Beach," *Tatler*, March 19, 1904, 8.

33. "Dinner at Whitehall," *Tatler*, February 27, 1904, 7.

34. "Palm Beach," *Tatler*, March 5, 1904, 7.

35. "Miami," *Tatler*, March 12, 1904, 16.

36. Kenan, *Incidents: More Recollections*, 40; Campbell, *Across Fortune's Tracks*, 132, 147.

37. Sarah D. Roosevelt Diary, Franklin D. Roosevelt Library, Hyde Park, New York; "Ponce de Leon," *Tatler*, March 12, 1904, 4; Geoffrey C. Ward, *Before Trumpet*, 330.

38. "Ponce de Leon," *Tatler*, April 2, 1904, 5; "Improvements at Palm Beach," *St. Augustine Record*, April 13, 1904, 4; "Personal," *St. Augustine Record*, April 15, 1904, 8.

39. "Local News of Interest," *St. Augustine Record*, April 19, 1904, 2; "Notes of Local Interest," *St. Augustine Record*, May 4, 1904, 2; "St. Augustine Memorial," *Mr. Foster's Travel Magazine*, 10.

40. "Mr. Flagler's Party Leaves," *St. Augustine Record*, May 4, 1904, 1.

41. Flagler to James McGuire, May 20, 1904; "Local Notes of Interest," *St. Augustine Record*, June 18, 1904, 2; Flagler to McGuire, September 1, 1904, HMFP.

42. Frank Lovering, "One Line After Another," unidentified newspaper clipping, Marsh Scrapbook 14, SAHS.

43. "Are Ready for the Races," *St. Augustine Record*, January 21, 1905, 1.

44. "Automobile Chat," *Daytona Gazette-News*, October 8, 1904, 2; "Flagler Converted to Autos," *New York Times*, October 4, 1904, 2.

45. Flagler to McGuire, September 1, 2, 1904, HMFP.

46. "Local Notes of Interest," *St. Augustine Record*, December 17, 1904, 2; "Alcazar," *Tatler*, January 7, 1905, 3; "Local Notes of Interest," *St. Augustine Record*, December 22, 1904, 2; Anderson to Harriett, December 24, 1904, AP.

47. "Palm Beach," *Tatler*, January 7, 1905, 12; "Northern People at Palm Beach," *New York Tribune*, January 14, 1905, 8; "Key West Extension," *St. Augustine Record*, February 9, 1905, 1.

48. "Palm Beach," *Tatler*, February 4, 1905, 7; "On Florida East Coast," *New York Tribune*, February 12, 1905, 3; "Washington's Birthday Ball," *Times-Union*, February 16, 1905, 3; "Palm Beach," *Tatler*, April 1, 1905, 7; "Hotel Project for Cuba," *St. Augustine Record*, March 4, 1905, 1.

49. "Ormond," *Tatler*, January 7, 1905, 10; "He Beat the Train," *St. Augustine Record*, January 9, 1905, 1.

50. "Mr. Flagler at Ormond," *St. Augustine Record*, January 20, 1905, 1; "Are Ready for the Races," *St. Augustine Record*, January 21, 1905, 1; "From Friday's Daytona Gazette News," *St. Augustine Record*, January 21, 1905, 3.

51. "Coker Died of Injuries," *St. Augustine Record*, January 23, 1905, 1; "Gossip," *Tatler*, January 28, 1905, 1; "Automobile Road," *Times-Union*, January 26, 1905, 3; "New Association at Ormond," *St. Augustine Record*, January 31, 1905, 8; "Ford's Automobile," *Times-Union*, March 7, 1905, 3.

52. "Local Notes of Interest," *St. Augustine Record*, January 23, 1925, 2; "Gossip," *Tatler*, January 12, 1901, 5; "Private Car Parties," *Times-Union*, February 9, 1905, 3; "Notes of Palm Beach," *New York Tribune*, February 11, 1905, 8.

53. Edel, *Henry James*, 274; "Social Life at Palm Beach," *Times-Union*, February 19, 1905, 3; "At the Hotels," *St. Augustine Record*, February 18, 1905, 6; Edel, *Letters*, 352.

54. Edel, *Letters*, 352.

55. Ibid.

56. James, *American Scene*, 459.

57. "At the Hotels," *St. Augustine Record*, March 22, 1905, 6; "Ponce de Leon," *Tatler*, March 25, 1905, 3.

58. "Mrs. Roosevelt and Children Here," *St. Augustine Record*, April 6, 1905, 1; "News of a Day," *Times-Union*, April 8, 1905, 3.

59. "Ponce de Leon," *Tatler*, April 1, 1905, 2–3; "Mr. Flagler and Party at Ormond," *St. Augustine Record*, April 5, 1905, 8.

60. "Visiting the Canal," *St. Augustine Record*, April 8, 1905, 5.

61. "Local Notes of Interest," *St. Augustine Record*, April 11, 1905, 2; "Name Changed," *St. Augustine Record*, May 17, 1905, 6; Harvey, *Flagler Hospital*, 16; "Hospital Fair," *Tatler*, February 17, 1906, 21; "Hospital Receipts May Reach $5,000 Mark," *St. Augustine Record*, March 5, 1906, 8.

62. "Palm Beach," *Tatler*, January 7, 1905, 12; "West Palm Beach Loses a Benefactor," *West Palm Beach Tropical Sun*, April 26, 1905, 1.

63. "Body of Jefferson Passes through City," *New York Times*, April 27, 1905, 11; "Body of Dead Actor Passed through This City," *St. Augustine Record*, April 25, 1905, 1.

64. "The Waiter," *Indianapolis Freeman*, January 4, 1901, 3.

65. Malloy, "Birth," 6; Maccanon, *Commanders*, 13–22; "Change of Headquarters," *Washington Post*, October 16, 1902, 4.

66. Maccanon, *Commanders*, 18; "Annual Address of President F. P. Thompson," *Indianapolis Freeman*, November 18, 25, 1905, 3.

67. "Mr. Frank Thompson Is Ill," *Indianapolis Freeman*, April 30, 1904, 6; "Head, Second and Side Waiters National Association," *Indianapolis Freeman*, June 18, 1904, 3; "Annual Address of President F. P. Thompson," *Indianapolis Freeman*, November 18, 1905, 3; "F. P. Thompson Dead," *Indianapolis Freeman*, December 30, 1905, 3; "Ponce de Leon," *Tatler*, January 13, 1906, 3.

68. "Mr. and Mrs. Flagler Leave," *St. Augustine Record*, May 4, 1905, 4; "Flagler Car Hits Girl," *New York Tribune*, September 27, 1905, 1; Flagler to Ingraham, August 15, 1905, Ingraham Papers, UFL; Flagler to O. B. Smith, August 25, 1905, Flagler file, SAHS; Flagler to Roy F. York, August 16, 1905, Flagler Letterbook, HMFM; "The Crowning Work," *St. Augustine Record*, October 9, 1905, 2.

69. "Some Very Warm Talk," *Ocala Banner*, October 20, 1905, 6.

70. "Improvements on Railway Plant," *St. Augustine Record*, June 28, 1905, 1; "Large Addition," *St. Augustine Record*, October 7, 1905, 1; "New Coaches for F.E.C. Rwy.," *St. Augustine Record*, November 6, 1905, 1.

71. Flagler to O. B. Smith, November 4, 1908, Flagler Letterbook, HMFM.

72. Lefevre, "Flagler," 178.

73. Flagler to Julian T. Davis, March 11, 1909, Flagler Letterbook, HMFM.

74. Flagler to J. R. Parrott, November 7, 1901, Flagler Letterbook, HMFM.

75. "President Will Visit This City," *St. Augustine Record*, September 20, 1905, 1; "Will Attend Memorial Church," *St. Augustine Record*, October 7, 1905, 1.

76. "Cordial Welcome to the President," *St. Augustine Record*, October 23, 1905, 2; "President's Visit to the 'Oldest City,'" *Tatler*, January 6, 1906, 2.

77. "Cordial Welcome to the President," *St. Augustine Record*, October 23, 1905, 2.

78. "Address by the President," *St. Augustine Record*, October 23, 1905, 7.

79. "Cordial Welcome to the President," *St. Augustine Record*, October 23, 1905, 7; unidentified newspaper clipping, chronological file, SAHS.

80. "Roosevelt Goes for a Swim," *New York Sun*, October 23, 1905, 1; "President Dips into Atlantic," *Richmond Times-Dispatch*, October 23, 1905, 1; "President's Party Leave," *St. Augustine Record*, October 23, 1905, 1.

81. Kenan, *Incidents: More Recollections*, 36; Flagler to McGuire, October 25, 1905, HMFP.

82. "Mr. and Mrs. Flagler Arrive," *St. Augustine Record*, December 9, 1905, 2; "The Alcazar," *Tatler*, January 6, 1906, 6; "Mr. Flagler Returns," *St. Augustine Record*, December 20, 1905, 4.

83. "Society," *Tatler*, January 6, 1906, 16; Gibbs, interviews with author.

84. "Cotillion by Mrs. Flagler," *St. Augustine Record*, December 30, 1905, 8; "Cotillion at the Ponce de Leon," *Tatler*, January 6, 1906, 3; "Interesting Order to GAR," *Times-Union*, March 1, 1905, 3.

85. The autographed copy of "You Alone" is preserved in the Palm Beach County History Museum. "Alcazar Notes," *Tatler*, January 6, 1906, 12; "Hotel and Society Locals," *St. Augustine Record*, December 10, 1906, 7.

86. "Society," *Tatler*, January 6, 1906, 18; "Dance at the Casino," *St. Augustine Record*, January 9, 1906, 5; "Yacht Club Reception," *Tatler*, January 13, 1906, 20; "Via Ostrich Express," *St. Augustine Record*, January 10, 1906, 5.

87. "Mainly about People," *Tatler*, January 13, 1906, 15.

88. "Palm Beach," *Tatler*, February 10, 1906, 7; "Palm Beach," *Tatler*, February 17, 1906, 8; "Visit to Key West," *Tatler*, February 17, 1906, 24; "Ponce de Leon," *Tatler*, March 10, 1906, 3; "Palm Beach," *Tatler*, March 17, 1906, 7.

89. "Automobile Show Ends," *New York Times*, December 9, 1906, SN14; "Automobile Notes of Interest," *New York Times*, December 25, 1905, 5; "New Year," *Tatler*, January 6, 1906, 2; "Palm Beach," *Tatler*, January 6, 1906, 14; "State's Bad Roads," *St. Augustine Record*, March 27, 1906, 2; "An Automobile Trip," *New York Tribune*, April 22, 1906, 4; "Palm Beach," *Tatler*, January 19, 1907, 7.

90. "Special Train to Ormond," *St. Augustine Record,* January 19, 1906, 1; "Ormond," *Tatler,* January 20, 1906, 5; "World Record," *St. Augustine Record,* January 23, 1906, 1; "Palm Beach," *Tatler,* January 27, 1906, 7.

91. "Ready for the Great Automobile Races," *St. Augustine Record,* February 10, 1906, 1; "Inclement Weather," *St. Augustine Record,* February 13, 1906, 1; "Automobile Races at South Beach," *St. Augustine Record,* February 19, 1906, 1; "Interesting Races at South Beach," *St. Augustine Record,* February 20, 1906, 1; "Exciting Races on Beach," *St. Augustine Record,* February 21, 1906, 1.

92. "Was Brilliantly Successful," *St. Augustine Record,* March 10, 1906, 1; "H. M. Flagler's Notable Speech," *St. Augustine Record,* March 12, 1906, 1.

93. "General Schofield," *St. Augustine Record,* March 5, 1906, 1; "Funeral Services," *St. Augustine Record,* March 8, 1906, 1; "Lieutenant-General Schofield," *Tatler,* March 10, 1906, 4; "Palm Beach," *Tatler,* March 10, 1906, 7; Gibbs, interviews with author.

94. "Former President Cleveland," *St. Augustine Record,* March 12, 1906, 8.

95. "Cleveland Comes North," *New York Times,* March 22, 1907, 1.

96. *New York Times,* June 25, 28, 1908; Dunlap, *Frank,* 120, 139.

97. "Ponce de Leon," *Tatler,* March 31, 1906, 3.

98. "Alcazar," *Tatler,* March 24, 1906, 5.

99. Flagler to Carrère, October 23, 1902; Flagler to McDonald, November 17, 1902; Flagler to McGuire, March 18, 1906, HMFP.

100. "Work Has Commenced," *St. Augustine Record,* April 9, 1906, 1; "Local Notes," *St. Augustine Record,* November 6, 1906, 5.

101. "Laying of Corner Stone," *St. Augustine Record,* February 26, 1906, 1; "Corner Stone Laid," *St. Augustine Record,* March 1, 1906, 5; "This Issue," *St. Augustine Record,* August 8, 1906, 4; "Record Kept Open House," *St. Augustine Record,* October 9, 1906, 1.

102. Dale, *St. Augustine Boy,* 20, 94.

103. "Notice!" *St. Augustine Record,* March 20, 1906, 2; "Local Notes of Interest," *St. Augustine Record,* April 26, 1906, 4; "Local Notes of Interest," *St. Augustine Record,* May 15, 1906, 4.

104. "Mr. Henry M. Flagler a Resident of St. Augustine," *St. Augustine Record,* May 17, 1906, 1.

105. Flagler to Ingraham, April 24, 1906, HMFP.

106. "Eight Hour Day," *Florida Times-Union,* April 15, 1905, 3; "Local Notes of Interest," *St. Augustine Record,* December 29, 1905, 2; "Local Notes of Interest," *St. Augustine Record,* March 26, 1906, 4.

107. Ingraham to Flagler, June 27, 1906, HMFP.

108. Parrott to Flagler, July 6, 1906, HMFP.

Chapter 21. Returning to St. Augustine, 1906–1911

1. "Electric Lights," *Times-Union,* March 31, 1905, 3; "Easter Sunday," *Times-Union,* April 24, 1905, 3; "Negotiations Are Closed," *St. Augustine Record,* January 9, 1906, 2; "Electric Current," *St. Augustine Record,* February 16, 1906, 5; "Lighted by Electricity," *St. Augustine Record,* March 16, 1906, 1; "Electric Light Service Permanently Installed," *St. Augustine Record,* April 2, 1906, 1.

2. Randolph, "Street Railways," 85–93.

3. M. R. Cooper et al. to Flagler, August 28, 1886, SAHS; Flagler to M. R. Cooper, September 30, 1886, SAHS.

4. "Midwinter in St. Augustine," *Times-Union,* January 26, 1890, 2; B. C. Rude to Flagler, December 25, 1891, HMFP; "Affairs at St. Augustine," *Times-Union,* October 5, 1894, 3.

5. "Preliminary Work Begins," *St. Augustine Record,* September 25, 1906, 6; "South Beach Plant," *St. Augustine Record,* September 27, 1906, 1; "South Beach Plant Sold," *St. Augustine Record,* October 1, 1906, 5; "Construction on Street Railway Has Commenced," *St. Augustine*

Record, October 29, 1906, 8; "Local Notes," *St. Augustine Record*, November 8, 1906, 4; "Progress of the St. Johns Light," *St. Augustine Record*, December 11, 1906, 8.

6. "Local Notes," *St. Augustine Record*, March 14, 1907, 4; "Improvements," *St. Augustine Record*, April 1, 1907, 2.

7. "Asheville Citizen Pays a Tribute to Mr. Flagler," *St. Augustine Record*, May 25, 1906, 1.

8. "White Mountains," *New York Times*, August 5, 1906, SM11; "Bridge Whist Has Great Vogue," *New York Tribune*, August 26, 1906, 3.

9. "Bretton Woods," *New York Tribune*, August 26, 1906, 3; "Autumn Coolness," *New York Tribune*, September 15, 1907, 7; "At Briarcliff Manor," *New York Tribune*, October 21, 1906, 5.

10. Flagler to Samuel Clemens, October 4, 1906, Mark Twain Papers, University of California, Berkeley.

11. Flagler to Ingraham, November 19, 1906, Ingraham Papers, UFL.

12. "Alcazar," *Tatler*, January 5, 1907, 5.

13. "St. Augustine Is Glad," *St. Augustine Record*, December 7, 1906, 2; "Mr. Flagler Visits the Extension," *St. Augustine Record*, December 20, 1906, 4.

14. Flagler to Harry H. Flagler, December 23, 1906, HMFP.

15. "Christmas Party," *St. Augustine Record*, December 24, 1906, 1; "Personals," *St. Augustine Record*, December 26, 1906, 4; "Personals," *St. Augustine Record*, December 29, 1906, 4; "Ponce de Leon," *Tatler*, January 5, 1907, 3.

16. "Mr. and Mrs. Flagler Cordially Welcomed," *St. Augustine Record*, January 2, 1907, 1.

17. Akin, *Flagler: Rockefeller Partner*, 228.

18. "Personals," *St. Augustine Record*, January 2, 1907, 1.

19. "Mr. Flagler Has Become a Citizen," *St. Augustine Record*, April 15, 1908, 8.

20. "Society," *Tatler*, January 5, 1907, 15; "Society" *Tatler*, January 19, 1907, 2–4.

21. Arthur Spalding to Ma, January 9, 1907, HMFP.

22. Spalding to Ma, no date, HMFP.

23. Spalding to Ma, January 20, 1907, HMFP.

24. Spalding to Ma, no date, HMFP.

25. "Mr. Henry M. Flagler," *Ocala Banner*, February 19, 1909, 2.

26. "Marriott's Condition," *St. Augustine Record*, January 26, 1907, 1; "Palm Beach," *Tatler*, February 2, 1907, 8; "Society," *Tatler*, February 23, 1907, 3; "Palm Beach," *Tatler*, March 2, 1907, 7; "Miami," *Tatler*, March 16, 1907, 7.

27. "Florida and Keys Joined," *New York Times*, February 10, 1907, 20; "First Passenger Train on Keys," *St. Augustine Record*, February 11, 1907, 1.

28. "Alcazar," *Tatler*, January 5, 1907, 6; "Alcazar," *Tatler*, January 26, 1907, 5; "Ponce de Leon," *Tatler*, February 23, 1907, 8, 17.

29. "Planning Program," *St. Augustine Record*, March 14, 1906; "League Arranging for Ponce de Leon Celebration," *St. Augustine Record*, December 15, 1906, 8; "F.E.C. Railway's Generous Offer," *St. Augustine Record*, January 19, 1907, 1.

30. "Ponce de Leon Costumes Arrive," *St. Augustine Record*, March 23, 1907, 1; "Magnificent Decorations," *St. Augustine Record*, April 4, 1907, 1.

31. "Ponce de Leon and His Retinue Land," *St. Augustine Record*, April 3, 1907, 1; "Local Notes," *St. Augustine Record*, March 30, 1907, 8.

32. "City of St. Augustine Is Founded," *St. Augustine Record*, April 4, 1907, 1; "Affairs in St. Augustine," *Times-Union*, March 4, 1894, 2.

33. "United States Now in Full Possession," *St. Augustine Record*, April 5, 1907, 1.

34. Ibid.

35. "On Florida's East Coast," *New York Tribune*, March 31, 1907, 5; "Dear Sir," *St. Augustine Record*, April 5, 1907, 1.

36. "Mr. Lewis' Dinner," *St. Augustine Record*, April 6, 1907, 1; "Mrs. Flagler's Dance," *St.*

Augustine Record, April 8, 1907, 4; "Gone to the Extension," St. Augustine Record, April 29, 1907, 4; "Mr. and Mrs. Henry M. Flagler," St. Augustine Record, May 13, 1907, 1.

37. "Canal Cut Is Completed," St. Augustine Record, May 14, 1907, 1; "Mr. Ingraham Made First Trip," St. Augustine Record, June 6, 1907, 7.

38. "Social Notes," New York Times, August 7, 1907, 7; "Henry M. Flagler Ill," Washington Post, September 27, 1907, 1.

39. "H. M. Flagler Not Ill," New York Times, September 27, 1907, 1; "H. M. Flagler Not Ill," Washington Post, September 28, 1907, 5; "Mr. Flagler Is Not on Sick List," St. Augustine Record, September 28, 1907, 1.

40. "News in Brief," Gainesville Sun, December 25, 1907, 4; Ingraham to W. R. Kenan, Jr., November 18, 1921, Ingraham Papers, UFL.

41. Ingraham to W. R. Kenan Jr., November 18, 1921, Ingraham Papers, UFL.

42. "Florida East Coast Railway Shops Close," St. Augustine Record, August 1, 1907, 1.

43. "Means Retrenchment and Rigid Economy," St. Augustine Record, August 8, 1907, 1.

44. "H. M. Flagler Not Ill," Washington Post, September 28, 1907, 5; "Extension Work to Cease Jan. 1," St. Augustine Record, October 4, 1907, 1.

45. "Extension Work Will Not Be Stopped," St. Augustine Record, October 8, 1907, 1.

46. "Checks Issued by FEC Ry Co.," St. Augustine Record, November 11, 1907, 1.

47. "Mechanics for R.R. Shops Arrive," St. Augustine Record, November 22, 1907, 4; "Whistle Calls R.R. Men to Work," St. Augustine Record, November 25, 1907, 8.

48. "Local Notes," St. Augustine Record, December 11, 1907, 4; "Personals," St. Augustine Record, December 23, 1907, 4; "Ponce de Leon," Tatler, January 4, 1908, 2.

49. "Society," Tatler, January 4, 1908, 2; "Ponce de Leon," Tatler, January 4, 1908, 3; "Christmas at the Ponce de Leon," Tatler, January 4, 1908, 3; "Ponce de Leon," Tatler, January 18, 1908, 3.

50. "Flagler's 'Folly,'" Washington Herald, August 18, 1912, 6.

51. "Gossip," Tatler, January 4, 1908, 10; "Cuba By Rail Will Soon Be a Reality," St. Augustine Record, January 27, 1908, 7.

52. "Miami," Tatler, February 8, 1908, 6; "Extension Train Service to Knights Key," Tatler, February 1, 1908, 17; "Sunshine Lane," advertisement, Tatler, February 1, 1908, back cover; "Solid Train," St. Augustine Record, April 23, 1909, 1; Flagler to J. P. Beckwith, July 30, 1909, Flagler Letterbook, HMFM.

53. "Opening Dinner at Ponce de Leon," St. Augustine Record, January 8, 1908, 1; "Ponce de Leon," Tatler, January 11, 1908, 3; "Leap Year Dance," Tatler, January 18, 1908, 2.

54. "New Management of Alcazar Hotel," St. Augustine Record, December 2, 1907, 5; "Alcazar," Tatler, January 4, 1908, 5–6; Carrère to Anderson, February 24, 1908, HMFP.

55. "Good Roads Party," St. Augustine Record, February 18, 1908, 1.

56. Saint Augustine Pictorial Edition, 5; McGuire to H. E. Bemis, January 29, 1908, McGuire Letterbook, FC; "Society," Tatler, February 1, 1908, 7.

57. "Electric Cars Running to Beach," St. Augustine Record, October 3, 1907, 4; "New Attractions at South Beach," St. Augustine Record, January 10, 1908, 1; "Whitney's Alligator Farm and Zoo," St. Augustine Record, February 2, 1910, 8; "Largest Alligator Farm," St. Augustine Record, February 5, 1910, 4.

58. "Everett Whitney Burned," St. Augustine Record, March 11, 1912, 1.

59. "Personals," Tatler, March 14, 1908, 4.

60. "Branch YMCA," Times-Union, February 19, 1905, 3; "Magnificent Club Building," St. Augustine Record, August 28, 1905, 1; "Work Begins," St. Augustine Record, January 19, 1906; "Local Notes," St. Augustine Record, November 23, 1906.

61. "Ormond on the Halifax," Times-Union, August 30, 1890, 2; Thompson, God's Church, 40; "Presbyterian Church," Tatler, February 10, 1900, 15; "Royal Poinciana," Tatler, January 27, 1898, 8; "St. Augustine Hotels," St. Augustine Record, March 20, 1903, 5.

62. "Will Open YMCA," *St. Augustine Record*, January 15, 1907, 5; "YMCA Notes," *St. Augustine Record*, June 5, 1907, 5; "Membership in the YMCA Extended," *St. Augustine Record*, August 13, 1907, 1.

63. "Dedication of YMCA," *St. Augustine Record*, January 10, 1908, 1; "Success Attended YMCA Dedication," *St. Augustine Record*, January 11, 1908, 1; "Dedication of YMCA," *Tatler*, January 11, 1908, 15.

64. "Palm Beach," *Tatler*, February 22, 1908, 7; "Palm Beach," *Tatler*, February 29, 1908, 7; "Palm Beach," *Tatler*, March 14, 1908, 7; "Ponce de Leon," *Tatler*, March 28, 1908, 3.

65. "Personals," *St. Augustine Record*, April 1, 1908, 4; "Ponce de Leon Lands," *St. Augustine Record*, April 1, 1908, 1; "Menendez Arrived Here," *St. Augustine Record*, April 2, 1908, 1; "Settlers Massacred," *St. Augustine Record*, April 4, 1904, 1.

66. "Moat Conveyed to School Board," *St. Augustine Record*, April 23, 1907, 1; "Filling in Moat," *St. Augustine Record*, February 14, 1908, 1; "Save the Bastion," *St. Augustine Record*, May 20, 1908, 5.

67. "Local Notes," *St. Augustine Record*, April 10, 1908, 4; "Delightful Days at Hot Springs," *New York Tribune*, April 27, 1902, 6; Flagler to George Ward, June 4, 1908, HMFP; "Great Tide of Travel," *New York Tribune*, August 2, 1908, 5; "White Mountain Resorts Change," *New York Tribune*, September 6, 1908, 5.

68. Flagler to John Archbold, April 21, 1909, Flagler Letterbook, HMFM.

69. "H. M. Flagler Quits Standard Oil Co.," *New York Times*, June 20, 1908, 11; "Trust Idea Not His," *New York Tribune*, November 24, 1908, 1; "More Millions for John D," *Washington Post*, August 20, 1909, 6.

70. Flagler to George Ward, October 1, 1908, HMFP; Flagler to Shelton, November 18, 1908, HMFP; "F. T. Martin Gives a Big Reception," *New York Times*, November 25, 1908, 9.

71. "Mr. Flagler and Party Leave," *St. Augustine Record*, December 14, 1908, 1; "Mr. Flagler Goes to Key West," Titusville *Florida Star*, December 18, 1908, 5; "Good News," *St. Augustine Record*, December 19, 1908, 1; "More about the Extension Work," *St. Augustine Record*, December 21, 1908, 1.

72. "Social Life in the Ancient City," *St. Augustine Record*, January 5, 1909, 1; Flagler to George Shelton, January 5, 1909, Flagler Letterbook, HMFM; "Personals," *St. Augustine Record*, January 7, 1909, 4.

73. "Messers. Flagler and Parrott on Inspection Trip," *St. Augustine Record*, January 25, 1909, 1; "Many Private Cars Go South," *St. Augustine Record*, January 18, 1909, 1; "Colonel Harris Tells about It," *St. Augustine Record*, January 27, 1909, 1.

74. Lefevre, "Flagler," 180; Akin, *Flagler: Rockefeller Partner*, 221; "Society at St. Augustine," *Washington Post*, March 7, 1909, 3; "Feting Bridal Couple," *Washington Post*, March 14, 1909, ES7.

75. "Local Notes," *St. Augustine Record*, May 2, 1907, 4; "Handsome Dwelling Sold," *St. Augustine Record*, July 10, 1907, 8.

76. Lefevre, "Flagler," 178.

77. "Ponce de Leon Landing," *St. Augustine Record*, April 1, 1909, 1; "Change of Flags," *St. Augustine Record*, April 2, 1909, 1; "Regatta during Ponce de Leon Week," *St. Augustine Record*, April 6, 1909, 1.

78. Flagler to Andrew Anderson, April 2, 1909, Flagler Letterbook, HMFM.

79. "Personals," *St. Augustine Record*, December 22, 1908, 4; "Personals," *St. Augustine Record*, April 23, 1909, 4; "Scattered for Summer Months," *St. Augustine Record*, August 18, 1909, 1.

80. "Ponce de Leon Moving Pictures," *St. Augustine Record*, May 13, 1909, 5; "Celebration Pictures," *St. Augustine Record*, May 14, 1909, 4; "Pictures of the Celebration," *St. Augustine Record*, May 14, 1909, 5.

81. "A Few Weeks Ago," *St. Augustine Record*, March 26, 1910, 10.

82. "Jefferson Name of New Theater," *St. Augustine Record*, October 21, 1907, 1; "Creatore

Opened New Theater," *St. Augustine Record*, February 23, 1909, 1; "Jeffersons Formally Open Jefferson Theater," *St. Augustine Record*, September 24, 1909, 1.

83. "Important Change," *St. Augustine Record*, April 12, 1909, 1; "F.E.C. Elects Officers," *St. Augustine Record*, April 8, 1910, 1.

84. "Local Notes," *St. Augustine Record*, April 13, 1909, 4; Flagler to Beardsley, May 1, 3, 1909, HMFP; "Mr. and Mrs. Henry M. Flagler," *St. Augustine Record*, May 19, 1909, 4; "Courtesy to U.D.C.," *St. Augustine Record*, May 8, 1909, 8.

85. "Henry H. Rogers Died," *St. Augustine Record*, May 19, 1909, 1; "Briarcliff Manor," *New York Times*, July 25, 1909, PX6; "Bretton Woods," *New York Times*, August 22, 1909, PX1; Ingraham to Maria Ingraham, September 7, 1909, Ingraham Papers, UFL; "Mr. and Mrs. Flagler," *Ocala Banner*, September 24, 1909, 4; "Hotel Stands Filled," *New York Times*, October 1, 1909, 2.

86. "Mrs. Flagler Entertains," *St. Augustine Record*, December 27, 1909, 1; "Wizard of Finance," *Daytona Daily News*, January 17, 1910, 5; "Extension Plans," *St. Augustine Record*, January 28, 1910, 3; "Mr. and Mrs. Flagler Leave," *St. Augustine Record*, January 31, 1910, 1.

87. "150 Doves Flutter," *New York Times*, February 23, 1910, 9; "Personal Mention," *St. Augustine Record*, March 12, 1910; "Society at Palm Beach," *New York Times*, March 20, 1910, X3.

88. "Social Happenings at Palm Beach," *New York Times*, February 20, 1910, X12; "Social Happenings at Palm Beach," *New York Times*, March 6, 1910, X12.

89. Anderson to Harriett, May 13, 1910, AP; "Henry M. Flagler Blind," *Washington Post*, March 19, 1911, E4.

90. Gibbs, interview with Jean Parker Waterbury.

91. Gibbs, interviews with author; "The Rights of Women," *Ocala Banner*, February 5, 1909, 7.

92. McGuire to Seavey, June 6, 1910, McGuire Letterbook, FC; "Off on Inspection Trip," *St. Augustine Record*, May 26, 1910, 4.

93. James McGuire to Herman Schladermundt, August 6, 27, September 7, 8, 1910; McGuire to L. C. Haines, September 23, 1910, McGuire Letterbook, FC.

94. McGuire to Ingraham, no date, page 481; McGuire to Flagler, July 4, 1910; McGuire to William McAuliffe, August 22, 1910; McGuire to L. C. Haines, September 2, 1910; McGuire to Flagler, October 3, 1910, McGuire Letterbook, FC; "Steam Heat for the Cordova," *St. Augustine Record*, October 10, 1910, 1.

95. McGuire to Southern Clay Mfg. Co., January 10, 1910; McGuire to Baker and Holmes Co., October 12, 1914, McGuire Letterbook, FC; "Scott Co., TN History of the Southern Clay Manufacturing Company," www.tngenweb.org/ . . . /fnb_v07n4_southern_clay_manufacturing.htm.

96. "First Asphalt Material Arrives," *St. Augustine Record*, October 20, 1909, 1; "Asphalt Repair," *St. Augustine Record*, November 9, 1909, 8; "Brick Paving of Sevilla," *St. Augustine Record*, December 9, 1909, 1; "Asphalt Repair Work," *St. Augustine Record*, February 9, 1910, 1.

97. Flagler to McGuire, July 6, 1910, HMFP; "Social Notes," *New York Times*, August 12, 1910, 7; "J. D. Archbold a Climber," *New York Tribune*, December 1, 1910, 2; Smith, qtd. in Chandler, *Henry Flagler*, 259.

98. "City Recovering from the Storm," *St. Augustine Record*, October 20, 1910, 1.

99. "Local News," *St. Augustine Record*, December 3, 1910, 4; "Season at Alcazar Opens," *St. Augustine Record*, December 12, 1910, 1; Campbell, *Across Fortune's Tracks*, 157; Gibbs, interview with Walker; "Mr. and Mrs. Flagler at Palm Beach," *St. Augustine Record*, December 31, 1910, 4.

100. "Personal," *St. Augustine Record*, January 11, 1911, 8; "Marriage Was Brilliant Event," *St. Augustine Record*, January 13, 1911, 1; "In Honor of Mrs. Flagler," *St. Augustine Record*, January 27, 1911, 7; "Personal," *St. Augustine Record*, January 28, 1911, 4.

101. Albert Silber, "Personal Recollections," *Times-Union*, May 24, 1913, 9; Flagler correspondence, July 11, 1911, Flagler Letterbook, HMFM.

102. "Society at Palm Beach," *New York Times*, March 13, 1911, 9; "Palm Beach," *New York Times*, March 26, 1911, X7.

103. "Palm Beach," *New York Times*, March 26, 1911, X7; "Florida Tourists in Need," *New York Times*, March 25, 1911, 1.

104. "Mr. H. M. Flagler Gives Interview," *St. Augustine Record*, April 7, 1911; "Henry M. Flagler's Vision of the South," *St. Augustine Record*, May 30, 1913, 8.

105. "Movement Being Laid for Capital Removal," *St. Augustine Record*, March 21, 1911, 1; "Capital Removal," *St. Augustine Record*, March 22, 1911, 2; "McWilliams Paves Way," *St. Augustine Record*, April 12, 1911, 1.

106. "Despite Stiff Breeze," *St. Augustine Record*, April 5, 1911, 1.

107. "Half Rates for Aviation Meet," *St. Augustine Record*, March 28, 1911, 6; "Aeroplanes Will Fly," *St. Augustine Record*, April 1, 1911, 1; "Aviation Flights Seen by Crowds," *St. Augustine Record*, April 3, 1911, 1.

108. "Mrs. Deborah Shedd Dead," *St. Augustine Record*, December 19, 1910, 4.

109. "John Anderson Passed Away," *St. Augustine Record*, February 20, 1911, 1; "Death Takes J. D. Price," *St. Augustine Record*, November 17, 1911, 1.

110. "W. H. Pell," *St. Augustine Record*, May 3, 1911, 8; "Gossip," *Tatler*, March 10, 1894, 5; "Tablet Unveiling Well Attended," *St. Augustine Record*, February 26, 1912, 1.

111. *New York Times*, February 13, 14, 28; March 2, 3, 1911.

112. "Local Personals," *St. Augustine Record*, March 30, 1911, 4; Campbell, *Across Fortune's Tracks*, 174; "Florida's New Sea Railroad," Fort Pierce *St. Lucie Tribune*, June 2, 1911, 1; "Locals and Personals," *St. Augustine Record*, April 21, 1911, 4; "Ry. and Hotel Companies Meet," *St. Augustine Record*, May 13, 1911, 1.

113. "Alfalfa, King of Forage Crops," *St. Augustine Record*, May 29, 1911, 7; "Proposes Tribute to H. M. Flagler," *St. Augustine Record*, July 7, 1911, 1.

114. Flagler to James McGuire, July 6, 1911, HMFP; Flagler to C. H. Greenleaf, July 31, 1911, Flagler Letterbook, HMFM.

115. Flagler to James McGuire, September 25, October 2, 1911, HMFP; Gibbs, interviews with author.

116. "Flagler Party Coming," *St. Augustine Record*, December 2, 1911, 4; "Inspection Trip to Key West," *St. Augustine Record*, December 9, 1911, 1.

117. "Col. Kenan Dead," *St. Augustine Record*, December 26, 1911, 1; "Purely Personal," *St. Augustine Record*, December 29, 1911, 5; Campbell, *Across Fortune's Tracks*, 158.

Chapter 22. Final Days, 1912–1913

1. "Mr. Flagler 82," *St. Augustine Record*, January 2, 1912, 1; "Visited Daytona in Special," *St. Augustine Record*, January 3, 1912, 4; "Ponce de Leon Opens," *St. Augustine Record*, January 9, 1912, 1; "At Palm Beach," *St. Augustine Record*, January 22, 1912, 4.

2. Flagler to Parrott, August 26, 1909, Flagler Letterbook, HMFM; "Congressional Delegation," *St. Augustine Record*, January 19, 1912, 1.

3. "Many Special Trains," *St. Augustine Record*, January 22, 1912, 1.

4. Graham, *Awakening*, 216; "Second Day of Celebration," *St. Augustine Record*, January 23, 1912, 1.

5. "Henry M. Flagler Cheered to the Echo," *St. Augustine Record*, January 24, 1912, 1; "Mr. Flagler's Address," *St. Augustine Record*, January 31, 1912, 8.

6. Flagler to Parrott, January 27, 1912, HMFP; "Mr. Flagler Applauded," *St. Augustine Record*, March 12, 1912, 1; "Mr. Flagler Highly Pleased," *St. Augustine Record*, April 4, 1912, 1.

7. Flagler to McGuire, April 4, 1912, HMFP.

8. "Personal Mention," *St. Augustine Record*, May 20, 1912, 8; Flagler to Mrs. George W. Gibbs, August 12, 1912, Ingraham Papers, UFL.

9. Frederick Townsend Martin, *Things*, 275.

10. Flagler to McGuire, September 16, 1912, HMFP; "Funeral for Mrs. A. Anderson," *St. Augustine Record*, September 23, 1912, 1.

11. Anderson to Clarissa Anderson, November 7, 1912, AP; "Inspecting Extension," *St. Augustine Record*, December 4, 1912, 4; "With Auspicious Opening," *St. Augustine Record*, December 9, 1912, 1.

12. "Kenan-Kenan," *St. Augustine Record*, December 18, 1912, 1; "Life among Palm Beach Guests," *Times-Union*, January 18, 1913, 13; Andrew Anderson to Clarissa Anderson, January 26, 1913, AP; "Henry M. Flagler," *St. Augustine Record*, February 21, 1913, 2.

13. "President Taft," *St. Augustine Record*, December 28, 1912, 1; "President and Party City's Guests," *St. Augustine Record*, December 30, 1912, 1.

14. "Miss Annie MacKay Taken by Death," *St. Augustine Record*, January 6, 1913, 1; "Annie MacKay's Death," *Times-Union*, January 8, 1913, 15; "Miss Annie MacKay Is Laid to Final Rest," *St. Augustine Record*, January 10, 1913, 8.

15. "At Palatial Palm Beach Hotels," *Times-Union*, February 14, 1913, 14; "Life at Gay Palm Beach," *Times-Union*, February 24, 1913, 15.

16. "Landing Great P.D.L. Exposition," *St. Augustine Record*, May 8, 1911, 1; "Impetus Given to Great Exposition," *St. Augustine Record*, May 10, 1911, 1; "Will Propose Plans for Next Celebration," *St. Augustine Record*, April 1, 1912, 1; "Ponce de Leon Celebration May Not be Held This Year," *St. Augustine Record*, January 2, 1913, 1; "Citizens in Great Mass Meeting," *St. Augustine Record*, January 4, 1913, 1.

17. George Morgan Ward, *In Memoriam*, 19.

18. Ibid.; Frederick Townsend Martin, *Things*, 274; Lefevre, "Flagler," 186.

19. "Mr. Flagler Reported Injured," *St. Augustine Record*, March 5, 1913, 1; "Henry M. Flagler Injured by Bad Fall," *St. Augustine Record*, March 6, 1913, 1; "Flagler's Injury Serious," *New York Tribune*, March 18, 1913, 1.

20. "Mr. Flagler Better," *St. Augustine Record*, March 18, 1913, 1; Ingraham, "Speech to Miami Women's Club, Nov. 12, 1920," Ingraham Papers, UFL.

21. "Mr. Flagler Better," *St. Augustine Record*, March 22, 1913, 1; "H. M. Flagler Now at Villa on Oceanfront," *Times-Union*, April 1, 1913, 15.

22. Gibbs, interview with Walker; "Condition of Henry M. Flagler This Afternoon," *St. Augustine Record*, April 2, 1913, 1.

23. Andrew Anderson to Clarissa Anderson, April 10, 1913, AP.

24. Andrew Anderson to Clarissa Anderson, April 27, 1913, AP; "Copy of Original Code," HMFP.

25. "Flagler's Death Near," *New York Tribune*, May 16, 1913, 1; H. H. Flagler comments on Martin; *Flagler: Visionary*, HMFP; "No Hope for Mr. Flagler," *New York Tribune*, May 18, 1913, 1.

26. "Henry M. Flagler Has Passed Away," *St. Augustine Record*, May 20, 1913, 1; "Death Claims Florida's Best Friend," *St. Augustine Record*, May 21, 1913, 1; John D. Rockefeller to Mary Lily Flagler, May 20, 1913, Rockefeller Papers, part 3, Rockefeller Archive Center, Tarrytown, New York.

27. "Body of Henry M. Flagler Lies in State," *St. Augustine Record*, May 22, 1913, 1; "Final Arrangements," *Times-Union*, May 23, 1913, 13; "Recollections," *Times-Union*, May 24, 1913, 1; "His Life Work Finished," *St. Augustine Record*, May 30, 1913, 4.

28. "His Life Work Finished," *St. Augustine Record*, May 30, 1913, 1.

29. Ibid., 4.

30. "Many Here for Flagler's Funeral," *St. Augustine Record*, May 30, 1913, 4; "Body Laid to Rest," *Florida Times-Union*, May 24, 1913, 8.

31. Campbell, *Across Fortune's Track*, 162; Gibbs, interviews with author; "Flagler Party Leaves," *St. Augustine Record*, May 26, 1913, 4; "Purely Personal," *St. Augustine Record*, May 26, 1913, 8.

32. Akin, *Flagler: Rockefeller Partner*, 227; "Last Will and Testament of H. M. Flagler Made Public," *St. Augustine Record*, May 27, 1913, 1.

33. Punnett and Punnett, "Mysterious," 4, 5–7.

34. Cam, *Old Seaport*, n.p.; Lefevre, "Flagler," 170; McGuire, *Howells*, 7.

35. McGuire, *Howells*, 39, 49.

36. McGuire to Beardsley, May 5, 1914, McGuire Letterbook, FC.

37. "Hotel Properties under New Management," *St. Augustine Record*, May 3, 1915, 1; "Joseph McDonald Dies," *Miami Herald*, November 16, 1918, 1.

38. Depew to Frank B. Matthews, November 22, 1918, SAHS.

39. "Superb Golf Course," *St. Augustine Record*, January 21, 1911, 1; "John D. Rockefeller Ends Stay in Seabreeze," *Times-Union*, March 20, 1913, 2; "Ormond Beach," *New York Tribune*, January 17, 1915, 4.

40. Campbell, *Across Fortune's Track*, 164, 173, 177, 182–88.

41. Campbell, *Across Fortune's Track*, 183; "Mrs. Lewis, Heiress to Flagler Fortune, Weds," *New York Herald Tribune*, March 25, 1931, clipping, Marsh scrapbook, SAHS; "Death Claims Mrs. Francis," *St. Augustine Record*, May 30, 1937, 1.

42. "Miss Flagler Left $1,844,000," *New York Times*, October 25, 1917, 24.

43. "Flagler Estate," *Wall Street Journal*, May 24, 1913, 6; "Flagler Ill," *New York Times*, October 4, 1934, 18.

44. "Mrs. H. H. Flagler Is Dead Up-State," *New York Times*, December 29, 1939, 15; "H. Flagler Dies," *New York Times*, July 1, 1952, 23.

45. "Captain Marcotte Dead," *St. Augustine Record*, January 22, 1923, 1; "Mrs. Marcotte Goes to New York," May 8, 1925, clipping, SAHS; "Mrs. Henry Marcotte," *New York Times*, November 11, 1935, 23.

46. "St. Augustine," *Times-Union*, February 22, 1913, 15; Anderson, Memorial Flagpole dedication speech, AP.

47. Ponce, interview with Frankie Walker; "Dr. Andrew Anderson is Claimed by Death," *St. Augustine Record*, December 1, 1924, 1; "Hundreds Attend Funeral," *St. Augustine Record*, December 4, 1924, 8.

48. "Thomas Hastings," *St. Augustine Record*, January 21, 1924, 1.

49. Hewitt et al., *Carrère*, 1:102.

50. Gray, *Hastings*, 222.

51. "Thomas Hastings," *New York Times*, October 23, 1929, 27; "Thomas Hastings," *New York Times*, October 24, 1929, 25.

52. "$25,000 a Year for Care," *New York Times*, November 21, 1901, 9; "Mrs. Flagler Now Has $9,000,000," *New York Tribune*, January 20, 1920, 1; "Mrs. Flagler Dead," *New York Times*, July 14, 1930, 18; "3 Flagler Heirs to Share $12,000," *New York Times*, July 17, 1930, 24.

53. Campbell, *Across Fortune's Track*, 199, 301, 332.

54. Graham, *Hotel Alcazar*, 29–32.

55. Campbell, *Across Fortune's Track*, 199; Lewis, interview with Robert Neeland.

Bibliography

Primary Sources

Anderson, Andrew. Flagpole Dedication Speech. St. Augustine Historical Society, St. Augustine.

———. Papers. St. Augustine Historical Society, St. Augustine.

Anderson, John. Papers. George A. Smathers Libraries, University of Florida, Gainesville.

Bruce, Frederick. Letterbook. Copy. St. Augustine Historical Society Research Library, St. Augustine.

Carrère and Hastings Digital Collection. George A. Smathers Libraries, University of Florida, Gainesville. http://ufdc.ufl.edu/caha. (Includes drawings and blueprints.)

Carroll, Lilian. Interview with the author. June 20, 1975.

Deforest, Julia Weeks. "Travel Diary." Biographical file, St. Augustine Historical Society Library, St. Augustine.

Edison, Thomas A. Papers. Rutgers University, Piscataway. http://edison.rutgers.edu/NamesSearch/SingleDoc.php3?DocId=CA022B and http://edison.rutgers.edu.

Flagler, Harry Harkness. "Misstatements and Inaccuracies in Prof. Sidney Walter Martin's book *Florida's Flagler*." Typescript and marginal notes. Henry Morrison Flagler Museum, Palm Beach.

Flagler, Henry M. Papers. Henry Morrison Flagler Museum, Palm Beach.

Gibbs, Clarissa Anderson. Interviews with the author. January 12 and 14 and February 12, 1977.

———. Interview with Frankie Walker. Undated. St. Augustine Historical Society Library, St. Augustine.

———. Interview with Jean Parker Waterbury. May 1, 1987. St. Augustine Historical Society Library, St. Augustine.

Gilpin Family Collection. Historical Society of Palm Beach County, West Palm Beach.

Hadley, Anna Fremd. Interview. 1962. Historical Society of Palm Beach County, West Palm Beach.

Ingraham, James E. Papers. George A. Smathers Libraries, University of Florida, Gainesville.

Lewis, Lawrence, Jr. Interview with Robert Neeland. November 31, 1985. St. Augustine Historical Society Library, St. Augustine.

MacWilliams, William A. "Recollections." Typescript. St. Augustine Historical Society, St. Augustine.

Martin, Sidney Walter. Papers. George A. Smathers Libraries, University of Florida, Gainesville.

McAloon, Joseph. Interview with the author. August 2, 1974.

McGuire, Robert E. "My Family." Typed manuscript. 1940. St. Augustine Historical Society, St. Augustine.

Payne, Ted M. "Cultural Resources Monitoring for Excavation at Fort Mose State Park." American Preservation Consultants, 2006. St. Augustine Historical Society Library, St. Augustine.

Plimpton, A. L. "Florida, 1889: A Trip Taken by Arthur Leslie Plimpton." Copy of typed manuscript. St. Augustine Historical Society Library, St. Augustine.

Ponce, James. Interview with Frankie Walker, February 25, 1990, St. Augustine Historical Society Library, St. Augustine.

Secondary Sources

Abbott, Karl P. *Open for the Season.* New York: Doubleday, 1950.
Akin, Edward N. "The Cleveland Connection: Revelations from the John D. Rockefeller–Julia Tuttle Correspondence." *Tequesta* 42 (1982): 57–61.
———. *Flagler: Rockefeller Partner and Florida Baron.* Kent, Ohio: Kent State University Press, 1988.
Albion, Michele Wehrwein. *The Florida Life of Thomas Edison.* Gainesville: University Press of Florida, 2008.
"The Amazing Story of Henry Flagler's Yacht *Alicia*." *Inside Whitehall* 19, no. 3 (Fall 2012): 5–9.
Armstrong, D. Maitland. *Day before Yesterday.* New York: Charles Scribner's Sons, 1920.
"Artesian Well Engineering." *Scientific American* 62, no. 25 (December 17, 1887): 1.
Barghini, Sandra. *Henry M. Flagler's Painting Collection: The Taste of a Gilded Age Collector.* Palm Beach: Flagler Museum, 2002.
———. *A Society of Painters: Flagler's St. Augustine Art Colony.* Palm Beach: Flagler Museum, 1998.
Barnes, Margaret A., and Janet A. Fairbanks, eds. *Julia Newberry's Diary.* New York, 1993, 1933.
Barrett, Nathan Frank. "Fifty Years of Landscape Modeling." *Art World* 1, no. 3 (December 1916): 180–85.
Baxter, Albert. *History of the City of Grand Rapids.* New York: Mansell and Company, 1891.
Birmingham, Stephen. *Our Crowd: The Great Jewish Families of New York.* New York: Harper and Row, 1967.
Blake, Curtis Channing. "The Architecture of Carrère and Hastings." Ph.D. diss., Columbia University, 1976.
Blouet, Paul (Max O'Rell). *Jonathan and His Continent: Rambles through American Society.* New York: Cassell, 1889.
Bowen, Beth Rogero. "Usina's Original North Beach." *El Escribano* 47 (2010): 93–120.
Boyer, Willet A. "Flagler At Law." *El Escribano* 40 (2003): 49–67.
Boykin Hayter, Kennette. "The 'Ultimate' in Spa Resorts: The Renaissance of the Alcazar, St. Augustine, Florida." Master's thesis, University of Florida, 1988.
Braden, Susan. *The Architecture of Leisure: The Florida Resort Hotels of Henry Flagler and Henry Plant.* Gainesville: University Press of Florida, 2002.
Bradley, Fred T. *The Class of '83 Sheff, Yale University.* New Haven: Fred T. Bradley, 1908.
Bramson, Seth. *Speedway to Sunshine: The Story of the Florida East Coast Railway.* Boston: Boston Mills Press, 2004.
Brooks, Abbie M. (Sylvia Sunshine). *Petals Plucked from Sunny Climes.* 1880. Facsimile edition Gainesville: University of Florida Press, 1976.
———. *The Unwritten History of St. Augustine.* Trans. Annie Averette. N.p., n.d.
Browne, Jefferson B. *Key West the Old and the New.* 1912. Facsimile edition Gainesville: University Press of Florida, 1973.
Cam, Mildred. *Old Seaport Towns of the South.* New York: Dodd, Mead and Company, 1917.
Campbell, Walter E. *Across Fortune's Tracks: A Biography of William Rand Kenan, Jr.* Chapel Hill: University of North Carolina Press, 1996.
Cardwell, Kenneth H. *Bernard Maybeck: Artisan, Architect, Artist.* Santa Barbara: Peregrine Smith, 1977.
Carrère, John M. "Referred to Our Readers." *American Architect* 17, no. 493 (June 6, 1885): 274.

Carrère, John M., and Thomas Hastings. *Florida: The American Riviera; St. Augustine: The Winter Newport*. New York: Gilliss Brothers and Turnure, Art Age Press, 1887.

———. "The Illustrations." *American Architect and Building News* 24, no. 661 (August 25, 1888): 87–88.

Castleden, Louise Decatur. *The Early Years of the Ponce de Leon*. N.p., 1958.

Chandler, David Leon. *Henry Flagler: The Astonishing Life and Times of the Visionary Robber Baron Who Founded Florida*. New York: Macmillan, 1986.

Chernow, Ron. *Titan: The Life of John D. Rockefeller, Sr.* New York: Vintage, 1998.

Clark, Susan L. "Franklin W. Smith: St. Augustine's Concrete Pioneer." Master's thesis, Cooperstown Graduate Programs, 1990.

Coghlan, Derek. "Theodore Whitney, Boy Publisher." *El Escribano* 44 (2007): 97–106.

Collier, Peter, and David Horowitz. *The Rockefellers: An American Dynasty*. New York: Holt, Rinehart and Winston, 1976.

Condit, Carl W. *American Building Art: The Nineteenth Century*. New York: Oxford University Press, 1960.

———. "The Pioneer Concrete Buildings of St. Augustine." *Progressive Architecture* 9, no. 71 (September 1971): 128–33.

Cook, Walter. "Obituary of John Merven Carrère." *Brickbuilder* 20, no. 3 (March 1911): 45.

Covington, James W. *Plant's Palace: Henry B. Plant and the Tampa Bay Hotel*. Louisville: Harmony House, 1990.

Crawford, William G. *Florida's Big Dig: The Atlantic Intracoastal Waterway*. Cocoa: Florida Historical Society Press, 2006.

Crespo, Rafael A. "Florida's First Spanish Renaissance Revival." Ph.D. diss., Harvard University, 1987.

Crocker, Ruth. *Mrs. Russell Sage: Women's Activism and Philanthropy*. Bloomington: Indiana University Press, 2006.

Dahl, Curtis. "Lincoln Saves a Reformer." *American Heritage* 23, no. 6 (October 1972): 74–78.

Dale, Russel Edward. *St. Augustine Boy*. Bloomington, Ind.: Xlibris, 2009.

Dennett, Tyler. *John Hay: From Poet to Politics*. New York: Dodd, Mead and Company, 1933.

Dinnerstein, Leonard. *Antisemitism in America*. New York: Oxford University Press, 1994.

Drysdale, William. "Some Big Florida Hotels." *New York Times*, April 28, 1889, 11.

Duncan, Alastair. *Tiffany Windows: The Indispensable Book on Louis C. Tiffany's Masterworks*. New York: Simon and Schuster, 1980.

Dunlap, Annette. *Frank: The Story of Francis Folsom Cleveland*. Albany: State University of New York, 2009.

Dunne, Finley Peter. *Dissertations of Mr. Dooley*. New York: Harper and Brothers, 1906.

Edel, Leon. *Henry James: The Master*. New York: J. B. Lippincott, 1972.

———, ed. *The Letters of Henry James*. Vol. 4, *1895–1916*. Cambridge: Harvard University Press, 1984.

"Examples of Roof Gardening." *Harper's Weekly* 32, no. 1645 (July 21, 1888): 528.

Favis, Roberta. *Martin Johnson Heade in Florida*. Gainesville: University Press of Florida, 2003.

Field, Henry M. *Bright Skies and Dark Shadows*. Freeport, N.Y.: Books for Libraries Press, 1970.

Fosdick, Raymond B. *John D. Rockefeller, Jr.: A Portrait*. New York: Harper and Brothers, 1956.

Garratt, Allan V. "Elements of Design Favorable to Speed Regulation in Plants Driven by Water Power." *Transactions of the American Institute of Electrical Engineers* 16 (June 26, 1899): 361–406.

Gipson, Richard M. *The Life of Emma Thursby, 1845–1931*. New York: New York Historical Society, 1931.

Graham, Thomas. *The Awakening of St. Augustine: The Anderson Family and the Oldest City: 1821–1924*. St. Augustine: St. Augustine Historical Society, 1978.

———. *Flagler's Grand Hotel Alcazar.* St. Augustine: St. Augustine Historical Society, 1989.

———. "Flagler's Grand Hotel Alcazar." *El Escribano* 26 (1989): 1–32.

———. "Flagler's Magnificent Hotel Ponce de Leon." *Florida Historical Quarterly,* 54, no. 1 (July 1975): 1–17.

———. *Flagler's St. Augustine Hotels.* Sarasota: Pineapple Press, 2004.

———. "Henry Flagler's St. Augustine." Special issue, *Henry Flagler: Florida's Foremost Developer,* ed. Jean Parker Waterbury. *El Escribano* 40 (2003): 1–24.

———. "Henry M. Flagler's Hotel Ponce de Leon." *Journal of Decorative and Propaganda Arts* 23 (1998): 96–111.

Graham, Thomas, and Leslee Keys. *The Hotel Ponce de Leon: The Architecture and Decoration.* St. Augustine: Flagler College, 2013.

Gray, David. *Thomas Hastings, Architect.* Boston: Houghton Mifflin, 1933.

Gregory, Alexis. *Families of Fortune: Life in the Gilded Age.* New York: Rizzoli, 1993.

Gunter, Archibald Clavering. *A Florida Enchantment.* New York: Hurst and Company, 1892.

Hanks, David A. "Pottier & Stymus Mfg. Co.: Artistic Furniture & Decorations." *Art & Antiques* (September–October 1982): 84–91.

Harvey, Karen. *America's First City: St. Augustine's Historic Neighborhoods.* Lake Buena Vista, Fla.: Taylored Tours Publications, 1992.

———. *Flagler Hospital: A Gift for Life.* St. Augustine: Flagler Hospital, 1990.

Hastings, Thomas. "John Merven Carrère." *New York Architecture* 5, no. 53 (May 1911): 65–72.

———. "A Letter from Thomas Hastings." *American Architect* 96 (July 7, 1909): 3–4.

———. "Relations of Life to Architecture." *Harper's New Monthly Magazine* 88 (May 1894): 957–63.

Heade, Martin J. (Didymus). "Notes of Florida Experience." *Forest and Stream* 20, no. 17 (May 24, 1833): 324.

Heaphy, Leslie A. *The Negro Leagues.* Jefferson, N.C.: McFarland, 2003.

Hewitt, Mark Alan, Kate Lemos, William Morrison, and Charles D. Warren. *Carrère & Hastings, Architects.* 2 vols. New York: Acanthus Press, 2006.

Howells, William Dean. "A Confession of St. Augustine." *Harper's Monthly Magazine* 134 (April 1917): 680–88; 135 (May 1917): 877–85.

Hunt, Douglas L. *The Life and Work of Charles H. Hoyt.* N.p.: Douglas L. Hunt, 1945.

Israel, Paul. *Edison: A Life of Invention.* New York: John Wiley and Sons, 1998.

James, Henry. *The American Scene.* New York: Harper and Brothers, 1907.

Jones, Robert O. *D. Maitland Armstrong, American Stained Glass Master.* Tallahassee: Sentry Press, 1999.

Kenan, William Rand, Jr. *Incidents by the Way: Lifetime Recollections and Reflections.* Self-published, 1946.

———. *Incidents by the Way: More Recollections.* Self-published, 1949.

Kerber, Stephen. "Florida and the World's Columbian Exposition of 1893." *Florida Historical Quarterly* 66, no. 1 (July 1987): 25–49.

King, Pauline. *American Mural Painting.* Boston: Noyes, Platt and Company, 1901.

King's Handbook of New York City. Boston: Moses King, 1893.

Kirwin, Bill. *Out of the Shadows: African-American Baseball from the Cuban Giants to Jackie Robinson.* Lincoln: University of Nebraska Press, 2005.

Knetsch, Joe. "One of Flagler's Men: William W. Dewhurst." *El Escribano* 30 (1993): 16–32.

Koch, Robert. *Tiffany: Rebel in Glass.* New York: Crown Publishers, 1972.

Lanier, Sidney. *Florida: Its Scenery, Climate and History.* Philadelphia: J. B. Lippincott, 1876.

Lardner, Ring. *Gullible's Travels, Etc.* New York: Charles Scribner's Sons, 1925.

Lefevre, Edwin. "Flagler and Florida." *Everybody's* 22 (February 1910): 168–86.

Lehr, Elizabeth Drexel. *"King Lehr" and the Gilded Age.* Philadelphia: J. B. Lippincott, 1935.

Levenson, J. C., ed. *The Letters of Henry Adams*. 4 vols. Boston: Massachusetts Historical Society, 1982–88.

Levy, Eugene. *James Weldon Johnson: Black Leader, Black Voice*. Chicago: University of Chicago Press, 1973.

Maccanon, E. A. *Commanders of the Dining Room*. New York: Gwendolyn Publishing Company, 1904.

"A Magnificent Hotel." *Washington Post*, April 19, 1891, 13.

Malloy, Jerry. "The Birth of the Cuban Giants." In *Out of the Shadows: African American Baseball*, edited by Bill Kerwin, 1–14. Lincoln: University of Nebraska Press, 2005.

———. "The Truth about the Cuban Giants." Typescript of draft of "The Birth of the Cuban Giants," with additional information. St. Augustine Historical Society Research Library, St. Augustine.

"Marcotte, Henry." In Guy V. Henry, *Military Record of Civilian Appointments in the United States Army*, vol. 2 (New York: D. Van Nostrand, 1873), 137.

Martin, Frederick Townsend. *Things I Remember*. New York: John Lane Company, 1913.

Martin, Richard A. *The City Makers*. Jacksonville: Jacksonville Sesquicentennial Commission, 1972.

Martin, Sidney Walter. *Henry Flagler: Visionary of the Gilded Age*. Lake Buena Vista, Fla.: Tailored Tours Publications, 1998. Originally published as *Florida's Flagler*. Athens: University of Georgia Press, 1949.

May, Jessica. "Ulysses S. Grant's Visit to Saint Augustine." *El Escribano* 46 (2009): 1–30.

McGuire, William. *William Dean Howells in St. Augustine*. St. Augustine: St. Augustine Historical Society, 1998.

Mead, William R. "Obituary of John M. Carrère." *Brickbuilder* 20, no. 3 (March 1911): 45.

"Monument to Be Erected at Woodlawn Cemetery, Mr. Thomas Hastings, NY." *American Architect and Building News* 12, no. 361 (November 25, 1882): 255.

Moore, Rayburn S. *Constance Fenimore Woolson*. New York: Twayne, 1963.

Morrow, James B. "Henry M. Flagler, Who Owns Half of Florida." *Washington Post*, December 23, 1906, A9.

Mueller, Edward A. *Steamships of the Two Henrys*. Jacksonville: Edward A. Mueller, 1996.

"Nathan Frank Barrett." *Landscape Architecture* 10, no. 3 (April 1920): 109–13.

Nevins, Allan. *John D. Rockefeller: The Heroic Age of American Enterprise*. 2 vols. New York: Charles Scribner's Sons, 1940.

———. *Study in Power: John D. Rockefeller, Industrialist and Philanthropist*. New York: Charles Scribner's Sons, 1953.

Nichols, Frederick D. "A Visit with Bernard Maybeck." *Journal of the Society of Architectural Historians* 2, no. 3 (October 1952): 30–31.

Nolan, David. *Fifty Feet in Paradise: The Booming of Florida*. New York: Harcourt Brace Jovanovich, 1984.

Ossman, Laurie, and Heather Ewing. *Carrère & Hastings: The Masterworks*. New York: Rizzoli, 2011.

Paine, Ralph D. "Over the Florida Keys by Rail." *Everybody's Magazine* 17, no. 2 (February 1908): 147–56.

———. *Roads of Adventure*. Boston: Houghton Mifflin, 1922.

Parker, Carl Rust, ed. *Transactions of the American Society of Landscape Architects*. Amsterdam, N.Y.: Recorder Press, 1922.

Parker, John H. *The Gatlings at Santiago*. 1898. Reprint Teddington, U.K.: Echo Library, 2006.

Paul, Tessa. *The Art of Louis Comfort Tiffany*. Baldock, Herts, England: Apple Press, 1987.

Pearson, H. C. "Charles H. Hoyt." *Granite State Monthly* 17, no. 3 (September 1894): 143–52.

Phillips, Morris. *Practical Hints for Tourists Abroad and at Home*. New York: Brentano's, 1891.

"Plan of the Hotel Ponce de Leon, The Alcazar, and the Methodist Episcopal Church." *American Architect and Building News* 24, no. 661 (August 25, 1888): 87–88.

Pollack, Deborah C. *Laura Woodward: The Artist behind the Innovator Who Developed Palm Beach.* Blue Heron Press with the Historical Society of Palm Beach County, 2009.

Pottier and Stymus. *King's Photographic Views of New York.* Boston: Moses King, 1895.

"Professionals in the South." *Frank Leslie's Illustrated Newspaper*, March 22, 1890, 164.

Punnett, Dick, and Yvonne Punnett. "The Mysterious Miss. A. M. Brooks, Unmasked at Last!" *East Florida Gazette* 18, no. 1 (February 1999): 1–8.

Ralph, Julian. "Our Own Riviera." *Harper's New Monthly Magazine* 86, no. 514 (March 1893): 489–510.

Randolph, Edward A. "Street Railways of St. Augustine." *El Escribano* 24 (1987): 85–101.

Reed, Henry Hope. *The New York Public Library.* New York: W. W. Norton, 1986.

Reiko, Hillyer. "The New South in the Ancient City: Flagler's St. Augustine Hotels and Sectional Reconstruction." *The American Hotel: Journal of Decorative and Propaganda Arts* 30 (2005): 105–35.

Robbins, Ellen. "Reminiscences of a Flower Painter." *New England Magazine* 14, no. 5 (July 1896): 532–45.

Rockefeller, John D. *Random Reminiscences of Men and Events.* New York: Doubleday, Doran and Company, 1933.

Saint Augustine, Saint Johns County, Florida, Illustrated. Pictorial Edition of the *St. Augustine Evening Record*, 1908.

Scharf, J. Thomas. *History of Westchester County, New York.* Philadelphia: L. E. Preston and Company, 1886.

Segall, Grant. *John D. Rockefeller: Anointed with Oil.* New York: Oxford University Press, 2001.

Sewell, John. *Miami Memoirs.* 1933. Miami: Arva Moore Parks, 1987.

Shand-Tucci, Douglass. *Built in Boston.* New York: New York Graphic Society, 1978.

Smith, Franklin W. *Design and Prospectus for a National Gallery of History and Art at Washington.* New York: Renwick, Aspinwall and Russell, 1891.

Smyth, G. Hutchinson. *Henry Brady Plant.* New York: George Putnam's Sons, 1898.

"St. Augustine, Florida." In *Picturesque America*, edited by William Cullen Bryant, 183–97. New York: D. Appleton Company, 1872.

"St. Augustine Lawn Tennis Tournament." *Outing Magazine* 16, no. 3 (June 1890): 180–82.

"St. Augustine Memorial." *Mr. Foster's Travel Magazine*, January 1922, 7–10.

Stebbins, Theodore E. *The Life and Works of Martin Johnson Heade.* New Haven: Yale University Press, 1975.

Stowe, Harriet Beecher. *Palmetto-Leaves.* Boston: J. R. Osgood and Company, 1873.

Summers, James C. "Com. E. C. Benedict." *Rudder* 32, no. 6 (June 1916): 261–66.

Swales, Francis. "Master Draftsmen VII, Emmanuel Louis Masqueray, 1862–1917." *Pencil Points* 5, no. 65: 59–67.

Tarbell, Ida M. *All in the Day's Work.* New York: Macmillan, 1939.

Thanet, Octave, comp. "Six Visions of St. Augustine: To the Memory of Helen Hunt Jackson." *Atlantic Monthly*, August 1886, 187–97.

Thompson, Sandra. *God's Church: Henry Flagler's Legacy.* Palm Beach: Royal Poinciana Chapel, 1998.

Torchia, Robert W. *A Florida Legacy: Ponce de León in Florida.* Jacksonville: Cummer Museum, 1998.

Travers, J. Wadsworth. *History of Beautiful Palm Beach.* Palm Beach: J. W. Travers, 1928.

Trovaioli, August P., and Roulhac B. Toledano. *William Aiken Walker, Southern Genre Painter.* Baton Rouge: Louisiana State University Press, 1972.

Upchurch, T. W. "Special Gifts and Acts of Charity: Buckingham Smith Benevolent Association, 1871–1894." *El Escribano* 47 (2010): 71–92.

Van Hook, Leila Bailey. "From the Lyrical to the Epic: Images of Women in American Murals." *Winterthur Portfolio* 26, no. 1 (Spring 1991): 63–80.

Ward, Geoffrey C. *Before the Trumpet: Young Franklin Roosevelt, 1882–1905.* New York: Harper and Row, 1985.

Ward, George Morgan, comp. *In Memoriam: Henry Morrison Flagler.* Memorials from various sources. N.p., n.d.

Waterbury, Jean Parker, ed. *Henry M. Flagler: Florida's Foremost Developer.* Special issue, *El Escribano* 40 (2003).

———. *Markland.* St. Augustine: St. Augustine Historical Society, 1989.

———. *The Oldest City: St. Augustine, Saga of Survival.* St. Augustine: St. Augustine Historical Society, 1983.

White, Joseph. *Reminiscences of Saratoga.* New York: Knickerbocker Press, 1897.

Wiggins, Larry. "The Birth of the City of Miami." *Tequesta* 55 (1995): 5–38.

William J. Hammer. N.p., 1914. Booklet in American Institute of Electrical Engineers Archives.

Winkler, John K. *John D. Rockefeller: A Portrait in Oils.* New York: Vanguard Press, 1929.

Woodbridge, Sally B. *Bernard Maybeck: Visionary Architect.* New York: Abbeville Press, 1992.

Woolson, Constance Fenimore. "The Ancient City. In Two Parts—Part 1." *Harper's New Monthly Magazine* 50, no. 295 (December 1874): 1–23, 296.

———. "The Ancient City. In Two Parts—Part 2." *Harper's New Monthly Magazine* 50, no. 296 (January 1875): 165–85.

"The Works of Messrs. Carrère & Hastings." *Architectural Record* 27 (January 1910): 2–120.

Index

Page numbers in italics indicate illustrations.

101; of Markland House, *xii*, 2, 3; of Presbyterian Church, 209–10; by Renwick, 16–17, 56–57, 106; of Royal Poinciana, 297; St. Augustine Hotel, 6, 54–55; of San Marco Hotel, 43–44, 54–55; of SS *Miami*, 351; for *St. Augustine Record*, 440; of streetcar system, St. Augustine, 443–44; Sunshine on, 15; of West Presbyterian Church, 56–57; of YMCA Building, 459, 459–60. *See also* Concrete; Coquina shells; Sand; Wood and woodworking; Workers

Business: of Anderson, Andrew, Sr., 3; of Anderson, Clarissa, 3–4; of Aspinwall, 17; of blacks, 19; of Flagler, Henry, ix–x, 22, 24, 25–29, 31, 45, 51, 76, 81, 183, 256–57, 277–78, 311–12, 323, 353, 373–74, 387–88, 390, 399–400, 454, 461–62, 476, 485–86; Florida enterprises in, 45–46; hotel, 45, 51–53, 76, 405–6; Hotel Alcazar and commercial, 139; invalid, 6; oil, 28–29, 34, 35–37, 399–400, 461–62; philanthropy and success in, 373–74, 378; staff and hotel, 405–6. *See also specific businesses*

Cake walks, 175–78
Call, Wilkinson, 85–86, 164, 348, 355
Campbell, Oliver S., 175, 204, 234, 253, 305, 306
Canfield, Heth, 309
Capponi, Joseph, 410
Caribbean, 416
Carrère, John, *58*, 135; background and personality of, 60, 62; in concrete controversy, 96–97; death of, 473; on Flagler hotel job, 62; Grace Methodist Church by, 140; Hastings, Thomas S., partnership with, 59–62, 67–68, 111, *307*; on Hotel Alcazar pronunciation, 457; hotel design by, 56, 62, 64–66, 69–72, 88–89, 111, 493; hotel research by, 69; Kirkside design by, 286; landscaping by, 119; marriage of, 97–98; Maybeck relationship with, 111; at McKim, Mead, and White, 60–61; Presbyterian Church design and interior decoration by, 209–10, 269; terra cotta used by, 109; Union Station design by, 201–2; Whitehall design by, 400; wood ornamentation used by, 109–10
Carriages and carriage drivers, 148–50
Casa Monica, *103*; architecture and design of,

146–47; concrete used in, 101–2; construction and completion of, 135–36, *136*, 146; economic limitations at, 147, 182–83; extension, 102–3; Flagler, Henry, purchase and impact on, 182–83, 184; furniture, 184; media on, 135–36, 182; occupancy, 146, 148, 182; opening of, 146; Sala del Sol of, *147*, 147–48; Seavey, Osborn, impact on, 184; of Smith, Franklin, 76, 101–2. *See also* Cordova

Cascade fountain, 128, *128*
Catholic cathedral, 15, 105, 106, 120, 233, 426, 450, 453, 491
Charity. *See* Fundraising
Charlotte Street, 320
Chewing gum, 381
Children: Flagler, Ida Alice, and lack of, 341; of Flagler, Henry, 27, 31–32, 39–40, 168, 207; marriage of Flagler, Henry's, 168, 307–8
City Building, 214–16, *215*, 240
City Gates, 14, 204, *305*, 306
Civics: Anderson, Elizabeth, involvement in, 393; for Anderson, Andrew, II, 6–7, 95–96, 216, 314–15, 490–91; in St. Augustine, 447–48
Civil War: for Andrews, Clarissa, 5; Flagler, Henry, and, 27–28; Marcotte, Anna, on experience during, 219–20; Smith, Franklin, during, 48–49; St. Augustine after, 1–2, 5–6; St. Augustine during, 5
Cleveland, 29, 32
Cleveland, Francis Folsom, 164, *165*, 271, 439
Cleveland, Grover: death of, 439; Flagler, Henry, and, 167–68, 205–6; Florida visit of, 205–6; Hotel Ponce de Leon visits by, 164–65, 205–7, 414–15, 427, 438–39
Clothing. *See* Fashion, dress, or clothing
Colee, Louis A., 149–50
Colonial Hotel, 369–70, 382
Communication and gossip, 407
Concerts. *See* Music and musicians
Concrete: in Casa Monica and Lyon Building, 101–2; composition and mixing of, 93–95; construction, 14, 47, *47*, 89, 101–2; controversy, 96–97; coquina shells and sand in, 89–90; expense of, 94; fire offset by, 106–7; in Hotel Ponce de Leon, 93–94, 95, 96–97, 118–20, 121–22; landscaping and fence of, 118–20

Connor, Joe, 248

Construction. *See* Building and construction

Coquina shells: Aspinwall quarry for acquisition of, 90–92; in concrete, 89–90; government in acquisition of, 90; St. Augustine resistance to acquisition of, 90; sources for, 89–90; transportation of, 92

Corbett, Jim, 299

Cordova: ancillary use of, 284, 325; balls at, 237, 311; dances at, 311; disease fears at, 274–75; electricity and, 298; furniture, 184; guest rooms at, 223; Hotel Alcazar connecting bridge to, 402–3, *403*; library, 223; occupancy at, 246, 307, 311; Randolph as headwaiter of, 200; renovations and opening of, 194–95, 222–23, 402–3, 413, 468

Cordova Street, 188

Cost. *See* Economy, economics, and cost

Country Club, 359–60, 383, 414

Crawford, William L., 82, 84, 86, 216, 217, 236, 263, 280, 288, 376

Crime and criminals: bunco team, 247; hotel detectives and, 248, 249; hotel guest, 249; hotels and education against, 247–48; media on, 249; nature and mechanics of, 247; in St. Augustine, 249–50, 314; staff, security, and, 249; among travelers, 246–47. *See also* Gambling

Cruft, Isaac, 53–54, 222

Cuba: Florida convention on crisis in, 342; resort impact of crisis in, 360–61, 362–63, 364; St. Augustine and crisis in, 360–61, 362–63, 364–65; travel to, 456–57

Cuban Giants, *178*, 179, 205, 227, 268–69

Cuban Relief Fund, 364–65

Dade County Fair, 438

Dale, Richard, 212, 282, 301

Dale, Russel, 301, 440

Dana, Charles A., 230, 255, 256

Dances. *See* Balls and dances

David Harum (Westcott), 30–31

Death. *See specific topics*

Decorative Stained Glass Company, 394–95

de Crano, Felix, 303

Deering, William, 335, 359, 418

Defense, 1, 14–15. *See also* Military

Democratic Party, 357

Depew, Chauncey, 450, 462, 471, 481, 487–88

Depression. *See* Anxiety and depression

Design. *See* Architecture and design

Development and exploration. *See specific topics*

Dewey, George, 385–87

Dewhurst, W. W., 338

Disease, illness, injury, or sickness: of Anderson, Andrew, II, 492; Bryan, 348–49; construction impacted by fear of, 186; divorce and mental, 396–97, 398; Flagler, Ida Alice, mental, 308, 315–16, 323, 324, 340–41, 349, 372, 493–94; Flagler, Henry, afflicted by, 300–301, 304, 305, 416, 445, 449, 452–53, 466–67, 474, 479–80, 482–83; Flagler, Henry, on, 275–76, 375–76; Florida travelers and fear of, 129–31, 133, 148, 185–86, 187–88, 202–3, 274–76, 368; Hotel Alcazar construction and, 138; marshland conversion and, 86–87; military and, 368; philanthropy and, 375–76; railroad travel and, 130–31, 185–86, 187; of Renwick, 316–17; St. Augustine fears and impact of, 185–88, 274–76; of Seavey, Osborn's wife, 304, 312; of Thompson, Frank, 430–31; tuberculosis, 6, 12–13, 250

Disston, Hamilton, 173, 184, 230, 321

Divorce, 396–97, 398, 399

Dix, Edwin Asa, 426

Douglass, Frederick, 409

Dragoon Barracks Lot, 209

Drown, W. Staples, 172

Drysdale, William, 151

Dunne, Finley Peter, 414

École des Beaux Arts, 58–59, 70, 158–59

Economy, economics, and cost: Casa Monica and limitations of, 147, 182–83; of Hotel Ponce de Leon, 160, 245–46; of Memorial Church upkeep, 396; occupancy and recession in, 297–98, 300, 307, 311, 338; railroad and recession in, 297–98, 453–54; St. Augustine impacted by recession in, 453; San Sebastian filling, 279; U.S. and recession of, 241, 297–98, 307, 311, 338, 453. *See also* Finances

Edison, Thomas Alva, 55, 125–26, 385

Edison Improved Phonograph machine, 234–35

Flagler, Henry Morrison, *cont.*

Hastings, Thomas S. (architect), *cont.*
by, 69; interior design by, 57–58; Kirkside
design by, 286; landscaping by, 118–19, 121,
122, 124; Maybeck relationship with, 59, 111;
at McKim, Mead, and White, 60–61; on
New York City development, 492–93; plaster murals from, 113; Presbyterian Church
design and decoration by, 209–10, 269; terra
cotta used by, 109; Union Station design
by, 201–2; Whitehall design by, 400; wood
ornamentation used by, 109–10
Hastings, Thomas S. (minister), 56–57, 144
Hathaway, J. S., 425
Hay, John, 29, 166, 167, 368
Haynes-Smith, William, 337, 346, 347
Heade, Martin Johnson, 170–71, 302–3, 418
Health: of Anderson, Elizabeth, 464, 479; of
Flagler, Henry, 33–34, 43, 416, 431, 445, 462,
466–67, 479–80; of Harkness, Mary, 25, 30,
33–34; marsh conversion and public, 86–87.
See also Disease, illness, injury, or sickness
Higbee, J. B., 83
Highway, coastal, 419
Hinckley, John Arthur, 32, 168
History: building and preservation of, 107; for
Flagler, Henry, 31; of Florida, 481; military,
491; of St. Augustine, 15, 107, 283, 450–51,
460–61, 481, 491; St. Augustine Institute
of Natural, 169. *See also* Family and family
history
Horses, 29, 33, 35
Hospital, Alicia or Flagler: Anderson, Andrew,
II, and, 212, 428; Flagler, Henry, creation of,
203; fundraising for, 203–4, 228–29, 250–51,
268, 318, 343–44, 428; notables involved in,
318; opening of, 228; philanthropy and, 375;
plans for, 203; women's association for, 203,
343–44. *See also* Florida East Coast Railway
Hotel Alcazar, 138, 496; alterations, renovation, and expansion of, 258, 259, 260, 325–26,
402–4, 457; as ancillary hotel, 325; atmosphere at, 169; balls at, 298, 343; Casino,
192, 196–97, 205, 206, 228, 251, 260, 283–85,
294–95, 307, 316, 343, 358; closing of, 494–
95; commercial business at, 139; completion
of, 136, *136*, 139, 168–69; construction of, *136*,
136–39, 168–69, 192; Cordova connecting

bridge to, 402–3, *403*; design, 492; dining
room, food, and meals at, 298–99, 403–4;
disease and, 138; electricity at, 197, 260, 294,
326, 385, 387; entertainment at, 251, 316, 363–
64, 387, 410, 439; exterior makeup of, 137,
194; fire at, 283–85; floor plan, 137; foundation, 137; guest activities and amenities, 316;
honored and famous guests at, 316, 363–64,
370, 385, 414, 450; Hotel Ponce de Leon and
ancillary, 77, 117, 136–37; land acquisition
for, 137; landscaping for, 117; media on, 169,
212, 242–43, 284–85; moving picture at, 358;
occupancy, 212, 222, 243, 344; opening of,
193–94; permanence of, 495; pronunciation
of, 457; Riding Academy, 334; St. Augustine Institute of Natural History at, 169; as
summer resort, 211–12, 242–43; swimming
pool, 137, 192–93, 205, 206–7, 251, 307; terra
cotta in, 139; Turkish bath, 251–52; workers
on, 258, 260
Hotel Continental, 389–90
Hotel Granada, *312*, 313–14, 459
Hotel Key West, 346
Hotel Ponce de Leon, 55, 494; art, artists,
and artists' studios at, *158*, 158–59, 169–70,
171–72, 271, 302–3, 375, 418; balls and dances
at, 162–64, *163*, 168, 172–73, 223, 228–29, 255,
266–67, 299, 301, 312–13, 317–18, 343, 363,
436, 457; building material for, 66–67; cake
walks at, 175–78; completion timetable
for, 99–100 134–35, 136, 141–42, 143–44; concrete in, 93–94, 95, 96–97, 118–20, 121–22;
construction of, 74, 88–100, *98*, 103–4, 108–
18, 130, 131–32, 134–35, 136, 141–42, 161; cost
of, 160, 245–46; courtyard, 122, 124, 132–33,
161, *161*; design of, 64–66, 69–72, *70*, 88–89,
111, 487, 492; Dining Room, *70*, 133, 145,
153, 160, 197, 295, 468; École des Beaux Arts
principles in, 70, 158–59; Edison Improved
Phonograph machine at, 234–35; electricity,
125–27, 167, 181–82, *183*, 294–95, *295*; elevation, 71, 71–72; entertainment, 175–78, 181,
183, 254, 291–92; entrance, 150; exterior style
and decoration of, 72; fashion and formal
dress at, 162, 173, 223, 381; finances of, 494;
Flagler, Henry, funeral and, *484*, 484–85;
Flagler, Henry involvement in, 67, 93, 97,

Ingersoll, Robert, 316

Ingraham, James, 45, 329, *488*; Flagler, Henry, business and, 277–78; on Flagler, Henry, philanthropy, and Florida, 374–75; Florida exploration by, 452; *Kathleen* engine explosion and, 326–27; on Kirkside and Flagler, Mary Lily, 448; on military in St. Augustine, 362; railroad involvement of, 276–78, 289, 297; on St. Augustine streets, 441

Injury. *See* Disease, illness, injury, or sickness

Interior design, 57–58

Invalids, 6, 12–13

Iron, 95, 192

Irwin, R. L., 191–92

Jackson, Andrew, 266, 267

Jackson, Arthur C., 280–82, 290

Jacksonville: hotels in, 53–54; railroad and resort status of, 217; railroad purchase, 82–83; railroad shortcomings, 82–83

Jacksonville, St. Augustine, and Halifax River Railway, 195–96, *196*, 212–13

Jacksonville, St. Augustine, and Indian River Railway, 279, 327

Jacksonville News-Herald, 354–55

Jail, St. Augustine, 96, 243–44

James, Henry, 426–27

Jefferson, Joseph, 412, *413*, 420–21, 428–29

Jews, 404–5

Johnson, James Weldon, 358, 381

Johnson, J. Rosamond, 358, 381

Jones, Charles H., 354, 355

Jones, Minor S., 398

Joyce's Military Band, 142, 144–45, 162; in hospital fundraising, 204; at Hotel Ponce de Leon balls, 173; at Ponce de Leon cake walk, 175–76; presidential visit and, 165

Kathleen. See Adelante or *Kathleen*

Kenan, Mary Lily, 250–51; family of, 390, 391, 447, 454, 462–63, 466, 475, 485, 489–90, 495; Flagler, Henry, marriage to, 396, 398, *417*, 467; Flagler, Henry, relationship with, 223–24, 350, 369–72, *371*, 372, 388, 391, 467. *See also* Flagler, Mary Lily

Kenan, William R., Jr., 495; Flagler, Henry, relationship with, 390; Flagler, Henry, business and, 390; marriage of, 421; on

Roosevelt, Theodore, visit to Hotel Ponce de Leon, 435

Kennish, William, 93–94, 96–97

Key West, railroad: completion of, 476–78; extension to, 346, 422, 424–25, 427, 435, 445, 450, 453–54, 455, 455–57, 456, 463, 465, 469–70, 475, 476–78; hurricanes and, 469–70; presidential visit to, 476, 480

King Street, 99, 117–18, 131–32, 188, 191

Kirkside, *285*, 285–86, 441, 448

Knott, Clarence B., 308, 327

Ladies Billiard Room, 156

Ladies Hermitage Association, 266, 267

Lake Worth, 289–91, 326. *See also* Palm Beach

Lamont, Anne, 268, 297, 300, 307–8, 317–18, 490

Land and property: Astor's, 17; of Ball estate, 345–46; for hotel, 51, 52–53; Hotel Alcazar and acquisition of, 137; for Hotel Ponce de Leon, 65–66, 73–76, 77–78, 332; marsh, 77–79, 82, 84–85, 86–87, 99, 107–8, 279; media on purchases of, 53, 78; for Presbyterian Church, 209; railroad and value of, 216–17; of Renwick, 16–17; resort plan and acquisition of, 85–86; St. Augustine and private *versus* public, 85–86; taxes, 240–41

Landscaping and gardens: Alameda plaza, 117; by Barrett, 120–21; concrete fence in, 118–20; courtyard, 132–33; geometrical, 120, *121*; by Hastings, Thomas S., 118–19, 121, *122*, 124; Hotel Alcazar, 117; Hotel Ponce de Leon, 117–22, *123*, 124, 132–33, *313*, 363; orange groves and, 118, 119; parties in, 363; plants in, 122, 124; for Presbyterian Church, 231–32; rooftop, *123*; streets and, 117–18; tropical, 122

Laundry, 186–87

Lawrence Park, 270–71

Lefevre, Edwin, 46, 278, 486–87

Leopold, Albert, 364

Lewis, Albert, 388, 393, 418, 419, 448, 450, 452, 458, 470

Lewis, Hugh, 393, 435, 489

Lewis, Lawrence, Jr., 489, 495–96

Lewis, Louise Wise, 369, 402, 418, 435, 445, 447, 454, 461, 466, 489–90, 495

Library, 223, 271

Presbyterian or Memorial Church, *cont.*
269–70; land for, 209; landscaping for,
231–32; marble renovation in, 395–96; media on, 230; music at, 448–49; ownership
of, 234; Paine, temperance, and controversy
at, 271–74; Roosevelt, Theodore, at, 434–35;
sand used for, 209–10; workers on, 210
President, U.S.: Key West visit by, 476, 480; St.
Augustine and Hotel Ponce de Leon visit
by, 8–9, 164–67, 205–7, 229, 321, 414–15, 427,
432, 433–35, 438–39, 480–81
Press. *See* Media
Prince, John S., 287–88
Privacy and private life: of Flagler, Henry, 21,
64, 399–400; railroad cars with, 195–96, *196*,
255, 326, 343, 360, *361*; Standard Oil business
and, 399–400
Prokaski, Julius "Count," 180
Property. *See* Land and property
Public health, 86–87
Public interest: in Hotel Ponce de Leon, 133,
145, 154–55, 183; SS *Miami* support and,
351–52
Pullman, George M., 120, 143, 173, 267, 298, 316

Race and racism: baseball and, *178*, 178–79,
205, 225, 227, 253, 268–69; for blacks, 358,
408–10, 430; cake walks and, 178; Cuban
Giants and, 227; entertainment and, 227,
387; for Flagler, Henry, 404, 408–9, 410;
in Hotel Ponce de Leon construction,
109; Jewish, 404–5; on railroad, 409–10;
Thompson, Frank on, 199; of whites, 18–19.
See also Blacks
Railroad: Anderson, Andrew, II, involvement
in, 83–84, 213–14, 267, 297; development
and extension of, 83, 84–85, 86–87, 187, 202,
212–14, 216–17, 238, 240, 278–80, 289–90,
291, 300, 321–22, 326, 327, 330, 346, 389, 422,
424–25, 427–28, 435, 445, 450, 453–54,
455, 455–57, 456, 463, 465, 469–70, 471,
475, 476–78; disease and travel on, 130–31,
185–86, 187; economic recession and impact
on, 297–98, 453–54; exploration and expansion by, 202; finances, 236; Flagler, Harry,
involvement in, 296, 297; Flagler, Henry,
involvement in, 82–84, 202, 212–14, 216–17,
235–36, 263–64, 277–80, 289–90, 321–22,

327, 342–43, 424–25, 427–28, 435, 445, 454,
455, 455–56, 463, 465, 474, 475, 476–78,
477; Florida hotel system and, 327; Florida
"Special" and, 221–22, 246, 380; gift of toy,
392–93; in Hotel Ponce de Leon venture,
81–82, 108, 142–43, 162, 165; hurricanes
damaging, 309; Ingraham involvement in,
276–78, 289, 297; Jacksonville, purchase
of, 82–83; Jacksonville, St. Augustine, and
Halifax River, 195–96, *196*, 212–13; Jacksonville, shortcomings of, 82–83; Jacksonville,
St. Augustine, and Indian River, 279, 327;
Jacksonville resort status and, 217; to Key
West, 346, 422, 424–25, 427, 435, 445, 450,
453–54, 455, 455–57, 456, 463, 465, 469–70,
475, 476–78; Long Key Viaduct and, 456,
456; management, 83, 84; in Maria Sanchez
marshland conversion, 79, *80*, 82; media
and, 353, 355–56, 453–54, 463; to Miami,
276–77, 280, 330, 416; Palatka, 84–85, 202,
212–13; Parrott involvement in, 465, 478;
Plant involvement in, 277–78; private cars
on, 195–96, *196*, 255, 326, 343, 360, *361*; property values and, 216–17; race and racism on,
409–10; riding experience, 84; through St.
Augustine, 216–17, 235–36; St. Johns Tocoi,
8, 11–12, 17, 34, 42, 81, 84–85, 202, 212–13, 380;
San Mateo oranges and, 263–64; San Sebastian marsh conversion and extension of,
84–85, 86–87; southern Florida and, 255–56;
Standard Oil and, 81; Union Station and,
201–2, 236, 279, 432; U.S. western expansion
and, 220; workers, 278, 279, 291, 297–98. *See
also* Florida East Coast Railway; Key West,
railroad
Ralph, Julian, 155
Randolph, C. C., 200, 227–28
Reading, 30–31
Religion: for Anderson, Andrew, II, 6–7, 216;
for Anderson, Clarissa, 6–7; Flagler, Henry,
beliefs and, x, 272, 394, 460, 482; in New
York City, 56; for Rockefeller, 30; in St.
Augustine, 96, 231–34
Renwick, James: architecture and construction by, 16–17, 56–57, 106; Catholic Cathedral redesigned by, 106; Flagler, Henry,
relationship with, 106; illness of, 316–17;
land of, 16–17

Thursby, Emma, 254
Tiffany, Louis C., 58, 111–13, 170, 303, 395
Tiffany Glass Company, 111–13, *112*
Tips, 200–201
Tocoi (St. Johns) railroad, 8, 11–12, 17, 34, 42, 81, 84–85, 202, 212–13, 380
Tojetti, Virgilio, *157*, 157–58
Tolomato Street, 51
Transportation: of coquina shells, 92; St. Augustine and local, 148–50; of sand, 93, 108; water, 238. *See also* Railroad
Travel: agency, first, 368–69; of Anderson, Andrew, II, 4; to Bahamas, 351, 352; to Cuba, 456–57; disease and railroad, 130–31, 185–86, 187; on Florida East Coast Railway, 342–43, 347; of Flagler, Henry, 23–24, 46, 343, 370, 382–83, 389; in Florida, 291, 452; St. Augustine, 202; by Smith, Franklin, 49; to South, 34. *See also* Florida
Travelers or visitors: criminals among, 246–47; entertainment for, 20, 337; Florida, disease, and, 129–31, 133, 148, 185–86, 187–88, 202–3, 274–76, 368; hotels and American, 153–54; from North, 15–17; and oranges, knowledge of, 19–20; St. Augustine for, 148, 155, 202, 237–38, 321, 329, 337, 402, 414, 415, 418, 421, 426–27; tuberculosis and, 12
Tropical Tennis Tournament: cancellation of, 287; City Gates trophy for, 204, *305*; honored guests at, 234; at Hotel Ponce de Leon, *175*, 175–76, 204, *206*, 305–6; Seavey, Osborn, involvement in, 253; St. Augustine support of, 252
Tuberculosis, 6, 12–13, 250
Turkish bath, 251–52
Tuttle, Julia, 151–52, 276–77, 322, 331
Twain, Mark, 402, 445
Typhoid fever, 274–76

Unions, 408, 430
Union Station, *480*; design of, 201–2; private cars at, 255; railroad and, 201–2, 236, 279, 432; St. Augustine entry through, *201*, 201–2
United States (U.S.): economic recession in, 241, 297–98, 307, 311, 338, 453; railroad and western expansion in, 220; "Star-Spangled Banner" as anthem of, 361–62

Usina, D. B., 327–28
U.S.S. *Hornet*, 366–67
U.S.S. *Maine*, 361

Vaill, Edward E., 79, 105, 106–7, 256, 331
Valencia Street, 188
Vanderbilt, George, 444
Vanderbilt, W. K., 32
Vardon, Harry, 383–84, *384*
Villa Zorayda, 46–47, *47*, 382
Visitors. *See* Travelers or visitors

Wages, 108–9
Walker, Lee A., 225
Walker, William Aiken, 303
Walkways, hotel, 468–69
Wanamaker, John, 229
Ward, George, 30, 378, 387–88
Ward, James J., 472
Warden, William G., 78, 98, 166, 168, 272, 300, 319, 410, 442
Washington, Booker T., 357–58, 410
Water and water supply: drilling and well for, 127–28; drinking, 129; fountains, *128*, 128–29; hotel, 205, 260–61; for Hotel Alcazar swimming pool, 205; for Hotel Ponce de Leon, 127–29, 260–61; for hydraulic elevators, 129; purification, 127, 128–29, 260–61; transportation, 238
Wealth: of Flagler, Henry, ix–x, 24, 373, 399, 454; government impact from, 399; Roosevelt, Theodore, on, 434; social condemnation of, 401
Webb, DeWitt, 50
West, 389
Westcott, Edward Noyes, 30–31
West Presbyterian Church, 56–57
White, Joseph, 245–46
White, Stanford, 60
White, Stephen V., 242
White, Utley J., 262
Whitehall, 396, 398; balls at, 412; design of, 400; entertainment at, 400–401, 420–21, 436–37, 460, 466; honored guests at, 420–21; in Palm Beach, 400–401; servants at, 408

White Motor Company, 423–24
White Mountains, 444–45, 465–66
Whites, 18–19, 253, 268–69. *See also* Race and racism
Whitney, Everett C., 415, 458–59
Whitney, John F., 10, 55, 166, 415
Whitney, Theodore H., 55
Whitney, William C., 165–66
Wills, 485–86, 489
Wilson, George W., 356
Wilson, Woodrow, 426
Women, 190–91, 203, 343–44
Wood and woodworking: Hotel Ponce de Leon use of, 103–4, 109–10; ornamentation, 109–10; South and fire risk from, 104–5; streets paved with, 188–90, 344–45; workers skilled in, 110
Woodward, Laura, 303–4

Woolson, Constance Fenimore, 11
Workers: electricity, 126–27; on Hotel Alcazar, 258, 260; on Hotel Ponce de Leon, 95, 141–42; murals and contribution from, 116; on Presbyterian Church, 210; railroad, 278, 279, 291, 297–98; rights of, 108–9; on St. Augustine projects, 241; wages of, 108–9; woodworking, 110
World's Columbian Exposition, 270, 280–82, 281
Writers, 10–14, 254–55

Yachting, 35, 49–50, 418–19
Yellow fever. *See* Disease, illness, injury, or sickness
Yellowstone, 220
YMCA Building, 459, 459–60
Youth, 41

Thomas Graham is professor emeritus of history at Flagler College in St. Augustine, where he taught full time for thirty-five years. Dr. Graham is author of *The Awakening of St. Augustine* and is a past president and life member of the St. Augustine Historical Society. A native Floridian, he is a lineal descendent of Francisco Xavier Sanchez of St. Augustine.